D0212178

DICTIONARY
OF
BRITISH
CHILDREN'S
FICTION

DICTIONARY
OF
BRITISH
CHILDREN'S
FICTION

Books of Recognized Merit

A–M

ALETHEA K. HELBIG

AND

AGNES REGAN PERKINS

Greenwood Press
New York • Westport, Connecticut • London

Library of Congress Cataloging-in-Publication Data

Helbig, Alethea.
  Dictionary of British children's fiction : books of recognized
  merit / Alethea K. Helbig and Agnes Regan Perkins.
    p. cm.
  Includes index.
  ISBN 0–313–22591–5 (set)
  ISBN 0–313–27239–5 (v. 1 : lib. bdg. : alk. paper)
  ISBN 0–313–27240–9 (v. 2 : lib. bdg. : alk. paper)
  1. Children's stories, English—Dictionaries. 2. Bibliography—
Best books—Children's stories. 3. Authors, English—Biography—
Dictionaries. I. Perkins, Agnes. II. Title.
PR830.C513H4 1989
823'.009'9282—dc19   88–17788

British Library Cataloguing in Publication Data is available.

Library of Congress Catalog Card Number: 88–17788
ISBN 0–313–22591–5 (set)
ISBN 0–313–27239–5 (v.1)
ISBN 0–313–27240–9 (v.2)

First published in 1989

Greenwood Press, Inc.
88 Post Road West, Westport, Connecticut 06881

Printed in the United States of America

∞™

The paper used in this book complies with the
Permanent Paper Standard issued by the National
Information Standards Organization (Z39.48–1984).

10 9 8 7 6 5 4 3 2 1

CONTENTS

Preface   vii

Abbreviations   xv

The Dictionary   1

Index   1421

PREFACE

The *Dictionary of British Children's Fiction: Books of Recognized Merit* contains 1,626 entries on such elements as titles, authors, characters, and settings based on 387 books published from 1678 to 1985. Like the two earlier companion volumes, *Dictionary of American Children's Fiction, 1859-1959: Books of Recognized Merit* and *Dictionary of American Children's Fiction, 1960-1984; Recent Books of Recognized Merit,* it is intended for the use of everyone who is concerned with children's literature in any way: librarians, teachers, literary scholars, researchers in comparative social history, parents, booksellers, publishers, editors--those to whom literature for children is of vital interest professionally or personally. A later reference will deal with award-winning books in Canada, Australia, New Zealand, and English-speaking countries of Africa and Asia. Periodic updates are planned.

We have long been aware of the need for such references, and a volume dealing with fiction from the British Isles was part of our plan from its inception. The response to the American volumes has shown that the need and interest which we had perceived is indeed real. Although we realized from the first that we could not include all the thousands of novels published for children, we hoped to present the best and those most representative of each period, and to do so, of course, we needed to consider the many fine books written by British authors.

Rather than depend upon our own subjective judgment about which books are best or most significant, we have included those books that have won or been finalists for major awards in children's literature, using the award lists in *Children's Books: Awards & Prizes* published by the Children's Book Council. We have not included translations or any strictly regional awards, nor those issued by organizations to their members only. We also excluded those given to books chosen by children, since the selection of books made available to the children who are polled is necessarily limited. For this book we have relied mainly upon the British: the Carnegie, the Whitbread, the Guardian, the Young Observer, and the Children's Rights Workshop Other awards. We have also included books by British authors appearing on lists that consider both American and British books, for example, the *Boston Globe-Horn Book* Award and the Children's Literature Association Phoenix Award.

Some books that clearly have become important as literature for children, however, were published before awards were given or were overlooked at the time of their publication by editors and award committees. Others, although perhaps of less-than-award quality, have become popular or have come to be considered standard novels that should be part of any representative collection for young people. We have, therefore, added several other lists that include both British and American books: the *Choice* magazine list of children's books for an academic library (1974, 1978, and 1983 editions); the lists of classics, both early and contemporary, published by *Horn Book* magazine; May Hill Arbuthnot's choices in *Children's Books Too Good to Miss* (1963, 1966, and 1979 editions); and the Children's Literature Association Touchstones. We have also included a type that has become increasingly important among books for young people, mysteries which have been nominated and selected as winners of the Edgar Allan Poe Award. Altogether, we have drawn books from twenty-one award and citation lists. A compilation of lists appears in the front matter.

While *Dictionary of British Children's Fiction* is not a history of children's literature

or even of fiction for children, these many
inclusions have given us a broad spectrum of the
fiction recognized for merit by a wide variety
of experts in children's literature. The awards
reflect contemporary critical attitudes toward
books for young people. Of course, the selec-
tions on various lists result from the application of somewhat different criteria, since the
purposes of the awards vary. Although the selection committees all want to provide interesting,
well-written books for children, some place more
emphasis on social or spiritual values, like the
Other, Christopher, and Child Study awards, and
others on entertainment, like the Edgar Allan
Poe Award.

Because our study is of fiction and not of
illustration, we have not included fiction in
picture book form, since the texts of such books
can seldom stand alone and their analysis
requires a consideration also of the illustrations. Somewhat arbitrarily, we have set 5,000
words as a minimum; most books need at least
that number to develop a story that can work
without pictures. Books of more than 5,000 words
are included, even if the illustrations are very
prominent.

Collections of short stories also require a
different sort of analysis and plot summary from
novels. Episodic books with the same characters
in each chapter, like A. A. Milne's Pooh books,
are included. Books of unconnected stories are
not, even if technically they are fiction. Retellings from the oral tradition are included if
the material has been developed like that in
novels. A few books by Australian, New Zealand,
American, and Indian authors have been included
when they have won British awards.

In our author entries, we have focused on
what in the author's life is most relevant to
children's literature and to the particular
books in the *Dictionary of British Children's
Fiction*. Although several other published sources give biographical information for authors,
none considers all the authors whose books are
in our study. Having the information in the same
volume is not only of convenience for researchers; it is of particular value for those areas
where libraries are on limited budgets and do
not own the other publications.

In presenting our entries we have tried to follow an arrangement that will be convenient for a variety of users. Entries are of several types:

A. Title entries. These consist of bibliographical information, including the American title if it is different from the British, and the publishers, the British title listed first even though the book may have been first published in the United States; the sub-genre to which the work belongs; the setting in time and place; a plot summary incorporating the plot problem (if any), significant episodes, and the denouement; a brief literary critical evaluation; sequels, if any; additional entries not mentioned in the summary, if any; and awards and citations in abbreviated form. A list of the complete names of the awards and citations appears in the front matter. Entries vary in length. Length in itself does not indicate the importance or quality of a book, since plots can be summarized more briefly and critical judgments stated more succinctly for some books than for others. Most readers will be acquainted with the terms we have used for sub-genres, but a few terms may need some explanation. By realistic fiction, we mean books in which events could have happened some time in the world as we know it, as opposed to an imaginary or fantastic world, and not necessarily that the action is convincing or plausible. Historical fiction includes those books in which actual historical events or figures function in the plot, as in *The Silver Sword* and *The Namesake*, or in which the specific period is essential to the action and in which the story could not have occurred in any other time, as in *The Iron Lily* and *The Eagle of the Ninth*. Books that are merely set in the past we have called period fiction.

B. Author entries. These consist of dates and places of birth and death, when available; education and vocational background; major contribution to children's literature; significant facts of the author's life that might have a bearing on the work; titles that

have won awards; frequently titles of other
publications, usually with brief information
about them; and critical judgments where they
can safely be made.

C. Character entries. These include physical and
   personality traits for important, memorable,
   or particulary unusual characters who are not
   covered sufficiently by the plot summary, and
   focus on such aspects as how they function in
   the plot, how they relate to the protagonist,
   and whether the characterization is credible
   and skillful. Characters are classified by
   the name by which they are most often referred to or by the name by which the protagonist refers to them, e.g., Uncle Andrew Ket-
   terly; Caxton, William; Red Queen; Smaug. The
   name is also cross referenced in the index
   under other most likely possibilities. If the
   character's surname does not often appear in
   the story, it will usually not appear in the
   index; when it is included, it is usually as
   a family name: Clock family, Dunham family,
   etc. If the plot summary gives all the significant information about characters, as
   with many protagonists, they are not dis-
   cussed in separate character entries. All
   major characters, however, are listed in the
   index.

D. Miscellaneous entries. These include particularly significant settings and elements that
   need explanation beyond mention in the title
   entry.

     Every book has title and author entries.
When a book has different American and British
titles, the complete entry appears under the
British title, but the book is also listed under
the American title, with a reference to the
British title. Unhyphenated two-word surnames
are treated similarly. Entries are in alplabeti-
cal order for convenience. Asterisks indicate
that the item has a separate entry elsewhere in
the book. Accompanying entries do not duplicate
one another. While a book's title entry gives
the plot summary and a critical assessment,
other entries provide additional information to
give a more complete understanding of the book.

Publishers' names have been abbreviated; a full list appears in the front matter. Similarly, the list of awards and their abbreviations appears at the front of the dictionary. A list of the books classified by awards appears in the index. The index also includes all the items for which there are entries and such items as cross references, major characters for whom there are no separate entries, specific place settings, settings by period, and such items as themes and subjects, books of first-person narration, unusual narrative structures, significant tone, authors' pseudonyms, illustrators, and genres.

The majority of the early classics for children and many of the strongest books in recent years are British. We have treated the American books in separate volumes from the British simply for convenience. Together they make up one large, significant, and cohesive body of literature in the English language. Most of the best books are eventually published in both England and the United States, and the children who read them are often oblivious of their origins, or accept foreign terminology and customs as naturally as those of an unfamiliar part of their own country, indeed often relishing unusual points of view and settings.

Some aspects of British fiction for children stand out. In the first place, many of the earliest novels on the British lists, and even some published in the twentieth century, were not originally intended for children, but have been widely read by them. *Pilgrim's Progress*, *Gulliver's Travels*, and *Robinson Crusoe* were adopted by children before imaginative literature was published for them. The works of Dickens and Tolkien's *The Fellowship of the Ring* are shared by young people, even though written for adults.

Fantasy has dominated British children's fiction. With a very few exceptions, all the major English-language fantasies for children are British and have come to be considered masterpieces of world literature, books that every educated person should know. Whereas in realistic fiction, children's literature has frequently borrowed from that for adults, in fantasy, children's literature has made a major contribution to imaginative writing. In recent

years, books of fantasy, although proportionate-
ly fewer in number, have continued to dominate
the British children's literature scene in quality, and many of the fantasies of the last two
decades are outstanding for their inventive concepts and their daring and skillful style.

At the same time, historical fiction has
been a less frequent but nevertheless strong
genre, coming into its own in the 1950s. It is
impossible to consider British historical fiction without thinking of such major figures as
Rosemary Sutcliff, Hester Burton, C. Walter
Hodges, and Barbara Willard, although others
have also made significant contributions. Settings range over the world and from ancient
times almost to the present, with a number of
fine World War II books having emerged twenty or
more years after the event, an interesting
literary phenomenon. Typically, the historical
novels reflect sound, accurate research that is
skillfully melded with interesting plots to
produce powerful stories. The result is that
British historical fiction has a solidity which
makes the books memorable.

Like historical fiction, realistic fiction
has appeared throughout the list, but only since
1960 has it led numerically. The influence of
Arthur Ransome, who wrote holiday adventures in
the 1930s, persisted for a long time, and
British writers were slower than Americans to
exploit social concerns. While some recent
novels have entered the realm of the gritty,
urban working class, the most memorable examples
of realistic fiction seem to be based on the
authors' own childhoods and have the genuineness
of lived experience, for example, *A Sound of
Chariots* and *A Long Way from Verona*.

An interesting aberration appears with the
works of Joan Aiken and Leon Garfield, which are
melodramatic, exaggerated representations of
their periods. Their convoluted structures,
playful use of conventions, and style full of
wit, irony, and humor produce entertainment with
unusual depth.

Overall, British children's fiction is
rich. It offers a great many examples of strong,
subtle characterizations and mature themes,
developed without didacticism. Plot structures
are often complicated, and style is frequently

sophisticated and demanding. It is safe to say that many of the best books remembered from the twentieth century, as with earlier periods, will be British.

As university teachers of literature for children and young adults for more than twenty years and as people trained in the study of literature as literature, we are dedicated to the idea that books for children must be judged by the same criteria as those for adults, keeping in mind, of course, that children are the intended audience. Our critical comments, therefore, judge each book as imaginative literature, not on other values, regardless of the particular emphasis of the award or list for which it was chosen.

As with the companion volumes on American children's novels, we ourselves have read every book included in *Dictionary of British Children's Fiction: Books of Recognized Merit* and have done all the research and writing in this volume. We have had some valuable assistance from a variety of sources. We wish to acknowledge the help of Eastern Michigan University and the Josephine Nevins Keal Fund with leaves and grants and to express our appreciation to the Eastern Michigan University Library and the Ann Arbor, Michigan, Public Library for the use of their extensive collections. Specifically, we thank Marcia Shafer of the Ann Arbor Public Library Youth Room and her staff for their encouragement and aid in research, Brian Steimel and his colleagues of the Interlibrary Loan Department of Eastern Michigan University Library for their invaluable help in obtaining obscure books, and Jennifer Striker for her expert assistance with computer programming.

ABBREVIATIONS

PUBLISHERS

Abelard	Abelard-Schuman Ltd.
Alden	Alden Press
Allen & Unwin	Allen & Unwin (Publishers) Ltd.
Allied Pub.	Allied Publshers, Private, Ltd., India
Allman	Allman & Son (Publishers) Ltd.
American Humane Ed.	American Humane Education Society
Anderson	Anderson Press
Angus	Angus & Robertson Ltd.
Appleton	Appleton-Century-Crofts
Arrowsmith	J. W. Arrowsmith Ltd.
Arts Council of Northern Ireland	Arts Council of Northern Ireland
Atheneum	Atheneum Publishers
Atlantic/Little	Atlantic Monthly Press in association with Little, Brown & Co.
Baker	J. Baker
Barker	Arthur Barker Ltd.
Barnes	A. S. Barnes & Co., Inc.
BBC	BBC (British Broadcasting Company) Publications
Beaufort	Beaufort Books Inc.
Bell	Bell and Daldy
Benn	Ernest Benn Ltd.
Bentley	Robert Bentley, Inc.

Blackie	Blackie & Son Ltd.
Blackwell	Basil Blackwell, Publisher Ltd.
Bles	Geoffrey Bles
Blond	Anthony Blond
Bobbs	Bobbs-Merrill Co. Inc.
Bodley	The Bodley Head Ltd
Boni	Boni and Livewright
Bradbury	Bradbury Press
Brockhampton	Brockhampton Press
Browne	Browne & Nolan
Burgess	W. F. Burgess
Burnham	T. O. P. Burnham
Cambridge U. Press	Cambridge University Press
Cape	Jonathan Cape Ltd.
Capricornus	Capricornus Press
Carey	Carey, Lea & Blanchard
Cassell	Cassell Ltd.
Century	The Century Co.
Chapman	Chapman and Hall Ltd.
Chatto	Chatto & Windus. The Hogarth Press.
Chetwood	W. Chetwood
Children's	Children's Press International
Civil and Military Gazette	Civil and Military Gazette
Colburn	H. Colburn
Collins	Wm. Collins Sons and Co. Ltd.
Constable	Constable Young Books
Cosmopolitan	Cosmopolitan Press Ltd.
Covent	Covent Garden
Coward	Coward, McCann
Criterion	Criterion Books
Crowell	Thomas Y. Crowell Co.
Crown	Crown Publishers Inc.
Daldy	Daldy, Isbister
David	David and Charles (Holdings) Ltd.
Davies	Peter Davies Ltd.
Day	The John Day Co.
Delacorte	Delacorte Press
Dennis Dobson	Dennis Dobson
Dent	J. M. Dent & Sons Ltd.
Deutsch	Andre Deutsch Ltd.
Dickson	Dickson and Thompson
Dobson	Dobson Books, Ltd.

Dodd	Dodd, Mead & Co.
Doran	G. H. Doran
Doubleday	Doubleday & Co. Inc.
Duckworth	Gerald Duckworth & Co. Ltd.
Duell	Duell, Sloan & Pearce
Dutton	E. P. Dutton & Co., Inc.
Edling	T. Edling
Eel Pie	Eel Pie
Elder	Elder & Co.
Elm Tree	Elm Tree Books
Elsevier	Elsevier-Nelson
Evans	Evans Brothers Ltd.
Eyre	Eyre & Spottiswoode (Publishers) Ltd.
Faber	Faber & Faber Ltd.
Farrar	Farrar, Straus & Giroux, Inc.
Fortune	Fortune Press
Funk	Funk & Wagnalls Co.
Gay Men's Press	Gay Men's Press
Gill	M. H. Gill
Gollancz	Victor Gollancz Ltd.
Greenwillow	Greenwillow Books
Grosset	Grosset & Dunlap, Inc.
Hamilton	Hamish Hamilton Ltd.
Harcourt	Harcourt Brace Jovanovich, Inc.
Harrap	Harrap Ltd.
Hawthorn	Hawthorn Books
Heinemann	William Heinemann Ltd.
Hill	Hill & Wang, Inc.
Hind Pocket Books	Hind Pocket Books, India
Hodder	Hodder & Stoughton Ltd.
Holiday	Holiday House, Inc.
Holt	Holt, Rinehart & Winston
Horn Book	The Horn Book, Inc.
Houghton	Houghton Mifflin Co., Inc.
Howe	Gerald Howe, Ltd.
Hurst	Hurst and Blackell
Hutchinson	Hutchinson Publishing Group Ltd.
Hyperion	Hyperion Press Inc.
India Book House	India Book House
Indiana U. Press	Indiana University Press
International	International Publishers Co., Inc.
Jack	T. C. & E. C. Jack, Ltd.

Jarrold	Jarrold & Sons Publishers Ltd.
Joseph	Michael Joseph, Ltd.
Kampmann	Kampmann & Company, Inc.
Kaye	Kaye & Ward Ltd.
Kenedy	P. J. Kenedy
Kestrel	Kestrel Books
Knopf	Alfred A. Knopf, Inc.
Lane	Allen Lane
Laurie	T. Werner Laurie, Ltd.
Lawrence	Lawrence & Wishart Ltd.
Lea	Lea and Blanchard
Lippincott	Lippincott & Crowell, Publishers
Little	Little, Brown & Co.
Lodestar	Lodestar Books
Longman	Longman Group Ltd.
Lothrop	Lothrop, Lee & Shepard Books
Lovell	Lovell, Coryell & Company
Lutterworth	Lutterworth Press
Macdonald	Macdonald & Co., Ltd.
Macmillan	Macmillan Publishers Ltd.
MacRae	Julia MacRae Books
Macrone	J. Macrone
Maunsel	Maunsel & Co.
McDowell	McDowell Obolensky
McGibbon	McGibbon & Kee
McGraw	McGraw-Hill Publishing Co.
McKay	David McKay Co. Inc.
Meredith	Meredith Corporation
Merrimack	Merrimack Publishing Corp.
Methuen	Methuen, Inc.
Michael Joseph	Michael Joseph Ltd.
Miller	J. Garnet Miller Ltd.
Morrow	William Morrow & Co.
Motte	Benj. Motte
Muller	Muller, Blond & White Ltd.
Murphy	J. F. Murphy
National Foundation for Educational Research	National Foundation for Educational Research
Nelson	Thomas Nelson Publishers
Newnes	Newnes Books

Norton	W. W. Norton & Co., Inc.
Novello	Novello
Nutt	E. Nutt
Oliver	Oliver & Boyd
Orient Longmans	Orient Longmans, India
Osgood	James R. Osgood & Co.
Oxford	Oxford University Press
Page	L. C. Page
Pantheon	Pantheon Books, Inc.
Parents	Parents' Magazine Press
Parrish	Max Parrish & Co., Ltd.
Pelham	Pelham Books Ltd.
Penguin	Penguin Books Ltd.
Peterson	T. B. Peterson and Brothers
Phillips	S. G. Phillips Inc.
Philomel	Philomel Books
Phoenix	Phoenix House Publications
Pitman	Pitman Publishing Ltd.
Ponder	N. Ponder
Prentice	Prentice-Hall Inc.
Putnam	G. P. Putnam's Sons
Rand	Rand McNally & Co.
Random	Random House, Inc.
Rebman	Rebman Ltd.
Redding	Redding & Co.
Religious Tract Society	Religious Tract Society
Reynal	Reynal & Hitchcock, Inc.
Rex Collings	Rex Collings
Robert Bentley	Robert Bentley, Inc.
Routledge	Routledge & Kegan Paul PLC
Roy	Roy Publications
Samson Low	Samson Low, Marston, Low, and Searle
Saunders	Saunders & Ottley
Scholastic	Scholastic Book Services
Scribner	Charles Scribner's Sons
Seabury	Seabury Press, Inc.
Secker	Martin Secker & Warburg Ltd.
Seizin	Seizin Press
Sheed	Sheed & Ward Ltd.
Sidgwick	Sidgwick & Jackson Ltd.
Small	Small, Maynard & Co.
Smith	Smith, Elder & Co.
SPCK	Society for Promoting

	Christian Knowledge
Stacey	Tom Stacey
Stanley Paul	Stanley Paul & Co. Ltd.
Stein	Stein & Day Inc.
St. Martins	St. Martin's Press Inc.
Stockwell	A. H. Stockwell, Ltd.
Stokes	Frederick A. Stokes Co.
Stone	Stone and Kimball
Strahan	Strahan & Co., Publishers
Taylor	W. Taylor
Thacker	Thacker and Spink
Ticknor	Ticknor & Fields
U. of London	University of London
U. S. Book	United States Book Co.
Vanguard	Vanguard Press
Van Nostrand	C. Van Nostrand Co.
Viking	The Viking Press, Inc.
Walck	Henry Z. Walck, Inc.
Walker	Walker Books Ltd.
Ward	Ward Lock Ltd.
Warner	P. L. Warner
Washburn	Washburn Press
Watts	Franklin Watts, Inc.
Wells Gardner	Wells Gardner, Darton & Co.
Wheaton	Wheaton Publishing
Wiley	John Wiley & Sons, Inc.
Winston	John C. Winston Co.
World	World Book Co.
World's Work	World's Work Ltd.

THE DICTIONARY

A

ABEL OAKES (*The Islanders**), old widower, who
occupies a cave near the shore of Halcyon*
Island and who takes in Otipo and Mua, whom he
treats like his own children. When the two
youths are transported to Kingfisher* Island
along with the other survivors from Rikofia,
Abel falls into a decline, to be restored in
spirit when Molly* Reeves gets the idea of
sailing to Kingfisher with supplies for the
exiles. Abel dies from a wound he receives when
the dissidents raid his cave, carry away the
treasure chest he has guarded for many years,
release Charlie* Herrick's pet rats, and steal
Abel's supplies. Except for a few passages in
which he is incongruously comic, Abel is noble
and stouthearted and wins the reader's sympathies. His name is probably intended to be
symbolic. He is a memorable character.

ADAM CODLING (*"Minnow" on the Say**), about
thirteen, grandson of old Mr.* Bertram Codling
and nephew of Miss* Dinah Codling, with whom he
lives. He has dark red hair and a pale face and
looks much like the Codling ancestor, Jonathan*,
whose lost treasure David* Moss helps him look
for. Although Adam wants the treasure very much,
he is inclined to give up and lose heart, and
David keeps him at the hunt. Adam never accepts
Betsy* Smith (Ashworthy-Smith), his counterpart
in looks and a distant cousin. He develops a
kind of leaf code with which he and David
communicate, to avoid trouble with Miss Codling,

who discourages the search. Adam is a much less convincing character than David, though both are stock for the genre.

ADAM FORREST (*A Grass Rope**), also called Forrest, Head Boy of the Grammar School which Nan* Owland attends and for which Peter* Dyson has just sat for examinations. About seventeen, Adam is polite, considerate, responsible, and hardworking. He is first seen on his bicycle coming up the grade to where Charley, the Owlands' hired hand is cutting trees to make a fence against the foxes. Adam is on his way to the Dysons' Unicorn Inn, where he is to paint trim after school for several days. He is very kind to the younger children and very helpful to the grownups, for example, even kneading Mrs. Owland's bread. He goes with Mr. Owland on the fox hunt and is very grateful when he realizes that it was not his shot that killed the mother fox. Mary* Owland later discovers one of her baby foxes in the glade of the old mineshaft. Adam goodnaturedly lets the children help him in redoing the signboard. It is through Adam that the plot problem develops. He has a bet going with his headmaster over the treasure that supposedly lies within Unicorn Yat, the great cliff that dominates the area, and his questions to Charley and efforts to uncover clues move the story along.

ADAM GOODALL (*The Islanders**), an obviously symbolic character; the young man who first questions the rightness of following tradition and transporting the young castaways to King-fisher* Island. He wonders whether the Law passed down by oral tradition has been accurately transmitted. That he should become the next Reader is simply not convincing. He marries Beth Reeves and chooses to remain on the island of Halcyon* after Charlie* Herrick returns on the schooner, because he feels a strong moral obligation to continue as Reader, since he accepted the position. He is patient, resourceful, sensible, and concerned with moral issues, as his name suggests.

ADAM SEYMOUR (*The Maplin Bird**), dashing young gentleman smuggler who has outwitted and escaped the revenue men until he and his small yacht, the *Maplin Bird*, have become a local legend. Bored and restless with the life his mother has planned for him supervising the building of houses on her property and attending social functions, he has taken to the illegal importing more for the adventure than for the profit, though he enjoys both. Another more ruthless side of his character is revealed when he acts as the Southend shark, looting a wrecked ketch and taking the opal necklace from the body of the captain's daughter instead of aiding the victims of the disaster. Although he is charming when he treats the housemaid, Emily* Garland, as an equal, he coolly uses both her and her brother, Toby*, to aid him and in the end doesn't bother to look at them when he is being taken away to prison.

ADAMS, RICHARD (GEORGE) (1920-   ), born in Newbury, Berkshire; civil servant and, since 1974, a full time, freelance writer, best known for his first published novel, *Watership Down** (Rex Collings, 1972; Macmillan, 1974), which won both the Carnegie and *Guardian* awards after being rejected by thirteen publishers and which reflects his interest in environmental concerns. About the hazardous journey over the English downs of a small number of male rabbits in quest of a new home, the book remains exciting and suspenseful and is filled with the sense of the natural world in spite of a density of detail. It has been translated into more than thirty languages and is considered a modern classic. *Shardik* (Allen-Rex Collings, 1974; Simon, 1975), set in an atavistic society whose god is a giant bear, is powerful in its intensity but lumbers along, and *The Plague Dogs* (Allen, 1977; Knopf, 1978), about how two dogs create a panic, seems overdone and message-laden. He has written verse, *The Tyger Voyage* (Cape, 1976; Knopf, 1976) and *The Ship's Cat* (Cape, 1977; Knopf, 1977), both published in picture book form, and has edited a collection of the tales of the Grimm brothers. Among his other publications are nonfiction and a novel for adults, *The Girl in a Swing* (Knopf, 1980; Allen, 1980). He attended Bradfield College, Worcester, and received his B.A. in modern history and his M.A. from

Worcester College, Oxford. After serving in the
British Army from 1940-1945, he held positions
in the Ministry of Housing and Local Government
in London and was Assistant Secretary of the
Department of the Environment until 1974. He has
also been writer in residence at the University
of Florida in Gainesville and at Hollins
College, Virginia, and has served as president
of the Royal Society for Prevention of Cruelty
to Animals. He and his wife have two daughters
and have lived in a cottage near the Berkshire
Downs and in London.

ADDIE JONES (*The Robbers**), Adelaide, black wife
of Bing* Jones, with whom Bing's brother,
Darcy*, and his father now live. Beautiful in a
regal way, Addie is acknowledged as almost
saintly in the way she cares for her crippled
father-in-law and copes with the problems of her
husband and young brother-in-law. She plays the
piano, mostly hymns, when her men sing with
their rich Welsh voices. Philip* Holbein, to
whom she is warm and gracious, loves her deeply.

ADMIRAL SIR JOHN BEAUCHAMP-TROUBRIDGE (*The
Grange at High Force**), retired naval officer
who rents Folly Grange and becomes involved in
the mystery of the missing statue. Called
"Trouty" by his faithful servant, Guns* Kelly,
the Admiral organizes the three boys in a
clean-up and repair of dilapidated Little St.
Mary's Chapel and arouses their interest in
seeing whether they can fire the eighteenth-
century cannon he has recently purchased. At
the end he arranges that the Grange be rented to
the Brotherhood of St. Francis, thereby
providing Miss* Cadell-Twitten with an income,
Little St. Mary's church with a congregation,
and the Grange with tenants who will maintain
it. In his relationship with the boys, he is
like the ideal British uncle, competent and
authoritarian but willing to join boyish games
with fervor.

ADMIRAL TWISS (*The Diddakoi**), Admiral Sir
Archibald Cunningham Twiss, shy, reclusive war
veteran who lives modestly in his mansion,
Amberhurst House, with his man Peters, and his
horseman, Nat. Until they find Kizzy* Lovell on

their doorstep, there have been no women in the house for years, because the Admiral is afraid of them, and his men take care of him with great skill. He has, however, allowed Kizzy's grandmother to camp in his orchard, as gypsies have for years, and he has a good deal of understanding of gypsy ways. His hobby is making very detailed miniature ships and other models, and he likes and keeps good horses. He shows Kizzy the portrait of his grandmother as a girl, and tells her that she may well be named for her, since this early Kezia was a friend of Kizzy's Gran.

THE ADVENTURES OF A BROWNIE (Craik*, Dinah Maria Mulock, Samson Low, 1872; Harper, 1872), episodic fantasy written with the cozy, Victorian tone exemplified in the subtitle, "As Told to My Child." In an old Devonshire house lives a Brownie, a small elf-man attached to a particular family for generations and given to pranks and mischief, mostly practiced on those who forget to leave him a bowl of milk behind the coal-cellar door or who are particularly slovenly or cross. In the household, set on a large farm or estate, are six little children, three boys and three girls, who sometimes play with the Brownie, their mother, a cook, a kitchen-maid, a gardener, and various other servants. In the first episode the Brownie punishes the new cook, who doesn't believe in him and fails to leave him the expected supper and who in addition is careless and sloppy, by tracking his coal-dust footprints all over her clean tablecloth and eating up the remains of the supper she has been too lazy to put away. After punishing the cat on the first night and the dog next, the cook takes the advice of the kitchen-maid, leaves the bowl of milk, and has no further trouble. In other episodes the Brownie, also referred to as Mr. Nobody, distracts the cross gardener so that the children can pick all the cherries without his surly supervision; he lures away the eight ducklings belonging to the gardener's wife and hatched by the old mother hen, then leads the children to a beautiful pond where the ducklings are swimming peacefully and the children can catch them and carry them home; he tricks Bill,

the lazy stable boy, who has locked the Shetland
pony in her stall and hidden the key so that he
will not be bothered by having to saddle her and
clean her   up   again after   the   children   have
ridden, by riding her at night and leaving her
with coat muddy and tangled, a full morning's
work for Bill; he tricks the gardener, who has
been assigned to watch the children slide on the
ice-covered pond, first to leave them to their
pleasure, then to crash through the ice and
stomp home, wet and crosser than ever; he pays
back the gardener's wife, who has stolen the
particularly large lump of coal under which he
makes his home, by tracking up the clean clothes
she has spread to dry and tying knots in the
sleeves. In each case, the erring servant is
reformed by the experience: the cook becomes
neater, Bill learns to work hard, even the
gardener mellows. The children are never named
or characterized, except that the two eldest are
boys and the youngest a remarkably sweet little
girl. The style is full of author intrusion--
"Where do you think he lived?" "Shall I tell
you all about it?"--and the children always do
just what they are told, never tell a fib, and
faithfully relate exactly   what happened to
their mother, but the author refrains from
drawing obvious morals and the mischief of the
Brownie makes lively, if old-fashioned, reading
for a very young audience. Children's Classics.

AFRICAN SAMSON. See *Black Samson*.

AGNES   CHISEL-BROWN   (*Charlotte   Sometimes*),
spinster daughter of the elderly, eccentric
couple with whom Clare and Emily* Moby lodge for
the several weeks that Clare and Charlotte*
Makepeace change places involuntarily   and
Charlotte is in the time-past part of the novel.
Agnes is conscientious, hardworking, eager to
please, kind, and sorrowful over the death of
her younger brother, Arthur, in the war. She
appears to feel no jealousy over the treasured
position Arthur held in their parents' regard,
but has always heroized him. Through her
stories, the girls learn what he was like, that
he loved to read stories of heroism and adventure, joined the army seeking to become a
hero himself, and returned on leave in dis-

illusionment. Agnes gives the girls his toy
soldiers, checkers, and marbles, among other
items, to play with. Emily keeps them and later
sends some of them to Charlotte in the time
present, a literary device that quite effectively builds credibility and provides unity.
Agnes is a convincing, attractive figure, one of
the more memorable characters in the book and
possibly an indicator of the kind of person
Charlotte may some day become.

AGNES MCSHANE (*A Sound of Chariots**), Bridie's
mother, a Scotswoman from Edinburgh, wife of
Patrick*. Strongly Presbyterian, she worries
about salvation, is a warm and affectionate wife
and loving and capable mother, and is highly
respected by her neighbors. After Patrick dies,
she earns money to keep her family together by
cleaning the houses of the wealthy people of the
area, chiefly the English, doing laundry, working as a maid, and taking in boarders. All this
becomes increasingly hard for her as the years
pass, because she has rheumatism, and she ages
rapidly. One of the book's most memorable scenes
is that in which Agnes forgets her coat and
Bridie delivers it to her at the house of
wealthy, haughty Mrs. Benson. Mrs. Benson ridicules Bridie, and for the first time Bridie
really sees what her father was striving for in
his efforts for "social enlightenment" and how
brave her mother has been.

AIKEN, JOAN (DELANO) (1924-   ), born in Rye,
Sussex; journalist, translator, and novelist,
best known in children's literature for her exuberant, Dickensian, wildly exaggerated melodramas. Daughter of writer Conrad Aiken, she was
educated privately at home by her mother, a
teacher, until she was twelve, and then at
Wychwood School, Oxford, from 1936 to 1940. She
married Ronald Brown, a journalist, who died in
1955. The couple had one son and a daughter. She
later married Julius Goldstein. She held several
positions before becoming a full-time writer,
working with the BBC, as a librarian for the
United Nations Information Centre in London, as
subeditor and features editor for *Argosy* in
London, and as copywriter for J. Walter
Thompson, also in London. A prolific writer,

daring in choice of subjects and technique, since 1953 she has published more than forty novels and books of short stories for young readers; a dozen plays for stage and television; a dozen and a half novels for adults; a collection of poems for children, the well-crafted and well-received *The Skin Spinners* (Viking, 1976); and a book of exposition, *The Way to Write for Children* (Elm Tree, 1982). Hers was a solitary childhood, without schoolmates or siblings, who were older and away at school. Her main amusements were reading and going for walks. She made up stories to entertain herself and began scribbling them down at age five. By the time she was seventeen she had had some fairy tales accepted by the BBC and had completed a novel, which was later published as *The Kingdom and the Cave* (Abelard, 1960; Double-day, 1974). Before her husband fell ill of lung cancer, she had started the novel that launched the series for which she is best known, *The Wolves of Willoughby Chase** (Cape, 1962; Double-day, 1963), the first of the Hanoverian, or Dido Twite, stories. It was postponed for almost ten years, but when published became a hit and is now listed in *Choice* and Contemporary Classics and was named to the Lewis Carroll Shelf. It is a wildly improbable take-off on Victorian melo-drama that offers plenty of excitement and chuckles in telling how the villains Miss Sligh-carp and Mr. Grimshaw attempt to usurp Sir Willoughby's estate. It is followed in the same vein by *Black Hearts in Battersea** (Cape, 1965; Doubleday, 1964), which introduces one of the most memorable heroines in contemporary chil-dren's literature, the clever, lively, and resourceful Dido Twite, and is listed in *Choice; Nightbirds on Nantucket** (Cape, 1966; Doubleday, 1966), another *Choice* book, which takes Dido to New England and involvement with Hanoverians who are attempting to overthrow nonhistorical King James III; and *The Stolen Lake** (Cape, 1981; Delacorte, 1981), a Fanfare book that is an astonishing conglomeration of improbabilities, finds Dido in South America, and adds Arthurian legend to the Hanoverian mix. Other novels that have won critical acclaim are *The Whispering Mountain** (Cape, 1968; Doubleday, 1969), a *Guardian* Award winner;

*Night Fall** (Macmillan, 1969; Holt, 1971), an Edgar Allan Poe Award winner; *Midnight Is a Place** (Cape, 1974; Viking, 1974), which was named to the Fanfare list; and *Arabel's Raven** (BBC, 1972; Doubleday, 1974), a *Choice* selection made up of three frolicsome short episodes featuring a clever and mischievous raven, the first of a series. Considered one of the leading children's writers of the late twentieth century, Aiken is widely admired for her versatility and inventiveness.

THE AIMER GATE (Garner*, Alan, ill. Michael Foreman, Collins, 1978; Collins, 1979), short, realistic, period novel of family and neighborhood life set during World War I, one of a quartet that "together form a saga tracing four generations of a working class family in Chorley, a small town in Cheshire, England." In Wicked Winnie, jerry-built of old oak planks and the frame of an old bassinet (probably the one that carried Uncle* Charlie in *Granny Reardun**), young Robert, Joseph's* son, conveys Faddock Allman to Leah's Hill, where Allman, a paraplegic from the Boer War, customarily chips stone for road flints. There he and Faddock watch while the village men, among them Uncle Charlie, now a soldier on the last day of his leave, reap the grain with scythes, because Leah's Hill is too steep for the self-binder, and the women bind the cuttings into sheaves and stack them in "kivvers." Robert fetches stone for Faddock, Faddock takes lunch with the reapers, and occasionally Uncle Charlie breaks, polishes, and sights through his rifle with evident pride, an attitude ironically shared by Faddock. Robert takes "baggin" (lunch) to his father, Joseph, the blacksmith, now making horseshoes for the war. Wicked Winnie rolls along splendidly, because Robert rubs the wheels with Uncle Charlie's fine oil, and arrives at the smithy in a good mood after a great run. His father absent and the clock striking ten, Robert knows Joseph is out checking the time of the village clock with the London telegraph, a serious task he does every day prior to adjusting and oiling the chapel clock. In the chapel, Robert climbs the ladder to his secret place inside the clock tower, past the pigeons up to the very peak, a dizzying height, where he discovers on the capstone his own name etched skillfully into the finely chiseled surface. Down again on the platform, he learns from Joseph that the name is that of his stonemason great-grandfather (Father*), and Robert is highly impressed by both the old man's skill and the care he took with a piece that no one would see, surely the sign of a true craftsman. At dinner, Uncle Charlie oils his gun while Faddock watches, Robert sings a popular war song while standing on the table, father gets out his cornet and plays a tune to which Robert sings, and Uncle Charlie accompanies them blowing on his rifle barrel. Robert thinks that maybe he'd like to be a soldier. Back at the hill, while Faddock chips stones, Robert fills in the place from which he has taken Faddock's stones so the carts will be able to bear away the grain, and watches as Charlie expertly shoots the rabbits forced out of the last stand of grain. All go home to supper, contented after the day's labor, the workers' "who-whoops" echoing through the village. Although less cohesive than its predecessors, like them this book about an important day in a youth's life has little plot. It derives strength from reve- lation of character and its themes of pride in craft and in family and of the importance of learning to know one's self. Style is tidy and spare to the point of crypticness, use of local terms is generous, and irony abounds. The reader never learns what the title refers to. Choice; Fanfare.

AJEET (*The Devil's Children**), cousin of Gopal* who becomes Nicky* Gore's best friend among the Sikhs. Though very quiet and small for her age, which is the same as Nicky's, she is self- possessed when she tells the stories that she has learned from her grandmother, and even the adult Sikhs respect her ability. She uses this talent on the night of the attack on the robbers who have terrorized the village. She tells a story to the hostage children who are so afraid of the Sikhs that they may scream and give away the surprise of the attack and keeps them enthralled while the fierce battle rages outside the barn where they are kept.

AKELA (*The Jungle Books**), great grey Lone Wolf who is the leader of the Seeonee Wolf Pack when Mowgli* is admitted to the group. With perfect impartiality he directs the meeting, ignoring Shere* Khan, the tiger, who seeks to interject himself into it, continually repeating the injunction, "Look well--look well, O wolves!" Some ten years later, Akela misses his kill, a signal that he is deposed as leader and will soon be challenged and killed. He seeks to save Mowgli by promising not to fight if Mowgli is allowed to go without harm. When Mowgli drives Shere Khan off with the blazing branches, he announces that Akela will not be killed as is the custom. In the fight in the shallows of the river against the Red Dog, Akela finally meets his end, first predicting that Mowgli himself will drive Mowgli back to man.

AL (*The Seventh Raven**), bearded priest, the least noticeable of the four terrorists who hold a group of 100 children and some twenty adults hostage in a Kensington church. Al gives an impassioned speech about the terrible oppression in his native Matteo, a South American dictatorship, during the mock trial organized by their leader, Danny*, but is asleep at the critical moment when Angel* starts to shoot and the police break in.

ALAIN DE FARRAR (*Lost John**), son of the outlaw, Sir* Ralf the Red, who, having run away from the monastery where his father sent him, joins his father's band in the Forest of Arden. A beautiful boy, he infuriates Sir Ralf by resembling his mother, whom the violent man killed, the act for which he has been outlawed. Alain suffers his father's contempt calmly and cheerfully preforms the demeaning tasks assigned him, showing remarkable maturity and self-control. When he is suspected of having betrayed the band, he and the other suspect, Simon, are tried by ordeal, each having to pick up a red-hot iron bar, their guilt or innocence being determined by which one God chooses to heal. Alain's hand is secretly treated by his father's non-Christian follower, Wolf, who despises Simon, and though the boy fears that God will condemn him for having allowed the

pagan to treat him, Alain is proved innocent,
and Simon confesses. Later Alain shows his great
courage by entering a castle dressed as a girl
and setting up the rescue of John* Fitzwilliam,
his father's young squire. With almost saintly
forbearance, he forgives John's slights and
surly temper.

ALAIN, DUC DE SAINT SERVAN-REZE (*Three Lives for
the Czar**), grandfather to Andrei* and Alix*
Hamilton, a French nobleman married to an
Austrian princess, whose daughter has married a
Russian noble of Scottish descent and who
thereby is intimately involved in the problems
that lead to the end of the Imperial Family.
Outspoken and ironically critical of the Czar,
the Czarina, and the incredible inefficiency of
Russia, Alain is forgiven much because he is a
foreigner, and he remains a favorite at court. A
great traveller, he is on the scene for much of
the action, and his wry comments, more frank
than those of most of the nobles with whom he
mingles, point out the insanity of much of the
policy.

ALAN-A-DALE (*Bows Against the Barons**), the one
of Robin Hood's outlaws who finds Dickon and
takes him to the outlaw leader, thus being most
instrumental in adding Dickon to the greenwood
band. A minstrel, he is presented as a merry,
happy man, whose music falls pleasantly upon the
ear. He is a master of disguises and dreams up
costumes for the outlaws and schemes for out-
witting the foresters and knights' men. He dies
in the battle against the barons, along with
Friar Tuck, Will Scarlet, and many others of
Robin's men. His most memorable scene is that in
which he sings a song containing instructions
for Dickon while Dickon is being held captive by
the foresters. Since the foresters are French
and not fluent in English, they do not understand what he is singing about. Although the
episode is unlikely, for indeed the foresters
seem to understand spoken English well enough,
the incident is amusing and exciting and is
typical of underdog humor.

ALAN BRECK STEWART (*Kidnapped**), Highland
Jacobite messenger whose boat is wrecked and who

is picked up by the brig *Covenant* off the
northern coast of Scotland.   A small man with a
pockmarked   face   and   a   penchant   for   fancy
clothes,   he is   very touchy   about any   real or
supposed   insult   to   the Highlands   or   to   him
personally and   comes near to dueling   more than
once. Because   David* Balfour   warns him   of the
crew's evil   intent and   aids in his   defense of
the roundhouse, Alan   Breck is protective toward
him and   insists on shepherding him   through the
Highlands,   apparently   not realizing   that   his
presence is a great danger to the boy, who might
travel   without suspicion   if he   were alone.   A
clever manipulator, Alan gets a girl to row them
across   the Firth of   Forth by   playing on   her
sympathy   for supposedly   ill David and   tricks
Uncle*   Ebenezer into   admitting that   he bribed
Captain Hoseason to kidnap his nephew.

ALAN HOBBS (*The Cave**), self-appointed leader of
the   expedition. Wealthy   and   bossy,   Alan   has
been president of the Tomahawk Club, but he is a
poor manager of other people and in a tight spot
loses   his nerve.   When   he kicks   out the   pins
holding the rope   on which two of   the boys have
been lowered down a   long shaft, thereby cutting
them off, he blames   Meaty* Sanders, and when he
drops his father's   expensive searchlight, taken
without permission,   he is   so scared   he breaks
down and   sobs. After   the boys are   finally all
reunited and see the   possible way out by diving
through   a syphon   where   the   river leaves   the
mountain, Alan   is terrified and admits   that he
can't swim,   so they have to   retrace a perilous
and difficult route.

ALASDAIR (*The   Kelpie's   Pearls**),   the   greedy
Scottish trapper and   poacher, who makes trouble
for   Morag* MacLeod   and   the kelpie*. He   tries
repeatedly   to steal   the kelpie's   pearls, and,
when prevented from doing   so, spreads the rumor
that Morag is a   witch. This leads eventually to
the kelpie's   decision to   take Morag   away from
the area. Although a type character, Alasdair is
boldly   and   interestingly   sketched, and   is   a
convincing if unsympathetic figure.

ALASDAIR MACASKILL (*The   Rough Road**), young man
from   Torrin who   moves   into the   Brae to   run

cattle on the forestry land and becomes an
object of hero worship to orphan Jim* Smith.
Alasdair Ban, as he is called by the Skye folk,
is a restless type, having gone to sea and been
a drover before moving into the Brae. He is also
a charmer, able to get his way by flattery and
smiles, and he takes Jim's service as his due,
ordering him about like a hired hand and giving
no thought to why the boy is not in school,
though teaching him a good deal in the process.
His betrayal of Jim when he brings the police is
so crushing that Jim makes no effort in his own
defense, and it is only after some time that
Alasdair begins to wonder about the truth of
Donald Bruce's story that Jim tried to kill his
foster mother. Good hearted but insensitive, he
tries to wipe out the wrong he has done by
finding Jim a good place to live, yet he never
realizes how deeply he has hurt the boy.

ALBERT SANDWICH (*Carrie's War**), fellow evacuee,
four or five years older than Carrie* Willow,
who is also one of the last chosen by foster
parents in the small Welsh mining town. With
typical calm, Albert calls it a cattle auction
and sits reading a book, while Carrie suffers
agonies of embarrassment and uncertainty. Later
she meets Albert at Druid's Bottom, where he has
been sent mostly because he is intellectual and
it has a fine library, but he has been ill
shortly after arrival and has not started school
by Christmas time. Albert wears glasses, and
seems very confident, but underneath he is shy.
He seems unaware of the conventions like the one
that decrees that older boys pay no attention to
girls as young as Carrie or kids like her
brother Nick*, and is just as friendly at school
as at home. Although Carrie is not aware of it,
he is an orphan, and he adopts Hepzibah* Green
and Mister* Johnny Gotobed as his family,
eventually buying Druid's Bottom so that they
will always have a place to live. Because Carrie
has said she will write first, he has refused to
write to her, not knowing that she has been
afraid to write, fearing those she loves have
been killed in the fire for which she believes
she is responsible. In the frame story, he is
expected for a visit that weekend, and it is
implied that, since he has never married and

Carrie is a widow, they will get together again.

ALCOCK, VIVIEN (DOLORES) (1926–   ), born in
Worthing, Sussex; artist and novelist. She
attended Devises High School, Wiltshire, and
Oxford School of Art and Ruskin School of
Drawing and of Fine Arts in Oxford. During
World War II she was an ambulance driver in the
Auxiliary Territorial Service in Belgium, and
later worked as a commercial artist in London.
She is married to novelist Leon Garfield* and
has one daughter. Since 1980 she has published a
number of fantasies for young people, the first
being *The Haunting of Cassie Palmer* (Methuen,
1980; Delacorte, 1982), a story of a phony
medium mother and her genuinely talented spirit-
daughter. This was followed by *The Stonewalkers*
(Methuen, 1980; Delacorte, 1983), about a
collection of statuary that comes alive, *The
Sylvia Game* (Methuen, 1982; Delacorte, 1984),
which has been described as an "uncomfortably
unforgettable nightmare", and *Ghostly Companions* (Methuen, 1984), a collection of ten ghost
stories. Her *Travellers by Night**, (Methuen,
1983; Delacorte), which was named to the *Horn
Book* Fanfare list, however, is realistic
fiction, a novel of circus children who kidnap
an aging elephant to save it from being slaugh-
tered. This, and *The Haunting of Cassie Palmer*
have been adapted for television. A more recent
title is *The Cuckoo Sister* (Methuen, 1985; Delacorte, 1986).

ALDO GAMBADELLO (*The King's Goblet**), short for
Rinaldo, Venetian boy, 15, who tries to hide
his sensitivity by joining the tough gang of
Gino the Fox. At one point he almost joins the
navy with a friend, but instead becomes guide to
a wealthy American boy, Al van Stratten, who has
been lamed by polio. The boys rehabilitate each
other, and Al arranges for Aldo to come with him
to Chicago, but Aldo realizes in time that he
would not fit into Al's wealthy world and stays
in Venice, joining his father at glass blowing.
His enthusiasm and his love of beauty give his
father the needed impetus to return to his
craft, at which he is extraordinarily skilled.

ALESHA HAMILTON (*Three Lives for the Czar**),

Alexander, father of Andrei* and Alix*, who is killed by an assassin bent on destroying the Grand Duc Serge, uncle of the Czar. Because he has attempted to persuade the Czar that the army must be updated, Alesha falls out of favor and is dismissed from his cavalry command when he attempts to avert the massacre of peasants marching to see the Czar. Serge, though an archconservative, tries to counteract this insult by requiring Alesha to accompany him, a post that Alesha accepts though he knows it is tantamount to suicide.

ALEXANDER OLDKNOW (*The Children of Green Knowe**), musical middle child of the three who died in the Great Plague of 1665 and whose spirits live on in the ancient house. Discovered by the organist when he is experimenting with sounds and echoes in Greatchurch, Alexander is impressed into the part of Cupid for the masque to be given for the king. His success is so great that the king sends for him and, when he asks Alexander what he desires for a gift and the boy names a flute, sees that he gets it. A bookish boy, Alexander has planned to go to the University and become a poet. He is not as close to Tolly* as Linnet* Oldknow or as much admired as Toby* Oldknow, but he seems to play through Tolly when the modern boy plays his flute.

ALFRED DANE-LEG (*The Namesake**), so called because his wooden leg is made from a Danish spear. Raised in a monastery, where he was brought as a young child after his leg had been injured and amputated, he acts upon his dreams or visions that he must take a harness and give it to his namesake, Alfred of Wessex, later known as Alfred* the Great. Just as the news comes to Alfred that his brother, King Ethelred, is dead, young Alfred has laid the harness about his shoulders. Later, at King Alfred's suggestion, he is taught to read and becomes the king's secretary.

ALFRED GRAVES (*The Winter of the Birds**), Edward Flack's Uncle Alfie, the not very close brother of Edward's foster-mother, Lily* Flack. An accountant, Alfred has grown weary of his mundane existence and plans to drown himself but

is rescued by Patrick Finn*, the giant of an
Irishman who takes Alfred to Haunton and Lily's
house and whose efforts to help Mr.* Rudge
combat the steel birds inspire the siblings to a
new appreciation of each other. Alfred takes on
some of Finn's confidence and cheery attitude
and begins to see new possibilities in life. He
even begins to dress like Finn, as a hippie. One
of the story's ironies is that Mrs. Flack had
hoped that Alfred would inspire Edward to enter
his profession. Alfred changes predictably and
is never a strong figure in his own right, being
merely the device by which Finn arrives in
Haunton. Alfred and Finn live in the abandoned
church of St. Savior's while they are in
Haunton.

ALFRED OVERS (*A Likely Lad**), officious father
of Willy*, and shopkeeper in Ardwick, a lower-
class section of Manchester. A self-made man,
he is very positive in his opinions about the
uselessness of education, the blight of
aristocracy, the value of being a "thruster" and
working your way up in the world. He is inclined
to lecture his family and his customers and has
grandiose, unrealistic ambitions for his older
son, Willy, without bothering to notice what the
boy is really like. Having married above
himself, he is sometimes uncertain when his wife
feels strongly about something, and he shows his
vulnerability by his strong competition with her
sister's family, who look down upon the Overses.
His purchase of a tandem bicycle is ostensibly
to improve Willy's health, but it is clear that
it is something he covets himself, and when
Willy has little interest, he takes his younger
son, George, on biking expeditions. Although he
often declaims about the parasitic qualities of
nobles, when he gets a letter from Lord de
Staseley that praises Willy and comments on the
value of education, he is remarkably pleased and
does a complete turnabout in his plans for his
son, deciding that Willy should continue in
school and try to go to a university, typically
acting as if this has been his own idea all
along.

ALFRED SMIRK (*Black Beauty**), lazy, foppish,
conceited, deceitful groom, who makes a great

show of taking care of Beauty when his master is around but who doesn't feed or clean him properly. As a result, Beauty gets sore feet from standing in a foul stall. Smirk is a type figure, used to illustrate how horses should not be handled.

ALFRED THE GREAT (*The Namesake**), historical king of Wessex in the years 871-899, the youngest of the four sons of Ethelwulf, who helped his brother, Ethelred, against the invading Danes and became king at Ethelred's death. In the novel he is pictured as a comparatively small man who is highly intelligent, able to devise plans to defeat the much larger Danish forces without engaging directly in battle. He has a recurrent illness that makes him weak and causes great pain, but he wraps himself in a fur robe and continues to work. Though devout, he is not as blindly religious as his brother and saves the day at Ashdown by leading the forces while the king hears mass.

ALICE (*Alice's Adventures in Wonderland**; *Through the Looking-Glass**; *Alice's Adventures under Ground**), direct, forthright, little English Victorian girl of seven and a half, who, in the first and third titles named above, falls asleep and dreams she tumbles down a rabbit hole into Wonderland, where she has unsettling adventures with the zany creatures she meets there. She considers the creatures generally rude, often bites her tongue, sometimes talks up to them, is often nonplussed by them, and finally, at the trial, simply calls them as she sees them--a pack of playing cards--and takes charge. Her many size-changes and eventual growing large and taking over may be a metaphor for growing up and being grown up. In *Looking-Glass*, Alice falls asleep and finds herself in the world behind the mirror over the mantel. There she has similar experiences with odd and eccentric beings in a world laid out like a chessboard, until she crosses to the eighth square and becomes a queen in her own right, probably also a symbol of growing up. Alice is the only character with whom the reader can identify and seems to represent conventional

logic and order in worlds that apparently operate under quite different, seemingly irrational
laws. She is one of the most memorable and
famous characters in English literature.

ALICE BASTABLE (*The Story of the Treasure
Seekers**), ten-year-old, spirited, warmhearted,
lively second daughter among the Bastable children, twin of Noel*, to whom she feels particularly close. She wears her hair short so she
can play boys' parts in plays the children put
on and often comes up with ideas for activities. Though she is assertive and outgoing,
she is also a peacemaker and tries to work out
compromises when the children dispute over something. The episode in which she plays the
greatest role is the one where the children
divine for treasure. She is the leader in this
venture. Alice is a strong figure, likeable and
interesting.

ALICE'S ADVENTURES IN WONDERLAND (Carroll*,
Lewis, ill. Sir John Tenniel, Macmillan, 1865;
Appleton, 1866), episodic dream fantasy, an
often-quoted and much-referred-to masterpiece of
English literature, in which almost all the
action takes place in the dream world of
Wonderland. Alice*, 7, is sitting on a river
bank, reading ("and what is the use of a book...
without pictures or conversations?"), when she
falls asleep, follows an anxious White* Rabbit
down a rabbit hole and finds herself in a land
of strange happenings and odd creatures. She
enters a long, low hall out of which open many
locked doors. One of these, about fifteen inches
high, leads into a very lovely garden, but
Alice is unable to enter the garden either
because she is too large or too small for the
door, depending upon what she has been eating or
drinking. The loose plot revolves around her
frustrated efforts to enter the garden and her
relations with the creatures she meets before
and after she gets there, most of whom treat her
badly. After a period of pondering her identity,
since she changes size so often and abruptly and
is at this point nine feet tall, Alice bursts
into tears, which create a large pool about four
inches deep, then picks up a fan the White
Rabbit drops as he skitters through, and

promptly begins shrinking in size again. Tiny now, she falls into the pool of tears she wept when giant-sized, encounters a Mouse*, a Duck*, a Dodo*, and some other birds and animals paddling about, who shortly assemble on the shore and engage in a "caucus-race" to dry off, which is engineered by the Dodo. This involves much running about every which way, after which the Mouse tells a long, sad tale that is printed in the shape of a mouse's tail. The hall vanishes, and Alice goes to the White Rabbit's house, where she drinks from a bottle she discovers, grows so immense she becomes stuck fast in the house, swallows some little cakes, shrinks, leaves, and finds herself in a wood and in the scary situation of facing a Puppy much larger than she. She next encounters a big, blue Caterpillar* sitting on a mushroom and smoking a long hookah. The Caterpillar rudely engages her in an extensive, circular conversation, which tries her patience sorely, then orders her to recite the poem that begins, "You are old, Father William," to prove her identity, a recitation which turns out to be very different from that intended and further confuses the girl. Alice's size continues to change as she nibbles from one side or the other of the mushroom, and, nine inches high, she visits an ugly Duchess*, who beats her baby and speaks in morals and whose cook casts pans and plates furiously about the place. The Duchess tosses her baby to Alice. To Alice's surprise, it turns into a pig and runs off. Alice next encounters the Cheshire-Cat*, which disappears leaving only his grin. She visits the March* Hare, where she participates in the never-ending tea-party of the Hare and his friends, the Mad* Hatter and the Dormouse*. Offended by their rudeness, she leaves and soon enters the little garden, which she discovers is the croquet-ground of the testy Queen of Hearts. The Queen, her more concil-iatory husband, the King of Hearts, their chil-dren, and numerous courtiers and soldiers are playing-cards engaged in a perpetual game of croquet, using hedgehogs as balls and flamingoes as mallets. The Queen orders everyone who of-fends her executed and takes Alice to the blunt-speaking Gryphon*, who escorts her to the lachrymose Mock* Turtle. The Turtle describes his schooling at the bottom of the sea in a long, nostalgic, pun-filled conversation and with the Gryphon's help demonstrates an energetic dance called the Lobster-Quadrille. The visit concludes when they hear that a trial the Queen has ordered is beginning. The Knave of Hearts is being tried for stealing tarts. Alice, who is called as a witness, can make little sense of the proceedings, feels herself growing to normal size and correspondingly more sure of herself, and, when the Queen imperiously shouts, "Sentence first--verdict afterwards," Alice reacts. She forthrightly declares, "You're nothing but a pack of cards," and the whole assembly flies up at her. She beats them off and awakens back on the river bank, where she relates the story of her dream adventures to her older sister, who then falls asleep and dreams much the same dream. Almost all the characters are humorous caricatures of common types. The only figure with whom the reader can identify is always-rational Alice, who represents conventional logic and order in a world apparently operating under quite different rules and whose carefully focused point of view provides unity for the loosely related episodes. Many critics have seen Alice's experiences in changing size and in coping as a metaphor for growing up, while others have also regarded the book as a shrewd description of what it is like to dream. Both theories are supported by apt psychological touches. Carroll appears also to comment on or poke fun at such aspects of contemporary life as educational practices and curricula, bringing up children, politics, manners, English idiom, cultural practices, traditions, recreations, logic, time--a multiplicity of ideas appears, especially in the conversations, deftly conveyed with wit and whimsey and without explicit statement. Humor arises not only from the zany characters and ridiculous situations but also from puns and wordplay, parody, logical contradiction, literal misunderstanding, taking remarks literally, unexpected gravity, inside jokes, non sequiturs, insults, overstatement, understatement--a clever combination of modes, unlabored, unstrained, superbly controlled. The tea-party, Mock Turtle, Cheshire-Cat, and trial scenes are most often referred to, and many phrases from the exceptionally skillful dialogue have entered common speech, among them, the Queen's favorite "Off with his head!"; the Mock Turtle's "No wise fish would go anywhere without a porpoise"; the Mad Hatter's "If you knew Time as well as I do...you wouldn't talk about wasting *it*. It's *him*"; and the Duchess's "Everything's got a moral, if only you can find it." The first great original novel for children, *Alice* is the measuring rod by which all subsequent fantasies have been judged. Many illustrators have decorated editions of the book, Arthur Rackham, Tasha Tudor, and Michael Hague, to name a few, but Tenniel's drawings are considered classic. Books Too Good; Children's Classics; ChLA Touchstones; Choice; Fanfare.

ALICE'S ADVENTURES UNDER GROUND (Carroll*, Lewis, ill. Lewis Carroll, Macmillan, 1886; Macmillan, 1886), facsimile of the first known manuscript of the fantasy masterpiece of English literature later published as *Alice's Adventures in Wonderland**. Carroll handprinted this version, adorned it with an epigraph page inscribed, "A Christmas Gift to a Dear Child in Memory of a Summer Day," decorated it with thirty-seven of his own drawings, and presented it to Alice Liddell, for whom he originally told the story, on November 26, 1864. The story was subsequently revised, expanded to almost twice the length, and published by Macmillan in book form with illustrations by Sir John Tenniel on July 4, 1865, the anniversary of the first telling to Alice and other friends. The handprinted manuscript was published in 1886 in facsimile form. The ninety-page, handwritten version consists of four long chapters--the beginning, end, and two middle portions of the later, expanded version--and demands comparison with its successor. Alice* falls asleep, tumbles down a rabbit hole, meets a nervous White* Rabbit, changes sizes frequently, enters and gets stuck in the White Rabbit's house, weeps a pool of tears over her predicament, encounters the Mouse*, Dodo*, Lory, and some other creatures in the pool, meets and engages in a circular conversation with a blue Caterpillar*, repeats a poem about Father William and his son

in an unsatisfactory attempt to verify her
identity, enters the croquet-ground garden of
the Queen of Hearts and participates in her zany
game, is taken by the termagent Queen to meet
the brusque Gryphon*, who escorts her to the
nostalgic Mock* Turtle, watches in amazement as
the two demonstrate a wild dance called the
Lobster-Quadrille for her, and attends the trial
of the Knave of Hearts, a mixed-up affair that
she brings to an abrupt conclusion by logically
and boldly declaring it all nonsense and the
participants just a pack of playing-cards.
Significant additions to this manuscript found
in the expanded 1865 version include the episode
about the Mad* Hatter's Tea-Party, involving the
Hatter, March* Hare, and Dormouse*, and the Pig
and Pepper scene, involving the Duchess*, her
cook, and her pig-baby. The trial has been
expanded from two pages into two chapters, the
drying off episode, where in version one the
Dodo takes everyone to a cottage to get dry,
becomes the famous "caucus-race" in the later
version, and the Gryphon-Mock Turtle scene has
been enlarged to admit the charmingly funny,
pun-filled account of the Mock Turtle's
schooling at the bottom of the sea. The Duchess
(merely referred to as the Marchioness in the
earlier account) and the Cheshire-Cat* are
completely new characters, and there are a few
other less important changes in characters and
plot. Some verses have been added and others
altered, most significantly the Mouse's tale,
and dialogue is more extensive in the second
version. Although Carroll's illustrations have
interest because they give insights into how he
visualized characters and situations, they are
stiff, angular, and one-dimensional compared to
Tenniel's. The manuscript version has a certain
charm arising from its provenance, but its main
value is as a historical artifact: it sheds
light on its justly more famous and accomplished
successor. Children's Classics.

ALISON JOHNSTONE (*The Battle of Wednesday
Week*), wife of Murdo*, middle-aged Scotswoman,
who lives near the Lattimer croft, keeps an eye
on the children, helps with housework when
needed, and is a kind of mother advisor. The
Lattimers have known her from early childhood.

In telling Charlotte* Lattimer that Scots clans often quarrel, she gives the girl the idea of how to cope with their tendency to bicker without feeling guilty. Charlotte then suggests that, like the clans, the Lattimers and Grahams may not be able to work out all their problems, but they can still be united under their shared Laird, Robert Graham.

ALIX HAMILTON (*Three Lives for the Czar**), Alexandra, younger sister of Andrei*, who dies at twelve after being injured by an assassin's blast meant for the Russian Chairman of the Council of Ministers, at whose home she is attending a children's party. Bright, frank, lively, and fun-loving, she has been one of the few friends allowed to Olga, daughter of the Czar, and her sparkling, cosmopolitan understanding of the world contrasts to the austere, repressed attitude forced upon the royal children.

ALLAN, MABEL ESTHER (1915–   ), born in Wallasey, Cheshire; author of novels, short stories, historical fiction, romances, Gothic fiction, and autobiography, mostly for children and young adults. The daughter of a merchant, she was educated in private schools. During World War II she served as a warden of a wartime nursery for children aged two to five and then served in the British Women's Land Army. Before 1939 she wrote short stories for younger children and had completed a novel but put it aside because of the war. Since 1948, she has published more than 140 books, mostly for children of different ages and on varied themes, at first for younger readers, in the middle period mostly mysteries and romances for older girls, and then problem stories and stories of the inner-city working class for both older and younger audiences. The latter are represented by the Wood Street series (Methuen), which deals with police encounters and gang rivalries in Liverpool. She has traveled extensively in Great Britain, Europe, and the United States, and most of her books have a travel interest. *Climbing to Danger** (Heinemann, 1969; published in the United States as *Mystery in Wales*, Vanguard, 1970), which was nominated for the Edgar Allan

Poe Award, is typical of her fast-action novels for older readers. It combines mystery and mountain climbing when some young people holiday in the Snowden peaks of northern Wales. *An Island in a Green Sea** (Dent, 1973; Atheneum, 1972) departs from the norm. A *Boston Globe-Horn Book* Honor Book, it is a sensitive and convincing account of two hardscrabble years in the life of the crofter Gilbrides in the Outer Islands of Scotland (Hebrides) in the late 1920s as seen by the daughter, eleven-year-old Mairi. Allan has had a long-standing interest in Scotland, perhaps because her grandparents were from that country, and she taught herself some Gaelic at sixteen. Allan has also written under the pseudonyms Jean Estoril (the series about Drina published mostly by Hodder), Anne Pilgrim (travel novels), and Priscilla Hagon (mystery-suspense novels). For adults, she wrote *Murder at the Flood* (Stanley Paul, 1957), *The Haunted Valley and Other Poems* (privately printed, 1981), and *To Be an Author: An Autobiography* (privately printed, 1982). She has made her home in Cheshire.

ALLEN, ERIC (ERIC ALLEN BALLARD) (1908-1968), born in London; jazz promoter, freelance writer, novelist. He has also used the pseudonymns Paul Dallas and Edwin Harrison. In the 1930s he founded *Hot News*, a jazz magazine published in London, and in the 1940s was a freelance writer in the Middle East. From 1946 to 1948 he wrote in South Africa, and from 1952 to 1959 in Spain, Morocco, and Italy; from 1959 until his death in 1968 he was a freelance writer in London. Besides *The Latchkey Children** (Oxford, 1983), a realistic story of working-class youngsters that was named a Carnegie commended book, he wrote a number of others for children, including *Pepe Moreno* (Faber, 1955; Barnes, 1960), a novel for younger readers set in Spain, which was followed by four sequels, and *The Incredible Adventures of Don Quixote: A Retelling* (Faber, 1958). He also published ten novels for adults.

ALLISON (*The Owl Service**), teenaged daughter of Margaret* Bradley, stepdaughter of Clive* Bradley, stepsister of Roger* Bradley, and the English girl that Welsh Gwyn* is sweet on.

Allison is not a strong figure and is more acted
upon than acting. When she is with Gwyn, she
appears to encourage him, or at least to like
his attention and to understand his aspirations,
but she readily yields to her mother's demands
that she keep away from him. When Gwyn challenges her about this, she defends herself by
saying that she doesn't want to distress her
mother. She loses the reader's sympathy when she
says that she is afraid her mother will punish
her by making her drop choir or will cancel her
tennis club membership. She seems childish,
spoiled, and shallow, brought up to please and
be attractive--a modern-day Blodeuwedd*. The
house in which the story takes place belongs to
her; she inherited it from her deceased father.
Previously it belonged to Bertram, Nancy's*
English lover.

ALMEDINGEN, E. M. (MARTHA EDITH VON ALMEDINGEN)
(1898-1971), born in St. Petersburg, Russia,
died in England, where, in 1932, she had become
a naturalized citizen; novelist, biographer,
scholar of medieval and Russian history and
literature. She was of Danish and Austrian
ancestry on her father's side, though the family
had for generations been part of the Russian
upper class; her mother was the daughter of an
English woman and a wealthy Russian nobleman.
She was educated privately and at Xenia Nobility
College and Petrograd University, and she
lectured in English and medieval history and
literature at the university in 1921-22, until
she was able to leave Russia. Later she
lectured on Russian history and literature at
Oxford University and became a fellow of the
Royal Society of Literature. In 1941 she
received the *Atlantic Review* prize for the
first book of her four-volume autobiography,
Tomorrow Will Come (Lane, 1941; Little, 1941),
which tells of her strange, impoverished
childhood, her wretched life during World War I
and the revolution in Russia, her near
starvation and illness, and her escape from
Russia in 1923. For adults, she wrote some
twenty-seven other works of nonfiction, as well
as seventeen novels, one play, and four books
of verse. For children, she is best known for
her novels based on the lives of her ancestors.

*Young Mark** (Oxford, 1967; Farrar, 1968), which was a *Boston Globe-Horn Book* Honor book and on the Fanfare and *Choice* lists, tells of her great, great-grandfather, an eighteenth-century runaway from the Ukraine, and his rise to the nobility through good fortune and a beautiful singing voice. *Little Katia** (Oxford, 1966; Farrar, 1967), the only book based on her paternal family, is about Catherine von Almedingen, 1829-1893, her great-aunt, who wrote the story of her childhood for Russian youngsters, translated a number of English children's classics, and started a magazine for young people. Others are *Anna* (Oxford, 1972; Farrar, 1972, about her intellectual great-great-grandmother; *Ellen* (Oxford, 1971; Farrar, 1970), about the English girl who married Mark's grandson; and *Fanny* (Oxford, 1970; Farrar, 1970), about Ellen's daughter, the author's aunt. These books give a panoramic view of Russian life, of the great and lavish estates on which the children lived relatively austere lives, of the social distinctions that could be bridged, infrequently, by musical and intellectual gifts. Among her other books for children are several historical novels including *A Candle at Dusk* (Oxford, 1969; Farrar, 1969), set in early eighth-century France; a retelling of the medieval story of Gudrun; a retelling of the *Nibelungenlied*: *The Treasure of Siegfried* (Bodley, 1964; Lippincott, 1965); and a retelling of the legends of the Russian Prince Vladimir, who corresponds to King Arthur, in *The Knights of the Golden Table* (Bodley, 1963; Lippincott, 1964). She also published biographies of Pavlova, Leonardo da Vinci, and Catherine the Great, three books of Russian history, and a collection of Russian fairy tales.

ANADYOMENE (*Emma Tupper's Diary**), two-man submarine invented by the Victorian who was Emma* Tupper's great-grandfather and grandfather to the McAndrew cousins whom she is visiting. The name means "coming up from the waves." She is about fifteen feet long and made of bronze, like a fat sausage with pointed ends and a small conning tower squatting on top. It becomes apparent that she was built to explore the loch for the creatures which call like wildcats and seem to be a species that has survived the ice age in the hot springs at the loch head.

ANDREI HAMILTON (*Three Lives for the Czar**), son of a Russo-Scottish father and a French-Austrian mother, both of the nobility, who sees the great powers move blindly toward conflict in the first years of the twentieth century. An intimate of the Grand Duchess Olga, eldest daughter of the last Czar (Nicholas II), Andrei is a cosmopolitan child and youth, used to traveling to France and Austria and to visiting the rulers of Austria, Russia, and Germany. In a sequel, *My Kingdom for a Grave*, he makes a last, unsuccessful attempt to rescue the Imperial Family from execution.

ANDRES LARRETA (*Talking in Whispers**), son of musician Juan Larreta, who is openly in opposition to the ruling Junta in Chile and who is taken prisoner and disappears after playing at a rally for a democratic candidate. Andres, a musician himself, has good reason to hate the party in power. Juan was picked up earlier and tortured, and Andres's British-born mother was shot for her outspoken views some seven years earlier, when he was nine. Though officially dead in the "accident" in which Juan is captured, Andres survives and feels a duty to try to alert Juan's friends, hoping somehow to apply pressure for his father's release. After being taken prisoner and tortured himself, he sees that it is unlikely that his father has survived, and he takes it as his own responsibility to work against the government. He is much attracted to Isa*, one of the twin performers in the marionette show, who returns his affection.

ANDREW MITCHELL (*Thunder and Lightnings**), city youth who becomes friends with Norfolk schoolboy Victor* Skelton after his family moves to the countryside. Events are seen from Andrew's vantage point, though they are not related by him, and his character is revealed through his developing relationship with Victor. Andrew discovers that, though Victor is considered slow and can barely read and write, he has a passion for airplanes and is very knowledgeable about them. Andrew exhibits a sincere concern for Victor, trying to help his friend with a school project on planes, helping him meet the disappointment of learning that his favorite plane, the Lightning, is to be phased out, and allowing Victor to house his pet guinea pig at Andrew's since Victor's mother, who is house-proud, forbids him to keep a pet. A well-drawn figure, Andrew is a consistently pleasant child, warm and sensitive, never mean or bad-tempered, much like his easygoing parents. With his mother's help, Andrew learns to keep an open mind about Victor's abilities. He is a good foil for Victor.

ANDY (*Sea Change**), first mate of the *Langdale*, a crusty, no-nonsense man who usually talks in a throaty whisper but can bellow to be heard over a high wind when the need arises. A short, barrel-chested man with huge hands, he is compared to an old tortoise for the way he jerks his head forward to peer from his ice-blue eyes. Although he seems unfavorable toward the young apprentice, Cam* Renton, he is really keeping a close eye on his development and guiding him in a quiet way.

ANDY MCANDREW (*Emma Tupper's Diary**), 22, clever, autocratic elder brother in the family where Emma* Tupper spends her holiday. Andy adopts the plan to fake a monster in the loch mostly because he wants to trick the television people whom he blames for the failure of a romance he has had with an assistant producer. Once started on the project, he shows amazing ingenuity and drive. Needled by his younger brother, Roddy*, Andy loses his temper easily. He shows little appreciation of the demands he is making upon Emma, but he forgives her for wrecking the two-man submarine, *Anadyomene**.

ANGEL (*The Seventh Raven**), fiery revolutionary terrorist, only woman of the four people who hold a group hostage in a Kensington church. Able to understand very little English, she is ironically the judge in the mock trial, but at the end she condemns Mrs.* Jacobs and starts to execute her, precipitating the confusion that gives the police a chance to enter. According to

her fellow terrorist, Chip*, Angel is the only
true Mattean of the group; a half-Indian
peasant, she is an unreasoning activist in every
way.

ANGELO GOES TO THE CARNIVAL (Fletcher*, David,
ill. Doritie Kettlewell, Hutchinson, 1956; *CON-
FETTI FOR CORTORELLI*, Pantheon, 1957), realistic
novel for younger children set in the city of
Syracuse in Sicily in the mid-twentieth century.
Angelo, a bright, resourceful ten-year-old, was
abandoned when he was three on the doorstep of
Pippo Bertoni's restaurant. Although they
already have eight children, the Bertonis take
in the orphan, but he is not on an equal footing
with their own offspring. Since he must act as a
slavey in the restaurant, Angelo has not been
sent to school, and he is not taken along when
the family goes to Palermo for a wedding.
Angelo's great desire is to get a costume for
the annual Carnival, which features a Children's
Fancy Dress Parade and which he has never before
attended. The plot concerns his acquisition of a
costume, piece by piece, while the Bertonis are
gone. Through the instigation of elderly Signora
Cortorelli, the next-door hatmaker, who gives
him his meals while the restaurant is closed, he
works for Signora Mortadello at the Hotel
Miramare and is paid with a marvelously
embroidered bandit's shirt, with full sleeves
and frilled wristbands. Corrado, a hotel handyman who tells him stories, gives him a red
leather belt with a silver buckle and silver
studs. In exchange for walking Magda, an
overweight dog, grocer Signor Guidone gives the
boy a white goat's-hair cape. Some ropemakers he
helps give him a length of rope and teach him to
throw the lasso. Two boys, strolling players,
give him a knife and a red-and-white bandana
when he lassos a thief stealing their accordian.
A pastamaker gives him two tickets to the
carnival when Magda drives away goats that are
eating his drying spaghetti. A young fisherman,
Nino, makes him a pair of dark blue canvas
trousers after he swims and recovers the man's
drifting fishing boat. A letter from the
Bertonis, saying that they are selling the
restaurant and moving to Brazil and that he must
join them immediately, almost ruins his plans

for the Carnival, but Signora Cortorelli decides
to take him in permanently. At the Carnival his
costume is given the title, The Spirit of
Sicily, and, since he has no last name, he tells
the judges his name is Cortorelli. When his
costume wins the first prize, a donkey and cart,
he and the hatmaker ride home pelted with
confetti by the cheering children. The story is
simple but pleasant and gives an uncomplicated
picture of life in Sicily. Angelo has an amusing
mixture of determination and naivete. Fanfare.

ANNA (The Other Way Round*; When Hitler Stole
Pink Rabbit*), daughter of a distinguished Jewish anti-Nazi Jewish writer who escapes from
Germany as Hitler comes to power. Through years
in Switzerland and France, Anna adapts quite
easily. In England, she does not fit in well
with the snobbish girls and teachers at Miss
Metcalfe's Boarding School for Girls, where she
is known derogatorily as "that clever little
refugee girl." Later she shows stout spirit to
get a job and support herself at sixteen and to
go to art school at night. As she matures, she
shoulders more and more of the family problems
that her refugee parents are unable to cope
with.

ANNA CLARE (Sisters and Brothers*), jealous sister who finds it difficult to accept Teresa*
Giselli, the adopted cousin now part of their
family. Immature for her age, Anna is given to
stormy rages and then sincere contrition. With
long blond braids and what is described as an
uncomplicated nature, she is good at heart.

ANNA-MARIE MURGATROYD (Midnight Is a Place*),
orphaned daughter of Sir Denzil* Murgatroyd,
about eight years old. She was born in France,
where her father moved after he lost Midnight
Court and Murgatroyd's Carpet, Rug, and Matting
Manufactury to Sir* Randolph Grimsby in a bet.
Anna-Marie is brought to Midnight Court by Mr.*
Julian Oakapple after Denzil's death. Sometimes
babyish and sulky, she sucks her thumb when
tired or frightened. She has, however, true
grit, a strong survival instinct, and a lively
wit. Although she and Lucas* Bell get on poorly
at first, when need afflicts them they work

together to solve their common problems. Anna-Marie comes up with most of the ideas that prove beneficial, for example, selling cigars and moving to the icehouse, and as the story progresses she often seems older than her years. At first she speaks only French and can converse with no one but Lucas and Mr. Oak-apple, but after Midnight Court burns, she quickly picks up English, speaking it fluently and liberally sprinkled with French words and expressions. Anna-Marie is a lively, well-drawn character.

ANNA TATE (*Wall of Words**), 7, pretty, golden-haired, youngest daughter in the Tate family. The scene in which she is introduced is typical: Anna is on the front lawn on a hot July after-noon, "busy being beautiful. More precisely, she was being a golden sun-kissed summer princess." Spoiled and willful (she throws fits to get her way), an exhibitionist, always conscious of appearances, she longs for a threatrical career, to go to a stage school, to be featured in ads on boxes, to be on television, to be on the radio--anywhere where she can have an audience. A clever child, she has a natural sense of how to appeal to viewers, can think on her feet, and is articulate. When interviewed by phone for the Kidsline position, she projects such a lively sense of self that she easily gets the position. What seems at first to be obnox-iousness is really self-confidence, and she very nearly steals the book. She is a round, dynamic figure, who learns that she can't always expect her sisters to defer to her wishes and aspirations.

ANNA VOGEL (*Children of the Book**), respectful, somewhat shy, capable, seventeen-year-old daughter of Herr* Jakob Vogel, a Viennese baker. She gradually assumes more responsibility as the siege wears on, and, when her mother is ill, she runs the house. She also gains in self-con-fidence, and, when soldiers come to arrest her father for not regularly attending the militia meetings, she stands up to them until they listen to the explanation. At first she is adolescently shy about and around Kaspar Haller, her fiance, but by book's end she also shows much social maturation.

ANNE MELTON (*The Watch House**), teenager who gets caught in the conflict between two ghosts who inhabit the old Watch House of the Garmouth Volunteer Life Brigade. Unhappy at leaving her father, Anne sees through her mother's pretense of being ill-used and resents being dumped on Prudie for the summer. Perhaps because she is in a lonely and vulnerable state, she attracts the energy of the two ghosts and becomes involved in trying to rescue the Old Feller, whose spirit is being harassed by that of Major Hague. In the real world Anne is a bright, somewhat insecure girl, easily embarrassed and uncomfortable with new people. With the help of her friends in Garmouth, she is able to stand up to her mother and return to her father, who was so caught up in a business crisis and so used to giving in to his wife's wishes that he hadn't thought of fighting for Anne.

ANNE ROSLEY (*The Member for the Marsh**), David's younger sister, who helps the boys of the Harmonious Mud Stickers investigate the marsh. She is a lively, inquisitive little girl, with many fine features, affectionate, supportive, agreeable, and never silly, and David likes her a lot. Sometimes she talks too much attempting to please him, however, and occasionally she lets out secrets and pesters him. Well-rounded, she appears as more than a typical little sister, with distinct likes and dislikes. She likes to brush David's hair, stands guard as he walks through the marsh to the bus, and is concerned that everyone chew his food sufficiently. She doesn't mind having to pretend to be a dog in order to engage in club activities.

ANNERTON PIT (Dickinson*, Peter, Golancz, 1977; Atlantic/Little, 1977), adventure thriller dealing with terrorists, set in the old coal-mining country north of Newcastle in the 1970s. Although Jake* Bertold, 12, has been blind from birth, he is far from helpless, in many ways being more level-headed and capable than his seventeen-year-old brother, Martin*. He has been particularly close to his Granpa* Uttery, 63, a retired mining engineer who spends his time traveling around investigating and debunking reports of ghosts and other paranormal occurrences. While their parents are away and the regular, carefully written Braille postcards from Granpa have failed to arrive, both boys are concerned, and Martin proposes riding his newly acquired BMW motorcycle from Southampton to Newcastle, where the last card had been posted, to see if they can find him. As they arrive in Newcastle, they are pulled over by police who have been alerted by a friend's mother. Although Martin nearly explodes at this interference, it turns out to be good luck, since Sergeant Abraham, the woman police officer, takes their story of Granpa's disappearance seriously and helps by checking accident reports and hospitals and by finding the boys a room in a church hostel. They get some leads by checking the local newspaper office, as Granpa had done, and from one of these leads they get three others. One is the Annerton Dike Disaster of 1837, in which forty-seven miners were found dead after a rock slip, but were not crushed, burned, starved, nor, evidently, gassed. The single survivor, found wandering the beach in a daze, was assumed to have been washed down the drainage audit, but he never regained his wits to tell his story. The first two of these leads having proved useless, they ride the bike to Annerton Dike and start poking around a small summer hotel, which is supposedly closed. The first man who intercepts them says a group of archeological students are doing research, and he curtly tries to send them off. When they persist, another man takes over, invites them with false cordiality to have tea, questions them closely and then signals to confederates to capture them and lead Jake away to a caravan, a house trailer. There he finds Granpa a prisoner, fastened with a chain and evidently ill from the cold. Because Jake pretends to be far more helpless than he is, they don't chain him, and that night he escapes out a trailer window but is apprehended and knocked out. He comes to in a tunnel of the abandoned mine, and with him are Granpa and Martin. Their captor tells them that they are behind the store of explosives, which is concealed from the outside by a shed that looks as if it is built against the cliff. When

the group leaves, they will rig enough
explosives to blow up if they are touched, and
will radio the police telling them where the
safety switch is located only after their
mission is accomplished. After they are left
alone, Martin is able to tell the other two
about the mission. Their captors are members of
the Green Revolution. Martin is a junior member
of this group which is dedicated to fighting
those who are ruining the environment. Their
captors are the very top, inside, senior group,
which is planning to hijack an oil rig in the
North Sea, employing a helicopter and a very
complex plan. Although one of the "propositions"
to which all members agree is nonviolence, they
have already admitted that maybe this time they
will have to kill. Martin is torn between
loyalties. At first he was willing to join the
conspiracy and had even called Sergeant Abraham
to say they were all right and would be gone a
few more days, so no search would be made for
them, but when he saw one of the men slug Jake,
he protested and landed in the tunnel with his
brother and grandfather. Worried about Granpa,
who seems feverish and is cold despite an air
mattress provided by their captors, Jake begins
to explore the tunnel, hunting for a dryer
place. He discovers a hollow spot in the floor,
with the sound of water beneath. Using
soft-drink cans as trowels, he and Martin dig
away at the floor and finally manage to pry
loose a flagstone, and Martin drops through,
thinking he can follow the stream down to where
it comes out and perhaps climb the cliff to get
help. After some initial exploration, with Jake
leading since he is used to traveling without
sight, they find the way barred by a grill. Jake
realizes that this must be the audit (or water
tunnel) down which the one survivor of the
disaster was washed, and that by following it in
the other direction they will reach the main pit
and be able to escape by the rescue shaft. They
return, pry out some more flagstones, and lower
Granpa on his mattress into the water, then
painfully drag it up the stream to a pool,
beside which is the floor of a regular mine
tunnel. Martin's plan is to go back and rig a
deadfall that will set off the explosives,
thereby aborting the hijacking mission without

abandoning his former comrades to the police.
Before they can get back down the tunnel, they
discover that they are being pursued by two of
the men with flashlights and guns. They fight
them by throwing lumps of coal, but as the men
retreat they threaten to block the tunnel so the
water will pile up and the boys and Granpa will
drown. Leaving Granpa, the boys explore the
tunnel, with Jake leading, until they come to a
shaft. In climbing it, they break the ancient
iron ladder but still manage to reach the top
and, eventually, the rescue shaft. By standing
on Jake's shoulders, Martin is able to get to
the part where he can climb out to the old mine
opening, and, they hope, to safety. Jake turns
back to find Granpa again, but because of the
broken ladder has to take a different route. He
has felt a presence in the mine, a presence that
gets stronger until he literally sees as if he
is the mine itself and is watching a blob that
is Jake crawling down the tunnel, until he comes
to the spot where the miners, men, women, and
children were huddled. Jake then passes out. The
story picks up with the two boys riding south on
the motorcycle, leaving Granpa recovering in a
hospital, where Jake was a patient for three
days. The police, already beginning to zero in
on the Green Revolutionaries, have captured them
all except for one zealot who deliberately dies
by setting off all the explosives in the tunnel.
Martin is miserable because he will have to
testify against the cause he has believed in,
and Jake is left wondering how much of his
experience with the presence in Annerton Pit was
real and how much was hallucination. The entire
story is seen through Jake's perceptions,
although it is not a first-person narrative. The
author skillfully evokes sounds, smells, and
sensitivity to changes in air pressure to make
the reader sense the world as Jake senses it and
to believe in Jake's ability to judge character
and intentions from the way a person talks. The
two boys and Granpa are clearly differentiated
and emerge memorably, and several of the minor
characters are well drawn. The scenes within the
mine are particularly strong. Choice; Fanfare.

ANNE SEKAR (*Hobberdy Dick**), noble-born orphan
girl who is hired by Mrs. Widdison to be her

"gentle-woman," a companion-servant. Because the
Culver and Sekar families have intermarried for
centuries, Anne is entitled to the Culver
treasure, which has been hidden for generations
in the manor. Her patience, efficiency, and
gentle ways endear her to everyone there except
her employer, who is jealous of the attention
Anne gets from the neighboring gentry.

ANNE-SIGRI NYGAARD (*When Jays Fly to Barbmo**),
aunt who has raised Ingeborg* Nygaard and
whose brother, Arne, has scarcely spoken to her
for fourteen years, though the three of them
share an isolated farm. A rigid and conventional
woman with a passion for house cleaning, she was
unable to accept the different ways of Arne's
Lapp wife and, after a disagreement, told the
young woman to go back to her tent if she
didn't like the way the house was run. The
pregnant girl took her at her word, left, and
died in the snow after giving birth to
Ingeborg. Always inflexible, Anne-Sigri feuds
with the hired man, Per, the "Wood* Troll," and
thinks that because he is German-born, he is a
spy. When soldiers come to arrest him as a Jew,
she tries to conceal his presence and later
grieves that she has misjudged him.

ANN RIDLEY (*The Dark Behind the Curtain**),
classmate of Colin Jackus* and Colin Marshall*
at Mr.* Garner's school. She plays the part of
the baker woman in the class play, *Sweeney
Todd, the Demon Barber of Fleet Street*. She is
heavy and plain, but she is intelligent. At
first she is attracted to Marshall and doesn't
think much of Jackus, but later she changes her
mind when she realizes Marshall is really disagreeable, mean, and manipulative. She is the
first to figure out that the footprints belong
to mistreated Victorian children.

ANN TARRANT (*The Summer People**), Philip*
Martin's summer romantic interest, daughter of
the receptionist at the hotel in Linley Bottom.
She is plain, small of build, a little shy, and
easily bullied. She initiates the game of
"playing house" to ease her self-consciousness,
and Philip soon falls in with the pretense. She
has been in a sanitorium, and word is out in the

village that she suffers from TB, a feared
scourge at the time. Phil is sure, however, that
she is telling the truth about having pleurisy
instead. Both realize from the onset that they
are too young for serious love, and they know
that Phil's family would never allow them to
marry because Ann is considered working class.
She is the book's best-drawn and most memorable
character.

ANTHEA (*Five Children and It**), sometimes play-
fully called Panther and called Panty by Lamb,
second eldest of the five children and the elder
daughter of the family. Anthea is direct and
candid, can be stubborn, is usually patient and
thoughtful, and is something of a "general,"
like her mother. She is responsible for the wish
that results in several adventures, among them,
episodes where she asks that the children be
made beautiful and be given wings. She also
concludes the adventures by bargaining with the
Psammead* to set things right. In the episode
with the Red Indians, she bravely gets Martha
the nurse and Lamb to safety and then, as Black
Panther, becomes the children's leader in
negotiating with the Indians. Anthea is the most
clearly drawn of the four older children.

ANTHONY HUNTERLY (*The Far-Distant Oxus**), a
middle child in age. Along with Peter* Cleverton
he is one of the six children who launch an
"expeditionary force" down the Oxus to the sea.
Except that he is described as having a superior
knowledge of animals and hence is best with them
of the six and can identify birds by their
songs, he is indistinguishable from the other
boys.

ANTONIUS (*The Dancing Bear**), Slav who inhabits
the tower of the ancient Roman garrison and
upholds the values and traditions of Rome,
claiming to be descended from the last of the
great emperors of old Rome. Physically he is
ugly--squat, square-headed, grizzled--but he
wears a pure white toga edged with a triple line
of purple, and he rules the Slavic village in a
lordly manner. He is apparently attracted to
Silvester because the boy can read and speak
Latin and because he can trust him to arrange

the proper funeral pyre when he dies, but after Antonius's death it becomes apparent that part of the attraction is that he, too, was a slave--or at least the descendant of a Greek slave and a line of Slavic women, and not a Roman at all. This explains his preoccupation with slaves and slavery whenever he drinks too much. He is a character about whom a reader feels ambivalent: too imperious and autocratic to elicit sympathy but nonetheless instrumental in Silvester's growth from a slave to an independent man.

AQUARIUS (Mark*, Jan, Kestrel, 1982; Atheneum, 1984), fantasy novel set in a mythical world, where the people believe in magic and the king is the ritual scapegoat. In childhood, Viner is washed downriver along with his mother by a torrential rain, is rescued by villagers, whom he calls Webfeet, and is despised and abused by them and his mother for his dowsing ability, a talent obviously unnecessary in a country where it always rains. At sixteen, fed up with their cruelty, he runs Over the Top and finds himself in rocky, desert country, where he is taken captive by four cutthroats, Cleaver, Anvil, Catskin, and Hern, who ironically are nobles from the King's court out looking for the source of their dried-up river. When they learn of his power to locate water, which they misunderstand as the ability to bring water, they take him back with them to the palace, intending to use him to their own political advantage. The palace is a strange, tumble-down, immense near-ruin, a warren of decrepit rooms fronted by a vast stone facade and featuring a large open terrace. Viner views the terrace in astonishment, as the silver-garbed King dances there, performing a strangely graceful yet feverishly labored rain dance, assisted by his seven-months pregnant queen. Viner learns that King Morning* Light is a figurehead ruler who really has only two main functions: to bring rain and to father a daughter to be the next queen and wife of the next king and rain-bringer. Since Morning Light has achieved neither of these objectives, he is viewed with derision, and his wife, Queen Mere, openly despises him. Viner's ability to locate water soon brings him power and prestige among these people, whom the prolonged drought has brought close to famine. Viner enjoys the position of respect he has yearned for and his self-esteem rises considerably. But he finds the rampant intrigue at the court and the open ridicule disquieting, at the least, and, when the Queen bears a daughter, finds that he fears for the safety of the King whom he now values as a friend. When the King's frenzied efforts to bring rain continue to come to nothing and the Queen runs off, Viner realizes that he himself could easily become the next king. He also discovers that he has no ambition for it, and he, Cleaver, and Hern persuade Morning Light to run away with them. They take the baby princess, Dark Cloud, along. Not wishing to spend his life on the run and realizing that Morning Light is a bringer of sun, not rain, Viner decides to go back to the Webfeet. He takes Morning Light captive, gives the courtiers the slip, and undertakes the long, hard, problem-riddled journey over the desert, rocks, and mountains back to his former country. The three arrive in the land of the Webfeet during a torrential storm. As they cross the swollen river, the bridge collapses, and Morning Light, Dark Cloud, and Viner are fished out of the river by villagers, an ironic repeat of Viner's original entry into the village. Viner convinces the people that Morning Light can stop the rain, convinces Morning Light he is a sun dancer, not a rain bringer, and persuades him to dance lest he lose his daughter to the villagers. The book concludes with Morning Light dancing to the rhythm of the villagers' clapping. The rain clouds are fleeing, the sky is lightening, and the reader is left with the expectation that Morning Light will become their king and that Viner will enjoy a well-deserved position of respect among these people. The book, however, paints a bleak picture of unrelieved societal corruption on all levels, and thus the conclusion may not be as rosy as it seems. The story is slow in starting, overly extended, and held up by long conversations that contribute little but intrigue. The courtiers are not sufficiently developed to be interesting as individuals, the voice is toneless, and the effect is as though the author were holding the reader at arm's length. Viner's struggle is less moral than pragmatic, and, if the reader is sympathetic with any character, it is probably the feckless Morning Light. The desert people's ways--choosing names for the babies, selecting a king in this essentially matriarchal society, the rain dance, the social patterns--and Viner's dowsing procedures are described in sufficient detail to be credible and interesting. Young Observer.

ARABEL'S RAVEN (Aiken*, Joan, ill. Quentin Blake, BBC, 1972; Doubleday, 1974), three frolicsome fantasy episodes set in Rumbury Town, London, in the 1960s, involving a family who acquires a clever and mischievous raven. One stormy night in March, Ebenezer Jones, taxi driver, respectable and conscientious to a fault, drives through the wild and sinister district of Rumbury Waste, rescues a raven that has been struck by a motorcycle, and carries it home to feed and comfort. His daughter, Arabel, a precocious, strong-willed preschooler, takes a fancy to the creature, which recovers quickly and soon reveals a cheeky nature. She claims him for her own, names him Mortimer, and pulls him about house and yard in her little red wagon. Before long, Mortimer's insatiable curiosity, collecting tendencies, and voracious appetite have dramatically altered the Jones's way of life, in particular, his propensity for answering the telephone with a loud, sharp "Nevermore!" and his habit of devouring staircases. Mrs. Jones loses her job at the Round and Round record shop because he chews up the stairway there, but this idiosyncrasy proves beneficial later when he devours the escalators and the lift at the Rumbury Tube Station, enabling the police to capture the Cash-and-Carat boys, a duo of local jewelry thieves and coincidentally the owners of the motorcycle that had nicked him on the Waste. Although his second and third adventures are even more filled with action and incident, they seem less inventive and are more cartoon-like. When Arabel goes roller-skating with bossy Auntie Brenda and her three disagreeable daughters, Mortimer creates havoc by skating through the car park, among other activities, and later, in Auntie Brenda's

house, hides in the chimney, making it
necessary to summon a sweep. He escapes, however, leaving "a scene of such blackness and
muddle behind him that I do not really think it
would be worth trying to describe it."
Attempting to catch Mortimer, Arabel takes a
chill and must be hospitalized. It falls to Mr.
Jones to locate the bird and bring him to the
hospital to comfort his despairing daughter. In
the final episode, Mrs. Jones's tendency to lose
her head creates a comedy of errors. After
Mortimer breaks all the bottles of milk in the
house, Arabel persuades her young, guitar-
playing baby-sitter, Chris Cross, to take her
and Mortimer to the High Street milk machine for
more. When Mrs. Jones calls home but receives
no answer, she comes home, sees broken glass
and blood, imagines the worst—maybe deadly gas
or an escaped black mamba—and soon arouses
friends, neighbors, and authorities. Rumors
escalate, and the chase is on. The zaniness that
ensues concludes with the children and the raven
foiling two thugs who mistake Mortimer for a
valuable mynah. Aiken romps through Mortimer's
escapades with tongue in cheek, piling hilarity
upon hilarity. Humor also comes from the funny
names and consistently interesting language
(the lift cable has been "haggled through";
old, irresponsible Mr. Gumbrell, the ticket
clerk at the tube station, complains that
someone has taken his "escatailors"), and wordplay is extensive (Mortimer is "flyjacked" by
jewel robbers, the Cash-and-Carat boys). Behind
the tomfoolery, however, appears some subtle
social commentary. Quentin Blake's scrappy
cartoons add to the silliness. Further adventures appear in *Arabel and Mortimer* and other
books in the series. Choice.

ARABIS DANDO (*The Whispering Mountain**), girl of
perhaps fourteen, who is Owen Hughes's friend
and the motherless daughter of old Tom* Dando.
Her character as presented exaggerates the stock
heroine of adventure. Arabis is quick-thinking,
resourceful, pretty, understanding, warm-
hearted, and impulsive. She is a skilled herbal-
ist, can play the lute and run like a deer, and
owns a falcon, Hawc, which perches on her
lustrous dark knob of piled-up hair and affects

the story occasionally. Forthright and candid,
Arabis speaks with fluency and an Irish brogue,
generously sprinkling her astute comments with
Irish terms. Her mother was a gypsy who came
from the island of Melita and who died through
the cruel action of Lord* Malyn, upon whom she
placed a curse in return.

ARAVIS (*The Horse and His Boy**), brave and
assertive girl of twelve or fourteen whom
Shasta* encounters while he is running away to
Narnia* and who joins him in his flight. She is
the daughter of a Calormene noble who to advance
his political interests has betrothed her to an
elderly noble and advisor of the Tisroc of
Calormen. To avoid the marriage, she runs away
on Hwin*, a talking Narnian mare. At first,
Aravis is haughty and scornful of Shasta, but
her attitude toward him changes, in particular
after he risks his life to rescue her from the
attacking lion they both later learn is Aslan*.
Aslan wounds her to punish her for leaving her
maidservant behind to take the blame for her
flight. At the end of the book, the reader is
informed that she settles at the Anvard court
and later marries Shasta, who has been revealed
as Crown Prince Cor of Archenland. She is
predictably a more attractive figure at the end
of the novel than she is at the beginning.

ARCHER (*Archer's Goon**), eldest of the seven
wizards who control the city. He "farms" power
and banks. He lives in a vast room full of
fantastic technological wonders. A real megalo-
maniac, he wants to farm the world, but in
appearance he is very attractive, with dark hair
and luminous blue eyes, and he is able to look
innocent and honest. He does seem to have a
genuine attraction to Fifi.

ARCHER'S GOON (Jones*, Diana Wynne, Methuen,
1984), fantasy of a seemingly ordinary family
caught up in the machinations and rivalries of
seven wizards who control their city. Howard*
Sykes, 13, comes home to find a huge,
stupid-looking man sitting in the kitchen,
terrorizing Fifi, the college girl who lives in
to help, by his very presence. He also
terrorizes Howard's little sister, highly

assertive and spoiled Awful* (Anthea), 8, by
throwing his knife at her, but he explains
agreeably that he was sent by Archer* because
Howard's father, Quentin*, owes "2,000" for
protection. To get him out of the kitchen before
his mother comes home, Howard proposes that they
go to the Polytechnic, where his father teaches,
and they all trek off, with the Goon*, as they
all soon call him, firmly holding Awful by the
hand. There they interrupt Quentin's literary
criticism class, the first of many such scenes
of which Howard and the Goon are a part. It
turns out that what the Goon has come to collect
is 2,000 words, which Quentin has been sending
quarterly to a Mr. Mountjoy for the past
thirteen years and the last installment of which
seems to have gone astray. Quentin quickly types
out a copy of what he sent earlier, as nearly as
he can remember, and the Goon goes away happy,
but the next day he is waiting as Howard gets
out of school, saying that the words are no
good: they have to be new each time, not
something Quentin has written before. To keep
him away from the house and his strong-willed
but sensitive mother, Catriona, who is a music
teacher, Howard persuades the Goon to take him
to see Mr. Mountjoy. After tramping through and
disrupting numerous offices in city hall, they
find Mountjoy, who disclaims any knowledge of
who gets the words, which he mails to a box
number, except that it is one of the seven
wizards who control the city. The Goon returns
to the Sykes house, so infuriating Quentin that
he refuses to type any more words. In the weeks
that follow, the house is periodically without
heat and electricity, since Archer, who controls
or "farms" power, shuts it off erratically. They
are also tormented by music that comes
simultaneously from the various instruments
around the house, from the television, and from
a series of bands that parade down their street,
since Torquil*, who farms music, also wants the
words. The street itself is continually torn up
with jack hammers by workmen controlled by
Hathaway*, who farms transport as well as
records and archives. The Goon continues to live
with the Sykes family, often escorting Howard
and Awful to school to protect them from a gang
of young hoodlums sent by Shine*, who farms

crime. In a series of expeditions, mostly
hilarious but sometimes frightening, Howard goes
to see Dillian*, a beautiful blond female wizard
who lives in a palacial house and farms law and
order; Archer, whom they reach through the bank
and who presides over a vast room full of
advanced technology; Hathaway, who lives in the
past (in the sixteenth century), and whom they
reach through the museum; and Shine, a vast
female wizard clad all in black leather, from
whom Howard and Awful are saved by the Goon when
she sets her young hoods on them. Torquil comes
himself, interrupting an orchestra practice
directed by Catriona and leading a cathedral
choir and a troupe of disco dancers. Though
none of them knows exactly how the words work,
and all claim not to have been the recipients of
the words for the past thirteen years, they all
say that somehow the words have kept them
confined to the city for that period, making it
impossible for them to travel or to take over a
larger territory. Archer, in particular, wants
to take over the world. Each of them wants
Quentin to write the words for him, and Quentin
gets more and more stubborn, now feeling it is a
matter of principle to refuse. He gets a bill
for thirteen years of back taxes, which he had
thought he was paying with the quarterly words.
In the meantime, Fifi has fallen madly in love
with Archer, the Goon has fallen in love with
Fifi, and Howard is upset by having learned from
Hathaway that he was adopted, though Awful is
pleased to learn that she is a descendant of
Hathaway through both Quentin and Catriona.
When they can no longer buy food (Torquil also
farms shops) and are running out of friends to
borrow from, Quentin and Howard, with Awful
tagging along as usual, persuade the Goon to
take them to Erskine, who farms drains, and whom
they approach through a sewage tunnel. There
they realize, with a shock, that the Goon is
Erskine. He shuts them into a hole amid a pile
of rubble, the dungeon of an ancient castle,
from which they are saved by Ginger Hind, the
leader of the young hoods, who has had a
falling-out with Shine and who has come to
admire Howard while trailing him for weeks.
After a wild chase by a big sewage tanker and
two rubbish trucks, Howard is rescued by a bus

sent by Hathaway, a shoot-out sent by Shine, a
musical diversion from Torquil, and police cars
sent by Dillian. Realizing that the real
receiver of the words must be Venturus, the
youngest of the wizards, who farms schools and
lives in the future, Howard sets out to find him
by going to the partly constructed building on
the Polytechnic campus, where, as he pushes his
way in, the structure shapes into a finished
Greek-type edifice around him, and he grows and
ages. When the Goon appears, having followed
him, Howard realizes with a shock that he,
himself, is Venturus. When he sees the marvelous
space vehicle in the building, he begins to
remember that his parents enjoined all the
others, with powerful magic, not to leave the
baby, Venturus, until he came into his powers,
after the age of thirteen, and that he had
arranged to live in the future so that he would
have the technology to build his dream spaceship
Then, when he came back into the present, he
lost his thirteen years and turned into a baby
that was found and adopted by Quentin and
Catriona, thereby holding his siblings in the
city for thirteen years. He has, in fact, done
this twice, to have time to perfect the
spaceship, so that they have lived the same
thirteen years twice. To try to undo some of the
harm he has caused and also to keep Archer,
Dillian, or Shine from taking over the world, or
a large part of it, he contrives with the other
wizards to lure these eldest three, along with
Fifi and two of Shine's guards, into his
spaceship, which he has programmed to take off
for a distant star and to be unable to return.
This leaves Erskine free to travel as he wishes,
Torquil to make friends again with Hathaway and
possibly to live in the past with him, and
Hathaway to carry on his happy family life
without having to worry about controlling
transport. Howard is determined to grow up into
a much better Venturus than he was before and to
see that Awful grows up with decent principles,
too. The story is so complex and the denouement
so frenzied that it takes a careful second
reading to realize that all the ends are tied up
neatly, including allowing Quentin to think his
words have actually been powerful rather than a
red herring, and providing him money for his

back taxes. Individual scenes are vividly
realized, and if the total is far from
believable, characters are full of interest and
the whole is so funny and spirited that one can
hardly expect it to be plausible. Boston Globe
Honor.

ARCHIE MEIKLE (*The Third Eye*), blacksmith in
the village near Ballinford Hall, whose smithy
is the center of village life. There Jinty
learns about what is going on in the village
and, in particular, learns from Archie about the
Ballinford doom. Archie is a squat, gnome-like
man, dark and swarthy, with great shoulders and
muscled arms. His son, Tom, is tall and blond
like a Viking, Jinty thinks, strikingly different in appearance from his father but also
strong in character. Archie is a well-rounded
figure, serious and laughing, capable and commanding, often intrusive, inquisitive, the self-
appointed and accepted leader-figure in the
village. He is the Earl's best friend, and the
two often converse about old times and make
plans for the present together. Archie
influences the action on many occasions, the
most notable being when he informs Jinty and the
girls that Mam's* dead soldier lover, Roger
Belaney, was distantly related to the Earl.
When Belaney was killed in the war, his family
turned their backs on Mam, and the Earl hired
Dad, who had in the meantime married Mam and
given a loving home to Meg* Morrison, who was
the dead man's daughter. Archie helps Jinty to
see the Earl as something more than a robber
baron, as a man, father, and benevolent spirit
in the village.

ARIADNE (*The Dancing Bear*), called Addie by
Silvester, only daughter of Lord Celsus, Count
of the Outfields, one of the most wealthy and
prominent of the nobles of Byzantium. In the
city she is a tense, doll-like figure, stammer-
ing badly except with Silvester* (Sillo, as she
calls him), the slave whose mother nursed them
both. She does not protest her betrothal to a
young noble of another prominent family, but she
dreads marriage, which will make her life even
more restricted than that of a slave. In the
Huns' camp she has not been mistreated sexually,

since the Kutrigurs scorn Greek women, and when she becomes the Khan's slave she is happy to be assigned duties as a herd girl, skillfully riding their wild horses. When Silvester gets her back to the Danube and explains that he dare not go back to the city with her because he is on the emperor's wanted lists, she refuses to go back herself to claim her great inheritance and orders him to take her to the tower of Antonius*. She is completely happy in her new life.

ARMSTRONG, RICHARD (1903–   ), born in Northumberland; laborer, sailor, novelist. The son of a blacksmith and a miner's daughter, he was educated at Walbottle Primary School and went to work in the steel plant at Tyneside at thirteen, where he was successively errand boy, laborer, greaser, and crane driver. From 1920 to 1937 he was a sailor and radio operator in the Merchant Navy, and from 1937 to 1954 he held an assortment of jobs, including typist, secretary, architect's assistant, and undertaker's laborer. Since 1956 he has been a full-time writer. For adults, he has written four novels and a biography of Grace Darling. For children, he has published more than twenty novels, a three-volume history of seafaring, and two other books of nonfiction. His early novels, about boys in heavy industry, for instance, *Sabotage at the Forge* (Dent, 1946) and *The Whinstone Drift* (Dent, 1951), were praised for showing a complete knowledge of scene. Most of his other novels are sea stories, including *Sea Change** (Dent, 1948; Bentley, 1950), which won the Carnegie Award. He also won the New York *Herald Tribune* Festival Award in 1956 for *Danger Rock* (Dent, 1955; as *Cold Hazard*, Houghton, 1956). His *The Mutineers* (Dent, 1968; McKay, 1968) is similar to Golding's *Lord of the Flies* in plot, but ends on an optimistic rather than pessimistic note. A number of his books have been translated in Japan, Germany, Brazil, Denmark, and Poland.

ARNOLD LUCKETT (*The Ghost of Thomas Kempe**), youth who came to visit his Aunt Lucy Spence in East End Cottage, Ledsham, in the mid-1800s, received notes from Thomas Kempe in antique

script, and became the object of pranks as does
James* Harrison 100 years later. The rector
lured Thomas into a bottle, which was then put
in a crevice below the window in the attic
bedroom that later becomes James's room. In
James's time, a workman renovating the room
smashes the bottle, releasing Thomas, who begins
to plague James as he did Arnold. James finds
out about Arnold in a small leather-bound diary
written by Arnold's Aunt Lucy which he discovers
in the rubbish heap behind the house. Since
Arnold seems to be a boy much like himself,
James carries him around in his head as a kind
of imaginary play- and soulmate, making up conversations and activities with his counterpart
of the mid-nineteenth century. Discovering that
Arnold had been able to exorcise Thomas encourages James to believe that Thomas can again
be gotten rid of if he just persists in his
attempts. Arnold later grew up to become an
important man in Ledsham; James finds his picture in a school storeroom. James's relationship
with Arnold supports the theme that past and
present are inseparably linked.

ARRIETTY CLOCK (*The Borrowers**; *The Borrowers*
*Afield**; *The Borrowers Afloat**; *The Borrowers*
*Aloft**; *The Borrowers Avenged**), spirited,
thirteen-year-old daughter and only child of
Pod* and Homily* Clock, a family of pencil-sized
people called Borrowers, and heroine of a highly
regarded series of fantasies. In *The Borrow-*
ers, she prefers emigration to continuing to
live alone away from others of their kind and in
constant fear of being "seen" by humans. Her
sense of adventure and need to take control of
her life motivate her to make friends with the
boy*. This friendship leads to Mrs.* Driver discovering the Borrowers, their subsequent emigration to avoid extermination, and all the
other adventures. She later makes friends with
Miss* Menzies, with similar disastrous results.
She enjoys the outdoors and is glad when the
family decides to leave Uncle* Hendreary's
family in *Afloat*, because she has felt penned
up in their upstairs apartment in Tom*
Goodenough's grandpa's cottage, and she likes
the freedom of the trips on the river. Her
romantic attraction to Spiller*, which never

goes anywhere, adds a dimension to her character, as does her tender relationship with
little Timmus in *Avenged* (he is called Timmis
in *Afloat*), Aunt* Lupy's youngest son. Arrietty
is a well-drawn, engaging character, who exemplifies the continuing theme that survival and a
good life depend upon initiative and personal
responsibility.

ARTHUR BARNARD (*The Devil's Children**), the
Master in the village of Felpham. A huge fellow
who used to be a cowman, he drove out a band of
ruffians who were terrorizing the villagers and
then set himself up as a sort of feudal baron,
acting as judge of the court and doling out jobs
and privileges to consolidate his power. He sees
the advantage of dealing with the Sikhs; he does
not believe that they are supernatural beings,
as most of the superstitious villagers do, but
he also sees that his power will be dissipated
if the other villagers contact the Sikhs
individually, so he lets them keep their
terrified notions. When the mounted young
hoodlums come to Felpham, the other village
people expect him to take care of them as he did
the earlier ruffians, but the newcomers spear
him through, cut off his head, and mount it on a
pole as a lesson to the rest of the villagers.

ARTHUR PRUDIE (*The Watch House**), old caretaker
of the Garmouth Volunteer Life Brigade Watch
House, who lives with his sister in the Brigade
Cottage. A lifelong bachelor, he lets himself be
bullied in some small things by his sister, but
maintains a fierce independence in others,
particularly about the Watch House collection of
miscellanea and artifacts, much of which is junk
but which contains some interesting items.
Partly to be one up on his sister in the
continual game of wills they play, he welcomes
Anne* Melton's interest in the collection and
allows her to dust it and write a guide book for
it. He supplements his navy pension by helping
at the fish market in exchange for the freshest
of the fish, which he barters with neighbors and
nearby farmers for groceries and other
necessities and delivers in a two-wheeled cart
pulled by a bad-tempered Galloway pony. When the
pony is killed, Timmo* Jones goes to a good deal

of trouble and expense to make another one available in a way that will be affordable to Arthur, since a gift would hurt the old man's pride. Arthur treats the Old Feller (the ghost of the Watch House) indulgently, as one might treat a slightly naughty child. A sharp judge of people, he clearly dislikes Anne's mother, but he enjoys Timmo, partly because of the boy's intense interest in the Watch House.

ARTHUR RAMSGILL (*The Grange at High Force**), son of a sheep farmer, the wittiest of the three good friends who become involved in the mystery of the missing statue. Largest and perhaps oldest of the three, he was formerly the head choir boy but as he aged his voice broke. Though a joker and happy-go-lucky about school, he is all business and responsibility when his father's sheep need to be rescued in the storm. He talks with a mixture of slang and dialect which is much more pronounced than that of the other boys.

ARTHY ROLLER (*The Piemakers**), proud piemaker of Danby Dale in preindustrial England, father of Gravella* Roller and husband of Jem*. Husky and red-haired, he is a steady, hardworking man who is very proud of his ability to produce savory, finely textured, beautifully decorated meat pies. He considers himself an artist in pie crust and often says that piemaking is in the family blood and that piemakers in his family probably go all the way back to Adam and Eve. His favorite recreation is reading meat pie recipes, which, he says, are "like poems." Though his failure with the King's pie and his arson weigh on his mind, his spirits lift at the prospect of winning the King's pie contest, and he sets to with a will, confident that with his own Standard Meat Recipe he will triumph. Although Jem suspects that his brother, Crispin, and Crispin's wife, Essie, spy on them and would do anything to cause Arthy to fail, Arthy keeps an open mind and acts as peacemaker. He is a well-drawn figure, comic yet too well rounded for caricature.

ASHLEY, BERNARD (1935–   ), born in London; teacher and writer of children's fiction re-

volving around social and psychological prob-
lems. He was educated at Roan School in
Blackheath, London, and Sir Joseph Wlliamson's
School in Rochester, Kent, and went from there
to Trent Park College of Education and Cambridge
Institute of Education. He also served in the
Royal Air Force from 1953-1955. He has held
teaching positions in Kent, Hertfordshire, and
London, and since 1977 has served as head
teacher at Charlton Manor Junior School in
London. He and his wife and three sons have made
their home in London. His experiences in teaching and working with children and families in an
urban environment have provided the subjects and
settings for his novels. They reflect the
tensions of the working class under stress, and
his characters confront internal and external
conflicts resulting from interpersonal relationships, racial prejudices, emotional illness, gangs, irresponsible parents, alcoholism,
and physical abuse. *The Trouble with Donovan
Croft** (Oxford, 1974), about a ten-year-old
black Jamaican boy's problems when he goes to
live with a white foster family, received the
Other Award, and *A Kind of Wild Justice** (Oxford, 1978; Phillips, 1979), about a street-wise
boy whose mother abandons him after his father
gets picked up for theft, was commended for the
Carnegie Award. Of his some dozen and a half
other books, *Terry on the Fence* (Oxford, 1975;
Phillips, 1977) and *Break in the Sun* (Oxford,
1980; Phillips, 1980) are for older children,
Linda's Lie (MacRae, 1982) and a collection of
short stories, *I'm Trying to Tell You* (Kestrel, 1981) are for younger children; and *The
Men and the Boats: Britain's Life-Boat Service*
(Allman, 1968) and *Weather Men* (Allman, 1970)
are nonfiction. He has also written several
readers.

ASK ME NO QUESTIONS (Schlee*, Ann, Macmillan,
1976; Holt, 1982), historical novel based on a
real case of large-scale child abuse in the
village of Tooting in 1849. Because cholera has
struck the London parish of their minister
father, Laura* and her younger brother, Barty*,
are sent to stay with their mother's sister,
Aunt* Bolinger, in Tooting, a village in the
countryside. From an upstairs storeroom window,

Laura sees over the high fence into a large,
bare yard next door and watches a poorly clad
child jumping rope. Later she and Barty,
visiting a new calf, are horrified to see the
girl and two boys snatching food from the pigs'
trough. Although Aunt Bolinger forbids the
children to speak of the house next door, they
gradually learn that it is Mr. Drouet's school
for children from the workhouses. Laura
accompanies her aunt to the parsonage where the
ladies are sewing for charity, but when she
innocently asks whether it is for Mr. Drouet's
children, the women are shocked. She does meet
one friend, the schoolmistress, Miss* Margaret
Roylance, who suggests that the Ladies Committee
at least make some contact with Mr. Drouet, so
they may see whether there is any truth in the
rumors of mistreatment. This suggestion is met
with scorn and a barely veiled threat that Miss
Roylance will lose her position if she persists.
Both Barty and Laura see the children in the
barn again and soon know them as Lizzie* Brown,
Jamie* Andrews, 6, and his protective older
brother, Will*. Barty takes three eggs from the
hen house for them, and this starts a pattern in
which Laura saves and even steals food every day
for them, all the while hating the obligation
she has somehow contracted. She sees hope in her
Cousin* Henry Bolinger, a young man home from
studying at Oxford to be a minister. She thinks
she can tell him and be free from the problem,
which is tormenting her conscience. Before the
opportunity arises, she hears him trying to
dissuade Miss Roylance from calling on Mrs.
Drouet, as she has suggested, and, since he is
obviously in love with the schoolmistress,
promising that he will look into the situation
at the asylum. When on Christmas Eve Laura sees
him going to Mr. Drouet's house, she is greatly
relieved, not knowing that he is actually going
as an agent for his father, who wants to get the
contract for selling potatoes and cabbages.
Realizing that nothing will be done for the
children until after Christmas, Laura takes the
splendid meat pie that her mother has sent in a
gift hamper and gives it to the children in the
barn, though she finds Lizzie too ill to enjoy
it. The next day her aunt accuses her of
thievery in front of guests, including Miss

Roylance and the kindly, senile wife of the
parson, and she runs crying from the room.
Seeking refuge in the barn, she finds Lizzie
there dead, and comes screaming for Cousin
Henry. Henry carries the body to Drouet's and
discovers the extent of the horror: dozens of
children dying of cholera, starving, and lying
three to a filthy bed. Laura's father, summoned
hastily, takes Laura and Barty home, but first
they catch a glimpse of Jamie and Will being
loaded with other children in a bus to go to the
hospital. They do not know that Jamie dies and
is chosen as the victim for whose death Drouet
is tried. Drouet is acquitted, however, because
it cannot be proved that the cholera is the
result of his mistreatment. Laura seems
strangely passive, but underneath she is
troubled by the memory of Lizzie, and at a more
conscious level she is upset at having lied and
stolen. When her father asks her why she didn't
tell anyone of the abuse she knew about at
Drouet's, her answer is simple and devastating:
"There was no one to tell." The point of view is
almost consistently Laura's, with the resulting
irony of a terrible situation seen through
innocent eyes while all the adults are deliberately avoiding the knowledge. Characterization
is strong, not only of the children but of
mean-spirited Aunt Bolinger; weak, idealistic
Cousin Henry; Amy, the maid; Mrs. Rees-Goring,
the imperious head of the Ladies' Committee;
the aging pastor--all convincing and memorable.
The claustrophobic piety and self-righteousness
of the village is well evoked, as is the horror
of the situation at Drouet's, a horror increased
by but not dependent on the historical note at
the end discussing the actual case that caused
some reform in workhouse conditions. Boston
Globe Honor; Fanfare.

ASLAN (*The Magician's Nephew**; *The Lion, the
Witch and the Wardrobe**; *The Horse and His
Boy**; *Prince Caspian**; *The Voyage of the "Dawn
Treader"**; *The Silver Chair**; *The Last Battle**),
majestic, golden lion of resonant tones and
penetrating eyes, who is Lord of the Whole Wood
of Narnia*. Son of the great Emperor-beyond-
the-sea, he is not often in Narnia but has a
strong and abiding concern for it and its

inhabitants, all of whom he created in *Nephew*. He is held in high esteem by them, and they look to him as the source of good. He determines who shall enter the land and how long they shall remain, assists in righting wrongs there, and is ultimately the one who brings the land to an end. He is not all-powerful and needs help in accomplishing his ends. He appears most often to Lucy* Pevensie, the youngest child, and even suffers by giving his life for his creation. He may represent the Christian God and does exhibit Trinitarian features, appearing variously as creator (*Nephew*), savior and redeemer (*Lion*), punisher (*Horse*), guide and sustainer (the middle books of the sequence), and the one who brings all things to fruition in *Battle*. Certainly, he is a great good force. The only character who appears in all the novels, he unifies the series.

AT THE BACK OF THE NORTH WIND (MacDonald*, George, ill. Arthur Hughes, Strahan, 1870; Routledge, 1871), story of little Diamond, son of a London coachman, whose friend, the North Wind, takes him on a number of adventures, realistic and mystical. The little boy sleeps in a loft above the horses, one of which, Old Diamond, he has been named for. One night the wind blows a knothole out of the wood near his head, and he hears a voice and sees the North Wind, in the shape of a beautiful lady, who urges him to come out. Because he stops to pet Old Diamond, he cannot find her when he gets outside, and, after wandering about in his nightgown, he is found in the garden belonging to his father's employer, whose daughter, Miss Coleman, takes him in and eventually home, thinking he has been sleepwalking. Another night the North Wind returns, makes a nest in her hair to carry him, and whirls all over London. When Diamond sees a little girl, a crossing sweeper, being blown about, he insists on getting down to help her. They wander about for much of the night, since Old Sal, with whom she lives, will not get up to let her in. Finally they come to his own house again, and she runs off to be early at her crossing. Sometimes the North Wind appears as a tiny, fairy-like creature and sometimes in a fearsome form, like a wolf, but

usually she is a beautiful woman who lets
Diamond ride in her hair or holds him to her
bosom. Once when she must sink a ship, work
which will distress him, she leaves him in a
great cathedral. He goes to visit an aunt in
Sandwich and is delighted that the North Wind
finds him there. He asks her to take him to the
land from which she comes, which is referred to
as "at the back of the north wind," and she
complies somewhat sadly, taking him first to a
boat going north, then to an iceberg, and
finally to the doorstep of the land, where she
seems pale and weak and where, at her direction,
he must go through her to enter. There he finds
an idyllic life, but he worries about his mother
and eventually returns to the doorstep where the
North Wind waits and takes him back to Sandwich.
He returns to find that he has been very ill,
that Mr. Coleman, who owned the wrecked ship,
has been ruined, and that his father no longer
has a job. After some time his father finds
Diamond, the horse, and sets up as a cabman. As
he recovers, little Diamond helps his mother
with the new baby brother that has arrived in
his absence and, when his father grows ill,
drives the cab himself, becoming a favorite with
the other drivers and meeting many people,
including Mr. Evans, who was Miss Coleman's
young man; Mr. Raymond, a wealthy man who lives
nearby; and Nanny, the sweeper girl. Diamond is
instrumental in reuniting Miss Coleman and Mr.
Evans, and with encouragement and books from Mr.
Raymond he learns to read. When Nanny is missing
for several days from her crossing, Diamond goes
to Old Sal's and finds the girl too ill to know
him. He enlists the interest of Mr. Raymond, who
has Nanny taken to the children's hospital,
where Diamond visits her as she recovers. Since
sending her back to Old Sal does not seem a good
idea, and her crossing has already been taken by
another child, Mr. Raymond arranges that, while
he goes abroad, he will leave his horse, Ruby,
with Diamond's father, in exchange for which the
cabman will agree to feed the horse well and
take in Nanny, who learns housework from
Diamond's mother and helps with another new baby
that has arrived. Although Diamond's father gets
rather the worst of the bargain, since Ruby is
lazy and feeding the extra horse and child is

expensive, Mr. Raymond is so pleased when he
returns that he hires Diamond's father as his
coachman, and they all go to live in the
country, including a crippled boy, Jim, who is
Nanny's friend and for whom Diamond has made a
special plea. Diamond becomes a page in the
household and meets the author, with whom he
discusses his adventures with the North Wind.
One night Diamond sees the North Wind looking
white and weak, as she was at the doorstep to
the idyllic land, and the next morning he is
found dead by Mr. Raymond's wife, having gone
again to the back of the north wind. The
author's sudden appearance is startling, and the
story is frequently slowed by songs and poems
either made up or read by Diamond, as well as
stories and dreams he is told. He is a beautiful
and impossibly good child, sweet-tempered even
though Nanny and others consider him a bit weak
in the brain. The novel exemplifies MacDonald's
quasi-religious mysticism but lacks the action
that holds the interest in his stories of Curdie
and the Princess, and it is very sentimental by
modern standards. Children's Classics; Choice.

AUDREY PARTON (*The Machine Gunners**; *Fathom
Five**), strong-willed friend of Chas* McGill.
Called by Chas's mother "a fine, strapping
lass," she is at fourteen bigger and stronger
than any of the boys, whom she has been known
to fight and beat. In the fortress, she takes
the traditional woman's role, making the tea,
distributing the food, and comforting weeping
Nicky* Nichol, but she also has a strong streak
of independence. When her well-to-do father
thinks the Germans are invading and starts out
for the Lake District using black-market gas,
she jumps out of the car in protest and heads
for the fortress. Though she disapproves of his
action, she is appalled and hurt that he continues trying to flee without her. In *Fathom Five*
she has left school and works for a newspaper,
where she has access to some secret information
about ships' cargoes. She is more sophisticated
than Chas and seems more mature, but she is
still willing to be part of the gang's wild spy
chasing. Furthermore, she is the only one who is
at all convincing in their sallies into the
bars of Low Street and the only one able to

fight off the Maltese toughs who attack them. When Sheila* Smythson has been carted off to boarding school, Audrey goes out with Chas and comforts him.

AUGUSTUS GLOOP (*Charlie and the Chocolate Factory**), self-willed, greedy youth of nine, so enormously fat from overeating that he looks as though he has been "blown up with a powerful pump." He is the first child to find a ticket to Willy* Wonka's chocolate factory. Inside the place, he disobeys Mr.* Wonka's command to stay away from the river of melted chocolate, begins to gorge himself on the savory syrup, falls into the river, and is drawn through the connecting pipe into the Fudge Room, where he lands inside a mixing barrel. When he leaves the factory to go home at the end of the tour, he is thin as a straw from having been sucked through the pipe. He is a caricature of a selfish, greedy child, and his experiences are like the satirical distortion of the old-time, moralistic, cautionary tale.

AUNT BETH (*The Watcher Bee**), Kate's* father's sister, who brings Kate up. Although she and Kate's mother's brother, Uncle* Ben, were friends as young people, they agree that they probably wouldn't have married if orphan Kate had not been left on their hands. Aunt Beth has been a teacher and now is a registrar, a position she takes very seriously. She is a proper, tight-lipped woman, inclined to be acerbic in her comments about her husband and given to occasional bouts of depression which Uncle Ben refers to as "the Haggard Mountains." It is Aunt Beth who suggests that Charlie's mother rent her front rooms to Lucy* Denham-Lucie, but she always refers to this old acquaintance in satirical tones, and the latter's arrival is the catalyst for conflict between Aunt Beth and Uncle Ben. She is very proud of Kate, thinking her more clever and talented than Kate herself does, and in the end Kate realizes that perhaps her aunt is bitter that her own life has been so narrow and uneventful.

AUNT BOLINGER (*Ask Me No Questions**), sister of

Laura's* mother with whom Laura and Barty* must stay when cholera sweeps their father's parish. A spiteful, mean-spirited woman, she does her best to break up her son's romance with the schoolmistress, drives her husband to sit in the kitchen to find peace, treats the children unkindly, and exhibits self-righteous piety and snobbishness. She resents the presence of the Drouet school for workhouse children next door. She refuses to discuss it, much less investigate the rumors of abuse there, and forbids Laura and Barty to speak to any of the children.

AUNT GWEN KITSON (*Tom's Midnight Garden**), Tom* Long's well-meaning but inept aunt, with whom he stays while his brother, Peter, is quarantined with measles. In her sincere attempts to make Tom feel wanted and at home, she smothers him with attention and food. She runs interference between Tom and his pedantic, opinionated Uncle* Alan, her husband.

AUNT HARRIET GREENGRASS (*The Peppermint Pig**), the younger of two aunts the family goes to live with in Norfolk. Aunt Harriet is tall, bony, red-faced, and merry, with a loud, masculine laugh. She teaches the youngest children in the school, romps with them, brings potatoes to bake in the ashes so the poorest will at least have a good lunch, and is affectionately called Miss Harry to her face and Old Harry behind her back. She has a sudden temper but also is perceptive about people's feelings. She is the one who realizes that sending Johnnie, the pet pig, to the butcher is going to be a shock to Poll* Greengrass, and she tries to ward it off by giving her a puppy.

AUNTIE JOAN MYHILL (*Handles**), Erica Timperley's mother's sister, an acid-tongued, almost shrewish woman. Overly indulgent of her lumpish son, Robert*, she does many things on the vegetable farm that he could do more easily than she, yet she will not tolerate criticism of him from Erica. She always seems to be about some task, and she has a tendency to look down upon neighbors, particularly those who "hent local." She is a dyed-in-the-wool country person who maintains that her city sister lives under dangerous, unwholesome conditions. She is a strongly drawn, surprisingly sympathetic character.

AUNTIE LOU (*Carrie's War**), Louisa Evans, much younger sister of Councillor Evans with whom Carrie* Willow and her brother, Nick*, are billeted when they are evacuated from London during World War II. Continually hectored and bullied by the brother who raised her after their mother's death, Auntie Lou has become timid and nervous, and though the children love her, they are occasionally annoyed by her lack of spunk. When she has seen her friend, Major Harper, she seems to glow, and her happiness is so transparent that Carrie despairs, certain that Mr.* Evans will become suspicious, discover what his sister has been doing, and forbid her to see the American man again. Nick guesses Auntie Lou's intentions, and she admits to him that she plans to elope, but they keep it a secret from Carrie. Auntie Lou has red hair and bright eyes, and Carrie thinks she looks a bit like a squirrel.

AUNTIE MAGGIE CHAFFEY (*A Likely Lad**), Willy* Overs's eccentric great-aunt, who opposed her niece Ellen's* marriage to Alfred* Overs and took to her bed, vowing never to rise or to see Ellen again. With her house literally falling to pieces around her, she lives in squalor with one grouchy servant and two vicious guard dogs, keeping her money in banknotes under her pillow and a jug of water beside her bed so she can douse any boys who dare come to the doorway below her window. For years she has let the Sowter family think that she will leave her money to their lumpish son, Stan*, and is gleeful when she decides to give it to Willy instead, mostly because it will make them so angry. In the end, the dogs she keeps to guard her money eat it all, and the shock kills her.

AUNTIE MOLLY BELL (*No End to Yesterday**), Gran's unmarried daughter, who still lives at home and is one of Marjory's chief detractors. She has some sort of responsible job working with jewelry. Although she routinely steals and discards her sister Ada's admirers, her steady

man is "Uncle" Fred Barnes, who owns a
Rolls-Royce and showers her with gifts--silk
stockings, pound notes, a player piano. Though
everyone in the family seems to know that Barnes
is not his true name, that he is really married,
and that he shares Molly's bed, no one admits
it; this points up the hypocrisy of their
condemnation of Marjory's mother and her
father's self-righteous break with Marjory when
she falls in love with a married man.

AUNT LUPY (*The Borrowers Afield**; *The
Borrowers Afloat**; *The Borrowers Avenged**),
heavy, sharp-tongued, bossy, easily flustered
Borrower woman. Wife of Uncle* Hendreary, she
dominates him and gives herself airs. She is a
concerned mother and loyal wife throughout all
the Borrowers' tribulations, looking out for
Hendreary and the children's best interests.
The Hendrearys live in a badger's set in the
field called Parkin's Beck and then in the
cramped upstairs room overfurnished with objects
that Tom* Goodenough brings from Firbank Hall
and which once belonged to the Clocks. Aunt Lupy
shares it all with the Clocks, with reluctance
but not selfishness, because she feels she must
provide first for her own family. At the end of
the series we see her living with Hendreary and
Timmus in the vestry of the old Fordham church,
where Lupy, having "found the Lord," seems
calmer, less quick to pass judgment, and more
accepting of Homily* Clock. She is an interesting, well-drawn figure, not merely a type,
and serves as a foil for Homily.

AUNT POLLY DUNHAM (*Gran at Coalgate**), vivacious
wife of Uncle Davie, who has led a procession
in London and made a speech at Albert Hall.
Although Jinnie, who often thinks in capitalized
words, realizes that Aunt Polly is No Better
Than She Should Be, she is not quite sure what
this means and does not immediately connect it
with her going around in public with Tot Bourke.
A dramatic woman, Polly relishes the limelight
and enjoys being the center of a shocked crowd
at the Pictures and the dance. When she is found
nearly murdered, her son and her husband are the
main suspects, but there are suggestions that it
might be Tot or any number of other men she has

been involved with. Gran-at-Coalgate* knows that
Polly's son, Will, might not be the child of
Davie and that Polly neglects her younger
children, yet even she admits that there is
something about Polly that people can't help
being attracted to.

AUNT SARAH GREENGRASS (*The Peppermint Pig*),
elder sister of Poll* Greengrass's father,
headmistress of the Norfolk school. Tall and
solemnly pretty, she has high ideals and a
dignified demeanor. She has given up her own
chances of marriage or a more distinguished
career because her father deserted the family
and she had to care for her mother and help her
younger brother and sisters to get an education.
Now she has aspirations for Poll's brother
George, who is intelligent, and for Lily, who
wants to be an actress. She knits pink under-
vests to protect Theo's* delicate chest, much
to his horror. Poll is a little too outspoken
and adventurous to meet with Aunt Sarah's
approval. Her sense of duty is also hard on
Poll's mother, Emily*, who is in the uncomfortable position of being dependent upon her.

AUNT SUSAN AND AUNT ANNE MAYFIELD (*The House in
Norham Gardens**), Clare Mayfield's great-aunts,
with whom she has lived since the death of her
parents in a plane crash when she was nine. The
aunts are spry, maiden ladies of eighty and
seventy-eight respectively and well-educated
("degrees and then more degrees"), although so
vague and unconcerned about practical, everyday
matters like bills and house repairs that Clare
has already begun to manage the household with
the help of Mrs.* Hedges, the day-lady. Clare
has great respect and affection for the two old
women, and her relationship with them is one of
the finest aspects of the book. She feels they
are "not fenced off," that is, they are very
adaptable and able to adjust to whatever they
must do, like taking in boarders, though they
are not given to fads and fashions. For Clare,
they and the house represent reality and
normalcy in life. The aunts are convincingly
drawn as old persons but are not individualized
from each other.

AVERY, GILLIAN (ELISE) (1926-   ), born in
Reigate, Surrey; novelist, specialist in
Victorian life and literature. She attended
Dunottar School, Reigate, became a junior reporter on the *Surrey Mirror*, a staff member on
Chambers Encyclopedia, and assistant illustrations editor for Clarendon Press in Oxford. In
1952, she married A. O. J. Cockshut, who has
taught at Oxford, the setting for a number of
her more than fifteen novels for children.
These include *The Warden's Niece** (Collins,
1957), which was commended for the Carnegie Med-
al and which introduces the Smith brothers and
Mr.* Copplestone, a most unconventional tutor.
Some characters appear in several of her novels;
the Smith boys, for instance, reappear in *The
Elephant War* (Collins, 1960; Holt, 1971), and
Mr. Copplestone reappears in *To Tame a Sister*
(Collins, 1961; Van Nostrand, 1964), all novels
set in Victorian England. *The Greatest Gresham**
(Collins, 1962), which was commended for the
Carnegie Medal, is set in London. *A Likely Lad**
(Collins, 1971; Holt, 1971), which won the
Guardian Award and was highly commended for the
Carnegie, and *The Call of the Valley* (Collins,
1966; Holt, 1968) are set in Manchester. All
these books are in the late Victorian era and
all are distinguished by convincing recreation
of the period, good characterization, and lively
humor. Avery is also well known for her studies
of nineteenth-century children's literature and
social history in *Nineteenth Century Children:
Heroes and Heroines In English Children's
Stories 1780-1900* (with Angela Bull, Hodder,
1965);, *Childhood's Pattern: A Study of Heroes
and Heroines of Children's Fiction 1770-1950*
(Hodder, 1975); *Victorian People in Life and
Literature* (Collins, 1970; Holt, 1970); and *The
Echoing Green: Memories of Victorian and Regency
Youth* (Collins, 1974; Viking, 1974). She has
also written a biography of Mrs. Ewing and two
novels for adults, and has edited a number of
collections, many of them early children's
stories.

AVOYE HAMILTON (*Three Lives for the Czar**),
mother of Andrei* and Alix*, an Austrian
princess married to a Russo-Scottish nobleman,
whose husband and daughter are both innocent

victims of assassination attempts on other
people. A beautiful woman, she can bring out
chivalry in the most stern soldiers and
bureaucrats and is chosen companion of the
Czarina, whom she pities even though she sees
how disastrous the woman's attitudes are for
Russia.

AWFUL SYKES (*Archer's Goon**), nickname for
Anthea, Howard's* little sister who gets her
way by screaming, biting, little sister who
gets her way by screaming, biting, and otherwise
asserting herself. Though she talks insultingly
to her father, he is able to quell her much
better than can her mother. Awful is given to
sudden enthusiasms, like her crush on Hathaway*,
but she is also shrewd and is the only one who
doesn't fall under Dillian's* spell. In the way
she continually insists on coming along and must
frequently be extricated from the trouble she
causes, her relationship to Howard resembles
that of Venturus, the youngest wizard, to his
siblings. In the episode set in the future, she
appears as a beautiful woman, but looks so
much like Shine* that Howard is determined to
stick around and help her grow up into a more
decent person.

B

BABE, THE GALLANT PIG. See *The Sheep-Pig.*

BADGER (*The Wind in the Willows**), reclusive but highly respected friend of the river-bankers, who makes his home in the tunnels and rooms of an ancient city buried in the Wild Wood. Although he loathes society and is rather uncouth in his speech and manners, Badger is intelligent and concerned for his friends, and when Mole* and Rat* seek refuge with him in the winter storm, he is a generous and gracious host. Because Toad's* father knew his son was frivolous and volatile in character, he confided only in Badger the existence of a secret passage into Toad Hall, to be revealed if great need demanded; and it is through this passage that the four friends attack the banqueting weasels and rout them from the premises.

BAGHEERA (*The Jungle Books**), Black Panther, inky black all over but with the panther markings showing up like the pattern of watered silk. Bagheera provides the second voice to speak up for the man-cub at the pack meeting, offering to buy Mowgli's way into the pack with one bull, newly killed. He looks after Mowgli* as devoted but in a much less doting way than Baloo*, and helps rescue him from the Bander-log. When Akela* has missed his kill and Shere* Khan is about to challenge Mowgli, it is Bagheera who advises the boy to steal fire from the village and explains how he knows so much about man: he himself was born in captivity in the king's palace at Oodeypore and broke out when he became full grown. Bagheera figures in most of the later stories, substituting for Messua and her husband after the villagers have locked them up, and he is still with Mowgli at the end, after the spring running.

BAKER, M(ARGARET) J(OYCE) (1918–   ), born in Reading, Berkshire; author of some three dozen books of fiction for young readers. Her father was a sales manager, and the family lived in the country until Baker was nine, when they moved to London, remaining there throughout her school years. She attended a private day school, Roland Houses in Rosary Gardens, and studied journalism at King's College, University of London. After the family moved to Marlow in Buckinghamshire, she began to write in earnest and soon placed her first article in the *Guide*. During World War II, she was a mobile canteen driver for the Church Army, and, after the war, she lived in an old country house called the Hare and the Hounds. She wrote adult stories for *The Lady* and other magazines and then in 1943 sold a children's story to *Child Life*. Much encouraged by editor Wilma K. McFarland, she wrote mainly for children after that. The stories published in *Child Life* were later collected and put out in two books, *Treasure Trove* (Brockhampton, 1952) and *The Young Magicians* (Brockhampton, 1954). Her novels fall into two main groups: fantasies for younger readers and family adventures for children from ten to fourteen. In the former are fantasies about talking animals including Homer, a turtle who belongs to three small English girls, *Homer the Tortoise* (McGraw, 1950; originally *"Nonsense," Said the Tortoise*, Brockhampton, 1949) and *Homer Goes West* (Brockhampton, 1965), and a bear family, *The Shoe Shop Bears* (Harrap, 1964; Farrar, 1965), who leave their shop and have adventures. The bears' story is continued in *Bears Back in Business* (Harrap, 1967; Farrar, 1967) and *Hi-Jinks Joins the Bears* (Harrap, 1968; Farrar, 1969), among others. For older readers, she wrote novels about children in family situations, coping with animals, people, and nature, like *Castaway Christmas** (Methuen,

1963; Farrar, 1964), a mildly suspenseful, incident-filled book about three children alone in a flood, which attained Carnegie Commended status, and *Cut Off from Crumpets* (Methuen, 1964), about a terrible blizzard. Two of her books were serialized on BBC-TV, and ten have been translated into other languages. She has also written a reader, *The Fighting Cocks* (Pitman, 1949), and a biography, *Anna Sewell and Black Beauty* (Harrap, 1956; Longman, 1957). She has said that she strives for both humanism and realism in her books for young readers.

BALDERSON, MARGARET (1935-   ), born in Sydney, New South Wales, Australia; librarian and novelist. She attended high school in Sydney and worked there as a librarian and a house mistress in a girls' school. Her travels have taken her to Greece, India, and Norway, where she was a resident worker for two years, living for autumn and part of winter in Tromso, the largest town north of the Arctic Circle. This experience is reflected in *When Jays Fly to Barbmo** (Oxford, 1968; World, 1969), about a girl during World War II who, having discovered her relationship to the Lapps, makes an arduous journey to find and live with her nomadic grandfather. This novel won the Australian Children's Book Council Book-of-the-Year Award and was highly commended for the Carnegie Award. Among her other publications are *A Dog Called George* (Oxford, 1975), set in Canberra, Australia, and highly commended for the Book-of-the-Year Award, and *Blue and Gold Day* (Angus, 1979), about two sisters who visit a beach before breakfast. She has been praised for her ability to evoke a sense of place.

BALDMONEY (*The Little Grey Men**), second eldest of the three gnomes who go upriver, the others being Sneezewort* and Dodder*, and the leader when Dodder is not around. He is their spokesman and mapmaker. Always restless, a doer, maker, and mender, he takes the initiative in preparing for the journey. Like the others, he is almost a caricature of a gnome, though not as cute as a Disney figure.

BALLANTYNE, R(OBERT) M(ICHAEL) (1825-1894), born

in Edinburgh, Scotland; fur-trader, publisher, novelist. He worked for the Hudson Bay Company as a trader, writing his first book (for adults) when he was isolated at an outpost in the far Canadian Northwest, then returned to Scotland to work for the publishing firm of Thomas Constable. His first novel for young people was *Snowflakes and Sunbeams* (Nelson, 1856; Nelson, 1856), later retitled *The Young Fur Traders: A Tale of the Far North*. This and many of his more than 100 books are based on firsthand experiences in Canada and the frozen North, but his most famous novel is *The Coral Island: A Tale of the Pacific Ocean** (Nelson, 1857; Nelson, 1857), a story of castaways on a South Sea island. He is remembered as one of the half dozen best writers of adventure stories for boys in the second half of the nineteenth century, producing novels of manly young fellows helping to extend the British Empire and Christian influence, often with a lack of sensitivity for native populations and ecology that is quite foreign to modern readers. Robert Louis Stevenson* acknowledged his debt to Ballantyne in his development as an adventure writer. Ballantyne was also an artist and exhibited water colors at the Royal Scottish Academy. He died in Rome, where he had traveled to improve his health.

BALLET SHOES (Streatfeild*, Noel, ill. Ruth Gervis, Dent, 1936; Random, 1937), career novel set in London in the early 1930s, dealing with the training of three little girls for the stage. Pauline, Petrova, and Posy Fossil are all orphans, acquired as infants by Great-Uncle Matthew, a scientist who has named them for his interest in fossil collecting, and who has turned them over to his great-niece, Sylvia Brown, to be raised while he goes off on expeditions. She is aided by her old nurse, Nana, and by Cook and Clara the housemaid. Great-Uncle Matthew departs for places unknown leaving money enough to last five years. When he fails to return and the money runs out, Sylvia, whom the girls call "Garnie," short for Guardian, decides to take in boarders. Among them is Miss Theo Dane of The Children's Academy of Dancing and Stage Training in Bloomsbury who, concerned that Sylvia cannot afford schools for

the girls, gets them accepted as nonpaying
students at the Academy, pointing out that they
will be trained there and by age twelve can
start earning money to help out. Pauline, ten
when she starts at the Academy, is a beautiful,
blond child, rescued as an infant from a sinking
ship. She loves acting from the first and is
moderately good at dancing and adequate at
singing. Petrova, 8, who was left at a hospital
when her Russian parents both died, is dark
complexioned and very bright, inclined to
mechanical interests, and utterly bored with
acting and dancing, though she applies herself
and does adequately. Posy, 6, is the red-haired
daughter of a ballerina too busy to raise her.
Even before starting at the Academy she has
danced at every opportunity, and she treasures
her only legacy from her mother, a pair of pink
dancing slippers. Among the boarders are Doctor
Jakes and Doctor Smith, retired professors of
literature and mathematics, who undertake to
teach the girls academic subjects, and Mr. and
Mrs. John Simpson, who drive a Citroen and are
strongly sympathetic to Petrova. Pupils at the
Academy are expected to work very hard, and all
three girls do, but with different results.
Pauline is recognized for her acting ability,
and even before she is twelve (the first legal
age that a child can go on the professional
stage), she is chosen to play the part of Tyltyl
in a benefit performance of Maeterlinck's *The
Blue Bird*, and as soon as she can get a license
she wins the part of Alice in a theater
production that runs for some weeks. Petrova,
though she dislikes dancing and is afraid of
acting, knows that Sylvia is worried about money
and gamely keeps from complaining, except to Mr.
Simpson, who lets her work every Saturday in the
garage he owns. Sometimes he takes her to an
airfield and even up for flights, making her
life bearable. Posy, who is absolutely confident
and single-minded about her dancing, has such
talent that she is taken as a private pupil by
Madame Fidolia, the director of the school, who
was once in the Russian Imperial Ballet. The
girls suffer a number of realistic problems.
When Pauline goes for the audition for the part
of Alice, she has no suitable dress, having
outgrown her dress-up clothes. After much secret

discussion, since the girls don't want to worry
Sylvia further, they pawn the neclaces that GUM
(as they call Great-Uncle Matthew) gave them, to
Mr. Simpson (who allows Pauline to purchase them
back from her earnings), and they buy a black
velvet dress that each will use in turn for
auditions. When their friend from school,
Winifred, whose family badly needs the money and
who also auditions for Alice, is turned down in
favor of Pauline, they are sad for her and
genuinely glad when she is made Pauline's
understudy. After some weeks as Alice, Pauline
gets a swollen head and becomes snippy at the
theater; she is punished and cured of her
conceit by having to act as understudy while
Winifred acts Alice for one performance. Pauline
easily gets the part of Pease-blossom in *A
Midsummer Night's Dream*, and then, when the
child auditioning for Mustard-seed does not show
up, talks the director into trying Petrova for
the part. Unfortunately, Winifred is the child
late for the audition and is again beaten out by
a Fossil. Petrova has difficulties, but muddles
through. Pauline goes on to act as young King
Edward in *Richard the Third*, for which Petrova
is an unspeaking page, and then as Charles the
Second's sister in a movie, but the money is not
enough to keep them all, and Sylvia decides she
must sell the house, which is fortunately in her
name. When Madame Fidolia becomes ill, Posy is
disruptive in the school classes until Pauline
bribes her to be good by promising to buy her a
ticket, with the last of her own money, to the
ballet featuring a great artist from Czechoslo-
vakia. Just as they are about to move from the
house, Pauline is offered a five-year movie
contract in Hollywood, the Czech artist agrees
to take Posy for a pupil, and GUM returns. It is
decided that Sylvia will go to Hollywood with
Pauline, Nana will go with Posy to Czechoslova-
kia, with her lessons paid for by Pauline, and
Petrova will go to live with GUM, with Cook and
Clara to work for them, and will learn to fly
and perhaps fulfill the vow the three girls made
and renewed on each birthday, to make the name
of Fossil famous. Although the successes are not
very realistic, the hard work of the children
aspiring to stage careers is lifelike, as is
also the copious and interesting information

about theaters and productions that forms a
solid background for the story. The idea of a
family being poor while having a cook, a nurse,
and a housemaid may seem odd to modern children,
and the way the children are brought up, being
chaperoned everywhere and regimented on a strict
schedule, is a far cry from the life of most
Americans even in the 1930s; however, the girls
themselves, with their squabbles, fears, hurts,
and triumphs, are true to children of any
period. Choice.

BALOO (*The Jungle Books**), sleepy brown bear who
teaches the Law of the Jungle to the wolf cubs.
He is one of the two voices to speak for
Mowgli*, outside the immediate family, as
required when there is some question of the
right of a cub to be admitted into the pack.
Because he knows Mowgli will need more
protection than most wolf cubs, he teaches him
the master words of all the animals in the
jungle. Baloo, along with Bagheera* and Kaa*,
rescues Mowgli from the monkey people. He is a
loving, almost doting teacher and friend of the
boy, but he disciplines him firmly when
necessary.

BARNABAS (*The Writing on the Hearth**), lazy,
inept clerk of about Stephen's age, who provides
an occasional touch of comic relief to the
novel. In service to Dame* Alice in London, he
disobeys and seeks out entertainment on the
South Bank of the Thames, where he catches the
plague and soon dies. Stephen does his work
throughout most of the book. Barnabas is a foil
for the conscientious, reliable Stephen.

BARRETT, ANNE (MAINWARING) (1911-   ), born in
Southsea, Hampshire; filmmaker and freelance
writer for children and adults. She attended
Sherborne School for Girls in Dorset, married
Hugh Miles Boxer, was divorced; then married
Wilfred Kenyon Tufnell Barrett, was again divorced; had one daughter; was an associate of
and story editor for Children's Films Foundation in London from 1959-1964, and has made
her home in Sussex. Of her half-dozen novels,
most are realistic stories of children in
family and neighborhood situations. *Stolen*

Summer (Collins, 1951; Dodd, 1953) is about a summer in a beautiful country house; *The Dark Island* (Collins, 1952) is a suspenseful story set in Ireland; and *The Journey of Johnny Rew* (Collins, 1954; Bobbs, 1955) concerns a boy's search for his father. She has also written a career novel, *Sheila Burton, Dental Assistant* (Bodley, 1956), and a screenplay, *Treasure in Malta* (1963). Her first published novel is the time fantasy, *Caterpillar Hall* (Collins, 1950). Her best-known books are *Songberd's Grove** (Collins, 1957; Bobbs, 1957), a lively story commended for the Carnegie Award in which a new family must deal with neighborhood toughs; and *Midway* (Collins, 1967), about a boy who tries to elevate his self-esteem by inventing a tiger, Midway, with whom he converses and has imaginary adventures.

BARRIE, JAMES M(ATTHEW) (1860-1937), born in Kirriemuir, Fofarshire, Scotland; playwright, critic, novelist. One of a weaver's large family, he attended Glasgow Academy, Fofar Academy, Dumfries Academy, and Edinburgh University, where he received an M.A. in 1882. He married actress Mary Ansell in 1894 and was divorced in 1909. He was drama and book critic for the *Edinburgh Courant* from 1879 to 1882 and leader writer for the *Nottingham Journal* in 1883 and 1884. After 1885 he lived in London; he was knighted in 1913. Of his forty-five plays, some are still performed, notably *Dear Brutus* (Hodder, 1922), first produced in London in 1917. He wrote seven novels for adults, among the best known being *The Little Minister* (Cassell, 1891; Lovell, 1891) and *Sentimental Tommy: The Story of His Boyhood* (Cassell, 1896; Scribner, 1896), and twenty-one other volumes. For children, he is known essentially for one story, that of Peter Pan, though it has appeared in several forms. It first was part of a book for adults, *The Little White Bird* (Hodder, 1902; as *The Little White Bird; or, Adventures in Kensing ton Gardens*, Scribner, 1902), which later was revised for children as *Peter Pan in Kensington Gardens* (Hodder, 1906; Scribner, (1906). He then used the character as the central figure in a popular play, and finally wrote him into a novel, *Peter and Wendy** (Hodder, 1911; Scribner,

1911), later called *Peter Pan and Wendy*. The boy
who refuses to grow up is said to have been inspired by Barrie's friendship with the five
sons of Sylvia and Arthur Llewellyn Davies, to
whom he became honorary uncle and later guardian.

BARRY MORTIMER (*Noah's Castle**), sixteen-year-
old second child and elder son of Norman
Mortimer, called Father*, and May Mortimer,
called Mother*. Barry tells the story of the
fateful eight months when Father out of noble
motives to provide for his family violates moral
and social laws and hoards food. Barry is an
intelligent, aware, and candid observer who
avoids harsh judgments, self-righteousness, and
self-pity. He tries to remain loyal to Father,
even though he suffers misgivings about
Father's methods; however, after he becomes
friends with Wendy Farrar, a schoolmate, and her
dying mother, he is moved by moral concerns to
take them food, which he does over Father's protests, and to serve the community through volunteer work with Share Alike. When he realizes
that Father by his very nature will not be able
to turn over the food voluntarily to Share Alike
and that militants will come and steal it, Barry
arranges with the Share Alikers to come and take
it in the middle of the night by leaving a door
unlocked for them.

BARRY PADGITT (*Hal**), over-protected boy who,
after a long illness, has become so withdrawn
that he is afraid to leave his slum apartment
without his mother. An intelligent, rather
romantic boy, he has been fascinated by the game
he sees played in the waste area overlooked by
his fourth-floor window, a sort of war between
groups of neighborhood children in which he
recognizes sexual undertones and has named the
leaders of the two factions The Indian Queen and
The Spaniard. Drawn into the action by the West
Indian girl, Hal*, he gradually grows stronger
physically and psychologically, so that he becomes less dependent upon his mother and less
manipulative about his illness. Although he is
fascinated by Hal, he senses her ambivalence
about him and is truly sympathetic when she
discovers that her favorite teacher and Tim

Black, on whom she has a crush, are engaged. With Hal's two younger sisters and in the warm Georgiou family Barry is relaxed and at ease.

BARTOLOMEO CORDOBA (*No Way of Telling**), huge sailor who has come into possession of information vital to the security of a foreign country and who is trying to get it to London, although he has been badly wounded in the arm and is being chased by terrorists. At first he is so confused that he appears to be a madman when he comes to Gwyntfa, the isolated cottage of the Bowens, but he shows his true goodness by rescuing a ewe caught in a snowdrift, saving Amy when her toboggan goes into the ravine, and turning back to rescue Amy's grandmother, though his own life is endangered by each of these acts.

BARTY (*Ask Me No Questions**), younger brother of Laura*, who with her goes to stay with their Aunt* Bolinger in Tooting. A quiet, self-contained boy, he is very interested in bones, and when a bird-catcher gives him a dead bird, he decides the way to get the bones is to put some maggots in a box with it and wait. He stores the box in his aunt's lower kitchen cupboard near the stove and is outraged when she discovers and throws it away; he refuses to be cowed even though she is furious and strikes him. He is not nearly as much affected by the condition of the children from the workhouse school as Laura is, though he is the first to steal food to feed them.

BASIL DUFFIELD (*Dogsbody**), elder of Kathleen* O'Brien's two cousins, a disagreeable boy given to teasing her and making unkind jokes about the Irish. One of the pressures on Sirius to find the Zoi (a very powerful force that could be mistaken for a meteorite) is that Basil and a friend are hunting for artifacts and for the meteorite that is thought to have fallen in the area, and Sirius knows that it will be very dangerous if Basil gets hold of the Zoi. Basil is somewhat shamed by the revelation that he watched Kathleen being bullied by a crowd of boys while he waited across the street, but he admits it so that the police will know that the

complaining father is not accurate when he says
that Sirius attacked his boys without provocation. Although Basil continually has made scornful remarks about the dog, referring to him as
Shamus Rat and other derogatory names, he gradually has come to admire Sirius, and when his
mother has Kathleen take Sirius to the vet to
have him destroyed, Basil flares up and leaves,
intending to stay away for good and eventually
tracing Kathleen to Miss* Smith's house. He is
with Kathleen and his brother, Robin*, when they
join the Wild Hunt, and in his request to the
Master he asks for the Zoi, thinking it is an
ordinary meteorite. He is fighting with Kathleen
for it when she loses her grip on it and Sirius
catches it in his mouth, thereby turning back
into a luminary and leaving his dog nature dead
on the ground.

BATES (*Pennington's Seventeenth Summer**; *The
Beethoven Medal**), John Bates, weedy, self-
effacing friend of Pat* Pennington, who has a
beautiful voice for singing folk songs but such
a lack of confidence that he will sing only
after being well primed with beer. Not a
fighter, Bates is an odd person to be a buddy to
belligerent Pat. He usually cowers out of the
way when fists begin to fly and suffers agonies
of apprehension when Pat defies his schoolmasters and others in authority. Coerced by Pat
into his first public performance, he becomes a
successful folk singer. In *The Beethoven Medal*
he has gone on the road as a performer, but
Pat, unable to endure his own parents any
longer, has moved across the street to live
with Bates's mother during vacations from
college. In a sequel, *Pennington's Heir*, Bates
turns up and helps Pat and Ruth* Hollis
financially during a period when Pat has broken
his hand and can't play. Skinny, scared, unsure
of himself, and unable to lie convincingly, he
is a foil for the aggressive Pat, to whom he is
devoted.

THE BATTLE OF BUBBLE AND SQUEAK (Pearce*,
Philippa, ill. Alan Baker, Deutsch, 1978),
short, realistic novel of contemporary family
life in an unspecified English suburb in which
members of a family squabble over pet animals.

When Jimmy* Dean's cousin leaves with his family
for Australia and gives his two pet gerbils to
Sid* Parker, Sid's mother, Mrs.* Sparrow, a
tense, commanding woman, insists they be taken
to the local pet center. Her husband and Sid's
stepfather, Bill* Sparrow, volunteers to return
them, but, recalling the pet white mice of his
own childhood, is unable to leave them there.
Over the next several weeks, several outright
confrontations and subtle maneuvers occur as
Mrs. Sparrow tries to get rid of Bubble* and
Squeak and the rest of the family gamely tries
to keep them. Bubble and Squeak are soon
cherished openly by Peggy and Amy Parker, Sid's
younger sisters, and less demonstrably appreciated by Sid, who, however, is even more emotionally involved with them, while Mr. Sparrow
attempts to mediate without bringing the full
force of his wife's wrath down upon himself.
When the animals gnaw holes in Mrs. Sparrow's
red living room curtains, she posts an ad on a
local bulletin board and gives the gerbils away
to two little boys who show up to claim them.
Unable to find the boys to get his gerbils back,
Sid runs away in anger and despair to what the
children call the "awful place," the local
dump, where Bill finds and placates him. The
next evening the two little boys bring the
gerbils back, having been forced by their mother
to return them, a situation that prompts Mrs.
Sparrow to put the gerbils out early the next
morning for the dustmen to cart away. To her
intense chagrin, one of the dustmen notices the
animals and curtly returns them, cage and all.
In response to the children's horrified howls
when they discover what she has done this time,
Mrs. Sparrow promises not to send the gerbils
away again. Sid and Peggy mistrust their
mother's motives, however, and Peggy convinces
Sid to board the animals for a couple of weeks
with the Mudds, family friends, until Mum
regains her calm. The turning point in Mrs.
Sparrow's attitude toward the gerbils comes when
Mrs. Pring's cat, Ginger, mauls Bubble, and the
children can't manage to administer the
antibiotic the vet has prescribed. Mrs.
Sparrow's maternal instincts are aroused, she
helps them, and Bubble is soon on the road to
recovery. The final threat to the Parker-Sparrow

ownership of Bubble and Squeak comes from an unexpected source: Jimmy Dean's cousin shows up and wants his gerbils back, his family having decided that Australia is not for them. Little Amy saves the day by suggesting that they need more gerbils to go around, a point that gives Peggy the idea of breeding them. When Jimmy Dean's cousin says he's afraid his parents won't take to the plan, in a speech that indicates her change of heart, Mrs. Sparrow says that Jimmy Dean's cousin's parents will just have to make the best of things. Firm characterizations, just the right number and kind of complications, natural dialogue, well-drawn scenes, and flashes of sensory imagery to support emotions make for an unpretentious, quite memorable slice of real life that revolves around the importance of family sharing and communication and that works very well within the limits the author has set for herself. (Dawn* Mudd) Carnegie Com.; Choice; Whitbread.

THE BATTLE OF ST. GEORGE WITHOUT (McNeill*, Janet, ill. Mary Russon, Faber, 1966; Little, 1966), realistic novel set in a run-down area of an English city probably in the 1950s. Dove Square, once a fashionable area, has deteriorated so much that the large houses no longer hold wealthy single families and their servants, but, now in shabby disrepair, each contains a number of families. Matt* McGinley, 13, who has moved here with his mother from the country after his father's death, sometimes feels a need to be alone. He discovers a way into the overgrown grounds of the old church of St. George Without in the center of the square, a church long abandoned and locked up. When old Mr. Harrison dies and the children of the area are shooed away, Matt shares his secret with the others-- Henry* Mickle, who sings in the cathedral choir; Henry's younger brother Bill, known only as The Trailer; red-haired Madge*, who lives with her eccentric Cousin Maudie; Sidney Lumba, a Jamaican; and pretty Gwen*. While they are in the ante-room of the church, which they have entered through a window, they discover that Eddie Flint, 13, and a group of the younger Flint children are on the roof. A wild battle and chase ensues, leading right into the prim funeral crowd leaving Miss* Queenie Harrison's. Forced by their parents to call on Miss Harrison the next day and apologize, they are surprised to be invited to tea and to find her eager to tell them about the old days, to show them pictures of herself and various neighbors when they were young, and to explain how she still happens to have keys to the church. Her father was a sort of caretaker and was the last to lock up after it was damaged in the war and closed. She even tells them where she hid a little key she used to have when she dusted in the church. At the first opportunity they get into the church grounds, find the key, and enter the church. Again they hear someone on the roof and pretend they are a choir practicing. Eddie, who is on probation after being arrested for shoplifting, admits he was there before because he was forced by Dan-boy, the new boyfriend of Gwen's big sister, who wants to steal the lead from the roof. Outraged, the youngsters decide to fight this threat, and they enlist Shaky* (Charlie) Frick, onetime gardener for one of the wealthy families of the square, who was left his employers' two Pekinese dogs and a living wage to care for them. Dan-boy and his friends play rough, but the youngsters are clever: when Dan-boy steals Miss Harrison's church keys, Henry, Sidney, and Matt trail him to a swimming pool, where Sidney pretends to be drowning to distract the attendants while the others steal the keys back from the locker room. The night of St. George's Eve, having cleaned the church, they plan a celebration but find that Dan-boy and his friends have stripped the roof and, they think, kidnapped The Trailer. They call the police and are discovered--by their assembled parents, the police, Shaky Frick, and the bishop--singing St. George's hymn. The Trailer, they later find, was sleeping in the laundromat. The bishop has a long talk with them, pointing out that they have been trespassing but that their desire to save the church is commendable. He admits that the church will probably be torn down. Their momentary triumph, however, is worthwhile. The youngsters seem rather innocent and younger than their given ages; still, they are believable as individuals and the action is fast-paced. Choice.

THE BATTLE OF WEDNESDAY WEEK (Willard*,
Barbara, ill. Douglas Hall, Constable, 1963;
STORM FROM THE WEST, Harcourt, 1964), episodic,
realistic family novel, with contemporary-
problem story aspects, set mostly near the
village of Kilmorah on the coast of Scotland,
in which two sets of bickering children merged
by marriage are left on their own to work out
how to get along. In London, the Lattimer
children, Charlotte*, 14, and Nicholas*, 16, and
in America, the Graham children, Nan*, 16,
Lucy*, 10, Alan, 12, and Roderick, 13, receive
with mixed emotions the news of the marriage of
the formers' mother, widowed painter Sarah
Lattimer, and the latters' widower father,
Robert Graham, an American lawyer. The vacation
the parents plan for the combined family at
Sarah's croft at Kilmorah has plenty of ups and
downs before they arrive at a satisfactory
working relationship. Lucy, at first the most
opposed of the Grahams to the marriage but
needing a mother's love, accepts Sarah but still
stubbornly goes her independent way, while Nan,
demonstrably affectionate like her own dead
Southern mother, soothes ruffled feelings but
sometimes in her eagerness to do the right thing
inadvertently adds to the tension. Alan and
Roderick, who make up a kind of "double-boy,"
are so engrossed in their own interests that
they have little to do with the story.
Reconciled to making the best of things,
Charlotte and Nicholas vary in attitude
throughout the story. Charlotte gives her room
to the Graham girls as a gesture of welcome,
while Nicholas assumes playacting postures to
mask his uneasiness, making it hard for the
others to get to know him. The children resent
differences in speech and ways, the disruption
of their lives, having to share their parents,
and the uncertainty about the future. After a
particularly pleasant day on the beach, Nicholas
generously suggests they picnic at Ardtorquil,
the Lattimers' favorite spot for an outing.
The day goes splendidly until the Graham
children, Scotsphiles and descended from Scots,
suggest getting tartans for everyone, which
offends the Lattimers, who, though they live in
Scotland, have no Scots blood; the children go
home angry and quarreling. Robert Graham makes a

decision: he will take Sarah away for a vacation from this fractious brood and leave the children to work out their problems alone. With neighbors Alison* and Murdo* Johnstone in the background keeping an eye on them, over the next several weeks the children come to terms with one another, though they never completely overcome their uneasiness. The best adventures involve the girls, especially headstrong Lucy, but Nicholas plays a strong role, too. In pairs, as individuals, and as a group, they do chores and go on outings, have good times and tackle ticklish ones, routinely taking two steps forward and one back. After Lucy falls into a small chasm on the mountainside and the children unite to rescue her, an especially amusing and memorable scene follows in which they celebrate by drinking ginger beer to "the Graham" (Robert), whom they decide to address as the Laird (leader of a Scots clan), thus resolving the knotty problem of what to call him. The book concludes with a raging storm, during which Murdo, Nan, and Nicholas rescue Lucy and others whose school bus has become stranded on the return from an outing. The next morning the children learn their parents are returning. Charlotte, who has been discussing Scots clans with Alison, suggests that the group think of themselves not as a family but as a clan, a group of families who don't always get along but who still owe loyalty to one another and to their Laird. Considered in a 1980s context, this Arthur Ransome*-like novel sugarcoats the tensions that uniting two families can create, especially when the children are in the middle years and from such different backgrounds. Characters are distinctively drawn, except for the parents who are vague and shadowy and on the fringes. The episodes are well-paced and developed, there is generous dialogue, and, though there is an underlying note of seriousness, the tone is mostly light and upbeat. The theme that give and take are essential for a relationship to work develops gradually through the action. The sense of the Scots physical setting is strong; descriptive terms evoke the smells and sounds of the coast, and the flavor of Scots life comes through. (Geordie* Monroe) Fanfare.

BATTY (*Kept in the Dark**), Mrs. Battle, housekeeper who comes four days a week to cook and
clean in the grandparents' large home where the
children are staying temporarily while their
father is ill. Resentful of the "airs" put on by
the grandmother, Liz*, Batty has been playing a
mean game of repeatedly hiding some article and
pretending that Liz has forgotten it, making the
old woman doubt her own memory or, when she has
accused Mrs. Battle of stealing, having to
apologize. Although she is a slovenly housekeeper and she seems sinister at first, the
children are scared when their half-cousin
David* fires her and they realize that no more
outsiders will be coming into the house he has
begun to terrorize.

BAWDEN, NINA (MABEY) (1925-   ), born in London; novelist for both adults and children.
She attended Ilford County High School, received
her B.A. and M.A. degrees from Somerville
College, Oxford, and has done graduate work at
the Salzburg Seminar in American Studies. She
has served as Justice of the Peace for Surrey
and as a reviewer for the *Daily Telegraph*, London. Her early books for children, though full
of exciting episodes, are not always entirely
plausible. These include *The Witch's Daughter**
(Gollancz, 1966; Lippincott, 1966), a mystery
set on a Scottish island, but with *Squib*
(Gollancz, 1971; Lippincott, 1971), a story of
children who rescue, somewhat clumsily, an
abused child, her accounts of contemporary life
became more probable, and both *The Robbers**
(Gollancz, 1979; Lothrop, 1979), which was a
Horn Book Fanfare choice, and *Kept in the Dark**
(Gollancz, 1982; Lothrop, 1982), which was an
Edgar Allan Poe Award nominee, depend more upon
character than plot and are thoroughly
convincing. During World War II, she and her
younger brother were evacuated to a small mining
town in Wales, an experience that serves as the
background for her best-known book for children,
*Carrie's War** (Gollancz, 1973; Lippincott,
1973), which, among other honors, has been named
a Contemporary Classic. She won the Guardian A-
ward for *The Peppermint Pig** (Gollancz, 1975;
Lippincott, 1975), a story Jill Paton* Walsh has
called "a small masterpiece." In this, and to

some degree in all her other books, she demonstrates a rare ability to see events through the
eyes of a child who perceives things clearly but
lacks the maturity to understand the full situation, thereby producing a story readable on two
levels at once. Among her more recent books are
The Finding (Gollancz, 1985; Lothrop, 1985), a-
bout an adopted child who inherits money and
runs away when it disrupts his happy home, and a
picture book, *Princess Alice* (Duetsch, 1986),
illustrated by Phillida Gill. She has also written a large number of novels for adults.

BAYLIS, SARAH (1956-1987), born in London; artist, illustrator, and author. She attended private schools in London, a small co-educational
school and St. Paul's Junior School for Girls,
then the Godolphin and Latymor state grammar
school for girls and later Sussex University,
where she read English literature and obtained a
second class honors degree. For several years
she did community work with children and
illustrated a number of books, among them *Three
Rainbows* by Tenebris Light (Brilliance, 1982),
Sappho: Poems and Fragments translated from
Greek by J. Balmer (Brilliance, 1984), and the
Alice B. Toklas Cookbook (Brilliance, 1983). Her
first published work, *Vila* (Brilliance, 1984),
won the Children's Rights Workshop Other Award.
It is an adventure story with feminist themes,
set in a forest in Slavonic lands and containing
elements from the folklore of the area. She
wrote a second book for older children, *The Tomb
of Reeds* (MacRae, 1987). Her first novel for a-
dults, *Utrillo's Mother* (Pandora Press, 1987),
was published shortly after she was killed in a
road accident on her bicycle in June 1987.

BB (D(ENYS) J(AMES) WATKINS-PITCHFORD) (1905-
), born in Lamport, Northamptonshire; art
teacher, freelance illustrator and author of
fiction and nonfiction books about wildlife and
nature for both adults and children. After a
private education, he studied art for a year in
Paris and then at the Royal College of Art in
London. He took his degree from the Royal
College of Art Painting School in 1928. From
1927 to 1929, he served in the Royal Horse
Artillery territorial army; he became a captain

in the home guard in World War II. He was an art
master at Rugby School in Warwickshire from 1930
to 1947. He inherited a gift for drawing from
his parents and his love for the countryside and
wildlife came from his maternal grandfather. He
began writing at ten, illustrating his stories
with his own drawings. The son of a country
clergyman, he often played by a brook called
Folly that ran near his house. He imagined that
little men who were hunters and wore clothes
made of mouse skins lived there. These eventually became *The Little Grey Men** (Eyre, 1942;
Scribner, 1949), a nature fantasy that won the
Carnegie Medal. This is a lively tale of three
gnomes, Sneezewort, Baldmoney, and Dodder (wild-
flower names), who leave their home under an oak
to go up Folly River in search of their lost
brother and have hair-raising adventures along
the way. On publication it was praised as being
fresh and inviting and for projecting a clear
and attractive sense of the English countryside. Its sequel is *Down the Bright Stream*
(Eyre, 1948). After he retired from teaching in
1947, he became a full-time writer and illustrator, publishing thirty novels and books of
short stories for children that reflect his
knowledge and affection for the outdoors, among
them the books about the fantastic forest of
Boland and the Bill Badger series for younger
readers; also *Stories of the Wild* (Benn, 1975)
and *More Stories of the Wild* (Benn, 1977). Before he retired he published *Wild Lone* (Eyre,
1938; Scribner, 1938), about a fox, and *Sky
Gipsy: The Story of a Wild Goose* (Eyre, 1939;
published by Scribner, 1939, as *The Sky
Gipsy*). He also published twenty books of observation and personal experience in nature and
short stories for adults. His writings have
appeared in such periodicals as *Country Life*,
Field, and *Shooting Times*. Several books have
been dramatized for radio and television, and
some were translated for publication in Germany,
Holland, Yugoslavia, Israel, and Switzerland. In
addition to illustrating all his own writings in
black and white and color, he illustrated many
books for others, including editions of *Prince
Prigio** by Andrew Lang* and *The Lost Princess* by
George MacDonald*, and some books by William
Mayne*. He also wrote under the pseudonym

Michael Traherne. He married and made his home
in Northhamptonshire.

A BEAR CALLED PADDINGTON (Bond*, Michael, ill.
Peggy Fortnum, Collins, 1958; Houghton, 1960),
episodic, talking toy fantasy, in which the
stuffed animal protagonist converses and inter-
acts with humans, set in London in the mid-
1900s. On the platform of the Paddington railway
station, Mr. and Mrs. Brown discover a small,
rather dirty, brown stuffed bear, sitting on a
battered suitcase (which he takes wherever he
goes), wearing a wide-brimmed hat, and carrying
a label that says, "Please look after this bear.
Thank you." Promising to give him marmalade for
breakfast every morning, they take him home and
name him Paddington after the place where they
found him. Soon, they and their daughter, Judy
(about ten) her brother, Jonathan, and Mrs.
Bird, the housekeeper, become quite fond of the
earnest, bun-loving fellow in spite of the
predicaments he causes, and treat him like one
of the family. Paddington's several adventures
are self-contained and relate to one another
only through involving the same characters.
Paddington almost drowns in the Browns' bathtub,
which fills to overflowing when he fails to turn
off the taps and doesn't think to pull the plug;
he loses his way and creates a commotion in the
underground; he goes with the Browns on a
shopping trip to Barkridge's, where he gets a
blue duffle coat and a green pom-pom cap and
blunders into the shop window, demolishing the
marmalade can pyramid displayed there; he
destroys a painting done by. Mr. Brown while
searching for an "old master," which his
friend, Mr.* Gruber, has told him sometimes
appears beneath old pictures, but redeems himself by creating a new one which wins first
prize for originality for Mr. Brown at the
Kensington handcrafts exhibition; he accompanies
the family to the theater to see the world-
famous actor, Sir Sealy Bloom, where he drops a
marmalade sandwich on a bald spectator's head,
mixes fantasy and reality when between acts he
visits the leading lady's dressing room to
offer her his services against the villain, and
acts as Sir Sealy's prompter; at the seashore
he builds a sand castle, falls asleep beside it,

and is carried off by the tide but sails back
later safe and sound in his sand pail; and, in
the final episode, he celebrates his two months'
anniversary with the Browns at a party, where he
enjoys a birthday cake of marmalade and cream
filling and entertains his guests with a series
of calamitous disappearing tricks. Paddington's
escapades are fast moving and funny, and the
reader never doubts that the well-meaning bear
will surmount all the problems that confront
him. Human characters are cardboard and almost
interchangeable, the tone is loving if a bit
condescending, and occasionally plot details
are missing. Paddington recalls Pooh* Bear, but
Bond lacks A. A. Milne's* skill with whimsey and
character, nor does the book reveal human
nature as does its justly more famous predecessor. Even the spare line drawings recall
Shepard's. Sequels. Choice.

BECKETT (*Windfall**), villainous captain of the
fishing smack *Charity*, who practices scavenging
from wrecked vessels and smuggling on the side.
To Matt* Pullen he is an implacable enemy for
several reasons: he knows Matt resents the way
he failed to help his drowning father, Tom
Pullen, and suspects that he stole the money
from Tom's body; he has been forced by Matt's
knowledge that he planned to throw the race
against the *Juno* to sail the *Good Fortune* to a
win, thereby losing his own wagers and those of
his friends; and he has lost the smack race to
Matt's old *Fathom*. When he is skipper of the
Good Fortune and therefore in authority over
Matt, one of the crew, he rides the boy hard and
does what he can to humiliate him but is
prevented from actual violence by the presence
of Francis* Shelley and his father. In the end
he is drowned because he wears the heavy money
belt he stole from Tom Pullen's body.

THE BEETHOVEN MEDAL (Peyton*, K. M., ill.
author, Oxford, 1971; Crowell, 1972), modern
romance told from the point of view of quiet,
intense Ruth* Hollis of *Fly-by-Night* and *The
Team**, who turns her emotional attention from
horses to the new baker's boy, Pat* Pennington
(of *Pennington's Seventeenth Summer**). Although
every day she has stationed herself with the

lawn mower or rake where she can see the bakery
truck arrive, Ruth has never had nerve to strike
up a conversation with the big, sullen,
aggressive young man until she impulsively
hitches a ride with him into Northend and is
then too tongue-tied to learn more than that he
is a student--of zoology, he says. A few days
later she is astonished when he asks her to go
up to London on Sunday, as he has tickets for
"work-cum-pleasure," and, having assumed he
means a day at the zoo, is further astonished
when he takes her to a concert at Festival Hall.
Not until the next week, when she responds to
his offhand message that he will be at a certain
coffee-bar at seven, does she learn that he is a
pianist in a pub on Saturday nights and, from
his friend Maxwell (who takes her under his wing
while Pat works), she also learns that he is
studying music at a London college. When they
borrow the bakery truck and are questioned by
the police, she sees another side of Pat's
character, a defiant anger toward authority that
frightens her. Each time they meet she learns
something new and startling about him: he lives
with the parents of John Bates* on vacations
since he can't stand his own; he has served
three months in jail for inflicting "grievous
bodily harm"; he had been going out with a
beautiful, wealthy girl named Clarissa Cargill-
Smith, a fellow student, toward whom he now is
bitter; he accepts only the authority of his
music teacher, Professor* Hampton, a man of
implacable demands. When he takes her to
Clarissa's home to practice a duet and then to
turn pages for him at their performance, she
sees the elegant life Clarissa is still willing
to offer him. Later that same night, with
Maxwell and his girlfriend, they sneak into a
public pool for a swim after hours, are chased
by the police, and Pat hits his old enemy,
Officer Mitchell, and is carted off to prison.
Ruth calls on Professor Hampton to tell him of
Pat's plight, and with a good lawyer the
professor is able to get Pat out of prison for
the one night of the important concert with a
German symphony (which Ruth's whole family
attends), and where Pat plays a Rachmaninov
concerto. A few days later Ruth sits in the
hearing at magistrate's court, where Pat is let

out on bail in the professor's custody until his trial. His lawyer is sure he will get a nine-month sentence. While the lawyer and the professor have lunch, Pat and Ruth walk out on the dock. Pat goes swimming, and then in his inarticulate way he tells her of the horror of his last jail term, of his determination to get through this one and continue his music, and of his love for her. She assures him that she will wait for him, and he gives her the medal he wears on a chain around his neck, an image of Beethoven, old and finely graven. Though not particularly original in plot, the novel is moving with its strong presentation of Ruth's emotions, her doubts and self-scorn, her ecstacy when Pat smiles, her anger at the police and the professor, and her more mature acceptance of the difficult role she is taking on as Pat's girl. Characterizations of the complex boy, of Ruth, and of her worrying mother are strong, and even minor characters are well differentiated and convincing. Sequels. Fanfare.

BELINDA FELL (*Little Plum**, *Miss Happiness and Miss Flower**), lively eight-year-old who carries on an unusual competition with the wealthy little girl newly moved into the House Next Door, Gem Tiffany Jones, which is focused on Gem's neglected Japanese doll. Although Belinda herself cares little for dolls, preferring to roller skate, play ball, or climb trees, she takes up the cause of the neglected doll mostly to tease Gem and to get access, somehow, to the fascinating house where she has been forbidden to go uninvited. A friendly, open child, she is humiliated and furious when Gem's aunt invites her cousin, Nona, to tea but pointedly excludes Belinda because she is "impossibly rough." In the earlier book, *Miss Happiness and Miss Flower*, Nona is the main character, but Belinda figures as her foil, being active where Nona is quiet and confident where Nona is insecure, and she is scornful of Nona's weeping and homesickness. She is also jealous of the attention given to her cousin's project of the Japanese house for the two dolls and spoils the celebration by insisting that Miss Flower is hers and then throwing the doll carelessly into her own neglected dollhouse.

BELLE CARTER (*Black Jack**), girl whose family is sending her to a private madhouse in Islington so that the titled family into which her older sister is marrying will not know of her insanity. When her coach overturns Belle is thrown out. Tolly* Dorking finds her, they join forces, and soon, as Belle improves, they fall deeply in love. At first she is given to wildly changing and unpredictable moods, from childish brightness to screaming fury and back. She repeats phrases she has overheard from servants: "I would be better off dead, you know," "I'm a curse to the master and mistress, God's punishment," and "Wouldn't it be a blessing if I was to do myself a mischief and come to a merciful end?"; but she doesn't seem to understand the significance of what she is saying until under good treatment she gains control and appears sane again. She also has a sort of vision in which she sees a tall black tower with white angels flying around it, "and all the world's singing a lullaby--for the sun's gone to bed in a blanket." She becomes violently angry when her companions do not see it, but in the end, when they are on Tolly's uncle's ship, she points to the mast at sunset, with gulls flying around it and the setting sun seeming to sink into the sails, and Tolly sees it as she does. It is not clear whether she has been a victim of real insanity or of misunderstanding and bad treatment, but it is clear that the power of love has cured her.

BELLE MARRIOT (*Travelers by Night**), young circus performer who has fallen while she is showing off on the high wire and, in being rescued by her cousin, Charlie* Marriot, as she clings to the wire, has badly injured one side of her face. The resulting scar has disfigured her but, more disastrously, has made her extremely self-conscious. She can still perform her Star Spinner tumbling act with Charlie, in which she plays a ballerina and wears a golden mask, but she has lost her nerve and can no longer even balance on a large ball or walk the low wire, acts she used to do with ease. When she decides to save the aging elephant, Tessie, from the slaughter house, she willingly gives up the money she and Charlie have been saving for

plastic surgery to repair her face and even
agrees to tie her hair back and show her scar,
the one condition Charlie makes in agreeing to
help her. Less practical and cautious than
Charlie, she is manipulative and gets along by
being a clever actress. Although she treats
Charlie imperiously, as her ballerina character
treats his clown, she depends on him and is, in
her own way, as devoted as he is.

BELL TEESDALE (*The Hollow Land**), Cumbrian boy
who, at age eight, becomes a friend of four-
year-old Harry* Bateman and who understands what
the place means to the London child. When Bell
is older, he marries Poppet, daughter of the TV
personality, the "Household Word," and grows
"over the years more like his father than his
father had ever been."

BEN GUNN (*Treasure Island**), slightly demented
pirate who has been marooned on the island for
three years, ever since the crew of a ship in
which he sailed listened to his story of buried
treasure, failed to find it, and left him there
in revenge. Ben was on the *Walrus*, the ship of
Captain* Flint, when the notorious pirate buried
the treasure, but he appears to have been more
simple-minded than villainous even then, and the
other pirates, though highly superstitious, are
scornful even of what they think is his ghost.
Ben has managed rather well on the island,
living on the meat of wild goats, berries, and
oysters, but he dreams of cheese, "toasted,
mostly." In his years alone, he has found the
treasure and laboriously carried it to the cave
where he has been living. He returns to England
with the honest men in the *Hispaniola*, but
within nineteen days he has lost or spent his
thousand-pound share. He ends up keeping a lodge
and singing in church.

BENTLEY, PHYLLIS (ELEANOR) (1894-1977), born in
Halifax, Yorkshire, England; lecturer, bio-
grapher, literary critic, and writer of books
mostly for adults and mostly regional. She
attended Halifax High School and Cheltenham
Ladies' College and received her B.A. from the
University of London in 1914. During World War
I, she taught in a boys' grammar school and then

became a secretary in the Ministry of Munitions in London. After the war, she catalogued for three West Riding, Yorkshire, libraries and wrote in her spare time. In the mid-1920s, she was asked to give a lecture, chose for her topic the regional novel and then realized that her main interest lay in the history and people of her native county. This fascination with the activities and development of, in particular, West Riding resulted in her becoming a leading regional writer. Both sides of her family came from Yorkshire and were engaged in the woolen industry. They and their work provided characters and background for such adult novels as *Carr* (Benn, 1929) and *Inheritance* (Gollancz, 1932; Grosset, 1932), her best-known novel, which deals with the effects of the Industrial Revolution on West Riding. *Environment* (Sidgwick, 1922) and its sequel, *Cat-in-the-Manger* (Sidgwick, 1923), are stories of a Yorkshire girl much like Bentley herself. Her deep sympathy for the plight of the people of her area in the post-World War I recession produced *A Modern Tragedy* (Gollancz, 1934; Macmillan, 1934). She also wrote for adults several books about the Brontes and Gothic mysteries. She created the character of Miss Marian Phipps, an elderly spinster detective, who stars in such short stories as "A Midsummer's Night Crime." For children she wrote five historical and adventure novels, among them, *Sheep May Safely Graze* (Gollancz, 1972), about the Wars of the Roses; *The New Venturers* (Gollancz, 1973), about the Pilgrims; *The Adventures of Tom Leigh* (Macdonald, 1964; Doubleday, 1966); and *Ned Carver in Danger* (Macdonald, 1967). *Gold Pieces** (Macmillan, 1968; published in the United States as *Forgery!*, Doubleday, 1968), combines her talents at writing historical fiction and mystery. Set in Yorkshire in 1769, it revolves around coin "clipping," a kind of counterfeiting prevalent at that time. It was nominated for the Edgar Allan Poe Award. She also wrote for the British Council and the Bronte Society, contributed to periodicals, published books of nonfiction, and wrote television plays for children. During World War II, she served in the American Division of the Ministry of Information. She traveled extensively and

lectured also in the United States. She received an honorary D.Litt. from the University
of Leeds in 1949 and was awarded the Order of
the British Empire in 1970 for her contribution
to literature. She made her home in Halifax in
an old master clothier's house.

BEORN THE PROUD (Polland*, Madeleine A., ill.
William Stobbs, Constable, 1961; Holt, 1962),
historical adventure of the ninth century in
Ireland and Denmark. Overlooked in the slaughter
of her Irish village by Viking raiders, Ness is
found and claimed by Beorn, the son of Anlaf, a
Viking chief. Although no other prisoners are
taken, Anlaf indulgently lets his son keep Ness
for his slave, even when she spiritedly fights
the idea that she will be subordinate. Her
feelings toward Beorn begin to warm when he
gives her back her mother's gold chain and
cross, which had been his share of the loot, but
she fears his foster cousin, Helge, the second
in command of the *Great Serpent*. Before returning to Denmark, they raid a monastery and
capture an old hermit, whom Helge insists on
taking along, though Ness warns that God will
punish him for such an act. Anlaf, wounded in
the raid, becomes worse and dies, making Helge
leader. Bad luck dogs them until Helge puts the
old man ashore to die. In Denmark, Ness is
treated far better than most slaves, partly
because the old slave, Macha, who has raised
Beorn, is an Irish Christian. It soon becomes
apparent that Helge plans treachery, but only
when Ness overhears him talking with some
visitors from Scania do they realize that he
plans an expedition to overthrow Eyvind the
Ancient, high king of Denmark. With the help of
Ragnar, a loyal older warrior, Beorn plans
diversions for the visitors to distract them
while preparations are made for the loyal people
of Anlaf's homestead to leave. They get to the
mainland and warn the king. Old Eyvind is much
attracted to Beorn. His chief war leader, Leif
the Giant, pretends to be friendly, but Ness
realizes that he resents the king's attentions
to the boy. Beorn has an idea of cutting loose
blocks of ice from the crossing so that Helge's
expedition drowns, and when the plan is
successful the king promises that Beorn will be

his heir. In his pride the boy will not listen
to the warnings of Ness, Ragnar, and Macha, and
is unprepared at the king's death for Leif's
action: he gives them one hour to leave Denmark
forever. With no home to return to, Beorn takes
Ness's suggestion that they go to her uncle in
Ireland and beg him, for her sake, to take them
in. To make their case stronger, Beorn agrees to
become a Christian. Their plan works and, in
addition, they discover that Ness's mother is
still alive and will join them to start a new
life in the place where their old village was
destroyed. The role of religion is prominent in
this novel and may seem overstated to
non-Christians. Ness is a girl of spirit, but
her treatment is more considerate than is quite
believable considering the harsh realities of
Viking life and attitudes toward slaves at the
time. Fanfare.

BERNARD HUNTER (*The Girl in the Grove**), father
of Paul* and, eventually, second husband of
Jonquil* Darley's mother. Bernard is loud,
overconscious of money, and proud of the way he
has been able to buy up the land of the local
gentry, the Seccombes, in whose manor his mother
was a nursemaid. Despite his bluster, he is an
expert manager of his orchards and a fond father
and son.

BERT ELLISON (*The Ghost of Thomas Kempe**),
carpenter in Ledsham, reputed to be skilled in
wart removing, water divining, and exorcising.
James* Harrison learns about him from Mrs.*
Verity, who lives next door to the Harrisons and
is an old acquaintance of Bert. Bert is a blunt,
competent man, who takes James's story about the
poltergeist at face value and helps him plan the
exorcism. The scenes in which he and James try
to get rid of Thomas are among the novel's most
vivid, done with a light but not satiric touch.
Bert is working on the church when James
searches unsuccessfully in the churchyard for
Thomas's grave. James takes his problem to Bert,
who remembers discovering a crypt under the
floor and concludes that Thomas might have been
buried there. When James ponders why a sorcerer
buried there. When James ponders why a sorcerer
should have been buried in the church, Bert

surmises that it was probably because some people like "to hedge their bets" and not put all "their eggs in one basket." Bert is an interesting, well-drawn figure.

BERTRAND STUDDARD (*The Wind Eye**), Cambridge professor, father of Beth* and Sally and step-father of Mike* Hendrey. Unlike his second wife, Madeleine*, Bertrand is careful, scholarly pedantic, and nonemotional, and his tendency to instruct at every opportunity is infuriating to both Madeleine and Mike. A rationalist and an atheist, he is scornful of the superstitions about St. Cuthbert, and he refuses to believe in the fantasy experiences that he and his children experience on the boat, *Resurre*. Even when Sally's burned hand is cured, he is more angry at what he thinks is some sort of trick than he is thrilled that she will not go through life crippled. A pacifist, he dislikes physical conflict though he is an expert at judo. He is not above sparring with words, however, and even getting into shouting matches with his wife. Even Beth realizes that he should have had an affair with Madeleine rather than a marriage, but although he believes in Free Love in principle, he is uncomfortable with it in practice. When he finally must admit the power of St. Cuthbert, he wants to strip all religion from it and scientifically examine Supernature as a force that can be controlled and explained.

BETH STUDDARD (*The Wind Eye**), teenaged daughter of Bertrand*, a stuffy Cambridge professor, and stepdaughter of his clearly nonintellectual second wife, Madeleine*. Unlike her atheist father, Beth is religious, "a pious little prig," Madeleine calls her. Beth often hates Madeleine, but she has a genuine attachment to Madeleine's teenaged son, Mike* Hendrey, and she is protectively fond of her little sister, Sally, 6. She also loves her father deeply, though she sees his faults and understands why both Madeleine and Mike frequently find him unbearable. Mostly, Beth wants the family to be happy, a hope that seems doomed even before their encounters with St. Cuthbert.

BETO (*Talking in Whispers**), one of the twins

who run the marionette show and who pick up and shelter Andres* Larreta. More impetuous than his sister, Isa*, Beto usually lets her take the lead in their activities. Because their own parents are among the "disappeared," he does not hesitate to support Andres in his desire to expose the brutal regime in power in Chile, but he is a little jealous of Isa's growing attraction to Andres, whom he calls, in a mixture of contempt and affection, "Towny."

BETSY ASHWORTHY-SMITH (*"Minnow" on the Say**), a beautiful, sweet, well-mannered girl of about sixteen, who is used by her greedy father, who calls himself Mr.* Smith, to advance his interests. David* Moss trusts her, thinks of her as an elder sister, takes her for a ride in the *Minnow*, and shows her the old bridge where Jonathan* Codling hid the family jewels. Adam* Codling, however, continues to distrust her to the end and refuses to accept her.

BETSY FARR (*Castors Away!**), neat, orderly farm girl, who serves Aunt Julia Henchman as a maid and becomes Nell* Henchman's best friend. She is a sturdy, sensible girl of about Nell's own age, which is twelve. She has little formal schooling but has picked up a good deal of practical information and knows more about the ways of the world than Nell. The Henchman children accept her as one of them, and, when she and they are together without adults around, she contributes equally to the conversation and activity. She assists the Henchmans in reviving Sergeant James* Bubb and helps the children manage his escape from the military authorities. Years later, she marries him. She is a well-drawn, engaging figure in whom the reader can see growth.

BEYOND THE WEIR BRIDGE. See *Thomas.*

BIDDY (*Great Expectations**), good, intelligent village girl who loves Pip* but who marries Joe* Gargery, Pip's blacksmith brother-in-law. Biddy has been a helper at the village school which Pip first attends, and after Pip's sister is attacked and injured, Biddy comes to live at their house and care for her. Pip's rise in

fortune makes him scorn her and treat her in a
patronizing and condescending way, but she
doesn't berate him for that or for neglecting
Joe as he does, nor does she object when Joe
spends the money they have been saving for their
future in paying off Pip's debts. They name
their first child for Pip. Biddy is a foil for
heartless Estella*.

BIGWIG (*Watership Down**), one of the largest and
staunchest of the Watership Down rabbits, a
strong and loyal fighter. Previously a member of
the Owsla (peace force) at Sandleford Warren, he
becomes a major figure and fighting mainstay of
the new warren under Hazel's* leadership. He can
be testy and inclined to throw his weight around
and to rough the others up a bit, particularly
at first, but he mellows through his experiences. At the end he serves as trainer of young
rabbits for the warren Owsla, a kind of beloved
senior citizen, an old-soldier type. His biggest part in the story involves entering Efrafa
to get doe rabbits, an assignment that requires
not only physical strength but a cool head and
great courage. His name derives from a curious
growth of fur on the crown of his head and is a
translation of Thayli, which means, literally,
"Furhead." Though an obvious type, he has
distinctiveness and depth.

BILBO BAGGINS (*The Hobbit**; *The Fellowship of
the Ring**), hobbit* who joins thirteen dwarfs in
an expedition to regain their ancestral home
and wealth from the dragon Smaug*. At first
rather timid and conventional, Bilbo grows in
character and confidence as the adventure
progresses until when the spiders of Mirkwood
attack, he is instrumental in saving the dwarfs,
and when they are in the elven prison, he works
out their escape. Before the final battle, he
gives the Arkenstone of Thrain to the men of
Laketown, knowing that greed has made Thorin*
Oakenshield unreasonable and that only with some
bargaining chip of great value to him can he be
brought to see that all the forces for good must
join. Thereby Bilbo plays an important role in
the final victory, though he does no real
fighting. Bilbo returns to The Shire, where he
is almost forgiven for having an adventure

because he is very generous with his wealth, and there he lives for sixty years, physically almost unchanged, until the start of *The Fellowship of the Ring*, being visited occasionally by elves, dwarfs, and the wizard, Gandalf*, and often writing songs and poems, but otherwise leading a respectable hobbit life. He remains a bachelor but adopts his young cousin, Frodo* Baggins, as his heir, and on his "eleventy-first" birthday throws a big party, makes a speech of farewell, and disappears, having slipped on the ring which he found in the orc mountain where he played the riddle game with Gollum*. He then goes home, collects a few things to travel with, and, leaving all his other possessions to Frodo (including the ring), departs. Frodo finds him again at Rivendell, home of the half-elves, where he has been living and writing the story of his adventures for nearly seventeen years. There, at the council of Elrond, when it becomes clear that the ring must be taken to Mordor, Bilbo courageously volunteers to try, but his offer is fondly rejected because his great age makes it impractical. He gives Frodo his sword, Sting, and his priceless mail corselet made of mithril, and promises to write the story of Frodo's endeavor if he lives long enough. When Frodo returns to Rivendell in time to celebrate Bilbo's 129th birthday, Bilbo gives him his manuscript and all his notes, and Frodo himself finishes most of the story, leaving only the final chapter to Sam* Gamgee, when, a year later, he joins Bilbo, Gandalf, and the last of the elves who are leaving Middle-earth and going across the sea, into the West.

BILGEWATER (Gardam*, Jane, Hamilton, 1976; Greenwillow, 1977), realistic novel set in a Yorkshire boys' boarding school in the mid-twentieth century, about a generation before the time of the publication. The narrator, "Bilgewater" or "Bilgie", 17, is really named Marigold Daisy Green, but has received her nickname from the boys of St. Wilfrid's where her father is a Housemaster. There he is known as Bill, and she is always referred to as "Bill's daughter," as if she has no identity of her own. Her mother having died at her birth, she

has led an odd life with her eccentric father, a
sweet-tempered, abstracted man, and the house
matron, Paula* Rigg, a whirlwind of energy and
common sense from a farm in Dorset, who is
young for her job, strikingly good looking, and
essential to the welfare and comfort of
Bilgewater, her father, and the boys. For years
thought to be retarded or mentally disturbed
because a visual problem kept her from reading,
Bilgie has grown up solitary and convinced that
she is ugly, awkward and, though brilliant,
unlovable. Among the boys she has always been
taken for granted, though she is often
tormented by Tom Terrapin*, a boy whose family
problems have kept him at school during the
holidays, and condescendingly tolerated by the
head boy, Jack Rose, whom she adores from afar.
At the Comprehensive school in town, which she
attends, she is friendless until the
Headmaster's daughter, Grace Gathering, returns,
having been expelled from her latest boarding
school. A beautiful, confident girl, Grace takes
Bilgie in hand, gets her very nice red hair cut
and shaped and chooses some stylish clothes for
her to replace the outlandish castoffs that
Paula has casually provided. Still, Bilgie is
astonished when Jack Rose asks her to visit at
his home between terms, saying that his mother
knew her mother in school. The invitation fills
her with both delight and consternation, and she
almost backs out, but finally with the help of
Paula and two other masters who act as her
uncles--old Hastings-Benson*, who teaches
English and maths and is always falling in love,
and Puffy Coleman, who teaches history and is
partial to the pretty, little, new boys--she
goes off on the right bus and makes the
necessary changes. Her arrival at Jack Rose's
home is a terrible disappointment, since it is
not the country house she has been led to
expect, but a suburban dentist's office, with
family living quarters above and behind. Jack's
parents, who are both dentists, have forgotten
she is expected, and the crowning blow is that
when Jack arrives he has brought Grace Gathering
with him. The weekend is a nightmare, with
everyone, including Bilgie, drinking too much.
At one point she discovers Jack and Grace
amorously entwined on the kitchen floor. She

goes off by herself to church and has a pleasant
conversation with the   rector, but later, unable
to bear the situation any longer, she climbs out
a window and catches a bus   toward home, though
she   doesn't have   enough   money for the   whole
fare. With   a vague   idea that   she will   try to
borrow money from a grossly overweight woman who
earlier sat next to her on the bus, she heads in
the cold and dark for Marston Hall, where the
woman   works,   and   finds   a   huge,   seemingly
deserted,   run-down country   house.   To   her
amazement, Terrapin answers the door   and takes
her up to his room in the tower, gives her hot
soup, and   tells her a little   about his strange
family circumstances.   They are in   bed together
when the   crude elephantine   woman bangs on the
door.   Bilgie has   second   thoughts and   insists
that Terrapin take her back to the Roses'. There
she writes a note to the rector, asking him to
call Hastings-Benson to come and get her as soon
as possible. To her great relief, he rescues her
the next morning, and they spend a marvelous day
with the rector, an old friend of his, and his
son, who turns out to be Boakes, another boy
from the   school, visiting cathedrals   and other
points of interest with Bilgie still wearing the
long   black   dress   belonging   to   Terrapin's
deceased grandmother, which he had provided
instead of her soaked clothes the night before.
When they   return to the school, they find that
Paula has left and Miss Bex, a teacher from the
Comprehensive whom Bilgie despises, is very much
in evidence, fussing over her father and acting
quite   possessive.   The   boys   returning   from
holiday   are all in need of Paula, and Bilgie
takes over, only to   discover that a number of
them are really ill, some with measles and some
with flu.   Although both Bilgie and Boakes are
about to   take their   Oxbridge exams,   they find
themselves in charge of a whole sick bay of
boys, and the entire   school in crisis, Terrapin
having run off with Grace Gathering and Jack
Rose with Grace's mother. Frantically, Bilgie
hunts for an address where Paula might be found
and discovers that Paula's private drawers are
full of little momentoes of her father and of
her own childhood. As the sick boys are
beginning to mend, Bilgie finds herself in bed
with Boakes but again saves her virginity by

suddenly realizing where she has seen Paula's
address and impulsively jumping up to write a
desperate plea to her to come back. With almost
no concentrated preparation, Bilgie takes her
Oxbridge exams and finds things to do to keep
her out of the house, where Miss Bex is more and
more prominent. Just as it looks as if the
teacher is about to nail down her claims to
Bilgie's father, Paula arrives, routs Miss Bex,
and brings with her the mail with invitations
for both Bilgie and Boakes to Cambridge. The
story is told with a frame scene of an interview
with the principal at the Cambridge college,
cleverly designed to seem at the beginning that
Bilgie is the interviewee but revealed at the
end of the book to be the interview of
Terrapin's daughter, conducted by Bilgie (now
Lady Boakes), the first woman principal of the
college. Though the coincidences rather boggle
the mind, they somehow seem appropriate, since
Bilgie sees the world with the disorganized
perceptions of an adolescent who is brilliant
but unworldly, and the epigraph of the book is a
quotation from Disraeli, "Youth is a blunder."
Bilgewater's extreme naivete at seventeen is
also plausible, since she has spent her
childhood in very strange surroundings. The
story is full of her clever, usually impertinent
thoughts. The result is a novel with an unlikely
plot but strong, interesting characterizations.
Choice; Fanfare.

BILL COWARD (*The Nature of the Beast**), son and
grandson of mill workers, a boy still in school
and therefore about fourteen. Around the house
he does most of the cooking and clean up, such
as it is, and has a sense of responsibility for
the two rough men who have raised him. Unlike
either of them, he does not have a sudden
violent temper, but rather what he describes as
a slow fuse, leading eventually to a bigger
explosion. It is in an effort to get enough
money to enable his jobless father to come home
that he takes his teacher's camera and hunts the
Haverston Beast. His future, at the book's end,
looks grim, but his teacher may be right when he
describes Bill as a survivor.

BILL SPARROW (*The Battle of Bubble and Squeak**),

stepfather of Sid*, Peggy, and Amy Parker.
Pleasant, mild-mannered, and soft-spoken, he
seems a milquetoast at first but really has a
mind of his own. Realizing that confrontation
with his emotional, strong-willed wife will not
accomplish anything productive, he defers to her
on the surface but does what he thinks right in
the long run. He knows she finds change hard to
accept. When Sid runs away after Mrs.* Sparrow
gives away his gerbils, Bubble* and Squeak,
Bill goes after Sid and demonstrates his sympathy to the boy by informing him that he
himself had white mice as a child. He suggests
that Mrs. Sparrow might eventually be "talked
round" into keeping the gerbils. At the end, in
a pleasant scene that appears to celebrate Mrs.
Sparrow's having indeed "come round," Bill
brings home a bag full of white sugar mice for
the children. He is a thoroughly likeable and
convincing character.

BILLY BONES (*Treasure Island**), old buccaneer
who comes to the Admiral Benbow Inn, calls
himself "the captain," and terrorizes the
proprietor and the local people with his rough
ways, drunken rages, and the old sea song,
"Fifteen men on the dead man's chest--/
Yo-ho-ho, and a bottle of rum!" The mate of the
notorious pirate vessel, the *Walrus*, he was
with the leader, Captain* Flint, when Flint died
of rum at Savannah, and, having made off with
the map to Flint's buried treasure, has been
fleeing his old shipmates ever since. When they
catch up with him and slip him the black spot,
the ultimatum that tells him he must give up the
map by ten o'clock, he dies of a stroke brought
on by fear and too much rum. His description in
the second paragraph of the book is one of the
most famous openings in all literature: "I remember him as if it were yesterday, as he came
plodding to the inn door, his sea-chest
following behind him in a handbarrow; a tall,
strong, heavy, nut-brown man; his tarry pigtail
falling over the shoulders of his soiled blue
coat; his hands ragged and scarred, with black,
broken nails; and the saber cut across one
cheek, a dirty, livid white." Although he is
dead by the end of the third chapter, he sets
the tone of terror in the book and is remembered

by the other pirates as a rough hand who would
"cut men down like that much pork."

BILLY BYRNE (*The Green Bough of Liberty**), middle brother in the family at Ballymanus, destined to be a priest before the rebellion of
1798 changes his life. When he is condemned to
be hanged for his part, he is offered a way out
if he will implicate the other leaders by saying
that they seduced him into the rebel organization of United Irishmen, but he refuses to bear
false witness. In his prison cell he admits to
Ned that he is terrified of the pain of hanging,
though he still believes in God and heaven. A
real historical figure, his goodness became
proverbial in the country, where a saying
developed, "As innocent as poor Billy Byrne."

BING JONES (*The Robbers**), older brother of
Darcy* Jones. He has a stall in the antiques
market and is imprisoned as a receiver of stolen
goods. In court he pleads guilty, proudly
admitting that he had reason to believe that at
least some of the goods he has bought at the
early-morning "market" might have been stolen.
Cheerful and hard working, he is trying to save
enough money to start a regular antique store.
He laughs at his father's assurance that their
coming baby will be a boy and admits that he
hopes it will be a girl, who will be tall like
his black wife. Although he clearly knew that it
was risky to buy from the back of trucks and
make whispered deals with shady characters, the
implication is that he is no more guilty of
wrongdoing than Henry* Holbein, who buys plates
cheap from Bing's stall, knowing they were
probably stolen.

BIRDIE PLANTAGANET (*The Dolls' House**), celluloid doll who acts as mother in the doll family
Originally part of a party cracker with a
feather skirt, she has been dressed in a red
skirt with blue rickrack braid on the hem and a
blue blouse with red pin spots that on her look
as large as buttons. Something in her celluloid
head rattles, and her thoughts also seem to
rattle around, so that she has trouble remembering that her son, Apple, has been given to
haughty Marchpane. She tries to save him from

the candle, burning herself up in the attempt.

THE BLACK ARROW: A TALE OF THE TWO ROSES (Stevenson*, Robert Louis, Cassell, 1888; Scribner, 1888), swashbuckling historical novel and adventure story set in England in the 1460s during the Wars of the Roses. Dick* (Richard) Shelton, 17, has been ward of Sir* Daniel Brackley since the death of his father in his infancy and has been taught by the priest, Sir* Oliver Oates. When Sir Daniel, for the moment on the Lancastrian side, is summoning his men for a foray, old Nick Appleyard, a veteran of Agincourt, is killed with a black arrow to which is attached a message threatening death also for Bennet Hatch, Sir Daniel's right-hand man, for Sir Oliver, and for Sir Daniel, in revenge for their oppression and foul deeds, and signed Jon* Amend-All. It also names Sir Oliver as the murderer of Dick's father. This arouses his suspicions, since Sir Oliver is Sir Daniel's tool, and Sir Daniel has made a handsome profit serving as Dick's guardian. That same day, after delivering a note from Bennet to Sir Daniel, he is asked by a boy called Jack Matcham for directions to Holywood and sees him creep from the room. On his return trip he overtakes Jack, and though he finds him a weak and unmanly boy, he listens to his story of being taken by force by Sir Daniel, and he agrees to see him to sanctuary at Holywood. On their way they run into the outlaw band under Ellis Duckworth, who, it turns out, is Jon Amend-All (and among them Will Lawless*, their cook), all preparing to ambush Sir Daniel. In trying to warn his guardian's men, Dick kills a man. He and Jack quarrel about it but then trudge on together until they come upon a blind leper, who turns out to be Sir Daniel, fleeing home disguised because the Yorkist forces have prevailed for the moment. He forces them to go on to the Moat House at Tunstall. There Dick bravely but unwisely asks questions about his father's death. Sir Daniel swears that he had nothing to do with it and forces Sir Oliver to take the same oath, but the priest's trepidation in swearing confirms Dick's suspicions. Sir Daniel realizes that he is not convinced and orders him to change his room to the one above the chapel.

Later, Jack Matcham, having overheard that Dick
is to be killed, comes to warn him, and as they
wait together, Dick realizes that Jack is really
Joanna* Sedley, the young woman Sir Daniel
planned to have him marry in order to get her
fortune in his control. They escape through a
trap door down a secret passage until they come
to an exit blocked by an unmoveable stone.
Bennet Hatch, sent to apprehend them, tells him
the secret of lifting the stone and lets them
get away into another chamber of the house.
Joanna is recaptured but Dick escapes down a
rope into the moat and thence into the forest.
There he collapses, is picked up by Ellis
Duckworth's band, and joins them. After some
months, during which the tide of the war has
turned from York to Lancaster again and Dick has
become one of the leaders in Duckworth's band,
he learns that Joanna is being held in a
dilapidated house on the beach not far from
Shoreby-on-the-Till and that Sir Daniel is now
planning to marry Joanna to old Lord Shoreby, a
man of infamous reputation. To try to free her,
Dick joins forces with Lord Foxham, her rightful
guardian. A daring rescue attempt by sea in the
Good Hope, a small ship Lawless has stolen for
the venture, is unsuccessful and leaves the ship
wrecked and Lord Foxham badly wounded. Dick
goes with Lawless to his hideout, a snug den
under the roots of a huge fallen beach tree.
There he buries the letter given him by the
(evidently) dying Lord Foxham to Richard* of
Gloucester, leader of the Yorkist forces (who
afterwards becomes King Richard III), and
Lawless, who once was a novice, provides friars'
robes for both of them and cleverly disguises
Dick's face. Together they go to Sir Daniel's
mansion, where a celebration has begun for the
wedding of Joanna and Lord Shoreby the next day.
A handmaiden helps him get to Joanna's room,
where they are briefly reunited, but later Sir
Oliver recognizes him. His old tutor does not
betray him but insists that he stay beside him
in the chapel praying all night, and Dick fears
that he will be witness to Joanna's wedding in
the early morning. Even as the procession is
going down the chapel aisle, however, Duckworth's men shoot Lord Shoreby and escape. At
Sir Oliver's direction, Dick and Lawless are

seized, but Dick speaks up boldly, and Lord Risingham, one of the guests, takes them captive while he sorts out the story. Dick convinces him by giving him an earlier letter from Sir Daniel to a Yorkist noble, written when Lancaster seemed to be losing, which not only proves his former guardian is a turncoat but also shows that he offered Risingham's estate as a bribe. Dick and Lawless are allowed to escape. The next morning Dick goes to St. Bride's cross as he has promised Lord Foxham and arrives just in time to aid a young man set upon by eight assailants. He helps stand them off until they are joined by men at arms. The noble proves to be Richard of Gloucester, who, upon hearing Dick's information, decides to attack Shoreby at once. In the ensuing battle, Dick holds one of the key streets with great courage and, when later knighted and offered a reward by Gloucester, asks for the life of Arblaster (the owner of the *Good Hope*), who has been captured, since his conscience has bothered him for ruining the poor shipmaster. Gloucester is disgusted with his choice, but he releases the old sailor, who is not grateful, and sends Dick on with a small troop to catch the escaping Sir Daniel. He is able to find Joanna, again dressed as Jack Matcham, but in the snow and dark Sir Daniel escapes him, and he loses most of his men. He finds Lord Foxham, partly recovered, with Gloucester. Foxham agrees to a marriage between Dick and Joanna the next day. Early in the morning, Dick runs into Sir Daniel in the woods, but rather than getting revenge, lets him go; before he is out of sight, however, Sir Daniel is shot by Duckworth's black arrow. Gloucester, meeting Joanna, offers her marriage to a much higher noble, but she insists on marrying Dick. They live quietly apart from the strife between York and Lancaster, and out of conscience support Arblaster. Lawless becomes a friar. The novel is divided into five books, each of which has enough action for a novel itself, and has a full canvas of characters, few of which are developed. Since there are any number of murders, besides men killed in battles and skirmishes, Dick's contrition for stealing and wrecking the *Good Hope* seems selective. The conflict between the two sides is not explored in any political or philosophical way but serves as background for action and intrigue. The resulting picture is more one of a violent and lawless period than of historical reasons or occurrences. Individual scenes of action are memorable, and Dick is an adequate hero, naive but upright and brave. Children's Classics.

BLACK BEAUTY: THE AUTOBIOGRAPHY OF A HORSE (Sewell*, Anna, Jarrold, 1877; *BLACK BEAUTY: HIS GROOMS AND COMPANIONS*, Am. Humane Ed., 1890), classic horse novel about the trials, tribulations, and varying fortunes of a black riding and carriage horse from earliest memories to late middle age as told by Black Beauty himself. One of six colts on a contemporary English horse farm not far from London, Beauty is instructed by his sweet-dispositioned mother, Pet, always to remember that he is well-bred and well-born and to grow up to be gentle and obedient. His good and kind master calls him Darkie because of his dull black color. At four years of age, he is gently broken to the bridle, saddle, and harness, and often pulls with Pet, who continues her moral training--"Do your best, keep up your good name." Bought by Squire Gordon of Birtwick Park not far away, he makes friends with Merrylegs, a little, fat, gray pony; Ginger*, a tall chestnut mare of changeable disposition and sordid history; Sir Oliver, an old, brown hunter; and Justice, a roan cob, who tell him stories of such cruel human practices in the name of fashion as tail docking and extremely tight checkreins. Mrs. Gordon renames the sturdy horse with one white foot and a star on his forehead Black Beauty, and he is gently used by Squire, John Manly*, the groom, and James Howard*, the stable boy, who strive to eliminate cruelty to horses. Beauty serves these kind people well and is valued by them. On one occasion he saves the lives of his master and John when he refuses to cross a flooded bridge, which they later learn is washed out. When James takes a new position, he is replaced by young Little Joe Green, willing but unskilled, who doesn't take proper care of Beauty after a long, hard ride, and the horse catches pneumonia. Three years after Beauty arrives at the Gordons', Mrs. Gordon must go abroad for her

health, and the master sells Black Beauty and
Ginger to his friend, the Earl of W----- at
Earlshall Park. Although the Earl forbids it and
York, his groom, protests, the Countess insists
that Beauty and Ginger be severely checkreined
to keep their heads up and necks highly arched
in the current London mode. Ginger rebels and is
given to the Gordon's son for a hunter, but
Beauty gets a new mate, Max, and suffers
altogether four months of the checkrein until
another riding horse runs away, injuring the
Gordon's daughter, and the gentle Beauty, now
called Black Auster, becomes her special mount.
Beauty's good fortune fails to last, however,
for Reuben Smith, a substitute groom given to
"demon drink," overdrives Beauty one night. He
loses a shoe, stumbles and falls to his knees,
throwing Smith to his death. Beauty's recovery
is long and painful, and his knees are so
scarred that the appearance-conscious Earl decides the horse must be sold. Beauty is
purchased by a master of livery stables, the
first in a succession of cruel masters, under
whom he is abused, underfed, and neglected.
Beauty continues to give good service anyway,
and luckily he is sold at a horse fair to kind,
good Jerry* Barker, a London cabbie, whose
family renames the horse Jack. Comfortable and
well-treated again, though he has to work very
hard, Beauty becomes friends with an old
war-horse named Captain* and sees much bad
treatment of cab and cart horses, especially by
the butchers. Beauty's three happy years with
the Barkers end when, one cold New Year's Eve,
Jerry picks up a cough that turns into
bronchitis and is ill for a long time. On
doctor's advice he gives up his cab to work as a
coachman. Beauty is sold to a corn dealer and
then to the owner of a cab company, both of whom
overload him and beat him until he wishes that
he might "drop down dead at my work and be out
of my misery." One day he is struggling to haul
a much overloaded cab up Ludgate Hill from the
railway station, goaded by chucks of the rein
and lashes of the whip, when he slips and
collapses to the ground. A kind man helps him to
a stable close by, and a farrier prescribes
rest. Twelve days later he is taken to a horse
sale, where an old gentleman farmer, Mr.

Thoroughgood, realizes he is a horse of high
quality fallen on hard times and buys him. The
gentleman's grandson, Willie, renames the horse
Old Crony. At Mr. Thoroughgood's home, perfect
rest, good food, soft turf, and loving care
build up Beauty's body and spirits, and he pulls
Mr. Thoroughgood and Willie in a phaeton with
ease and joy. Mr. Thoroughgood finds Beauty his
last home, a country place with three gentle-
women who take him on trial, are pleased with
his paces and gentle mouth, and promise he'll
never be sold again. Their groom turns out to be
Little Joe Green, once Squire Gordon's stable
boy, who recognizes Beauty by his star and white
foot. Beauty, now thirteen or fourteen years
old, looks forward to giving good service and
receiving gentle treatment for the rest of his
life. Sentimental, moralistic, and overex-
tended, the novel is a tract, an open protest
against cruelty to horses, which succeeded in
promoting more humane treatment of animals. The
novel gains force from its detailed descriptions
of horse behavior and the use of horses in those
days, which carry the conviction of experience
and observation. Some scenes are exciting; many
are moralistic and preachy. The point of view
remains carefully focused, but Beauty reveals
more than equine knowledge, and, along with the
other horses and some human characters, he
mouths the author's humanitarian concerns, particularly in the stories they tell within the
larger story. Beauty is a plucky protagonist,
who ironically seems more feminine than masculine. He lives up to the highest standard of
horse behavior. He is a model equine: earnest,
modest, intelligent, obedient, willing. A martyr among horses, he is occasionally a little
smug about his goodness. The style is quaint,
the conversation wooden, and the large cast of
characters features many obvious types, often
in cameo appearances. (Seedy* Sam; Alfred*
Smirk) Children's Classics.

BLACK HEARTS IN BATTERSEA (Aiken*, Joan, Cape,
1965; Doubleday, 1964), broadly humorous,
realistic novel with fantasy aspects. It purports to be historical and to take place in
England during the reign of James III near the
beginning of the nineteenth century, while the

country is still plagued by wild, ravenous
wolves. Orphaned country boy Simon*, about fifteen, travels to London where he is to study
art. When he arrives at the boarding house of
his mentor, Dr. Gabriel Field, he learns to his
surprise from the landlords, Mr.* and Mrs.
Abednego Twite (whom, along with their family,
Simon considers a "shifty, havey-cavey lot"),
that the doctor has never lived there. Simon is
accepted right away at the Riviere Academy by
its peppery principal, Dr. Furneaux, also known
as Dr. Furnace. There he encounters feckless
Justin, Lord Bakerloo, who is heir to the
Battersea dukedom, and helps him with his
drawing; gets a job near by with wheelwright,
Mr. Cobb; meets his old friend from the
orphanage, Sophie* (now maid to the Duchess of
Battersea), who embroiders tapestries; befriends
scrawny, abused, tart-tongued Dido Twite,
daughter of his landlord; accepts an invitation
to the castle to play chess with the eccentric
Duke, who studies molds in his spare time; and
finishes cleaning an heirloom picture that Dr.
Field had been working on for the Duke. In
addition to being perplexed over the disappearance of his friend, Simon discovers that
the Twites and some of the Battersea retainers,
notably Justin's tutor, Buckle, are involved in
a plot to overthrow King James and put Bonnie
Prince Georgie of Hanover on the throne, and
that the Twites have an arsenal of weapons
stored in their cellar. Fearing Simon knows
their plans, the Twites have the boy kidnapped
and taken aboard the *Dark Dew*, commanded by
conspirator Captain Nathaniel Dark and bound
for Bremen. Dido, now grown fond of Simon, who
has taken her to a fair, informs Sophie of the
kidnapping by note and then with Justin stows
away on board the *Dark Dew* hoping to rescue
Simon. When the ship catches fire, the three
make for a nearby island, but Dido is lost. On
Inchmore, Simon and Justin discover Dr. Field,
marooned there by the conspirators because he
knew their plans, and Mrs. Buckle, who informs
them that Justin is really her son and that
Simon is the rightful heir to the Battersea
dukedom. While this is going on, the Duke and
Duchess head for the King's country estate at
Chippings, taking Sophie with them. They hope to

find Justin there. Along the way they stop at
the rude forest hut of Sophie's now deceased
foster father, old Turveytop, the glass burner.
After fighting off an attack of wolves with
billiard balls, they discover in Turveytop's
secret tree hiding-place a chain bracelet that
proves Sophie is also a Battersea. Some weeks
later, Simon, Justin, Mrs. Buckle, and Dr. Field
turn up at Chippings, Dr. Field having doped
some sailors with a soporific seaweed so that
the quartet could escape from the island. Mrs.
Buckle relates her story about Simon's identity
and soon all take off for London in the Duke's
rose-colored air balloon, landing in the Cobbs'
yard, arriving just in time for the Duke and
Duchess to give their annual Christmas Eve mince
pie dinner for King James. Simon discovers that
the Twites' arsenal has been moved to Battersea
Castle and that the conspirators plan to dynamite the castle that evening. Simon engineers a
daring and timely rescue of the good people by
balloon, and the bad people are blown up along
with the castle. The plot is drawn with a full
palette of melodramatic Dickensian incidents
and amazing characters. It moves rapidly, offering plenty of action, tongue-in-cheek humor,
and lots of twists, turns, and lighthearted
villainy. This book follows *Wolves of
Willoughby Chase**, which also concerns Simon,
and precedes *Nightbirds on Nantucket**, which
features Dido. Choice.

BLACKIE (*A Chance Child**), so called because
half her face is blackened and grotesquely
deformed by having been burned when she fell
forward, exhausted and asleep at the bellows,
into the fire. At age seven, she was sold for
ten shillings by her mother to the nail and
chain maker, who brutally overworks her, spends
most of his pay on drink, and keeps her awake by
showering her with sparks from the anvil. When
Tom* Moorhouse callously rejects her because of
her appearance, she cries bitterly, but after
Creep* brings her back she sings and never
mentions the incident again. Though very small
and ill-used, she has a tough spirit and an
optimistic outlook; she is a survivor among the
abused child laborers. In the pamphlet about his
life Creep says that he returned to the mill

town on "mischief night," when young men leave
tokens on doorsteps of the girls they are
interested in, so he leaves on her doorstep a
holly bush, signifying one loved in secret, and
a sprig of birch, signifying a pretty wench.
Creep is afraid she will not want to marry a
cripple, but she is willing, and he says they
have never a hard word between them, good times
and bad. As an adult, she is called her by her
real name, Lucy.

BLACK JACK (*Black Jack**), huge ruffian who has
tricked the gallows by sliding a silver tube
down his throat. He regains consciousness in
the home of the Tyburn widow who has left Tolly*
Dorking to watch the corpse while she dickers
with buyers from the Surgeons' Hall and College
of Physicians. Nearly seven feet tall and broad
to match, Black Jack is an imposing figure of
great strength and complete ruthlessness, who
insists that Tolly accompany him but scorns the
boy's compunctions and calls him derisively, "my
little saint." Since he has been stripped by the
hangman, Tolly takes a voluminous nightgown from
a clothes line for Black Jack to wear, and he is
often taken for some sort of monk. Black Jack's
weak point is his fear of madness, which keeps
him from simply picking up Belle* Carter and
taking her back to the madhouse for the reward
offered by Dr. Jones. He does hang about the
traveling fair to keep track of her, and when
she seems cured he sees his chance and tells her
that her father has gone mad and shot himself,
thereby proving that her madness is inherited
and, according to the wisdom of the day, will
come back to her. To spare Tolly further grief,
she goes willingly with Black Jack to the
madhouse, where he collects the reward and she
is chained in the squalor with the other insane
women. Later, the fear that the end of the world
is approaching, combined with the evidence of
Tolly's great devotion to Belle, affects the
great ruffian, and he becomes the instrument to
free Belle, prove her father a murder victim,
and get the two young people onto the ship bound
for New England.

BLACK JACK (Garfield*, Leon, ill. Antony Maitland, Longman, 1968; Pantheon, 1969), involved

melodrama about an innocent apprentice, a huge murderer revived from the gallows, and a mad girl from a wealthy family, set in eighteenth century England. When Mrs. Gorgandy (a "Tyburn widow" who makes a good living of claiming bodies of those hanged without any true grieving family and selling them to physicians) needs help handling the huge body of the ruffian Black* Jack, she calls on the pity of a young draper's apprentice, Tolly* (Bartholomew) Dorking, 14, and then tricks him into sitting with the corpse while she rushes off to dicker with prospective buyers. To Tolly's horror, the body begins to move and make choking noises and, using signs, persuades him to pull from its throat a silver tube, which Black Jack himself had inserted to thwart the hangman. From then on Tolly is in the power of the giant, linked to him by mutual fear: Black Jack's fear that Tolly will turn him in to be hanged properly, and Tolly's fear that Black Jack will murder him or other innocent victims if he tries to get away. Together they help an overturned coach back onto the road and are rewarded handsomely. This gives Black Jack the idea of placing a large stone in a turn of the road where it will certainly cause further coach upsets. The first to overturn, however, spills out an unusual cargo, a Dr. Jones, who runs a private madhouse in Islington; Parson Hall, his chaplain and adviser; Mitchell, his coachman; and their newest inmate, a girl about fourteen named Belle* Carter, who is being sent by her wealthy Reigate family to be kept out of sight so that her older sister can marry into a titled family without their secret being discovered. Belle escapes into a nearby wood, and Tolly is sent to find her. Belle alternates between sweet, childish prattle and fits of violent anger, and by the time Tolly gets her back to the scene of the accident the coach and all the men are gone. Together he and Belle wander on until they reach a traveling fair, where Dr. Carmody, who sells the "Elixer of Youth," takes them in, convinced that his quack medicine can cure the girl. Before long, to Tolly's horror, Black Jack joins the group, becoming part of the midgets' show since his size makes them look unusually small; actually Black Jack plans to take Belle to the madhouse

in Islington to collect the reward of ten
pounds. Tolly discovers Black Jack's weak point,
however: since he is terrified of madness, he
doesn't dare take the girl by force. The giant
makes a deal with Dr. Carmody's apprentice,
weasely Hatch, to take the news of Belle's
whereabouts to Islington. Hatch, who knows a
good thing when he sees it, blackmails both Dr.
Jones and Belle's father. As the caravan rattles
on from town to town, Black Jack keeps
disappearing and reappearing, and Tolly keeps
vowing to himself to write an explanation to his
much admired uncle, a sea captain, and to ask
his advice. He keeps putting it off as Belle's
health improves and her mind clears. In the
meantime, Mr. Carter, whose older daughter,
along with her husband and Mrs. Carter, has set
off for Europe, decides to face his situation
and writes to Dr. Jones, telling him to send
Belle back. He also keeps a pistol by his side,
determined to kill Hatch when he returns for
more money. Hatch, however, kills him instead,
and Dr. Jones, arriving at the same moment,
conspires with the blackmailer to make it look
like suicide. Hatch is taken into Dr. Jones's
employ as keeper of the men's side in place of
Mitchell (who has become a street preacher,
predicting the imminent end of the world). When
they reach Reigate, which Belle now remembers is
her home, Dr. Carmody prepares to present the
cured girl to her father, only to learn that he
has shot himself. Black Jack uses this
information to convince Belle that her madness
is hereditary and will, therefore, certainly
return. To save Tolly grief she goes off with
the giant man to the institution in Islington.
In headlong fury Tolly follows, and, when he
can't gain entrance to the madhouse, he takes a
job as potboy in the inn and continues to try to
see the girl. An unusual display of Northern
Lights and a couple of earthquakes convince the
populace that Mitchell's apocalypse is at hand.
Black Jack, in awe of the natural phenomena, the
terror of the populace, and Tolly's single-
minded devotion to Belle, breaks into the
madhouse and brings the girl out, and then sends
her with another friend from the fair on to the
river's edge, where Tolly's uncle's ship *The
Philosopher*, is at anchor. Black Jack and Tolly

go to the graveyard and dig up Mr. Carter's coffin. They discover it is empty, set off to confront the undertaker, and find Mrs. Gorgandy there, awaiting another corpse to sell. Under pressure from Black Jack she takes him and Tolly to the College of Physicians where she sold Mr. Carter's body; records there show that he was shot in the back. With this great news Black Jack carries Tolly through the swarming crowds to the river, where he and Belle board *The Philosopher* and set off for life together in New England. A brief retelling does not do justice to the complexity of the plot or the cast of bizarre characters that people the story. The grim scenes of London slums and the foul and abusive madhouse contrast with the seedy but cheerful life of the traveling fair. Throughout, the author uses irony and striking figures of speech to produce a style that in some ways mimics eighteenth-century novels and that moves with compelling action and humor to a satisfying conclusion. Carnegie Com.; Fanfare.

BLACK SAMSON (Harman*, Humphrey, Hutchinson, 1965; *AFRICAN SAMSON*, Viking, 1966), story based on a legend but told as a novel, set in the nineteenth century in the Kano valley on the eastern shores of Lake Victoria. The Joluo people, who inhabit the valley, are preyed upon by their neighbors, particularly the Nandi tribe of the hills, who raid the villages, burn the huts, and drive off the cattle. One day Opio*, about ten, son of the clan head, is out tending the family herd of goats and comes upon a band of Nandi returning from a raid who are hiding through the daylight hours with their stolen cattle among some huge stones. Opio runs home and tells his young uncle, Magere*. The peaceful Joluo discuss for hours what is to be done, until Magere rouses them to attack the Nandi. Led by Opio, they surprise the raiders, killing most and scaring off the others, and acquire the cattle, of which Magere insists that Opio get his share. This incident starts Magere's career as a war leader, attacking and raiding even as far as the Masai. He gains a reputation for being immune to harm by knives and spears, and wins the name of Magere the Stone. Opio, called Opio the Fish from an incident in his early

childhood, is still too young to be chosen for
Magere's raiding band, but he joins an ill-fated
raid led by a malcontent against the Masai, in
which Odhiambo, goaded by being called a coward,
goes berserk and kills almost the entire band,
leaving only Opio to bring home what cattle he
can. As Opio grows older he becomes known as a
fine storyteller, a position of some prestige
among the tribes. One day a wounded young man
named Oronde from Sakwa on the lakeshore is
brought to Opio's house, is tended there,
becomes a fast friend to Opio, and falls in love
with Opio's sister, Andito. After they are
married, Opio visits them, wins a storytelling
contest, and at the market meets a girl named
Teri from an island tribe, the Wafango or Snake
people. Because the Wafango are a proud people
who consider themselves rightful heirs to the
throne of Uganda, everyone is surprised that
they accept Opio's offer to her uncle of a
bride-price of sheep and goats. After the
marriage feast, however, the Snake people
disappear with the bride-price and the
prospective bride, who is able to leave Opio a
message that it is none of her doing. Opio
enlists reluctant Oronde and two piratical Samia
fishermen to retrieve her in an exciting but
nearly disastrous expedition. Teri makes a good
and loving wife, and they have several children.
Magere has never married, despite the urging of
his old mother. One day a delegation of Nandi
arrive, talk peace, and bring a beautiful Nandi
girl who, they say, will marry no one but
Magere. Flattered and smitten by her beauty,
Magere marries this girl, who is named
Tapkesos*. He is a doting husband, and she
appears an adoring wife, but she is treated with
suspicion and jealousy by all the women except
Teri. After a hunting expedition in which their
band joins some Nandi and have a close scrape
with a leopard, Magere falls ill and all
Tapkesos's nursing and the efforts of the witch
doctors cannot cure him. Finally, while Opio
watches through a crack in the wall, Magere begs
Tapkesos to bleed him a little and tells her his
secret: his body is invulnerable, but his shadow
can be wounded or killed. Armed with this
knowledge, Tapkesos goes back to her own people.
The Nandi attack, Magere is killed in single

combat by a warrior who spears his shadow, and
when Opio, wounded, comes back to hunt for his
body, he can find only a strange black stone,
different from and harder than any of the
surrounding rock. The detailed treatment, with
the focus on Opio, makes this story from the
African oral tradition into a novel, but the
style, full of sentence fragments that give a
sense of oral transmission, retains some of the
flavor of legend. Opio is a warm, human
character, as are Oronde and Teri. Magere is
believable as a natural leader, strong in his
ability to plan and direct men, but vulnerable
to flattery. Though the story is parallel to the
Biblical Samson story, in an epilogue the author
says it is not derivative. Fanfare.

BLAI (*Warrior Scarlet**), foster sister of Drem*
and a couple of years younger. The daughter of
a traveling smith, she was born in the village,
and her mother died at her birth. Her father
left her, and Drem's mother has taken her in,
but her status is ambiguous, not that of a
servant but not quite that of a daughter. As a
young child she fiercely insists that her father
will come back for her, but when he does pass
that way, he treats her with contempt and
scornfully tosses her a trinket as a "dowry."
She runs off, taunted by the other children, but
when Drem follows and tries to comfort her by
saying that her father is not a nice man and it
is good that she doesn't have to go with him,
she spits on the brooch and throws it angrily
into the river. She declares that the smith was
not her father and that her father will never
come for her now. When Drem is banished from the
tribe, Blai comes up to help with the shearing,
brings him word of his family, and offers to
hike up to the high pastures to bring him news
during the summer, an offer he at first
welcomes, but then bluntly refuses. Although she
stays loyal even under his rude rejection, she
is a girl of spirit and compassion, understanding Drem's hurt perhaps even better than he
does.

BLODEUWEDD (*The Owl Service**), one of the main
characters in an ancient, romantic Welsh myth.
She was a beautiful woman fashioned of the

flowers of the oak, the broom, and the meadow-
sweet by the wizard, Gwydion, to be the wife of
Lleu Llau Gyffes, to whom she is unfaithful with
Gronw Pebyr. She and Gronw plot Lleu's death.
Blodeuwedd persuades Lleu to tell her the one
way in which he can be killed, and the lovers
make their preparations. Lleu is struck by the
fatal poisoned spear in the manner he has
divulged and is changed into an eagle. Gwydion
searches for him and restores him to human form.
He punishes Blodeuwedd by turning her into an
owl. Lleu then slays Gronw in the manner in
which Lleu was slain. Before Lleu throws the
spear, Gronw asks a boon: that he be allowed to
stand behind a huge stone. The blow pierces the
stone and breaks Gronw's back. According to the
myth, the stone still stands there on the bank
of the Cynfael in Ardudwy, with the hole through
it. It is called Gronw's Stone. Blodeuwedd's
story forms the crux of the novel.

BLOOD FEUD (Sutcliff*, Rosemary, ill. Charles
Keeping, Oxford, 1977; Dutton, 1977), historical
novel starting in southwestern England and
ending in Constantinople in the last two decades
of the tenth century, concerning a feud which
follows a Viking faring through the Baltic Sea,
down the great rivers of Russia, to the fabled
capital of Byzantium. Telling the story as an
old man, Jestyn the Englishman remembers his
childhood in the land of his father, a British
blacksmith, the death of his Saxon mother, and
his wandering, after being turned out by his
stepfather to the Saxon-held land by the
seacoast, where he becomes a cattle-herd. He is
captured in a Viking raid, taken to Dublin where
there is a large Norse settlement and garrison,
and sold to one of the young Viking soldiers,
Thormod Sitricson, as his slave. After a long
winter of polishing weapons, running errands,
and translating for Thormod and his friends
(since the Irish tongue is close enough to his
father's and the Viking to his mother's to be
comprehensible), Jestyn becomes much attached to
Thormod, and one night when he finds his
master's amber talisman, which is shaped like
Thor's hammer, caught in his discarded clothes,
he worries that without his good-luck piece
Thormod might come to harm. He sets out to find

him, comes upon him in a ruckus with half a
dozen Irishman, and dives in to stand shoulder
to shoulder with him to fight them off. In
gratitude, Thormod has his thrall ring cut off
and offers him the chance to join the crew of
the *Sea Swallow* as a free man when they leave
Dublin. They come home to Thrandisfjord on the
east coast of Jutland, then walk inland to
Svendale, Thormod's family steading, only to
find that his father has just been killed by his
best friends, Anders and Herulf Herulfson, in
retaliation for the death of their father, whom
Sitric killed accidentally. Rather than wait for
the ruling of the Thing, the judicial council
which will levy a payment of Wyr Geld to the
wronged party, they have murdered Sitric and
left word that they have set off for Miklagard,
or Constantinople, to take the blood feud away
from the home place to be settled by the two
sets of brothers on foreign soil. Thormod,
however, persuades his older brother to stay to
care for the farm and the families and swears
blood-brotherhood with Jestyn, thereby making
him party to the feud as they follow Anders and
Herulf. They take passage on the *Red Witch*
under Hakon Kitelson, known as Hakon One-Eye,
cross the Baltic, beat their way up the Dvina,
make a gruelling portage to a river that flows
south into the Dnieper, and eventually reach
Kiev, which, like the other cities and
settlements they have passed, is a mixture of
the Vikings and the Rus who have intermarried to
start a new people, the forerunners of the
modern Russians. There they learn that Basil II,
Emperor of Constantinople, beset by rebel
commanders, has sent for help from Khan Vladimir
of Kiev, asking for 6,000 fighting men, in
exchange for the Princess Anna, Basil's sister,
as his fourth wife. Having caught up with Herulf
and Anders, Thormod arranges a Holm Ganging, a
fight to the death, first between him and
Herulf, then between Anders and Jestyn, and
finally between the winners. In a knife fight
at dawn, which is watched by half of Kiev,
Thormod kills Herulf, but as Jestyn and Anders
are about to start, Khan Vladimir rides up and
announces that the War Hosting has been called
and all private feuds must be postponed, and he
makes them swear that their feud will not be

picked up until the end of the fighting in the
south. All that terrible winter and most of the
summer they build war ships as the great force
gathers; then they sweep down the Dnieper to
Constantinople. For two years Jestyn serves in
the emperor's mercenary army and then in his
barbarian or Varangian Guard, sometimes in the
field and sometimes in the city. Accompanying
the emperor on a hunting afternoon with his
trained cheetahs, Jestyn is sent to round up one
of the great cats that has strayed and finds it
mauling a girl, who is trying unsuccessfully to
protect a pregnant pet deer. He kills the
cheetah, and, calling on his training as a
cattle-herd, cuts the fawn from the body of the
dead doe, and then goes to the farm and helps
the girl (obviously an upper-class woman) to
bind her wounds and start the fawn sucking milk
from a bowl. When he returns to the city, he
finds that Thormod has knifed Anders and knocked
him off the quay, their oaths being no longer
operative now the war host has broken up, but
Anders is pulled from the water half dead and
the feud continues. The Varangian Guard is sent
to fight the Bulgars in Thrace, and there, in
the middle of a conflict, Anders kills Thormod,
and Jestyn's knee is smashed. After several
months in the military hospital, Jestyn is
released with a stiff knee, no longer any use in
the guard. Very much at loose ends he walks out
to the farm where he killed the cheetah, vaguely
hoping that he may be taken on as a cattle-herd.
There the suspicious servants say their mistress
is in the city, but they give him directions to
the house of her father, Alexius Demetriades, a
physician. Though hesitant and too proud to
accept help in payment for having saved the
girl, Alexia, Jestyn is talked into staying and
serving as a dresser for the physician. More
than a year goes by, during which he learns many
skills to aid the physician and also, from
Alexia, how to read Greek. Though Demetriades
offers to teach him all he knows of medicine,
Jestyn hesitates, feeling that he still is bound
by the feud if Anders lives. One night Anders
appears at the door, having been a Bulgar
prisoner, escaped, and traced Jestyn. He nearly
kills Jestyn but is too ill with lung fever
caused by Thormod's knife wound. Jestyn is torn

between his dedication to the feud and his training as a healer, but his medical calling wins out, and he tries desperately to save the Viking. When Anders dies despite Jestyn's best efforts, he accepts the offer of Demetriades and becomes his student, eventually marrying Alexia and staying in Constantinople. The historical background of the Viking voyages through Russia and the Byzantine conflicts are well handled, though they have been told before in novels by Henry Treece*, and the perspective of the old man, once an English herd-boy and a slave, gives them a special flavor. As always, Sutcliff creates a feeling of the culture about which she is writing, from the binding obligations and the ways of viewing life to the more superficial customs and dress. Boston Globe Honor; Fanfare.

BLUDWARD, BOB (*Midnight Is a Place**), vicious, wheelchair-bound leader of the Friendly Association at Murgatroyd's Carpet, Rug, and Matting Manufactury, racketeers who prey upon the workers and demand protection money from them. Those mill-hands who refuse to pay meet with such "mishaps" as getting rammed by presses or tumbling into glue pots. Bludward lost his legs in a factory accident, but after working out a new dye process and inventing a steam wheelchair, he was given the run of the place. He becomes Anna-Marie's* enemy at the mill and tries to murder her when she defies him. At the book's end, he duels with Davey Scratcherd, killing Scratcherd and then rolling to his own death in the icy lake at the edge of Midnight Court park.

THE BLUE BOAT (Mayne*, William, ill. Geraldine Spence, Oxford, 1957; Dutton, 1960), gently amusing realistic novel of domestic adventures set in an English seaside village near which lies a shallow lake surrounded by woods. Two young brothers, Christopher* and Hugh*, who are perhaps nine and eight respectively, devise games of their own imagining while they stay with the authoritarian Mrs. Wrigley in the village of Withern until their parents return from working in Africa. Chafing under her fussiness, instructed to play on the beach, they begin to think of Mrs. Wrigley as a witch who

will gobble them up unless they take pre-
cautions. They explore in the opposite direction and discover a lake they call the Mere.
It is surrounded by trees and brush and
encloses a small island. With a blue rowboat
Hugh finds, they paddle about the lake for hours
on various occasions, always managing to return
to Mrs. Wrigley's in time for meals (except
once, when they get spanked) and creating out
of their new surroundings an exotic realm of
enchantments in which every tree, every sound,
and every creature has some new special meaning
mostly related to old hero or folk tales they
have read or heard. For example, they wander in
a maze they pretend is Old England. A good third
of the book is given over to such meanderings of
feet and fancy. The low-keyed plot starts when,
as they are pottering about with the boat, they
encounter a "giant," an extremely tall man, who
"roars" and throws stones at them as they
hastily paddle retreat. The next day they
encounter a "goblin," a little man who stands
shoulder-high to Hugh and who lives in a little
house he calls his "cave" in the woods with
kittens, a trained and friendly bear, and talking ravens. The goblin entertains them, warns
them against the giant, calls them princes, and
joins them in exploring for spring water to
supply the "palace" they pretend their father,
the "king," will build in the open area overlooking the lake owned by the giant. Later the
goblin's full-sized adult friend, the
"alchemist," also joins in the make-believe
games. The book comes to a climax with a battle
against the giant. After luring the giant from
his dry-moated "castle," the good army, which
also consists of the bear and the ravens,
attacks with loud challenges, and, after much
feinting and parrying of makeshift weapons on
both sides, the good side forces the giant into
the lake, which renders him powerless. As a
term of surrender, he must sign his "X" to a
document granting the open land to the king.
After he signs, all become friends immediately,
and the adults escort the boys back to Mrs.
Wrigley's for tea. The boys learn that the giant
is John March, the goblin is a dwarf named
Howard Gray, and both are circus performers not
accepted in the village; the alchemist is

John's cousin, Peter, a teacher. All are on summer holiday. The boys also learn that their
parents have arrived from Africa to collect them
for a family vacation before school starts
again. Although doughty Mrs. Wrigley strongly
disapproves of the boys' lark with the performers, the parents are grateful for the good
times the circus men have provided their sons.
The power of this quietly engaging story
springs from the author's fidelity to the
imaginative child's way of seeing and behaving
when allowed to act out fancies as he or she
wishes. Hugh and Christopher are misfits in the
Wrigley household, as the circus people are
misfits in the community, and both find comfort
in imaginative games, which both children and
adults acknowledge are only games and hence for
the utmost pleasure must be kept secret.
Characterization of the boys is deft and subtle,
that of the circus men less keen. They are
choral figures, differentiated by size and their
outsider status. Mrs. Wrigley remains an
unsympathetic, unimaginative type. The boys'
speech carries an authentic ring, and the
unforced and quiet humor arises from situations,
language, irony, and character. The physical
setting becomes clearer as the boys meander and
poke about and become more familiar with it:
the shallow lake with the island hill in the
center, the once almost impenetrable "passage-
ways" of the maze, the currents that become
springs, the fields and cliffs upon which the
boys scramble and bestow exotic names--the
reader sees it all through the eyes of the
enterprising boys as they liven up what could
otherwise have been a boring stay with dull Mrs.
Wrigley. Carnegie Com.

THE BLUE HAWK (Dickinson*, Peter, ill. David
Smee, Gollancz, 1976; Atlantic/Little, 1976),
fantasy set in a country much like ancient Egypt
in an unspecified time, possibly in the far
future. At the ceremony of the Renewal, when a
blue hawk is sacrificed to give new strength to
the king, young Tron*, 13, one of the novice
priests dedicated to the hawk god, Gdu, feels
the god speak through him when he looks at the
drugged hawk. Because he found the goat-stone in
his morning bread, Tron has the right to do

whatever he wishes for the day without
punishment, and he exercises that right by
stepping forward, taking the hawk from its
perch, and walking out of the temple. In the
turmoil that follows, Tron is taken to the
secret room of the high priests, where he
realizes his life is forfeit, and he sees the
priests in a new light, not in solemn holy
agreement but as individuals struggling for
power and wrangling among themselves. For their
own political reasons, they decide to poison the
king immediately as he is sleeping but to send
Tron to the deserted Temple of Tan to train the
supposedly untamable hawk, which they plan to
let him fly at the ceremony of the Showing of
the New King, thereby discrediting the whole
royal line. As he is hunting in the empty land
near the temple, Tron comes upon a party of
horsemen including the new king, who sends the
others away and talks with Tron as they hunt
together, explaining the war of wills between
the priests and the royal house. Tron shows the
king the secret passages in the Temple of Tan,
which correspond to those in the temple where he
has grown up and by which the king can gain some
advantage over the priests. Although the other
priests are delighted to learn that Tron has
tamed the hawk, the One of Gdu is furious, and
Tron knows that whether or not their plot works,
he will be killed after the Showing. The king,
however, has worked out a plan to hide Tron in
his father's coffin, which will be floated on a
barge down the river many miles to the great
falls, the Jaws of Alaan, which mark the
southern boundary of the kingdom. The king's
most faithful follower, Kalavin, whose father is
general of the Southern Levies, is charged with
rescuing Tron before he reaches the falls.
Hidden inside the coffin are food and water and
implements for propping the lid and cutting the
linen bands that bind it. Day and night the
barge carrying the coffin journeys down the
river, propelled back into the current by
villagers whenever it might stall along the way.
Tron escapes the coffin and, with his hawk,
hides in one end of the barge, concealed by some
draperies. As it passes the last village, Tron
sees Kalavin, who is unable to help him, make
the motions of swimming. Since he is unable to

swim, Tron is carried almost to the lip of the falls; then he throws his hawk upward and flings himself to a rock ledge beside the river. From there he painfully climbs an almost ruined stairway cut in the cliff, coming out at last on a high plateau, where he meets a girl, Taleel, about ten, herding her sheep. With her help he finds a cave and survives several days of fever, then makes his way to the neighboring village of Lower Kalakal, where the priest is Odah, one who was also once the Goat and who exercised his right by singing a hymn he had composed. In his ensuing years as a novice he was punished so severely that he is now badly crippled, yet, in this out-of-the-way place, he still commits the sacrilege of composing and changing the rituals. After living peacefully for some time at Kalakal, Tron comes upon a hunting band with a prisoner, Onu Ovalaku, an emissary from a country south of the border, carrying the Red Spear which by ancient treaty calls the king to bring troops to help them. Tron takes him to Kalavin's father, and as they travel by chariot to the main temple, Onu tells them by pictures of the savage Mohorrim, naked blue-painted horsemen with war dogs, who have been pilaging his country. At the temple, the priests, most of whom want to avoid war because it will increase the king's power, delay the group, try to discredit the emissary, drug the priest of the war god, Sinu, and almost defeat the mission, but Tron is able to alert the king and in the battle of wills and intrigue which follows, the king's faction wins temporarily. The priests, however, have closed the pass of Gebindrath with a powerful ritual and send a body of priests to renew the ritual so that the king cannot get his troops through. Knowing that the curse cannot be lifted except by priests of three orders performing a ritual under the full moon, the king gets Tron, dedicated to the hawk god Gdu, Odah, a priest of O, the sun, and the old blind One of Sinu, the war god, to journey to the pass. There, as they hide in the brush, they see the Mohorrim pour through, and later they come upon the whole contingent of priests, murdered and beheaded. Led by Odah, the three perform a ritual that lasts through the night and, they all feel, lifts the presence and the curse of

Aa, the moon goddess, from the pass. The next day the One of Sinu dies, and Odah and Tron, who are ill, are left with two hunters. Hiding in a cave, they see the retreat of the Mohorrim and the suicide of the savage men, women, and children when they cannot escape the soldiers of the kingdom. As they perform the ritual for the dead Mohorrim, a wounded savage kills Odah and shoots Tron in the back with an arrow. As he recovers at Kalakal, Tron realizes that the gods have left the kingdom, as if the ritual at the pass of Gebindrath opened a way for them to leave. He tries to make sense of his ideas and to tell Taleel that he thinks perhaps the Wise, those ancients who built the great temples and the now ruined bridges, may have somehow bound the gods to their service and that now the gods are free. As a symbol of the freedom, Tron releases his hawk. Intertwined with the exciting adventure story and the tale of intrigue are some difficult and rather obscure ideas of humanity's relationship to its gods and the true powers of ritual. On a more approachable level, Tron is an appealing character, and the details of this priest-ridden kingdom are strong and convincing. Carnegie Com.; Fanfare; Guardian.

BOBBIN RAMSAY (*The Thursday Kidnapping**), Robert, youngest of the four siblings and the least worried about the disappearance of Bart. His main contribution to the search is to rush off to the church while the others are in the police station, where he lights two candles, one to get Bart back and the other, while he's about it, to retrieve his bow and arrow that he thinks Kathy* Fisher took. He has seen Marika Kodaly lighting candles and is confident that the saints will help him, though he has to promise he'll pay the money for the candles when he gets his allowance. When he sees the carriage in their garden, he is rather frightened to have a personal miracle work so rapidly. In Kathy's home he seizes the opportunity to explore the toy cupboard and finds his long-missing bow and arrow. Kathy breaks it as she wrests it from him, knocking down the Christmas tree, with its real lighted candles, in the process. Twice, his thoughtless dashing across a street causes difficulty for the others, but in general he is

a cheerful, good natured, always hungry nine
year old.

BOB WHITE (*Ravensgill**), younger brother of
Dick, grandson of Grandma* Lizzie, and the one
who is chiefly instrumental in solving the
puzzle of the murder of Abraham Dinsdale and
reconciling the Chapmans of New Scar House and
the Whites of Ravensgill. Bob is an observant,
intelligent youth, a little pampered by and a
little afraid of his strong-minded, imperious
Grandma, who has raised him. A good swimmer, he
decides to practice for a coming meet in the
nearby gill (river), a challenging location. He
gets swept over rocks and into a tunnel, is
badly battered and bruised, and almost loses his
life. On his return to Ravensgill, he finds
Gran Chapman's letter to Grandma, which whets
his curiosity to learn more about the White
family history. His investigations and his swimming bring him into conflict with Mick Chapman,
who also swims competitively at school and who
has strong feelings against the Whites because a
White is supposed to have killed his great-
grandfather, Abraham Dinsdale. A mean, somewhat
rebellious boy, he picks on Judith and beers it
up with the local youths. One night, he and his
gang attack Bob and Dick, Bob's older brother
and Mick's foil, but luckily do not succeed in
harming them. At the end, because Bob has
apparently uncovered the truth about what happened to Dinsdale, Mick is more friendly toward
the Whites.

BOLINGBROKE, ROGER (*The Writing on the Hearth**),
historical master of arts from Oxford, the
villain of the novel. He is a large, heavy man,
with a pale, flabby face, described in cliches
as having "hair like faded straw and eyes like
cold steel." He wears a fine gown of red wine
color, a silk hood, and an ornament of twisted
metal about his neck that Stephen recognizes as
a magical symbol. Bolingbroke is in service to
Duchess Eleanor, called "the witch," and Duke
Humphrey of Gloucester, the king's uncle, who is
building a library at Oxford. Deep in the
political intrigues of the day, Bolingbroke is
convicted of conspiracy against the king and of
witchcraft and is executed. As presented, he is

a type figure.

BOND, (THOMAS) MICHAEL (1926-   ), born in
Newbury, Berkshire; television cameraman, director, author best known for his highly popular
series of books for younger readers about the
teddy bear named Paddington. He grew up in
Reading with lots of animals, including newts,
guinea pigs, and a dog, and was educated at
Presentation College in Reading. During World
War II, he served first as a navigator in the
Royal Air Force, then in the Middlesex Regiment
of the British Army. While on duty in the Middle
East, he wrote a short story which was accepted
by *London Opinion*, his first publication. After
the war, he took a position as cameraman for
BBC-TV in London, retiring to full-time writing
in 1965. The origin of the Paddington books is
now legendary. At Christmas in 1957, he discovered a left-over toy bear on a shop shelf,
bought it as a stocking stuffer, and christened
it Paddington because he was living near the
Paddington station in London at the time. The
subsequent book, *A Bear Called Paddington**
(Collins, 1958; Houghton, 1960), now a *Choice*
listing, was finished in ten days. The immensely
popular series resulted in some two dozen books,
plays, and picture books and their spinoffs into
pop-ups, and the like. Many of the books have
been translated into other languages for
distribution abroad. Paddington is fat, lovable, and prone to situation-comedy accidents.
In the novel, Paddington is found, small,
abandoned, rather dirty, and wearing a label
that says, "Please look after this bear. Thank
you." He is taken in by the Brown family, and
hilarious, rapid-action, calamitous adventures
follow. In 1966, Bond created a new character,
an orphaned mouse named Thursday, in *Here Comes
Thursday* (Harrap, 1966; Lothrop, 1967), the
first of a series. Later he initiated another
set of novels featuring a pretty, proud,
romantic guinea pig in *The Tales of Olga da
Polga** (Penguin, 1971; Macmillan, 1973), also a
Choice book and a similar domestic, talking
animal, episodic, sitcom story. Although Bond
created other characters, too, the Paddington
books remain the great favorites, comfortable if
condescending in tone, filled with incident,

affectionate toward readers and subject matter.
The lovable bear has even lent his name to the
film business in which Bond is a director, Paddington and Company Ltd., of London. Bond has
also written many plays for radio and television, articles, short stories, and a novel
for adults, *Monsieur Pampelmousse* (Hodder,
1983). He has two children and has lived in
Surrey and in London.

THE BONGLEWEED (Cresswell*, Helen, Faber, 1973;
Macmillan, 1974), lighthearted fantasy novel set
somewhere in England in the late twentieth
century. Loyal, hardworking, thorough, inarticulate, green-thumbed Albert Finch serves Dr.
Harper, a scientist, as head gardener of Pew
Gardens, an experimental botanical laboratory
consisting of several greenhouses and outdoor
planting areas. He, his equally hardworking,
more articulate wife, Else, and their only
child, willful, intelligent, morally ambivalent
Becky, about twelve, occupy a flat in the
Harper house, where Else is employed as housekeeper and cook. Becky, from whose vantage
point events are seen, often spies into the
Harper living room through a tiny peephole
concealed behind a picture in the Finches'
adjacent living room. When the Harpers' nephew,
tall, thin, bespectacled, "posh-voiced" Jason,
arrives for a few months in the country "to
build him up" and Becky is expected to socialize
with him, she takes an immediate dislike to him
and sets him up for trouble. Told by Finch to
tend Else's garden, she maliciously neglects to
tell Jason that Else thinks weeds have a special
beauty and lets him pull them all out. Then she
gives him a packet of seeds with which Dr.
Harper is experimenting, which he acquired
mysteriously at a recent conference, and which
have already in only two days produced an
unusually large and exotic tropical plant in the
greenhouse. Jason plants them, and the next
morning the children discover to their mutual
amazement that the seeds have sprouted into
giants, whose foliage is "dense and tangling,
intricate as ivy." Her animosity toward him
dispelled by their shared anxiety over this
phenomenon, Becky apologizes, and the two uproot
most of the South American Bongleweed, as Becky

terms it, casting the plants on the compost heap
adjacent to the local cemetery. Some, however,
continue to grow in Else's garden and soon burst
into "wickedly beautiful" bloom, and the Finches
thrill to the glory of their new horticultural
development. Real trouble comes when the compost
heap plants survive their uprooting, take over
the cemetery, and even climb up the church
tower. When the vicar complains and status-
conscious Mrs. Harper orders Finch to chop them
down, Finch gives notice rather than comply,
asserting in his characteristically laconic way
that nature will take its course. Guilty but not
sorry for her part in the dilemma, Becky discovers she can communicate with the plant. She
thrills to its uninvited beauty, feels a strange
kinship to it and power to influence it, and
doesn't want to move from Pew Gardens or see
the Bongleweed injured. A sudden April frost
supports Finch's conviction. Overnight it
blackens the tropical Bongleweed stalks like
fire. Becky weeps tears of grief for its loss
but discovers she can conjure the plant up in
her mind's eye whenever she wants. Though Jason
thinks that magic was at work, Becky has learned
something about the nature of beauty and the
power of the imagination and has discovered
that even the impossible can be possible. At
times it seems the author is trying to make the
slight story do more than it has strength for,
to explore in addition, for example, adolescent
growing pains and the ordering power of nature.
Much of the narrative is taken up with Becky's
thoughts and feelings about the other characters, life in general, and the weed and with
considering alternative courses of action. There
is a pleasing relationship between Becky and her
parents, especially Finch, whose love for
growing things she shares. Characterization is
skillful, humor contributes credibility, tone
is light, word choice is distinctive, double
entendres add spice, and style is highly metaphorical, drawing upon nature for figures.
Incidents do not relate well to one another,
however, and Becky's role with respect to the
growth and spread of the Bongleweed is left
open. It is hard to see just how much of the
weed's peculiar behavior can be traced to her
influence. Carnegie Com.

THE BONNIE PIT LADDIE (Grice*, Frederick, ill.
Brian Wildsmith, Oxford, 1960; *OUT OF THE MINES:
THE STORY OF A PIT BOY*, ill. Brian Wildsmith,
Watts, 1961), historical novel set for about a
year and a half at an indeterminate time in the
late nineteenth or very early twentieth century
in the coal mining town of Branton Colliery in
Durham County in northern England and focusing
on strife between coal miners and their oppressive bosses. Kit Ullathorne, about fourteen, and
his brother, Dick, 12, are the only chidren of
respected, hardworking miner Davy Ullathorne and
his wife, Hetty. The despair of his earnest
parents, mischievous Kit often plays hookey
from school for days, preferring jaunts about
the countryside with one or another itinerant
stranger to lessons behind the four walls of
the colliery school. Severely caned following
his latest escapade, he quits school and happily takes a job as pony boy and then miner in
the pit. Dick, on the other hand, loves books
and learning and is encouraged by family and
friends to stay in school as long as he can. The
first third of the novel establishes these
characters and the setting and places Dick in
situations that will later prove important in
the plot. While poking about the hills, Kit
discovers a boarded-up "staple," or entrance to
a pit, that he and Dick subsequently explore in
an exciting episode. Later, while on an errand,
Dick discovers the mine boss, Mr. Sleath, ill in
his trap and takes him home. Naive about mill
life, Dick is puzzled by his father's remark
that Sleath is "just about the worst master that
ever walked the face of this earth." Relations
between miners and Sleath become increasingly
strained over one problem after another. The
miners stage a last-straw strike over a speedup.
Mr. Sleath insists on invoking the "rocking-
rule," that is, he orders the men to rock or
shake the coal in the tubs down to a certain
level so that the tubs will hold more, an
extremely difficult thing to do in the low-
ceilinged mines, but he refuses to pay more for
the added coal. After four weeks of the walkout,
Sleath hires "candymen," thugs from the docks of
Newcastle and Sunderland to strong-arm the
miners from their company-owned homes. A long,
hard winter follows for the miners and their

families. They camp out on Rushy Field, which is
common ground, in tents provided by the union.
At first this new life seems to Dick a great
adventure like those in the storybooks his new
teacher, young Mr. Bradwell, provides for him;
but his attitude begins to change when the
strike pay stops, and food and fuel run out. The
miners are forced to capitulate, and Mr. Sleath
vindictively blacklists the leaders so they
can't get jobs in any of the mines in the area,
Davy Ullathorne among them. Dick's schooldays
are over; he enters the pit to help support the
family, working as a trapper, or door opener,
and then as a pony boy. The problems with Sleath
come to a dramatic climax less than a year after
the strike began, when his negligence about
complying with a new law that stipulates certain
repairs to the pit results in a terrible
accident. The pithead caves in, and 200 men and
boys are entombed far below the surface of the
earth, Kit and Dick included. After three days,
almost everyone above and below ground has given
up hope that the miners will ever be rescued.
Dick, however, suspects there may be a way out
through the seam he and Kit explored inside the
old staple months before. After hard digging and
shoring up the old walls, all the trapped miners
make their way through the outlet to safety, in
pitiful shape physically but alive. Dick
develops rheumatic fever, is told he must leave
the pit, and experiences a long convalescence.
Mr. Sleath is replaced by more humane bosses, to
the miners' relief, and the needed repairs are
made. Mr. Ullathorne is taken off the job
blacklist and happily returns to mining, an
occupation he thoroughly enjoys, physically
demanding as it is, and life becomes easier for
the family economically. Then, to Dick's
surprise, the doctor reverses his opinion and
says that Dick has recovered completely and can
return to the mine. Dick, however, finds that he
no longer wants to be a miner. He confides in a
community friend, Mr.* Candlin, a historian and
archaeologist. With the secret help of Dick's
grandmother, Mrs.* Ullathorne, Mr. Candlin
arranges for Dick to become journeyman apprentice to Mr. Dorman, the local chemist, or
pharmacist, and thus Dick escapes the pit and
the fate of most of the men of Branton Colliery.

The author early enlists the reader's sympathies for these decent, hardworking people, who are victims of circumstances and the whims of malicious, exploitive bosses and who struggle to make the best of their hard lot. Most of the time the setting blends well with the plot, but occasionally the author's voice can be heard stridently advocating miners' rights. Sleath and his underlings are typecast as villains, and bullish, tough Headmaster Allcroft ("he always gave two little snorts" before speaking) and supercilious, snobbish Dr. MacIntosh (he "pushed open the doors of his patients' houses as if he were entering a byre or a stable") exemplify the educated but ill-bred, as compared to the Ulla-thornes and their neighbors, who lack education but are profoundly decent. The author paints a clear if overly pleasant picture of colliery life, the work in the pit, the digging, the shoring up, the school, the recreation, the hymn singing, and the sharing of bread and stealing of coal during the strike. Little details add authority to the loose narrative, for example, how the idled miners must keep their hands calloused so they don't bleed when they return to the pickaxe. Some use of dialect supports the setting. (Jossie* Milburn) Carnegie Com.; Fanfare; Other.

BOROMIR (*The Fellowship of the Ring**), son of Denethor, Steward of Gondor, a strong, valiant man who has come north to Rivendell seeking advice and, if possible, help against the might of Sauron, which is growing and threatens to overwhelm his country. Boromir chafes at some of the decisions of Gandalf* and at having Strider* assume leadership when Gandalf is lost, and even at the first he does not really understand or agree with Elrond's decision that the ring should be destroyed, but it is not until the fellowship has left Lothlorien that he begins to come under the power of the ring and desire it. He tries at first to persuade Frodo* that it is madness to destroy a power that could be used for good, and when the hobbit* shrinks from him, he tries to take the ring by force. Frodo slips on the ring, disappears, and escapes, but Boromir's action precipitates Frodo's decision to go off to Mordor alone.

Boromir dies shortly thereafter defending Merry*
Brandybuck and Pippin* Took from orcs.

THE BORROWERS (Norton*, Mary, ill. Diana
Stanley, Dent, 1952; ill. Beth and Joe Krush,
Harcourt, 1953), suspenseful and humorous fantasy novel about pencil-sized people who live
under the floor of an old Georgian country house
in Bedfordshire about 1910 and exist by
"borrowing" from humans. The first of a series,
the book has the status of a classic in children's literature. Kate, the narrator, repeats
a second-hand story told her when, a spoiled and
willful little girl of ten, she would visit old
Mrs.* May, a relative of sorts, and they would
do handwork together in Mrs. May's sitting room.
The story Mrs. May tells Kate came to her from
her brother, a lonely and imaginative boy* of
nine, who was sent away to Firbank Hall, the
country house of his Great* Aunt Sophy, to recover from rheumatic fever. He becomes involved
with the Clock family of Borrowers, so named
because the entrance to their home lies under
the hall clock: Pod*, the practical, philosophical father; Homily*, the nervous, house-
proud mother; and their daughter, Arrietty*, 13,
obedient, loving, spirited, and adventurous.
They are the last of their kind in the house,
the others all having left because they were
"seen" by humans. When Pod is seen by the boy in
the upstairs nursery while borrowing a teacup,
the Clocks are faced with the prospect of
"emigrating" to the countryside, a proposal that
Homily, who is very pleased with her comfortable quarters, vetoes. They decide that Pod
should teach Arrietty the rudiments of borrowing
so she can fend for herself if need be. Three
weeks later, Arrietty accompanies Pod outside
the house on her maiden borrowing expedition and
is enjoying the freedom of the azalea bank under
the cherry tree when she encounters the boy.
They strike up a friendship, and Arrietty, in
discussing with him the nature of Borrowers and
human beings and their relative numbers, makes
a famous speech, "Human beans are *for*
Borrowers--like bread's for butter!," in
response to his assertion that Borrowers don't
borrow, they steal. He offers to carry a note to
emigrated Clock relatives, Uncle* Hendreary and

his wife, Aunt* Lupy, who are thought to be
living in a badger's set in the field called
Parkin's Beck, in return for Arrietty reading
books to him. He delivers the letter, provoking
suspicion among the servants when Crampfurl, the
gardener, sees him poking about, and brings back
a reply from Uncle Hendreary for Arrietty. When
Pod and Homily learn of the friendship, they are
even more frightened and uncertain about what to
do, with Pod asserting that "no good never
really came to no one from any human bean."
Ironically, with the best of intentions, the boy
becomes a kind of Borrower himself, and a golden
age sets in for the little people, soon to be
concluded by terrible misfortune. That night,
the boy lifts a floorboard in the kitchen
(catching appearance-conscious Homily in bed in
her curlers, to her immense chagrin) and presents his diminutive friends with the first of a
series of elegant and useful furnishings from
the dollhouse in the schoolroom, and later from
shelves in the drawing room. The last gifts produce trouble, since Mrs.* Driver, the
sharp-eyed, defensive housekeeper, misses the
objects, suspects the boy, keeps an eye on him,
and discovers the Borrowers' quarters. Frightened and upset by the presence of creatures
whose nature she does not understand, she causes
a ruckus, and, even though the boy insists the
Borrowers are harmless and begs her not to hurt
them, she sets extermination proceedings in
motion. She summons police and the ratcatcher,
who brings a lad with a ferret. While the boy
awaits the cab which is to take him to the
station to return to his family in India, the
exterminators arrive and plug up all the floor
exits in preparation for their task. Stealthily,
the boy knocks a hole in the hallway
wainscoting and then dislodges the grating
outside at the base of the house near the
Borrowers' home before he departs. Focus shifts
at this point, and the reader is brought back to
the frame story and conversation between Mrs.
May and Kate. Mrs. May says she is sure the
Borrowers escaped, that she smelled hot-pot and
found important objects in a certain place in
the countryside, including Arrietty's
"Memoranda" book. Then she says that her
brother's writing was much like Arrietty's.

Consequently, the reader never learns whether or not the Borrowers got away, and is indeed left in doubt about whether they even existed. Perhaps Mrs. May made up the story, or perhaps her brother did. So strong is the emotional appeal generated by this engaging family and their unfortunate plight, however, that most readers would align themselves with Mrs. May's hopes and imagine the Borrowers safe and sound, well out of the reach of Mrs. Driver and her cohorts. Strongly delineated characters; important themes of initiative, independence, and survival; ironic humor; a charming, amusing style detailing the Borrowers' attitudes, home, way of life, and methods of borrowing; a skillfully constructed plot based on experience (common objects get lost), observation (this happens to everyone), and logic (these things can't just disappear; someone must take them); and a point of view that remains unerringly that of the miniature beings combine to make this an outstanding book of its type. Books Too Good; Carnegie Winner; Children's Classics; ChLA Touchstones; Choice; Fanfare; Lewis Carroll.

THE BORROWERS AFIELD (Norton*, Mary, ill. Diana Stanley, Dent, 1955; ill. Beth and Joe Krush, Harcourt, 1955), suspenseful fantasy that continues the story begun in *The Borrowers** of the pencil-sized people in the English countryside about 1910, who live by borrowing (or gleaning) from human beings what they need to survive. A year later, Kate, now eleven, accompanies her elderly relative, Mrs.* May, to Leighton Buzzard, Bedfordshire, to inspect a cottage the old woman has inherited on the Studdington estate near Firbank Hall, the scene of the Borrowers' disaster. Kate is disappointed to learn that Firbank Hall is now a school, but becomes interested in Tom* Goodenough, the aged gamekeeper, who has lived for eighty years in the cottage that is now Mrs. May's. Kate learns from Tom that he was the boy with the ferret who was present on the fateful occasion when the Clocks leave to escape the exterminators. Tom also possesses Arrietty's* diary and heard from Arrietty what subsequently happened. Kate persuades him to tell her Arrietty's story and later writes the narrative down for her own four children. The Clocks flee in terror up the azalea bank and into the woods, and then, under Pod's* calm leadership and constant admonitions to beware, trudge along the trench workmen had made for a gas pipe and over three fields to the one called Perkin's Beck, where they are sure the Uncle* Hendrearys are living in a badger's set. Arrietty delights in her new-found freedom, in the possibilities for adventure, and in the beauty of nature, but Homily* is as complaining and piously self-righteous as ever, only now and then allowing a tiny spark of the spirit of adventure to glow. They find an old boot, outfit it as a home as best they can with the minimal possessions they have brought along, and settle in. They meet with numerous difficulties, including mice in their nut storeroom, the theft of their nail-scissors knife and hat pin, and an attack by an owl, in addition to the vagaries of the weather. Their fortunes take a turn for the better after Arrietty discovers a brown-faced, moleskin-clad Borrower youth named Spiller*, who takes a special interest in them and brings them meat he has hunted and items he has borrowed from gypsies encamped near by. Things go well for about six weeks, but at the end of October, Spiller leaves to get winter clothing, frost comes, the food runs out, and the Clocks' situation becomes desperate. Before they find appropriate quarters, Mild* Eye, a big, burly gypsy, finds and carries their boot-house, with them in it, back to his caravan, where they are trapped under his bunk until rescued by Tom Goodenough, the gamekeeper's boy, and taken to the cottage Tom shares with his grandpa. There, to their great surprise and relief, they dis-cover their Uncle Hendreary, Aunt* Lupy, and the children, including cousin Eggletina, whom they thought had been eaten by a cat, living com-fortably in an overfurnished upstairs room inside the cottage wall, well-provided with items Tom has brought from the dollhouse in Fir-bank Hall. The book's end finds the Clocks joyfully welcomed and taken in, safe and sound at last. The power of this consistently inter-esting Robinsonnade comes from the carefully worked out and inventive details of survival and the vivid descriptions of the landscape. The narrative has a very strong visual quality, and it is easy to see what is going on and understand the Borrowers' situations. The author is careful to keep the reader looking at things from the point of view of the tiny beings. Story complications are interjected skillfully at critical points to maintain maximum interest, and there are moments of humor and poignancy as well as plenty of suspense and excitement. The story answers the burning question with which the reader was left at the end of the first book concerning whether or not the Borrowers escape the exterminator's smoke, but this book can stand alone and is not dependent upon the earlier one for effect. The Clocks' bravery and perseverance under conditions that would try the staunchest spirits win admiration. Choice; Fanfare.

THE BORROWERS AFLOAT (Norton*, Mary, ill. Diana Stanley, Dent, 1959; ill. Beth and Joe Krush, Harcourt, 1959), fantasy novel, third in the series about the Clock family of Borrowers: Pod*, Homily*, and Arrietty*. This one begins, like its predecessors, with old Mrs.* May and her niece, Kate, discussing the miniature people. Kate then begins to describe more adventures of the family, but stops and says that old Tom* Goodenough, the gamekeeper, is the one to tell what happened next. Presumably, then, Tom continues the narrative, but that is not clear. The story picks up events at the very end of The Borrowers Afield*, where the Clocks are living upstairs in the home of Uncle* Hendreary and Aunt* Lupy, located inside the wall of the gamekeeper's cottage, near the fireplace. Personality conflicts between Lupy and Homily, in particular, and jealousy over borrowing prerogatives and ability among the men create tension. Some months pass, and spring approaches. Arrietty has formed a friendship with Tom Goodenough, at that time the gamekeeper's grandson, who had helped the family escape from Mild* Eye, the gypsy, in the previous book. She learns from him that the cottage will soon be closed because his grandpa must go to the hospital. Since the survival of Borrowers depends upon having humans to borrow from, Pod and Homily realize that they will soon be a burden on the Uncle Hendrearys and decide to move.

Tom leaves them a loophole under the door for escape, but his ferret lurks outside, and, when they are almost in despair, Spiller* turns up and helps them get out through his customary avenue, the drain under the mangle in the washhouse. The dramatic departure is described in generous, easily visualized detail, in particular the very exciting scene when they get washed down the subterranean drainpipe by an unexpected and unexplained rush of bath water from the cottage. Spiller agrees to take them by river to Little Fordham, a model village of which they have heard, but he has important errands to complete first. Awaiting his return, they outfit for minimal habitation an old, enameled teakettle and are fairly comfortable when hard rains dislodge the kettle and carry them on a swift and scary ride downriver. Fortunately, the kettle catches on sticks and netting that form a kind of island in the river near a bridge and not far from shore. Mild Eye, who is poaching for trout, spies them and almost captures them before Spiller, who has returned and been awaiting the chance to help them, cuts the rope-line that Mild Eye, who can't swim, has fashioned to get out to where the Borrowers are. At the same time, Ernie Runacre, the policeman from Leighton Buzzard appears, and Mild Eye has to answer for poaching. When last seen, the Borrowers are in Spiller's cutlery-box boat, and Spiller is poling them in the direction of Little Fordham. At novel's end, the reality of events is reinforced by a conversation about the Borrowers between Mrs.* Driver, the cook and housekeeper, and Crampfurl, the gardener, in the kitchen at Firbank Hall, during which the reader (but not Mrs. Driver) learns that Crampfurl saw the miniature people floating downriver. Like those of the other books, the plot is uncomplicated and easy to follow. The characters, still interesting, are much the same. The main interest in this Robinsonnade comes not from plot, though there are several suspenseful episodes, but from seeing how the Borrowers and Spiller manage to manipulate found materials and their physical environment to suit their purposes and evade danger, all of which are worked out in very carefully delineated, generous, imaginative detail. Choice; Fanfare.

THE BORROWERS ALOFT (Norton*, Mary, ill. Diana
Stanley, Dent, 1961; ill. Beth and Joe Krush,
Harcourt, 961), fantasy novel, fourth in the
series about the Clock family of Borrowers,
pencil-sized people who live by gleaning what
they need from human beings. When met, in late
1911, Pod*, Homily*, and Arrietty* Clock, with
Spiller's* help, are settled comfortably in the
thatched and secure Vine Cottage in Little
Fordham, the model railway village by the river,
for which they were headed in Spiller's boat in
the previous book, The Borrowers Afloat*. The
first third of this book is devoted to the
history and description of Little Fordham and
its counterpart across the river, Ballyhoggin,
which is not far away as the crow flies. Little
Fordham, a tidy and loving construction, was the
conception of kind, gentle, softspoken Mr.* Abel
Pott, a former signalman, for his own amusement,
after he lost his leg in an accident and was
retired by the railroad company. His project
has garnered so much interest in Fordham
village that several craftspeople have contributed to it, including sweet, talkative,
elderly Miss* Menzies, who writes children's
books and enjoys woodworking and weaving.
Avaricious, unscrupulous Mr.* Sidney Platter and
Mrs.* Mabel Platter, on the other hand, have
made their Ballyhoggin a plastic, gimmicky
tourist trap, hoping it will entice patrons to
their second-rate tearoom. For a while, the
Clocks are very happy in Vine Cottage. Practical
Pod can polish his skills at borrowing again,
Homily rejoices in having a proper house once
more, and Arrietty can explore to her heart's
content. Unbeknownst to her parents, she makes
friends with Miss Menzies, who provides additional items to make them comfortable. Things
seem ideal, until terrible trouble arises from
an unexpected quarter. Mr. Platter, who has a
habit of spying on Mr. Pott's village, discovers
that among the figures Mr. Pott has made to
people his village some are actually alive, the
Clocks of Vine Cottage. In October, Mr. and Mrs.
Platter kidnap the little people with a net and
a cardboard box and imprison them in their
attic, intending to display them at Ballyhoggin
in the spring in a glass-enclosed cage-house.
At first, the miniature people are confused and

frightened, but before long their customary
good sense and resourcefulness return. Pod lays
down strict rules (absolute obedience and not
speaking a word when the Platters are around),
and they investigate their surroundings, noting
many useful items, like raffia, wheels, and
pins. Arrietty spends hours poring over old
issues of the *Illustrated London News*. Winter
passes, spring nears, and they realize that time
is running out. From articles in the old
newspapers about free ballooning, Arrietty gets
the idea of making a balloon. She reads the
articles to Pod who translates them into practical action, and the result, after many days of
experimenting and trial and error, is a large
purple, gas-powered balloon (ironically advertising the Platters' village), covered with
netting from the shrimp net with which the
Clocks were captured, to which is attached a
berry basket. On The Day, March 28, 1912, they
take off, heading in the direction of Little
Fordham across the river, and, after a
relatively pleasant ride, make a rough landing
in the river just outside the fence that now
surrounds Little Fordham. They get back safely,
however, and discover Spiller in the cottage,
which Mr. Pott has outfitted with running water
and electric lights for their greater convenience. All are happy to be home again, in
particular, Homily, who joyfully tidies and
shoves around furniture. Arrietty then confesses
to her parents that she has made friends with
Miss Menzies, and that Miss Menzies and Mr. Pott
have provided the conveniences because they are
fond of the Borrowers and wish them to stay.
Pod wisely points out that by accepting this
help they are exchanging one kind of imprisonment for another, that Borrowers by their
very nature must be independent and fend for
themselves. The book's end finds them planning,
with Spiller's help, to move to the mill down by
the river. The Platters have a touch of the
comic about them that reduces their villainy,
and they are obvious foils for Mr. Pott and
Miss Menzies. Ironically, however, the author
uses the latter to support the continuing theme
of the series of independence and initiative
being necessary for survival and a good life.
Arrietty's romantic interest in Spiller adds an

interesting new dimension and shows she is
growing up. Pod is the real hero, however; without his calm, good sense, practical aptitude,
and resource, the little family would not have
made it out of the clutches of their kidnappers. The plot is overly foreshadowed, and,
as is true with the other books in the set, the
details of situations and procedures have
greater appeal than the story. The comments the
Borrowers make about human ways have remarkable
accuracy. By this book, however, the main charm
is the little family; the reader has developed
an affection for them and simply wants to find
out what life holds for them next. Choice;
Fanfare.

THE BORROWERS AVENGED (Norton*, Mary, ill.
Pauline Baynes, Kestrel, 1982; ill. Beth and Joe
Krush, Harcourt, 1982), fantasy novel, sixth
book and last novel published in the series
about the Borrowers, the five- or six-inch-high
people who live in odd nooks and crannies and
take what they need from the humans who live
around them. On March 31, 1912, three days after
their dramatic escape by balloon from the attic
in which they have been imprisoned by Mr.* and
Mrs.* Sidney Platter, who planned to exhibit
them for money, the Clock family of Borrowers
are again on the move. To remain independent of
well-meaning Miss* Menzies and out of the
clutches of the greedy Platters, they leave Vine
Cottage in Little Fordham model village, not for
the old mill down by the river as hoped (Pod*
and Spiller* deem it unsuitable for habitation),
but for the Old Rectory upriver. This is now
unused except for a small part inhabited by Mr.
and Mrs. Whitlace (called Witless by Pod),
caretakers of the famous, historic Fordham
church, where Pod and Spiller have found the
Uncle* Hendrearys living in the vestry. After
dark, the Clocks pile their household items and
personal possessions, all the nice things Miss
Menzies had given them and Homily* delights in,
into Spiller's knife-box boat, and depart, under
the very noses of the Platters, who keep vigil
in their rowboat hoping in vain to snare the
miniature people as they come down the path to
the river from Vine Cottage. Spiller poles them
along skillfully, while Homily and Arrietty*

(who delights in the open air and the adventure)
nap, and dawn sees them arrived at the Rectory
bank, where they put in, move essentials into
Spiller's soap-box punt, and drag it up the
slope and over the dewy grass to the con-
servatory door. They live briefly in the con-
servatory stove and then, after Arrietty
discovers and makes friends with the sole
Borrower left in the place, an affected but
helpful lame youth named Peagreen* (Peregrine)
Overmantel, in his house under the windowseat in
the library. He has moved for ease of living to
the aviary over the larder, and Pod, whose tools
Spiller throughtfully retrieved from the
gamekeeper's cottage, soon renovates the little
apartment into very comfortable quarters that
please Homily greatly. The Clocks exchange
visits with the Uncle Hendrearys, and Aunt* Lupy
and Homily get on better, the physical distance
of the lawn between them and Lupy's new, milder
personality (she has found religion in the
church) improving their relationship considerably. Arrietty soon comes to love the
place, reveling in the sense of freedom she gets
from the airiness of the old house with its
many, large windows and its gardens, lawns, and
bushes to climb. She enjoys the company of
Timmus, the Hendrearys' youngest, who is a
lively little fellow, and their borrowing trips
aid both families. The Whitlaces follow a steady
routine, and overhearing their conversations on
the telephone in the hallway helps the Borrowers
keep easy track of them. Six golden weeks pass,
and mid-April and bright spring arrive. Unknown
to the Clocks, however, the Platters are making
plans to get them back. They break into Little
Fordham, and, finding the Clocks gone, wreck it
in their clumsiness and disappointment. Next,
they consult Lady Mullings, the local "finder."
The dramatic and comically humorous climax comes
in the old church on Easter Saturday, while Lady
Mullings and other ladies are arranging the
Easter flowers. As they confer with Lady
Mullings, Mrs. Platter spots Timmus watching the
activities from the top of the historic old rood
screen. He flees for safety into the collection
box, which Mrs. Whitlace locks in the vestry
cupboard for the night. The Platters break in
after dark, and, in trying to catch Timmus, get

tangled in the bell ropes. The Whitlaces, Mr. Pomfret the constable, the Clocks, and the Uncle Hendrearys witness the calamity, the former with considerable puzzlement, the latter with relief, as the Platters attempt to explain their presence and the forced-open cupboard. No longer do the Clocks need to worry about these enemies. The conclusion leaves the reader satisfied that the brave and charming little Clock family has the comfortable home it deserves after its many vicissitudes and pleased that the greedy Platters have gotten their much deserved come-uppance. Arrietty's developing skill in borrowing gives scope for her to mature, helps satisfy her need for freedom and accomplishment, and makes way for Pod's semiretirement in that occupation and his return to the handcrafts he loves. Lupy's religious awakening is amusing, convincing, and appropriate, and the improved relationship between the two women is satisfying. Peagreen is an interesting, new character. The book seems less effective, however, than the previous ones, in particular than the first two. It seems wordier and slower, and there is less action to hold the interest, most it being devoted to description and conversation not much connected with plot. Fanfare.

BOSIE (*Kept in the Dark**), Ambrose, 10, youngest of the three children who go to live with their grandparents and are terrorized by their half-cousin, David*. At first he is completely taken in by David's charm and even willing, when David fires the housekeeper, to do all the cooking, since he likes to cook. He does a complete turnaround after he sees David fight Noel* and really hurt him. Always fond of money himself (he cheerfully admits that he used to steal), Bosie sees that money is the way to control David and, to get a fund to bribe him to leave, starts a scheme where he takes pay from his fellow students to alter the principal's conduct book.

BOSTOCK (*The Strange Affair of Adelaide Harris**; *Bostock and Harris; or, The Night of the Comet**), faithful friend and schoolboy companion of the quicker-thinking Harris*, whose sister he yearns for and upon whom he depends for leader-

ship and advice in romance. In *The Strange Affair of Adelaide Harris*, Bostock is an admiring
and unquestioning follower who actually carries
off the baby and then helps Harris in all his
plans to retrieve her. In *Bostock and Harris* he
has a more central role. At thirteen and a half,
Bostock is large and thick in both body and
mind, and he lets himself be persuaded to
exchange his father's telescope for the surefire aid Harris guarantees to attract the
attentions of Mary Harris. In following the
advice of his friend, he manages to ruin several
items of his father's best clothes, lose the
ivory-handled knife presented to his father by
the Brighton Exploring Society and inscribed
with his name, and destroy the lovely wine jelly
which is the centerpiece of Mrs. Harris's
lavish tea. When, in the end, he is able to
dance with Mary at Devil's Dyke, it is because
his friend has given up and told his sister that
Bostock's affections are set on another girl,
thereby causing her to turn her interest to the
boy for the first time. Bostock is also the main
character in the title story in *The Restless
Ghost*.

BOSTOCK AND HARRIS; OR, THE NIGHT OF THE COMET
(Garfield*, Leon, Kestrel, 1979; *THE NIGHT OF
THE COMET, A COMEDY OF COURTSHIP FEATURING
BOSTOCK AND HARRIS*, Delacorte, 1979), sequel to
*The Strange Affair of Adelaide Harris** set in
eighteenth-century Brighton. Bostock* and Harris*, the two boys who kidnapped Harris's infant
sister and thereby started a chain of hilarious
misadventures, are now thirteen and a half, and
reappear in a tangle of love affairs. Everyone
pines: Bostock for Mary Harris; Dorothy Harris
for her music teacher, Philip Top-Morlion;
Michael Cassidy*, an Irish roofer, for his
former sweetheart, Mary Flatley, whom he and his
partner, O'Rourke, have been seeking throughout
England; and Harris for the telescope owned by
Bostock's father. In exchange for the promise
of obtaining Mary's favor for Bostock, Harris
persuades his friend to swipe the telescope,
pointing out that Bostock's father is so plagued
by gout that he is unable to ascend to the third
story where the telescope is kept. With the help
of Cassidy, who is working on the Bostock roof,

they smuggle it out. Cassidy finds his Mary, only to lose her temporarily to a fishmonger's son. Harris directs Bostock's courtship, basing his advice on a treatise he has read on animal courtship, and fails to recognise that every move ends in disaster. The many plot-lines culminate on the top of Devil's Dyke, where the whole town goes to dance and view Pigott's Comet. Despite complex misunderstandings, all the affairs turn out well. Even Dorothy's jealous friend, Maggie Hemp, ends up happy with the fishmonger's son. Although the plot is a romp much like a stage farce, Garfield's style, full of startling metaphor and tongue-in-cheek humor, raises the hilarity to a higher level and introduces a wickedly clever satire. Fanfare.

BOSTON, L(UCY) M(ARIA WOOD) (1892-   ), born in Southport, Lancashire; author of the Green Knowe books, which are usually acknowledged to be a-mong the twentieth-century classics for children. One of six children in an intensely evangelical family, she had a repressed and old-fashioned childhood, even for the 1890s, but it did not dampen her spirit of adventure. Her autobiography, *Perverse and Foolish: A Memoir of Childhood and Youth* (Bodley, 1979; Atheneum, 1979) shows her as a lively and unconventional girl. She attended Downs School, Seaford, Sussex, and Somerville College, Oxford, until 1914, when she went into training with the Volunteer Aid Detachment at St. Thomas Hospital, London, and then served as a nurse in France in World War I. Her marriage to a cousin in 1917 was dissolved in 1935 but produced one son, Peter Boston, an architect who has illustrated many of her books. For some years she lived on the continent and concentrated on painting, but later she returned to England and bought the old manor house at Hemingford Grey, near Cambridge, which was built in 1120 and is the model for Green Knowe. Her first book for children, *The Children of Green Knowe** (Faber, 1954; Harcourt, 1954), was published when she was sixty-two, and its gentle and haunting fantasy of the seventeenth century children who still inhabit the house won it a place on the Lewis Carroll shelf and listings as a commended book for the Carnegie Award and in *Children's Books Too Good* *to Miss*. It was followed by *The Chimneys of Green Knowe** (Faber, 1958; as *Treasure of Green Knowe*, Harcourt, 1958), in which the earlier children, a little blind girl and a black boy, are from the eighteenth century, and *The River at Green Knowe** (Faber, 1959; Harcourt, 1959), a less unified book of several remarkable fantasy adventures. *A Stranger at Green Knowe** (Faber, 1961; Harcourt, 1961), the only one of the series to contain no fantasy elements, is about the friendship of a lonely boy and a gorilla. It won the Carnegie Medal and was named a Contemporary Classic. The last of the original series is a chilling story of witchcraft, *An Enemy at Green Knowe** (Faber, 1964; Harcourt, 1964). It was followed some twelve years later by *The Stones of Green Knowe* (Bodley, 1976; Atheneum, 1976), which brings the children from various centuries together in a climactic scene. Boston has also written some books for younger children, including *The Castle of Yew* (Bodley, 1965; Harcourt, 1965), *The Guardians of the House* (Bodley, 1974; Atheneum, 1975), and *The Fossil Snake* (Bodley, 1975; Atheneum, 1976), of which *The Sea-Egg* (Faber, 1967; Harcourt, 1967), a story of a polished stone from which hatches a triton, is usually considered the best. For adults she has published two novels and a play.

BOWS AGAINST THE BARONS (Trease*, Geoffrey, ill. Michael Boland, Lawrence, 1934; International, 1934), historical adventure novel set in England, which blends details of an actual fourteenth-century insurrection of peasants against the barons with the Robin* Hood legends. Dickon, 16, a serf on the manor of hard-fisted Sir Rolf D'Eyncourt and the sole support of his mother and younger brothers, rashly kills a king's deer that is browsing their meager vegetable patch. He flees for his life to Sherwood Forest, which borders his village of Oxton, to join the band of outlaws headed by the notorious Robin Hood. He soon becomes involved in advancing Robin's grand plan for uniting the exploited and abused peasants, craftsmen, and townspeople against the hated overlords of manor, church, and state. After a period of training with the bow, Dickon is disguised as a weaver's apprentice and sent by

Robin to Nottingham with a message that Robin
will come to the aid of the townspeople in demanding that the villainous sheriff release
prisoners unjustly held. In the ensuing battle,
Dickon is almost captured, makes a perilous escape through an underground passage, and then
falls into the hands of the king's foresters.
Almost turned over to Sir Rolf as a runaway
serf, he escapes when Alan-a-Dale*, Robin's minstrel, and nearby villagers set upon the
foresters. Back in Sherwood, he makes friends
with Martin, a runaway apprentice, helps Robin
and his men intercept a punitive force headed
for the village that defeated the foresters, and
sees Robin's band grow to more than seventy
angry and disillusioned men bent on revenge and
the acquisition of what Robin has convinced them
are rights usurped by the lords. Before long,
Robin's silver horn is often heard echoing
throughout the woods, fields, towns, and hills
of the region, and a tidy price is posted for
his head as the barons react to his raids for
material, money, and harassment. Sir Rolf scours
the forest in search of Robin and his men, an
effort easily foiled when Robin cleverly
stations his bowmen in the trees and instructs
them to fire upon the knight's men from the
rear. Certain that by winter the entire Midlands
will be in revolt, Robin, Little* John, Friar
Tuck, and others leave on various errands, while
Dickon assists Alan in robbing a traveling
abbot. On Christmas Day, disguised as a page,
Dickon enters D'Eyncourt Castle to spy, is
almost caught, and escapes by lying flat along a
ceiling beam in the church and then lowering
himself over the wall with the church bell rope.
Soon Robin's men, in various disguises, enter
the castle, attack, and seize and burn it,
slaying Sir Rolf. Sir Rolf's death arouses the
ire of neighboring barons, who conspire among
themselves and with the clergy to capture Robin.
They surround Sherwood, intending to starve the
outlaws into submission. After several efforts
to break the cordon fail and their cause appears
doomed, Robin's band makes a grand foray, is
attacked by forces far superior in number, and
is systematically cut down. Robin, Little John,
Dickon, and a few others fight their way valiantly back into Sherwood and from there flee

northward into Yorkshire. When Robin's wounds
worsen, Little John takes him to the convent at
Kirklees, where the Prioress proves treacherous
and bleeds him too much. Although he blows his
silver horn for help and Little John responds,
the famed outlaw dies. After burying him in an
unmarked grave in a nearby wood, Little John and
Dickon head into Derbyshire, certain that some
day Robin's vision of an England without masters
will become reality. The characters are the familiar flat ones of adventure story and legend,
except for Robin himself, who is presented as a
visionary born too soon and hence doomed to
defeat. Fast-paced action and a lively writing
style result in a story that not only holds the
interest well for what happens in the plot and
convinces in spite of many unlikely coincidences, but also skillfully weaves details of
social, economic, and political history into
Dickon's experiences without sounding didactic.
Life in the greenwood is more realistic than in
the legends. Choice.

THE BOY (*The Borrowers**), nine-year-old lonely
and imaginative child, who is sent to recover
from rheumatic fever in the old, Georgian country house of his bedridden Great* Aunt Sophy,
where he has adventures with the Clock family
of Borrowers, Pod*, Homily*, and Arrietty*. He
passes these along to his elder sister, Mrs.
May, and many years later she repeats them to
Kate. The reader is left in doubt about the
truth of the tale. Mrs. May says that he was a
tease and habitually told "impossible stories,"
"such strange imaginings," probably because he
was jealous of his older siblings. He died many
years before Mrs. May tells Kate about him, "a
hero's death," as a colonel of his regiment. In
the Borrowers' story, he becomes a kind of Borrower himself, taking things for the Clocks
because he is fond of them. His generosity leads
to their discovery by Mrs.* Driver, the housekeeper. When he first meets Arrietty, he thinks
she is a fairy. A realist in some respects, he
tells Arrietty that borrowing is actually stealing. After they are discovered, he offers to
carry the Borrowers away, tries to persuade Mrs.
Driver that they are harmless, then compensates
for his part in their predicament by creating

avenues for possible escape. Mrs. May tells Kate that he told her the Borrowers were "touchy and conceited and thought they owned the world." He thought that underneath they were frightened and that that was why they had grown so small. He thought that "each generation had become smaller and smaller, and more and more hidden." Though he plays an important role in the story, he is a relatively uninteresting character.

BRAN (*The Stronghold**), fourteen-year-old younger brother of Coll, who, when orphaned by Roman slave raiders, was taken in by Domnall* the Druid, whose pupil he now is. He is a lonely, self-mocking, cynical youth, who affects the action chiefly by giving Coll information about Taran* and by throwing himself under Domnall's knife as Domnall is about to slay Fand*. He also gives Coll the idea for saving Fand, by suggesting that she is not a true virgin. He is somewhat of a mystic and insists that he does and says only what his destiny decrees. As a character, he wins and holds the reader's attention and sympathy.

BRAN DAVIES (*The Grey King**), white-haired youth of mysterious background, who has been raised as the son of Owen Davies, farmhand of Will* Stanton's Welsh uncle. Brave, intelligent, and talented on the harp, he helps Will win the golden harp with which the Six Sleepers are awakened by correctly answering a riddle put to him by a lord inside the mountain. He and Will learn that he is the son of King Arthur, brought forward in time along with his mother, Guinevere, for their protection by Merriman* Lyon. Bran's dog, Cafall, shot by Caradog Prichard, the agent of the villainous Grey King, was named by Owen after Arthur's dog. Bran also appears in *Silver on the Tree*, the last book in The Dark Is Rising set, where he cuts the mistletoe from the Midsummer Tree with the shining sword to defeat the Dark. He chooses to continue to live with those he has come to love in the twentieth century rather than to return to Arthur's time. As a character there is a certain modern-fantasy stereotyping about him, but he still is a more interesting figure than Will, the protagonist.

BRANFIELD, JOHN (CHARLES) (1931-   ), born in
Burrow   Bridge,   Somerset; educator,   novelist.
He attended Drax Grammar School, Yorkshire,
received his M.A. degree in English from Queens'
College,   Cambridge,   in   1953   and   his M.Ed.
degree from the University of Exeter, Devon, in
1972. Most of his teaching career has been at
Camborne Comprehensive School in Cornwall, where
he has made his home and where many of his books
are set. Most of his novels are problem stories
treated without sensation in which characterization and   setting are important. His first book
for young people, *Nancekuke* (Gollancz, 1972; as
The Poison Factory, Harper, 1972),   explores attitudes toward military research and investiga-
tive reporting. *Sugar Mouse* (Gollancz, 1973; as
Why Me?, Harper, 1973) is about a diabetic and
her rebellion against   the restrictions of her
disease. *The Scillies Trip* (Gollancz, 1975) is
concerned with teenage drug use. *The Fox in
Winter** (Gollancz, 1980; Atheneum, 1982), which
was commended for the Carnegie Medal, deals with
the problems of aging in a story of the
friendship between a girl and a manipulative and
irascible but courageous old man. Branfield has
also written a television play, *The Day I Shot
My Dad*, which was produced in 1976, and three
novels for adults. He won the English Speaking
Union Page Scholarship in 1974 and the Arts
Council Award in 1978.

BRANWELL, SAM (*Brother in the Land**), old
"smallholder," owner of a goat and chicken farm,
who becomes the leader of the resistance group
following the nuclear disaster that ruins
Skipley and turns the soldiers into dictatorial
fascists. A seemingly harmless old fellow who
wanders around the devastated area with a
donkey, Branwell is the spirit behind the group
that eventually takes over Kershaw Farm, and it
is he who stands up to the Swiss military people
when they arrive. At their first meeting, when
Danny* Lodge is showing his little brother, Ben,
their mother's grave, Branwell quotes, "He who
places his brother in the land is everywhere,"
and then explains that it means that everyone
now is burying family members and loved ones. He
depends on the bravery and guerrilla skills of
Rhodes*, but he deplores the man's insensitivity

and refers to him as a barbarian. When Danny is sliding into deep pessimism and cynicism, Branwell points out to him that along with the horrors that have followed the nuclear exchange, there is good that has survived, as exemplified in the love that he feels for Kim* Tyson and for Ben. His choice of the term Masada for the resistance group is symbolic, although he says it stands for Movement to Arm Skipley Against Dictatorial Authority.

BRAQUE, CARMODY (*The Changeover: A Supernatural Romance**), evil owner of an antique shop who seizes Jacko Chant's life force in order to sustain his own. He has almost drained the boy of life by the time Laura* Chant succeeds in breaking his power. After she uses her witch power against him, all that remains of him is a pile of clothes around a rotting mass of dead leaves. He is a flat, functional figure.

BREE (*The Horse and His Boy**), proud, talking Narnian horse stolen away as a foal and taken to Calormen, where he is a war horse when Shasta* encounters him. His comments about Narnia* induce Shasta to seek refuge in that country. Bree, whose full name is Breehy-hinny-brinny-hoohy-hah, loses much of his arrogance and self-conceit as the tale proceeds. At first he is the leader of the expedition, but Hwin* gains in importance along the way. Bree adds some humor to events, in addition to playing a strong role in the plot, especially at the beginning.

BRIDGET HUNTERLY (*The Far-Distant Oxus**), one of the six children who undertake an "expeditionary force" by raft and pony down the Oxus to the sea. Though shallow, she and Maurice* are the best characterized of the lot. She shares the leadership with him, serving in the maternal role to his paternal one, and is largely responsible for the cooking. She is athletic, however, on her long, stick-like legs easily winning the high jump contest at a fete they attend; she is also a crack climber and rider. Her age is not specified, but she prefers active pursuits and is unhappy at receiving a mauve manicure set in the contest. Without any re-

luctance, she "sacrifices" the set to Ahura
Mazda to insure a successful journey.

BRIGGS, K(ATHERINE) M(ARY) (1898-1980), born in
London; scholar, folklorist, writer. She was
educated at Lansdowne House and at Lady
Margaret Hall, Oxford, where she received her
M.A. degree in 1923 and a Ph.D. in 1952, with a
doctoral thesis on folklore in the seventeenth
century. This interest in folklore permeated
almost all her writings, including her five
books of fiction for children. These are *The
Legend of Maiden-Hair* (Stockwell, 1915), *The
Witches' Ride* (Capricornus, 1937), and *The
Prince, the Fox, and the Dragon* (Capricornus,
1938), as well as the two that have been
republished in the United States, *Hobberdy
Dick** (Eyre, 1955; Greenwillow, 1977) and *Kate
Crackernuts** (Alden,1963; revised, Kestrel,
1979; Greenwillow, 1979). *Kate Crackernuts* is a
retelling of a folktale, but with strong elements of characterization and seventeenth-
century setting. *Hobberdy Dick* tells of the
influence of a resident hobgoblin on a Puritan
family, despite their official disbelief in any
such creatures. Both are cited by *Choice*
magazine as books to be included in an academic
library. She also wrote a three-volume book of
plays for children and two books of verse. For
adults she wrote two novels, four plays, and
twelve other long works, mostly studies of
folklore, including the four-volume *A Dictionary
of British Folk-tales in the English Language*
(Routledge, 1970-1971; Indiana U. Press, 1970-
1971). Others include *A Dictionary of Fairies:
Hobgoblins, Brownies, Bogies, and Other Supernatural Creatures* (Lane, 1976; as *An Encyclopedia of Fairies...*, Pantheon,1976) and *Abbey
Lubbers, Banshees, and Boggarts: A Who's Who
of Fairies* (Kestrel, 1979; Pantheon, 1979). Her
last book, published the year of her death, is
Nine Lives: Cats in Folklore (Routledge, 1980;
Pantheon, 1980). During World War II, she was in
the Women's Auxiliary AirForce, and in the 1970s
she spent one year each as visiting professor at
the University of Pennsylvania and at the
University of California at Berkeley. She also
headed an amateur theatrical touring company for
fifteen years and served as president of the

Folklore Society of London from 1967 to 1970. Among her many awards is an honorary doctorate from Oxford University.

BROCK (*Owlglass**), badger also known by his hyphenated surname, Meles-Brock, who hosts the club meetings. A sort of elder statesman type, he organizes the deputation to the owl, provides the gift, and calls on Old* Beak and Claws to inform him of the plan when the animals decide to get spectacles for the bird. Very much a gentleman of the old school, Brock provides generous repasts for his guests and passes on to the younger members the traditions of the club and such information as how Foxy* got the name of Mr. Williams.

BRONIA BALICKI (*The Silver Sword**), fair-haired youngest of the Balicki children, three years old when she enters the story, sister of Ruth* and Edek* and fellow-refugee of Jan*. All four make their way from war-torn Poland to Switzerland at the end of World War II in search of the Balicki parents. Since Ruth mothers her tenderly, Bronia seems less affected than other refugee children by the difficulties of life during the war and on the trek to Switzerland. Artistic, she draws with ease, covering their rude living quarters with charcoal pictures, and becomes an accomplished artist after the war. Bronia is less developed than the other characters.

BROOKE (*The Sentinels**), first lieutenant on the *Sentinel*, under Captain James Murray*. Tory in politics (while Murray is Whig) and a social snob, he looks down on Murray at first, thinks the captain is too lenient with the men, and often disagrees with his policies, although he is always obedient and dutiful. He tends to be more pragmatic and aware of appearances than Murray, for whom the well-being of the men is always paramount. He comes to see that Murray knows his business and to respect him professionally. Brooke can be capricious and cruel, as when he sends Spencer up the masthead merely out of spite. The flogging Brooke orders sickens the watching Spencer; it is the boy's initiation to harsh discipline at sea. Brooke is a complex, interesting figure.

BROTHER DUSTY-FEET (Sutcliff*, Rosemary, ill. C. Walter Hodges, Oxford, 1952), historical novel set in Elizabethan England dealing with life among a troupe of strolling players. Since the death of his father, a vicar in a poor Cornish village, orphan Hugh Copplestone, 10, has lived with his mother's brother, Uncle Harry, and Harry's shrewish wife, Aunt Alison. His only heritage from his own family is his love of learning, gained from his father, a pot of periwinkle, his mother's favorite flower, and his big dog, Argos, who is part deer-hound. When Aunt Alison plans to have Argos killed, Hugh steals off in the night with the dog, hoping to get to Oxford, which he knows from the stories of his father's Oriel College days, when he acted as servitor, a sort of servant-companion, to a wealthy fellow student, Anthony Heritage. After a couple of days of eating little and sleeping in the open, he comes upon a group of traveling players who accept him, with little question, being in need of a new boy to play the female parts. The troupe consists of the leader, Tobias Pennifeather; the romantic lead, melancholy Jasper Nye; the comic, Benjamin Bunsell; young Nicholas Bodkyn, who must be promoted to male roles since his voice is changing; Jonathan Whiteleafe, tumbler and repairer of costumes; and the little mare, Saffronilla, who pulls the tilt-cart carrying their props. With them, Hugh (usually called Dusty, short for the generic traveler's name, Dusty-Feet) wanders for more than a year, acting in inn-yards and at the foot of market crosses, on good nights feasting in inns and sleeping in warm stables, on poor nights tightening his belt and sleeping in ditches. They have many adventures along the way. At one point a Palmer joins them, a man who has been on pilgrimages to many far places, and he takes Hugh with him on a cross-country jaunt through fields and woods where he plays his pipe and draws wild animals to him in such a magical way that Hugh suspects he might be one of the fairy people. At Stourbridge Fair, the first fair Hugh has ever seen, he saves an old friend of the players, Zackary Hawkins, a quack doctor illegally

selling his wares, by warning him of the
approach of the Steward's officers. That night a
Tom-o'-Bedlam, one of the harmless, wild-looking
madmen who live on the roads, joins their
campfire and performs the ancient ceremony of
the Seisin for Hugh, making him one of the
Brotherhood of the Road, a ceremony the others
half ridicule and half believe. Just before
Christmas, Argos, chasing a rabbit, is caught in
a trap, and, though they search diligently for
him, they fail to find him. Unknown to them, the
Palmer with the pipe finds and releases the dog,
and he makes his way on three legs to the
cathedral where he finds Hugh attending
Christmas Eve service. Toward the end of winter,
heading for Rye, they get lost in a heavy mist
beyond Burmarsh and eventually blunder upon the
hall of Thomas Trumpington, a huge and hugely
generous man who feeds them lavishly and summons
all his household and close neighbors to enjoy
the performance they give in return. At one
point, down on their luck, they perform without
the required license, resist arrest in a grand
fight, and are locked in the stocks for the
night awaiting trial, only to be secretly
released by a fine gentleman who has joined the
fray on their side and whom they afterwards
learn is young Sir Walter Raleigh. At Exeter, to
his astonishment, Hugh runs into Uncle Jacob and
eludes him only by the quick thinking of the
actors, who have Nicky exchange clothes with him
and then pretend that one of their number is
stricken with plague so that he will not
investigate too carefully. As they play at
Sherborne, a man in the audience watches Hugh
closely and later sends for him. This turns out
to be Anthony Heritage, his father's old friend,
who proposes to take Hugh in and let him become
servitor to his son, Martin, who attends Oriel.
At first Hugh refuses, out of loyalty to the
players, but Jonathan, who has been his best
friend and father figure, persuades him to take
advantage of the opportunity. The players
promise to act in Sherborne each summer so Hugh
can see them again, and Hugh is accepted into
the Heritage family, along with Martin and his
sisters, lively Tiggy (Antigone) and toddler
Meg. Hugh is a polite boy, adequate for his part
but not memorable. The plot has little tension

and employs coincidence blatantly without much attempt at foreshadowing; characters are flat, with only slight development; and the tone sometimes dips into the condescending, story-telling attitude of earlier books for rather young children. The main interest is in the life of the sixteenth-century strolling players. Those in this group seem to get along with remarkable accord. There is not much suggestion of the danger, dirt, and discomfort such a life must have entailed. A couple of digressive stories within the story about St. George are interesting in themselves but slow the action. The strength of the novel is in its plentiful and convincing detail of the period. As a whole, this is a pleasant tale, but there is little suggestion of the skill Sutcliff later developed in structure and style. Fanfare.

BROTHER ERNULF (*One Is One**), grouchy old monk of Richley Abbey who is a fine artist and who recognizes talent in Stephen* de Beauville that surpasses his own. When Stephen returns to the abbey as an adult, Brother Ernulf asks him whether his manner drove the boy to run away and whether, had he not been so chary with his praise, Stephen might have been happy enough to stay at Richley. Stephen answers honestly that he might have stayed but that he is not sorry he left. Satisfied, Brother Ernulf turns over the remaining Gospel of John to Stephen to complete, his own eyesight having failed.

BROTHER IANTO (*The Whispering Mountain**), an old monk of the order of St. Ennodawg, an almost extinct group whose monastery lies in ruins near Pennygaff. He lives in a cave on Whispering Mountain where he makes lenses for eyeglasses for the people who live round about, a trade he learned while serving in China. He once saved the life of the Seljuk* of Rum, pulling the noble out of the Oxus River. It is because of Brother Ianto that the Seljuk has come to Wales in search of the lost tribe of Yehimelek*. Brother Ianto and irascible old Mr. Hughes, Owen's grandfather, were friends in their youth, when Brother Ianto was Ianto Richards.

BROTHER IN THE LAND (Swindells*, Robert, Oxford,

1984; Holiday, 1985), profoundly pessimistic novel of the aftermath of nuclear war, set in England sometime in the not-far-distant future. Teenager Danny* Lodge, the first person narrator, caught in a thunderstorm while riding his bike, crawls into a pillbox left from World War II and from there witnesses the brilliant flash and the mushroom cloud of the nuclear explosion that destroys Branford and most of his home town, Skipley. Before he can make his way back, he is stopped near Kershaw Farm by a man, evidently a soldier, in a black rubber suit, who beats him up and confiscates his bike. In the rubble of their small grocery store, he finds his father and little brother, Ben, 7, who were in the basement at the time of the strike, but his mother, like most of the people in the town, has been killed. At first they live in hope that the government will follow the preannounced plans for action in such a disaster, meanwhile living on the canned foods and water from the one uncontaminated source, an old well uncovered in a tavern yard. While getting water, Danny saves a girl (whom he later knows as Kim* Tyson) from a thug, and immediately becomes infatuated. Kim, who lives in a ruined basement with her sister and her sister's husband, is cynical, harder, and more clear-sighted than Danny. The weeks following bring one shock after another. When the trucks from Kershaw Farm do come, with loudspeaker announcements that all those who are ill must be carried to the curb to be taken to the hospital, the survivors are greatly relieved and bring out their dying relatives, only to learn, later, that the ill have been carted off, shot, and buried in a mass grave. Various new elements in the population appear: Spacers, whose minds have been damaged by the horrors and who wander about unaware of the situation; Badgers, who have holed up in underground shelters and are smoked out and killed for their stores of uncontaminated food; Terminals, who are dying of radiation sickness; Goths, gangs of hoodlums from outside the area; Purples, cannibals who get their name from the song about "Purple People Eaters." Danny and his father take turns standing guard with guns over their supplies, which they dole out to old customers. A second loudspeaker announcement tells them all

to register for food and fuel cards. Though
skeptical, Danny takes Ben, but is appalled when
the crowd is separated into two lines to get
handouts of stew, one line of ordinary people
and the other of Spacers, who receive poisoned
portions and die horribly. Not long afterward,
the soldiers raid their store and take Danny's
father prisoner in a vehicle that blows up a few
yards down the street. Danny learns that the
explosion was engineered by Rhodes*, his former
Physical Education teacher, a macho, fascist
type who is part of a resistance group led by
Sam Branwell*, an old farmer who wanders around
with a donkey, and who has quoted to him, at his
mother's grave, "He who places his brother in
the land is everywhere." Branwell takes Danny
and Ben in at Masada, which stands for Movement
to Arm Skipley Against Dictatorial Authority and
which is headquartered at his smallholding, his
little goat and chicken farm. Though she does
not live at the farm, Kim is part of Masada.
When an order comes out that all able-bodied
adults are to report to Kershaw Farms and build
what amounts to their own concentration camp,
the members of Masada become outlaws, raiding
the army trucks and sabotaging wherever
possible. On one mission, Danny is captured,
pretends to be a Spacer, and is ordered shot by
a soldier he recognizes as Alec Booth, a bully
from school. Surprisingly, Booth roughs him up a
bit, shoots into the air, and lets him escape.
When the soldiers poison the town's only well,
Masada mobilizes all its forces and attacks
Kershaw Farms and, through a series of
fortuitous events, captures the place and sets
up its own survival colony, open to all who show
up. In the deep shelters, where the soldiers
survived the blast, they find seeds, and they
optimistically set out to clear off the
contaminated topsoil and plant beans, potatoes,
and turnips. Kim's sister is pregnant, another
omen of good to most of the people, although Kim
herself has read of deformed babies at Hiroshima
and is apprehensive. In August, they discover
that all their plants have been affected by the
radiation and have failed to produce. Just as
they are about to despair, they hear a
helicopter, and they are wildly hopeful that the
government has sent a rescue mission. The next

day a Swiss army group arrives, announces that
the British government is a thing of the past,
counts the people at Masada, condemns their
group as a commune, demobilizes their vehicles,
and confiscates their weapons. Rhodes, who all
along has fought the humanitarian principles of
Branwell, has already left with a group
ostensibly to hunt supplies, but as Kim clearly
sees, with no intention of returning. Danny
waits until the baby is born, deformed, to live
only a few minutes, and Branwell dies, then he,
Kim, and Ben take the donkey and set out for the
castle at Holy Island, which is joined to the
mainland by a causeway and where he hopes they
may be safe. On the way they are attacked by
Rhodes, whom Kim is able to kill, and then are
snowed in at an isolated farmhouse, where Ben
dies from spreading radiation. The story is, not
too plausibly, supposed to be what Danny writes
and leaves in the house before he and Kim move
on. Although the characters are not highly
developed and Danny's love for his little
brother is not entirely convincing, the novel is
compelling, getting its power from the grim
circumstances and its refusal to soften the
horror by a hopeful ending. The picture of the
betrayal of the people by duly constituted
authority is especially chilling. Carnegie
Highly Com.; Other.

BUBBA (*The Dancing Bear*) she-bear for whom Silvester* is warden. When Ariadne* was an infant,
her careless father let her fall into his
bear-pit, and Bubba, then a young female, picked
her up and cuffed away the hungry male, who was
ready to devour her. Because of this and because
Bubba was born the same day as Ariadne and
Silvester, Lord Celsus has her trained as a
dancing bear and makes Silvester her warden as
soon as he is old enough. Unlike most trained
bears, she has not been maimed by having the
bones in her arms and chest smashed to prevent
her from crushing men in her hug, and she has
grown up friendly, handsome, and devoted to
Silvester and Ariadne. On their journey north
she is frequently the cause of their
difficulties, but with the Kutrigers she gives
them a special advantage, since the word for
bear, "Kuttri," is associated with their name

and the bear is a specially honored animal among them. After Silvester and Ariadne go to the tower of Antonius*, Bubba escapes and mates with a wild bear, but she returns to have her cub, which they name Terence.

BUBBLE AND SQUEAK (*The Battle of Bubble and Squeak**), the two gerbils the Parker children acquire from Jimmy* Dean's cousin and that precipitate a battle with Mrs.* Sparrow, their mother, over whether or not the children may keep them. Sid* Parker calls them by the English term for a meal of cabbage and sausage.

BUCHAN, JOHN (1975-1940), born in Perth, Scotland, died in Montreal, Quebec, Canada; novelist, biographer, historian, lawyer, and government official. He tells of his religious background in the family of a minister of the Free Church in his autobiographical work, *Memory Hold-the-Door* (Hodder, 1940; as *Pilgrim's Way: An Essay in Recollection*, (Houghton, 1940). He studied theology at Glasgow University and history at Brasenose College, Oxford, where he took first class honors and won the Stanhope Historical Prize and the Newgate Prize for Englsh Verse. He later studied law and at the end of the Boer War went to South Africa for three years as private secretary to Lord Alfred Milner, the high commissioner. For twenty years, from 1907 to 1927, he was a partner in the publishing firm of Thomas Nelson and Sons; during World War I he was the director of Reuter Press Agency and war correspondent in France for the *Times*, and then became Director of Information under the Prime Minister. From 1927 to 1935 he was a Conservative Member of Parliament and became Lord Tweedsmuir, and from 1935 to 1940 he served as Governor General of Canada. During all these years he was a prolific writer, mostly of novels of adventure and suspense, biography, and history. Among his famous adventure novels published for adults but often read by children are *Prester John* (Doran, 1910), and *The Thirty-Nine Steps* (Doran, 1915). In 1931 he was voted the most popular living writer for young people in Britain. Among his books published for children are fantasies, like *The Magic Walking Stick* (Hodder, 1932; Houghton,

1932), novels like *The Long Traverse** (Hodder, 1941; as *Lake of Gold*, Houghton, 1941), biographies of Sir Walter Raleigh, Andrew Jackson, Lord Ardwell, Sir Walter Scott, Julius Caesar, and Oliver Cromwell, and a number of histories, many of them about World War I. Some of his books for teenaged boys are set in Canada, including *The Long Traverse*, selected under its American title for the *Horn Book* Fanfare list, which gives scenes from the history of that country. His wife, Susan Charlotte Grosvenor, aided in the research for his books.

BUD RILEY (*Danger at Black Dyke**), Hart Riley, rich youth, whom Geordie* Bickerson, Tim* Charlton, and Hamish* MacLeish shelter at the old farmhouse called Black Dyke. He becomes fond of the boys, and, while he is grateful for and needs their help, he also worries about endangering them. He understands Geordie's need for security and for stability in his friendships because he also comes from a broken home. He is a sympathetic character, even though his reasons for not explaining to the boys why he is running are unconvincing.

BUMPO KAHBOOBOO (*The Story of Doctor Dolittle**; *The Voyages of Doctor Dolittle**), Crown Prince of Jolliginki, who leaves his African kingdom to attend Oxford, and then leaves Oxford to accompany Doctor* Dolittle to Spidermonkey Island. When Bumpo's father imprisons the doctor and his friends, Bumpo allows them to escape in return for being made white (temporarily) so that he can win the affections of a Sleeping Beauty, whom he afterwards makes the first of his many wives. In the second book he is less ridiculous, though his malapropisms make his ornate language amusing and his bare feet contrast with his otherwise impeccable dress. In the many trials of the voyage he is a hard worker, loyal, and a formidable fighter when necessary.

BUNTY (*Charlotte Sometimes**), really named Marjorie, one of the girls at the boarding school that Clare and Emily* Moby attend. She is Emily's friend, a lively, energetic, mischievous child, who thinks up things for the girls to do.

Her father is killed at the end of the war, dampening the spirits of the girls even though they are glad that the long conflict is finally over. Her character adds dimension by contrast to those of Charlotte (Clare) and Emily.

BUNYAN, JOHN (1628-1688), born at Elstow in Bedfordshire; Puritan clergyman and writer of religious works. He had little formal education and followed in his father's footsteps, becoming a tinker. During the English Civil War, he served as a soldier from 1644-1646; then he settled again at Elstow, married, and had six children. Greatly influenced by his wife, he experienced a spiritual conversion from his previous high living, joined a Nonconformist church, and became a preacher. Arrested for preaching publicly without a license in 1666, he spent most of the next fifteen years in jail, where much of his writing was done and where he began his most famous book (and the most important work to come out of the Puritan period), *The Pilgrim's Progress* (Ponder, 1678). An allegory of the journeys of Christian and his wife toward heaven, it has been translated into 100 languages and has the status of a world literary masterpiece. Intended for adult encouragement and instruction, it appealed to children in the days before there was an established literature for the young, and continues to be appreciated today in a condensed version by Mary Godolphin, entitled *Pilgrim's Progress**. This edition was published in 1884 and reissued by Lippincott with illustrations by Robert Lawson in 1939. The Godolphin retelling pares away the extraneous and moralizing material and makes the story accessible and appealing to modern tastes; it is listed in *Children's Classics*. Bunyan noted his book's popularity with young readers and wrote another expressly for them, *A Book for Boys and Girls, or Country Rhymes for Children* (Ponder, 1686), later entitled *Divine Emblems, or Temporal Things Spiritualized*. This consists of versified sermons in which Bunyan draws morals from common human experiences. Though heavy with lessons, the sharply depicted scenes and the music of the meter and rhyme give the verses a certain charm; nevertheless, they never became as popular with

the young   as the religious novel   that made him
immortal   in   the   world of   literature.   Bunyan
wrote many other works for adults, was pastor of
Bedford, and continued to preach until his death
in London.

BURTON, HESTER (WOOD-HILL) (1913-   ), born in
Beccles, Suffolk; editor, author of historical
novels for   older readers. She often   builds her
stories   around   specific historical   incidents,
such as a battle, riot, or natural disaster, and
then peoples them with   ordinary persons to show
how   these   events   might   have   affected   the
everyday   lives of   common people.   Her thorough
research and her intelligent and responsible use
of   her source   material produce   vivid and   realistic reading that never glamorizes or softens
the past. *The Great   Gale** (Oxford, 1960; as *The
Flood at   Reedsmere* by   World, 1968),   which was
her first   novel and commended for   the Carnegie
Award, gives   a clear   sense of   the excitement,
terror, and   sheer helplessness   of experiencing
a home- and life-threatening   flood. *Castors
Away!** (Oxford,   1962;   World,   1963),   which
appears   on both   the Fanfare   and the   Carnegie
Commended lists, is a slice   of life at home and
in battle   during the   Napoleonic Wars.   *Time of
Trial** (Oxford, 1963;   World,   1964), her Carnegie Award-winning third   novel, finds the heroine's father imprisoned   for libel   during the
wars with   France. This   novel, the   most highly
regarded critically   of her books,   appears also
on   the Fanfare and *Choice* lists. Holding *Boston
Globe-Horn Book* Honor status is *Thomas** (Oxford,
1969;   as *Beyond   the   Weir   Bridge* by   Crowell,
1970), which   focuses on   the persecution   of the
Quakers   and the   plague that   struck London   in
the mid-1600s following the defeat of Charles II
(Charles Stuart)   at Worcester. She   wrote about
the   evacuation of   Dunkirk in   *In Spite   of All
Terror* (Oxford,   1968; World, 1969) and   about a
girl growing up during   the English Civil War in
Kate   Rider (Oxford,   1974; as   *Kate   Ryder* by
Crowell, 1975), and   about poverty among English
farm workers   in the early nineteenth   century in
No   Beat of   Drum (Oxford,   1966; World,   1967).
Burton's father was   a   quiet, unassuming, un-
worldly country doctor, the prototype of many of
her elderly characters,   including the father in

Time of Trial. Her upbringing in a quiet
Suffolk coastal market town provided the background for *The Great Gale, Castors Away!*, and
Time of Trial, among others. She was educated at
Headington School, Oxford, and took an honors
degree in English literature at Oxford University, where J. R. R. Tolkien* was her teacher
in Anglo-Saxon and C. S. Lewis* one of her
literature teachers. She married Reginald W. B.
Burton, a teacher of Latin and Greek at Oxford,
who shared her love of history. The couple and
their three daughters made their home in Oxford.
Her work as a part-time grammar school teacher
helped her to understand what young people
enjoy in a story--excitement and the sense of
important things happening. She was also an
assistant editor for *Oxford Junior Encyclopedia* in London from 1956-1961. In addition
to several more novels and some nonfiction, she
also published a radio play, *The Great Gale*,
1961, and a television play, *Castors Away!*,
adapted from her own books, and for adults she
edited the works of Coleridge, the Wordsworths,
and Tennyson for Oxford University Press. She is
considred a leading writer of historical fiction
for youth.

THE BUS GIRLS (Harris*, Mary K., ill. Eileen
Green, Faber, 1965; Norton, 1965), realistic
story of the off-again, on-again friendships of
a group of teenagers who ride the bus together
to their Suffolk girls' high school. Hetty Grey,
13, has just moved from the city to Pilot's
Cottage in Pebblecomb, which was willed to her
mother by her great-uncle, but has been unable
to start the spring term because of bronchitis.
Her nervous, timid, widowed mother, who barely
earns a living as a seamstress, arranges with
the vicar's wife, Mrs. Daring, for Hetty to call
at the vicarage on the first day back to school
so that the vicar's oldest daughter, Davina, can
shepherd her to the bus and her classrooms in
Barbridge. Hetty, very bright and confident, and
inclined to domineer over her uneducated mother,
sees at once that this is a bad plan, but she is
not prepared for the confusion she encounters at
the vicarage entrance nor the deliberate
rudeness of Davina as soon as they are out of
her mother's sight. On the bus she is approached

by Amabel Lee, a rather stupid, doll-like girl
with china blue eyes and permed hair, who
proposes that they be best friends, but Hetty is
wary. She soon realizes that Davina bullies and
manipulates the other girls and most of the
teachers. Some of the other girls are friendly,
but the only one Hetty sees as a potential
friend is a tough-looking, frowning little girl
named Bernie whose parents run the local pub,
The Fighting Cocks. In their class, Form Lower
IVA, Davina is the dynamic force, showing off,
joking, sulking, being warm and insulting by
turns, and full of vitality and anger. She
frequently neglects her homework, particularly
her Latin, though she is obviously highly
intelligent. Unlike American teenagers, these
girls do not talk or appear to think much about
boys. Three incidents give Hetty more insight
into Davina's problems. On the way to the hockey
field, Davina realizes she has forgotten a book,
tries unsuccessfully to persuade selfish Amabel
to lend her bicycle so she can ride back and get
it, then rushes off and returns just in time on
another bicycle, which she drops in a nettle
thicket and forgets. A few days later the whole
school is told in assembly about the stolen
bicycle, and the thief warned that she must come
forward that day to confess. All the girls know
it is Davina and watch apprehensively as she
leaves to see the headmistress; then they turn
furiously on Amabel, accusing her of being mean
and reciting a litany of her past stinginess. To
Hetty's surprise, Davina calls them off. Some
days later, Davina phones Hetty in panic, as she
does not understand her Latin assignment. Hetty
volunteers to come around to the vicarage to
explain it to her, but when she arrives, the
vicar himself answers the door, is extremely
rude to her, and sends her on her way without
seeing Davina. The next day on the bus Davina
accuses Hetty of bungling and, when Hetty
answers back sharply, admits that her father was
listening in on the call. The most revealing
incident occurs in connection with the Sale of
Work, an annual money-raising event at the
school. Lower IVA is in charge of the baked-
goods table and when Rachel, the head girl,
tries vainly to pin the others down about what
their mothers will contribute, Davina takes

over, proposes that they do their own baking in
the Domestic Science Kitchens, gets permission
from the teacher in charge, and organizes with
whirlwind efficiency. Hetty is dismayed when her
mother insists that she come home on the regular
bus rather than stay to help, so that she will
not be overtired and become ill again. Feeling
like a traitor, Hetty comes home and grudgingly
attends a Lenten evening service with her
mother, where she is astonished to see Davina.
The next day, helping with the sale, Hetty sees
how overbearing the vicar and his wife act, and
she realizes that Davina had been forbidden to
miss the service, had decided to stay at school
in defiance, and had been picked up and forced
to go home by her father. The next school day,
the other girls turn on Davina, who manages to
shift the attention by grabbing Bernie's rosary
which has fallen from her pocket, ridiculing it,
and tossing it on the floor. In the confrontation that follows, Hetty steps in on Bernie's
side, but she understands Davina's need to
create the diversion. She sees a new side of
Davina when a Shakespearean actor gives a
program at the school, and the two girls share a
glowing, almost hypnotized appreciation. In her
happy daze after the program, Davina loses a
valuable map that her father has loaned to a
teacher and she was to bring home. That evening
she calls Hetty in panic, saying she has to find
it before her father returns, and Hetty
remembers seeing it in the luggage rack of the
bus. Hoping to retrieve it before the vicar
knows it is missing, Hetty sets off on Amabel's
bicycle, arrives at the bus terminal too late,
and, realizing that her effort is in vain,
starts back in the beginning of a snow storm.
Just as the going is getting too difficult for
her, Davina appears, having set out to find her.
Without Davina's urging and physical help, Hetty
would have collapsed before they get to the road
but together they reach it. There Davina flags
down the first car, which turns out to be that
of the grim-faced vicar, coming out to find
them. Hetty is very ill and doesn't know what
has happened for some time. She eventually
learns that Davina has come to visit, only to be
severely scolded and sent off by her mother.
When Bernie comes to visit, she confesses to

Hetty that she and Rachel saw the map on the bus
and that she took it, intending to return it to
Davina after she had had time to worry for a
while. Before Hetty can start back to school,
she has another visitor, the vicar himself, who
takes the opportunity to tell her what a trial
Davina is and that he intends to ship her off to
boarding school. Hetty sturdily defends Davina,
pointing out that only his daughter's sense of
responsibility made Davina come out in the storm
to rescue her, and, surprised at being opposed,
the vicar agrees to think it over. Hetty returns
to school for the last of the term, and now
clearly will have Davina's friendship, though
it is not certain yet what the vicar will
decide. The novel does a remarkable job of
making the friendships and quarrels of thirteen-
year-olds important to the reader. This is
accomplished partly by telling the story
through the point of view, though not in the
voice, of Hetty, but mostly through strong
characterization. The parents and teachers are
believably drawn as real people, not stereotypes, and even the minor characters are well
differentiated, but Hetty and, to a far greater
extent, Davina, are really memorable. Although
it is easy to see how exasperating Davina would
be to adults and often to her peers, she emerges
as a sympathetic character, sensitive, clever,
and courageous in her fight against the
suppression of her true nature. Carnegie Com.

C
___

CABBY (*The Magician's Nephew**), when first seen, a red-faced man in a bowler hat, who is angry because Queen* Jadis, the Witch, has stolen his hansom cab and horse, Strawberry. He and his horse accidentally accompany Polly* Plummer and Digory* Kirke into the world that becomes Narnia* and are present at its creation. There he appears as a kind, brave person, younger than he seemed in London, a fond husband, minus his cockney accent and worried ways. Aslan* makes him and his wife the first rulers of Narnia, King Frank and Queen Helen, a sweetly charming, good-hearted couple. They demonstrate how Narnia can relieve tension and bring out the best in good people. He appears briefly as King Frank at the end of *The Last Battle**, along with Helen and other characters from previous Narnia books including Fledge, the winged horse who was once Strawberry, his cab horse.

CADELLIN (*The Weirdstone of Brisingamen**), wizard hundreds of years old, whose responsbility is to guard the 140 Sleeping Knights until the time to rouse them and send them forth to conquer the evil Nostrand, who dwells in the Abyss of Ragnorak. Cadellin provided the knights' pure white steeds, and, having only 139, took a farmer who owned a horse inside the cave called Fundindelve, where the Sleepers lay. In return for the farmer's white steed, Cadellin allowed him to take all the gold, silver, and jewels the man could carry.

Unknown to Cadellin, the farmer, an ancestor of Bess Mossock, took with him Firefrost*, which then came down in Bess's family and finally into the possession of Susan through her mother, whose nurse Bess had been. Cadellin is the stereotypical good wizard, wise, kind, brave, caring, white-bearded, and ancient yet seemingly ageless.

CALCIFER (*Howl's Moving Castle**), fire demon who has entered into a contract with Howl* and who persuades Sophie* Hatter to try to break it in return for finding a way to raise the enchantment that makes her an old woman. Calcifer appears as a face with green eyebrow-like flames over orange flames with a little purple glint in each, like an eye with a pupil. When he can be persuaded, he bends his head forward, so that only a ring of curly green flames shows, on which a cooking pan can be balanced. Calcifer has actually designed the castle and keeps it moving; in fact, he does most of the real magic for which Howl gets credit, and, though he complains, he is bound to the fireplace. He comments ironically on Howl and events throughout the story. It is not until the end of the book that it is revealed that he is really a falling star, to which the compassionate Howl has given his heart so that it may live, in exchange for its magic services. When Calcifer is released from the contract, it flies away, but then returns of its own accord to the castle grate.

CALEB (*The Night Watchmen**), impatient, suspicious, and less outgoing than his brother, Josh*; one of the two tramps whom Henry* helps to escape from the Greeneyes and catch the night train to There, where the do-as-you-pleasers live. Caleb feels he must protect Josh because he thinks his brother is too trusting. He is the cook and takes a great deal of pleasure in preparing gourmet meals for the two.

CAM RENTON (*Sea Change**), apprentice who ships aboard the *Langdale* and, during an action-filled voyage, changes from a discontented little boy to a responsible and competent young man. Early in the voyage he badly misjudges the first mate,

Andy*, and develops an antagonism that nearly
ruins his voyage. Through a series of episodes,
particularly the boarding and repairing of the
abandoned *Arno*, Cam comes to see his mistake,
and when circumstances put him in a position
where he must assume responsibility, he responds
in a mature way.

CANDIDATE FOR FAME (Jowett*, Margaret, ill.
Peggy Fortnum, Oxford, 1955), historical novel
of the rise to stardom of a young actress in
the eighteenth-century theater of Sheridan and
Mrs. Siddons. The story starts in Yorkshire when
Deborah Keate, eldest daughter of the manager of
a troupe of strolling players, is twelve.
Although she has acted and worked in the theater
from her earliest memory, she has also spent two
years at a boarding school, where she found that
the girls snobbishly looked down upon actors.
Now, in 1788, back with the players while the
second daughter, Elizabeth, is at school and the
youngest, Sarah, waits her turn, Deborah is well
aware of the difficulties of such a troupe. They
are subject to the whims of local magistrates,
to whom they must apply for a license to
perform, and forced to travel in even the worst
weather, often short on comforts and even food
if the audience is sparse. She is, however, an
ambitious girl, and she is coached by her
father, who was once a London actor with David
Garrick. Her first big part comes at Beverley,
when the leading actress decamps without notice
to follow a departing actor, and Deborah fills
her part playing Juliet, to resounding applause.
A year later she is saved from being run down by
the carriage of two gentlemen, one of whom turns
out to be Tate Wilkinson, manager of the Theatre
Royal at York. Having seen her act, he proposes
to her father, whom he knew in London, that she
come to his troupe for a season. There she finds
Peter Etty, grandson of Mr. Constable, the kind
old magistrate at Burlington, who has run away
to join the players and is known by them as John
Edmunds. They are old friends, and she does not
give him away, but later in the season he is
recognized by some friends of his mother and
sent home in disgrace. At the end of the season
Deborah is offered a place in the theater in
Bath, where she meets Mrs. Siddons, already a

famous actress, and becomes a good friend of her
younger sister, Frances Kemble. She is well
received in supporting roles and, occasionally,
in a lead in a farce on Wednesdays, when the
company travels to Bristol, but she has two near
disasters that teach her much. In Bristol she
strolls off by herself after a performance, is
abducted by a couple of drunken thugs, shut in a
filthy room, and finally escapes by using her
gold chain to bribe a woman to unlock the door.
Overconfident with her modest stage success, she
begins to slack off at practice and one night,
having failed to learn her lines well in a new
play, has the humiliating experience of having
to apologize to the audience. Reformed, she
works hard and at the end of the Bath season is
asked, along with Frances Kemble, to join the
company at the Drury Lane theater, which, along
with Covent Garden, is one of the two licensed
theaters in London. The manager, Richard Sheridan, is charming, but unfortunately he is more
interested in Whig politics than his theater and
so short of cash that his actors are frequently
unpaid. For the next summer season she goes to
Weymouth, where she again finds Peter Etty, who
has deliberately failed at law so that his
mother will give up and let him become an actor.
At the end of the season there, when she returns
to Drury Lane, Peter goes to London with her.
With a higher salary, at least on paper, she
invites her family for Christmas and spends most
of her savings for their visit. Then, because
poltics demand most of Sheridan's money, she is
unable to collect what she is owed. She gives up
her nice lodgings to take a cold, bare room and
eats as little as possible to make her small
funds last. She becomes ill, and Peter, who has
been getting on in small theaters in the
suburbs, suggests that he could marry her and
they could live cheaply. Deborah is insulted at
the suggestion of being married out of pity and
refuses. Sheridan solves her problem by arranging that she go for the summer as companion to
Lady Fanshawe, a Whig supporter with a country
home. There she gets involved in politics and
sees high society for the first time, but at
the end of the summer when Lady Fanshawe asks
her to stay on and travel with her, she decides
to go back to the theater. Lady Fanshaw suggests

that Sarah, now sixteen and dying to get away
from the strolling company and to get a taste
of high life, become her companion instead.
Elizabeth having married a decent schoolmaster,
their parents agree. Deborah, now twenty, goes
back to Drury Lane, where the actors are being
paid, at least partially, works hard in
secondary roles, and finally gets a chance at
her first big London lead as Perdita in *A
Winter's Tale*. Her father comes from Yorkshire
to see her brilliant performance, and Peter,
now a rising actor at Covent Garden, suggests
that he ask Mr. Keate for permission to marry
her. The story is full of details of theater
life--of the rivalries, the benefits, the green
room gossip, and the hard work required--and
almost every famous person of the period,
including Dr. Johnson, appears in at least a
cameo role. There is also a great deal of
information about the politics of the period
and life in London and the provinces, all very
detailed and authentic, but the story never
rises above the research, and the characters,
even Deborah, never seem real. Carnegie Com.

CAPTAIN (*Black Beauty**), Jerry* Barker's other
cab horse, who works with Black Beauty. Old,
proud, well-mannered, high-bred, once a war
horse, Captain tells Beauty a long story about
his service in the Crimean War, during which he
lost his master, an officer, who was killed
while riding Captain into battle. Captain's
story illustrates the horrors war service brings
to men and animals. Dragged down and injured by
a runaway team, Captain fails to recover and is
put down. He is replaced by a former coach horse
named Hotspur.

CAPTAIN FLINT (*Pigeon Post**; *Swallows and Amazons**), Nancy* and Peggy* Blackett's Uncle Jim
Turner, called after the pirate because he has a
parrot and lives on a houseboat where he is
writing a book. In *Swallows and Amazons*, he mistakenly accuses John* Walker of meddling with
his boat, so that the Walker children willingly
join the Blackett sisters, who are feeling
neglected by their uncle, in a plot to storm the
houseboat and make him walk the plank. This is
all done in a jolly spirit of make believe,

after which he serves them a feast aboard and plays sea songs on his accordian. In *Pigeon Post* he is expected back from South America momentarily. The gold mining expedition, which involves the Walkers, the Blacketts, and the two Callum children, is undertaken in the belief that, if they find gold, Captain Flint will stay in the locality for a while to mine it.

CAPTAIN FLINT (*Treasure Island**), pirate leader who buried the treasure, then died raving with delirium tremens, calling, "Darby M'Graw! Fetch aft the rum, Darby!" at Savannah. Although he has been dead several years and never appears in the novel, he is still a presence, since he is frequently mentioned by the men who were crew on his ship, the *Walrus*. He is characterized by the way he killed all the six men who helped bury the treasure and used one of their bodies stretched out as a pointer. Long* John Silver's parrot is named after him.

CAPTAIN HOOK (*Peter and Wendy**), elegantly dressed and elaborately coiffed captain of the *Jolly Roger*, the only man Barbecue feared, and leader of the pirate band in the Neverland. His right hand was devoured by a crocodile, which so enjoyed the snack that it has followed him everywhere, hoping for more. Although the hand has been replaced by a hook, ever so much more convenient in everyday life and terrible to enemies, the captain fears the crocodile and is able to avoid it only because it swallowed a clock, which ticks a warning as it approaches. Hook is obsessed by the idea of good form and has a last triumph because he dies, with his shoes right, his waistcoat right, his tie right, and his socks right, while Peter* Pan shows bad form by kicking instead of stabbing him.

CAPTAIN OLDKNOW (*The Chimneys of Green Knowe**), father of blind Susan*, who buys a black slave boy, Jacob*, in Barbados to be her companion. Though loving and understanding with Susan and convinced that she is being over-protected, he is home from sea duty so little that he cannot change the pattern of her treatment until he brings Jacob to Green Knowe. Captain Oldknow realizes that Susan is very bright, and he hires

Jonathan* Morley, the parson's son, to come and teach her and later to teach Jacob, too.

CAPTAIN VANSITTART DARKNESS (*The City of Frozen Fire**), small, foppish officer of the *Ursula Howell*, a sometime pirate ship that runs guns for South American revolutions. Viciously bad tempered, Darkness carries knives in both sleeves, which he throws at any real or imagined insult. He bullies all his associates except Charlie Yemm*, his former schoolmaster, who continues to exert some restraining power over him. In the end he is killed by one of the convicts he has enlisted in Quivera to aid him in his plot to steal all the treasure.

CARBONEL (*Carbonel, The King of the Cats**), big, black cat bought by Rosemary Brown at the Fairfax Market, the lost King of the Cats. He has a superior, all-knowing attitude and is bossy and easily offended, quite in keeping with the conventional image of cats. He and Rosemary are able to converse when she holds the witch's broom. Carbonel speaks in a lofty manner, sometimes quoting from Shakespeare, and browbeats Rosemary whenever he can. He was stolen from the cradle by the witch, Mrs. Cantrip, who wanted a cat to run errands for her. She put two spells on him to keep him from escaping. The first spell is broken when Rosemary buys him for three farthings. The second spell, a far more complicated one, involves a combination of the broom, the witch's steeple hat, the cauldron, and Silent Magic. Rosemary and her friend John acquire all the objects and knowledge of the Silent Magic. Thus they release Carbonel from the second spell and enable him to return to claim his cat kingdom from the usurper, who turns out to be John's aunt's runaway ginger tom, Popsey Dinkums.

CARBONEL, THE KING OF THE CATS (Sleigh*, Barbara, ill. V. H. Drummond, Parrish, 1955; Bobbs, 1957), lighthearted fantasy involving talking animals and magic set probably in London in the mid-1950s. Goodhearted, congenial, obedient Rosemary Brown, about ten, lives alone with her widowed mother, a seamstress, in three sparsely furnished rooms at 10 Tottenham Grove.

Hoping to add to the family's meager income by
cleaning houses during her summer holidays,
Rosemary goes to Fairfax Market to buy a broom,
and there meets a strange, untidy, old woman
named Mrs. Cantrip, who sells her a rickety,
wispy one and a huge black cat for just the
amount of money Rosemary has with her. Rosemary
soon discovers that she and the cat can converse
as long as she holds the broomstick. The cat,
Carbonel*, informs the girl that he is royal,
that he was stolen by the old woman, who is a
witch, and that now he must belong to Rosemary
until the spell that binds him to her is broken
and he can return to his royal duties. Breaking
the spell involves finding the witch's hat and
cauldron and learning the special Silent Magic.
Rosemary agrees to help imperious, crotchety
Carbonel, and the two return to the market where
a wheezy, old second-hand man informs them that
a youngish man bought the pointed hat from Mrs.
Cantrip. Before seeking out this buyer, Rosemary
accompanies her mother to Tussocks, the mansion
of wealthy, snooty Mrs. Pendlebury Parker, for
whom Mrs. Brown sews. There she meets John, Mrs.
Pendlebury Parker's nephew, a sensible, regular
sort of boy, who likes adventures and joins the
quest. The Parker chauffeur takes them to the
youngish man, whom they call the Occupier*. He
is an actor, who at the urging of a fellow
performer agrees to loan the children the hat
once they have found the cauldron. Told by the
wheezy man that the cauldron was purchased by an
artistic, gray-haired lady, the children search
fruitlessly and then take tea in a tiny shop,
Miss Maggie's Copper Kettle, where they discover
the cauldron being used as an umbrella stand.
With Carbonel's help, the children make a Rainbow Spell that brings all the china from the
Fairfax Museum so that Miss Maggie can handle
the extra trade brought in by the Women's
Institute Rally, and as reward they receive the
cauldron. Back at the market, the children find
Mrs. Cantrip operating a run-down candy shop.
Because she could not break his proud spirit,
she is still so angry at Carbonel that she
refuses to divulge the Silent Magic spell, but
John finds and carries away her battered, old
magic book under his coat, and thus the children
secure the necessary spell. At a fete to which

Mrs. Pendlebury Parker has instructed Mrs. Brown
to take the children, Mrs. Brown saves the day
by making replacement costumes for the actors,
and the Occupier loans the children the witch's
hat. They perform the necessary magic with
appropriate rhyming spells and flights on the
broom, and Carbonel is freed. The next night
Carbonel returns to fetch Rosemary and John to
attend his Lawgiving on the roof of the Town
Hall, where at full moon he defeats the usurping
ginger cat and is hailed by his subjects as
Carbonel X, King of the Cats. Rosemary scoops up
the defeated ginger cat, which John identifies
as Mrs. Pendlebury Parker's lost Popsey Dinkums,
and the children return him to his mistress, who
rewards them handsomely. The broom is accidentally burned up in a bonfire, Rosemary is
invited to join John and his family at the
seashore, and Mrs. Brown accepts a permanent
position as wardrobe mistress for the Occupier's
traveling players. Told in third person from the
children's point of view, with frequent
interjections by the author, the story is entertaining but overly extended. The abundant
conversation is filled with talk about magic and
spells, and numerous magical rhymes add interest. Characters are types; there is much humor,
some of it adult; the tone is condescending and
arch; and one is always conscious of the
author's presence, hand, and voice. Choice.

CAROLINE TEMPLETON (*We Couldn't Leave Dinah**),
one of two English schoolchildren left behind
during the evacuation of Clerinel, an island in
the English Channel, during World War II, and
who become involved in intrigue with the German
occupation forces. Lively, active, and outgoing, Caroline thinks quickly, is very observant, and initiates activities. Although she
tends to have a queasy stomach under stress, she
always comes through. She is the figure to whom
the reader is first introduced, whose activities
the reader mostly follows, and with whom the
reader's sympathies mainly lie.

CARRIE (*Up the Pier**), ten-year-old English
schoolgirl who has come with her mother to live
with her Aunt Ester in a Welsh seaside town
while her father, who has secured a new posi-

tion, finds a house for them to live in. Bored with the dreariness of the tasks set her by "Aunt Pesty" and unhappy and hurt that she and her mother must be separated from her father, she spends more and more time on the pier, conversing with the Pontifexes and shopping for them. After two weeks, the pier is closed to sightseers, and Carrie realizes that she will not be able to visit with the family much longer. About the same time, Gramper* Pontifex tells her that they need her help in returning to their own time dimension; then her father arrives with the news that he has found a place to live. Carrie decides it is time to give up the Pontifexes and wills them home again. Her strong desire that they be allowed to go back to their own time and place prevents Samuel* Pontifex from keeping them on the pier.

CARRIE'S WAR (Bawden*, Nina, ill. Faith Jaques, Gollancz, 1973; Lippincott, 1973), story of two children evacuated from London during World War II to a small mining town in Wales. Carrie* Willow, 11, and her brother, Nick*, 9, are among the last to be chosen from their evacuee train when Miss Louisa Evans hesitantly agrees to take them, though she has been looking for two girls. She bustles them along the street and through a shop to the living quarters in the back, stands nervously over them as they eat, and rushes them upstairs and into bed, where they cling together listening to the loud, hectoring voice of Mr.* Evans, her brother, whom she obviously fears. With the flexibility of children, they soon adjust. Mr. Evans is not an ogre, just a thin, cross man who bullies his much younger sister and even his female customers, and who is much aware of his own importance as a store owner, being also a Councillor and very strong Chapel, and they soon come to love "Auntie* Lou," though they are a bit scornful of her timidity. Nick, a beautiful but greedy child, is caught swiping cookies from the store, but when Mr. Evans starts to beat him with his belt, Nick threatens to tell at school that he was hungry, and the storekeeper backs down. Carrie, a conscientious girl, worries that Nick would tell a lie, but Nick gloats cheerfully that he has won and asserts, as he has before, that he hates Mr.

Evans. By the time their mother comes to visit,
they are so used to life in the dark, cold house
and the rigid rules--making only one trip up and
down stairs a day, for fear of wear on the
carpet, using the privy in the garden during the
day rather than the upstairs bathroom, having no
games or books on Sunday--that they don't think
of complaining, for fear of embarrassing Auntie
Lou. Just before Christmas they discover a real
haven. They have been sent by Mr. Evans to the
home of his estranged older sister, Dilys
Gotobed, a decaying mansion at Druid's Bottom,
to pick up a goose, which he will accept though
he has not spoken to his sister for years. Dilys
is an invalid, cared for by Hepzibah* Green, a
warm, competent woman who also cares for Mister*
Johnny Gotobed, a retarded man or "innocent," a
cousin of Dilys's husband, and, to Carrie's
surprise, Albert* Sandwich, a bespectacled boy
of fourteen whom she met with the evacuee group.
Although they are frightened at first of the
strange, dark area and of Mister Johnny, whose
speech is an incomprehensible gobble, they soon
look forward to a chance to go to Druid's Bottom
where Hepzibah gives them good meals, tells them
stories, and provides relaxed, accepting love
which is lacking even in Auntie Lou's nervous
affection. One of Hepzibah's stories involves a
skull which is still in the house, supposedly
that of a ten-year-old slave boy who cursed the
family as he was dying and directed that his
skull be dug up and kept, lest, if it ever be
removed from the house, the walls will crumble.
Eventually Carrie meets Dilys, who talks calmly
of her approaching death and gives Carrie a
message to take to her brother when it happens,
saying that she has not forgotten him but that
she owes more to strangers. In the meantime
Auntie Lou has been ill and has gone for a visit
to a friend where she has attended a dance and
met an American soldier, Major Cass Harper. When
he comes to visit, both Mr. Evans and Auntie Lou
are out, and Carrie sends him away, explaining
that Mr. Evans disapproves of Americans,
dancing, frivolous women, and having anyone call
at the house, and that he would make Auntie Lou
cry if he found out she had a visitor. Nick is
outraged, and runs off, followed by Carrie, to
the chapel where Auntie Lou is scrubbing the

floor. Together they bustle her off to the pub, where they have seen Major Harper turn in, and finish scrubbing the floor. When Dilys dies, Carrie hurries to give Mr. Evans her message, thinking he will be comforted, and is appalled that he is furious at Hepzibah, calling her a viper who has done him out of his rights. At Druid's Bottom, Albert is also angry at Carrie for rousing Mr. Evans's ire before they have been able to find a will and motivating him to rummage through Dilys's things and to give Hepzibah and Mister Johnny one month to pack up and be gone. Since no will can be found giving the house to Hepzibah, as Dilys intended, Albert believes it was in an envelope Mr. Evans took from Dilys's jewel box. Word comes from Carrie's mother that she has found a place for the children to live with her on a farm near Glasgow. Carrie is torn at the prospect of being uprooted again, but Nick seems quite happy. On their last afternoon at Druid's Bottom, Carrie, upset that Mr. Evans will inherit what should be Hepzibah's, takes the skull and throws it into the horse pond with some vague idea of destroying his legacy. When they return home, Auntie Lou is not there, and Nick tells her with delight that she has run off to marry Major Harper, a secret Nick has shared. Early in the morning Carrie confronts Mr. Evans, who has been up all night, intending to throw back at him the ring of Dilys's he has given her as a goodbye present, but before she can, he shows her what was in the envelope. It is not a will but just a picture of him and Dilys as children and the ring, which he gave his sister from his first wages. Flooded with relief that he has not stolen and destroyed the will, Carrie leaves feeling quite warm toward him, but from the train she glimpses with horror that the house at Druid's Bottom is in flames. The main story is encased in a frame, in which widowed Carrie, some thirty years later, returns with her children to the little town and walks out along the railway track, but, still feeling guilty for the destruction of the mansion and possibly the death of those she loved, she can't bring herself to go down through Druid's Grove to the ruins of the house. The children return the next morning and find Hepzibah and Mister Johnny still there, living now in a rebuilt outbuilding and expecting a visit from Albert, who has bought the place from Auntie Lou, Mr. Evans having died of a heart attack shortly after the fire, and they run to meet their mother, who Hepzibah knows has followed them down. The novel has a strong sense of place but an even stronger sense of character, with all the main figures beautifully realized and convincing. The only false note is in the skull episode, a melodramatic and unnecessary addition, which is well enough explained and integrated into the main story but lacks the plausibility and sense of genuineness that permeates the rest. Carnegie Com.; Choice; Contemporary Classics; Fanfare.

CARRIE THATCHER (*Good Night, Mr. Tom**), one of the twin girls who are part of the group of youngsters which includes the evacuee child, William* Beech, in the village of Little Weirwold. Unlike her domestic twin, Ginnie, Carrie is interested in books and education, and with the encouragement of Zach* Wrench, she applies to go to high school, which is rare for a village boy and unprecedented for a girl. Despite the protests of her mother and with the grudging approval of her father, she is accepted and sticks it out, although she is at first ostracized for her countrified speech and village ways. Because she has been close to Zach, she and Willie are drawn together after his death.

CARRIE WILLOW (*Carrie's War**), Caroline Willow, eleven-year-old who, with her brother, Nick*, 9, is evacuated to a small Welsh mining town during World War II. A worried, conscientious girl, she tries hard to take care of her little brother and to be no trouble to Mr.* Evans and his sister, with whom they are billeted. Sensitive to other people's feelings, she suffers agonies of embarrassment when anything goes wrong and is so concerned to avoid conflict that she tries to cover up Nick's frankness and placate Mr. Evans so he won't bully Auntie* Lou, but she is not timid and she has a strong sense of what is right and fair. Hepzibah* Green refers to her as "Miss Heart" in contrast to Albert* Sandwich, whom she calls "Mr. Head." Even after thirty years, Carrie is afraid to face the remains of the burned-out house; she feels that she caused the fire, though her mind tells her this is impossible. Her oldest boy, who has bright green eyes like hers, seems to have the same sort of sensitivity to people's emotions.

CARROLL, LEWIS (CHARLES LUTWIDGE DODGSON) (1832-1898), born in Daresbury, Cheshire, the son of a vicar; author renowned for *Alice's Adventures in Wonderland** (Macmillan, 1865; Appleton, 1866), and *Through the Looking-Glass, and What Alice Found There** (Macmillan, 1871; Macmillan, 1871), two of the most famous and often-quoted books in English literature. A lecturer in mathematics at Oxford University, Carroll and a friend, Robinson Duckworth, took the three small daughters of Henry Liddell, Dean of Christ Church, on a boating trip up the River Isis, a tributary of the Thames, on the hot afternoon of July 4, 1862. On the way, Carroll entertained the group with stories, making them up as he went along. The three girls were Lorina, Alice, and Edith Liddell; of them, his favorite was ten-year-old Alice. She later asked Carroll to write the stories out for her, and *Alice's Adventures under Ground** (Macmillan, 1886; Macmillan, 1886) resulted, neatly written and illustrated in his own hand, which he gave her early in 1863 "in Memory of a Summer Day." Urged by George MacDonald*, among others, to publish it, Carroll revised and expanded the adventures, and the book came out with illustrations by Sir John Tenniel in mid 1865. It and its sequel became milestones in children's literature. Filled with zany characters, slapstick humor, and clever wordplay, they marked a strict departure from the sentimental, religiously oriented, didactic, and sombre children's literary fare of the day. The second book followed six years later, and in 1886 Macmillan brought out *under Ground* in facsimile form. All appear in Children's Classics, and the first two books appear also in *Choice*, ChLA Touchstones, *Books Too Good to Miss*, and Fanfare. Carroll published a fourth and final version of *Alice* in 1889, also with Macmillan. This was *The Nursery Alice*, with the text rewritten for very young children--"from Nought to Five," Carroll announced in his preface--and decorated with twenty of Tenniel's pictures enlarged and colored. Carroll was educated at Richmond Grammar School in Yorkshire, where he grew up, and at Rugby in Warwickshire and Christ Church, Oxford, from which he graduated in 1854 with high honors in mathematics. He began teaching at Oxford the next year and stayed there the rest of his life. He was ordained an Anglican deacon but did not pursue that career, preferring to teach instead. He published several works on mathematics and also enjoyed doing nonsense verses. For the latter, he invented his pen name, translating his first two names into Latin as Carolus Ludovicus, reversing them, and then translating them back into English as Lewis Carroll. He first used this pseudonym in 1861 for his long poem, "The Path of Roses," and employed it subsequently for his nonscholarly writings. None of his several other published works for children became as popular or as influential as the *Alice* books, and they mainly have antiquarian value today. These include *Sylvie and Bruno* (Macmillan, 1889; Macmillan, 1889), a long fairy tale in prose and verse; its sequel, *Sylvie and Bruno Concluded* (Macmillan, 1893; Macmillan, 1893); and *The Hunting of the Snark: An Agony in Eight Fits* (Macmillan, 1876; Osgood, 1876), a long nonsense poem. Carroll was also very interested in puzzles, games, and logic and was an accomplished amateur photographer. In later life he suffered from ill health and died in January, 1898, of bronchitis, which resulted from a cold he caught while spending Christmas with his sisters in Surrey. He is buried in Guildford, Surrey.

CARTER, PETER (1929-   ), born in Manchester, Lancashire, the son of a seaman; teacher, freelance writer, translator, author of books for older children. After an apprenticeship in the building trades from 1942-1949, he held a wide variety of jobs ranging from construction worker to road builder to office worker to schoolteacher. He received his M.A. from Wadham College, Oxford, in 1972, and married Gudrun Willege, a photographer, in 1974. He has traveled extensively in the United States, Canada, Europe, India, and the Middle East. His books are ambitious in their choice of subject matter and their approach, are carefully researched, and at their best reveal strong characterization, much drama and suspense, and a forceful style. Most are historical fiction and show his concern for moral issues, in particular as they appear at crucial moments in history. His first novel, *The Black Lamp* (Oxford, 1973; Nelson, 1975), revolves around the mechanization of the textile industry in Lancashire in the early 1800s that culminated in the Peterloo massacre. *Matadan* (Oxford, 1974; Oxford, 1979) concerns a Celt captured by Vikings and converted to Christianity, and *The Sentinels** (Oxford, 1980; Oxford, 1980), winner of the *Guardian* Award, is a dramatic and action-filled story of the Royal Navy's antislave patrol along the West African coast in 1840. *Children of the Book** (Oxford, 1982) has at its center the siege of Vienna and is of near-epic dimensions, encompassing the viewpoints of inhabitants, attacking Turks, and relievers. It won the Young Observer Teenage Fiction Award. *Under Goliath** (Oxford, 1977; Oxford, 1979), a Carnegie Commended book, has a contemporary setting. It describes the ill-fated friendship between two boys, one Catholic and the other Protestant, during the religious strife in Belfast, Ireland. He also published *Mao* (Oxford, 1976; Viking, 1979), a biography, and a translation of the tales of the Brothers Grimm (Oxford, 1982); his *The Gates of Paradise* (Oxford, 1974; Oxford, 1979) is a fictional life of William Blake.

THE CASE OF THE COP CATCHERS (Dicks*, Terrance, Blackie, 1982; Lodestar, 1982), seventh in a series of detective novels starring the Baker Street Irregulars and set in England in the modern period. Dan Robinson, a Sherlock Holmes enthusiast and leader of the group of youngsters that calls itself by the name that Holmes's young friends used, discovers that Detective-Sergeant "Happy" (Herbert) Day has disappeared under suspicious circumstances and that an anonymous tip to the police station has implicated him in what looks like a bribe for secret police information. Since Happy has been a good friend of the Irregulars and they are

sure he is innocent, they start an investigation, going first to the house where he lodges.
There they find a rough notebook, obviously
used to keep notes which would later be copied
more carefully into the formal day book. From
it they find that he was involved in three
separate investigations: (1) a series of truck
hijackings, (2) a disappearance of a local
businessman, and (3) a theft of a diamond
necklace from a jewelry company. There is also a
scrawled note about "failing to give due
precedence," with a license number and the name
Domingues. Dan directs each of the Irregulars to
investigate the crime that seems to him most
likely to be connected with Happy's disappearance. Mickey Denning, small, impetuous, and ever
hungry, goes to Anderson Transport, Ltd., where
he gets the approval of the boss, Mr. Anderson,
and a chance to look around but is nearly killed
when a truck chassis is dropped on him as he is
examining its underside for some device to mark
the valuable loads, as he assumes someone in
league with the hijackers has been doing.
Cautious, skeptical Jeff Webster gets an
introduction from his banker father to Mr.
Caraboose, the French-born owner of the jewelry
store. There he learns of the "impossible"
crime, the disappearance of a diamond necklace
from its box in the safe where it was placed in
the presence of Caraboose, his two sons, and his
nephew, Bruno. After some humiliating condescen-
sion from the sons and Bruno, Jeff leaves,
still unable to figure out the crime. Liz
Spencer, the only female Irregular, calls at
the home of the vanished businessman, a Mr.
Fillmer, who sells garden supplies and plants.
His elegant wife shows her about their
expensively decorated house. Later Liz calls at
the nursery and talks to both Old Sam, the
watchman, and Mr. Patterson, Mr. Fillmer's
partner. By deduction Dan solves all three
crimes, proving that the security man and the
mechanic who tried to kill Mickey are conspiring
to mark the trucks with valuable shipments for a
share in the hijackers' loot, that Bruno placed
the necklace in a false-bottomed box, which he
hid in the storeroom to be retrieved later, and
that Old Sam is really Mr. Fillmer in disguise,
hiding out to escape his demanding wife. Since

none of these lead to Happy, he follows the clue in the scrawled note and discovers that Happy was almost run down in a crosswalk by a car really belonging to Mr. Marko Santos (an international swindler) who is supposedly in South America. They realize that Happy must have discovered that Santos was still in England and that Santos had kidnapped him to keep him quiet. The four manage a daring rescue of Happy from the yacht where Santos has been hiding, and once more they are heroes. The plot unfolds at a rapid pace, with enough complexity to keep middle-grade readers breathless. Characterization is minimal, and the style is not difficult. The chief appeal comes from the young people being more clever than the adults. Poe Nominee.

THE CASE OF THE SECRET SCRIBBLER (Hildick*, E. W., ill. Lisl Weil, Hodder, 1978; Macmillan, 1978), mystery set in what appears to be an American town in the mid-twentieth century, one of a series about crimes solved by the McGurk Organization, a group of ten-year-olds led by assertive Jack P. McGurk. Told in the first person by Joey Rockaway, this tale concerns a scrap of paper he has found in a library book on Morocco which his father has borrowed from the public library. The paper itself shows part of a diagram, but marks of something written on another sheet show through and, though not a complete message, seem to indicate that a robbery is planned. Brains (Gerald) Bellingham, whose expertise in handwriting analysis they seek, recognizes the diagram as a particular kind of burglar alarm. The organization, which includes Willie Sandowsky and Wanda Grieg as well as McGurk and Joey, follow a number of leads. The note is fortuitously written on a special type of paper sold by Willie's father to only a few business establishments. This leads them to a jewelry store, where the clerk, Carol Rodriguez, is their first suspect. Her handwriting, however, does not match the original note, while that of the store owner, Mendoza, does. At the library they trace the books on Morocco and find that one has been taken out by Terry Burch, a teenaged neighborhood boy who has a reputation for trouble-making. They discover that he had tried to pass a bad check in the jewelry store and that Mendoza has blackmailed him into agreeing to rob the store for the insurance money. Lieutenant Kaspar of the police department finally takes their evidence seriously, swears them all in as deputies, and then orders them to stay at home, where they listen to the arrest on a police shortwave radio. The style is aimed at readers as young or younger than the young detectives, with a large percentage of dialogue, rapid action, and minimal development of character and setting. The plot is consistent, though it might not stand close scrutiny. Poe Nominee.

CASPIAN (*Prince Caspian**; *The Voyage of the "Dawn Treader"**; *The Silver Chair**), prince of Narnia* and true king, whose wicked uncle, Miraz, has killed his father and usurped the throne, and who is restored to his rightful position through the efforts of the four Pevensies, Peter*, Susan*, Edmund*, and Lucy*, and the powerful lion, Aslan*. Caspian is characterized at the beginning of *Prince Caspian* as an earnest lad who delights in learning about Old Narnia. His life endangered by the birth of a son to Miraz, he is helped to escape from the palace by his wise, half-dwarf tutor, Doctor* Cornelius. He leads the fighting until Peter arrives. In *Voyage*, after he has been ruling Narnia for three years in Narnian time, he leaves the realm in Trumpkin's* charge and sails in the *Dawn Treader* to seek the seven nobles his uncle had exiled. Caspian is a conscientious king, capable in battle, who tries to be fair and just and is liked by his subjects. He probably represents the right kind of monarch. In *The Silver Chair*, seventy years later, he has been ruling worthily as Caspian the Tenth, Navigator and Seafarer, but, mourning the loss of his kidnapped son, Rilian*, and realizing he has not long to live, he once again leaves the realm in Trumpkin's care and sails off to consult Aslan. He makes one brief appearance, when, after his death at the very end of the book, he is revived by Aslan, blown to England along with the children, and given the glimpse of the children's world that he requests.

CASSIDY, MICHAEL (*Bostock and Harris; or The

Night of the Comet*), Irish roofer who wanders
into Brighton with his gloomy partner,
O'Rourke, hunting for his love, Mary Flatley,
who left Dublin in a huff after finding him with
another woman. Cassidy is "a liar, a rogue, and
so light-fingered it was a wonder that, while he
slept, his hands didn't rise to the ceiling of
their own accord," but he has vowed to reform to
merit Mary's love. Unfortunately, he is
constitutionally unable to refrain from chatting
up any pretty girl (or any plain one) who
happens to cross his path, and several times
when he seems on the point of winning Mary back,
she catches him pouring his charm and his
flattery on some other woman. He aids Bostock*
and Harris* by smuggling out the telescope owned
by Captain Bostock partly because he has
sympathy for Bostock as a fellow lover and
partly because Harris pays him fourpence
ha'penny (of Bostock's money), though he
refrains from pawning the telescope because he
is determined, at the moment, to reform.

CASTAWAY CHRISTMAS (Baker*, Margaret J., ill.
Richard Kennedy, Methuen, 1963; Farrar, 1964),
realistic family novel with survival story aspects set in Somerset in western England in the
late 1950s. On December 22, the three Ridley
children, Miranda*, 15, Pinks*, ten and a half,
and their older brother, Lincoln*, along with
their bull terrier, Oliver Cromwell, and Siamese
cat, Sheba, travel by train from their boarding
schools, anticipating a joyful Christmas reunion
with their traveling businessman father and
concert pianist mother at Little Topsails, a
cottage rented just for the occasion. The children have paid little attention to reports
about the rainstorms that have been buffeting
southern England. When their parents fail to
meet them at Duckford station, they trudge the
deserted roads to the cottage, arriving rain-
soaked and chilled to a house that stands cold
and empty and lacks electricity and phone.
Having no other choice, they settle in for the
night, lighting fires, drying their clothes, and
eating a dinner of half-done macaroni and stale,
dry cheese. Later Lincoln discovers a telegram
from their parents with the information that the
parents have been detained in Paris by an

airline strike. In the morning, after scouting,
Lincoln informs the girls that they are
marooned, the waters of the two rivers on either
side of Little Topsails having burst their
banks, and the children realize they are on
their own. They search the house for food and
useful items, like candles, one of which Pinks
hides for Christmas Eve. Lincoln discovers some
potatoes, and outside they find some brussels
sprouts. Pinks wanders off and finds a hen house
with five chickens and some eggs. For safety
from the still rising waters, they move the
chickens to the stable, which is on higher
ground. For two days the children manage to meet
all obstacles and stay warm, dry, and fed, like
the paradigm of a nuclear family, with Miranda
seeing to the housekeeping, Lincoln shooting a
rabbit and seeing to their safety by keeping an
eye on the waters, and Pinks decorating the
house for Christmas. Late on the second day, the
girls discover that Lincoln has been gone a long
time, hunt for him in the fading light, discover
he's been marooned on a bit of land while trying
to reach a cottage whose light he has seen
across the deeper water, and rescue him by
attaching a line to Oliver who swims over to his
young master. On the way back to the house,
Pinks stops off at the stable for Sheba and
discovers that she has been sleeping in a box of
groceries their parents had ordered for them.
Their spirits considerably raised by the
groceries, which to them represent the presence
of their parents, they go to bed full, after
singing Christmas carols before the fire. On
December 24, Pinks is the first to come down
from upstairs and discovers water flowing
through the lower story. Much of the day is
spent sandbagging the back door, sweeping and
siphoning water out, and clearing the debris
from the arches of the bridge nearby to prevent
further flooding. They rescue a sheep that is
being swept downstream and put her in the shed
to recover. That evening, in anticipation of
Christmas, Pinks puts her candle in the window
to usher in the holiday season and soon is
awakened by the sound of a car horn signaling an
SOS. She rouses Miranda and Lincoln, and the
three rescue the Hunters, a man, woman, and
baby, whose car has been disabled by the waters.

The Hunters have been living in a caravan near the cottage Lincoln saw. Their caravan destroyed in a sudden landslide, they were attempting to get to Little Topsails when the waters caught their car. Mr. Hunter is a shepherd, and the sheep the children rescued belongs to him. The Hunters also bear a message from the Ridleys, informing the children that they are in the area and will come to Little Topsails as soon as they can. During the night, the ewe gives birth to twin lambs, which Mr. Hunter gives to the children for looking after the sheep so well; however, the children decide to give the lambs to the baby as a Christmas present. On Christmas afternoon the Ridleys arrive, the family is joyfully reunited, and the Ridleys and their guests enjoy a Christmas lunch of the rabbit Lincoln shot earlier. The novel moves at a good pace. It is more a domestic adventure story than a novel of suspense, since the children never seem to be in any real danger, although there is some sense of the potential for destruction of the storm and the messiness of a flood. The weather and temperature seem inconsistent. The author depicts the rain as cold and describes the waters as raging or flowing heavily, yet the children seem to manage for long periods of time striding about, clearing away debris, or performing rescues without the intense discomfort one would expect from cold December waters. Some story details seem fortuitous (Pinks just happens to have a line in her pocket, the children's raincoat belts are just long enough to reach to the Hunters' car, Lincoln finds a rabbit in spite of the waters, and the rabbit's carcass remains good without refrigeration) or vague (they fill bags with soil and "anything they could find"). The children are individualized but stay the same and seem young for their age. Here and there sentimentality intrudes, and the theme of members of a loving family caring for one another depicting the true spirit of Christmas is important but obvious. Carnegie Com.

A CASTLE OF BONE (Farmer*, Penelope, Chatto, 1972; Atheneum, 1972), fantasy set recently in an urban area in England, which examines the concepts of dreaming and time. Dreamy Hugh, about twelve, likes to read and paint. Because his mother insists he tidy his messy, cluttered room and he lacks a cupboard for storing his things, he and his father set out to buy one. In an antique shop run by a mysterious old man they find a cupboard that holds a curious fascination for the boy. After the hefty, inelegant old piece arrives, each night for several weeks Hugh dreams of being on a strange, wooded landscape, where stands a turreted, ivory-colored castle. After every dream, he awakens with some tangible evidence of the experience. He, his sister, Jean, and their friends, Penn, an outdoors, games-loving youth, and Penn's sister, Anna, are intrigued with the cupboard. After Jean accidentally places Hugh's pigskin wallet in the cupboard and a full-sized sow runs out, they realize that this is no ordinary wardrobe. Although puzzled and disconcerted at first, they have some light and ticklish moments testing its powers before concluding that anything placed in it reverts to an earlier state. When Jean's cat wanders in and comes out a kitten, tension takes over. Then Penn falls into the cupboard and reverts to infancy, and things become serious. The day in which the youths must care for him, while keeping what has happened secret from their mothers and attempting to restore him to his proper state, offers excitement, suspense, and a little humor. They consult the old man, whose oblique advice perplexes them, but Hugh eventually realizes that they can rescue Penn only by voluntarily entering the cupboard's dimension. They enter and find themselves in the castle of which Hugh dreamed. Hugh discovers Anna, like goddesses of mythology, trying to give Penn immortality by placing him in fire. Though afflicted by vague, visionary, monstrous beings, Hugh insists that the procedure stop. The spell is broken, all return to reality, and Penn is restored to normalcy. The plot moves slowly and without much impact on the emotions until the metamorphosis of the cat clearly foreshadows a similar danger to humans. The dreams knit poorly with reality, and their world is simply too monochromatic and obscure in meaning to grip, though they evoke psychological interest in their blend of realistic and surrealistic details. The mythological motifs seem superfluous, the meaning of the statement near the end that Hugh remains imprisoned in his own castle of bone is obscure, and the reader is left to ponder the meaning of it all. The old man is too enigmatic, and Jean and Anna never emerge as distinct characters, but Hugh and Penn are clearly drawn, their personalities quite deliberately offsetting and complementing each other. Style is sure and diction deft; action and dialogue are convincing and apt in the realistic portions but colorless and lifeless in the fantasy ones; and tone is contemporary. Fanfare.

CASTORS AWAY! (Burton*, Hester, ill. Victor G. Ambrus, Oxford, 1962; World, 1963), historical novel about how a British family saves the life of a soldier during the latter part of the Napoleonic Wars, based on an actual incident. On the day in September of 1805 that widower Dr.* William Henchman and his children leave their home in Rushby and arrive in Walsingby in Suffolk to stay with Aunt Susan Henchman, whose husband, Captain Simon Henchman, is away on the *Pericles*, a terrible storm batters the coast, wrecking the Twenty-Eighth Regiment transport ship. The next morning, little Martin, 4, discovers the body of a sergeant cast up on the shore, apparently dead. Dr. Henchman finds faint signs of life, however, and for several harrowing hours, he; Nell*, 12; her twin, Tom*; their brother, Edmund*, 16; Aunt Susan; and Betsy* Farr, their maid, labor over the body on Susan's kitchen table and miraculously revive the soldier. Elated with their success, they are shocked and dismayed when they learn that James* Bubb had been drunk on duty, was washed overboard, and has been sentenced to 300 lashes in punishment. Grown fond of the modest, cheerful man, they help him escape from authorities by hiding him in a field of uncut wheat. When Tom leaves to serve Captain Henchman on the *Pericles*, Bubb goes along as ship's carpenter. The story reaches its climax in October with the famous, hard-won victory at Trafalgar, during which Captain Henchman sustains a fatal wound. James, who is missing, is later found by Edmund among the wounded brought back to Portsmouth. James regains his health, but remains deaf from

a severe head wound. Tom is despondent for weeks
from the horrors he has witnessed and from Uncle
Simon's death, but Nell and Aunt Susan help him
come back to himself. Subplots concern serious-
minded, responsible Edmund, who is apprenticed
to a London surgeon; blunt, impetuous Nell, who
chafes under her rigid, stern, proper Aunt
Julia's efforts to make her into a lady and who
longs to explore new lands; and practical,
orderly, wise-beyond-her-years Betsy, who becomes Nell's closest friend and who falls in
love with James. This ambitious, well-crafted
novel combines fine characterization; excitement; action; and carefully researched, appropriately detailed views of domestic, farm,
medical, military, and naval life for both a
good story about a warm, close, attractive
family and a rich picture of a turbulent,
significant period. The title is a nautical term
of the times, an expression that distorts the
command, "Cast us away," meaning to shove the
boat off. Some of the characters really lived,
but the Henchman children, other relatives, and
the servants are fictitious. (Monsieur* Armand)
Carnegie Com.; Fanfare.

CAT CHANT (*Charmed Life**), Eric, an apparently
normal boy in a world much like ours was in
Edwardian England. Cat is dominated by and often
a victim of his older sister, Gwendolen*.
Although both are fair-haired, blue-eyed, and
seemingly innocent orphans, Gwendolen is a
witch, and patient Cat, without knowing it, is
an enchanter with nine lives and far more
potential power than his sister. An earnest,
well-meaning boy, he feels responsibility for
Janet* Chant, who is pulled from another world
by Gwendolen's magic to take her place when she
leaves, and he involves himself in a series of
predicaments trying to protect her.

CATE, DICK (RICHARD EDWARD NELSON CATE) (1935-
     ), born in Durham, England, the son of a
shopkeeper; teacher and writer of fiction for
middle-grade readers. He was graduated from
Leeds College of Education, Goldsmiths' College
in London, and from Bretton Hall College, with
diplomas in teaching, speech, drama, and English. He served in the Durham Light Infantry in

the British Army from 1950-1953. He taught for
twenty years before he began writing for young
people. From 1961-1970, he was a resident
teacher in a services school in Hamm, West-
phalia, Germany, and then became a remedial
teacher and administrator in the English
Department of the Grammar School in Barnsley,
England. He has written scripts for plays and
stories on BBC, poems, and articles for educational journals. Some of his short stories
have been published in *On the Run* (Macmillan,
1973). He is best known for his amusing, contemporary, domestic novels about Billy and his
coal mining family in northern England which are
intended for younger readers; among them are
Old Dog, New Tricks* (Hamilton, 1978; Elsevier,
1981), in which Billy's out-of-work Dad doesn't
think he can learn a new trade and which won the
Other Award; *Flying Free* Hamilton, 1975; Nelson, 1976), where Billy's family is brought
closer together when his future brother-in-law
suffers a mining accident; *Funny Sort of
Christmas* (Hamilton, 1976; published as *Never
Is a Long, Long Time* by Nelson, 1976), where
Billy's family copes with the death of the
family dog, the birth of his sister's baby, and
his grand mother's illness; and *A Nice Day
Out?* (Hamilton, 1979; Elsevier, 1981), in
which the family has an eventful but pleasurable
day at the beach. He and his wife, also a
teacher, have four children and have made their
home in Huddersfield, Yorkshire, where he is
active in miners' organizations and educational
movements.

CATERPILLAR (*Alice's Adventures in Wonderland**;
Alice's Adventures under Ground*), the big, blue
Caterpillar whom Alice* meets in her dream
fantasy in Wonderland, one of several characters
who treat her rudely. When she meets him, he is
sitting on a mushroom smoking a long hookah. He
engages her in a lengthy circular conversation
about her identity that frustrates her because
it comes to nothing and seems intentionally
irritating. The Caterpillar tells her to recite
the familiar poem that starts "You are old,
Father William" to verify her identity: is she
who she thinks she is? It comes out wrong (being
one of Carroll's several parodies on well-known

poems of the day), which perplexes her considerably. The Caterpillar finally instructs her
to eat of his mushroom to adjust her size.
Perhaps the way he treats Alice is intended to
show how children feel they are treated by
adults, or at least how Victorian children were
treated.

CATHERINE MOMPHESSON (*A Parcel of Patterns**),
lovely young wife of the new parson, who wins
the hearts of the villagers when he cannot, by
good sense and good will and such acts as
grabbing her new calico curtains to serve as
rope to help a miner trapped in a fall, and by
playing with the man's children in her kitchen
so they will not see their father brought out
dead, if that should be the outcome. Consump-
tive, she nonetheless insists on staying with
her husband in the plague-ridden village, though
she does agree to send their two young children
away. Ironically, it is a parcel of patterns for
her new dress which the tailor has sent for
that brings the plague to Eyam. Catherine dies
toward the end of the plague year.

THE CAVE (Church*, Richard, Dent, 1950; *FIVE
BOYS IN A CAVE*, Day, 1951), holiday adventure
novel set in some hilly country area of England
in the mid-twentieth century. Nearing the end of
a vacation he has spent with his uncle and aunt,
John Walters discovers the opening of a cave and
the chance to add thrills to a dull holiday. He
enlists four local boys, all adolescents of
unspecified ages who with him have formed the
Tomahawk Club, and they collect the gear they
will need for exploring. The only adult to know
is John's Uncle George, a doctor, who insists
that he draw a map so a rescue party can find
them if they fail to return, but promises not to
look at it unless need arises. The boys are
stock types: John is thoughtful and scientific;
Lightning* (Harold) Soames is small and
reckless; Meaty* (Cuthbert) Sanders is heavy and
easygoing; Alan* Hobbs, their self-proclaimed
leader, is bossy but proves to be a coward; and
George* Reynold, poor and uncared for by his
parents but sensitive, shows his true mettle in
a crisis. They have a series of near disasters,
when John and Lightning, having been let down a

nearly 100-foot shaft, are separated from the others because, in the confusion of Alan's contradictory orders, Meaty lets the end of the rope drop. Later, Alan, having dropped the expensive searchlight he took without his father's permission, blames Meaty and furiously throws Meaty's flashlight after it, leaving them only a weak kerosene dark lantern brought by George. They negotiate dangerous turns on narrow ledges, follow an underground river, chip away a rock screen to free the stranded boys, and find a skeleton, perhaps of primitive man, before they finally emerge. The adventure itself is exciting and the sensory detail builds a feeling of reality that adds greatly to the suspense. The psychological responses of the boys, however, are predictable. Alan's breakdown and George's development of confidence are conventional story elements; they are not especially convincing, nor is the attitude of John's uncle, a former mountain climber, who allows these untrained and ill-equipped boys to undertake the dangerous exploration even though he doubts Alan's character. Sequel is *Down River*. Fanfare.

CAWLEY, WINIFRED (COZENS) (1915-   ), born in Felton, Northumberland; teacher, novelist. She attended Western Elementary School, Wallsend, Northumberland, and Wallsend Secondary School, the University of Durham at Newcastle, and University College, London. Married to a university professor whose work took them frequently overseas, she has taught English in Roumania, Yugoslavia, Egypt, and Brisbane, Australia, as well as in several schools and colleges in Leeds. Her parents were a housemaid and a butler turned shopkeeper; she drew on their characters and her own life in Wallsend-on-Tyne for her best-known novel, *Gran at Coalgate** (Oxford, 1974; Holt, 1975), a novel commended for the Carnegie Medal. It is set in the 1920s and tells of Ginny, whose restrictive life is opened to new ideas by a visit to her relatives in Coalgate, which is based on Leadgate in County Durham. *Silver Everything and Many Mansions* (Oxford, 1976) contains two novellas about Ginny when she was younger. Among her other novels are *Down the Long Stairs* (Oxford, 1964; Holt, 1965), a story set in 1648

in border country concerning life in the mines,
and *Feast of the Serpent* (Oxford, 1969; Holt,
1970), starring the daughter of a gypsy mother
and concerning the border country witch hunts
of 1649.

CAXTON (*The   Chimneys of Green   Knowe**), corrupt
manservant for the Oldknow family of the late
eighteenth century, who has grandiose plans for
his   future. He   systematically involves   the
Oldknow's son, Sefton*, in   scandalous and
illegal schemes, gambling, and even catching
boys to sell to the press gangs. With this hold
on the family heir, he plans that at the death
of Captain* Oldknow, who leads a dangerous life,
he will   marry the Captain's widow, Maria*, or,
preferably, little blind Susan*, for whom he can
then arrange an accident. Smarmy and flattering
in front of his employers, he is surly when no
one is watching and says in Susan's presence
that "it [Susan] should have been drowned at
birth, like a kitten." Since he prefers Susan to
remain   helpless, he   resents and ridicules
Jacob*, the black boy who is companion to her.
After he is dismissed by Captain Oldknow for
involving a local boy in poaching, Caxton steals
Maria's jewels. When the house is burning, he
rushes back in, evidently to get the hidden
treasure, and is never seen again.

CAXTON'S   CHALLENGE. See   *The   Load of   Unicorn*.

CAXTON, WILLIAM (*The Load of Unicorn**; *The
Writing   on the   Hearth**), England's first
printer, presented in *Unicorn* as an elegant
dresser, fond family man, master of Bendy
Goodrich (the protagonist), friend of Bendy's
father (scribe John* Goodrich), and lover of
stories of adventure and romance. When he is
unable to secure the paper he needs for his
press by the usual merchant routes, he seeks
help from John and thus meets Bendy. Impressed
by the youth's ingenuity, he asks John to
apprentice the boy to him. Caxton's need for
paper and his desire to print Malory's stories
about King Arthur bring him into contact with
such important figures of the day as Robert
Tate, Sheriff of London. Through Bendy's
association with Caxton, the reader gets

fascinating glimpses into the difficulties and challenges of early publishing in England and, in particular, of the Westminster section of London. In *Hearth*, he appears briefly as a rising young businessman and lover of books, who shows Stephen around London.

CEFALU (*The Moon in the Cloud**), Reuben's haughty, black cat, who figures importantly in the plot and provides some comic humor. When Reuben and his animals are captured on the way to Kemi (Egypt), Cefalu hides and then creeps out at an opportune moment to preen himself. Although really just an ordinary cat, he is black and hence is immediately regarded as sacred by the men from Kemi. An amusing scene follows as courtiers and servants hasten to prostrate themselves on the sand to do obeisance to the cat, lest he be displeased. Later, in the temple of the goddess Sekhmet, to whom cats are sacred, Cefalu meets and falls madly in love with Meluseth, a proud and beautiful aristocrat cat, and makes a fool of himself over her. Thus, Reuben acquires the two sacred cats he needs to satisfy Ham and, he thinks, buy passage on the ark.

CELIA WITHENS (*Hell's Edge**), beautiful, haughty, young heiress to the fortune of Sir George Withens, against whom Caradoc Clough unsuccessfully led a rebellion in the early nineteenth century after Sir George simply fenced in for his own use the land of the Hallersage Common. Celia believes firmly in the Withens's motto, *Teneo tenebo*, "What I have I hold," and refuses to give any thought to selling the land back to the people of Hallersage. Since she is afraid people will think she is soft, she acts tough. She is susceptible to flattery, however, and falls for Roy Wentworth, a slick-talking, local car salesman. When she realizes he is out for her money, she becomes even more adamant about not parting with any Withens land. She and her affair with Roy are unconvincing, too obviously contrived to complicate the plot. She serves as a foil for Ril* Terry.

CEM JONES (*The Machine-Gunners**; *Fathom Five**),

Cyril, called Cemetery because his father is caretaker of the graveyard. In *The Machine Gunners* he is sidekick to Chas* McGill and provides the orginal hiding place for the machine gun in the leg of his Guy Fawkes dummy. He gets the plan for the machine gun emplacement from his sister's boy friend as a bribe for leaving them alone in the living room. In *Fathom Five* he is sixteen, a harebrained lad, given to hamming around and drinking and smoking. He is far less stable than Chas and can't be trusted to keep a secret, but he enjoys being part of any wild adventure. He is mentioned but does not appear in *The Watch House**.

A CHANCE CHILD (Paton* Walsh, Jill, Macmillan, 1978; Farrar, 1978), unusual time fantasy revealing the abusive child labor of the late eighteenth century and the different, but equally appalling, child abuse today. When the row house next door is demolished and a hole is knocked into the wall, a nameless illegitimate or "chance" child called Creep* escapes from the closet where he has been shut most of the time. He makes his way through the Place, the site of an old foundry that has become a dump among industrial buildings, and goes to a rusting derelict boat on the remains of a canal. Told by a workman (who helps him free the boat from surrounding weeds) that the canal goes on or back from that point, he chooses to go back, and tugs the boat along by the towpath in a world where everything is strange to him, so that he does not realize that he is going back in time. After a while his boat seems to go of its own accord. Creep is invisible to most adults, though children see, talk with, and accept him naturally, like the little girl who teaches him to use the locks and another who gives him a tow with her barge through a tunnel. His boat takes him, to his consternation, into a coal mine, deep into the hill, where he hears a child crying and helps to rescue a lost girl, a tiny trapper, one who sits to open and close the doors that keep the ventilation moving. He then comes upon a miner beating his apprentice, a boy named Tom* Moorhouse, a poorhouse boy who has been bound to a brutal master. Creep helps Tom

to his boat, which takes them through the night
far enough so that Tom will not be traced and
dragged back, and leaves them on the hillside
above a foundry. There Tom gets work with a nail
and chain maker who also employs a little girl
called Blackie*, 7, half of whose face is
grossly deformed and blackened from having been
burnt when she fell asleep and tumbled into the
fire. After a particularly cruel double shift,
they run away back to the boat, Blackie with
them. Together they scratch the word CREEP into
the stone of a bridge over the canal as a sign
to Creep's half-brother, Christopher*, who, he
worries, might be looking for him. The boat then
carries them on to a place where pottery is
made, and both Tom and Blackie are taken on
while a regular boy is ill. The work again is
cruel, with long hours and heavy loads to be run
from the potter's wheel through the cold yard
into the intense heat of the drying kilns, but
they have a happy time living on the boat, with
Blackie even planning ahead for the time when
she and Tom can be married, an idea that Tom
rejects with scorn because of her appearance.
When the regular boy returns, Blackie is taken
on as a liner in the shop where they paint the
pottery, a place that seems like heaven to her
because there is a fire for the workers' comfort
and they are allowed to sing or have an old man
read to them as they work, and Tom is
transferred to running for the dippers; by then,
however, Tom is so ill from the constant
exposure that he falls and smashes a load. He is
fired, and Blackie loyally joins him. The boat
goes only a short time, stopping at another
mine--a more modern and, apparently, more humane
place than the one in which Creep found Tom--and
there Tom gets a job and leaves the other two,
who travel on to a textile mill. There Blackie
gets a job as a piecener in the spinning room,
crawling under the moving machinery and twisting
together the broken threads. Although the heat,
humidity, noise, and long hours are exhausting,
Blackie does well with Creep to help her, though
many children are beaten if they slack off from
weariness. Creep is not seen by the grownups
until the mother of one of the most cruelly
treated boys storms in and beats the overseer
with the same billy rolly with which he had

belabored the boy, and Creep, watching with the other workers, laughs aloud, the first time he has ever laughed. Suddenly, he is visible and famished, though previously he has needed to eat none of the food Blackie and Tom shared. Realizing that Blackie's wages can't buy food for both of them and that she had best stay with the kind woman whom she helps in the mill, Creep takes the boat and goes on to a place where he gets a job as a navvy, building an extension to the canal. In the meantime, as told in alternate chapters, Creep's half-brother, Christopher, is searching for him, sometimes accompanied by his younger sister, Pauline*. Following the canal along an overgrown and refuse-filled branch, he sees the word "CREEP" in large, crooked letters scratched into the stones of a bridge arch. A workman points out to him, from the wear of the tow ropes on the stone, that the letters must have been there many years. Some weeks later Christopher hangs around the entrance to a posh school and accosts the history teacher, asking him how to find someone in the past. At his suggestion, Christopher doggedly reads through the Parliamentary Papers at the public library, causing some concern to the librarians. At last one of the Papers, which record the interviews with workers that eventually led to some reform laws, mentions a Nathaniel Creep, who was crippled in an accident in canal building, learned to read as he lay ill, and became a printer. It also mentions a pamphlet written and printed by this man, telling of his own life. With the librarian's help, Christopher finds this obscure pamphlet and is convinced that it was written by Creep, as it tells of his start as a chance child whose mother "took against" him. He says that he left a message on a bridge for those who might be seeking him. With reluctant Pauline, Christopher retraces his way to the bridge where he saw the word CREEP, clears away some nettles below it, and finds a quotation about the transience of time cut in neat, regular letters. The fantasy has a beautiful inner logic arising out of Creep's abused condition in the modern world and its parallel to the child labor abuse of the Industrial Revolution. Scenes in the mines and mills are devastatingly vivid, yet the total tone is not depressing. The oppressed but staunch children, particularly Creep, Blackie, and Tom, are appealng and believable survivors. Choice; Fanfare.

THE CHANGEOVER: A SUPERNATURAL ROMANCE (Mahy*, Margaret, Dent, 1984; Atheneum, 1984), mystery of the supernatural with girls' growing-up story aspects covering about a week's time in a middle-class suburb of a New Zealand city not long ago. Plain, intelligent Laura* Chant, 14, lives with her divorced mother, Kate*, who manages a book shop, and her little brother, Jonathan, 3, called Jacko. Laura loves them both dearly and is mostly satisfied with her life, except that she regrets her plainness and is a little afraid of the changes her body is experiencing. She also fears the "warnings" that occasionally come to her, bringing with them a sense of impending disaster. One of these occurred just before her father walked out and another when Sorry* Carlisle, prefect and model student, arrived in school eighteen months earlier. Only to Laura does Sorry show a less than perfect face; only she recognizes him for what he really is: a witch. One school-day, after Laura collects Jacko from his sitter, the two visit an antique shop where the owner, disagreeable Carmody Braque*, rudely stamps Jacko's hand with his own picture. Jacko complains of pain which persists in spite of Laura's repeated efforts to wash off the mark. Coincidentally, that evening Kate arrives home with a new man friend, Chris Holly, a Canadian librarian, of whom Laura immediately feels jealous. Although the stamp mark disappears, Jacko has a bad night, and worsens the next day. Laura fears witchcraft, especially when she detects in his room the same peppermint odor she smelled in Braque's shop. She decides to consult Sorry, who lives with his mother and grandmother, Miryam* and Winter*, also witches, in the old Carlisle mansion. Though Laura insists Jacko must be the victim of a vampire, Sorry and his relatives refuse assistance. The next morning Jacko has a convulsion, but before he is taken to the hospital, Sorry arrives to make peace and confirm Laura's suspicions of foul play. He suggests that Braque is a lemure, a

wicked spirit of the dead who maintains his own
life by absorbing the energy of living beings
whom he has managed to get into his power.
Sorry says that Laura can save Jacko's life only
by forcing Braque to let the child go. While
Jacko is in the hospital, where doctors despair
for his life, Laura stays with the Carlisles,
who persuade her to undergo a "changeover," that
is, to go through the ritual to become a witch
herself. They maintain that this should be
entirely possible since Laura is already a
"sensitive." A long passage involves the intricate ritual that the three Carlisles conduct. It
recalls descriptions of rites of passage of
primitive societies. Once a witch, Laura quite
boldly seeks Braque, tricks the man into
extending his hand to her, marks it quickly with
a stamp bearing her own likeness, and, with him
thus in her power, causes him to fade away to
nothingness. Jacko recovers quickly. Laura feels
more content with herself and less afraid of her
changing sexuality, and discovers she is no
longer resentful of her mother's relationship
with Chris or of her father's new wife. She and
Sorry agree to put their own blossoming romance
on hold, at least until both have finished
school. Laura and her family are thoroughly
likeable, but the Carlisle women seem shallow
and made to order. The author's suspenseful
plotting, touches of humor, snappy dialogue,
engaging and real-seeming main characters, and
the literate, imagistic style lift the book
above average for its type. The carefully worked
out details about witchcraft keep the story
interesting and contribute to the suspense.
Laura's feelings about her mother's boyfriend
seem legitimate, and Sorry's levelheadedness is
a refreshing feature. Laura's evolvement into a
young lady from a petulant child and Sorry's
gradual acceptance of his own ambivalent nature
are completely believable. Boston Globe Honor;
Carnegie Winner; Fanfare.

CHARLEE LOON (*The Silver Curlew**), fisherman
friend of Poll*, who helps her triumph over the
Spindle-Imp* by learning his name. Charlee is an
enigmatic figure, not entirely convincing, a man
of indeterminate age with whom the wild
creatures, particularly puffins, are friends. Of

changeable temperament, he can be accommodating
and perceptive sometimes and at other times
peevish, aloof, and slow. He plays tunes on his
whistle and sings little ditties whose words,
when put together (the reader learns at the
end), contribute to his life story. He is really
the Man in the Moon and his story is a play on
the old nursery rhyme. He has come down too soon
to Anglia, England, to ask his way to Norwich,
leaving his wits behind and soon followed by the
Lady in the Moon, who becomes the Silver Curlew.
It is never clear why they have been enchanted
or what breaks the spell and restores them to
their previous forms and to their home in the
moon.

CHARLIE (*The Watcher Bee**), boy next door to
Kate*, his family having rented the house and
farm belonging to Kate's mother's family, and
thereby obtaining the trees, barn, and pony
which Kate insists are rightfully hers. Since
her maternal grandmother has been reluctant to
leave her home, they have also inherited her,
and she is cared for by Charlie's mother and
claimed by Charlie, too, as his Granny. From
infancy, he and Kate have been companions, but
quite early she realizes that he isn't the good
little boy their parents think. He is continually making derogatory remarks about her, calling
her "warble-lip" and "beanpole," since he is
short and stocky while she is tall and thin. She
comes upon him and Ivy Holt making love in the
barn before he is fifteen, and she realizes
that he and Zoe* Vardoe are not practicing
French language during the many evenings they
spend in her "boudoir." Always fond of tinkering
with motors, he becomes enamoured of planes
when one lands by accident in his father's field
and he is given a ride, on which he gets Zoe
rather than Kate to accompany him. When Kate
observes that he has trifled with Ivy just as
Zoe has with him, he hits her and lets her ride
off on her bicycle alone in the dark. After she
has an accident and is bedridden for some weeks,
he apologizes somewhat awkwardly. At one point
he is engaged to the daughter of the Lincolnshire farmer for whom he works, but he has
willingly broken off that entanglement before
he enters the air force. Kate realizes sadly

that she loves him but that nothing will come of that love since they are too different in height and interests.

CHARLIE AND THE CHOCOLATE FACTORY (Dahl*, Roald, ill. Joseph Schindelman, Allen, 1967; Knopf, 1964), comic fantasy with satirical overtones set in the contemporary period in England. Five children win Golden Tickets for a tour of the fabulous Willy* Wonka's Chocolate Factory: greedy, fat Augustus* Gloop; sassy, spoiled Veruca* Salt; brassy, gum-chewing Violet* Beauregarde; bratty, television addict, Mike* Teavee; and respectful, conscientious, skinny, little Charlie Bucket. Charlie lives in a two-room, tumbledown, wooden house on the edge of a great city with his underpaid, overworked father, who makes toothpaste, his sacrificing mother, and his four old grandparents, who never leave the only bed in the house, all of whom live mostly on boiled cabbage. While the other children acquire their tickets fairly easily, poor Charlie, who had despaired of being lucky enough to get one, secures his when he buys a candy bar with some money that he has found and then only when he is rescued from grasping, greedy crowds by a kind storekeeper. These five children are ushered inside the wonderful building, where mysterious Mr.* Willy Wonka makes his mouth-watering candy bars and other extraordinary, world-renowned confections. The first four children bring their parents with them. These adults are almost as obnoxious as the children. On the other hand, Charlie, by common consent of his close and loving relatives, brings only his old, wise Grandpa* Joe, who had given Charlie the very last of his money in a futile effort to secure a ticket for his beloved grandson. Garrulous, sprightly, garishly garbed Mr. Wonka welcomes the little party of fourteen spectators into his factory, an amazing underground labyrinth of countless workrooms and complex passages. Three thousand Oompa-Loompas*--energetic, always laughing pygmies, who dance about and speak in rhyme--create the exotic, savory sweets. One by one the first four children disobey Mr. Wonka's orders and come to grief in poetically just ways, leaving only little Charlie and his Grandpa Joe to finish the grand tour. In reward for his patience, obedience, and all-round virtue, Mr. Wonka makes Charlie his heir. The whole family, both Charlie's poverty-stricken parents and his wizened, aged grandparents (these latter transported in their bed by Mr. Wonka's great glass elevator), all come to live with Charlie in the factory. His elders will run the place until Charlie is old enough to take over operations himself. Never again will the Bucket family want for the necessities of life, because Charlie has been virtuous (and lucky). The book is all plot, and everything for predicting the outcome is right before the reader. Dialogue and style are contemporary in tone and language, and the social commentary is also obvious. Characters are flat, distorted types, distinguished by one feature; some are made angular to such absurdity that they offend, for example, the four old people and the pygmies; and the handling of both groups has aroused the ire of many social and literary critics. Although it is clear that the author ricidules and lectures modern children for their narcissistic ways and excessive wants, the book has remained extremely popular, probably because the preposterousness alleviates the cautionary content and keeps the book from sounding cynical and preachy. Choice.

CHARLIE HERRICK (*The Islanders**), survivor of a shipwreck, who leads a Robinson Crusoe existence for two years on Kingfisher* Island before being discovered by Adam* Goodall and his friends. Charlie is living in a hut constructed of ship's timbers and furnished like the dead captain's cabin. A sensible, self-controlled man, he bides his time and acts when the time is right. At Adam's request, he reads the Book of Teaching to the islanders, warning them first that they might not like what they will hear. The reading leads to the rebellion of those who believe a better life awaits them in England, and they stealthily depart, taking away with them the island's only canoes and most of the supplies. Charlie, who is forced to go with them, returns as soon as he can to the island with supplies much needed by that time.

CHARLIE MARRIOT (*Travelers by Night**), young

circus performer who has been somewhat in the shadow of his talented cousin, Belle*, until her fall on the high wire from which he saves her but in which she injures and disfigures her face. Charlie came to live with Belle's parents, a knife thrower and his partner, after the death of his own parents when he was five, and has been devoted to Belle ever since. When the circus breaks up, Mr. Schneider, the trainer for the performing children, offers him a job during school holidays, an offer that causes some tension between the cousins. It is partly this offer that makes him hesitate to join Belle in her harebrained scheme to kidnap Tessie, the aging elephant, since he doesn't want to queer the deal by getting into trouble, but he also sees much more clearly than she the many difficulties her plan presents. Nevertheless, his devotion to Belle wins out, and he helps her, though at first he hopes they will be apprehended. Before the circus goes bankrupt, he has sneaked out with Belle and performed their Star Spinners tumbling act along the highway to earn money for a fund for plastic surgery to repair her face. In the act he is a clown, hopelessly in love with the ballerina who rejects and ignores him, just as in real life Belle bosses Charlie and takes him for granted.

CHARLIE WHITELAW (*A Kind of Wild Justice**), big, broad-shouldered, tough bus driver who runs his own bus company and who occasionally transports school children. He is a heroic figure to the children, who are in tremendous awe of him because he is reputed to have suffered severe back injuries at the hands of the feared and hated Bradshaws. Ronnie learns later that Charlie's back was actually broken in a truck accident. Charlie likes Steve and Ronnie and knows Val is sweet on Bernie Bradshaw, and, when Steve is arrested, Charlie offers unsuccessfully to help Ronnie. When later Ronnie moves in with Charlie, Charlie gives the boy opportunities to develop self-respect, for example, putting him to work cleaning buses for pay. Charlie is the stereotypical "good guy forced to go wrong" whose goodness is recognized in the end.

CHARLOTTE LATTIMER (*The Battle of Wednesday*

Week*), occasionally called Charley by Nicholas*
Lattimer, her older brother. She keeps the
house going with Nan* Graham's help while their
parents are away. Even before Robert Graham and
his children arrive, she has decided she will do
her best to accept them, and with Alison*
Johnstone's help, she makes bedroom curtains
with a flying gull pattern for her new sisters
to show her friendly intentions.

CHARLOTTE MAKEPEACE (*Charlotte Sometimes**; *The
Summer Birds**), elder sister of Emma and, in
Charlotte Sometimes, also Clare Moby, while she
is in the time-past story of the fantasy. As
Charlotte and as Clare she is a quiet, somewhat hesitant, reserved child, who likes order
and calm, lives up to her surname by trying to
avoid conflict and by smoothing things out when
it occurs, and tries to keep her sister and
Emily* Moby out of trouble and on the right
track. The other children and her boarding
school mates call her a prig. She matures somewhat because of her experiences in the two
books, but remains essentially the same in personality and attitude toward life. In *Charlotte
Sometimes*, Emily, like Emma, is the more
resourceful and inventive of the two girls. The
author expresses Charlotte's point of view well
and conveys her feelings and reactions with
accuracy and conviction; this is one of the
strongest aspects of the two books.

CHARLOTTE SOMETIMES (Farmer*, Penelope, ill.
Chris Conner, Chatto, 1969; Harcourt, 1969),
fantasy of well-sustained if mild suspense,
which begins in the world of reality somewhere
in England about 1960 and in which characters go
back and forth in time. In September, conscientious, responsible Charlotte* Makepeace of
The Summer Birds*, now thirteen, leaves her
younger sister, Emma, and Aviary Hall for
boarding school. A prefect, Sarah Reynolds,
shows her to her bedroom and encourages her to
choose the bed by the window, the only one with
wheels. The next morning, Charlotte awakens in
the same bed and the same building but as Clare
Moby in the year 1918. Clare and her sister,
Emily*, motherless children whose father is
fighting in France, are day students living

temporarily at the school until lodgings can be
found for them. Clare, who has also slept on the
wheeled bed, awakens as Charlotte, but the story
proceeds from Charlotte's point of view. She
encounters many problems: gaining Emily's confidence, maintaining continuity in schoolwork,
and not arousing suspicion. She and Clare,
about whom we hear very little, communicate by
leaving notes in a diary and exercise book.
When the Moby girls are transferred to lodgings
away from school, Charlotte is trapped in 1918
(and Clare in the time present), and the most
interesting part of the novel takes place. The
girls live with grumpy old Mr. Chisel-Brown and
his abstracted wife, who sits all day surrounded
by pictures of her son, Arthur, who was slain
in the war, and their spinster daughter,
Agnes*, who shares memories of her brother with
the girls. She gives them some of his toys, and
they read his books and climb the monkey puzzle
tree that he used to climb. They observe a
seance in which Mrs. Chisel-Brown attempts to
contact him and during which, to everyone's
consternation, Clare speaks from the "other
side." Weeks pass, and Charlotte finds herself
actually feeling she is Clare, and even
sometimes Agnes. Interestingly, Emily becomes
more concerned about returning Charlotte to her
own time, in order to get Clare back, than
Charlotte is to go back. Because at Armistice
the two girls join revelers in the street
without permission, the headmistress recalls
them to school. This gives Charlotte the
opportunity to sleep again in the wheeled bed
and to return to her own time. She learns that
Sarah had given her the bed on orders from her
mother, once Emily Moby, who knew she would
enroll in the school, and that Clare died in the
flu epidemic that followed the war. Charlotte
returns to Aviary Hall and Emma and is delighted
to be celebrating Christmas in her own time. Although it flags at times, the plot is inventive,
carefully crafted, and moves with just enough
complications to hold the reader's attention.
The Chisel-Browns are eccentric but not
outlandish, and Agnes is strongly drawn. Charlotte becomes more adventuresome as a result of
her experiences and association with Emily, and
her fears that she may never quite be herself

again are convincing and prove true, though she remains essentially a passive figure. Except for the lively Bunty*, the schoolmates are wash-outs as characters. Sarah's part of the plot is anticipatory, and she herself is too shadowy to be convincing. Style is descriptive if mono-chromatic. It is sure and literary, but never stiltedly formal, and filled with the small details of feeling, action, and everyday life that create credibility and provide interesting texture. The book gives some views of boarding school and domestic life during World War I, such as attitudes toward Germans (one of the schoolmates is half-German) and the diffi-culties of everyday existence caused by short-ages of food and energy. Fanfare.

CHARMED LIFE (Jones*, Diana Wynne, Macmillan, 1977; Greenwillow, 1978), fantasy set in another world very like Edwardian England. Since the untimely death of their parents, Cat* (Eric) Chant depends on his sister Gwendolen*, a talented young witch. They live, supported by the town of Wolvercote, with Mrs. Sharp, a Certified Witch, who arranges lessons for Gwendolen with Mr. Nostrum, a local necromancer. At his suggestion, Gwendolen writes to Chresto-manci*, a figure the witches and warlocks hold in some awe and letters from whom were found among their parents' effects. He arranges that they live with him in the castle at Bowbridge. There they meet Michael Saunders, the tutor; Miss Bessemer, the housekeeper; Chrestomanci's wife, Milly; his two plump children, Julia and Roger; and the maids, Euphemia and Mary. In the unaccustomed luxury Cat is at first miserable; Gwendolen is initially thrilled, but then becomes resentful at the lack of attention given to her gifts of magic. She decides to force them to notice her superiority and produces one mean trick after another--ruining the lawn with molehills, summoning an apparition to the window during dinner, turning the castle dark at intervals, transforming Julia's skirts to snakes, making the stained glass figures in the church windows dance and fight during service, bringing all the nearby trees to crowd close around the castle and seal the entrances--all without seeming to disturb Chrestomanci in the

least. At last, when visitors are expected for
dinner, she uses dragon's blood she has
purchased, summons up a procession of horrible
creatures, and sends them to the dining room.
This brings both Chrestomanci and Saunders, who
spanks Gwendolen soundly with his shoe and takes
away her magic, winding it like a string around
his wrist. In fury, Gwendolen makes master
magic, which sends her to another world and
pulls one of her several doubles from coexisting
worlds into her place. This child, Janet* Chant,
seems to have come from our modern-day world
and is a mater-of-fact good sport, differing
from Gwendolen in everything except appearance.
Cat finds that he must protect both Gwendolen
and Janet by keeping the transfer secret, a
problem complicated by the fact that Gwendolen
has turned Euphemia into a frog. When Cat takes
responsibility for this spell, he becomes involved in a string of difficulties: Chrestomanci
forces him to turn her back into a woman and, to
his surprise, he can; Euphemia's intended husband threatens him; the dealer in exotic supplies demands payment; Janet, knowing nothing of
the history of this world, is in constant need
of his ingenious cover-ups. Although the tone of
the book as a whole is light, the adventures
climax in a terrifying scene in Chrestomanci's
garden (which has doorways to other worlds),
with witches, warlocks, necromancers, and other
workers in magic pitted against Chrestomanci
and his household in a struggle in which Cat
will be sacrificed (as an innocent child) to
give the evil forces power over the transitions.
It is discovered that Cat is really an enchanter
with nine lives, that Gwendolen has been using
his magic and squandering his lives to get power
for her major spells, that she has bound his
lives into a book of matches, several of which
are now burnt out, and that he is really nephew
to Chrestomanci and destined to become his
successor. Although the plot complications are
difficult to unravel, the general spritely pace
and tone keep the reader from dwelling on this
problem. Cat is a believable little boy,
Gwendolen a villainess with a flair, and minor
characters are memorable. Carnegie Com.;
Guardian.

CHAS MCGILL (*The Machine Gunners**; *Fathom Five**), working-class boy who has adventures in wartime Garmouth, a grimy Northumberland port. In *The Machine Gunners*, he acquires a German machine gun as part of his collection of war souvenirs and is the major force in building the underground bunker they call the Fortress Caparetto. Though fourteen, he is still considered a child by his parents, but because both are overworked and weary, he gets little supervision. His teacher recognizes his ability and thinks of him as a boy to like but not to trust. In one interesting scene, he goes with his father to see if his grandparents have survived the bombing, and finds his grandfather, a veteran of World War I, having a recurrence of his war-induced mental illness, thinking he is shooting at the Germans in the trenches. Chas is mainly interested in getting his grandfather's souvenir German helmet into his collection. In *Fathom Five*, Chas (now sixteen and in the sixth form) and his friends, Cem* Jones and Audrey* Parton, attempt to catch a spy who is alerting German U-boats to ships leaving Garmouth with strategic cargoes. Chas has become tall and gangling, but is attractive to the upper-crust girl, Sheila* Smythson, as well as to several older women. Despite his resentment of the airs and snobbishness of schoolmasters and public officials, he is very bright and seems destined to go to the university on scholarship. In *The Watch House**, the solicitor is named McGill, and although he is not identified by first name, his appearance and his unconventional attitude seem to indicate that he is Chas as an adult. The title story of *The Haunting of Chas McGill and Other Stories* is about Chas as a younger boy, in the opening days of World War II, some time before *The Machine-Gunners*.

CHEE-CHEE (*The Story of Doctor Dolittle**; *The Voyages of Doctor Dolittle**), monkey whom Doctor* Dolittle rescues from an unkind organgrinder. A message from Chee-Chee's cousin telling of an illness among the monkeys triggers the doctor's first voyage to Africa, where Chee-Chee remains when Doctor Dolittle goes home. Chee-Chee becomes so homesick, however, that he dresses like a woman, stows away on a ship to England, and makes his way across the country to Puddleby, still dressed in women's clothes. He accompanies the doctor on the voyage to Spidermonkey Island.

CHESHIRE-CAT (*Alice's Adventures in Wonderland**), pet of the ugly Duchess*, in whose kitchen Alice* first meets him. His outstanding trait is his ability to disappear, leaving only his grin behind. He attempts with marvelously clever illogic to convince Alice that he's mad. Later, in the garden of the King and Queen of Hearts, he disappears, leaving only his head visible. This offends the king and queen. The latter orders him beheaded, and a spirited disagreement erupts over how to behead something that possesses only a head. The cat settles the argument by simply disappearing altogether. A flat and distorted character like most in the novel, he is one of its most famous figures.

THE CHILDREN OF GREEN KNOWE (Boston*, L. M., ill. Peter Boston, Faber, 1954; Harcourt, 1955), first of a series of fantasies set in an old house in England in the mid-twentieth century. Toseland, a lonely, young schoolboy, whose father and stepmother are in Burma, comes to spend his winter holidays with his mother's grandmother, Mrs.* Oldknow, whom he has never met, at her house, Green Noah, which dates back to the time of the Crusades. He arrives in a flood, which has made Green Noah an island, and at the lane's end his taxi is met by the gardener-handy man, Boggis, in a row boat. He immediately loves the house and his small, imaginative great-grandmother, and feels that he belongs there as he has not belonged anywhere since his mother died. Over the fireplace is a strangely realistic portrait of three children and their mother and grandmother, the Oldknow family of the seventeenth century. There are two boys, Toby* (Toseland), about thirteen, who wears a sword and has his hand on the collar of a tame deer, and Alexander*, a younger boy, who carries a book and a flute, and a little girl, Linnet*, 6, who holds a chaffinch. The present-day Toseland, whom his great-grandmother calls Tolly*, learns that the names recur in the family; Granny's name is Linnet, as was Tolly's mother's name, and there has always been a Boggis in the gardens or stables. Tolly sleeps in the room that still holds the rocking horse and other toys of the children in the painting. Gradually, he begins to hear them laughing and talking and then to catch glimpses of them in the mirror. Granny sees them, too, and tells Tolly stories about them: about Toby's horse, Feste*, whose stall is still kept vacant in the stables; about how the gypsy, Black Ferdie, tried to steal the black mare, and how Feste, now long dead, thwarted him; about how Alexander sang for the king at Greatchurch and was given his flute as a reward; about how Linnet saw the great stone St. Christopher carrying the Christ Child to Midnight Mass. She also tells him that the children died in the Great Plague of 1665, all on the same day. Together the boy and the old woman feed the birds, plan and decorate for Christmas, and walk to Midnight Mass at the local church. Tolly finally comes upon the children in the snowy garden under a spreading yew tree, with the deer, and Watt, their hare, Truepenny, their mole, Orlando, their little dog, and a variety of other pets. They talk, and he soon becomes used to seeing them for brief snatches of time, particularly Linnet, though it is Toby he most admires. Among the yew trees trimmed into fancy shapes is one, he discovers, no longer trimmed but retaining the rough shape of a man, and in a gardening magazine he reads an article about the curse placed on the house, formerly called Green Knowe, by Old Petronella, Black Ferdie's mother, that the yew trimmed to be Noah should take on the Devil's image. The house has since been known as Green Noah. Tolly hears Linnet singing a taunting song to Noah and copies her, and that night, going in the dark to put a sugar cube in the empty stall for Feste, he sees Green Noah move, reaching out blindly with its branches. Terrified, he cries out for Linnet and hears her calling to St. Christopher. A great flash of lightning answers, and Tolly runs back to the house and faints. Later Boggis discovers that Green Noah, the tree, has been destroyed. He also says that he met his long-dead grandfather, roaring drunk, in the garden. On Christmas morning Tolly puts on Toby's coat, and feels and hears, though he doesn't actually see, Feste nudge the pocket for an apple and crunch it up. That day he gets a puppy, his Orlando, and Boggis's great-grandson, Percy, comes to play with him. There is a suggestion that with the real boy and the dog for friends, Tolly will need the ancient children less. The house reverts to the name Green Knowe. Tolly's age is not given, but he seems closer to Linnet than to the boys. There is not a great deal of action, but the story is lively with Tolly's delight in his many discoveries. The book's strength is in the evocation of mood and setting, which makes the presence of the children seem very real, though there is always the possibility that both he and his grandmother are imagining them or even that old Mrs. Oldknow is pretending to believe to amuse him. The relationship between the lonely boy and the old lady is especially appealing, warm, and affectionate, as they both accept the unusual presences with pleasure but no doubt or fear. Part of the conviction comes from a blurring of the generations, with the recurring Toselands, Linnets, and Boggises, and with the many objects in the house that date back to the time of the children or earlier. The stories within the story are skillfully blended to enhance rather than to slow the action. Sequels. Books Too Good; Carnegie Com.; Choice; Fanfare; Lewis Carroll.

CHILDREN OF THE BOOK (Carter*, Peter, Oxford, 1982), historical novel set in 1682–1683 about the second attempt by the Ottoman Turks to capture Vienna from the Children of the Book, as the Turks call the Christians. The story opens at the Turkish court in Istanbul in August of 1682 as conniving, power-hungry, ambitious Kara Mustafa, the Grand Vizier, persuades Sultan Mehmed the Fourth to break his treaty with the Austrians and wage "Holy War" for the glory of Allah to capture Vienna, the Golden Apple. Kara Mustafa reports that his sources assure him that the Europeans are divided among themselves and that none will come to the aid of the Austrians, least of all the "barbarous" and "backward" hard-fighting Poles. In addition, the enormous army that maintains the Ottoman empire has to be used in order to keep the men from becoming

mutinous. War declared, the novel shifts from
Turks to Christians and back, advancing the
reader's understanding of what is going on by
focusing on one family or group in each major
sector and setting up as foils several adults
and youths: war-eager, seventeen-year-old Timur*
Ven, a raw recruit in the Twenty-Eighth Orta in
the Turkish Janissaries (the infantry), under
the command of hard-bitten Colonel Vasif*;
Stefan Zabruski, a Polish youth of about
seventeen, eager to win honors on the field to
impress his bride-to-be; his father, Ladislau, a
huge, brutish man called "The Wild Boar," who
has been ennobled for previous war service to
the Polish king; and short, honest, Viennese
baker Herr* Jakob Vogel; his wife; their
dutiful, pretty daughter, Anna*, 17, who comes
to womanhood during the siege of the city; and
her staunch, hardworking sweetheart, Kaspar
Haller, 21, a carpenter. In addition to the
Sultan (who prefers "to hunt, make money, and
avoid being assassinated") and Kara Mustafa,
other historical figures include urbane, · diplomatic King Leopold of Austria, who is
determined to protect the heart of his realm,
Austria, at any cost; mountainous, practical,
good strategist King John Sobieski of Poland;
and war-wise, skillful Austrian General Count
Starhemberg. While the Viennese hurriedly but
systematically fortify the city for siege, lay
in extra food and other supplies, and bribe,
cajole, and blackmail support among the
Christian nations of Europe, the Sword of Islam,
as the Sultan's army is known, ploughs through
southern Europe, 150,000 Turks, Syrians,
Egyptians, Tartars, and others from throughout
the broad empire, ravaging and pillaging an
eighty-mile-wide swathe as it advances on
Vienna. The Turks cross the Drava River in June,
1683, rapidly push back the Austrian forces, and
soon begin the siege of the city. At tremendous
cost in lives from Austrian guns and cannon,
from disease, from overwork, and even from
exemplary executions, the Turks continue to make
slow, steady, bitter, bloody progress and have
almost breached the city walls, when in
mid-September King John Sobieski arrives with a
combined army of about 100,000 Poles and other
Christians from Central Europe. Kara Mustafa

chooses both to continue the siege and to send an army to deal with the defenders. Ironically, it is the Polish armored knights on horseback who break and rout the Turkish line. In the battle, which occurs on September 12 and lasts only about an hour, "ghostly camels," as the Turks say, come for Vasif and Timur Ven, and young Stefan dies, too. Kara Mustafa escapes and leads the remnants of his army south. Before long, he pays the price of defeat: he is garroted at the Sultan's command. A rich and substantial picture of a brutal and turbulent period, the book is a harsh indictment of the era, of the Turks, and of the war itself, which is shown as an utterly irrational enterprise, wasteful of life and resources on both sides, and promoted by inhumane, callous, selfish men, who, while not oblivious of the cost, completely disregard it. The author occasionally over-writes, and his interest in the period runs away with his ability as a storyteller to the extent that the amount of background detail sometimes becomes ponderous. The several main characters are individualized with telling touches and seem real, the style is vigorous, and the narrative advances through the cinematic techniques of rapidly shifted, carefully counterposed scenes with lots of action and dialogue. The Viennese family is presented with faults but also as warm and caring. They contrast favorably with the brutish Poles and hardened Vasif, and young Timur's slowly dawning realization that war holds little advantage for anyone is very convincing. Young Observer.

CHILDREN OF THE RED KING (Polland*, Madeleine A., ill. Annette Macarthur-Onslow, Constable, 1960; Holt, 1961), historical novel set in what is now County Galway, Ireland, in the early thirteenth century. Cormac*, the Red King of Connacht, is one of the few remaining Irish leaders who have not been subdued by or made peace with the Normans under King John. In 1209, his people gather to choose the new heir, a choice between Cormac's younger half-brother, Felim, and Cormac's seven-year-old son, Fergus*. The child, however, who has been sent to the Abbey of Athenmore to be educated, is not present for the Gathering, because the abbey has

fallen into Norman hands. In a daring night
rescue, the wounded king and his daughter,
Grania*, 9, ride to the abbey and, while their
soldiers cause a distraction that draws the
guards, enter the grounds. Grania climbs through
a window, wakes Fergus in the midst of the
sleeping boys, and they escape to Duncormac. In
the election of the tribe, Fergus is chosen
overwhelmingly over Felim, who becomes a bitter
enemy as a result. Before they leave Duncormac,
Felim's daughter, Mairi, steals the Circlet of
Deirdre, which is rightfully Grania's, breaking
the law of peace of the Gathering (an offense
punishable by death), and Felim is proved to
have shot at Fergus during the escape, but
Cormac sends them both off without punishment.
Some time later, riding in the forest with their
father's faithful follower Dermot, Grania and
Fergus find a secret trail to the Norman-held
castle of Androhan. With this knowledge, Cormac
seizes a pack train carrying bags of precious
jewels. The result is an attack on Duncormac by
the Normans that destroys the Great Hall and the
village and kills most of the people. Grania
rescues the Book of Gospels, which is sacred to
her people, and she and Fergus escape with their
nurse, Eithne, to a hermit's hut in the forest.
The next day they return to Duncormac and are
intercepted by Sir* Jocelin de Courcy Rohan,
Norman holder of Androhan, who sends word to
Cormac that they are not hostages and will be
well treated, and takes them to his castle.
There Grania learns to love his gentle young
French wife, Lady Blanche, and Fergus, at first
resentful, becomes happier when he is allowed to
go, under escort, to study painting and Irish
lore with a hermit. After three years a message
comes through the hermit, Brother Colman, that a
rescue attempt is planned. Fergus is torn, since
he has given Sir Jocelin his word that he will
not try to escape, so he keeps silent. The
attempt proves to be treachery by Felim, who
wounds Fergus but is killed in the attempt. Soon
after, a visit from King John, who is critical
of Sir Jocelin for not capturing Cormac and
wants to use the children to force the Red King
into submission, precipitates the climactic
adventure. Grania, who has known all along where
her father is hiding, makes a deal with Sir

Jocelin that if she and Fergus are allowed to go alone, they will return and will try to persuade Cormac to make peace. They cross a swamp by night, but, as Grania suspects, Sir Jocelin's follower Guilbert and his men, in a secret deal with King John, trail them. Grania leads them into the treacherous bog and takes Fergus, still weak from his wound, to Cormac's camp on the island in the middle of the swamp. Because of his children's bravery, the good treatment they have received, and Sir Jocelin's generous terms, Cormac returns with them and makes peace with the Normans. The main outlines of the story and the places are historical, but the romantically adventurous novel contains more brave deeds and narrow escapes by Grania than are credible, even in such unsettled times and even among among the descendants of Deirdre and Cuchulain. The pace is rapid, however, and the costumes and customs are presented as essential parts of the action, not mere stage dressing. Fanfare.

THE CHIMNEYS OF GREEN KNOWE (Boston, L. M., ill. Peter Boston, Faber, 1958; *TREASURE OF GREEN KNOWE*, Harcourt, 1958), second fantasy in a series set in Green Knowe, an old English house dating from the medieval period. Tolly*, returning to spend summer holidays with his great-grandmother, Mrs.* Oldknow, is disappointed to find that the portrait of the seventeenth-century Oldknow children is no longer hanging above the fireplace, having been loaned for an exhibit, and he no longer feels the children's presence in the house. The painting's place is taken by a picture of an eighteenth-century woman in a carriage driving toward a rather different and larger Green Knowe, a picture embroidered with human hair. Mrs. Oldknow is repairing the patchwork quilts which she uses for draperies and which also date from the late eighteenth century, and she tells Tolly stories of the Oldknow family of that period. Besides the strict, religious grandmother who made the quilts, there was a father, a captain of a sailing ship, his silly, frivolous wife, Maria*, his spoiled, self-important son, Sefton*, and his blind daughter, Susan*, ten years younger than her brother. In Barbados, Captain* Oldknow buys a little slave boy,

Jacob*, and brings him home to be a companion to
Susan, now eight, who has an adventurous spirit
but has been neglected by her mother and kept
virtually a prisoner by her well-meaning but
stupid nurse. Although Sefton orders a monkey
suit for Jacob, and his mother and most of the
servants, including the wicked manservant,
Caxton*, think it is a huge joke, Jacob is
immediately able to introduce freedom and
adventure into Susan's life with his imagination
and quick understanding. The parson's son,
Jonathan* Morley, has been able to think of no
way to teach Susan to write, but Jacob suggests
using dough, so she can feel the marks she
makes and even mold letters. He teaches Susan to
somersault and to climb trees, and he catches
frogs, a moorhen chick, butterflies, worms, and
fish--all so that Susan may feel and know them.
Sefton continues to torment Jacob when he thinks
of it. After he has been shooting with a friend,
he pretends that a bird fell down the chimney
and sends Jacob up to look for it. The boy is
amazed at the interlocking chimneys and flues
and eventually finds his way to his own closet,
runs outside to find a recently killed chicken,
climbs back up the chimney, and drops it down to
Sefton as his "game," thereby getting the best
of the arrogant older boy. Tolly gradually
begins to see Susan and to sense Jacob's
presence, but their lives do not really
interconnect until he finds the tunnel under
what used to be the old chapel and learns that
Jacob has hidden young Fred Boggis, the
gardener's son, there after Fred was caught
poaching and escaped from the gamekeeper, an
offence for which he could be hanged. Because
Caxton and Sefton are involved with getting boys
to poach for their profit, and then selling them
to the press gang, Susan and Jacob dare not take
food or reassurance to Fred lest Caxton see
them, but Tolly takes the basket they have
prepared. Later, when Captain Oldknow returns,
Susan and Jacob tell him the story, and, with
the help of Jonathan and the parson, he has Fred
smuggled out to his ship, the *Woodpecker*,
where he can become part of the crew. He
dismisses Caxton, but the servant gets revenge
by stealing Maria's jewels. While the Captain
and Sefton are away, Green Knowe catches fire,

and Susan, forgotten by everyone but Jacob, is caught in her room, fortunately in the old part of the house. Jacob goes up the chimney to reach her room and brings her down to Jonathan. Caxton, evidently trying to find the jewels he has hidden, is either killed or escapes; he is never seen again. The stylish new section of the house is destroyed, but the older portion is repairable. Maria, prompted by one of her silly friends, consults an old gypsy about finding her jewels and is told she must embroider a picture of the house on the day of the fire, using the hair of all the people present at the time. She has most trouble with Jacob's short, crinkly hair. Excited by the story of the jewels and worried that the portrait of the Oldknow children may have to be sold to pay for needed repairs to the house, Tolly searches for the lost treasure. Exploring the space above the ceiling, he opens an iron door to a flue and pulls up a sack containing silver spoons, golden sovereigns, and the missing jewels. The mixture of the characters from the past and present is not as convincing as in *The Children of Green Knowe**, the present-day plot with the discovery of the treasure is less likely, and the structure is more awkward, with most of the story of Susan and Jacob coming in tales by Mrs. Oldknow, but the story of the little blind girl and her ingenious black companion is in itself so interesting that the novel overcomes these liabilities. Characters and setting are both strong. The outstanding feature is the sense of how the world must be to a sightless child, a world of smell and sound and touch strongly evoked by vivid sensory descriptions. Carnegie Com.; Choice; Fanfare.

CHIP (*The Seventh Raven**), attractive youngest terrorist, who holds the cast and orchestra of St. Andrew's Church Christmas opera hostage after a bungled attempt to kidnap the Mattean ambassador's son. A Texan by birth and only half-Mattean, Chip has been a student activist and a prisoner of the repressive dictatorship and is trying to get the British to apply pressure to free prisoners in Matteo. At a crucial point, he moves to prevent the woman revolutionist from executing Mrs.* Jacobs and, in leaving the children momentarily unguarded, he allows the police to shoot and bring an end to the siege.

CHIPPERFIELD, JOSEPH E(UGENE) (1912-1976), born in St. Austell, Cornwall; prolific and popular novelist of animal stories for middle-grade readers. Educated privately, he grew up on a farm in Cornwall and later lived in Surrey. He was a newspaperman, writer for a magazine that specialized in dogs, editor for Author's Literary Service in London, and editor and scriptwriter for documentary films. In 1940 he turned to freelance writing. He married, traveled in Ireland and England, and always enjoyed dogs and being outdoors. Two of his thirty novels were named to the Fanfare list by the editors of *Horn Book*: *Windruff of Links Tor** (Hutchinson, 1954; Longman, 1951) and *Wolf of Badenoch: Dog of the Grampian Hills** (Hutchinson, 1958; Longman, 1959). Both are dog stories, conventional in plotting and characterization but vivid in their affectionate description of moors, highlands, animals, and those who care for them. Chipperfield once said that almost every one of his titles was based on some personal experience. *Storm of Dancerwood* (Hutchinson, 1948; Longman, 1949), his favorite book and considered by many his best, is highly autobiographical, being for the most part the story of his own German shepherd, Max, and their travels about Exmoor. He also used some of his experiences while tramping with Max for *Windruff* and *Rex of Larkbarrow* (Hutchinson, 1969). *Grey Chieftain* (Hutchinson, 1952; Roy, 1954) and *Sabre of Storm Valley* (Hutchinson, 1962; Roy, 1965), on the other hand, were based on movie dogs. His horse stories are also filled with action, among them, *Ghost Horse: Stallion of the Oregon Trail* (Hutchinson, 1959; Roy, 1962) and *Checoba, Stallion of the Comanche* (Hutchinson, 1964; Roy, 1966), set in the Old American West. He also wrote of other creatures in nature in such books as *Greeka, Eagle of the Hebrides* (Hutchinson, 1953; Longman, 1954) and *Rooloo, Stag of the Dark Water* (Hutchinson, 1955; Roy, 1962). For the former work, he spent many hours studying an eagles' nesting site on the Isle of Skye. He wrote a book of nonfiction, *The Story of a Great Ship: The Birth and Death* *of the Steamship Titanic* (Hutchinson, 1957; Roy, 1959) and, under the name John Eland Craig, *The Dog of Castle Crag* (Nelson, 1952) and two collections of short stories.

CHITTY CHITTY BANG BANG. See *Chitty-Chitty-Bang-Bang, the Magical Car*

CHITTY-CHITTY-BANG-BANG, THE MAGICAL CAR (Fleming*, Ian, Cape, 1964; *CHITTY CHITTY BANG BANG*, Random, 1964), light adventure fantasy starring a touring car endowed with a mind and abilities of its own. When inventor Commander Caractacus Pott, known locally as Commander Crackpott, sells his idea for whistling candies, which change tone as they are sucked, to Lord Skrumshus, the candy magnate, he decides his family needs an automobile. He and his wife, Mimsie, and their eight-year-old twins, Jeremy and Jemima, look at a great many cars and finally see an old wreck in a broken-down little garage run by a once-famous racing driver. Although it is rusty and broken, with moths in its upholstery and beetles under its carpets, they all know immediately that the four-seater open motorcar is exactly what they want. Jemima even notices that the license plate, GEN 11, spells Genii. While the children are at boarding school, Commander Pott works very hard on the car, and when they return they find a beautiful, completely refurbished, twelve-cylinder, eight-liter, supercharged Paragon Panther, with an array of dashboard knobs that even the Commander doesn't fully understand. The next day, a hot August Saturday, they head for the Dover beach, but, although the car (that Jeremy has named for the noise she makes, like two sneezes and two thumps) can go well over 100 miles per hour, they are soon stalled in traffic. A light on one of the dashboard knobs reads, "Pull," and when they hesitate, adds, "Idiot!" When the Commander obeys the directions, the big front mudguards swivel outward, so that they stick out like wings; the car undergoes other automatic transformations and then takes off like an airplane. They look down at crowded beaches, but Chitty-Chitty-Bang-Bang flies right past them and out to the Goodwin Sands, acres of sand out in the channel exposed

at low tide, and lands them there for their
picnic. While they are all dozing on the sand,
however, the tide begins to come in, and by the
time they notice it, Chitty-Chitty-Bang-Bang's
wheels are nearly submerged. On the dashboard a
light blinks urgently, showing the words, "Turn
the knob." When the Commander obeys, the wheels
turn sideways and act like propellers, and
Chitty-Chitty-Bang-Bang moves through the water
like a motorboat. Instead of steering for Dover,
however, Commander Potts opts for adventure and
heads the vehicle toward France. In the fog they
are nearly run down by a big ship, but they
avoid disaster as they make for Calais. The
strong current keeps pushing them southward so
that they touch the beach at the base of
gigantic French chalk cliffs. Jeremy explores
for a way to get up before the tide reaches them
and finds the mouth of a cave above the high
water mark. They drive Chitty-Chitty-Bang-Bang,
now transformed again to an automobile, into the
entrance. By her powerful headlights they see
that the cave extends far into the cliffs, then
curves and climbs. Although the cave is
booby-trapped with a hanging skeleton, a live
wire, and a false door that looks like a cliff
wall, they drive upward, avoiding the obstacles,
until they come to a room full of packing boxes
that contain arms and explosives. From a slip in
a packing box they discover that these belong to
Joe the Monster, a notorious gangster who
operates on both sides of the English Channel.
The Commander sets a fuse, and, after driving
the car a good distance away, lights it, blowing
up the cave and a large chunk of the cliff in an
exciting display of fireworks. Unfortunately, a
car coming toward them contains Joe the Monster
with his sidekicks, Man-Mountain Fink, his
muscle man; Soapy Sam, his explosive expert; and
Blood-Money Banks, a blackmailer. Just as these
villains are about to set a fuse in the gas tank
and light it, Chitty-Chitty-Bang-Bang again
takes charge, changes into an airplane, and
whisks the Potts off to the main road into
Calais, where they stop at the Hotel Splendide,
lock the car in a garage, and enjoy a delicious
dinner. Joe the Monster, however, is not so
easily foiled. In the middle of the night he and
his cohorts climb a ladder to the room where

Jeremy and Jemima sleep, tie the corners of their sheets together, and scoop them up like bundles of laundry. The twins soon discover that they are to be part of Joe's next holdup, of a famous candy store in Paris run by Monsieur Bon-Bon. Joe gives them a 5,000-franc bank note and tells them they are to go into the store just at closing time and ask for a 4.000-franc box of chocolates. Together the children figure out that then Monsieur Bon-Bon will have to go to his till to change their note, and that the gangsters will dash in and take the keys to the safe from the till. Jeremy prints "Gangsters" with holes made by his knife in the bank note, hoping that Monsieur Bon-Bon will notice the odd feel and, holding the note up to the light, will be warned. Their plan works beautifully. Monsieur Bon-Bon sees the word on the note, dashes to slam and bar the door, lowers the steel shutters, and phones the police. In the meantime, Chitty-Chitty-Bang-Bang has been aware of the kidnapping and has shot up her radar antenna to track the gangsters and then sounds her klaxton horn until the Commander and Mimsie wake. They speed to Paris, leaving the direction to the car's radar, and are able to apprehend the villains as they are trying to escape. The next day, Chitty-Chitty-Bang-Bang flies the family back to Dover. The story is all plot (not very convincing even on the level for younger readers), and, despite the abundance of action, the style is strangely ponderous, with much author intrusion and paragraphs of information interspersed throughout, telling why ships are spoken of in feminine gender, how football matches are played on Goodwin Sands, how wreckers operate from Dover to strip wrecks on the Sands, what sort of vessels are to be found on the English Channel, and so on. The appeal of the book is in the concept of a wonderfully versatile and intelligent car, a surefire popular idea and certain to be filmed, as it was by the United Artists studios. Choice.

CHORISTERS' CAKE (Mayne*, William, ill. C. Walter Hodges, Oxford, 1956; Bobbs, 1958), realistic school novel, the second of Mayne's Canterbury Choir stories, set in late October and early November in the 1950s, following the

plot pattern of the first book, involving the
same adults and some of the same boys, and featuring a new protagonist. When Dr. Sunderland,
the amiable and portly organist who swallows
the ends of his words, decides to appoint
another Chorister and pointedly remarks it is
high time Peter Sandwell, called Sandy, becomes
one, and when Head Boy Trevithic agrees, that's
enough to make stubborn, often inattentive,
underachiever Sandy rebel. To "chiz" Trevithic
and curry favor with Michael Stanhope, already
chosen as Chorister but not yet installed, Sandy
cooks up a plot to pit the two groups of
singers, Decani and Cantoris, against each
other. After a complicated series of comic opera
conversations and acts culminates in fisticuffs
between the rival sets of boys, Head Master Mr.
Ardent investigates the shameful incident, and,
to the boy's credit, Sandy owns up. Mr. Ardent
lectures him on his responsibility to the
school (school comes first, self last) and is
willing to drop the matter at that, but the boys
invoke the rule of silence to bring Sandy in
line: no one speaks to him directly; everyone
ignores him as much as possible. Trevithic tells
him bluntly, "We're tired of your being such a
fool and not behaving properly," and says that
he's been a general nuisance. After several
days of the silent treatment, Sandy realizes
that the only way to get his life back to
normal is to pass Dr. Sunderland's test and
become a Chorister. Since he is deficient in
musical theory, he borrows a copy of *Exposi-
tions of Musical Theory* from Dr. Sunderland but
refuses Trevithic's help with theory, because he
feels Trevithic isn't interested in helping him
but is only concerned about the Cathedral. To
spite Trevithic, he accepts Stanhope's offer of
help and then in turn helps Paterson, another
candidate, who has started to speak to him. At
the same time as the boys look forward to the
Chorister examination, they prepare for Guy
Fawkes Day. Again to spite Trevithic, who, with
Prefect Madington, is to construct the guy,
Sandy collects and hides shavings for stuffing
the guy from the Pergales, three generations of
the same family who operate the Cathedral
carpentry workshop. On October 29, Dr. Sunderland examines the several boys who are up for

Chorister in both voice and theory. Sandy passes, is chosen for the position, and discovers to his amazement that he's glad he is good enough to occupy the office. The traditional Choristers' Cake is provided for the boys in honor of Sandy and Stanhope, and of Paterson, who is to receive a badge, and Sandy contributes a guy he has made with the Pergales' help for the annual celebration on November 5. Almost a carbon copy in plot of *A Swarm in May**, *Choristers' Cake* is less dramatic and slower moving but shares its predecessor's rich local color and subtle humor. It is often hard to follow, however, being highly understated, and in some parts is almost incomprehensible for one unfamiliar with life in an English boys' school. Carnegie Com.

CHRESTOMANCI (*Charmed Life**), enchanter who takes an interest in Cat* and Gwendolen* Chant and proves to be their uncle. A tall, lean, elegantly dressed man, he contrasts with his pleasant, dumpy wife and two plump children. His name proves to be a title, signifying an office whose obligation it is to keep the witches, warlocks, and other magicians in check and restricted to their own worlds. Unsure of whether or not Cat is aware of how Gwendolen is using his power to produce nasty occurrences, Chrestomanci ignores her actions until she goes too far and causes almost irredeemable trouble.

CHRIS FAIRFAX (*The Plan for Birdmarsh**), older brother of Paul*; he has invented an inflatable survival suit and is more intent on testing it than he is on the prospects of Birdsmarsh being exploited for commercial reasons. Although Chris is not completely callous, he does not share Paul's love for the farm, and he is single-mindedly set on proving his invention and making his fortune. Twice he is nearly drowned. Because he is so wrapped up in his own interests, he refuses to put any credence in Paul's doubts about the good intentions of Peter Winnington.

CHRISTIAN FANSHAWE-SMITHE (*A Long Way from Verona**), immature but intense son of a rural dean who despises his family's bourgeois pretensions and Christianity, considers himself

a communist, and admires Fred Vye, father of
Jessica*, extravagantly. He is very good-
looking, with longish blond hair. Jessica thinks
he looks just like Rupert Brooke, and her father
refers to him as, "That Adonis. That Romeo. That
fellow who can't stop talking about setting the
world to rights." Though he takes Jessica to see
"real life," Christian is completely distraught
by the bombing in Dunedin Street, and Jessica
has to get him onto a bus headed for his home
and then get herself back alone. Some weeks
later he appears across the street from
Jessica's home with his brother, Giles,
obviously trying to get up nerve to call. She
marches out to see him with her brother, Rowley,
under her arm, and, while Giles entertains
Rowley, she discovers that Christian feels he
has somehow called down the destruction on
Dunedin Street and is responsible for the
bombing. She scolds him for not using his head.
Her crush on him has disappeared, but evidently
he is still interested in her: when her poem
appears in *The Times*, he sends a card signed,
"love, Christian" and her only comment is, "very
childish writing."

CHRISTINA PARSONS (*Flambards*; *The Edge of the
Cloud*; *Flambards in Summer*), orphan who goes
to live at the estate of her Uncle* Russell
and becomes involved in his discordant family,
and later wife of William* Russell. At twelve,
when she first is summoned to Flambards,
Christina is a quiet girl who has learned to fit
into households where she is not much wanted by
making herself useful and inconspicuous, and she
is appalled by the neglect at Flambards and
violent emotions that are the norm there. It
does not worry her much that her uncle wants her
only because she will inherit a small fortune
when she is twenty-one and that he plans to have
Mark*, his older son, marry her, since this all
seems to be in the unreal future. She pleases
her uncle by becoming a superb rider, better
even than reckless Mark, but her sympathies are
mostly with William, the younger son, who has,
like his father, been crippled in a hunting
accident. She quarrels frequently with Mark and
is much attracted to the gentle, sensitive
stable boy, Dick* Wright, but she thinks the

gulf between the family and the servants so
great that she cannot imagine really loving
Dick. By going to the Hunt Ball with Will, who
has been forced to leave home, she incurs Mark's
fury, and when she refuses the same night to
consider marrying him, she realizes that she
can't go back to living at Flambards. Her love
for Will is, she realizes, greater than his love
for her, since his first devotion will always be
to airplanes and flying. In *The Edge of the
Cloud*, her main role is enduring her worry for
his safety and her terror when he insists that
she fly with him, and concealing her true
emotions so that he will not scorn her. In
Flambards in Summer, she is more assertive and
seems to have more genuine emotion in her
antagonism to Mark and her love for both Tizzy*
and Dick Wright. A sequel published some twelve
years after the trilogy, *Flambards Divided*,
tells of the breakup of her marriage to Dick
after Mark comes home wounded and of her prospects of marriage to Mark, but has never been
as popular as the original books.

A CHRISTMAS CAROL (Dickens*, Charles, ill. John
Leech, Chapman and Hall, 1843; Routledge, 1843),
fantasy detailing the rehabilitation of an old
miser through the spirit of Christmas. Ebenezer*
Scrooge is a grasping, disagreeable, mean-
spirited old skinflint who underpays his clerk,
Bob Cratchit. One holiday he refuses to
contribute to a fund for Christmas food for the
poor and answers his nephew's good wishes of the
season with, "Bah! Humbug!" That very evening
when he approaches his gloomy dwelling, he sees
in the knocker the face of his partner, Jacob
Marley, dead seven years. Startled but refusing
to be dismayed, he enters, double-locks the
door, and is eating his evening bowl of weak
gruel when Marley's ghost appears coming through
the closed door, dragging a great chain made of
money boxes and ledgers. He predicts that
Scrooge will be visited by three spirits, his
only chance to escape a fate like that of
Marley, whose spirit must travel through the
world in misery, through the world tormented by
remorse. As the clock finishes striking
midnight, the first spirit appears, a figure
like both a child and an old man, wearing a

crown from which springs a jet of light and carrying an extinguisher, like a cap, under its arm. It introduces itself as the Ghost of Christmas Past and takes Scrooge to scenes from his earlier life. Two are at his old school, the first when he is a lonely boy deserted there at Christmas, comforted only by the characters from books he is reading, and later when he is almost a young man and is fetched by his sister, little Fan, his father having relented and allowed him to come home for the holiday. The next is a festive occasion at the business where he is apprenticed, a dance given by Old Fezziwig*. The last two are with Belle, the girl to whom he was engaged, when she says that she has been replaced in his heart by a golden idol and she releases him from his promise, and years later, when her husband tells her he has seen Scrooge, quite alone in the world, working on the night his partner is dying. The second spirit, the Ghost of Christmas Present, is an ample, jolly giant dressed in a robe of green trimmed with white fur and wearing a wreath of holly. The spirit takes him through the streets, both rich and poor, where people are rejoicing, and then to the Cratchit home where the large family is preparing dinner and Bob comes in from church, carrying his little crippled son, Tiny* Tim, on his shoulder. Despite a rather small goose and pudding, they have a joyous time, the only sour note coming when Bob proposes a toast to "Mr. Scrooge, the Founder of the Feast," and the family responds with a trace of bitterness. Next they go to the home of Scrooge's nephew, Fred, and his pretty wife, where a group is playing parlor games with such zest that Scrooge enters into the game, unseen and unheard. Before he disappears, the ghost reveals two emaciated children clinging beneath his robe, the boy Ignorance and the girl Want. The Ghost of Christmas Yet To Come is a tall, silent figure shrouded in a black garment. Without speaking, he leads Scrooge through the business district, where he overhears a couple of conversations regarding a recent death that obviously causes no grief to the speakers. From there they go to a foul, wretched part of town where three people, a charwoman, a laundress, and an under-taker's man, sell the possessions, bedclothes,

and even the shirt that they have scavenged
from the dead man's rooms to a junk dealer. When
Scrooge asks if there is no one who shows
emotion at this death, the spirit takes him to
a young couple for whom the death gives them a
reprieve from a foreclosure and who cannot help
feeling happiness. When he begs the spirit to
show him some tenderness at a death, he is taken
again to the Cratchit home, where the family is
bravely trying to bear up after their loss of
Tiny Tim. Before the ghost parts from him,
Scrooge is escorted to a churchyard, where he
sees a neglected stone bearing the name Ebenezer
Scrooge. He pleads with the ghost to say that
these are not necessarily images of what will
happen, only of what might happen, and as he
grasps the spirit in entreaty, he finds he is
holding his own bedpost. Relieved, in fact
delighted to find that the curtains and
bedclothes are still there, he frisks about his
rooms, then throws up the window and calls to a
passing boy to ask what the day is. When the
lad, amazed, says it is Christmas Day, Scrooge
sends him off to the poulterer's to buy the
biggest goose and has it sent to the Cratchit
family. He then goes to church and walks about
the streets and, coming upon the men to whom he
rudely refused a contribution for the poor the
day before, insists on making a very generous
donation. Although he must whip up his courage,
he then goes to his nephew's house, apologizes
for his former attitude, and accepts the
invitation to dinner that he scorned before. The
next morning he sets a trap for Bob Cratchit,
catches him coming in late, pretends severity,
and announces that he plans to raise his salary
and help his struggling family. He is as good as
his word, becomes like a second father to Tiny
Tim, and keeps Christmas in the true spirit ever
after. Although not written for children, the
book has been a seasonal favorite for many years
with the young as well as with their elders,
frequently dramatized on stage and film, and
often recited as a "reading" for Christmas
programs. If its story is rather sentimental, it
redeems itself with a wealth of memorable
characters and with rich language in a
storytelling style full of wit and vivid
metaphor. Books Too Good; Children's Classics;

Fanfare.

CHRISTOPHER (*The Blue Boat**), English schoolboy, who with his brother, Hugh*, paddles about in a blue rowboat on a shallow lake near the coast and encounters two circus performers, with whom the boys play imaginative games. Christopher is an earnest youth, who has a strong sense of right and wrong and an understanding of the importance of rules. He justifies not obeying Mrs. Wrigley, however, by pretending along with Hugh that she is a witch. He misses his parents, who are in Africa, but is resigned to not living with them any longer, since he knows he will have to return to boarding school. He also is resigned to not understanding everything he is asked to do, for example, in church. He is very understanding with Hugh, and, when Hugh says he feels the need to cry, he just lets him cry until he feels better. Christopher is less imaginative than Hugh, and a good deal less adventuresome, but he is also more responsible. He is a well-drawn, likeable figure who changes little, but in the context of the story his lack of dynamism makes no significant difference.

CHRISTOPHER (*A Chance Child**), older brother of Creep*, who has fed him, mostly from his own plate, tried to teach him and tell him something of the world outside his closet, and who tries passionately to find him after he escapes. Although he has insisted to the welfare worker that he is hunting for his brother and she has pointed out that he has never had one, after he has seen the letters CREEP scratched into the bridge arch and realized that they are very old, he gives up for a while and meekly agrees that he has no brother. However, he cannot sleep for worrying about what had happened to Creep, and eventually consults the history teacher and, walking the long way to the central library at every opportunity, starts reading the Parliamentary Papers, the records of investigations in the 1830s and 1840s into the conditions of factory work and child labor. Though poorly educated and scruffy, Christopher has been better treated by his mother and is torn by his compassion for his abused half-brother and his

fear that his mother will get into trouble if
he tells about Creep.

CHRISTOPHER, JOHN (CHRISTOPHER SAMUEL YOUD)
(1922-   ), born in Knowsley, Lancashire; author
who popularized science fiction for middle-grade
readers with, in particular, his Tripods and
Sword trilogies. He attended Peter Symonds's
School in Winchester. After serving in the Royal
Signals from 1941-1946, he worked as a freelance
writer for two years with the aid of a Rocke-
feller-Atlantic Award. He then worked in the
information bureau of a diamond cutting firm,
leaving there in 1958 to write full-time on his
own. He has written novels of several kinds for
adults, comedy, detective stories, sports
novels, and also published poetry under the name
Anthony Rye, but he is best known for his
fantasies and science fiction. His earliest
books were published under his own name of
Samuel Youd. Later, he wrote also as Peter
Graaf, Hilary Ford, William Godfrey, and Peter
Nichols. He came to writing for children and
young people after becoming well established as
an author for adults. He was asked by an editor
at Hamish Hamilton to do an adventure story for
adolescents, refused the commission, but then
finished the book. After several revisions, the
novel was published as *The White Mountains**
(Hamilton, 1967; Macmillan, 1967), the first of
the Tripods or White Mountains trilogy, and was
followed by *The City of Gold and Lead** (Hamilton, 1967; Macmillan, 1967) and *The Pool of
Fire** (Hamilton, 1968; Macmillan, 1968). About
efforts to destroy powerful and tyrannical
extraterrestrial invaders called Masters who
have conquered Earth and have no regard for
human life and filled with excitement and conflict, all three appear on the *Choice* and George
G. Stone lists, and the initial book also is
included in *Books Too Good to Miss*. His fifth
book for young readers, *The Guardians** (Hamilton, 1970; Macmillan, 1970), set in a twenty-
first-century England that is sharply divided
into County and Conurbs and is under the control
of an elite governing class who regard themselves as benevolent dictators, won the
Guardian and Christopher awards, and, translated
into German, received the German Children's

Best Book Prize in 1976. He has completed two more trilogies: the highly regarded Sword series, *The Prince in Waiting* (Hamilton, 1970; Macmillan, 1970), *Beyond the Burning Lands* (Hamilton, 1971; Macmillan, 1971), and *The Sword of the Spirits* (Hamilton, 1972; Macmillan, 1972), concerning a youth, Luke, who is destined to become ruler of a city-state in an England that has reverted to feudalism; and the recent Fireball set, *Fireball* (Gollancz, 1981; Dutton, 1981), *New Found Land* (Gollancz, 1983; Dutton, 1983), and *Dragon Dance* (Viking, 1986; Dutton, 1986), in which two youths are drawn by a fireball into societies at different periods. *Empty World* (Hamilton, 1977; Dutton, 1978) postulates a future earth depopulated by a deadly virus, and *Wild Jack* (Hamilton, 1974; Macmillan, 1974) features a Robin Hood-like figure who urges resistance against tyrannical overlords of the future. Christopher's characters are usually shallow and passive, his incidents are underdeveloped, and his recurring themes of freedom of thought and action and the role of authority are easily grasped, but the books exude excitement, are often thrilling, and are less dependent on technology and gadgetry than most books of the genre. He has called his books "adventure stories involving a study of human reactions to severe environmental stresses." He married two times, has four daughters and a son, and has made his home in Guernsey in the Channel Islands.

CHRISTOPHER ROBIN (*Winnie-the-Pooh**; *The House at Pooh Corner**), little boy patterned on Milne's own son, who is the only human in a series of episodic adventures with various animal characters based on his stuffed animals. Christopher Robin is clearly the most efficient and sensible character in the forest. On most occasions he is the one who solves the problem or gets his friends out of their difficulties, and they rightly look up to him. He is especially close to Pooh* Bear, of whom he frequently says, fondly, "Silly old bear!" At the end of the second book he is about to leave the charmed circle of his nursery friends and go off to school. He is also a character in Milne's two books of verse for children, *When We Were Very*

Young and *Now We Are Six*, but there he is more more often in a realistic setting with other humans.

CHUNDER (*The Nature of the Beast**), Charles Ernest Coward, grandfather of Bill*, who has helped raise him from infancy. A man with a sudden, violent temper, he rows continually with his son, Ned*, yet is really dependent on him emotionally and is shattered when he learns that Ned is in prison. The grandson of a gypsy woman and a fiery-tempered man who was hanged for killing the gypsy's husband, he has some acquaintance with gypsy lore, particularly in folk medicine and in raising fighting cocks. He is only two years from his retirement and pension when the mill closes, and he is ashamed of going on the dole.

CHURCH, RICHARD (THOMAS) (1893-1972), born in London; editor, journalist, poet, novelist. He attended Dulwich Hamlet School, London, and was a civil servant from 1909 to 1933, when he became an editor at the publishing house of J. M. Dent, where he worked until 1951. He was cofounder of *The Criterion*, London, in 1921, was a regular contributor to *The Spectator* and *New Statesman*, and for forty years contributed to the "Home Forum Page" of the *Christian Science Monitor*, Boston. Among his many honors was the Fayle Poetry Prize in 1957, fellowship in the Royal Society of Literature, 1950, and in the Royal Society of Art, 1970, and being named Commander, Order of the British Empire, in 1957. He wrote seven novels for children and for adults thirteen novels, one play, nineteen books of poetry, a biography of Mary Shelley, and many books of essays and criticism. The story of his life is told in *Over the Bridge: An Essay in Autobiography* (Heinemann, 1955; as *Over the Bridge: An Autobiography*, Dutton, 1956); in *The Golden Sovereign: A Conclusion to "Over the Bridge"* (Heinemann, 1957; Dutton, 1957); and in *The Voyage Home* (Heinemann, 1964; Day, 1966). Among his adventure books for young people is *The Cave** (Dent, 1951; as *Five Boys in a Cave*, Day, 1951), about a group of boys who get lost exploring a large underground network of caverns, and its sequel, *Down River* (Heinemann,

1958; Day, 1957). Others that received critical acclaim are *A Squirrel Called Rufus* (Dent, 1941; Winston, 1946), about a battle of red squirrels against a horde of invading gray squirrels, which can be viewed as allegory, and *The White Doe* (Heinemann, 1968; Day, 1969), a story of complex human relationship, set in the context of a forest and concern for a deer. *The Cave*, originally written for a grandson, has been selected for the *Horn Book* Fanfare list and translated into many languages.

CICELY BRADSHAW (*The Wool-Pack**), daughter of a Newbury clothier, 11, and betrothed to Nicholas* Fetterlock. Lively and high-spirited, she is obedient in most respects and aware of her place, but she still makes certain she knows what's going on so she can influence things to her best interests. She keeps an eye on the Lombards and passes information along to Nicholas. It is her idea to put hen feathers in the bales of wool so that they can be iden- tified as Fetterlock property. Cicely is a type, but an interesting one.

THE CIRCUS IS COMING (Streatfeild*, Noel, ill. Clarke Hutton, Dent, 1938; *CIRCUS SHOES*, Random, 1939), realistic career novel set in England in the mid-twentieth century in a traveling circus Peter* Possit, 12, and his sister, Santa*, 11, are orphans raised in London by their Aunt Rebecca, who has been lady's maid to a duchess and has acquired all her employer's snobbish attitudes and imposed them upon Peter and Santa, dressing them in fashionable clothes and isolating them from other children. When she dies, the inept tutors she has employed arrange to send the youngsters to orphan homes, but the idea of being separated so appalls them that they run away to an uncle that they know only from a postcard that says, "Cob's Circus." Though totally ignorant of the world away from Aunt Rebecca's, they find helpful people and arrive at the circus as it is setting up in Bridlington. To their surprise, since they've always assumed that they are related to the duchess, they find that Uncle Gus* Possit is a clown who lives in a caravan. Gus is equally surprised and somewhat dismayed to have these two dressed-up, glove-wearing children on his hands, and he finds it difficult to keep his patience with them, particularly with Peter, who seems to him a milksop. Compared with their previous dull, restricted life the circus is fascinating to Peter and Santa, and after a few unfortunate incidents they soon acquire their first friends, Olga and Sasha Petoff, whose father has performing horses; Fifi Moulin, whose mother has trained poodles; Fritzi and Hans Schmidt, whose family own the sea lions; and old Ben Willis, who cares for the stables. In the ensuing weeks they have some problems, mostly because they are ignorant of circus ways and because they can't seem to please Gus, but they become very attached to the way of life, and Peter loves the horses. Old Ben gives him riding lessons early in the morning when Gus will not know and no one is around to laugh, and Ted Kenet, partner to Gus on the trapeze, starts teaching Santa tumbling. The children worry about what will happen at the end of the summer, since Gus has only said that they can travel with him during the tenting season. A few things go right. Peter is the one who figures out that the best poodle is ill and that one of the elephants has turned rogue because they have been separated in the menagerie, but the elephant trainer takes credit for the insight. The celebration for Gus's birthday, which they feared had gotten out of hand, turns out to be successful. As the summer ends, Gus announces that he has arranged for them to go live with one of Aunt Rebecca's friends and go to school. Peter and Santa are miserable, but, since it is generous of Gus, they try to cover up. The last night a bad windstorm rips the big top and as the men are frantically getting out the horses, Peter sees a fire from a cigarette butt starting in one of the stalls. He gets the horse out, and he and Santa put out the flames with their coats. Mr. Cob, the owner, persuades Gus to change his mind and keep the children with him. Ben has trained Peter enough so he can soon take the place of an older Petoff boy, who wants to go to France with an acrobatic troupe. Ted says he will train Santa, who has a natural aptitude to be an acrobat. Many details of circus life are carefully woven into a predictable story

with an earnest tone. Both Peter and Gus are
believable characters, and their well-meaning
conflict provides most of the plot interest.
Carnegie Winner; Fanfare.

CIRCUS SHOES. See *The Circus Is Coming.*

THE CITY OF FROZEN FIRE (Wilkins*, Vaughan,
Cape, 1950; Macmillan, 1951), adventure novel
set in Pembrokeshire, England, and in the
fictional country of Quivera in South America in
1826. A strangely dressed gentleman speaking an
unfamiliar language arrives at the country home
of teenaged Christopher "Tops" Standish,
introduces himself as Prince Madoc of Quivera,
presents a letter to Tops's historian father,
and collapses. Tops's Aunt Penelope Standish,
24, known as Tuppenny*, cares for the wound
which has severed the man's left hand while Kit
Standish reads to Tops the letter from a judge
in New Orleans. From this and later questioning
of Madoc they learn that the prince is the
present ruler of a kingdom founded by the Welsh
under a Madoc who emigrated in the twelfth
century and prospered, enslaving the native
Indians and mining gold and extremely valuable
rubies. Later volcanic action cut the country
off from all outside entrance except the secret
Gate of Vapour. Recently, a convict ship was
wrecked on their shore and when the Quiverae
rescued them, the influenza of one stranger
spread through the country, killing many. The
foreigners then armed the Indians, seized the
City of Cibola, and are now raiding the other
settlements. The present Madoc set off to seek
help but was shipwrecked and taken to New
Orleans. There the judge learned some of his
history from the limited Latin Madoc could speak
and sent him on the barque *Ursula Howell* to
consult Standish, a scholar of Welsh history.
The crew, being little better than pirates,
robbed and wounded Madoc, but he escaped with
his ruby diadem. Three sinister characters
arrive, a dapper, evil little man, Captain*
Vansittart Darkness; a huge Negro named Baby;
and a grotesque man with a large hooked nose,
Mr. Charlie Yemm*. They kill a servant, steal
the diadem, and escape in the *Ursula Howell*.
The good characters, including Tops, his father,

Tuppenny, her gallant admirer, Sir Richard Gayner, and an old shipbuilder and munitions-maker, set off with Madoc in the steam-vessel *Volcano*, heading for the island of Natividad where Madoc was wrecked and where he buried the gold plates giving directions to Quivera. There they find Yemm, ostensibly marooned by Captain Darkness, who has already seized the plates, and they take him aboard. In the country of Quivera, Tops meets a fiery princess about his age, Olwen*, who converses with him in Latin and insists on learning to shoot his gun. While the adults recapture Cibola, Tops and Olwen adventure on their own and are captured by Darkness, who was not drowned as had been reported but is in league with Yemm and uses them as hostages aboard the *Volcano*, which he captures, expecting to get all the treasure aboard, and then do them in. Along with Aunt Tuppenny and the munition maker's assistant, Li Ching-ku, they turn the tables, fake an explosion of the boilers with the fireworks made by Li, and recapture the ship. Captain Darkness kills Yemm in a fit of anger and is himself killed by one of his former allies. The pirates who escape are later hanged for gunrunning. A deliberate explosion seals off the only entrance to Quivera from the outside world, but Olwen is discovered to have stowed away on the *Volcano*. The romantic story is fast-paced and full of action. In comparison to *Treasure Island**, with which it has many things in common, it is less convincing and overplotted. Yemm, the good-bad character, is not as believable or likable as Long* John Silver, but the bizarre characters and setting are interest-ing and the whole swashbuckling adventure is fun. Slavery in Quivera is not criticized. Fan-fare.

THE CITY OF GOLD AND LEAD (Christopher*, John, Hamilton, 1967; Macmillan, 1967), action-filled science fiction novel set 100 years in the future in northwest Europe; second in the Tripods or White Mountains series narrated by Will Parker. The story begins six months after Will leaves Wherton, England, where his father is the village miller. He, Beanpole (Jean-Paul Deliet), and his cousin Henry Parker are now living inside the White Mountains somewhwere in central Europe along with other refugees from the Tripods. Their commander is wise, elderly, lame Julius, who devised the scheme of using pseudo-Vagrants (Vagrants are social misfits) like Ozymandias to win recruits to the cause of destroying the Tripods. The three youths become part of a small cadre being trained to participate in the annual summer athletic games in Germany. Traditionally, the winners are feasted and then taken to live in the Tripods' City. It is hoped that at least one of the White Mountain youths will be among the victors, will be taken into the City, and will be able to escape and bring back information about the Tripods. Julius chooses Will, a boxer, to compete (though he cautions the youth about his rashness), and Beanpole, a hurdler, but chooses instead of Henry a taciturn and withdrawn German boy named Fritz, whom Will does not much like at first, but later comes to appreciate as steady and levelheaded. The boys travel to a large river, where they join a friendly, bargeman named Ulf and proceed downstream. When Will and Beanpole become separated from Ulf and Fritz, they trudge the river path to catch up, then build a makeshift raft out of an old hut, and, cold, hungry, and wet from cloudbursts, are borne downstream until a Tripod discovers them and steps on their raft, dumping them into the river. They struggle to an island where a hermit named Hans feeds them and gives them shelter. When they realize he intends to force them to stay and work for him, they steal his rowboat and depart hastily. At the games, Fritz and Will win their respective contests and along with several other victors are soon taken inside Tripods and transported into the City, where they will have the "privilege" of serving the Tripods as slaves. The boys discover that the City is an immense structure consisting of many pyramid-shaped buildings surrounded by a golden wall and enclosed by a green crystal dome. The atmosphere is light green, extremely hot, and so heavy that the human slaves soon become old from the leaden weight of the gravity on their limbs, and their skins soon become pallid and unhealthy from the greenish light. The average life expectancy of a slave is two

years, in spite of their air helmets and rooms
specially equipped for their needs. The boys
also discover that the Tripods are merely
devices of transportation for the Masters who
rule the City. The Masters are huge, green,
reptilian creatures with stumpy legs and no
necks, which spend many hours soaking in pools.
The boys also make the horrifying discovery
that, even though their lives are wretched, the
human slaves consider themselves a select,
honored group. In the slave choosing, Fritz is
taken by a cruel Master who often beats him, but
Will is more fortunate, being chosen by one who
is contemplative and interested in the history
and ways of humans. His Master often converses
with Will and grows fond of him, holding him and
petting him as though he were a dog. He also
suffers from a strange disease, the Curse of the
Skloodzi. To get relief, he inhales intoxicating
gas bubbles. Will's Master takes him on a tour
of the City, showing him the Pyramid of Beauty,
which is a kind of museum of the human world.
There Will is horrified to see preserved
specimens of girls who have been brought to the
City as slaves (among them, Will's friend,
Eloise), dressed in finery and lying like the
others in state in transparent caskets. Though
separated, Will and Fritz manage to communicate
and gradually collect information about the
Masters, a task at which Fritz is more zealous
than Will, whose life is considerably easier.
One day, in a fit of melancholy brought on by an
attack of the Sickness, Will's Master reveals
broad details of the Plan, by which in four
years the Masters intend to annihilate all
earthly life and set up conditions on the planet
suitable for them. He says that a spaceship with
the technology to accomplish this has already
left their home planet. A crisis occurs when
Will's Master discovers Will has been recording
information about the City and realizes Will is
different from the other slaves who have no
interest in books or writing and is not as
obsequious as the other slaves. As he is about
to discover that Will's Cap (headbands by which
the Tripods control human beings) is fake, Will
strikes him between the nose and mouth, the only
place, Will has learned, that the Masters are
vulnerable, and kills him. The two boys hastily

make their way to the wall by night and locate the outlet of the river that flows through the City. At the last minute, Fritz refuses to leave, choosing to stay to provide cover for Will, who is stronger physically and hence more likely to escape successfully. He says he will join Will in three days. If escape proves impossible, he will go to the Place of Happy Release, the room in which slaves voluntarily commit suicide when they feel they can no longer satisfactorily serve their masters. Will makes a harrowing escape by river under the wall and is rescued from the torrent by Beanpole, who has fortunately come to the City to see if he may be of help. The boys wait twelve days for Fritz, leave when he doesn't appear, assuming he is dead, and make for the White Mountains. The book is full of action and suspense and much more exciting than the other two in the trilogy, with event following event in rapid order. Will's objective, understated, reportorial style of telling what happens and of describing the Masters and their City makes them seem more real and terrible than would a more emotional account. The setting is worked out in precision, even to descriptions of the Masters' recreations, and small details add to the credibility: the slaves must suck on salt sticks because of the intense heat, their helmets need special sponges for filtering the air that must be replaced periodically, airlocks make it possible to pass from the slaves' cubicles to the Masters' atmosphere, and the Masters' illness induces melancholy and strange brown spots on their green hides. Characters are shallow types, though ironically Christopher gives Will's Master some roundness. Beanpole's appearance at the end is entirely too fortuitous, but Will's plight at that point is so dire and the fate that awaits him if he doesn't escape so potentially horrible that the reader accepts the conclusion in spite of its lack of invention. The first book in the trilogy is *The White Mountains**, and the third is *The Pool of Fire**. Choice; Stone.

CLARA (*Kept in the Dark**), at twelve a girl of strong emotions, quick temper, and warm sympathies, middle of the three children who go to live with their grandparents. At first attracted to their half-cousin, David*, because he is an orphan who says he always longed for a family and because he kisses and fondles her, she eventually sees through him and then has to force herself to be nice, hoping thereby to keep him from provoking Grandpa* into a heart attack.

CLARKE, PAULINE (1921-   ), born in Kirkby-in-Ashfield, Nottinghamshire, daughter of a clergyman. Journalist, lecturer, and poet and author of fiction for children, she is best known for her Carnegie Award-winning fantasy, *The Twelve and the Genii** (Faber, 1962; as *The Return of the Twelves*, Coward, 1963). An English schoolboy finds in the attic of his farmhouse the twelve soldiers immortalized by Branwell Bronte in *The History of the Young Men* and helps them return to their proper home at Haworth in Yorkshire. Original in concept, the book blends excellent characterizations with action, humor, excitement, and important themes of respect and concern for others. The book also appears on the *Choice* and Fanfare lists, was selected for the Lewis Carroll Shelf, in Germany received the Deutsche Jugend Buchpreis, and was an honor book in the New York *Herald Tribune* Children's Spring Book Festival of 1964. She has written several doll stories under the name Helen Clare (Lane; Prentice); *Silver Bells and Cockle Shells* (Abelard, 1962), a book of verse; and contemporary stories such as *Keep the Pot Boiling* (Faber, 1961), an episodic novel about a family's efforts to make money; and *The White Elephant* (Faber, 1952; Abelard, 1957), a thriller. For very young readers, she has written the stories of James, *James the Policeman*, *James and the Robbers*, *James and the Smugglers*, and *James and the Black Van* (Hamilton, 1957-63) and an alphabet book, *Crowds of Creatures* (Faber, 1964). More recently, for older readers she published a magic-fantasy, *The Two Faces of Silenus* (Faber, 1972; Coward, 1972), in which two teenagers become involved with characters from Greek mythology. She went to school in London and Essex, then received her honors degree in English from Somerville College, Oxford, in 1943. She married Anglo-Saxon historian Peter Hunter Blair in 1969, and the couple lived in Cambridge. He died in 1982. She has lived in Norfolk, which provided background for several of her books, among them *The Boy with the Erpingham Hood* (Faber, 1956), a historical novel set in the Middle Ages. Also historical is *Torolv the Fatherless* (Faber, 1959), set during the Viking period. After receiving her degree, she worked for a children's magazine, then wrote a story for an illustrator friend, Cecil Leslie, *The Pekinese Princess* (Cape, 1948), a dog fantasy, her first published book and the first of many that Miss Leslie would illustrate for her. In 1963, she directed a seminar for the British Council in Accra to teach Ghanians how to write children's stories in English with African settings. Her series of short plays about an African family written for the BBC Overseas Education Department was recorded for use in teaching English to African children. She has also lectured, reviewed books for notable publications, and written short stories, plays, and articles for adults.

CLIFF TRENT (*Noah's Castle**), assistant manager of the chain shoestore that Norman Mortimer, called Father*, manages. Cliff is a shy, diffident man, who is attracted to Nessie* Mortimer. She likes him, but not as a sweetheart. Cliff has been lodging with the Mortimers and must find another place to live when Father abruptly moves the family to the Mount. When Father suggests to Barry* that the Farrars take in a lodger to ease their financial problems, Barry arranges for Cliff to move in with them, a situation that proves beneficial to them all. Cliff is a volunteer at Share Alike, a social welfare agency committed to helping the poor, aged, and destitute, and he introduces Barry to the organization. It is Cliff's idea that Father can best avoid trouble with the government (which intends to prosecute hoarders) and with potential blackmailers, blackmarketers, and vandals by turning over his supplies to Share Alike, and he so suggests to Barry when Barry shares with him his dilemma of what to do about Father.

CLIMBING TO DANGER (Allan*, Mabel Esther,

Heinemann, 1969; *MYSTERY IN WALES*, Vanguard, 1970), realistic novel of mystery and suspense set in the Snowden peaks of northern Wales in the late 1960s. Bronwen Parry, 18, now of Norfolk, tells of the experiences she, her brother, Robert, and friends Adam and Tina Carson, brother and sister, have one August during a mountain-climbing trip in her native Wales. Right away strange happenings disturb their holiday. While hiking into Melynedd Valley, they are caught in a rainstorm and take shelter for the night in the area's now ramshackle manor house, where Robert discovers the body of a tramp, which then mysteriously disappears. Then the Owens, long-time family friends at whose farm the party have intended to stay, are strangely inhospitable. Mrs. Owen, usually warm and maternal, seems distant and jumpy, normally affable Mr. Owen is irritable and looks old and worn for his years, and Ceiridwen, the daughter, is sullen and sharp. While climbing, the four observe two police cars visiting the farm. Then Tina's radio disappears, Bronwen overhears the Owens arguing privately, and the four discover a postcard to the Owens, postmarked Manchester, from their son, Glyn, who Mrs. Owen has told the four has emigrated to Australia and who Bronwen remembers as rebellious, pugnacious, and out for easy money. Bronwen suspects that Glyn is in some kind of trouble and the Owens are shielding him. The next day on the mountain, the four encounter climbers who tell them that Glyn Owen is wanted for robbery and murder in Manchester. They realize that Owen was probably the tramp Robert saw in the old house, and Bronwen is convinced that he is hiding in the cave behind the waterfall along the path just over the stile. She ponders her dilemma of loyalty to her old friends and responsibility under the law. The four decide it best to leave the farm the next morning before trouble strikes, but late that night Bronwen is unable to sleep and goes for a walk. She encounters Glyn in the darkness as he comes from the cave to the house for his evening meal, and the Owens take her and the others prisoner. The next day Glyn holds the girls hostage behind the waterfall, while the boys, Robert with a sprained ankle and Adam ostensibly keeping him company, put the police off with the story that the girls are hiking in the mountains. The next night Bronwen tries to escape to the village, descending from her window on a rope made of sheets and a quilt, but along the way she is intercepted and recaptured by Glyn. Much later that night, Ceiridwen, fed up with her trouble-making brother, helps them all escape and in-structs them to flee to the abandoned mine up the mountain. There follows a tense chase with Glyn, and soon also Mr. Owen, both armed and pursuing the four along the misty and treach-erous mountain paths. Bronwen slips and falls down the precipice above a lake, her descent broken by a boulder. Seeing her so close to death, Glyn experiences a change of heart, heroically attempts a rescue, loses his footing, and falls to his death in the lake below. Adam bravely effects the rescue, and all return safely to the Owen farm. Adam declares his love for Bronwen, the two become engaged, and Robert and Tina also make plans to marry. Characters are types, interest lies in plot, and tension builds agreeably as the author combines mystery and mountain-climbing story conventions. Glyn's heroism seems incongruous with his character as revealed. Bronwen's theory that Glyn's going wrong is due to parental indulgence seems to voice contemporary opinions about rearing chil-dren. Poe Nominee.

CLIPPER (*The Member for the Marsh**), David Ros-ley's friend, the eldest of the four schoolboys in and the president of the Harmonious Mud Stickers. He has a reputation for cleverness, laziness, and breaking promises because he doesn't keep his mind on things. He is the keeper of the clove candies the boys are partial to, organizes their meetings, is more intel-lectual and well-read than the others, and often quotes from writers like Coleridge and Dickens, or whatever he happens to be reading at school. Since he is farther along in school, he knows about matters like neolithic villages and national monuments. He is an interesting figure, rounded but less attractive than the more lively Kitson*.

CLIVE BRADLEY (*The Owl Service**), almost the

stereotypical English businessman, secure in his position and means. Clive is eager that his new family gets on well together, however, and wants particularly that Margaret* not be aggravated by household problems. He tries to placate Nancy* with liberal gifts of money; she takes them but despises him for it. She compares him unfavorably with Bertram, the previous owner of the house and in her mind the finest example of an English gentleman. Clive is pleasant, innocuous, fond of his family, an aspiring sportsman, not too bright, and goodnatured. Allison* calls him a "rough diamond."

CLODHA (*The Stronghold**), daughter of Nectan*, the chief of the Boar people; sister of Fand*; foster-sister of Coll; betrothed of Niall*. As elder daughter, she is the one through whom the succession of the tribe passes; hence, it is expected that Niall will be the next chief. She is a proud, strong-minded, young woman of sixteen. She realizes that Taran* wishes to take over the headship of the tribe and knows that if he does, she will have to marry him. Since she despises him, she works to defeat him. She is sympathetic to Coll's plans for a stronghold, and, when the Romans attack, takes her place as a warrior among the men. Without hesitation, she deals the deathblow to Taran when he attempts to betray the tribe to the Romans. She is a strongly drawn character, likeable and interesting.

CLOGGER DUNCAN (*The Machine Gunners**), tough boy from Glasgow who becomes part of the gang that builds the fortress to house their German machine gun. Clogger is involved originally because he hangs around Chas* McGill, who makes him laugh, and because Chas needs him as an escort for timid Nicky* Nichol, who is being terrorized by Boddser Brown's gang. Clogger has come to Garmouth to live with an aunt but has no hesitation in leaving her and going to live in the fortress with Nicky, explaining that all she loves is her beer and her fags (cigarettes). When Boddser has held Chas's head under water and nearly drowned him, Clogger beats him up so badly that even Chas is shocked. While Chas is from the respectable working class, Clogger is from a much lower social stratum.

COCKLE-SNORKLE BUG (*The Song of Pentecost**),
malicious,   conniving,   orange-backed,   seven-
legged, flying insect, who deliberately incites
Owl* against the Harvest Mice just for the fun
of seeing what will happen. A terrible gossip,
he loves to play both ends against the middle.
His heartless nature is shown by his not having
told Owl that Owl wasn't responsible for his
brother's death, even though the Cockle-Snorkle
has known all along that Owl has been suffering
from grief and a guilty conscience. The Cockle-
Snorkle adds considerable spice to the story,
being a primary catalyst for tension. He is the
epitome of selfishness and deceit and the main
villain of the story.

COCK LOREL (*When Shakespeare Lived in South-
wark**), the "upright man" or captain among
beggars and thieves, who keeps a stable of boys
whom he trains as pickpockets and burglars at
the Hen Roost, a remote inn. Cock is brutal when
drunk and without compunction when sober, quite
willing to murder the nobleman who comes to the
inn lost, and insistent that the boys be found
and killed after they escape, lest they tell
authorities about the organization.

THE COLD FLAME (Reeves*, James, ill. Charles
Keeping,   Hamilton,   1967;   Meredith,   1969),
fantasy novel that improvises on "The Blue
Light," a tale from the collection of the Grimm
brothers. After five-and-twenty years and five-
and-twenty wounds in the king's service all over
the continent of Europe, a faithful soldier is
mustered out with only a single silver dollar in
reward. Bent, scarred, maimed, and resentful, he
trudges through a forest reputed to be full of
witches and outlaws. He spies a faint light,
"not warm, almost green in its coldness," and
follows it to the rude hovel of a wise woman. In
return for food and a bed, he digs her garden
and chops her wood. She induces him by the power
of her will to allow her to lower him in a
basket into her well to recover the blue-green
light she has dropped down there. When he
refuses to give her the light until he has both
feet firmly on the ground, she grabs at the

light, it falls back into the well, and she
lowers him down again. Despairing, he decides to
smoke his pipe and kindles it with the blue
light. A black and naked manikin appears, who is
cunning and innocent at the same time, and
awaits his command. Almost jestingly, the
soldier tells the manikin to destroy the witch
and get him out of the well. The imp leads him
along a passage to a treasure room, tells him to
help himself to whatever treasure he wishes out
of the witch's ill-gotten gain, and instructs
him to light his pipe with the blue flame
whenever he wishes the imp to return. His bag
loaded with gold, the soldier travels to The
Wanton Child, an inn in a nearby town, sells the
treasure and buys clothes, and learns that the
witch is to be hanged for her misdeeds. Musing
on the injustice done him by the king, he summons the manikin and commands him to fetch the
king's daughter. Although he warns that it will
bring trouble, the manikin obeys, and the soldier sets the princess to cleaning his quarters.
This happens on two more nights. The third
night, the princess, on the instruction of her
father, cunningly hides her slipper of white
silk underneath the soldier's bed. The king's
men discover it there, arrest the soldier, and
imprison him. Tried for treason in a kangaroo
court, the soldier is convicted, not of treason
but of endangering majesty and is condemned to
be hanged. Granted a last request, he asks for
his pipe, lights it with the blue flame, and
summons the manikin, who lays about him mightily
with his little blue sword, cutting down judge
and guards right and left. The king begs for his
life, offering the soldier in exchange either
the princess as wife or the kingdom. The soldier, at heart a moral man, chooses the kingdom,
because the princess has been betrothed to a
neighboring count. Ironically, he soon discovers
that he is too unsure of himself to be happy as
king and wishes he had chosen the princess
instead. Seeking advice from the manikin, he
accidentally drops the blue light into the
castle moat. He tells the princess he has made
the wrong choice, begs her pardon for the way he
forced her to perform menial tasks, and says he
wishes he had the old king to advise him in
governing. She says she holds no grudge, that

he asked her to perform no unworthy task anyway, and that her father is not a wicked man, but merely became unkind after the death of his beloved wife. Then the soldier learns from the princess's father that the count has rejected her since she no longer has a kingdom to inherit, and that she and her father are without asylum. When the old king asks for refuge, the soldier grants it freely, and the story ends with the soldier and his former master reconciled and the expectation that the soldier and the princess will marry. Though Reeves retains the basic plot of the source story, he exploits emotions and characters in greater detail and adds episodes and conversation. Imagery is used extensively, and language is more decorative. The theme stresses the importance of forgiveness and reconciliation, while the folktale emphasizes revenge. Fanfare.

COLLIN-SMITH, JOYCE (1919-), British writer, author of *Jeremy Craven** (Hodder, 1958; Houghton, 1959), a substantial and well-crafted historical novel, first published in England for adults, about a youth's involvement in the Mexican Revolution of 1910-1913. Although some critics complained about unconvincing characterizations, the book met with general approval for its clear picture of the impact of revolutionary activities upon both Indios and politicians and for its sensitivity in capturing the tenor of the period. It appears on the *Horn Book* Fanfare list.

COLM (*Old John**), talking pigeon rescued by Old John after he has been injured in a storm and healed by Bainen, the fairy doctor, who has assumed the shape of a small white cat. Colm influences the action several times. Most importantly, he discovers that the dwarf has imprisoned Bainen in his castle on Blue Mountain and leads the prince's archers there.

COMFORT HERSELF (Kaye*, Geraldine, ill. Jennifer Northway, Deutsch, 1984; Deutsch, 1985), realistic novel of family life set recently in London and southeastern England and in Ghana for one year recently in which a young girl learns that she herself can and must decide what to do

with her life. Loving, responsible Comfort
Kwatey-Jones, black daughter of a mixed racial
marriage, has been living with her divorced
mother, blonde, fun-loving Margaret, in a London
flat near Kensington Gardens. In June, just
after Comfort turns eleven, Margaret is struck
and killed by a bus. Miss Hanker, a kind,
dutiful social worker, arranges for Comfort to
be "taken into care" in a group home, Ivywood
Court, where Comfort's lack of tears embarrasses
the other girls and where Comfort decides that
she must follow resilient Margaret's example and
be adaptable, a survivor. She does, however,
find the pattern of her life, which had revolved
around Margaret and school (where she had won a
scholarship), so disrupted that she feels lost
and powerless. Though she hasn't seen her now
remarried father, Mante*, a black Ghanaian, in
years, she writes to him at the address of an
old letter she finds in her mother's purse. Miss
Hanker attempts to locate Mante, then takes
Comfort to her Barton grandparents, now retired
and living in Smithy Cottage in the village of
Penfold in Kent. Comfort tries hard to please.
She connects immediately with patient, accepting
Grandad*; though less well but satisfactorily
with demanding, judgmental Granny*; becomes good
friends with vibrant, lonely Lettie* Stamp, a
village girl who has yearned for a friend her
age; and gets along well with the other village
youngsters, who regard her blackness as exotic
but accept her without reservation. Then Mante
sends for her, and, although the Bartons protest
vigorously, Comfort chooses to fly to Accra in
Ghana. She moves in with her handsome, well-
educated father, who works two jobs, as a civil
servant by day and a taxi driver by night, in
order to make ends meet, and his very pregnant
and discontented wife, Efua, a former airline
hostess, in their modern apartment. Comfort discovers that the basic expectations of her
behavior that the Bartons had also apply here--
obedience, modesty, industry--and quickly adjusts to changed physical circumstances. Like
other Ghanaians, however, Efua retains some old
beliefs and doesn't want the daughter of her
predecessor around lest Margaret's ghost harm
her baby, particularly if it's a boy. Comfort is
taken by her father's sister, Aunt Ata, to live

with her father's mother, Grandmother*, her
daughters, and their large extended family in
their compound in the village of Wanwangeri,
where the manner of life has remained more
traditional, is based on agriculture and barter,
and involves strict routine and division of
labor. Again, she finds basic behavioral requirements much the same. She is surprised but
pleased to discover that cousins are considered
brothers and sisters, and she likes the
resulting closeness and support. She finds her
imperious Grandmother intimidating at first but
soon discovers that the old woman admires her
courage, quick mind, and adaptability. Before
long, she enjoys the position of favorite, to
the envy of her siblings. She discovers that
Grandmother is crafty and manipulative and that,
if she wishes to get her way with the old woman,
she must be wily, too, and make it worthwhile
for Grandmother to give her consent. She learns
to farm and receives her own plot and persuades
Grandmother to allow her to go to market by
agreeing to spy on an employee of Grandmother's.
She becomes adept at selling and bartering,
earns money of her own, and sees her
cousin-brother die from lack of medicines and
proper care. The days pass rapidly, and, though
she misses school at first, that fades from her
mind. Seeing an English tourist couple in the
market in March jolts her memory and con-
science--she has not kept in touch with the
Bartons. When cousin-sister Ama has her first
period and is sequestered, Comfort must stay
home from market to assume Ama's duties. She
feels restricted and begins to question the
propriety for her of remaining in Ghana. Even
though she has been receiving preferential
treatment, she finally decides her roots are in
England. When Grandmother protests vociferously,
insisting that Mante gave Comfort to her,
Comfort makes an important decision. She insists
she is no one's property to give or receive; she
belongs only to herself. Still not sure she has
made the right choice, she runs away to consult
first the village headman, the potter Sika, who
tells her to obey her Grandmother, then to the
chief of the area, who advises her to return to
England, noting, "The eagle that is reared as a
chicken will still be an eagle....Let the girl

take her eagle blood back to England." She
returns to Mante, whom she finds engrossed in
making money to satisfy material wants and
enjoying his new, longed-for son. The book's end
finds her back in Penfold joyfully celebrating
her twelfth birthday with the Bartons, Lettie,
and the village children. She knows she has many
friends in Penfold and can be herself there.
Scenes are well-drawn and easily visualized,
dialogue is generous, appropriate, and real
sounding. The book is substantial and remains
consistently interesting, with new complications
growing out of previous ones. The plot has gaps,
however; most notably, it is not clear why
Comfort decides to return to England: is it
because she has encountered the English couple,
because she is told she will probably be married
in a year or two, because she genuinely feels
life in England will be better for her, or
because she has come to feel life with the
Bartons will be better for her? That she comes
back implies that life in an English village is
preferable to that in Africa, at least for a
"been-to," one who has lived in England. Why
then does the author have the Bartons arrange to
send Comfort to boarding school shortly after
her return? The reader is given tantalizing
allusions to trouble between the Bartons and
Margaret and between Grandmother and Mante, but
these problems are never developed. Characters
and settings seem too deliberately contrasted,
and, except for Comfort, characterization is
shallow. Mante, potentially the next most interesting figure, disappoints, never rising above
stereotype. The reader is given hints about his
estrangement from Margaret and from his mother.
Comfort thinks he's brilliant and tricky, but
the reader is never given instances of either.
The book makes only a few references to Comfort's meeting racial prejudice in England. Her
carefully contrasted experiences indicate that
she is loved and wanted everywhere regardless of
her looks and origin. Intelligent and resilient,
she holds the novel together, and it is the
reader's sympathy for her invoked early on that
keeps the book from becoming a sociological
study of several different yet similar ways of
life. Point of view is tightly controlled,
almost as though Comfort were telling the

story. The author balances descriptions of life in inner London, Penfold, Accra, and Wanwangeri, details of everyday life, the world of work, and social attitudes. The use of typical proverbial expressions and metaphorical speech enhances the African setting and adds interest: Ama has her "out-dooring" when she is initiated into womanhood, an irrational person is "sky-sky," and Mante is "fridge-ful" and "carful." Other.

CONFETTI FOR CORTORELLI. See *Angelo Goes to the Carnival.*

CONORY (*The Mark of the Horse Lord**), cousin and best friend of Midir*. He recognizes Phaedrus* as an imposter but keeps silent about it rather than jeopardize the uprising that will throw off the cruel rule of the goddess-queen, Liadhan. Since he has been chosen to be the next king by Liadhan, he must kill the present king, only to be killed himself in seven years if she remains in power. A young man who at first seems effeminate, with bleached hair, dangling jewelry, and a tame wildcat, Shan, which he wears draped around his neck, Conory is really tough and steady, and he proves to be a true friend to Phaedrus. When Phaedrus doubts whether he will come back from his last battle, he asks Conory to take care of his wife, Murna*, and his unborn child. Conory, reminding him that he is of the Royal Blood himself and therefore might want to take the kingship from the child, insists on swearing that he will be faithful to the wishes of Phaedrus.

CONRAD'S WAR (Davies*, Andrew, Blackie, 1978; Crown, 1980), amusing dream fantasy, or perhaps a fantasy of time travel or telepathy, set in the late twentieth century in a middle-class family somewhere in England. The story explores the relationships between a father and son and can also be read as a satire on war and a spoof on contemporary family life. Events are seen from the viewpoint of but are not related by Conrad Pike, about twelve. Conrad is an energetic, imaginative youth at a stage of life where he finds fault with everyone around him, and, in particular, with his father, a novelist. Conrad sees him as an aging, bald, abstracted genius and thinks of him ironically as the "great writer." Keen on war, the army, killing, and guns, as well as on his dog, Towzer, one night Conrad unsuccessfully asks his father for help in building a model tank. Later, he apparently dreams that he builds a real one in the garage. Starting it up, he demolishes the garage and rams the tank into the living room, certain he has finally made an impression upon his usually distant father. To his amazement, he discovers that his father has dreamed the same dream, and curiously both detect the strong odor of diesel in the living room. The next evening at bedtime, Conrad keenly senses World War II "leaking" into his life. There follows a long, often amusing, sometimes suspenseful and action-filled dream sequence, peopled with assorted figures from Conrad's real life in various roles, filled with dialogue, and skillfully combining realistic and surrealistic details. Conrad pilots a Lancaster Avro (like the model at his bedside), with his father as bombardier and gunner and Towzer as passenger. They raid Nuremberg, are shot down, parachute to safety, and are captured, interrogated, and imprisoned in Colditz Castle. Disguised in German uniforms, they escape in a glider. Conrad enables his father to avoid capture and then commandeers a tank. He has the chance to kill the Germans operating the tank but doesn't, because he finds he's had enough of killing and violence. He falls in with the Resistance at a local farm-house, where his father has found safety. They reach the coast and embark on a motorboat to cross the Channel back to England. German guards spy them, and, when their Alsatian dog attacks Towzer, Conrad's father flies into a rage (what Conrad thinks of as the "Red Mist") and belts the Alsatian with a bottle of red wine. Conrad awakens to a new appreciation of his father, who strangely has again had the same dream. Conrad announces that he is through with war and killing, hears his father remark gratefully that another Difficult Phase has passed, and then asserts that he will now take up the study of electricity in order to make an electric chair. The humor of irony, situation, errors, insult, and character; the playful tone; the idiomatic style; the shrewd psychological details that accurately recreate the process of dreaming; the unerring point of view; and careful attention to home situations and the details of flying and World War II in long retrospect make this first-rate entertainment, without the horror and didacticism often found in stories of war or the sensationalism and unconvincing characterization of the New Realism novels of family life. Boston Globe Winner; Choice; Fanfare; Guardian.

CONSTANTINE (*The Emperor's Winding Sheet**), last emperor of the Roman Empire of the East, which fell to the Turks in 1453. He is pictured in the novel as a tall, dark, serious man, devoted to his people and dedicated to the preservation of the empire, although he has little hope against the Turks who are far greater in numbers and wealth. With dignity he settles quarrels, endures rituals, and prays frequently, but he lights up when he is in action and can drop the ceremonial aspects of his position. Among his own household servants, he is kindly, making sure that there is plenty for his inferiors to eat before he accepts his own, and toward the common people he has a special gentleness which endears him to them. When it becomes apparent that Constantinople will fall, he goes among the nobles of the City asking, "If ever I have wronged you, I pray you now, forgive me," and on the last day makes the same request of Vrethiki*, the English boy whom he has taken to be his constant companion to fulfil a prophecy which neither of them believes but which the common people think important. Although he is urged by his nobles to leave the doomed City, he quotes a saying that if he must die, the empire will make a splendid winding sheet.

COOPER, SUSAN (MARY) (1935-   ), born in Burnham, Buckinghamshire, England; journalist and author of books for adults and children. She grew up near London, spending time also with her grandmother in Wales. After taking her M.A. in English literature from Oxford, she worked as a reporter and feature writer for the London *Sunday Times*. In 1963 she married Nicholas Grant, an American college professor, and moved near Boston. The couple was divorced in 1982.

She has received high critical acclaim for her
series of five fantasies for middle-grade readers, called The Dark Is Rising, for which she
drew on the major English and Welsh myths to
produce an adventurous and suspenseful account
of the endless battle between good and evil.
The books, all of which have won many awards and
citations, move through various settings and
times and feature several modern children as
protagonists: *Over Sea, Under Stone* (Cape,
1965; Harcourt, 1966); *The Dark Is Rising**
(Chatto, 1973; Atheneum, 1973), which was commended for the Carnegie Medal, is a Newbery
Honor book, appears on the *Choice*, Fanfare, and
Contemporary Classics lists, received the Jane
Addams Award, and won the *Boston Globe-Horn
Book* Award; *Greenwitch* (Chatto, 1974; Atheneum,
1974); *The Grey King** (Chatto, 1975; Atheneum,
1975), which won the Newbery Award, appears in
Fanfare and *Choice*, and was commended for the
Carnegie Medal; and *Silver on the Tree* (Chatto,
1977; Atheneum, 1977). *Dawn of Fear* (Chatto,
1972; Harcourt, 1970), a powerful novel set near
London at the height of the blitz in World War
II, echoes her own childhood. More recently she
has published *Seaward* (Bodley, 1983; Atheneum,
1983), another fantasy that draws on Celtic
myths, and *The Silver Cow* (Chatto, 1983;
Atheneum, 1983) and *The Selkie Girl* (Hodder,
1987; Atheneum, 1986), both retellings of old
Celtic tales published in picture-book form and
illustrated by Warwick Hutton. She has also
written for adults a novel, *Mandrake* (Hodder,
1964); a play, *Foxfire*, with Hume Cronyn, that
was produced at Stratford, Ontario, and in New
York and Minneapolis; television plays; and
books of nonfiction.

THE CORAL ISLAND: A TALE OF THE PACIFIC OCEAN
(Ballantyne*, R. M., ill. author, Nelson, 1857;
Nelson, 1857), story of three resourceful young
castaways on a South Sea island in the mid
nineteenth century.The first-person narrator,
Ralph Rover, 15, son of a retired English sea
captain, sets sail in the *Arrow* for the South
Pacific and when it is driven onto a coral reef
and wrecked, trusts his luck not to the
overcrowded lifeboat but to hanging onto a large
oar with the other ship's boys, Jack Martin, 18,

and Peterkin Gay, a mischievous youth of thirteen. They are cast up on an island of great beauty and marvelous flora, much of which Jack, a great reader, is able to identify and put to use. Besides fish, oysters, whales, sharks, crabs, and other sea creatures, they also find pigeons, ducks, hogs, an old cat, and even penguins. The cat, they surmise, was a pet of the man whose skeleton, along with that of a dog, they find in a much decayed hut from which they take an ax, an iron pot, and various other items which prove valuable to them. For many months they live an idyllic life, building a boat and exploring nearby islands, and enjoying the fruits of the land, before they see their first humans, two canoe-loads of blacks, one in pursuit of the other. The boys hide and watch a bloody battle, which ends with the pursuers tying up the fifteen remaining men of the other party, cutting, roasting and devouring steaks from one of their dead enemies, and brutalizing the women and children who have been rounded up from their hiding places in the brush. When one young woman of lighter skin and "modest demeanor" is threatened, Jack sends the other two boys to release the captives from the first canoe while he leaps into the fight. In the end, the pursuers have all been killed or been taken prisoner, and the remaining natives, with their chief, Tararo, and the girl, Avatea, leave in a state of friendship with the boys, except for one warrior, who is hostile because Jack has prevented him from eating part of an enemy. Not long after, a pirate schooner appears. The boys hide in what they call the Diamond Cave, a limestone cave whose entrance is below the water level and to which Peterkin, who cannot dive, must be dragged by his companions. Ralph, who comes up to reconnoiter, is captured and taken to the ship. It masquerades as a trader in sandalwood, and Ralph learns from Bloody Bill, a taciturn but decent dissident in the crew, a great deal about the brutal customs of both the pirates and the natives. At one island he is watching natives riding surfboards and recognizes one of the visiting chiefs as Tararo. With Bloody Bill translating, he learns that Avatea is refusing to marry the man Tararo has chosen for her, and faces death as a result. Caught in double-dealing by natives, the captain and crew are wiped out, and Ralph (who has been left to guard the ship), joined by Bill (who has escaped with a serious wound), gets the schooner under way and sails off. Bill, brought to peace by Ralph's Bible quotations about divine forgiveness, dies, and Ralph sails single-handedly for the coral island, where he finds Jack and Peterkin overjoyed at his safe return. With a vessel at their disposal, Jack decides he must rescue Avatea, and the other two follow his lead enthusiastically. They sail for the south end of Tararo's home island of Mango, an area that has been Christianized, and obtain the aid of the local native missionary. There follows a series of descriptions of brutalities on other parts of the island by non-Christian natives, to each other and to enemies, while the three boys are captured, escape, and are recaptured. After a long imprisonment in a cave, they are suddenly released to discover that the natives have all become Christian, a conversion that entirely changes their characters. Avatea is allowed to marry her love, a handsome chief of another island, and the boys, with some native crew members, set sail for Tahiti and thence home. Although many of the adventures on the coral island are highly improbable, the early part of the novel is entertaining and full of lively action. Following the contact with the missionaries, the story loses conviction and becomes embarrassingly chauvinistic. The book is important historically as one of the early adventure novels intended for boys. Choice.

CORBETT, W(ILLIAM) J(ESSE) (1938–   ), born in Warwickshire, England; writer of fantasies for children. After he left school at fifteen, he held a variety of jobs, as factory worker, soldier, construction laborer, dishwasher, and merchant seaman, the tedium of which, he has said, was eased by his "life-long love of reading." In his forties and jobless, he began to write, inspired by the books his mother read to the family when he was a child. He first wrote poems and ghost stories, and then, prompted by memories of childhood trips to the Lickey Hills in the English Midlands, he began the story of a harvest mouse named Pentecost. His first

published   novel,   *The   Song   of   Pentecost**
(Methuen, 1982; Dutton,   1983), a talking-animal
fantasy about   the search   of some   harvest mice
for a new home, won   the Whitbread Award and was
hailed   by   some   critics   as   a   new   classic,
notable,   they feel,   for   its   brisk style   and
intriguing   mix of   comedy, pathos,   action, and
mystery.   Its   sequels   are   *Pentecost   and   the
Chosen One* (Methuen,   1984; Delacorte, 1987) and
Pentecost of Lickey Top (Methuen, 1987). He also
wrote *The   End of   the Tale* (Methuen,   1985). He
has made his home in Birmingham, England.

THE CORIANDER (Dillon*, Eilis, ill. Vic Donahue,
Faber, 1963; Funk, 1964), realistic novel set on
the most   westerly island off the   Galway coast,
probably   in the   first third   of the   twentieth
century, involving the   efforts of the islanders
to keep a shipwrecked   doctor   against his will.
The   people of   Inishgillan   think their   remote
island has   almost everything a man   could want,
and above all privacy, since it has a slip where
the currachs   can land but no   harbor for larger
boats   which might   encourage   more visits   from
Revenue   Men and   other officials   who would   be
poking   around.   They   do   feel the   lack   of   a
doctor,   however,   and   have   frequently   been
promised one by the   officials in Galway with no
result.   When   a   ship   from   Brazil,   the
Coriander,   founders   on   the   Three   Rocks just
off Inishgillan, Pat Folan, 16, the first person
narrator, and   his friend Roddy Hernon   rescue a
man trying vainly to crawl ashore and learn that
he is a doctor and   has a broken leg. They seize
the opportunity as one sent   by God and take him
to   the   isolated   house   of   Mamo,   their   old
schoolteacher, now   retired, who they   know will
take him in   and keep a secret.   At the doctor's
direction, Pat sets his leg, and Mamo brings out
for his use her embroidered sheets which she has
been saving   for her   funeral. Although   all the
other men   are saved and   sent to Galway   in the
Aran lifeboat   summoned   by   Luke   Hernon   the
postmaster on   his telegraph,   the boys   and old
Mamo do   not reveal   the doctor's   presence. The
island men have been too busy to notice anything
unusual, first hooking all their currachs to the
ship by night and pulling   her around to a safer
place   where   they   strip   her   of   cargo   and

everything movable, and then sink her, feeling
strongly that they have a right to whatever the
sea sends them. The leading men of the island,
Big John Moran, Bartley MacDonagh, and Pat's
father, Martin Folan, begin to have second
thoughts, however, particulary about the crates
of beautiful blue serge suits, and talk the
others into transferring much of their booty to
the post office and having Luke call the Revenue
Men from Galway to say that they have managed to
save some of the cargo, while hiding the rest in
secret caves they often use for salvage.
Because Mamo has an extra bedroom and they plan
to take two of the Revenue Men to her house, the
boys realize they can keep the secret no longer
and tell Pat's father. Soon he, Luke, Bartley,
Big John, and one or two others make their way
quietly to Mamo's, interview the doctor, and
explain why they can't let him go. He is
furious, but even Luke, as postmaster their only
government representative and a very law-abiding
type, agrees they should not send him away. When
the Revenue Men are safely gone again, they move
him down to the Folan house, where he takes
Pat's room while the boy sleeps on the settle in
the kitchen. Although he is polite to Pat's
mother, he tyranizes over Pat, berating him and
demanding he wait on him and serve as his chess
partner, since the other men avoid him. Only
Mamo is fully at ease with him, and when she
stops coming to call, Pat gets uneasy, runs up
to her house, and discovers she is very ill.
They transport the doctor to her house in a
cart, and he cares for her devotedly, also
teaching the other women nursing skills. When
his leg is healed, he seems to settle down on
the island, since he is a widower, was born in
Clare, and had already retired from active
practice before he went to Brazil. He takes Pat,
who is a clever boy and very interested, for his
assistant, and teaches him many practical
medical skills. In the meantime, the men of
Inishgillan are deeply worried about their
sheep, which have been disappearing from the
Grazing Island, an uninhabited but fertile area
between them and their nearest neighbor,
Inishthorav, with whom they have a long-standing
feud. The grown men are hesitant to spend a
night on the Grazing Island because of tales of

fairies and other supernatural beings there, but
they allow Pat and Roddy to stay when they take
the lambs over for summer pasture. The boys
pretend not to be frightened, and in the middle
of the night they hear voices and watch three
Inishthorav currachs approach and take away
eighteen of their young sheep. The Inishgillan
men are wildly angry and ready for a fight, but
Big John is determined that there shall be no
needless bloodshed. As he ponders the situation,
the boys meet an Inishthorav lad who has rowed
over in his currach and introduces himself as
Colm Cooney, son of the late King Cooney of
Inishthorav. Colm says he deplores the sheep
thievery, which his father would have prohibit-
ed, and volunteers to round up the eighteen
sheep and have them ready at a quiet beach that
night for the Inishgillan men to take back.
Though suspicious, the Inishgillan men trust
him, but that night find the beach at
Inishthorav lined with jeering men armed with
pitchforks. Humiliated, the Inishgillan men turn
home, furious at Colm for betraying them and
angry with Pat and Roddy for putting them in
that position. It is not until the next morning
that the boys remember that among the shouts
from Inishthorav were mentions of the doctor,
whose presence was not known to Colm, and they
realize that the doctor himself must have seized
the opportunity to telegraph Inishthorav of
their intended arrival, and that the Inishthorav
men have summoned the guards to take him to
Galway and arrest his kidnappers. When the news
gets around, Pat and Roddy realize that a couple
of the island men are thinking of murdering the
doctor and disposing of his body before the
guards arrive. They rush the doctor away to the
secret caves and hide him between a pair of
bunks from the *Coriander* until the Pilot Boat
arrives. Certain that the guards will want to
arrest someone, Big John and Pat's father
heroically agree to be the ones. As the boat
approaches, Pat sends Roddy to the cave to get
the doctor, while he sets off to try to distract
the would-be murderers. There is a wild chase,
ending at the beach where Big John is formally
welcoming the guards. As the doctor arrives, so
do a group of currachs from Inishthorav full of
gloating men, waiting to watch the arrests. When

he sees them and hesitates, old Mamo rushes at the doctor, kneels and kisses his hand, and thanks him for all the good he has done. Calmly he refuses to go with the guards, pointing out that no one is required to report his own shipwreck and saying that he believes he will stay on Inishgillan for the present at least. His efforts afterwards bring about a reconciliation between the two islands and send Pat to medical school in Galway. While the plot is exciting and hangs together well, the strength of the novel lies in the characterization of the islanders, with their suspicions and their loyalties, their natural greed and their strong sense of honor. Pat's voice is well sustained, but he and Roddy might be any boys, while old Mamo and half a dozen of the men are memorable characters. Fanfare.

CORMAC (*Children of the Red King**), Red King of Connacht in the early thirteenth century when the Normans under King John are gaining control of Ireland. A red-haired man of powerful build and fiery temper, he is unwilling to compromise with the Normans until his hall has been destroyed and his people decimated, and even then he carries out harassment raids for three years until his children come to him with a proposal from the Norman noble, Sir* Jocelin de Courcy Rohan, that will allow him to continue as king, ruling jointly with, not under, the Norman invaders.

COTTIA (*The Eagle of the Ninth**), British girl who lives with her Roman uncle and very Romanized British Aunt Valaria next door to Marcus's* Uncle Aquila. Although her aunt calls her Camilla and tries to make her act like a Roman girl, Cottia sticks fiercely to her Iceni heritage and hates living in a town and speaking in Latin. She has a great mass of red hair and reminds Marcus of a vixen, particularly when she is angry. Marcus leaves his military bracelet with her when he goes north and asks her to keep track of his pet wolf, Cub. When he returns and finds her much more grown up, he is at first shy of her, but she begs him to take her with him if he goes back to Rome, and it is partly for her sake that he decides to take up his land in

Britain and settle there.

COUSIN (*The Song of Pentecost**), fast-talking,
worldly, tough, slick, con man snake, who cheats
naive Snake* out of his inheritance, Oily Green
Pool, after the death of Snake's father in a
knotting accident. Cousin pretends that Snake's
father willed the pool to him and forces the
lying Frog* to uphold his story. After he takes
possession of Snake's pool, he throws wild
parties, and, when Pentecost* leads his mice by,
they see that the place has degenerated into a
swamp slum. His agreement to share the pool with
Snake is just one more example of his motto:
"Never give a sucker an even break." When last
seen, he is practicing the trick he calls his
"boomerang chuck" on Snake, flinging the youngster through the air in spite of the Snake's
despairing and frightened cries. Cousin is a W.
C. Fields type.

COUSIN HENRY BOLINGER (*Ask Me No Questions**),
idealistic but weak young man who has been
studying for the ministry at Oxford. Dominated
by his mean and petty mother, he usually
pretends to be reading when she starts her
spiteful comments on people he admires because
he is afraid to oppose her. He is in love with
Miss* Margaret Roylance, the schoolmistress, but
is not strong enough to stand up for her. Laura*
sees him as her only hope of help, but when she
tries to tell him of her troubles, he appears
distracted and pays no attention. It is he who
carries Lizzie* Brown's body back to Drouet's
and is shown by the doctor, who has been called
in, the children dead and dying in the crowded,
filthy rooms. He hopes to succeed the aging
parson in Tooting.

COUSIN ROBERT MCGILL (*Fathom Five**), Chas* Mc-
Gill's father's cousin from a more socially
acceptable branch of the family, who is
stationed in Garmouth as commander of a convoy
escort service. After the night when Chas and
his friends try to find the spy in the Low
Street bars and Chas, hearing the radio static,
realizes that another message is being sent to
the U-boat, Chas runs to the *Virago*, his cousin's ship newly come to port, to try to tell

him and prevent another disaster. Pleading a family emergency, he gets to the commander's office, only to find Cousin Robert, whom he has never met before, drunk and incoherent. His men try to cover for him. Later, when Chas has correctly identified Sven* as the spy and has nearly been drowned, Cousin Robert takes charge and cleverly sets a trap for the U-boat. Afterwards, although he cannot acknowledge Chas's part in the episode, he makes sure the boy is allowed to watch the ceremony and gives him a souvenir sea cap. Cousin Robert has contracted tuberculosis, and at the end is about to be sent to a hospital.

CRAIK, DINAH MARIA MULOCK (1826-1887), born near Stoke-upon-Trent, Staffordshire; writer of Victorian novels for both adults and children. Her father, an abusive and irresponsible clergyman, moved the family frequently during her childhood. At thirteen she taught Latin in a school run by her mother, and at eighteen she broke with her father, taking her mother and two younger brothers back to Staffordshire, where her mother and one brother died. In 1846 she moved with her remaining brother to London, where she began publishing a steady stream of books and was soon a highly successful novelist. Her best known work, *John Halifax, Gentleman* (Hurst, 1856), concerns the rise of a poor orphan to the gentry because of his honesty and hard work. Her children's books of this period were highly didactic, like *Michael the Miner* (Religious Tract Society, 1846). When she was thirty-nine, she married George Craik, a publisher eleven years her junior, and they later adopted a daughter, Dorothy. *Little Sunshine's Holiday* (Samson Low, 1871) is about taking her not yet three-year-old daughter to Scotland. Her only books that are read much today today are *The Adventures of a Brownie** (Samson Low, 1872; Harper, 1872), originally subtitled *As Told to My Child*, a fantasy written for Dorothy, and *The Little Lame Prince** (Daldy, 1875; Macmillan, 1875), originally published as *The Little Lame Prince and His Travelling Cloak*, about an abused prince who learns of the world by riding on a magic cloak supplied by his fairy godmother. Both have been named to the

Children's Classics list. Craik became active in helping the less fortunate, often giving pensions to needy authors. She saw her books as "tales to educate the emotions," and although today they seem sentimental and moralistic, they are distinguished by liveliness and sincerity from the average Victorian stories for children.

CREEP (*A Chance Child**), undernourished, abused, illegitimate child who has been kept in a closet under the stairs most of the time, fed and cared for only by his older half-brother, Christopher*. After he escapes and retreats into the past, he is at first apparent only to children, who help him and whom he is able to help, holding nails and chain links with a tongs while Blackie* beats them into shape with a hammer, sitting on the ladder in the drying kilns to stack pottery for Tom* Moorhouse, and climbing beneath the spinning machinery to twist broken threads together to keep Blackie from falling behind. After he is on his own, according to the pamphlet he printed up about his life, Creep at first leads a horse for the canal builders; then, as he gets stronger, he digs and shovels and runs the barrows until he falls beneath one and breaks his hip and back. Crippled so that he must use a crutch and a stick, he becomes involved with the Primitive Methodists and the Chartists, learns to read, and becomes a printer. Eventually he goes back to the mill town, finds Blackie, whom he calls by her real name, Lucy, and marries her. They have ten children, of whom four survive to adulthood, and none of whom, he says passionately, have been put to factory work. Though as a child he is spindly and naive, he is, as Christopher says, a "spunky little perisher, considering."

CREGAN, MAIRIN, born in Kerry, Ireland; writer and translator; educated by the St. Louis nuns in Ireland. She traveled extensively in Europe and had an enduring interest in music, especially Irish folk music, and in the theater. She married James Ryan, once Minister of Agriculture in the Irish Free State, and the couple lived in the country near Dublin with

their three children. *Old John** (Allen, 1937;
Macmillan, 1936), about a kindhearted Irish
shoemaker and his animals, began as stories made
up to entertain the two eldest of her children. Later her husband suggested she write the
episodes down, and her children helped remind
her of the incidents. James Carty of the
National Library at Dublin then suggested she
submit the manuscript to Macmillan. Well
received by most critics as inventive and
evocative of the spirit of old Ireland, the book
was selected for the Fanfare list by the editors
of *Horn Book*. Cregan also wrote the novel
Rathina (Macmillan, 1942) and *Hunger-Strike: A
Play in Two Acts* (Gill, 1933).

CRESSWELL, HELEN (1934-   ), born in
Nottinghamshire, daughter of an electrical engineer; prolific writer mainly of comic
fantasies for children. Before her marriage and
after her schooling at Nottinghamshire Girls'
High School and receiving her B.A. with honors
in English from King's College, University of
London, she held various positions, as a
literary assistant to a foreign author working
on a book on Van Gogh, a writer for BBC-TV in
Bristol, a teacher in Nottinghamshire, and a
fashion buyer. In 1962, she married Brian Rowe,
who was employed in textiles. The couple has
two daughters and has lived in Nottinghamshire
in a 200-year-old farmhouse on a hill at the
edge of Robin Hood's Sherwood Forest. She began
writing at six or seven, both verse and prose,
and continued through her teens, receiving the
Nottinghamshire Poetry Society Award for best
poem when she was sixteen. She has said that she
feels that the experience she gained from
experimenting with form and technique in this
early writing was invaluable in her development
as a writer. Of her over sixty published books,
a dozen have been readers, and some have been
series books, like those about Jumbo Spencer and
Lizzie Dripping, but humorous fantasy pre-
dominates and has received the most attention
from critics. The books have been praised for
their variety of tone and types of humor, their
originality of concept, their careful control,
their subtle revelation of human nature, and her
skill at making eccentrics and eccentricity

believable. Three were commended for the Carnegie Award, *The Night Watchmen** (Faber, 1969; Macmillan, 1969), a suspense fantasy which is light on the surface, serious underneath, about a boy's concern for two middle-aged tramps on the run from threatening Greeneyes; *Up the Pier** (Faber, 1971; Macmillan, 1972), a fantasy of time and magic in which a family from the past finds themselves on a pier in a Welsh seaside town, which is also a Fanfare book; and *The Bongleweed** (Faber, 1973; Macmillan, 1974), a tall tale about gigantic tropical plants. Also selected for Fanfare by the editors of *Horn Book* are *The Winter of the Birds** (Faber, 1975; Macmillan, 1976), a sober story about some potentially dangerous steel birds that deviates from her usual form, and the also quite different tall comedy of many domestic errors, *Ordinary Jack** (Faber, 1977; Macmillan, 1977), the first in a series about the only underachiever in a family of zany overachievers which is known collectively as The Bagthorpe Saga. *Ordinary Jack* is included in *Choice*, as is *The Piemakers** (Faber, 1967; Lippincott, 1968), a work that explores the theme of pride in craftsmanship in relating the hilarious, tongue-in-cheek adventures of a talented family of piemakers. One of Cresswell's early books and still one of her best, *The Piemakers* has been her own favorite because she feels it has most successfully "fused humor and fantasy." She has said she prefers working in the fantasy genre because "a very much deeper level of truth can be reached through fantasy than by any other form of writing...," and she sees her books essentially as inner journeys to solutions of problems. She has written television plays and contributed stories to magazines. Several of her children's novels have been televised in serial form on the BBC.

THE CRICKET ON THE HEARTH (Dickens*, Charles, Bradbury and Evans, 1846; Redding & Co., 1846), whimsically treated domestic story set in an English village in the mid-nineteenth century. John Perrybingle, a middle-aged carrier, and his pretty little wife, Dot (Mary), are as happy as can be with their two-month-old baby, their young servant, Tilly Slowboy, their active dog,

Boxer, and their snug cottage, even though the disparity in their ages is great. Then one night John brings home, along with various packages to deliver, a very deaf old gentleman whom he has picked up along the road. Since no one calls for the old gentleman, as he seems to expect, Dot makes him up a bed in the spare room. Among John's packages that night is a wedding cake for Mr. Tackleton, of Gruff and Tackleton, toymakers, the sight of which upsets Dot, since she opposes his marriage to her friend May Fielding. Mr. Tackleton is not only even older than John, he is also bad-tempered, sarcastic, and penny-pinching, but May's mother considers him a good match, and May has finally given in. Though John refuses an invitation to the wedding, since it is to be on the first anniversary of his own wedding, a date he and Dot plan to spend together in their home, Tackleton is eager to get his bride-to-be to see their domestic bliss, obviously thinking it might make her more resigned to him as a husband. The next day, therefore, when Dot makes her fortnightly visit to Bertha, blind daughter of Caleb Plummer (the actual maker of the toys), Tackleton turns up with May Fielding and her mother. Caleb, a devoted father, has deceived his daughter for years by descriptions of their hovel as a smartly painted little cottage, his own sackcloth coat as a handsomely tailored blue greatcoat, and, worst of all, Tackleton, their landlord, as a benevolent man, constantly talking in a rough, disagreeable way as a joke or to cover his noble generosity. Bertha greets May with loving best wishes but then breaks down and weeps, and Caleb realizes that she has been in love with the false picture of Tackleton which he had created. Dot helps smooth over the incident, though she herself seems nervous. Then John comes in to pick her up for the homeward journey, bringing the old gentleman with him. While John is warming himself by the fire and playing a game of cribbage with Mrs. Fielding, Dot and the old gentleman both disappear. Tackleton soon interrupts the game, insists that John accompany him across the courtyard, and look though the window into his counting house, where he sees Dot and a young, handsome man who is holding the old man's wig in his hand, in earnest conversation, with his arm around her waist. He watches as she helps him adjust the wig on his head once more. Without saying a word about the incident to Dot, John sits up all night struggling with his feelings. At one point he almost falls prey to Tackleton's suggestion that he "might do murder before you know it," and takes up his gun to destroy the imposter sleeping, still supposedly an old man, in the next room. At that point the cricket on the hearth, which has been a favorite of Dot's, begins to chirp and awakens the fairies of the chimney, the clock, the cradle, and other parts of the cottage, all of whom troop around him and remind him of Dot's good qualities and patient cheerfulness. Early in the morning, Tackleton pays a call to commiserate with him. They find the spare room window open and the "old gentleman" gone. When Tackleton starts to make disparaging remarks about Dot, John defends her vigorously and angrily, insisting that it has been his fault never to have realized that she must have given up a young love to become his wife, and saying that he will send her home to her parents that day without blame. Tackleton leaves, astonished by this reaction, but almost immediately Caleb appears with Bertha, wanting Dot's support while he makes a full confession of his deception to his daughter. With Dot's gentle guidance, the blind girl soon sees that all the good qualities she attributed to Tackleton were actually her father's, and she gladly gives up her delusion. The sound of wheels at the door is followed by the entrance of the handsome young man, whom Caleb recognizes as his long lost son, Edward, from the Golden South Americas, along with his newly wedded wife, May. Dot explains her suspicions when she first saw the old gentleman, her willingness to act as go-between because she remembered that May and Edward had loved each other dearly before he left, and her anguish at having to keep quiet, even when she knew John had seen and misunderstood her conference with Edward the previous night. Tackleton arrives to claim, he believes, his bride, but, apprised of the real situation, he apologizes brusquely to Dot for his suspicions of her virtue, and leaves. The assembled crowd has a great party, with Dot's parents, arrived for the anniversary, taking part, and in the middle of it Tackleton reappears with the wedding cake to contribute to the festivities, and to everyone's surprise, acts most pleasant and reformed. The story is sentimental, with coincidences and unlikely elements (Caleb's ability to deceive his daughter about their ramshackle home, for instance) and depends for its interest on a nostalgic view of the solid worth of village domestic love. The only character convincingly developed is John, who is slow, lumbering, and thoroughly honest. The style is that of the oral storyteller, with many author intrusions and comments, in a tone that is both jolly and cozy. While in some ways similar to *A Christmas Carol**, it is not as well developed, the language is not as rich, and the fantasy elements do not work as well. Children's Classics.

CROSS, GILLIAN (CLARE) (1945-   ), born in London, her father a scientist and musician, her mother an English teacher; author of a dozen novels for young people with diverse themes, periods, and modes. She was educated at North London Collegiate School, received her B.A. in 1969 with honors and her M.A. in 1972 both from Somerville College, Oxford, and her Ph.D. from the University of Sussex in Brighton in 1974. She has been a teacher; an assistant to an old-style village baker, which provided the description for the Victorian bakery in her novel *The Iron Way* (Oxford, 1979; Oxford, 1979); an assistant to a member of Parliament; and has worked with emotionally disturbed teenagers. She married Martin Cross, an examinations director for the Royal Society of the Arts, has two sons and a daughter, and has made her home in Gravesend, Kent. She had scribbled stories privately from early childhood but became serious about composition after she had children of her own, when she made up and decorated storybooks for their amusement. Her experiences in helping to start a children's book group in Lewes, where she was living at the time, also stimulated her urge to write. After five years and many rejection slips, two novels were accepted in the same year: *The Runaway* (Methuen, 1979) and *The Iron Way*, the latter a historical novel about railway expansion in the English countryside that was nominated for the Guardian Award. Now a full-time writer, she has said she feels free to write for young people about such important matters as love, death, moral decisions, and broader social implications because these are of prime interest to youth today. Her third book and her first to receive much critical attention was *Revolt at Ratcliffe's Rags* (Oxford, 1980; Oxford, 1980), a contemporary novel about labor problems that develop after three young people conduct a study of working conditions at a small factory in their English town and that lead to the closing of the factory. *A Whisper of Lace* (Oxford, 1981; Merrimack, 1982) involves lace smuggling in the eighteenth century. Other titles include *The Demon Headmaster* (Oxford, 1982; Merrimack, 1983), a contemporary tongue-in-cheek narrative about an evil schoolmaster who hypnotizes teachers and students to bend them to his will and plans to turn Britain into a robot society; *The Mintyglo Kid* (Methuen, 1983), about a cricket-league competition; and *Born of the Sun* (Oxford, 1984; Holiday, 1984), an adventure story about a girl and her archaeologist father on a search for a lost Incan city that combines mystery, danger, and girl's growing-up story aspects. Two of her novels have received critical citations: *The Dark Behind the Curtain** (Oxford, 1982; Merrimack, 1984), a Carnegie Highly Commended thriller in which teenagers preparing to present *Sweeney Todd* release the ghosts of abused Victorian children, and *On the Edge** (Oxford, 1984; Holiday, 1985), a story of terrorism that examines both the terrorist mentality and contemporary family structures and that was nominated for the Edgar Allan Poe Award. Critics have praised her ability to combine a good story with substantial background detail and to create and sustain tension without resorting to melodrama or sensationalism. She also regularly contributes reviews to *British Book News* and the *Times Literary Supplement*.

CULLEN (*The Silver Branch**), slave from an Irish tribe who has become Fool for Carausius, the self-proclaimed emperor of Britain. A very small man, with the facial tattoos of his

people, he serves Carausius devotedly, with
lithe, noiseless movements, and wears at his
belt a curved rod of bronze from which hangs
nine silver apples, each tuned to a different
note in a minor key, with which he makes strange
music. Hanging from his belt behind is a hound's
tail, which swings as he moves, and he sleeps
like a dog before the fire and calls himself
Carausius's "hound." To him Carausius has
entrusted a message to Justin* and Flavius, to
be delivered if Carausius is killed, that
explains to them why he acted as if he did not
believe their story of Allectus dealing with the
Saxons, and when Justin and Flavius come upon
Cullen in Calleva he has been hunting them
since the murder of Carausius. He becomes the
standard bearer of the ill-assorted band that
the cousins lead to join the forces of
Constantius, and in the last fight in the
burning basilica he climbs to the high cross-
beam to hold the eagle above the fighting men
and, caught by a thrown spear, props the eagle
there before he crashes down. He is not severely
wounded and insists on following Justin and
Flavius to their new posts in the north to be
their slave.

CULLY (*The Little Black Hen**), a hen that
belongs to Biddy Murphy. Cully is the mother of
Cossey Dearg, a central character in the novel.
When in the egg-laying way, Cully hid her nest
inside the *Coolah Vrac*, the little gray doorway
that leads into the fairy hill not far from
Biddy Murphy's cottage. Cully returned six
months later with a *leah-keown*, a sideways head
put on her by the fairies, and behind her a
little black chick, Cossey Dearg. Because Cossey
Dearg was born in Fairyland, the fairies "have a
call on her still," that is, whenever they send
the fairy cock to crow outside Biddy's window,
Cossey Dearg is obligated to answer his summons
and join the fairy kind. It is her refusal to
respond to the fairies' call that provides the
novel's central problem.

CYRIL (*Five Children and It**), slightly superior
eldest child in the family of four children who
discover the Psammead* and have adventures with
wishes the Psammead grants. Cyril, like his

brother, Robert*, tries to be manly, take care
of the girls, and be brave. He participates in
all the episodes, often taking the lead in their
play, but the one in which he figures most
prominently involves being imprisoned in the
church tower. It was his idea for the children
to help themselves to food from the clergyman's
larder, including soda water in a siphon con-
tainer. He has disconcertingly funny problems in
getting the siphon out of the tower without its
being discovered by the vicar. He is a well-
drawn but not memorable figure.

D

DAG (*The Queen's Blessing**), little brother of the Saxon girl, Merca*, who is orphaned and sold into slavery by Malcolm* III, king of Scotia. A dreamy and dependent child, six when the story starts, Dag follows Merca unquestioningly until after he has been in Dunfermline some time, and then he does not rebel against her but simply pretends he does not understand her fierce hatred of the Scots. When he is a ragged urchin, Dag comforts himself with the feel of a smooth shell that is his most precious possession; he is moved by color and beauty. At Dunfermline he is roused to rare excitement by the promise of the monks to teach him to read and paint.

DAHL, ROALD (1916-   ), born in Llandaff, Glamorgan, South Wales, his parents Norwegian immigrants and his father a shipbroker, painter, and horticulturist; writer noted for his novels, short stories, plays, and screenplays for adults, best-known in children's literature for his outrageously comic fantasies. He was sent to boarding school at seven, and his main schooling was at Repton School in Yorkshire, where his headmaster was Geoffrey Fisher, later Archbishop of Canterbury. At eighteen, he turned down his mother's offer of Oxford (his father was long deceased) and took a position with the Eastern Staff of Shell Company in London, then with Shell Company of East Africa in Dar-es-Salaam in Tanganyika (Tanzania). In 1939, he joined the

Royal Air Force and saw eventful service in the
Middle East, North Africa, and Greece, rising to
Wing Commander. In 1942, as an Assistant Air
Attache in Washington, D.C., he began writing
stories and published *The Gremlins* (Collins,
1944; Random, 1943), which was illustrated by
the Disney Studios but never filmed by them.
About little beings who deliberately cause
trouble for the sake of causing trouble, the
book started a fad of dolls, songs, and the
like, and attracted the attention, among others,
of Eleanor Roosevelt, who read the book to her
grandchildren and invited Dahl to dinner. The
war over, he wrote stories for adults that became popular for their invention, surprise
endings, and grotesquerie. Several books were
best sellers. Twenty years passed before he
again turned to writing children's books, motivated to entertain his own children. In 1967,
*James and the Giant Peach** (Allen, 1967; Knopf,
1961) came out. About the preposterous adventures of a boy, a huge peach, and an assortment of zany characters, it is included in
Choice. Since then, in addition to writing for
adults, he has published about twenty books for
young readers. His most popular novel has been
*Charlie and the Chocolate Factory** (Allen,
1967; Knopf, 1964), a satire on five awful
children that is filled with bizarre situations
and has provoked widely divergent critical
reactions. It has spawned such spin-offs as a
motion picture, play, filmstrips, and re-
cordings and has a sequel, *Charlie and the
Great Glass Elevator* (Allen, 1973; Knopf, 1972).
It is cited in *Choice*, as are *Fantastic Mr.
Fox** (Allen, 1970; Knopf, 1970), a slapstick
comedy in which clever animals outwit three mean
and grasping farmers, and *Danny, The Champion
of the World** (Cape, 1975; Knopf, 1975), about
the high jinks of a boy and his poacher father.
More recently, *The Witches** (Cape, 1983; Farrar, 1983), a coarsely humorous tale of a boy's
attempts to keep evil witches from getting
"rrrid of every single child in Inkland," won
the Whitbread Award. In 1953, he married actress
Patricia Neal, whom he met at the home of
playwright Lillian Hellman. The couple had five
children and for some years divided their time
between England and New York, finally settling

in Buckinghamshire. Unusually severe personal problems afflicted the family, including the death of their eldest daughter from measles encephalitis, the near-death of their only son from hydrocephalus, and Patricia's three cerebral hemorrhages, after which she gave birth to their fifth child, an event that made headlines. More recently, Dahl has published *Boy: Tales of Childhood* (Cape, 1984; Farrar, 1984), his autobiography; the story for a picture book, *The Giraffe and the Pelly and Me* (Cape, 1985; Farrar, 1985); and a book of short stories, *Two Fables* (Viking, 1986; Farrar, 1987). His books have evoked strong reactions, being variously termed ridiculous, highly amusing, strained, darkly entertaining, consciously cute, contrived, and inventively bizarre. He has done several screenplays for adults and for children and a play for adults, and contributes short stories to leading magazines.

DAISY PARKER (*Ordinary Jack**), Jack's little cousin, 4, the only child of Uncle* Parker and Aunt Celia. Already considered a genius by the Bagthorpe clan, she starts to set fires, and, at the beginning of the novel, she combines party crackers and fireworks for a sparkling blaze under the dining-room table during Grandma* Bagthorpe's seventy-fifth birthday party, rapidly accelerating the excitement and soon bringing the festivities to a conclusion. Her tendency toward pyromania thus encouraged, she sets fires throughout most of the book. Since her parents hope that saturation will cure her of her mania, they let her set as many as she wants. At the very end, she starts a fire just as Mr.* Bagthorpe arrives with Jack's notebook, drawing attention away from Jack and Uncle Parker's scheme and Mr. Bagthorpe's passion for comics.

DAME ALICE (*The Writing on the Hearth**), historical Countess of Suffolk, granddaughter of Chaucer and wife of William de la Pole, fourth Earl* of Suffolk. She is presented as a warm-hearted woman, loyal to her lord, a good wife and loving mother, kind to and deeply concerned about the welfare of all within her house, deeply religious, firm, and decisive. To

Stephen, she is the paragon of a virtuous lady, and he serves her diligently and affectionately. Early in the novel, she brings lists for him to copy, not realizing that she has included among them a letter to her stepdaughter containing acid comments about Duchess Eleanor, wife of a political rival of her husband. Stephen copies the letter with good motives, but upon the advice of Doggett* does not give the copy to Dame Alice, after he realizes that she had not intended for him to copy it. Later he loses the copy before he has a chance to destroy it, and thus the plot "pot" begins to boil.

DAME ELIZABETH FITZEDMUND (*The Lark and the Laurel**), aunt of Cecily Jolland and sister of Sir Thomas Jolland, Cecily's father; friend of Lewis* Mallory; and holder of Mantlemass* manor. Dame Elizabeth is on poor terms with her brother because he arranged her marriage to a cruel man of royal connections for his own political advantage. She was a friend of Cecily's dead mother and has resolved that Sir Thomas will not use Cecily as a political pawn as well. Dame Elizabeth is tall, straight, dark-browed, and strong-willed. She works along with her servants because she feels that no employer should ask of a servant what she herself could or would not do. She subtly and cleverly encourages the friendship between Cecily and Lewis Mallory that eventually blossoms into love and concludes with a wedding that reaffirms the marriage contract made years before when the two were children. She is a vividly drawn figure, a conventional strong woman in most respects, yet possessing a vulnerability and humaneness that individualize her and make her sympathetic to the reader.

DAN ALONE (Townsend*, John Rowe, Kestrel, 1983; Lippincott, 1983), realistic novel of family life set in 1922 in an English city that is never named but that is probably the Cobchester of Townsend's Jungle* series. Pale, thin Dan Lunn, 11, lives with his pretty Mum in a respectable neighborhood about half way up City Hill, not far from the equally respectable house of his highly regarded, very religious Grandpa, Percy Purvis. Dan dreams of having a perfect family, a handsome father, attractive mother, and bright and lively little sister. At his Grandpa's house one day, he overhears a conversation through which he learns that Jack Lunn, who sometimes lives with his mother and drinks too much, is not his real father, and takes the news to his mother. She angrily accuses her father of breaking confidence and soon thereafter runs off with another lover, a married man known to Dan as Uncle Alec, to the intense disapproval of, in particular, Grandpa's new wife, called Aunt Hilda, and Dan's real aunt, Verity, who are both mean-spirited, acid-tongued, judgmental women. Dan moves in with Grandpa and Aunt Hilda, who abuses him emotionally, for example, ignoring his birthday but extravagantly buying a honey-roast ham for the minister. Dan resentfully gobbles up the whole ham, but then, raised on Grandpa's moralistic admonitions and Victorian children's stories, he suffers severe guilt pangs. When Grandpa has a heart attack and Dan overhears Aunt Hilda talk about Broad Street Children's Home, anger and fear carry him back to Mum's house, where he finds Jack Lunn sprawled on a sofa. When he asks Jack what he knows of his father, Jack suggests that perhaps Daniel Hunter of the posh engineering firm might be the man, since Hunter is Dan's middle name. His head filled with Victorian notions, Dan seizes on the idea and dreams of wealth and luxury. Jack also tells Dan that he has been living in an attic above a row of derelict cottages on Canal Street in the Jungle (so called because the streets are named for exotic tropical flowers), the rowdiest, most unsavory part of the city. Jack also gives Dan twelve pounds from the proceeds of the sale of the house, purchased by Grandpa for Jack as an incentive to marry Mum when it was discovered she was pregnant. Dan then moves into the Canal Street attic, determined to search for his real father. He is soon joined by abused little Olive, about ten, who also doesn't know who her father is and who lives in the Shambles, the toughest part of the Jungle. Dan visits the Hunters, and, when they prove cold and unfeeling and threaten him with the police, informs Mr. Hunter that he wouldn't have him for a father. On the way back to the

Jungle, he encounters the Jewish glazier, whom
his mother always avoided, who coughs a lot, and
whom no one likes because he is Jewish. The
glazier tells Dan his Grandpa is very ill and
says he wishes he could offer Dan a home. On
the way to consult his amiable Uncle Bert,
Verity's husband, Dan bumps into his Grandpa's
funeral procession and returns to the Jungle.
For the next several weeks he contends with
thieves and thugs, eventually becoming a
professional beggar for a group that calls
itself "the family," fences stolen goods,
includes a cardsharp, a pickpocket, and two
young women in the "love business," and is run
by a slick-talking, rationalizing, Fagin-type
known as Pop, who claims that all they're doing
is redistributing the wealth. Though he feels
wanted and cared for by the family, Dan's
religious upbringing makes him uneasy about
their way of life, and he embarks unsuccessfully
on a plan to reform them. When police raid the
family, Dan gets away, then is caught by
another policeman as a vagabond and sent home to
Aunt Verity. One day while they are visiting the
cemetery, he spots his Mum by Grandpa's grave,
but she runs away before he can speak to her.
Then one of the family writes to Dan that he
has seen Mum working in a tearoom in City Park.
Dan goes there and tells her he has figured out
that Benjie, the Jewish glazier, is his real
father. He traces Benjie through a glass company
to the country cottage where Benjie now lives
for his health, travels there, and discovers
that Benjie has taken in homeless Olive. Benjie
and Mum patch up their broken love affair, and
Dan soon realizes that his fantasy family has
become a reality. The many characters represent
familiar types, and Dan's search for a home
seems a modern version of the Victorian domestic
stories he reads at Grandpa's house. Dan is a
sturdy, likeable fellow, particularly as compared with his snotty cousin Basil, who has sex
on his mind and delights in baiting Dan and
denigrating Mum. Dan's developing assertiveness
seems convincing, but the identity of Dan's
real father is overly obvious. Best are the
clear sense of contemporary prejudices and
mores, the ironical interpersonal relationships
within the different families, and the picture

of the struggle for survival and thieves' code
in the Jungle. Fanfare.

THE DANCING BEAR (Dickinson*, Peter, ill. David
Smee, Gollancz, 1972; Atlantic/Little, 1972),
historical novel set in 558 A.D., starting in
the city of Byzantium and traveling northward
across the Danube into what is now Romania. In
the middle of the betrothal feast of the Lady
Ariadne*, 14, daughter of Lord Celsus, Count of
the Outfields, a group of Kutrigur Huns who have
been brought into the city disguised as slaves
escape and raid his great house, killing,
looting, and burning. Silvester*, a slave born
the same day as Ariadne and raised with her,
whose special duty is to act as bear warden
while he studies to be a clerk and doctor, tries
to save the girl by taking her into the cage of
Bubba*, the dancing bear, but she is seized and
carried off by a Hun who leaves Silvester
injured and unconscious. He wakes to find almost
everyone slain except the young bridegroom (who
is badly injured) and Holy* John, the unwashed
household saint, who has spent the last ten
years on a pillar in the courtyard, mortifying
his flesh and expounding on the particular brand
of Christianity favored by Lord Celsus. When two
nobles, Lord Brutus from the family of Celsus
and a lord from the bridegroom's family, arrive,
their main interest is in the marriage contracts, and from their conversation it becomes
clear that if Ariadne is dead, Lord Brutus and
other heirs will get the huge estates, whereas
if she is living, the bridegroom's family will
get at least one third. Lord Brutus orders
Silvester to lie, to say that Ariadne was killed
in the fire, and a slave girl was carried off,
remarking that he will not have to lie long, a
comment that Silvester knows means that he will
be quietly killed before he can be tortured by
the courts. Lord Brutus also casually remarks
that Bubba's arms and chest will have to be
broken to make her less dangerous. In terror
Silvester tells Holy John, who takes it as a
sign from the Lord that the boy and bear should
go with him on a mission to convert the
Kutrigurs. At first their escape is agonizingly
slow because Holy John has scarcely walked in
ten years, though he was once a soldier. They

come across an injured Kutrigur named Urguk,
whom Silvester treats with his limited medical
knowledge and whom they then carry with them on
a litter dragged by his horse. Some time later
they discover that Silvester is not only wanted
by the two lords, but also that, evidently
because of a lie by Lord Brutus, his name has
been placed on the lists, the dread roll of
those who have committed offenses against the
emperor and who are hunted for years throughout
the kingdom and then tortured to slow death.
After that they travel by night, with Silvester
and Bubba taking long detours to avoid the road
and the cleared land. When they reach the
Danube, Holy John bribes the captain of a log
raft to take them on and later land them on the
north shore, beyond the jurisdiction of the
empire. On the river they are met by an official
rowing boat carrying a eunuch with the white
wand which signifies authority to arrest those
on the lists, but the raft captain cleverly
makes the boat go aground, and they escape down
the river. Silvester, with Bubba, is put ashore
on the north bank before the eunuch can get a
new boat, with Holy John and Urguk agreeing to
wait a fortnight for him before starting on to
the Kutrigur country. He finds a Slav village
where the people are delighted by the bear and
call the local noble to see him. This man,
Antonius*, lives in a restored Roman garrison
and considers himself the last true Roman,
upholding the standards and learning of the
great empire after its fall. He wants to keep
Silvester, who can read Latin, but since the boy
is intent on finding Ariadne and ransoming her
with the ruby he found in the raided house,
Antonius lets him go with the agreement that, if
he cannot find her, he will return to this
tower. When they finally reach the main
Kutrigur settlement, Urguk's home, Silvester is
ordered to have Bubba dance for the leader, the
Khan Zabergan, because bears have a totemic
significance to the Kutrigurs. Though Bubba is
upset, Silvester gets her to dance until she
smells the Hun who carried Ariadne away and
incidentally injured Bubba the night of the
raid, and she breaks away and kills him. At
first it seems as if Silvester will be killed in
revenge, but the Khan cleverly manipulates

things so that both young Greeks will be his
slaves. Silvester discovers that Ariadne is
quite happy, having become one of the herd girls
and an accomplished rider. With no duties except
to care for Bubba, Silvester is restless and
hides food in preparation for their escape. The
opportunity comes when another group of
barbarians attacks the Hun settlement. When the
two reach the Danube with Bubba, Silvester wants
Ariadne to go back to the city and claim her
inheritance, though he cannot go because he is
on the lists. She refuses, and together they go
to Antonius, who eventually adopts Silvester and
then dies. Among his things Silvester finds a
record showing that he was not a Roman at all
but the descendant of a Greek slave who escaped,
set himself up in the abandoned garrison, and by
claiming royal Roman blood started a family that
dominated the surrounding Slavs. With this
example, and with his manumission papers which
Ariadne makes him write out, Silvester starts a
life as a Byzantine noble who has, for some
reason, chosen to live in this Roman garrison as
lord of the village Slavs. He marries Ariadne,
who has no desire to return to the restrictive
life of a Byzantine lady. While the story is
full of action and colorful description of life
in Byzantium and among the barbarians of the
north, the main interest is in Silvester's
gradual change from a boy with a slave
mentality, unquestioningly following orders, to
an independent thinker and the concurrent change
of Ariadne from an unhappy doll-like figure to a
free and assertive young woman. The intrigues
and religious rivalries of the nobles in the
city are especially well evoked, and Bubba and
Holy John are memorable characters who are both
humorous and sympathetic. Carnegie Com; Contemporary Classics; Fanfare.

DANGER AT BLACK DYKE (Finlay*, Winifred, Harrap,
1968; Phillips, 1968), mystery-detective novel
set in the mid-1900s in the marshy country along
the Roman Wall in the north of England. A school
project so inspires three ten-year-old English
schoolboys, Geordie* Bickerson, Tim* Charlton,
and Hamish* MacLeish, with enthusiasm for local
history that they form a secret society to
reenact the rituals of Mithras, an ancient cult

brought to England by the Roman legionaries,
complete with masks, replicas of ancient implements, and passwords. One day, while playing at
Roman soldiers, Geordie and Tim come upon Bud*
(Hart) Riley, a youth who is fleeing from pursuers whose identity and purposes he persistently refuses to divulge. The boys offer him
sanctuary in the old, abandoned farmhouse, Black
Dyke, that serves as headquarters for their
society, and unwittingly become involved in
international intrigue. Geordie masterminds
their efforts not only to give Bud the protection he apparently needs but also to learn
why he is being pursued. The boys initiate him
into their society so that he can legitimately
remain at Black Dyke, provide him with food, and
even take him into their confidence about the
secret passage located off the cellar, which
they believe to be the escape route of robbers
who once made the farmhouse the center of their
operations and think may contain a buried
treasure. Although Bud realizes his presence
endangers the children, he recognizes that his
circumstances require their help. He cheerfully
goes along with their schemes, and he comes to
respect their ingenuity and resourcefulness. In
town, Geordie overhears a conversation between
two strangers that indicates that they are Bud's
pursuers and that they plan to locate him by
following two youths and a girl who earlier
helped Bud elude them. When the two men check in
at the local hotel, Hamish enlists the help of
the owner's daughter, Connie, in keeping tabs on
them. She proves gullible, however, and unwittingly leads them to the hideout. They take Bud
captive and imprison his friends and the boys in
the cellar passage. Geordie squirms his way
through its unexcavated portion to the other
end, where he attracts the attention of his
stalwart, peppery Gran*, who is bicycling by.
In a melodramatic scene, she releases King
Arthur, a great, white bull known for his
temper, who effectively foils the villains'
plans to escape with Bud. The two had intended
to use Bud to blackmail his father, a wealthy
businessman, into supporting a movement to overthrow a South American government, an effort
that in the meantime has been suppressed,
rendering their plans unnecessary. Although the

foreign agents are types, Geordie, Tim, Hamish, Gran, and Bud are interesting characters whom the reader gradually gets to know and increasingly likes. Like Geordie, the reader struggles, however, to understand why Bud does not go to the police with his problem, but the plot is otherwise well-knit, if constructed with genre conventions, and remains suspenseful to its rather flat conclusion. The story is rich in human interest with the themes of friendship, coming to terms with life, rapport between generations, and the pleasures of imaginative play. The setting is especially well drawn and plays a significant role in the story, and local history meshes well with the plot. The author aptly catches the flavor of regional dialect, and vocabulary is mature but not difficult. Poe Winner.

DANNY (*The Seventh Raven**), ex-drama teacher and terrorist from a South American dictatorship called Matteo, who blunders into taking a whole opera cast of 100 children and some twenty adults hostage in St. Andrew's church, Kensington, England. Leader of the four terrorists, he he is an amateur, and he seems to alternate between boredom and political fervor, possibly worked up more for dramatic effect than through conviction.

DANNY LODGE (*Brother in the Land**), teenager who survives the nuclear exchange that wipes out most of England and, presumably, most of the rest of the world. At first trusting and hopeful, Danny becomes increasingly hardened and cynical living in the ruins of his devastated town, where conditions turn decent people into thieves, killers, and worse. Danny is saved from despair by his love for Kim* Tyson and for his little brother, Ben, as well as by the wise counsel and practical activity of Sam Branwell*, leader of the resistance group called Masada. In the end, Danny has developed enough to offer comfort to Kim and to organize a brave but probably futile attempt to take her and Ben to an island where he hopes they may be safe.

DANNY, THE CHAMPION OF THE WORLD (Dahl*, Roald, ill. Jill Bennett, Cape, 1975; Knopf, 1975), realistic novel of exaggerated, mock-serious action set in the late 1900s in the English countryside. Danny tells how, since his mother died, he has been raised by his father, William*, a hardworking auto mechanic who runs a little filling station on the side. The two live simply in a gypsy caravan parked out in the back of the station under an apple tree. Danny and his father are very close, and William tells Danny stories that he makes up especially for him about a Big Friendly Giant (BFG), teaches him about car engines, and takes him kite and balloon flying. Danny loves life with father and yearns for nothing more than to continue the special relationship he has with his "sparky," life-loving father. One night when he is nine, he awakens to find his father mysteriously absent from the caravan, something that has never happened before in all his life. Later, he learns that his father, once an enterprising, adept poacher, has sneaked off to polish his rusty skills at the nearby estate of wealthy, grasping Victor Hazell, who employs sharp-eyed, armed keepers to mind the pheasant flocks he maintains for the annual shoots he puts on for socialites and cronies. Danny learns, too, that William longs to return to the sport he had been taught by his father, who was considered a master at it, and that he considers poaching the greatest of sports. On his next expedition to the Hazell estate, William falls into a pit dug by the keepers (considered a particularly terrible way to nab poachers) and breaks his ankle. In an exciting and suspenseful episode, Danny rescues William using a Baby Austin his father has just repaired, and Doc Spencer, beloved local physician and a poacher-sympathizer, helps with first aid and an ambulance. Danny learns that everyone around believes poaching a grand game and has a tacit or active interest in it. When William discovers that Hazell plans to hold a shoot to celebrate the opening of hunting season and ponders how to capture the 200 pheasants Hazell has accumulated, Danny suggests spiking raisins (William's father's favorite pheasant bait) with William's left-over sleeping powders. The trick works splendidly, and the two come away from the hazardous venture with 120 doped birds. Everyone in town is in on the scheme, including the local taxi driver, who transports the pheasants to the village vicarage where they are stored with the vicar's consent prior to being divvied out to deserving locals, and Doc Spencer declares Danny the champion of the world for his inventiveness. All goes well until the next day, when, just as Mrs.* Clipstone, the vicar's wife, is transporting the birds to William's garage in her baby carriage, one by one the birds come to and fly up, settling in the apple tree by the filling station. When Sergeant* Samways suggests that Hazell prove the pheasants are his by shooing them back to his land, the half-doped birds settle on Hazell's shiny silver Rolls Royce, leaving slimy messes all over it. Hazell angrily starts up the car and roars away, and the scared birds stream off in the opposite direction. All is not lost, however, because Doc Spencer has foreseen what might happen and has cleverly stored six birds in the garage. Everyone considers the exploit great fun and a "famous victory," and William and Danny, who wishes every child had a parent as "sparky" as his, make plans to poach trout next. The implied comments on the relationships between the classes would have more meaning for a British audience than an American one, but the adventures are rollicking good fun, are unpretentiously and cleverly worked out, and hold up to the very last page. Dahl skillfully enlists the reader's sympathy for father and son and builds credibility for the nonsense by his warm and affectionately detailed descriptions of their way of life before he launches into the tall-tale part of the story. The style is straight-faced, and Hazell is such an obviously overdrawn villain that the reader readily accepts the fun of it all and never questions the morality of the Robin Hood exploits of these latter-day "good guys." Choice.

DARCY JONES (*The Robbers**), Welsh boy who becomes a friend of Philip* Holbein in London and with whom he gets into trouble with the law. Red-haired, with freckles, Darcy has a cheerful temperament and a beautiful singing voice. Because his father is badly crippled by arthritis, the family live with Darcy's brother, Bing*, and

Bing's black wife, Addie*, and Darcy takes much
of the responsibility for feeding and helping
to nurse his father. Worry over their finances
when Bing goes to prison creates the situation
that gets Darcy and Philip into trouble. Darcy's
strong concern for Addie and her prospective
baby makes him turn down the prospect of going
to school to train his fine voice, but the
possibility that he may be able to change his
mind is left open.

THE DARK BEHIND THE CURTAIN (Cross*, Gillian,
ill. David Parkins, Oxford, 1982; Merrimack,
1984), novel of suspense involving ghosts and
confrontations with evil in two dimensions. The
teenagers in the school of Headmaster Mr.*
Garner prepare to present the musical *Sweeney
Todd, the Demon Barber of Fleet Street*. Since
producer-director Miss* Lampeter needs one more
actor, Mr. Garner impresses into service Colin
Jackus*, who was recently caught stealing school
tape recorders, in return for not prosecuting
him. The other youths accept Jackus reluctantly
because of his reputation for rebelliousness and
trouble making. As rehearsals continue, Colin
Marshall*, Jackus's childhood pal and the star
of the play, seems increasingly to embody the
evilness of the barber, even when not acting. A
series of unsettling and inexplicable events
occurs: books fall from shelves and open and
close by themselves, a pencil flies through the
air and almost hits Miss Lampeter, objects
disappear, and Jackus and fat, bossy Ann*
Ridley, who plays the baker woman, find child-
sized footprints in the paint on the prop room
floor. Suspecting ghosts, Jackus and Ann hold a
kind of seance in his garage, during which
small footprints are left by bodiless beings who
Ann is convinced are the spirits of abused and
hungry children from the Victorian era. She
persuades Jackus that they are seeking revenge
against those like Sweeney who oppressed them.
Suspense builds as two plot problems work themselves out: the spirits' activities and the
growing antagonism between Marshall and Jackus.
Events come to a head during the first night's
performance when Ann as baker grabs the knife
belonging to Marshall as Sweeney and tries to
kill him and thus to do away with the evil that

beset the children and send them back to their
dimension. Jackus intervenes at the critical
moment and dismisses the ghosts by convincing
them that killing will only perpetuate the evil.
Although Marshall gratefully offers to go to Mr.
Garner and explain that Jackus stole the
recorders on his dare, Jackus refuses to allow
him to do so, thus emancipating himself from
Marshall. He realizes that Marshall is probably
sincere at the moment about wanting to right old
wrongs but feels that he, Jackus, had better
recognize the other boy for what he really is,
selfish and manipulative, and sever ties
completely. This story about the importance of
forgiveness and being true to one's self is told
mostly in third person from Jackus's point of
view, becoming more tightly focused as the
reader learns more about the relationship
between Marshall and Jackus and hence becomes
more sympathetic to Jackus, who at first seems
quite reprehensible. Here and there appear
excerpts from Ann's diary. These serve to
clarify the characters of the two boys and
reveal the motives for Ann's behavior. The conclusion seems rushed, some mysterious events
are never satisfactorily explained, and the
spirits' objective is not clear. Do they wish to
kill Marshall/Sweeney, or just to disrupt the
play? The three main characters are flat and
symbolic, and the book's strongest element is
its atmosphere of impending danger, an aspect
created early and sustained well throughout the
book. The headmaster and Miss Lampeter are sympathetically and convincingly realized. Carnegie Highly Com.

THE DARK IS RISING (Cooper*, Susan, ill. Alan
Cober, Chatto, 1973; Atheneum, 1973), fantasy
set recently in a village in Buckinghamshire
during the twelve days of Christmas, the second
in The Dark Is Rising series, which also
includes *The Grey King**. For his eleventh
birthday, which falls on Midwinter Day, Will*
Stanton, seventh son of a seventh son, receives
from Farmer Dawson a circle of iron crossed by
two lines, an emblem which he is instructed to
keep with him at all times for his protection
and which he subsequently wears on his belt. In
evading a mysterious Black Rider, Will is

transported on a white horse back in time to a
great hall. There he meets a frail old lady and
a tall, imposing man, Merriman* Lyon, who informs Will that he is an Old One, one of those
immortals who are as old as the land, who represent the Light of Good, and whose responsibility
is to defeat the evil ones whose power is of the
Dark and who are attempting to bring all the
world under their control. The lady and Merriman
are also Old Ones, as are Farmer Dawson and two
of his men. Will learns that he is the long-
awaited Sign-Seeker and that, when he has
acquired the signs of wood, bronze, water, fire,
and stone to put with the iron circle and the
knowledge of the ancient Book of Gramarye, the
Old Ones will be able to overcome the forces of
the Dark. Going back and forth in time and
assisted by the Old Ones, especially Merriman
Lyon, all of whom also exist in the present as
well as in the past, Will gradually finds the
necessary signs, except for those of fire and
water, and gains the knowledge of the ancient
book by Twelfth Night. As the days pass the
weather worsens, until on Twelfth Night all
England is in the throes of the most terrible
snowfall and cold spell in recorded history.
When, on Twelfth Night, Will acquires the sign
of fire, a torrential thunderstorm occurs, melting the snow and causing a flood. The torrent
unearths the ship burial of an ancient king,
from whose body Will takes the last sign, that
of water, thus breaking the power of the Dark.
Characters are conventional good-versus-evil
types, and not even Will is well developed or
made sympathetic. The book's authority comes
from its atmosphere of impending doom which is
created early and is well sustained. Skillful
use of Celtic folklore strengthens the plot,
which follows the quest pattern familiar from
hero tales. Past and present are skillfully
intermingled to support the theme of the continuing conflict between good and evil, but it
is never clear why the Old Ones do not exert
more control over circumstances. Boston Globe
Winner; Carnegie Com.; Choice; Contemporary
Classics; Fanfare.

DAVID (*Kept in the Dark**), grandson by a first
marriage of the children's Grandpa* and

therefore their half cousin, who turns up and begins to terrorize the household. Presumably an American orphan, he speaks with a British accent. He has visited before and been demanding and unpleasant, but this time he seems to be planning to stay and to inherit the house, possibly even speeding the old people into the grave. Although too plump to be physically attractive, he can be charming and remains an ambiguous character, possibly just insecure and willful but well-meaning, or possibly an impos- ter, even criminal or insane, and a potential murderer.

DAVID BALFOUR (*Kidnapped**), son of a village schoolmaster who learns that he is really the heir to a large estate, which his Uncle* Ebenezer Balfour has falsely claimed and has allowed to deteriorate under his miserly management. Kidnapped, shipwrecked, and unjustly suspected of the Jacobite murder of the king's factor, David makes his way across Scotland in secret with many adventures on the way. Although he realizes that he would be safer alone, he cannot bring himself to point this out to fiery Alan* Breck Stewart, who solicitously accompa- nies him. While adequate in his role, David is more the typical boy hero than a well- developed character.

DAVID HOLDER (*Wall of Words**), youth of fourteen who lives next door to the Tates and is Kim* Tate's best friend. The two often converse while lying on their garage roofs, where they can exchange confidences in private. David's family is better off than the Tates, and he accommo- datingly and resourcefully but uncondescendingly assists Kim in her efforts to earn a little extra money for the family by doing odd jobs. Thus he affects the plot by helping to bring Kim into contact with Mrs. Hanrahan and to a solution to Kerry* Tate's problem. Before the novel begins, David and Kim quarrel over Mr.* Tate's going away to complete his novel, and David continues to be unimpressed by Kim's father's aspirations. He maintains that most people who write novels manage to do it without leaving their families. He thinks that Mr. Tate has simply deserted his family and neglected his obligations. Events prove him right. David is not as well drawn as are the Tate children.

DAVID HUGHES (*The Grange at High Force**), son of the Darnley carpenter. He is an imaginative boy, appreciating beauty and quality of craftsmanship, and is the one mainly interested in tracing what has happened to the statue of Our Lady. Having been crippled as a small child, a condition relieved by an operation, he has been bookish yet desirous of adventure. He consults Guns* Kelly about the advantages of joining the navy. The only one who can manage snowshoes, he goes ahead of the others to check on Miss* Cadell-Twitten, and when he finds her confused and near freezing, he competently gets her fire going, persuades her to eat, and is largely responsible for her rescue.

DAVID IN SILENCE (Robinson*, Veronica, ill. Victor Ambrus, Deutsch, 1965; Lippincott, 1966), realistic problem novel set in the mid-1900s in a working-class suburb of Birmingham, England. The story is told mostly from the vantage point of two thirteen-year-old youths, David Williams, deaf since birth, and Michael Guest, his first hearing friend. When David's family moves to Blackley, most of the children in the neighborhood regard him with suspicion and distaste because he seems aloof and makes animal-like sounds. Michael and his sister, Eileen, 14, make overtures of friendship, and Michael persists in learning to communicate with David by writing, sign language, and lip reading. The two work happily together for days on a model village David is making out of matchsticks. One day Michael attends a ball game in another part of the city. David leaves his house, and through signing manages to join a soccer game some younger boys are playing. Buoyed in spirits because they seem to accept him and recognize his playing ability, David responds with such exuberance that they turn on him, mistaking honest joy for the desire to dominate. They chase him into the hills overlooking the subdivision. Perplexed and terrified by their anger, he flees, taking refuge in a narrow, long, dark tunnel by a canal. For hours he makes his way through the darkness, panicky and puzzled, once falling into the cold and grimy water, before emerging at the other end in an unfamiliar part of the city. He has enough presence of mind to take a bus, but once back in Blackley is unable to get directions for home. He is in a state of panic and nearly exhausted when Michael happens to see him on his way home from his game. The story comes out, and the other children make a greater effort to understand David. He advances in their esteem when he corrects a defect in the rafts they build and later joins them for a trip up the canal. The book stops abruptly as the reader hears the youths express admiration for David's solo trip through the tunnel while they are paddling to its limit. The plot seems tailor-made to teach young readers about the problems of both the deaf and those who live with them. Some scenes have life, and David's feelings and hopes are made real and palpable, sometimes painfully so. Passages in which Eric, his older brother, discusses with the neighborhood youth his brother's handicap and the methods of communicating with the deaf have a particularly didactic flavor. Choice.

DAVID MOSS (*"Minnow" on the Say**), eleven-year-old son of a Barley bus driver, whose house stands on the River Say. He discovers the canoe called the *Minnow*, which the flooded Say has deposited at the Moss dock, and disobeys his mother's orders about not trying to find the owner by himself. He finds and makes friends with Adam* Codling, to whom it belongs. He and Adam use the canoe to recover the Codling family's lost jewels. David is a likeable, venturesome boy, good-natured, mostly obedient and helpful, and, like most boys of his age, somewhat unreliable and inclined to get caught up in schemes. He comes up with most of the ideas that lead to the discovery of the old treasure and the retention of the Codling ancestral house. Although upon reflection it seems unlikely that David would not have known Adam before the novel begins, the reader soon forgives the author this small implausibility as the adventures of detecting unfold.

DAVID WIX (*Earthfasts**), grammar-school youth,

son of the local physician in Garebridge, friend of Keith* Heseltine, who with Keith observes Nellie Jack John Cherry, an eighteenth-century army drummer boy, materialize from inside Haw Bank. David is the leader of the two boys and comes up with most of the ideas that motivate their activities in discovering what is behind the mysterious events that are occurring around Garebridge. For example, he suggests they hunt for giants' tracks after the local piggery is raided and that they write a book about their experiences, details that later substantiate Keith's story about giants and the unnamed witness's testimony about supernatural happenings associated with David's disappearance. David is more intelligent than Keith and seeks scientific explanations for things, while Keith is more clever and intuitive. David is also more concerned than Keith about John's feelings. Why the black rider kidnapped David is never explained.

DAVIES, ANDREW (WYNFORD) (1936-   ), born in Cardiff, Wales; teacher, author of novels, playwright. His books have all been for young readers. His first novel was *The Fantastic Feats of Doctor Boox* (Collins, 1972; Bradbury, 1973), a humorous story about a doctor who helps animals in trouble. His next novel, *Conrad's War** (Blackie, 1978; Crown, 1980), received the *Guardian* and *Boston Globe-Horn Book* awards and was named to *Choice* and Fanfare. A humorous, loosely autobiographical, satirical fantasy novel, with lots of wry comment and zany slapstick, it concerns a boy's problematic relationship with his writer father and was intended as an antidote to the sentimental, antiseptic portrayals of fathers and sons common in children's books. It was written to please his son, who is something like Conrad, and Davies's family refers to Davies as "The Great Writer," also Conrad's term for his father. To please his daughter, Davies wrote *Marmalade and Rufus* (Blackie, 1979; Crown, 1983), another hilarious fantasy-satire about an incorrigible girl and an intractable, chauvinistic talking donkey, the first of a series about the irrepressible duo. Until the early 1970s, Davies was known as a dramatist for radio

and television. He has authored many radio plays
and nearly twenty television plays for the BBC,
mainly for adults, including a highly regarded
trilogy on Eleanor Marx, daughter of Karl Marx.
For children's television he did "The Legend of
King Arthur" and some programs about Marmalade.
He has also written for the live stage. Davies
was educated at Whitchurch Grammar School,
Glamorgan, Wales, and received his B.A. degree
with honors in English in 1957 from University
College, London. From 1958-1963 he taught at
St. Clement Danes Grammar School and Woodberry
Down School in London, and after that he became
a lecturer at Coventry College of Education and
the University of Warwick. He married Diana
Hentley, also a teacher.

DAVY (*The Lark and the Laurel**), simpleminded
waif whom Cecily Jolland befriends after his
mother abandons him to run off with her lover.
Cecily's decision to care for him marks a
turning point in her development toward a
caring and responsible young woman and significantly affects the plot. When Sir Thomas
Jolland's messengers come for Cecily, Davy
cleverly leads them astray, enabling her to
escape to the forest.

DAWN MUDD (*The Battle of Bubble and Squeak**),
school friend of Peggy Parker. She realizes that
Mrs.* Sparrow, Peggy's mother, is slow to accept
change, gets a book about gerbils from the
library, and suggests that Peggy leave it for
Mrs. Sparrow to read. She thinks that by looking
at the pictures and reading bits of it Mrs.
Sparrow may become more receptive to keeping
Bubble* and Squeak. Her idea pays off. When Sid*
Parker hears his mother remark that since,
according to the book, gerbils have a short life
expectancy of three years, she will only have
to endure them that long, Sid remarks to his
sister that his mother appears to be facing up
to having them around, a step in the right
direction.

DAWN WIND (Sutcliff*, Rosemary, ill. Charles
Keeping, Oxford, 1961; Walck, 1962), historical
novel set in southern England in the late sixth
century, showing the beginnings of British-Saxon

understanding. When the last of the Roman-
British forces fall at Aquae Sulis (Bath), the
only two who wake and stagger from the battlefield are Owain*, 14, and a young war hound.
Owain finds the bodies of his older brother and
his father, and takes from his father's hand the
signet ring, with a dolphin carved on a flawed
emerald, which has been a family heirloom.
Then, wounded and confused, he starts with Dog
toward Viroconium, the mustering city, with some
vague idea that any survivors will gather
there. Somewhere north of Glevum (Gloucester) he
collapses on the threshold of a remote British
farm belonging to an old Christian couple named
Priscilla and Priscus, who nurse him back to
health and offer him a home, but when he is
strong enough he pushes on, only to find
Viroconium deserted and mostly destroyed. After
he snares a rabbit and builds a fire, he
discovers that he is not alone with Dog. A girl,
about twelve, grasshopper thin, in rags and
infested with lice, approaches and begs for some
of the meat. The child, Regina*, an orphan and
a beggar even before the Saxon coming, shares
his fire, and soon they have made themselves a
sort of home. They spend the winter together in
the ruins. Regina is afraid to leave the city
until cattle raiders, who are British renegades
and not Saxons, come through, stable their
stolen stock in the Forum, and capture her.
Owain starts the cattle stampeding as a
diversion, Regina breaks away, and together they
race through the dark alleys and overgrown
gardens, pursued by the raiders, until they
finally crawl, with Dog, into the hypocaust of a
collapsed house and wait through the night, in
horror, since they have found the bones of the
owner, who must have also hidden there from the
Saxons. Without any discussion, they agree that
they must leave Viroconium, and they set out
toward the southeast with a slight hope that
they may find a way to get to Gaul. Regina
sickens on the way and becomes very ill. Owain
buries his father's ring under a great thorn
tree and carries Regina to the nearest Saxon
farm, there offering to become a slave for them
if they will care for Regina. The farmer rejects
his offer but Beornwulf, a young Saxon from
Seals' Island on the Sussex coast several days'

ride away who happens to be spending the night,
buys him and Dog for one gold piece, and the
mistress of the house agrees to nurse Regina in
return. Owain spends more than the next six
years wearing the thrall ring at the coastal
farm, desperately lonely and depressed though
not badly treated. During that period Owain
becomes Beornwulf's trusted lieutenant,
separated by temperament and intelligence from
the other thralls. When a mare about to foal
breaks out one misty night, Owain finds her
already in labor on the land belonging to Vadir*
Cedricson, their neighbor, and he helps her
deliver a stallion colt which even at birth
shows that he will be white. Vadir, a bitter,
disagreeable man with a club foot, finds him
and, though insulting to Owain, is strangely
gentle with the foal, explaining to Owain that
such a horse is very rare and will be sent to
the stables of Haegel the King, foster brother
of Beornwulf, as a God-horse, sacred to the god
Frey, to be sacrificed at a time of need in the
kingdom. Called Teitri, which means simply
"foal," the horse is never broken to saddle but
only to the headstall, a job which Owain
accomplishes, and he helps Beornwulf deliver him
to the king's stables. On the day of his return,
Vadir allows his hounds to set on Dog and
watches the fight with amusement, and Bryni,
Beornwulf's ten-year-old son, rushes to get
Owain, who wades into the struggle and suffers
some bad bites but is unable to save Dog. Bryni
vows to kill Vadir, and Owain, despite his own
hatred for the man, tries to point out to the
boy that he could start a blood feud which would
ruin his family. Beornwulf goes with Haegel to
the court of King Aethelbert of Kent, taking
Teitri as a royal gift and leaving the farm in
Owain's hands. He returns by ship in a storm,
and Owain risks his life to save him as the ship
cannot get into the harbor and is wrecked on the
rocks near Seals' Island. For that service,
Beornwulf offers him freedom, but Owain bargains
with him to stay a thrall through the winter in
return for a sword to fight Caewlin, the Saxon
whose forces killed his father and brother, in
the conflict sure to come in the spring. At the
suggestion of Einon* Hen, the British envoy from
Wales, he serves as a messenger to the British

forces, who are joining with the Saxons against
Caewlin, and fights at Wodensbeorg, where
Beornwulf is mortally wounded. Before he dies,
Beornwulf asks Owain to stay with his family
until Bryni is fifteen and of age to carry a
sword. Though torn, Owain promises and serves
these four more years, managing the farm and
seeing the oldest daughter, Helga, married, but
just before he is ready to move on, Vadir asks
for Lilla, the younger girl, for his wife.
Beornwulf's widow is afraid to say no, but
Owain, who has always been fond of Lilla and
knows that she greatly fears Vadir, offers to
stay one more year if Vadir can be put off at
least that long. Before the year is up, Bryni
distinguishes himself by a rash but courageous
act in the king's boar hunt, and both he and
Owain are chosen to accompany Haegel to Cantis-
burg to answer a summons from King Aethelbert.
Vadir also is part of the company, and as they
all wait at the Kentish court, he and Bryni, who
have both drunk too much, quarrel and, to settle
it, Vadir choses to ride Teitri, a double danger
since he has never been ridden and it is a
sacrilege to mount Frey's Horse. Vadir is
killed, though Owain tries to save him. Relieved
at last of the threat to fearful Lilla and
impulsive Bryni, Owain leaves Seals' Island,
travels northward to the farm where he left
Regina, and learns that she has run away a month
before, after her old mistress died and her
young master wanted to take her for a second
wife. He goes to the thorn tree, digs where he
left the ring some eleven years before, and
finds a little clay pot containing a lock of
black hair tied with a strand of scarlet thread.
He rightly interprets it to mean that Regina has
returned to Viroconium, and there he finds her,
living once more in the little courtyard where
they made their home. He plans to take her to
Priscus and Priscilla and to start life anew.
The title comes from the words of the British
envoy, whom Owain meets again at Aethelbert's
court, who says that the reconcilation, the
light ahead, is not yet here but that the wind
before the dawn is rising. Owain's devotion to
the Saxon family is logical, as is his return to
Regina. The difficult political allegiances of
the period are made clear and are important to

the plot, and some of the scenes, like the
battlefield at the opening and the coming of
Augustine, the Christian missionary to the court
of Aethelbert, are memorable. Books Too Good;
Choice; Fanfare.

DAYA WANTI (*The Devil's Children**), grandmother
of Gopal*, mother of six of the adults in the
Sikh group, and great-grandmother of some of
the younger children. She is carried in a
cushioned cart and speaks no English, but she is
clearly the leader of the group, prevailing in
the noisy councils by her strong personality and
good sense. At first Nicky* Gore thinks that,
with her face shriveled into wrinkles and folds
and a thin, hooked nose standing out like the
beak of a hawk, she looks like a witch, but a
queen witch. She wears at least five necklaces
and two rings on each finger of her left hand.
Later Nicky becomes much attached to the old
woman, with whom she feels a special kinship,
and though they must always speak through an
interpreter, they seem to have a strong mutual
understanding. In the end, Daya Wanti persuades
Nicky to go to France to try to find her family
by telling her of her own experience when she
was married at twelve to a stranger and hardened
her heart as she has seen Nicky doing. She also
provides the bribe (probably one of her rings)
to the sailor who will take Nicky out to the
ship in the middle of the channel.

DEFOE, DANIEL (1660-1731), born in London; merchant, political pamphleteer, novelist. The son
of a butcher named James Foe, he changed his
name about 1703, perhaps as a return to a
version of an older family name, Du-foe. Defoe
was well educated for his day at the Reverend
James Fisher's school in Dorking and at the
Reverend Charles Morton's academy at Newington
Green, Stoke Newington. He originally intended
to become a clergyman but decided to be a
merchant, making and losing a number of fortunes
in his lifetime. Throughout his life he was
involved in politics. Originally he was a Whig
and a dissenter from the Church of England. In
1702 he wrote a pamphlet, "The Shortest Way with
the Dissenters," ironically advocating that all
dissenters should be hanged. Unfortunately, it

was misunderstood by Whigs, who took it at face
value, and also by Tories, who thought it
accused them unjustly of wanting violence, and
Defoe was arrested, fined, and sentenced to
stand in the pillory three times and to serve
seven years imprisonment. After several months
he was released, but his business had failed in
his absence, he needed money for his large
family, and he became a pamphleteer for both
sides, sometimes simultaneously. During the
reign of Queen Anne, he wrote and published the
Review, a thrice-weekly paper that was for ten
years the main government organ. In 1719 he
ventured into his first long fiction with
*Robinson Crusoe** (Taylor, 1719-1720), now named
a Children's Classic, originally titled, *The
Life and Strange Surprizing Adventures of Robinson Crusoe, of York, Mariner: Who Lived Eight
and Twenty Years All Alone in an Un-inhabited
Island on the Coast of America, Near the Mouth
of the Great River of Oroonoque; Having Been
Cast on Shore by Shipwreck, Where-in All the Men
Perished but Himself. With an Account How He Was
at Last Strangely Deliver'd by Pyrates.* It is
usually considered the first English novel and
been published in literally hundreds of editions
in many languages. In 1722 he published his two
other best-known novels, *Moll Flanders* (Chet-
wood) and *A Journal of the Plague Year* (Nutt).
Although most of his writings were unsigned and
the authorship of many are in scholarly dispute
the *Encyclopaedia Brittanica* says his published
works may exceed 545.

DEIRDRE (Polland*, Madeleine A., World's Work,
1967; Doubleday, 1967), fictionalized retelling
of the ancient Irish tale of the tragic and
beautiful daughter of Felim the Harper in the
days of King Conor MacNessa and the Red Branch
heroes. The novel follows the old story closely:
at Deirdre's birth, old Caffa the druid sees
disaster in her stars; to avert this fate, Conor
decides to raise her and marry her himself; so
that she shall not be attracted to a younger
man, he isolates her with her nurse, Lavercam,
in a distant and secluded place; nevertheless,
when she grows up she meets by chance Naoise,
son of Usna, and falls immediately in love with
him; to escape Conor's wrath, they flee with the

two brothers of Naoise, the twins Ardann and
Alainn, to Alba, present-day Scotland; after
some time Conor sends Fergus MacRoy to Alba to
ask the sons of Usna to return to his palace at
Emain Macha, promising forgiveness; though
Deirdre does not trust Conor's motives, they
return and are arrested at Conor's orders; when
the sons of Usna are slain, Deirdre also dies
and is buried in the same grave. The novel
departs from the best-known old versions in a
few places: as a young child, Deirdre is not
isolated with Lavercam but raised at Emain
Macha, where she knows Naiose, and is seven
before Conor builds for her not a simple hut in
the forest but a rather lavish hall surrounded
by a high fence and sends Caffa as well as the
nurse to see to her education. When the sons of
Usna first go to Alba, they take service with
the king, and it is not until an attempt is made
to kidnap Deirdre for the king of Alba that they
go off to the wilderness to live. Even there,
Deirdre and the three men have some servants.
After the sons of Usna are beheaded, Deirdre
simply dies and falls into the grave; she does
not, as in some versions, throw herself to her
death from Conor's chariot. The highly romantic
story, like many tales from the oral tradition,
is better in its original brief, spare version
than developed with the realistic detail of
Polland's fictional treatment. The dialogue of
Deirdre and Naoise, particularly when they are
being playful, is not convincing. Fanfare.

DEIRDRE (Stephens*, James, Macmillan, 1923;
Macmillan, 1923), fantasy novel involving magic,
which weaves together and embroiders various
oral traditions about Deirdre, beautiful tragic
heroine of Ulster. The night Deirdre is born,
Cathfa, poet and magician, predicts she will
bring evil to Ireland and names her Deirdre,
the Troubler. She is reared in seclusion in
Emain Macha, King Conachur's stronghold, with
faithful, opportunistic Lavarcham, the king's
"conversation-woman" or spy, as her nurse. When
Queen Maeve terminates her marriage by going
home to Connacht, Lavarcham, grown ambitious for
the fosterling she has lovingly raised, arranges
a meeting between Deirdre, now sixteen and
beautiful, intelligent, and resourceful, and

proud and willful King Conachur. As she hopes,
the king is so taken with Deirdre that he
immediately decides to make her his wife.
Unfamiliar with the ways of the world, however,
frightened of the self-important, overbearing
king, and in love with Naoise, one of the three
sons of Uisneac (a handsome young warrior she
has met quite by chance), Deirdre persuades
Naoise to run away with her, and together with
his two brothers, Ainnle and Ardan, they flee to
Scotland. The story then skips ahead seven
years. To salve his wounded pride, Conachur has
thrown himself into the work of kingship, and,
though he has become wealthy and powerful, the
loss of Deirdre still lies heavy on his heart,
and he schemes to bring the exiles home. His
yearning is ironically whetted by Lavarcham, who
longs to have her fosterling back. When he
learns that Naoise is under *geasa* (taboo) to
return only under the protection of Conall,
Cuchulinn, or Fergus mac Roy (all warriors), he
manages to get Fergus, who is very fond of him
and trusts him, to agree to fetch the exiles.
Then he arranges with another noble, Borach, to
invite Fergus to a feast when the exiles land,
knowing that Fergus is under a *geasa* never to
refuse such an invitation, thus making it
impossible for Fergus to protect the fugitives.
In spite of Deirdre's pleas that they not return
with Fergus, since she has had a dream of doom,
the sons of Uisneac trust Fergus and their king,
long to rejoin their fighting comrades at the
court, and they do come back. Fergus charges his
two sons to protect the exiles, and all proceed
to Emain Macha, where they are lodged in the Red
Branch rather than the Royal Branch, the king's
house. Portents of doom continue to haunt
Deridre, and Lavarcham warns them of treachery
and lies to the king that Deirdre is no longer
beautiful, hoping thus to save their lives. A
guard spies on them, however, and reports the
opposite, and the king orders his men to
attack. Cathfa makes magic against them,
Conachur has the hostel set afire, and, though
they fight valiantly, the sons of Uisneac are
captured and executed in a dramatic climax to
the story. In the brief and poignant conclusion, Deirdre keens the deaths, sips of
Naoise's blood, and dies upon his body. Stephens

retells the old tale of revenge, love, hatred, pride, and treachery with the force of a novel, exploring motivations and character and building suspense to hold the interest. Images and figures (usually drawn from nature and occasionally quite elaborate), lengthy descriptive passages, clever turns of phrase, and some use of Irish speech rhythms produce a literary tone. The leisurely pace can be deceptive, since details important to the story's plot appear unexpectedly in seemingly inconsequential dialogue or descriptions. Although predominately serious and romantic, there is occasional humor, some patter dialogue provides relief, and in a few places the author interjects moralistic or sententious comments. The edition cited by *Horn Book* was illustrated by Nonny Hogrogian and published by Macmillan in 1970. Fanfare.

DE LA MARE, WALTER (1873-1956), born in Charlton, Kent and buried at St. Paul's Cathedral, London; author, editor, poet. His early books were published under the pseudonymn Walter Ramal. His father died when he was four, and he was educated at St. Paul's Cathedral Chorister's School, London, where he founded the weekly *Choristers Journal*. For eighteen years, from 1890 to 1908, he was a clerk for the Anglo-American Oil Company, but he also wrote poetry and was a reviewer for *The Times* and *Westminster Gazette*. In 1908 he was granted a Civil List pension which enabled him to write full time. He produced fourteen books of fiction for children, one play, eleven books of verse, and retellings of various kinds, including folktales and *Stories from the Bible* (Faber, 1929; Cosmopolitan, 1929). He also compiled two major anthologies for young people, *Come Hither: A Collection of Rhymes and Poems for the Young of All Ages* (Constable, 1923; Knopf, 1923, revised 1928), a very large collection as notable for its voluminous and entertaining notes as for its wide-ranging selection, and *Tom Tiddler's Ground: A Book of Poetry for the Junior and Middle Schools* (Collins, 1932; Knopf, 1962, a shorter collection of somewhat easier poems. Although his forty-six books of poetry for adults are not attracting major critical

interest at present, those published for young
people clearly place him among the few top poets
for children. Notable among these are *Peacock
Pie: A Book of Rhymes* (Constable, 1913; Holt,
1917) and *Rhymes and Verses: Collected Poems for
Children* (Holt, 1947). His prose works, which
include for adults three novels, eighteen books
of short stories, and a large number of critical
works and editions, were highly acclaimed critically, with his *Memoirs of a Midget* (Collins,
1921; Knopf, 1922) winning the James Tait Memorial Prize for Fiction. For children, his most
notable novel is *The Three Mulla-Mulgars* (Duckworth, 1910; Knopf, 1919, republished as *The
Three Royal Monkeys; or The Three Mulla-Mulgars*,
(Faber, 1935), an unusual fantasy of a quest of
the royal monkey brothers, Thumb, Thimble, and
Nod, for the paradisal land of Tishnar. *Mr.
Bumps and His Monkey** (Winston, 1942), a shorter
fantasy named to the *Horn Book* Fanfare list, was
originally called "The Old Lion." It appeared in
The Lord Fish and Other Tales (Faber, 1933) and
reappeared in *The Old Lion and Other Stories*
(Faber, 1942) and in *Collected Stories for
Children* (Faber, 1947), which won the Carnegie
Medal. Among his other honors, De la Mare was
awarded honorary doctorates from Oxford,
Cambridge, Bristol, London, and St. Andrews
Universities. He was named a Companion of Honour
in 1948 and was awarded the Order of Merit in
1953. His writings for children show a strong
respect for the abilities of young people and an
ability to see from their point of view without
sentimentality.

DENZIL MURGATROYD (*Midnight Is a Place**), father
of Anna-Marie*, son of Lady* Eulalia and Sir
Quincy Murgatroyd, founder of Murgatroyd's
Carpet, Rug, and Matting Manufactury, also known
as Midnight Mill, central industry in Blastburn.
Considered brilliant, Denzil devised the process
that put Murgatroyd's in the forefront of the
carpet industry. He also had a beautiful singing
voice and won fame as a composer. Wild and
irresponsible, however, he left college at
twenty and fell in with a wild group called the
Devil's Roustabouts, among whom was Sir*
Randolph Grimsby. After a long period of trouble
with his family over his behavior, he acceded to

his sweetheart's wishes that he leave the group. At a farewell party he made the ill-fated bet that resulted in his losing the family mill and mansion to Sir Randolph. Denzil then moved to France where Anna-Marie was born and where he died. At the end of the novel, it is learned that Sir Randolph cheated to win the bet.

DEREK POOLEY (*The Devil on the Road**), enigmatic owner of the barn where John* Webster stays and becomes involved with seventeenth-century witch-craft. Often referred to by the local villagers as "Squire Pooley," Derek is from the family that has owned the land for centuries, and he appears to have inherited the admonition to keep the Vavasour house unchanged until a rightful heir returns to claim it. Like the villagers, he is expecting the "harb mother" to come, and he goes to considerable trouble to insure that John will be on hand to take his part in the reenactment of the witch trial. Derek has an abrupt, self-conscious way of speaking, and though he obviously is deeply involved in what, it becomes evident, is an attempt to keep Johanna* Vavasour satisfied by providing her with a young man, he is an educated person and does not admit to a belief in witchcraft. In doing what he sees as his duty to the past, he almost loses his wife, Susan*.

DESAI, ANITA (1937–   ), born in Mussoorie, India; writer for both adults and children. She received her B.A. from Delhi University, is married, and has four children. She has been a member of the Advisory Board for English, Sahilya Akedemi, New Delhi, India, has contributed short stories to many periodicals, including *Harper's Bazaar*, *Writer's Workshop*, and *Envoy*, and has published several novels for adults, including *Bye-bye, Blackbird* (Hind Pocket Books, and *Fire on the Mountain* (Harper, 1977). Among her books for children are *The Peacock Garden* (India Book House, 1974) and *Cat on a Houseboat* (Orient Longmans, 1976). Her *The Village by the Sea** (Heinemann, 1982; Allied Publishers, India, 1983), which won the Guardian Award in 1983, is a quiet, evocative story of a poor family in a changing India.

DEVIL-IN-THE-FOG (Garfield*, Leon, ill. Antony Maitland, Constable, 1966; Pantheon, 1966), period novel of mystery and suspense set in eighteenth century Sussex, dealing with a family of strolling players and a sinister figure who appears semiannually out of the fog with a bag containing thirty guineas. George Treet, 14, who narrates the story, is the red-haired eldest of seven children who make up the troupe of traveling actors led, since the death of their mother seven years before, by their father, the ever optimistic but improvident Mister* Treet, a genius, George assures the reader, and a man of dignity even in the stocks, where he frequently finds himself. His particular flair is for stage effects: flying hoists, cascades and fountains, visions and appparitions, and especially Lucifer's Smoke and the Devil's Fire, which often get out of hand since he keeps experimenting with proportions of the chemical ingredients. Though frequently low on food and other creature comforts, the Treets are a happy family, from seven-year-old Hotspur, who lisps; up through Nell; Henry; Rose, 10, who is very interested in money; Jane, 11, clearly George's favorite; and Edward, the scholar of the group. Their spirits dampen, however, on the third day of June and November, when the Stranger is due to appear, an event that casts even ebullient Mister Treet into rare gloom. It is in the middle of a demonstration of Lucifer's Smoke in the parlor of an inn, the Eloquent Gentlewoman, that the Stranger last appears and gives Mister Treet the fateful message, "My Principal bids me come no more." Mister Treet turns their wagon for the first time in memory to Sussex and explains to George the story of the mystery. Some thirteen years earlier, the Stranger appeared out of a stormy night with a weak, sickly child, and offered Mister Treet thirty guineas twice a year to keep the child, only insisting that he agree to stay out of Sussex and return the boy to his home there if the message ever comes. Thus George Treet becomes George Dexter, son of Sir John and Lady Dexter at the manor house near Fulking. They arrive to find Sir John dying of a wound acquired in a duel with his brother, Captain Richard Dexter. He does not die, however, but gradually grows stronger, and treats George with quiet, steady affection, quite different from that of his wife, which veers wildly from warmth to biting irony. George learns one version of the story of his abduction from the servant, Joseph, who blames Richard Dexter and explains the jealousy between the two brothers caused by an entail upon the property, by which it must go to the eldest male heir. Sir John's first two children had died, and George was a sickly infant, while Richard has several strong sons. George accepts this version at first until Mrs. Montague, a dumpy medium who has been comforting Lady Dexter by communicating with the supposedly dead infant George for years, summons him to a meeting in the nearby copse with his Uncle Richard, who has just escaped from debtor's prison and who borrows five shillings from the boy. Since it seems unlikely that Richard, perennially short of funds, would have come up with sixty guineas a year for Mister Treet, George begins to doubt the story and to wonder about the identities of the Stranger and the Principal. Mrs. Montague suggests that Mister Treet is the villain, but George finds this hard to accept. His suspicion shifts from one to another as a series of complications occur: Richard's wife and sons appear and move into the manor; Mister Treet comes and asks for seventy pounds so that his family can emigrate; Sir John sends George off with a full 100 pounds and a pistol to protect himself; Richard, met in the copse, borrows the extra thirty pounds and points out to George that his pistol has been tampered with so that it will blow up in his face if fired; the Treet family misses the boat on which they have presumably paid all seventy pounds for passage; on his return, George is accosted by a man who is about to shoot him but who is first shot by Richard; Richard, who undertakes to bury the body, finds the bones of an infant buried in the copse; and George recognizes Mr. Craddock, Sir John's attorney, as the Stranger. In the meantime, George has more than once humiliated his mother or his father by playing the actor in company, a background they think unfit for a gentleman, and his set of values has been thoroughly confused. Sir John insists on a hunt for Richard, as if he is a wild beast, and makes

sure that George has his pistol, not knowing
that he has exchanged the damaged one for
Richard's, which is its mate. In the hunt,
George tries to warn Richard, discovers that Sir
John is the Principal, now trying to kill him by
goading him to shoot his pistol, and finally,
having seized the damaged pistol from Richard,
he turns it on George and dies when it blows up
in his own face. The explanation is that Sir
John has been mad with jealousy of his younger
brother, has discovered his own infant son dead,
and has secretly buried him and spread the story
of his abduction, hoping to discredit his
brother, while at the same time arranging
through his attorney to have another infant,
George Treet, brought up as an alternate in case
of need. He had induced the duel, knowing he
will soon die of heart trouble and hoping to
have his brother hanged for murder or at least
jailed, and then sent for George; but he could
not bear to think that an imposter, however
innocent, should inherit, and so has tried to
arrange a fatal accident for George. Although at
first bitter at Mister Treet for selling him, as
it were, at the urging of Lady Dexter George
forgives him, after Mr. Treet has, somewhat
reluctantly, refused the offers of large sums
from both Richard and Lady Dexter to give George
up permanently to one of them. Lady Dexter
leaves the manor to the new Sir Richard and his
wife and takes up residence in London, where she
becomes benefactor to the Treet family. As a
mystery story, the novel has sufficient twists
of plot and red herrings to satisfy any thrill-
seeker, but it also has a steadily maturing
protagonist in George and a wealth of other
interesting characters set in a background of
intrigue and detail of eighteenth-century life.
There is also a good deal of humor, most of it
grim or ironic, and much vivid description that
contributes to the tone of danger and foreboding. Guardian.

THE DEVIL ON THE ROAD (Westall*, Robert, Macmillan, 1978; Greenwillow, 1979), fantasy set in
Suffolk, concerned with witchcraft in both the
seventeenth century and the 1970s. The narrator,
John* Webster, having just finished his first
year at University College, London, takes off on

his motorcycle, a Triumph Tiger-Cub, hoping to
get to the beach, but traffic keeps detouring
him until he finds himself at an annual reenactment of a battle from the English Civil War,
Roundheads against Cavaliers. Always ready for
a fight, he joins one of the Cavaliers manning
a brass cannon. After a company of Roundheads
from the Midlands turns the mock battle into a
real rumpus, John gets evicted, rides off, and,
when a very localized rain storm forces him off
the highway, seeks shelter in an old barn. There
he comes upon one of the Midland company, he
thinks, trying to kill a kitten with his
billhook. John attacks him, and the Roundhead
shoots him point-blank in the head with his
antique pistol. Dazed, John passes out and wakes
to find the owner of the barn and land around
it, Derek* Pooley, bending over him, and his
motorcycle helmet blown to smithereens by the
shot. Derek insists to his wife, Susan*, and to
the skeptical doctor that he saw John crash on
his bike, and he drives him back to the barn and
fixes him a bed of straw. The next morning Derek
brings him an elaborate breakfast, offers him a
job as caretaker for the barn, and buys him a
new crash helmet. Though dubious, John decides
to stay until he works off the cost of the
helmet. He becomes attached to the undernourished kitten, whom he names Daily News, takes it
to a veterinarian, who wants to destroy it, and
soon finds it to be his companion and main
interest at the barn. In the next few weeks he
has a series of strange experiences. Moving a
harness board, he discovers it is the rear of a
high-backed settle, hiding a huge fireplace, and
he realizes that what he thought was Vasers'
barn was really a seventeenth-century house. In
the nearby village, Besingtree, people treat him
with strange curiosity and deference and call
him "Cunning." He finds gifts of dead rabbits
dropped on his doorstep, and then vegetables and
honey, and a local girl brings him half a dozen
eggs and asks for something to get her young man
back. He gives her a bar of soap and advises her
to clean herself up and get a bra. Following
News on a walk, he comes upon a gibbet
containing a rotting body. When he tries to ride
away from the barn, his Cub stalls, but when he
turns back, it runs smoothly. Again following

News, he comes upon a field being reaped with
scythes and is warned by a girl he had seen at
the gibbet against letting himself be observed
lest he be hanged for a witch. She introduces
herself as Mistress Johanna* Vavasour, and he
begins to realize that she belongs to the
seventeenth century, to which he was somehow
transported by News, and that the barn was
really Vavasours' house. Back at the twentieth-
century barn, he discovers that News has caught
an unusual rat, which he takes to Susan who is
very interested in natural history. She
identifies it as a black rat, a plague rat,
thought to be extinct, and is furious when Derek
burns it so she will have no evidence to warn
people. Derek shows John how to blow tree stumps
up with plastic explosive and how to use his
shotgun, and he makes a point of giving him the
key to the shed where he keeps his equipment.
Johanna appears again the next day and takes him
to see Goody Hooper, a filthy, demented old
woman who lives, almost naked, in a dark cave.
He is repelled by her smell and her lice-ridden
hair, but Johanna gives her food, treats her
kindly, and warns her that Hobekinus* is coming.
The next day in the village John buys a book
that tells of Hobekinus, the name given to the
mid- seventeenth-century Matthew Hopkins,
self-styled Witchfinder General, who became
wealthy by instigating witch hunts for pay and
hanging dozens of old women as witches. In the
list of his victims, John finds Goody Hooper,
hanged, and Johanna Vavasour, hanged, but with a
question mark after the entry. Johanna appears
and takes him with her, ostensibly as a dumb
servant, to the witch trial at the inn of
Beesingtree, which in the modern period is
Derek's house. There Johanna bravely defends the
eight old women on trial, and it seems as if the
session will end in ridicule of Hobekinus until
a Trooper Collins testifies that he searched the
Vavasour house, fought the devil, and fired a
pistol at his head, and produces as evidence the
remains of John's shattered crash helmet. Since
the material is something no one can identify,
they take it as proof that it came from the
devil. Vacillating between the seventeenth and
the twentieth centuries, John works out a plan
to save Johanna, dressing in his motorcycle

clothes to impersonate the devil and using Derek's explosives. After a wild scene, it appears that they will retire safely to the Vavasour house when a single pursuer almost shoots John in the face and News leaps onto the pistol and is killed. Back in the present day, Johanna shares the barn with John and is obviously willing to share his bed, but he cannot bring himself to make love to her, guessing that it will tie him forever to the past. He becomes more and more uneasy, and finally, when he finds a replica of himself on his motorcycle made from bits of the cycle, his hair, finger nails, and other things belonging to him, he realizes she is putting him under a spell, and he breaks away. Before he leaves the barn, he puts his name on the wall beside that of a John Briarly, 1877, knowing that he is not the first one who has been drawn back into the seventeenth century to save Johanna nor the first to fail to love her enough to stay with her. The elements of time fantasy and witchcraft are skillfully manipulated to make a chilling novel, in which one is never sure how to evaluate Johanna's powers and motives, or those of Derek and the other twentieth-century villagers. The scenes of Goody Hooper's hovel and the witch trial are gripping, and the documents from actual seventeenth-century records add a feeling of authenticity. John's attachment to the idea of chance, which is credited with getting him into the situation, is less convincing but adequate to tie the elements of the story together. Carnegie Com.; Fanfare.

THE DEVIL'S CHILDREN (Dickinson*, Peter, Gollancz, 1968; Little, 1969), fantasy set in the future, shortly after the "Changes" have affected England. These are a mind-set that has made the inhabitants hate machines, forget much of modern history, and turn into a society in many ways like the Middle Ages. It is a companion novel to *The Weathermonger** and *Heartsease*. Nicky* (Nicola) Gore, 12, has somehow become separated from her parents in the madness of smashing and looting that first swept the country when the Changes came and has been left behind when they fled to France. For twenty-eight days she has waited at their home,

expecting someone to return for her, and has
existed by breaking into bars and taking the
soft drinks and packaged snacks, since
electrical and water systems have ceased to
function. When a group of strange people stop to
rest in the park where she waits, she suddenly
decides to go with them, even though they seem
foreign and are dark-skinned, with the men
wearing turbans and the women dressed in flowing
garments. At first they try to drive her back,
but she sees them turning down a street that
leads to a district where plague has killed off
all the people and calls out a warning, which
they heed. When she trails after them, they
ignore her until one of the young men tries to
start an abandoned bus. The sound of the motor
wakens the terrible fear and hatred of the
Changes in Nicky, and she tries to attack him
with a knife. After she has been pulled off and
the motor stopped, the strangers question her
and explain: they are Sikhs, originally from
India, and for some reason they have not been
affected by the Changes as have the English
people. They have, however, been attacked and
reviled for their actions, and are now seeking a
place where they can stay in safety. Since she
wants to go with them, they will take her as
their "canary," to warn them when they are about
to do something that will infuriate the English,
in the same way miners used to take canaries
into the mines to warn them if firedamp was
present. As the procession (which includes
babies in prams and moves at the pace of the
youngest child) ambles on, Nicky learns a few of
their names: Gopal*, 13, who becomes her chief
translator when the others talk in Punjabi;
Kewal*, his cousin, who tried to start the bus;
his Uncle* Chacha Rahmta, who clubbed her away
from knifing Kewal; his cousin Ajeet*, a quiet
girl of twelve; his Uncle Jagindar, the biggest
man in the group; and, most important, Daya*
Wanti, his grandmother, an ancient woman who
rides in a cart and always has the decisive word
in the noisy family discussions. Eight days
later they come to a deserted farm on a hill
outside of the village of Felpham, where they
pause while one of Gopal's aunts has a baby.
There they find a good well and storage silos
full of grain, as well as wheat standing in the

field. The barnyard is surrounded by a strong
brick wall, and there are several houses besides
the barns and sheds. They decide to stay and set
up a smithy directed by Uncle Jagindar, who used
to be a skilled metalworker in London, since
they will need hand tools and weapons and hope
to trade with the villagers for food and other
necessities. Because a double row of electric
pylons, under which the villagers dread to go,
separates the village from the farm, the Sikhs
have not been driven out, but the natives are
far from friendly. Nicky goes alone to the
village to see if she can set up trading. She
learns that the villagers call the Sikhs the
"Devil's Children," and most think they are some
sort of dwarfs or hobgoblins. The men she first
approaches bring Arthur* Barnard, a huge man
they call the Master, who smacks her head,
knocks her down, and shakes her almost senseless
because she mentions the word "tractor," but
agrees to try out the blacksmithing skills of
the Sikhs in exchange for milk, vegetables.
seeds, and other items necessary for farming.
She learns that Arthur drove out a band of
ruffians who were terrorizing the village and
now has set himself up as a sort of feudal
baron. They all work very hard through the
summer, but as fall approaches they have a
little more free time. Nicky, Ajeet, and Gopal,
exploring a deserted farm nearby, find a village
boy stuck in a loft with a badly cut foot. The
youngsters get him back to the Sikhs' farm,
where one of the cousins who had been studying
medicine gives him a tetanus shot and bandages
the foot. Though he is afraid to tell them his
name, Nicky discovers (when they carry him home
after dark to a mother who is terrified and not
grateful) that he is Mike Sallow. About a month
later Nicky finds Mike hiding in the tall grass
along the verge of the lane. Between his sobs
she learns that robbers have come to the
village, killed Arthur, and rounded up all the
children as hostages. Because he was still in
bed with the sore foot, he was not found
immediately, and his mother then smuggled him
out the door and told him to crawl to the Sikhs.
That night Nicky, accompanied by Gopal, sneaks
down to the village to find out more. From Tom
Pritchard, one of the men she has traded with,

she learns that some thirty new ruffians have
arrived, riding horses and dressed in armour,
that they have put the children in a barn loft
with hay and timber piled below and threatened
to set fire to it if the villagers give them any
trouble, and that they are planning to attack
the Sikhs' farm as soon as they are settled. The
noisy Sikh council of all the grown men and most
of the women discusses the problem and decides
to watch for two days, and then attack the third
night, before the robbers are organized to
attack them, even though they are outnumbered by
the robbers two to one. Nicky is taken along
since they must first capture the barn where the
children are kept hostage, and they will need
someone of whom the children are not terrified
to keep them calm. Ajeet secretly comes to help
her. When the sentries have been killed by the
uncles and the brazier to fire the barn has been
carried outside, Nicky climbs to the loft, but
cannot quiet the frightened children until Ajeet
calmly sits on a hay bale and starts telling a
story she has learned from her grandmother. As
Ajeet holds the children enthralled, Nicky
watches the fight between the mounted robbers
and the Sikh uncles from the loft window, and
after the fight has localized in the robbers'
headquarters house and Ajeet's story is done,
she leads the youngsters through the fields
toward their homes. She intercepts the enraged
villagers, who think the barn has been fired,
and is able to convince them that they must help
the Sikhs, not murder them. With the robbers
destroyed, the villagers make friends with the
Sikhs. In the spring, the grandmother pays the
cousin of a villager to take Nicky in a fishing
boat to France, where she hopes she can find her
parents. Because Nicky and the Sikhs are so well
characterized, the bizarre tale is convincing.
Details of the attempts to farm without modern
implements keep the fantasy well grounded in
reality, and the Sikh culture, shown from
Nicky's point of view, is presented sympathetically but also with humor. The theme of the need
for mutual understanding between different social groups is explicit, and a secondary theme
deals with Nicky's own psychological needs,
first to harden herself so that she can survive
emotionally and then to allow herself to care so

she won't be trapped in her hate and isolation.
Carnegie Com.

DIAZ, PORFIRIO (*Jeremy Craven**), President of
Mexico, an actual historical figure. He is shown
in his palace in Mexico City, just before he
resigns his office. He is a dejected, wavering,
old man, in great pain from a toothache, torn
between his own desires and the wishes of some
followers to fight for his position and the
advice of his loving wife, Carmelita, and other
counselors to surrender to the demands of the
revolutionaries and retire to France. He makes a
deal with Jeremy's Uncle Titus* Carver for guns
and then immediately changes his mind and
resigns from office, leaving Titus with a worthless check.

DICKENS, CHARLES (JOHN HUFFAM) (1812-1870), born
at Landport, Portsmouth; best-known of all
nineteenth-century English novelists and a master of characterization. As a boy of ten he
went to work in a warehouse, pasting labels on
blacking bottles, an experience reflected in his
most nearly autobiographical novel, *The Personal
History of David Copperfield* (Bradbury, 1850;
Burgess, 1850). His father was imprisoned for
debt in Marshalsea jail, the setting for his
novel *Little Dorrit* (Bradbury, 1857; Peterson,
1857), and served as a model for David
Copperfield's friend, Mr. Micawber. Later,
Dickens went to school for a couple of years,
worked in a lawyer's office, and became a
reporter in the House of Commons at the age of
nineteen. His first published book was a collection of pieces from magazines and newspapers
reprinted as *Sketches by Boz* (Macrone, 1836;
Carey, 1836), which was followed by the humorous
The Posthumous Papers of the Pickwick Club
(Chapman, 1837; Carey, 1836-1837), which made
him world-famous. In all, he wrote fifteen
novels, of which *Great Expectations** (Chapman,
1861; Peterson, 1861) is often said to be his
best-rounded story and *A Tale of Two Cities*
(Chapman, 1859; Peterson, 1859) his most dramatic. Many of his books described deplorable social conditions and led to reforms, notably *Oliver Twist, or The Parish Boy's Progress* (Bentley, 1838; Lea, 1838), about the abuse of

children in the workhouse system. Although the plots in most of his novels lean heavily on coincidence and sometimes fall into sentimentality, he is acknowledged to be a master at drawing memorable characters and writing with humor and wit. Two of his Christmas stories, *The Cricket on the Hearth** (Bradbury, 1846; Redding, 1846) and the longer and more artistic *A Christmas Carol** (Chapman, 1843; Routledge, 1843), though not written specifically for children, are popular with young people, widely read and dramatized each holiday season. Both have been named to the Children's Classics list.

DICK HEDLEY (*Gumble's Yard**; *Widdershins Crescent**), neighbor youth and good friend of Kevin* and Sandra* Thompson. He is a red-haired, well-built, helpful youth, good at football and hardworking. He is a take-charge sort, who, according to Kevin, likes to be the boss and run things, and, Kevin also admits, he does better at leading than Kevin does. Resourceful and daring, he initiates the sleuthing the two boys undertake, and the "flit" to Gumble's Yard is also his idea. In order that the children will have money to live while in the Yard, he voluntarily turns over his paper route to Kevin and suggests they chop and sell firewood. In *Widdershins Crescent*, he has left school and is working as a printer's apprentice. He helps with the move to Westwood Estates, assists the children in buying used furniture, suggests they consult Tony* Boyd, and pushes the unsuccessful investigation of Mr. Widdowson. His mother hopes that he and Sandra will form a twosome some day, and actually he is beginning to notice her. Dick is a thoroughly likeable, well-drawn figure.

DICKINSON, PETER (MALCOLM DE BRISSAC) (1927-), born in Livingstone, Northern Rhodesia (now Zambia); editor and novelist for both adults and children. His family returned to England when he was seven, and he attended Eton College and King's College, Cambridge, earning a B.A. degree in 1951. He served in the British army from 1946 to 1948 and was assistant editor and reviewer for *Punch* from 1952 to 1969. For adults he is ranked among the foremost writers of mystery thrillers in Britain, and for young

people he has published a wide variety of novels
and nonfiction which have achieved high critical
acclaim. The first of these is the Changes trilogy, set in a future when a sudden, mysterious
change has turned the population of Great
Britain violently against machines and back to
the superstitions and social patterns of the
Middle Ages. The series moves backwards in time,
with *The Weathermonger** (Gollancz, 1968; Little,
1969) telling of the end of the Changes, *Heartsease* (Gollancz, 1969; Little, 1969) telling of
life in the middle of this five-year period, and
*The Devil's Children** (Gollancz, 1970; Little,
1970), which was commended for the Carnegie
Medal, describing the early months. Several of
his other books have straddled the division
between fantasy and realistic fiction, including
The Gift (Gollancz, 1973; Little, 1974), whose
ironic title refers to the extrasensory perception that plagues a boy, and *Emma Tupper's Diary** (Gollancz, 1971; Atlantic/Little, 1971),
in which a Scottish family discovers prehistoric
creatures surviving in their loch. *The Blue
Hawk** (Gollancz, 1976; Atlantic/Little, 1976),
which won the Guardian Award and was a Carnegie
Commended book, is set in a priest-ridden land
rather like ancient Egypt, though perhaps really
in the far-distant future; it is a story of high
adventure and intrigue and gives a remarkable
sense of the power of ritual. Among his realistic novels are two dealing with modern-day terrorists, *Annerton Pit** (Gollancz, 1977; Little,
1977), in which a blind boy leads his brother
and his ill grandfather to escape through abandoned mine tunnels, and *The Seventh Raven** (Gollancz, 1981; Dutton, 1981), in which all the actors in a children's opera are held hostage in
an attempt to kidnap an ambassador's son. *The
Dancing Bear** (Gollancz, 1972; Atlantic/Little,
1973), listed as a Contemporary Classic and a
Carnegie Commended book, is a historical novel
set in the Byzantine Empire of the sixth century. *Tulku** (Gollancz, 1979; Dutton, 1979),
winner of both the Carnegie and the Whitbread
awards, starts with the Boxer rebellion of 1900
in China but is set mostly in mysterious Tibet,
at the time a land normally closed to all outsiders. Six of these books are on the *Horn Book*
Fanfare lists and two are on the *Choice* magazine

list for children's books in an academic librar-
y. In all his fiction, Dickinson is noted not
only for lively plot but also for interesting
characterization and a strong sense of place.
He has also won awards for two nonfiction
books for young people, the Carnegie award
for *City of Gold and Other Stories from the
Old Testament* (Gollancz, 1980; Pantheon, 1980)
and the *Boston Globe-Horn Book* award for *Chance,
Luck and Destiny* (Gollancz, 1975; Little,
1976.

DICKS, TERRANCE, television scriptwriter, novelist. He has been an advertising copywriter and
a radio scriptwriter, and has edited material
for the BBC. His best known television work is
as a scriptwriter for the science fiction series
Doctor Who. For children, his most popular books
are in the Baker Street Irregular series, starting with *The Baker Street Irregulars in the Case
of the Missing Masterpiece* (Blackie, 1978; Nelson, 1979), in which a young Sherlock Holmes
enthusiast and three of his friends form a
modern detective group and solve the crime of
the theft of an early painting by John Constable
from a private collection. The same four
children, three of them presumably early high-
school age and one younger, appear in at least
half a dozen more detective mysteries, including
a nominee for the Edgar Allan Poe Mystery Award,
The Case of the Cop Catchers* Blackie, 1982;
Lodestar, 1982), in which they rescue a
policeman friend who has been kidnapped and
solve, simultaneously, a series of truck hyjack-
ings and the theft of a diamond necklace. The
stories, for middle-grade readers, are full of
clever deduction, threats, and chases, but do
not involve actual murders. Dicks, who lives in
London, has also published some forty other
books for young people.

DICK SHELTON (*The Black Arrow**), Richard, ward
of the turncoat noble Sir* Daniel Brackley, who
switches loyalties from Lancaster to York and
back as the political fortunes of the two sides
change in the War of the Roses. Until he is
seventeen and the black arrow of Jon* Amend-All
kills old Nick Appleyard, Dick does not appear
to have questioned the good intentions of his

guardian or to have suspected that he had a role
in Dick's father's death; then, instead of being
crafty, he boldly challenges Sir Daniel and
demands an explanation. This same blunt honesty
characterizes all his actions and brings him
into severe difficulties in an era when intrigue
rules among the upper classes. Naive but brave,
he deliberately chooses the life of Captain
Arblaster as his reward from Richard* of
Gloucester, even though it annoys the prince and
destroys Dick's chances of further preferment,
all because he has suddenly realized that he has
ruined an innocent man by stealing and wrecking
his ship, the *Good Hope*, even though he had no
qualms at the time of the theft and has
cheerfully killed several men with no second
thoughts. Because he is opposed to Sir Daniel,
who at the moment is a Lancastrian, Dick becomes
a Yorkist; this is not done because of any
ideological conviction.

DICK WRIGHT (*Flambards**; *Flambards in Summer**),
steady, sensitive stable boy who teaches
Christina* Parsons to ride and falls in love
with her. Fair-haired, good-looking, and intelligent, Dick has more to recommend him than
Mark* Russell, but he has been born into the
servant class, as William* Russell points out to
Christina. Dick is dismissed from his job for
helping Christina save her favorite horse from
slaughter, and later he reappears and beats Mark
thoroughly for getting his sister, Violet,
pregnant. In *Flambards in Summer* he has been
invalided out of the army with a lung injury.
Though Violet is quite willing to sell her son,
Tizzy*, she hesitates, and only later Christina
realizes that it is because of Dick's affection
for the little boy. When Christina hunts Dick
up, he is sensibly reluctant to dredge up old
emotions, but he comes to Flambards and acts as
farm manager and is mostly responsible for
making the farm pay. He gradually drops his
subservient attitude, but doesn't presume to
show his love for her until she makes the first
move. In a sequel to the trilogy, *Flambards Divided*, Dick is married to Christina, but their
social positions and expectations are too different, and their marriage, already strained
when Mark comes home wounded, finally breaks up.

DICKY BASTABLE (*The Story of the Treasure Seekers**), the eleven-year-old second son and third child in the Bastable family. He "likes things settled exactly," according to Oswald*, to such an extent that "Father calls him the Definite Article." He likes to think things through before sharing them, and Oswald says that "Dicky never will show you anything he's making till it's quite finished...." Dicky says poetry is rot, which hurts Noel's* feelings, and he is the businessman of the family. He is an interesting figure, a foil for the more talkative Oswald.

THE DIDDAKOI (Godden*, Rumer, ill. Creina Glegg, Macmillan, 1972; Viking, 1972), realistic novel of a half-gypsy child and her difficulties fitting into a modern English village. Orphan Kizzy* Lovell, 7, has been happy living with Gran, her great-great-grandmother, in their wagon in Admiral* Sir Archibald Cunningham Twiss's orchard. Many gypsies used to camp there, but now they are the only ones. Her life changes drastically when busybody Mrs. Cuthbert investigates and arranges that she go to school. There her well-meaning teacher, Mildred Blount, makes the children promise not to tease her, but they keep their fingers crossed and secretly torment the child for her unusual looks and strange ways. Still, she has Joe, their old horse, to comfort her. Then Gran dies, and the gypsies summoned by the Admiral burn her body in her wagon, in the old way as she wanted (though they take her good china, which should have been smashed and left in the fire). None of them want to take Kizzy in, and they tell her she'll be found a good foster home, instead. This horrifies her, and when one of the children tells her that Joe will be sold to the knackers for dog meat, she sneaks out and rides him away. The next morning she is found by the Admiral's man Peters asleep on the doorstep, covered by snow, with the horse's rope in her hands. She begs the Admiral to keep Joe with his horses and then collapses with pneumonia. Though by far the best house in the village, Amberhurst House, the bachelor establishment of the Admiral, Peters, and Nat (who takes care of the horses) is not thought suitable for a child, but Kizzy is too sick to be moved. The three men take extremely good care of her and, from her delirious ravings, they learn a good deal about the misery she has felt in school. When she becomes better, Mrs. Blount calls with a gift of a coat, but Kizzy refuses to talk to her and throws the coat out the window. The Admiral and his men find the problem of clothes for Kizzy almost insurmountable. The Admiral himself goes to London with the measurements Peters has taken, but comes home in defeat, unable to decide what to get. He finally turns to the one person in the village who he knows will not gossip, Miss* Olivia Brook, who lives in a small cottage and has known much better days. Practical Miss Brook lists what the child should have and shops for the essentials, including some bright skirts that Kizzy can't refuse. The one child who has been nice to Kizzy, Clem Oliver (one of the big boys) calls to see her; this encourages the girls who are dying of curiosity to see Amberhurst, and Prudence Cuthbert, the worst of the tormentors, comes to the door demanding to see Kizzy, a call that ends in a scratching, biting fight. At the court hearing to decide what to do with Kizzy now that she is well, Miss Brook, who is a magistrate and has been a barrister, volunteers to take her in. As she expects, the child is hostile to anyone who will take her from Amberhurst, particularly to a woman, and Miss Brook is prepared to be patient; she is almost defeated, however, by Kizzy's clever stubbornness. On weekends, however, she is a different child, being allowed to go to Amberhurst and be with Joe and her male friends. At first she runs to Amberhurst every day after school, until Miss Brook tells her she must come to her cottage. When she arrives with torn hood and buttons missing, Miss Brook suspects the girls are after her, and the next day she is horrified to see fourteen little girls knocking Kizzy down, pouncing on her, and then dragging her up by the arms and running her like a battering ram into a tree trunk. By the time Miss Brook can reach her, Kizzy is unconscious, and the girls are suddenly terrified that they might have killed her. With unusual perception, Miss Brook insists that the girls' parents not be told and that the children be left to worry

about what will happen. Clem, however, finds out
from his sister and tells the boys, who shame
them. Kizzy has decided that as soon as she is
well enough, she will quietly go off with Joe,
and she has begun saving scraps and collecting
matches and other necessary items. The weekend
she plans to leave, however, the Admiral tells
her that Joe has died that morning. Kizzy is no
longer tormented at school, but she remains
aloof and lonely, though she has gradually
warmed up to Miss Brook and even seems happy
when they have tea by a fire in the garden,
sitting on a makeshift bench and an old box,
protected from the wind by a scrap sheet of
corrugated iron. The Admiral and his men bring a
child-sized gypsy wagon and rearrange Miss
Brook's small yard to accommodate it, much to
Kizzy's delight. She refuses to let anyone else
see it except Clem, until the night of the
village bonfire, when Clem persuades his sister
Elizabeth, along with Mary Jo and Prudence, to
ask her to come with them to the fireworks. When
she says that she has her own bonfire, they
doubt her; in fury she shows them, then heaps on
more wood and pours on some gasoline. The
resulting explosive flames catch the thatch of
the cottage roof. Kizzy dashes in to save Miss
Brook, who is asleep upstairs. With great
presence of mind, Prudence organizes the other
two girls to rescue both Kizzy and Miss Brook.
The Admiral, who has done a good deal of
conferring with Miss Brook over Kizzy's
problems, insists that they both come to Amberhurst and sweeps away Miss Brook's objections
that the neighbors will talk by proposing to
her. The story ends with a birthday party for
Kizzy, who has been adopted by the couple and
given the name of the Admiral's grandmother,
Kezia. The village children come with the gypsy
wagon, which they have secretly restored, and
the Admiral gives Kizzy a pony to pull it.
Despite sentimentality and some unlikely
occurrences, the story has charm, largely
because Kizzy is a genuine little girl, full of
hate and longing and defiance, and not some
cardboard Cinderella. The change of the
children's antagonism to fondness for Kizzy is
made to seem possible, but having Prudence be
the heroine of the fire is rather too fortui-

tous. The style is economical and clever. Whitbread.

DIGORY KIRKE (*The   Magician's Nephew**; *The Lion,
the Witch   and the   Wardrobe**), youth who, with
Polly* Plummer, is present when Aslan* creates
Narnia* in *The Magician's Nephew*. With Polly, he
is able to enter and return from other worlds by
using   rings his Uncle* Andrew Ketterley has
fashioned following an ancient magic formula.
Digory is a moral boy, whose sincere concern for
Polly's well-being sends him to the Wood between
the Worlds, whose   conscience moves him to
confess to Aslan that it was his act that
brought evil in the   form of Queen* Jadis into
Narnia, and whose love for his dying mother
prompts him to persist in the adventures in
hopes of finding a cure for her. Digory is a
real-seeming boy, a multi-faceted figure, with
whose dilemmas the reader can identify. In
Lion, he plays a smaller role. He is the
Professor Kirke in whose house stands the
wardrobe through which the Pevensie children,
Peter*, Susan*,   Edmund*, and Lucy*, enter
Narnia. He is presented as elderly and wise, a
ready listener who accepts what the children say
without question or judgment and tries to keep
them from lapsing into easy answers about what
constitutes reality. Of   course, they don't
realize that he once visited Narnia, too, and
that the wardrobe was made of wood from Narnia.
He appears very briefly as elderly Lord Digory
in *The Last Battle**, where he is one of the
Seven Kings and Queen of Narnia.

DILLIAN (*Archer's Goon**), beautiful, sophisticated wizard who "farms" law and order. Just as
ruthless as Archer*, she is better organized and
does not covet the whole world for her own, just
a manageable portion of it. She acts charming
when Fifi and the children come to see her, but
she tricks them by giving them the pages of
Quentin's* words and then making the words
disappear when they leave her house. In the end
she tries to shoot Venturus before she enters
the spaceship.

DILLON, EILIS (1920-   ), born in Galway, Ireland; novelist for both adults and children. She

was educated at Ursuline Convent, Sligo, and has taught creative writing at Trinity College, Dublin, although she started out to be a professional cellist. Her father was a professor at a university in Galway, and she grew up in the Irish-speaking village of Barna and spent summers in the Aran Islands. This area is the setting for most of her more than thirty books of fiction for children, but a few are set in Italy where she lived for six years, among them *Under the Orange Grove* (Faber, 1968; Meredith, 1969) and *The Five Hundred* (Hamilton, 1972; Nelson, 1977). The west coast of Ireland, particularly the remote islands running up the coast north of Galway, forms the background for many adventure stories featuring boys of fifteen or sixteen, usually allied with an old person, who work out a problem or resolve a misunderstanding of moral significance. In *The Singing Cave** (Faber, 1959; Funk, 1960), a boy and his lively grandfather discover ancient Viking relics in a coastal cave. In *The Coriander** (Faber, 1963; Funk, 1964), boys and their retired schoolmarm conspire to keep a shipwrecked doctor on their island, which badly needs medical service. Both these books were chosen for the *Horn Book* Fanfare list. In *The Sea Wall* (Faber, 1965; Farrar, 1965), some boys and an old woman work to get a wall built to protect their village from the periodic disaster of storms. In *The Island of Horses* (Faber, 1956; Funk, 1957), two boys take an ancient grandmother to the island where she grew up, which is now deserted by people but supports a band of beautiful wild horses. *A Herd of Deer** (Faber, 1969; Funk, 1970), though set on the same coast, departs from this pattern, being about a boy hired to ferret out the reasons for the hostility of local people to a man who is trying to raise deer on land he has bought. It was chosen for the Lewis Carroll Shelf Award. Although the adventures are satisfying and often exciting, her books are marked by restraint and understatement, with strong characterization of the Irish people, particularly the old ones, and a vivid sense of the hardships and beauty of life on the western islands. She has also written a play and about ten novels for adults, and has done some writing in Irish Gaelic. Many of her books have been translated into French, German, Dutch, Swedish, and Norwegian.

DINTIRION (*No Way of Telling**), farm in the Welsh marshes once owned by the Bowens but now owned and occupied by the Protheroe family. Both Amy Bowen and her father were born there, but when an accident killed Amy's mother, her father left the child to her grandmother, emigrated to Australia, eventually remarried, and started another family there. Old Mrs. Bowen has moved to Gwyntfa, an isolated cottage in the mountains beyond Dintirion, but the Protheroes are her closest neighbors and are not a great distance away by the dangerous path over the top of the mountain. Since Ivor Protheroe and Amy Bowen are classmates and best friends, there is some suggestion that the Bowens may eventually be part of Dintirion again.

DOCTOR CORNELIUS (*Prince Caspian**), tutor of Caspian* (who becomes Caspian the Tenth of Narnia*). Doctor Cornelius is half dwarf, a small, fat man with a long, silvery, pointed beard that comes down to his waist. His brown, wrinkled face looks very wise, ugly, and kind. He is not only a wise and learned teacher but also a good friend to Caspian. One of the Old Narnians, he realizes that with the birth of Miraz's son Caspian's life is in danger. He risks his own life to get the lad to safety. Later, when he learns that Miraz knows that Caspian is safe with the Narnians, he leaves the castle and joins them. He is responsible for their taking refuge in Aslan's* How. He is a consistently interesting if all-wise character.

DOCTOR DOLITTLE (*The Story of Doctor Dolittle**; *The Voyages of Doctor Dolittle**), John Dolittle, M.D., originally a physician for people, who learns the languages of animals and becomes a great naturalist. A rotund little man who always wears a top hat, Doctor Dolittle is brilliant, an accomplished flautist, and has many other unusual talents, but is impractical about money and undisturbed by such trifles as his ship being wrecked or his dinner burned. He is friendly, unpretentious, and cheerful, being aroused to fury only by such institutionalized cruelty as bullfighting.

DODDER (*The Little Grey Men**), the eldest, wisest, and shortest of the three gnomes who go upriver, the others being Sneezewort* and Baldmoney*. He has a wooden leg and is their leader. He invokes the aid of Pan, the woodland god, against Giant Crum and the wood dog (the red fox). Like the others, he comes just short of being a Disney-type figure.

DODO (*Alice's Adventures in Wonderland**; *Alice's Adventures under Ground**), one of the odd creatures Alice* meets while swimming in the pool of tears. In *Wonderland*, he organizes the "caucus-race" by which the swimmers dry out. They run around any way they like for a half hour or so until they are quite dry. The Dodo then declares the race over and everyone a winner, assuming Alice will provide prizes for the participants. Fortunately, Alice, though put on the spot, has enough comfits in a box in her pocket to go around. The Dodo presents her own thimble to her as her prize. The Dodo's role in *Alice's Adventures under Ground* is more limited and less imaginative. There he leads the swimmers to a nearby cottage where they dry out, wrapped up in blankets and sitting snugly by the fire. Some think the Dodo represents Carroll himself and the caucus-race is intended as a comment on the caucus as an inept and wasteful method of decision making.

DOGGETT (*The Writing on the Hearth**), old bedesman at the cloister in Ewelme, in whose school Stephen is a student and whose advice Stephen seeks on occasion. Doggett paints coats of arms for Dame* Alice. Stephen is on his way to get squirrels' hair from old Meg* for Doggett's brushes when he runs afoul of the Earl* of Suffolk's hunters. He flees to Meg and encounters Roger Bolingbroke*. Doggett advises Stephen to destroy the copy of Dame Alice's letter that the youth has well-meaningly made, advice which Stephen carelessly and unfortunately does not heed. Stephen helps Doggett paint coats of arms on the walls of their lady's solar. In doing so, Stephen (and the reader) learn about the coats of arms of important people in the region. Thus, Stephen is able later to recognize Duchess Eleanor's flag and to prevent Red* Jak from overturning her barge, earning the praise of the Earl for his quick action.

DOGSBODY (Jones*, Diana Wynne, Macmillan, 1975; Greenwillow, 1977), fantasy set mostly in and near a town in England in the late twentieth century. The luminary Sirius, a sort of spirit of the dog star, has been wrongly found guilty of misusing a Zoi (a very powerful force that could be mistken for a meteorite) and of murdering a minor luminary and has been condemned by the celestial Court to inhabit the body of a creature on the sphere where the Zoi fell and, unless he can find and retrieve the Zoi, to live and die as that creature. He wakes to find himself a puppy in a litter fathered by a dog quite different from the Laborador mother and therefore condemned to be drowned as mongrels. He struggles and scratches and succeeds in tearing a hole in the rotten burlap bag and is washed to the edge of the stream. There he is found, half dead, by Kathleen* O'Brien and her two cousins, Robin* Duffield, who is younger than Kathleen, and his disagreeable older brother, Basil*. Their mother, known as Duffie* (Daphne Duffield), who strongly dislikes Kathleen and resents having to take her in when her Irish activist father is sent to prison, lets her keep the puppy only because she promises to do all the housework, a bargain of which her aunt takes full advantage. Sirius, whom Kathleen calls Leo, grows rapidly into a typical large dog, but also retains some of his nature as a luminary. He realizes that he must find the Zoi, although he doesn't know what it is. Gradually, he also remembers that he had a Companion, who was somehow involved in the disaster with the Zoi. In order to get more control, he concentrates on learning human language, which he soon understands, but, with his canine mouth and throat, cannot speak. He also discovers that he has an ally in Sol, the luminary of the sun, who was once one of his underlings. His warm, stupid dog nature and his green luminary nature exist in him simultaneously, just as his affection and concern for

Kathleen exist at the same time as his growing
need to explore and find the Zoi. He figures
out how to slip out of his collar and open the
gate to the yard where he is tied while
Kathleen is in school, and he has several
run-ins with the police. He begins to discover
other things in the vicinity, among them four
dogs, all with the same creamy coat and red ears
that he has; they are a bitch named Patchie and
three males, Rover, Redears, and Bruce. He also
discovers a place where buildings have been
cleared off and where he feels a tingling that
indicates the Zoi is near, and a retired
schoolteacher, Miss* Smith, who saves him from
eating chicken bones and feeds him whenever he
turns up at her door. He learns a good deal from
books that Kathleen likes to read aloud,
including one on astronomy from which he gets an
idea that the Zoi might be on earth as a
meteorite, and one on mythology which describes
the hounds of Arawn, the king of the underworld,
which look remarkably like Sirius. His hunt for
the Zoi is interrupted for more than a week when
his dog nature responds and he waits with other
dogs outside Patchie's pen while she is in heat.
There he meets Yeff, one of Arawn's hounds, and
follows him at the call from Yeff's Master,
learning that only those who run with the pack
and share its duties are allowed to know about
the hounds. When he finally starts his hunt
again seriously, he goes back upstream to where
he was born and runs into the woman who
recommended that the puppies be drowned; to his
horror, he realizes that it is his Companion,
disguised as a person. After a wild chase, he
goes into a wood and dives into a fox's hole,
where he talks for the first time to Earth, who
is hiding the Zoi and says it belongs to her
most unhappy child, who must abide by the rule
told him by the hound. Crushed by his memories
and his realization that his Companion has
framed him and tried to destroy him so that she
could replace him with a blue-green luminary
from Castor, Sirius limps home, but that night
the Companion and the Castor luminary, now
New-Sirius come into the house in the form of
people and try to kill him. His dog nature
responds by barking and rousing the family, and,
afraid the Celestial beings might hurt Kathleen,

he leaps out and leads them away, hiding in a
culvert at the directions of Earth and Moon.
Later he runs into Bruce, the only one of his
siblings with any sense. They spend the night
together and plan to join the wild hunt the next
night, the last full moon for a month, but the
police capture Sirius, this time taking him home
as a lost heroic dog who has saved the house
from burglars. Later in the day Kathleen is
brought home from school because her father has
been killed following a prison break. When
Duffie is particularly mean to her she rebels;
she takes the broom and wildly smashes pots in
Duffie's pottery shop. Duffie hits her with the
broom, Sirius bites Duffie's calf, and, at
Duffie's threat to have him put down, Kathleen
drags him away, saying she herself will take him
to the vet to be destroyed. Once out of the
house, she tells Sirius she was lying so that
they could get away, and with relief he takes
her to Miss Smith's, where she can finally tell
her whole unhappy story to a sympathetic
listener. Before the evening is over, both Robin
and Basil have also run away and traced her to
Miss Smith's. When all the children fall asleep
and Sirius gets out, he finds that Bruce has let
out their siblings. Just as the Companion and
her New-Sirius are about to destroy them, the
Master of the strange dogs appears, a dark
figure with legs like a man and branching
antlers, who brushes them aside and leads them
on a thrilling Wild Hunt. Just before it ends,
Kathleen and the two boys, who have waked and
missed Sirius, appear and join in the chase,
which ends in the underworld. There the Master
must give each of them a request, since they
have run with the hounds. The sibling dogs want
only to get home without being in trouble.
Robin, seeing a mother dog and her litter, wants
one of the puppies. Basil wants the Zoi,
thinking it is a meteorite, but Sirius, who
knows it will either kill him or make him do
great harm, suggests to the Master that he can
make him another meteorite with the Zoi.
Kathleen wants to be able to understand Sirius's
language. To his dismay, the Master gives her
the Zoi, and when the Companion and New-Sirius
appear, she uses it to destroy them, without
realizing what she has done. When Basil tries to

take the Zoi from Kathleen, Sirius catches it in
his mouth and is transformed back into his
luminary self, while his dog self dies on the
ground. Though he tries to get back into the dog
to keep Kathleen from being too unhappy, he
cannot do it, and she partly understands. She
goes to live with Miss Smith and eventually
adopts one of Patchie's puppies, which was sired
by one of Arawn's hounds. Sirius returns to his
sphere, but will let no luminary be assigned to
his Companion dwarf star, hoping instead that
somehow he can have Kathleen in this role. The
unusual story is complicated by having most of
the explanations come gradually, as Sirius in
his dog nature discovers or begins to remember
them. The earthy details of his dog nature and
of the three cats in the family give the fantasy
its sense of reality. Although Duffie is
overdone as a wicked guardian figure, the other
human characters are interesting and believable,
and Sirius and his siblings are recognizably and
endearingly dog-like. The elements from mythology are cleverly intertwined in the plot. Carnegie Com.

A DOG SO SMALL (Pearce*, Philippa, ill. Antony
Maitland, Constable, 1962; Lippincott, 1963),
realistic novel of family life with animal story
aspects set recently in London, in which a boy
learns to be satisfied with what he has. On his
birthday, Ben Blewitt, ten or twelve, awakens to
find his yearning for a dog even keener than
usual, feeling that Grandpa* Fitch had practically promised him one. Ever-practical Granny*
Fitch, however, aware that Ben lives in a busy
part of south London, where his father works for
the Underground, has vetoed a real dog and sends
him a framed picture of a Mexican Chihuahua
embroidered in wool. Ben reacts with disappointment and anger and insists he will never
again visit his Fitch grandparents, but Mrs.*
Blewitt diplomatically persuades him otherwise,
and he spends a pleasant summer holiday with
them in their small cottage beyond Little Barley
on the River Say. He helps Grandpa about the
place and frolics with Young Tilly, Grandpa's
spaniel-like old dog, taking over her care and
entertainment. Vacation ended, he returns to
London by train, losing the picture en route. At

departure, he assures Grandpa that it would, of course, be impossible to have a dog in London, even one "so small you can only see it with your eyes shut." Ironically, his "misery of disappointed longing" finds release in imagining the Chihuahua of the picture to be real. He dreams about the dog at night, haunts the libraries for books about Chihuahuas, and makes up adventures that are more real to him than real life, finally becoming so obsessed with the dream dog that, while on a Christmas Eve outing with the family, he walks into the street with his eyes shut and is struck by a car. Hospitalized, he misses Christmas and also the wedding of his older sister. He recuperates during another visit to the Fitches, where he spends most of his time with Tilly's puppies, glorying in all nine of them, and becomes especially fond of one, the nondescript Brown, but, being essentially a realistic boy, he knows there's no hope of getting the pup for his own. The possibility, however, arises when Mrs. Blewitt suggests the family move to less congested north London, to be nearer her daughters, and, while the family inspects a likely apartment, Ben reconnoiters, discovers Hampstead Heath, persuades his parents to allow a dog, and travels to Little Barley to claim Brown, by that time the only pup left unplaced. In spite of Grandpa's efforts to help Ben see that he is being unrealistic, he calls Brown by the name he called the Chihuahua, Chiquitito, and disappointment sets in when Brown doesn't respond. Back in north London, Ben bitterly takes the dog to Hampstead Heath, removes the leash, and shoos the dog away. When the dog finally trots off, Ben suddenly realizes that "you can't have impossible things" and that "if you didn't have the possible things, then you had nothing." He remembers feeling the dog's warmth and softness and envisions the dog's potential for love and joy. He calls the dog back using the name Brown, thus accepting Brown for himself, and his reconciliation with self and dog is complete. Ben is an attractive, interesting character, a well-brought up, sensible child, whose hopes, longings, and disappointments are so accurately focused from his point of view that he totally wins the reader's sympathy. The family is likeable, too, projecting a pleasing give-and-take with the teasing younger brothers, Frankie and Paul, for whom life is appropriately simpler; the older sisters, May and Dilys, who are engrossed in preparations for May's wedding; Mr. Blewitt, a hardworking, practical family man who knows this will be the last Christmas they will all be together as Blewitts and whose love for them results in the outing on which Ben is injured; and maternal, nurturing Mrs. Blewitt, who is sensitive to the needs of them all. The grand-parents are especially well-drawn, individ-ualized and understandable in their attitudes and motives. The occasional humor probably has more appeal to adults than to children. Fanfare.

DOLL JACOBS (*The Seventh Raven**), seventeen-year-old narrator who is taken hostage along with 100 children and some twenty adults by a group of terrorists in a Kensington church. A girl of considerable spirit and presence of mind, she is able to understand the pressures that cause the Matteans to undertake their acts but is clear headed enough not to condone their violence.

THE DOLLS' HOUSE (Godden*, Rumer, ill. Dana Saintsbury, Joseph, 1947; Viking, 1948), doll fantasy set in 1946 in London, England. Tottie* Plantaganet is a "farthing doll," a very small, jointed wooden Dutch doll of a kind sold cheaply in the mid-nineteenth century. She had belonged to the great-grandmother and the great-great-aunt of Emily and Charlotte Dane and has come down to the little girls, who have provided her with a doll family, including Mr.* Plantaganet, a doll with a china face and a foot half bitten off by a puppy; Mrs. Plantagenet or Birdie*, a celluloid doll, who was once part of a party cracker; Apple, a plump plush doll with brown darning-wool hair; and a dog, Darner, who is made of clipped wool with a darning needle backbone and pipe cleaner legs. The doll family lacks a home, however. After a great deal of wishing by both the dolls and the girls, a dollhouse arrives. It was left by a great-aunt and is much the worse for its years in the attic, exposed to London grime. They also inherit an elegant little doll named Marchpane, made of kid and china, with real hair and eyes that will close, but before they seeher she is sent to be cleaned. The girls, with their mother's help, clean the dollhouse and move the family in, though the lace window curtains and the upholstery on the living-room furniture have rotted. When Mrs. Innisfree comes to tea, the girls stand Tottie under a sampler worked by their great-grandmother, and she suggests that they send Tottie, along with the sampler, for the exhibition "Dolls Through the Ages" for the Blind Children's Fund, and offers enough of a fee to pay for the new sofa and chairs they have seen in a toy shop. Tottie is dismayed, thinking she has been sold, but the girls are at first delighted. Later, however, their consciences tell them that they should have lent their doll free for a good cause, and they return the money to Mrs. Innisfree, who offers to make little petit-point covers for their present furniture and to get the wooden parts refinished. At the exhibition, Tottie is the smallest doll and attracts the attention of the Queen, who wants to buy her but is told that she is not for sale. There Tottie sees Marchpane, who has also been loaned, and dislikes the proud, vain doll as much as she did years before. At the end of the exhibition both dolls are returned to the girls, and Emily is entranced with Marchpane. She immediately moves her into the living room and the Plantaganet parents' bedroom, relegating the Plantaganets to a cotton-reel box in the attic. Soon she decides the Plantaganets and Tottie are Marchpane's servants, and that Apple is Marchpane's little boy. Marchpane maliciously encourages Apple to do dangerous things, and Birdie, who is literally rattlebrained but loves Apple dearly, finds him leaning over the candle-lamp, his hair already singeing. To save him, she throws herself at the lamp and, being celluloid, burns in a sudden flash. This brings Emily to her senses, and the girls decide to give Marchpane to a museum. The fantasy gets around the problem of how the dolls "come alive" by having them dependent on the girls for their action but able to speak to each other, to understand human speech, and to wish strongly, thereby putting ideas into the heads of the

girls. Sometimes, however, when the dollhouse is
closed, they move independently. Charlotte, who
is less innovative than Emily but more sensitive, is better able to understand their
desires. The story is told with frequent author
comments and questions to the reader in a cozy,
storytelling style, which is a bit too cute for
modern tastes. Choice; Fanfare.

THE DOLL WHO CAME ALIVE (Tregarthen*, Enys, ed.
Elizabeth Yates, ill. Nora S. Unwin, Day, 1972),
fantasy first published nearly fifty years after
the author's death in 1923, set in her native
Cornwall in an unspecified earlier period.
Little Jyd Trewerry is an orphan "starving for
want of someone to love her and something to
love," when a sailor gives her a Dutch doll he
has brought for a niece who, he finds, has moved
away. When Jyd tells him she will "love her and
love her till she was alive like me," he laughs,
gives her a silver penny to buy the doll a new
frock, and cautions her that she must teach the
doll to wash and scrub since she comes from a
country that prizes cleanliness. Jyd is
delighted with the doll. "You tender dear, you
elegant," she says, "I'm fine and glad you
belong to me," and she is not greatly surprised
when, about six months later, the doll blinks
her eyes, smiles, and begins to talk. Jyd calls
her Jane and teaches her to wash and scrub and
play the games she knows--Mop an' Heidy, Blind
Man's Buff, Here Comes Poor Nancy, and Pretend.
Pretend is handy at mealtimes, when they pretend
a small herring is pig-trotter pie and dry bread
is jam tart and cream. The next day Jyd goes to
the shop of Miss Orange Nankelly, who sells her
a lovely blue frock for the doll and gives her a
Red-Riding hood into the bargain. When she gets
back, she finds that the doll has greeted her
stepmother and scared the mean woman into
dropping a pasty, which they eat with pleasure.
But when the stepmother returns, however, she
orders Jyd to put the "bewitched" doll into the
fire. Jane suggests that they ride away from the
dreadful place "on Footman's horse," so they run
away to a beautiful wood near the sea. There
they stop and play "Here Come Three Knights
A-Riding." To Jyd's surprise, three "kinky
knights," small men on fairy horses, appear to

take the knights' parts in the game and at the
end ride off with Jane on the chief knight's
horse. Jyd tries to follow and catch up, but
they disappear in a pile of boulders, and after
hunting desperately, she falls down exhausted
and weeping. When she wakes, Jane is sitting
calmly beside her. Jane tells of her marvelous
experiences in fairyland, where the Small People
took her because they were curious to see a doll
that had been loved into life. Jyd is sad,
thinking she'll lose the doll she loves, but
Jane has no intention of leaving her. She has
brought some fairy food and tells Jyd that when
she puts it to her lips it will grant her
heart's desire. Jyd wishes the sailorman will be
on the ship she sees and that she and Jane will
"be the ones to keep his house for him, washing
an' scrubbing an' getting his fardels
[bundles]." They confidently run to the harbor
to meet him. The language of the story and its
characterization of stout-hearted little Jyd are
charming. It has much of the quality of the best
of Eleanor Farjeon's* stories. Fanfare.

DOMNALL (*The Stronghold**), Chief Druid of the
Boar people and main antagonist of Nectan*, the
chief of the tribe, and of Coll, the youth who
is convinced of the rightness of his scheme to
build a stronghold to defend his people from the
raids of the Roman slavers. Domnall is proud,
occasionally arrogant, jealous of his prerogatives, and determined to control the tribe
for its own good, at least at first. Gradually
his conflict with Nectan evolves into a simple
power struggle between the two men. After the
death of Bran, Domnall has a change of heart,
sees the direction in which his action is pro-
pelling the tribe, and turns his attention to
what is good for his people. He is quick to detect Taran's treachery and to denounce the
youth. He is the most interesting character in
the book, complex, ambivalent, a man of depth of
character and great intelligence, whom the reader both likes and dislikes.

DONG PE (*Tulku**), Tibetan monastery "clinging
like a line of wild bees to what seemed almost
vertical cliff," to which Theodore* Tewker,
Mrs.* Daisy Jones, and Lung are taken by the

Lama Amchi, who believes he has found the new incarnation of the Tulku of Siddha Asara in the unborn child of Mrs. Jones and Lung. The monastery is a place of both deep religious belief and ignorant superstition, of simple faith and cynical political intrigue.

THE DONKEY GOES VISITING. See *The Turf-Cutter's Donkey Goes Visiting.*

DORA BASTABLE (*The Story of the Treasure Seekers**), eldest child and elder sister among the six lively Bastables, she tends to "come the good elder sister over" the others, according to Oswald*, "a jolly sight too often." She participates in most of their money-seeking ventures, and the first one, digging for treasure, is her idea. A maternal child, she looks after the others and takes very seriously their mother's dying request that she take care of her siblings and teach them to be good. Sometimes they become very impatient with her moralism, but mostly they realize that she is on the right track and accept her admonitions. She is a good character, of whom the reader sees several sides.

DORIS (*Gumble's Yard**; *Widdershins Crescent**), common-law wife of Walter* Thompson. A fat, slovenly, lazy woman, she often quarrels with Walter over money, which he regularly squanders. After the family moves from the Jungle*, Doris begins to see different possibilities in life and yearns to have nice things as her new neighbors do. Although she seldom does much about the house, doesn't care well for Walter's children, Harold* and Jean*, and his orhpaned nephew and niece, Kevin* and Sandra*, and has a nasty mouth toward the family and the neighbors, one becomes more sympathetic toward her as one learns about her background and watches her aspirations change. A dynamic figure, she becomes gradually less repulsive and more likeable.

DORMOUSE (*Alice's Adventures in Wonderland**), one of the crazy characters with whom Alice* participates in a never-ending tea-party along with the March* Hare and the Mad* Hatter. The

Dormouse is a sleepy animal, being mostly in a daze, and the other two pinch and shout at him to keep him awake. At one point in the scene they rouse him and demand a story. He responds with a tale about three sisters who live in a well and eat treacle. Their names play upon those of Alice Liddell and two of her sisters. At the end of the scene the March Hare and the Mad Hatter are trying to stuff the Dormouse into the teapot.

DOROTHY SAUNDERS (*The Edge of the Cloud**; *Flambards in Summer**), beautiful, vivacious, flirtatious girlfriend of Sandy* Hardcastle. Dorothy is wealthy, the daughter of a man who owns several hotels, and willful, enjoying risks like learning to fly. She is a good friend to Christina* Parsons, but she urges her to have more fun and suggests that she can get William* Russell to pay more attention if she makes him jealous, not understanding the relationship of trust between Christina and Will. Though Dorothy genuinely grieves when Sandy is killed, she had already been looking beyond him to Mark* Russell. In *Flambards in Summer*, she reappears after being a nurse in France but does not seem much changed by the experience. After the war she and Mark plan to live in a hotel she owns in Northamptonshire, in good hunting country. She is a foil for steadfast Christina. In a sequel to the original Flambards trilogy, *Flambards Divided*, her marriage to Mark is unsuccessful, and she plans to divorce him and return to nursing.

DOYLE (*On the Edge**), the more vicious of the two Free People terrorists who kidnap Tug* Shakespeare and hold him prisoner for ten days in the Derbyshire countryside. Doyle was the victim of an abusive father. Tug is more afraid of him than he is of the Hare-woman* because Doyle is the leader and is less predictable. It is unclear what happens to him at the end, whether he is shot by police or merely captured. As a character he is less developed than the Hare-woman and seems less believable. Jinny* Slattery rightly fears him.

THE DREAM TIME (Treece*, Henry, ill. Charles

Keeping, Brockhampton, 1967; Meredith, 1968),
realistic novel set at the dawn of human history
among several Stone Age and early Bronze Age
tribes, presumably in Britain, and featuring
Crookleg, a misunderstood youth, who unlike his
peers, prefers drawing and sculpting to fighting
and feels words can achieve peace better than
weapons. Lamed in a fall, Crookleg becomes an
object of suspicion among the Dog Folk, his
Stone Age tribe, because of his skill at drawing
figures in the dust. Expected to become a
warrior like his father, he reluctantly accompanies the men against the Fox Folk. Once the
Fox village is left a smoking ruin and the Dog
leaders are slain, Crookleg sets out through
the forest for the seashore, along the way encountering Blackbird, a Fox girl for whom he
makes a owl neck-ornament out of clay and whose
father also had an arist's gift with charcoal
and clay. Blackbird shares his dream of a world
without blows and harsh words and accompanies
him to the Fish Folk. Attacked by brutal Shark,
the headman, and helped to escape by Blackbird,
who is herself taken captive by Shark, Crookleg
flees, eventually discovering the River Folk, a
peaceful people whose leader, a golden-haired,
red-cloaked woman named Wander, accepts him and
names him Twilight. He makes ornaments of bronze
for her people, which they regard as powerful,
good magic. He stays with the River Folk for
many months, and when the Fish Folk attack,
Twilight, now Wander's consort, insists the
River Folk try to make peace with words. When
this fails, he bests Shark with a spear. After
defeating Shark's war party, the River Folk wipe
out the Fish Folk village, taking a few
captives, among them Blackbird. When bad feeling
erupts between Blackbird and Wander, Twilight
leaves and goes inland, encountering in the
forest brutish, hairy Red Men, who speak only in
grunts and live in caves. When they see his
talent with charcoal and stick, they accept him
eagerly, proudly showing him their domed cave,
whose walls are covered with pictographs, and
even attacking the River Folk for him to free
Blackbird. For some time, Twilight and Blackbird
live happily in a cave of their own with the
kind Red Men. When the River Folk slay the
chief's daughter, the Red Men retaliate by

attacking, returning with Twilight and Wander's
child, a baby whom they name Linnet and who
becomes a favorite of the tribe. Then food grows
scarce, and, after three hard years, the Red Men
steal away one night, leaving the little family
to fend for itself. Fearing Linnet will die,
Blackbird and Twilight leave the forest for open
land. They push steadily on until they reach a
little village, one without a stockade, where
the people welcome them. One-dimensional characters, a severely understated style, a forest
setting tinged with the unreal and mystical, and
emphasis on action project the atmosphere of
legend. However, greater attention to facts of
setting such as beliefs and way of looking at
life, to message, and to literary touches mark
the story as the work of a single writer
voicing a philosophy. As an authored story, the
novel needs both plot and character development.
Rosemary Sutcliff*, writing in an afterword,
suggests that Treece deliberately blended
periods in order to emphasize the story's
universality: that in spite of circumstantial
change, human nature remains the same; peace
will remain elusive, and visionaries and
artists will continue to be misunderstood.
Looked at that way, the final scene in which the
pair come out of the dark forest into the light
of the open country and smiling hosts is clearly
symbolic. What is one to make, however, of the
passage with the Red Men, who take Twilight in,
cherish him and his gift, and then abandon him
and destroy the paintings in the cave? Such
ambiguities mar the novel, which was published
posthumously, and leave it too obscure for
satisfaction. Carnegie Highly Com.; Fanfare.

DREM (*Warrior Scarlet*), Bronze-Age boy of a
British tribe who is born with a withered right
arm. Although he easily compensates for it in
ordinary life and has learned to be the most
skillful spearsman among the boys, he misses his
wolf kill, the initiation feat of his people,
and is banished from his tribe. Partly because
his handicap has forced him to fight for his
place, Drem has developed stubborn courage, but
he also has gentleness and sensitivity that make
him a good worker with the sheep and make him
appreciate the beauty of nature. As a boy he has

seldom given any thought to the feelings of his foster sister, Blai*, and in his hurt, while he is living with the shepherds, he treats her curtly. When he has been initiated, he sees her with new eyes, realizing that they share not only the same childhood hearth but also the same experience of rejection and that they understand each other as no one else in the tribe can understand either of them. He is a complex character who grows through his experience.

DR. KERRIDGE (*Time of Trial**), handsome, cold man of proud bearing and imperious manner. He speaks effectively on behalf of Mr.* Pargeter at the trial, not out of affection, sympathy, respect, or agreement with the old bookseller's beliefs, but out of family loyalty. He treats Meg coolly because he thinks she has designs on his son, Robert*, as a way of elevating her position in life. Although he provides a place for her to live in his village of Herringsby, while her father is in prison for sedition and libel, he and Mrs. Kerridge do not receive her in their home, and Mrs. Kerridge, although a kind woman, is tardy in calling upon Meg. There is some suspicion that the doctor may be directing the smuggling operation in the area. At the end, he refuses to come to the aid of a dying smuggler who has been shot by the soldiers. His behavior shocks Robert and reveals the doctor's base nature. He is a one-dimensional, typecast figure.

DR. LIVESEY (*Treasure Island**), local physician and magistrate to whom Jim* Hawkins shows the treasure map and who goes along on the *Hispaniola* as ship's doctor. He is the only person to stand up to Billy* Bones at the Admiral Benbow Inn, and he warns the old buccaneer that rum will kill him if he keeps on drinking. A decent, honorable man and a dedicated healer, Dr. Livesey insists on treating the wounded pirates and those suffering from malaria even at the risk of his own life. Far more level-headed than Squire* Trelawney, he is nevertheless fooled by Long* John Silver at the beginning of the voyage. He is the narrator for the portions where Jim is absent from the action.

DR. MAUD BIGGIN (*The River at Green Knowe**), scientist who has rented the marvelous old house at Green Knowe and then invited her niece, Ida* Biggin, and two displaced boys to spend the holidays there. Intent on writing her book, *A Reconstruction of the Habits and Diet of the Ogru: A Summary of Recent Discoveries*, she pays very little attention to the children. She is described as dressed much as a chimpanzee would be, if left to choose its own clothes, and she often adds to the odd effect by donning a crash helmet and riding off on her motorcycle. One of a group of scientists who believe that there were giant people as well as giant animals in ancient times, she is delighted to find the giant's tooth that the children have left on the path for her, but when she actually sees a giant in the circus she refuses to believe he is genuine. She is a caricature of the woman in academe.

DR. MCINTYRE (*A Sound of Chariots**), the fuzzy-headed, high-speaking form master at Bridie McShane's secondary school. After he discovers Bridie's love of poetry, he encourages her to write and is yet another teacher who plays an important role in her intellectual growth and ambition to become an author. The other students make fun of him, but Bridie takes to heart his words that she does not have to rely on formal schooling to become an effective writer.

THE DRUMMER BOY (Garfield*, Leon, ill. Antony Maitland, Longman, 1970; Pantheon, 1969), grim and ironic novel of a group of survivors from an unspecified eighteenth-century war in France. The book starts with the "golden" idealistic drummer boy leading the red-coated troops up a hill into an ambush in which some 10,000 men are killed. The boy, Charlie Sampson, wakes to find himself apparently the only living thing on a field of desolation, but as he picks his way in the dusk back through the devastation, he is joined by others, the dregs of the army, those who hid out in ditches or in the quartermaster's wagons and have emerged to loot the corpses: Corporal Finch, a lean, spectral man from a baggage train who uses and

misuses bits of foreign languages in all his
conversation; Parsons, a private with fair hair
and bad luck; Edwards, a Welshman; and Mister
Shaw, a grey and fat surgeon who is collecting
teeth from the bodies. Charlie takes a note from
the hand of a corpse, a note asking that it "be
given into the hand of Sophia Lawrence of Bruton
Street, London, with the news of the death in
battle of James Digby who loved her with all his
heart and all his soul and all his might," only
to discover that the man is not dead or even
wounded, just asleep. To Charlie's disgust he
joins them, as does a Frenchman named Mushoo,
whose brotherhood in unsavory crime is stronger
than the fact of being from the enemy army. They
trudge toward the sea through a terrible
rainstorm and shelter in a derelict barn which
collapses in the night, wounding Edwards and
killing Digby. Charlie once again takes the note
to Sophia, debating with the spirit of Digby
which seems to be following him about whether he
will report that he died bravely in battle or
tell the truth. Another follower seems to be
trailing them as they slog their way over the
sixty miles to the sea, stealing food and
sleeping wherever they can. Mister Shaw sticks
close to Charlie, wanting to go with him to
Bruton Street, where he hopes to find wealthy
clients for his goulish dentures. At the coast
they enter a low inn, where they discuss in
English a plan to steal a boat, all the time
insulting the impassive Frenchmen in the room,
only to find that they are really English
smugglers, led by Isaac Gulliver, who is willing
to take them across to England on his fishing
vessel, *The Dove*, for part of their battlefield
booty. Just as they are about to board, the
figure that has been following them shows up,
gives his name as Maddox, and joins them. After
some time at sea, silent Maddox amazes them all
by leaping from the rail. Charlie jumps after
him, is saved because his drum floats, and
pulls Maddox with him as he is heaved aboard
again. Mister Shaw, who becomes suddenly
efficient and skilled when faced with a medical
emergency, revives Maddox, who turns on
Charlie, bitter at having been saved. By the
time they land, Gulliver has recognized the
kindred spirits among the group and hired them

to transport his cargo to some abandoned gypsy
cottages near Burley, in the New Forest not far
from Charlie's home at Lyndhurst, and to manage
a distribution depot there for him. Charlie and
Mister Shaw journey on to London, where they
find the house on Bruton Street to be the home
of General Lawrence, who was in command of the
disastrous advance, and in mourning for his
son-in-law, who was killed in the ambush. The
general, while ostensibly accepting responsibility, blames the dead man, Major Fitzwarren, for
the debacle, saying that he ordered Fitzwarren
to search the woods ahead and that the major
had skulked behind instead. Then his younger
daughter, Sophia, enters, and Charlie immediately falls in love with her. She is an invalid,
apparently so delicate that the disgrace and
courtmartial of her father will bring on her
death, and Charlie is faced with the temptation
to perjure himself, claiming to have heard the
General give Major Fitzwarren the order, in
order to save Sophia. After days of
vacillating, standing all night outside her
house and seeming to see the ghost of Digby
climbing into her window, he tells the fatal lie
in front of a group of officers making an
inquiry and then is forced to prove its truth by
picking the likeness of Fitzwarren from among a
number of miniatures of the Lawrence family. To
his horror, he recognizes Maddox and realizes
that he has saved from drowning the man
responsible for 10,000 deaths. Mister Shaw then
volunteers that the man is still alive and
offers to lead them to him. In horror, Charlie
runs out and takes a coach to the forest where
they left Maddox, hoping to warn him. He is
followed by the general, Shaw, Sophia, who
insists on coming along, and Sophia's maid,
practical Charity. There is a wild chase through
the forest, Charlie seeking to find Maddox,
Mister Shaw repenting and sure the general means
to kill his son-in-law rather than let him
testify, and the general determined to get rid
of Fitzwarren but also wanting to strike a noble
figure in front of his daughter. Maddox escapes,
another young officer is shot but not fatally,
and they end up at an inn where Sophia has an
attack, is assumed to be dying, and is examined
by Mister Shaw, whose fondness for Charlie and

annoyance at the general prompts him to give up his chances of a practice among the rich and to denounce the girl as a fraud, who pretends illness and sucks the life out of her admirers as a spider kills her mates. Charlie catches the look of fear and hatred in Sophia's eyes, realizes that Shaw is correct, and follows the surgeon back into the forest. After the general's party has left, he returns to the inn for his drum, finds that Charity is waiting for him, and goes off with her to his home at Lyndhurst. No one in the book, with the possible exception of Charity, is what he pretends to be, and all succumb to corruption in one form or another. The general cynical tone keeps a reader from liking even Charlie, the golden drummer boy, but the characters are memorable and some of the scenes, notably the glorious opening of the battle and the later desolate field strewn with corpses, are so vivid that they dominate the rest of the story. Carnegie Com.; Fanfare.

DR. WILLIAM HENCHMAN (*Castors Away!**), kind, solicitous father and knowledgeable and compassionate physician. A widower whose wife died a couple of years before the novel begins, he realizes that his children do not get on well with his imperious, rigid, status-conscious sister, Julia, who now runs his household. As a change in routine, he takes them for summer holidays to visit Aunt Susan Henchman, the wife of his brother, Simon, the captain of the *Pericles*, who is away fighting Napoleon. While the family is at Aunt Susan's, they rescue the shipwrecked soldier, Sergeant James* Bubb. Dr. Henchman is much concerned about the limits of current medical knowledge, and saving the sergeant's life lifts his spirits, especially since he was unable to save his wife's life when she caught diphtheria.

DUCHESS (*Alice's Adventures in Wonderland**), ugly, rude woman whom Alice* meets in her kitchen, which is filled with smoke and smells so strongly of pepper that the Duchess and Alice sneeze a lot. Her cook flings pots, pans, and plates around in a fury of activity, which the Duchess completely ignores, and her Cheshire-Cat* sits on the hearth and grins incessantly.

The Duchess speaks in morals and sings to her baby a parody of a once-popular poem, tossing the child violently up and down as she does so. She departs abruptly and hastily to play croquet with the Queen of Hearts, flinging her baby into Alice's arms as she leaves. She is an obvious caricature of a Victorian mother. The scene is hilariously slapstick on the surface, but some critics think it has latent, disturbing meanings.

DUCK (*Alice's Adventures in Wonderland**; *Alice's Adventures under Ground**), one of the odd creatures Alice* encounters while swimming in the pool of tears. Some think he represents the Reverend Mr. Robinson Duckworth, who accompanied Carroll*, the real Alice, and her two sisters on the trip down the Isis when Carroll first made up the story. The Duck contributes little to the plot.

DUFFIE (*Dogsbody**), Daphne Duffield, unkind aunt of Kathleen* O'Brien and mother of Robin* and Basil*. A thoroughly disagreeable woman, she resents Kathleen because her husband agreed to take the girl in when Kathleen's father, an Irish activist, was sent to prison, and because Kathleen is Irish and therefore to be blamed for the violence of Irish terrorists. Duffie's main interest is in making pottery, and she has a small shop attached to the house. When Kathleen begs to be allowed to keep the puppy she has found half-dead and promises to help with the cooking and cleaning if she can keep him, Duffie takes unfair advantage of the bargain and turns all the housework over to her, but continues to criticize and scold her and holds the threat of having Sirius destroyed over the girl's head. Her husband, though kinder and more appreciative of Kathleen, avoids confrontation and doesn't notice anything that might make him uncomfortable, so he doesn't stop Duffie from being mean. When Kathleen's father is killed, Duffie is particularly insensitive and goads Kathleen into rebelling and breaking her pots, then hits her with the broom until Sirius bites the calf of Duffie's leg.

DUNLOP, EILEEN (RHONA) (1938-   ), born in

Scotland; educator and novelist. She was
educated at Alloa Academy and Moray House
College of Edinburgh, where she received a
teacher's diploma in 1959. She has taught at
various schools in Scotland: at Eastfield
Primary School, Penicuik, from 1959 to 1962; at
Abercromby Primary School, Tullibody, from
1962 to 1964; and at Sunnyside School, Alloa,
from 1964 on. In 1979 she married Antony Kamm.
Her fantasy-mystery novel, *A Flute in Mayferry
Street* (Oxford, 1976; as *A House on Mayferry
Street*, Holt, 1977), was named an International
Reading Association honor book. *Robinsheugh* (Oxford, 1977; as *Elizabeth Elizabeth*, Holt, 1976)
is a time fantasy of a girl who is sent to stay
at an old Scottish mansion with an aunt, an
Oxford don, who is working on the family
papers. *Fox Farm* (Oxford, 1978; Holt, 1979) is
an appealing story of an orphan who has been
placed as a foster child on a Scottish farm and
how he and the son in the family keep a pet fox
cub in secret.

DURATHROR (*The Weirdstone of Brisingamen**),
dwarf, along with Fenodyree*, instrumental in
enabling Colin and Susan in getting Firefrost*
to Cadellin* before Selina* Place and Grimnir*
can get it and use it for their evil purposes.
Durathror is a great fighter and uses his sword
Drynwyn frequently on their behalf. He once had
the power of going unseen, called Tarnhelm,
which he exchanged for the power of flight,
Valham, and for doing so was cast out by his
father and has since wandered the earth, barred
from his people. He dies a Cuchullin-like death
at the end of the novel, having given his life
on behalf of the children and the cause of good.
He is a stereotypical heroic figure.

DUTIFUL PENITENCE CASKET (*Nightbirds on Nantucket**), nine-year-old daughter of Jabez
Casket, the morose Quaker captain of the whaler
Sarah Casket. Shortly after Dido Twite awakens
on the *Casket*, the captain enlists her aid in
persuading his daughter to end her self-imposed
isolation in his cabin. She has locked herself
in and refused to come out ever since the death
of her mother some months before. She has been
living on beach-plum jelly and sassafras. Dido

lures her out by arousing her curiosity with a
series of carefully executed, outlandish stunts.
For weeks Dutiful remains shy, fearful, and
whiny, a child who tries overly hard to be
good. When deemed negligent in some way, she
puts the blame on Dido. Gradually she grows in
self-reliance and self-esteem through association with and instruction from Dido, and,
after Dido is kidnapped, Dutiful manages quite
well to foil Aunt Tribulation. She is also referred to as Pen or Penny.

E

THE EAGLE OF THE NINTH (Sutcliff*, Rosemary,
ill. C. Walter Hodges*, Oxford, 1954; Walck,
1961), historical adventure novel of an
expedition to discover what happened to the
Ninth Roman Legion which marched north into what
is now Scotland in 117 A.D. and disappeared.
Some ten years after the loss of the Ninth,
Young Centurion Marcus* Flavius Aquila, fresh
from Rome, is wounded in his first command
during a native uprising at the frontier outpost
of Isca Dumnoniorum in an action that brings him
and his cohort honors but leaves him with a lame
leg and unfit for the legions. He goes to
Calleva to recuperate, to the home of his Uncle
Aquila, the much older brother of his father who
was second in command of the lost Ninth Legion.
He finds his uncle, whom he has never before
met, a quiet, scholarly man, retired from being
a post commander and living on a small property
at the edge of the city. During the next months
Marcus suffers considerable pain from his leg,
which is slow to heal, and worries about his
future, and to distract him Uncle Aquila takes
him to a circus, where he sees two gladiators
fight to the death. The bravery of one, a
tattooed Briton with the clipped ear of a slave,
so impresses Marcus that he jumps to his feet
and makes the thumbs-up sign to save the man's
life with an eagerness that infects the crowd to
follow his example. Then, realizing that the
fellow's career as a gladiator is over, he buys
him for a body slave and learns that he is

Esca*, son of Cunoval, of the tribe of Brigantes, a proud warrior who is willing to serve him because Marcus treats him with a certain respect. When Marcus allows him to join a hunt for wolves that are harassing the countryside, Esca brings him back a wolf puppy, which they call Cub and raise for a pet. Marcus also gets to know Cottia*, 13, a British girl who lives with her Roman uncle and very Romanized British aunt next door. Because Marcus's leg is not healing properly, Uncle Aquila sends for his old field surgeon, Rufrius Galarius, who examines it, discovers that splinters have been left in the wound, and opens it again to clean it thoroughly, an extremely painful operation but a successful one. Marcus gradually regains full use of his leg, though it tires easily. Uncle Aquila is visited by Claudius Hieronimianus, Legate of the Sixth Legion, who tells of rumors that the Eagle of the Ninth Legion has been seen receiving divine honors in some tribal temple in the far north. Since it is a symbol around which another uprising might rally, it worries him, but to Marcus the idea of recovering the Eagle means that there might be a chance of reconstituting the legion and restoring his father's reputation, and he begs to be allowed to go north in disguise with Esca, to ferret out news of what is happening. Before they start Marcus gives freedom to Esca, who has long been more friend than slave, and they travel as Demetrius of Alexandria, a Greek eye-healer, and his British servant-companion. They crisscross the Province of Valentia, long abandoned by the Romans, which lies north of Hadrian's Wall, without learning much until one night in the deserted fort at Trinomontium they come upon a hunter named Guern. He appears to be a painted Briton like Esca, but Marcus has heard him whistling a song from Roman barracks and sees the faint scar of the Raven order of Mithras on his brow. After some verbal skirmishing, Guern admits that he was a member of the Ninth Legion and tells of its end, of how it was rotten at the core and how through the deaths in sudden, rearguard raids and through desertion and mutiny the men were so demoralized that only a small force finally tried to fight its way back south.

They were hunted by tribesmen all the way until
they made a last stand and were wiped out
somewhere north of Trinomontium, a short time
after Guern dropped out. He cannot tell them
where the Eagle was taken, but he thinks it is
in Caledonia, in some Holy Place of the tribe of
the Epidaii. After weeks of wandering and
salving sore eyes, they run into a small group
of Epidaii led by Dergdian, their chieftain, who
has an infant son with the swamp opthalmia that
brings blindness to many. Marcus and Esca go
with him to his dun, treat the child, and stay,
hoping to hear some hint of the Eagle. They are
still there when the tribe gathers for the Feast
of the New Spears, at which the boys are
initiated into the mysteries of the tribe and
become men; they are invited to attend, not the
secret ritual itself but the celebration open to
all the men afterward. At the high point of the
ceremonies, a priest enters carrying what had
once been a Roman Eagle. Telling him about how
they acquired the Eagle, Dergdian's old father,
Tradui, also shows Marcus a signet ring set with
a flawed emerald on which is engraved a dolphin,
saying he took it from the body of the last man
to hold the Eagle aloft, and Marcus recognizes
it as his father's ring. The next night Marcus
and Esca enter the Holy Place, steal the Eagle,
and hide it under an overhanging bank in the
nearby lake. As they expect, they are followed
when they leave the next day and are searched,
but since they do not have the Eagle with them
the Epidaii let them go, shamed at having
treated guests so badly. As they come to a
remote village, Esca puts on an act of one
suffering a bout of malaria, and Marcus asks for
a hut apart from the others where he may cast
out the devils from his servant. The villagers
are glad to leave them alone, and that night
Esca slips out, backtracks by foot, retrieves
the Eagle, and after three nights returns. They
set off again toward the south, carrying the
Eagle, but they discover that when a bit of the
overhanging bank broke off, Esca must have
dropped the ring-brooch from the cloak in which
the Eagle was wrapped. Knowing that Dergdian's
men will soon be on their trail, they hurry, but
Marcus's leg weakens and they soon realize that
the hunt is catching up. Just as they are

surrounded, Guern appears. He knows about the hunt and leads them by a secret way across the bog as a way of redeeming his honor. With this breathing space they almost reach the Wall, but the tribesmen catch up again and surround them in an old Roman signal tower. Three young warriors, eager to be the ones to capture them, rush the tower, but Esca and Marcus are able to overpower them. They recognize one as Liathan, Dergdian's younger brother. Threatening to throw the Eagle into a lake below, Marcus forces him to call to those below that the tower is empty. Telling Marcus that old Tradui realized who he must be and sent the ring to be buried with him, Liathan gives him his father's ring. Binding and gagging the three young men, Marcus and Esca set off on their ponies and make it safely to the Wall. Realizing that the shame of the Ninth was too great for it ever to be reformed, they bury the Eagle under Uncle Aquila's house. The Senate makes Esca a Roman citizen and gives Marcus land as a reward. He plans to marry Cottia and become a farmer in Britain. After a rather slow start, the adventure becomes very exciting, but the book's great strength lies in making the time and place extremely believable, not only in the way people live and dress and act but also in how they think and feel. This is the first of a trilogy telling of the fortunes of several generations of the same family. It is followed by *The Silver Branch** and *The Lantern Bearers**. Carnegie Com.; Choice.

EARL OF SUFFOLK (*The Writing on the Hearth**), William de la Pole, historical English nobleman, husband of Dame* Alice of the Chaucer line, and Stephen's master in the novel. The Earl is depicted as a hard, quick-tempered, demanding, but fair man, a loving husband and worthy master. Politically ambitious, he is engaged in a struggle with Duke Humphrey of Gloucester for favor at court. The Earl is away during most of the book but appears in three particularly important scenes: first, that in which, while he is out hunting, one of his deer is shot by an unknown hunter and Stephen flees to Meg's* cottage to avoid being charged for the act of which he is innocent, there to encounter Roger Bolingbroke*; second, when, on the anniversary of the battle in France in which Stephen's father died protecting the Earl, the Earl takes Stephen on a ride in the countryside and speaks to him of important historical events; and third, when the Earl interrogates Stephen about his association with Meg, after which Stephen decides he will warn Meg of the accusation of witchcraft lodged against her.

EARTHFASTS (Mayne*, William, Hamilton, 1966; Dutton, 1967), fantasy set in a rural area on the Yorkshire moors in the 1940s or 1950s that improvises on the legend of King Arthur. Two intelligent, keen youths of grammar-school age, Keith* Heseltine and David* Wix, are out on Haw Bank overlooking the town of Garebridge at half-past eight one September evening. They have been investigating a strange sound and a ground swelling, when they observe Nellie Jack John Cherry, a uniformed, eighteenth-century, army drummer boy, materialize from the hillside, drumming and carrying a lighted candle. John, who speaks in a heavy, archaic version of the boys' own dialect, says that he belongs to the garrison stationed at Castle Wynd in Garebridge, that he has gone into the hillside to search for Arthur's treasure, and that it is the year 1742. John's efforts to place himself in time, his attempts to contact his relatives, sweetheart, and regiment, and his reactions to modern food and ways provide some humor. Within a couple of days, discouraged and perplexed, he decides to go back into the hill, lighting his way this time with David's bicycle lamp. The boys feel a strange sense of loss. They take home John's candle, which burns with a cold flame, cannot be extinguished, and is never consumed, and decide to record their experiences with John in a notebook. Three weeks later several more strange happenings take place: the boys read in the local paper that "many earthfasts are plough- ing"; they note that the Jingle Stones, huge natural pillars arranged in a special way on the moor, have moved; a boggart disrupts Frank Watson's farm; the boys see giants on a hillside not far from the town; all the pigs in the area disappear; the boys sense peculiar, invisible presences; and the candle exerts a curious power over David. Most disconcerting of all is

David's disappearance: one day at Watson's farm thunder claps, and a great black crack streaks across the sky, simply absorbing the youth. At the inquest, an anonymous witness attests to seeing a black rider swoop down and carry him off. The story now focuses on Keith, who misses his friend very much, feels drawn to the candle though he resists for a while, senses unseen beings about him on several occasions, and generally lacks enthusiasm for life. When he brings the candle, which he had buried for safety, into his room, he sees an army arrayed outside his window, and King Arthur appears to him, Excalibur in hand. Finally realizing what must be done, Keith, accompanied by the phantom army, carries the candle, now extraordinarily heavy, to Castle Wynd, through a tunnel into a cave beneath, where he replaces it in its socket, returning the king and his retinue to their previous form as stalactites and other rock formations. He realizes that when Nellie Jack John removed the candle to light his way on his treasure hunt, he disrupted time and the beings sleeping through it. Now that the candle has been replaced, they can continue to sleep until the candle is consumed and their time to reenter the real world has arrived (as the legend predicts). Keith encounters David and Nellie Jack John, still carrying David's bike lamp, and the three return to Garebridge, David and Keith to their respective families, and John to work as a hand on Frank Watson's farm, whose ancestral boggart has become peaceful once more. The townspeople seem to accept the fantastic happenings too calmly, strangely no one but the boys sees the giants playing ball on the hillside and stealing cattle, and the reasons for John's bursting into the present and David's disappearance are never explained. This is still a suspenseful, gripping tale, made so by the inventiveness of the plot, the strongly pictorial style, and careful attention to small details of story, place, and emotion. David and Keith are individualized and likeable, and minor characters have depth, including the seemingly omniscient Dr. Tate, the boys' Head Master; efficient, understanding Dr. Wix, David's physician father, who goes about his duties in spite of David's presumed death by lightning;

unfortunate Frank Watson, who gets on less well with the boggart than his easygoing wife; and the fair and practical coroner, who is more interested in getting what facts he can about David's disappearance than in prosecuting a witness who won't give his name because he has been poaching turf. Humor, strong local color, use of dialect, interesting metaphorical language, and careful pacing contribute to the effectiveness of the novel and make up for the rushed climax and loose ends. Choice; Lewis Carroll.

EBENEZER SCROOGE (*A Christmas Carol**), white-haired, sharp-nosed old miser who reforms after being visited by the Ghosts of Christmas Past, Present, and Future. Scrooge is a "tight-fisted hand at the grindstone" and "a squeezing, wrenching, grasping, scraping, clutching, covetous, old sinner!" He grudges the scanty wage and the tiny fire he provides for his clerk, Bob Cratchit; rudely answers, when two men collecting donations for the poor suggest that many would rather die than go to the workhouse, that "they had better do it, and decrease the surplus population"; and refuses his nephew's invitation to dinner by calling Christmas a humbug. The scenes introduced by the Ghost of Christmas Past, however, show that he was not always like this, though he was a neglected boy, and the last chapter, or "stave" of the book shows him in a new, generous, and loving transformation.

EDEK BALICKI (*The Silver Sword**), second eldest of the Balicki children, 11, brother of Ruth* and Bronia* and fellow refugee of Jan*, who journey from Poland to Switzerland at the end of World War II. He is intelligent, self-reliant, cheerful, and practical, the children's breadwinner during the war and until he is taken for the slave labor force. Tubercular and undernourished when discovered at liberation, he becomes increasingly ill as they travel toward Switzerland and Ruth sometimes despairs for his life. He is a moral strength on the journey, in particular trying to keep Jan out of trouble, and he serves as a level-headed spokesman. He is especially memorable in two scenes. He helps the

Bavarian burgomaster whose car has been wrecked because he feels it is the right thing to do, even though he knows it may, and eventually does, result in the burgomaster attempting to deport the children back to Poland. He also tries to keep Jan from wrecking a train, an act in which both boys are apprehended. Edek is a stalwart, well-developed figure.

THE EDGE OF THE CLOUD (Peyton*, K. M., ill. Victor Ambrus, Oxford, 1969; World, 1970), sequel to *Flambards**, set immediately before World War I mostly near London and involving the early development of aviation in England. The book covers about two years, starting with the arrival of Christina* Parsons and William* Russell, also known as Will, at the home of Aunt Grace in Battersea after they have eloped from Flambards, and ending with their marriage. Practical Aunt Grace, who knows her half brother, Christina's Uncle* Russell, and his violent temper, understands why they cannot return to his home, and she takes Christina in while Will hunts for a job as a pilot or even a mechanic at the developing airfields. Christina is worried and desperately bored helping in Aunt Grace's seamstress work, and when Will finally gets a job as mechanic at Elm Park through his acquaintance with the instructor, Sandy* Hardcastle, she is eager for an opportunity to find a job nearer to him. Through Sandy's girlfriend, Dorothy* Saunders, whose father owns several hotels, she gets a job in the office of The Bunch of Grapes in Kingston. There she is able to see Will by going to the airfield on her afternoons off, mostly handing him tools as he works in the hangar which also serves as living quarters. When a wire comes that Mr. Dermot has been killed trying to fly his homemade plane, *Emma*, Will, grieving as he would not have done for his own father, goes off to his funeral and comes back flying the plane, which Mr. Dermot has left to him. Now that he is able to fly again, Will feels the handicap of his stiff leg, the result of an injury in his last fox hunt, and flies off to Switzerland to the only doctor thought capable of repairing his knee. The operation works but leaves him heavily in debt, and he is soon doing all sorts of risky things,

instructing, entering races, giving exhibition
flights, and anything else that will bring in
money to pay the doctor and to get materials to
build the plane he has designed. In the most
exciting episode of the book, he returns a
Bleriot plane to the factory in France and flies
back a new one, taking Christina with him. The
motor springs an oil leak as they cross the
channel and they lose altitude drastically and
barely make the French coast. Christina, who
fearlessly jumps horses in fox hunts, is
terrified of flying, but she conceals her true
feelings from Will, and only Sandy, who is more
sensitive to her emotions, realizes how much
courage her apparently cheerful attitude in
flying and watching Will fly costs her. Once
Dorothy, a wealthy, vivacious, flirtatious girl,
rents horses and insists that the four of them
go riding, and Christina is able to regain some
self-esteem by clearly outriding the other three
and watching Will sweat with fear at the horses.
To take advantage of the growing interest in
aviation exhibitions, Will experiments with
looping the loop in *Emma*, and soon he and Sandy
are giving synchronized flight shows. To their
astonishment, Will's brother Mark* shows up in
uniform, having a commission in the Yeomanry.
He makes an immediate hit with Dorothy, who
begins to see him on the side. Having escaped
injury in wild stunts in planes, Will is
injured in a routine takeoff at the field, but
not seriously. As the plane he is building, the
Dermot, nears completion, a telegram comes saying that his father has died. Will refuses to go
to the funeral though Christina does, and he
views the death as a release, since his father
had refused permission for them to get married
and neither he nor Christina is yet twenty-one.
They set the wedding date for the first weekend
after the *Dermot* is completed and has been
put through her trials at Farnborough, the Royal
Aircraft Factory, where Will is offered a job
designing. A week before this, in Will and
Sandy's by now routine two-plane exhibition, one
of the crafts crashes. At first Christina thinks
it is Will, but it turns out to be Sandy, who is
killed. Although Christina has paid little
attention to the news, events leading to World
War I have occurred, and Will lets her know that

if war comes he will enlist in the Royal Flying
Corps. Despite their grief for Sandy and the
growing political uncertainty, they are married,
with Dorothy as bridesmaid and Mark, ironically,
giving Christina away. Details of the early
planes and the fever of interest in aviation
dominate the book, and descriptions of the
risky flights and dangerous tricks provide most
of the tension. Will is so intent on his efforts
to make his way and build his plane that he is
seldom shown in a more human role, and
Christina is characterized mostly by her
determined disguising of her own fear and
concern. This makes the human story less
compelling than in the two other books of the
trilogy, but as a picture of the daring young
men who experimented in frail, underpowered
aircraft, it has some fascination. The sequel
is *Flambards in Summer**. Carnegie Winner;
Choice.

EDMUND HENCHMAN (*Castors Away!**), at sixteen the
eldest child of Dr.* William Henchman, brother
of Nell* and Tom*. He hopes to become a
physician like his father. A steady, sober
youth, he looks after the younger children and
provides moral support and encouragement to his
father after his mother's death. He helps his
father the most in saving the life of Sergeant
James* Bubb, and later is mainly responsible for
the sergeant's escape. He goes to London to
study medicine. At Portsmouth after Trafalgar,
while he is helping his teacher, Dr. Coke, to
care for the wounded, he happens upon Bubb, who
has been reported missing in action. He is an
interesting, rounded figure.

EDMUND PEVENSIE (*The Lion, the Witch and the
Wardrobe**; *The Horse and His Boy**; *Prince
Caspian**; *The Voyage of the "Dawn Treader"**;
The Last Battle**), a major character in the
Narnia* books, second and younger boy of the
four Pevensie children. The other children are
Peter*, Susan*, and Lucy*. At first, in *Lion*,
he is a bad-tempered, willful child, who
grumbles a lot and is spiteful and selfish.
After he follows Lucy into Narnia and makes his
bargain with the Witch, or Queen* Jadis,
agreeing to bring his brother and sisters to her

in return for Turkish Delight and power as a prince, he pretends he hasn't been there, and the others think Lucy has lied about her experiences. He has a bad time of it while he is with the Witch, whom he comes to see cares nothing for him but indeed despises him and is only using him to advance her evil ends. He begins to change in character when he feels sorry for the animals she has turned into stone; this is the first time he thinks about somebody else. He redeems himself when he breaks the Witch's wand, thus enabling the good forces to triumph against her. He is much different at the end of the book and becomes a worthy ruler in Narnia. In the other books he occasionally shows a bit of his former self, as when he persists in calling Trumpkin* Dear Little Friend (in *Prince Caspian*), even though he knows the Dwarf doesn't like it, but on the whole he becomes a considerate, loyal lad, and as ruler he is a capable administrator and worthy warrior. In *Battle*, he appears among the Seven Kings and Queens of the everlasting Narnia.

EDWARDS, DOROTHY (BROWN) (1914-1982), born in Teddington, Middlesex, and died in Reigate, Surrey; broadcaster, lecturer, scriptwriter, and author, particularly noted for books for children under five. She was educated in schools in Teddington and Sunbury, and at one time served as secretary for Odeon cinemas; then for many years she was a freelance editor. She was producer of the "Listen with Mother" series on BBC, which gave rise to her best known stories, the Naughty Little Sister books, of which the first published was *My Naughty Little Sister: Stories from "Listen with Mother"* (Methuen, 1952) and which have made up eleven books, some in collections and some printed as separate picture books. Altogether she wrote twenty-five books of fiction for children, as well as radio plays, a cookbook, a garden book, and numerous others. Another series of books for children are the Joe and Timothy books, the first being *Tales of Joe and Timothy* (Methuen, 1969), followed by *Joe and Timothy Together** (Methuen, 1971), mild little stories full of domestic detail which won the Children's Rights Workshop

Other Award. She won a second Other Award for her one book for adolescents, *A Strong and Willing Girl** (Methuen, 1980); it is a realistic and humorous story about her aunt, who went out to do domestic work at the age of eight in the 1880s. Edwards also wrote for and ran a drama school for the Surrey Community Players.

EEYORE (*Winnie-the-Pooh**; *The House at Pooh Corner**), gloomy old gray donkey who lives in a swampy corner of the forest. Eeyore is a typical pessimist, querulous and moody. On a couple of occasions he brightens up briefly, as when Pooh* and Piglet* give him a Useful Pot and a burst balloon to put in it for his birthday, and when Pooh finds his lost tail and Christopher* Robin nails it back on, but his normal attitude is one of dejection. He is inclined to speak with sarcasm and to make his well-meaning friends so uncomfortable that they find excuses to make their visits short. He also has a way of not understanding the situation, as when he thinks Christopher Robin's party for Pooh is for him, and when he discovers the perfect home for Owl after the storm blows Owl's tree down and doesn't realize that it is Piglet's house.

EINON HEN (*Dawn Wind**), envoy from the Britons of Wales who join with the nephews of Ceawlin in taking up arms against him in return for a frontier guaranteed against Saxon invasion. A small, older man with only one eye, to Owain* he looks like a falcon. Owain is chosen to be his armor-bearer and serve him on the trip to Wodensbeorg, being the only other one of British descent, and also to be a messenger from Coel, King of Wessex, to the British camp to tell of the final arrangements for the attack. Einon Hen offers to become a hostage for his return to the Saxon camp, the only way they have of knowing that the message has gone through and that they can count on the British allies. Later, at the court of King Aethelbert of Kent, Owain meets him again, is introduced by him to the Christian queen, and has more than one talk with him about the possibilities of an accord between the Saxons and the British and about the meaning of Aethelbert's summoning the lesser kings at the time he expects the landing of the Christian missionaries. Einon Hen is wise enough to see it as calculated political maneuvering, but he also is hopeful that some real understanding may arise from it. Einon Hen is a character who articulates much of the historical background for the action and the deeper themes of the novel.

ELIDOR (Garner*, Alan, Collins, 1965; Walck, 1967), fantasy with adventure-story aspects set in contemporary Manchester, England, and in a medieval land of castles and armor, in which children on their own solve the problems. While searching for a mysterious Thursday Street, four children (siblings) explore side streets and blunder into a construction area. Roland, the youngest at about ten, finds a white plastic football (soccer ball), kicks it, and watches it crash, to his horror, through the window of a nearby church. When Helen, David, and Nicholas each go after it in turn and don't come back, Roland also enters the church, where he encounters a mysterious blind fiddler whom he follows into the land of Elidor. There the fiddler becomes a man with yellow hair who calls himself Malebron. He insists that Roland must "bring light to Elidor," a country once golden and thriving and now an arid wasteland. He says that his land and Roland's are connected, being really mirrors of each other, both devastated by great wars and waiting to be rebuilt. Roland enters a mound at Malebron's command, where he finds his brothers and sister, frees them, and recovers four magical, jeweled objects: a sword, a spear, a stone, and a cauldron. Malebron shows them an ancient vellum, *The Lay of the Starved Fool*. It mentions a certain Findhorn which, together with the four treasures, Malebron believes, can save Elidor. The children are strangely attacked and retreat to safety in their own dimension, bringing with them the treasures, which are quite ordinary in appearance. The children hide them first in the attic of their present house and later in the garden of the new house to which the family moves. In both places a series of odd and humorous electrical disturbances occurs, to the consternation particularly of the children's parents. More than a year later, things come to

a head. At New Year's, while returning from a
party, the children observe a unicorn, the
Findhorn of the lay, being attacked by the same
evil dark men who have on occasion attacked the
children's house. The children come to the unicorn's defense. Helen persuades the creature to
come to her, and when it lays its head in her
lap, Roland commands it to sing. An ancient
prophecy is thus fulfilled, and though the
unicorn dies, the children observe a sunburst
sweep over Elidor and reinfuse the land and its
castles with radiant color. Roland heaves the
four treasures back into Elidor, and it fades
from view, leaving the children standing alone
in a Manchester slum. The children are never
individualized, and other characters are either
good or bad types or stock functionaries. The
author has invested the story with so many
symbols that he leaves the reader in doubt about
what he intends the story to mean. At the very
least, it appears to say that the hope for a
better world lies in the best efforts of the
younger generation, an unoriginal concept. The
book's strong point is its action, which is
fast-paced, suspenseful, and often humorous.
Carnegie Com.; Contemporary Classics; Fanfare.

ELIJAH (*Time of Trial**), the orphaned waif whom
Mr.* Pargeter adopts and whose plight prompts
the old man to write "The New Jerusalem," a
manifesto that results in his conviction on
charges of libel and sedition. At first withdrawn, surly, and fearful, Elijah eventually
grows to be a very active and cheerful boy. At
Herringsby he makes many friends among the
local children and occasionally brings home news
of the goings-on among officials and smugglers.
An interesting character in his own right, he
sets the other characters in relief and helps
indirectly to advance the plot.

ELIZABETH BARNET (*Elizabeth's Tower**), girl of
eleven, whose tower room Lawrence* Willoughy
occupies while he is in the country. She is a
remarkably capable child, half-orphaned and very
close to her father, and lonely and maladjusted.
She grows close to Lawrence, who gives her a new
purpose in life. She is a round character, whom
the author puts through melodramatic and sen-

sational escapades, for example, climbing
through trees to escape the spies and rigging a
cart by which she pulls Lawrence through the
woods. As a character, Elizabeth has considerable potential for exploration, but the
author never exploits this, diverting the interest into conventional thriller avenues instead.

ELIZABETH'S TOWER (Stewart*, A. C., Faber. 1972;
Phillips, 1972), novel of suspense in a family
setting, which takes place somewhere in the English countryside during the middle-to-late
1900s. Intelligent, competent, practical Eliza-
beth* Barnet, 11, has difficulty getting along
with people. During her mother's terminal
illness, Elizabeth managed the house for her
soldier father, whom she cherishes. While her
father finishes his current tour of duty, she
lives with his sister, her Aunt Rose Andrayson,
and her cousin, Mike, 14, who consider her bossy
and pushy. Since Elizabeth finds them unsympathetic to her efforts to help around the
place, she goes off by herself and takes refuge
in the tower room of a nearby abandoned castle.
One day on her way to the tower, she encounters
a stranger, pleasant, understanding Lawrence*
Willoughby. Crippled in a freak car accident not
long before, the young man is a designer of
devices for controlling antiaircraft guns. He
wishes to live in the area while he finishes a
project he is working on and learns to use his
new crutch. Remembering her Girl Guide oath to
be helpful, Elizabeth offers him the tower room
and settles him there with blankets, food, and
other necessities. At first she officiously and
competently takes care of him by herself, simply
taking what he needs from her aunt's house, but
later, at Lawrence's suggestion, she tells the
family about him, and her aunt and cousin visit
him. He thinks them unsympathetic and unimaginative. When Lawrence disappears and the tower
room is ransacked, Elizabeth tracks her friend
to a cottage not far away, where she finds him
lying in front of the fireplace, tied up. It
turns out, not unexpectedly, that his assailants are foreign spies, to whom Elizabeth's
father smuggled plans because he needed money
to pay off her mother's medical bills and his
own gambling debts. The spies believe that

Lawrence has the drawings they need to complete the designs already in their possession. After the spies are captured and her father dies of gunshot wounds, the family decides to send Elizabeth to boarding school, but Lawrence offers to take her with him to Australia, where he plans to live on his brother's sheep ranch. This promising character study of a maladjusted child wavers between being an examination of a young-old girl extremely close to her father and a conventional melodramatic, spy thriller. The last half holds unlikely chases and hairbreadth escapes, obviously contrived for sensation. Style is descriptive, vocabulary is mature and literary, and many places are rich with imagery and charged emotion. Most characters are type-cast, and the themes of friendship, cooperation, and loyalty are handled in a mature fashion. At the end, the reader is left to ponder the relationship between Lawrence and his young ward. Poe Nominee.

ELLEN CHAFFEY OVERS (*A Likely Lad**), house-proud mother of Willy* Overs. Conscious that she came from a slightly higher social bracket than her husband and the people who live around her in Ardwick, she keeps her house meticulously neat and does not let her boys play with the rough youngsters of the neighborhood. Her main effort is to somehow outdo her sister, Auntie Kitty Sowter, who looks down upon the Overs family but nonetheless spends every first Sunday of the month alternately at Ardwick or at the Sowter home in Trafford. Her response to any crisis is consternation at what the neighbors might think. While she defers to her husband in most things, she sometimes tries to soften his treatment of Willy.

ELLEN PONTIFEX (*Up the Pier**), house-proud, easily upset mother in the displaced family that Carrie discovers on the pier and befriends. Ellen cries and talks a lot about having to live in the makeshift quarters of the old kiosk that Samuel* Pontifex has made available for them and about not having the things she needs to make a proper home. She first notes the footsteps at night, which the family later learns belong to Samuel. He spies on them and

tampers with the ingredients that Gramper*
Pontifex uses to make spells.

ELLEN RAMSAY (*The Thursday Kidnapping**), eldest
of the four children, a very responsible and
competent thirteen-year-old. Generally better
able to manage her siblings than her mother is,
she is not worried about being in charge of them
as well as their friends' baby for the whole day
and rather looks forward to doing things her own
way without her mother or Marika looking over
her shoulder. Her fear and guilt are the
greatest of anyone's when the baby disappears,
for she has some idea of what losing this child
will do to the Kodalys, whose first baby died in
a refugee camp. A girl with an active conscience, she even realizes in the end that she
will have to take Kathy* Fisher in hand and
somehow befriend her, disagreeable as she is,
because Kathy doesn't even have her own mother's
love.

ELLIE HARTHOVER (*The Water-Babies**), about ten,
pretty daughter of Sir John Harthover, at whose
mansion, Harthover Hall, Tom (the chimney sweep
who is transformed into a water-baby) is working
when he accidentally falls into her room and
awakens her. When Tom first sees her he thinks
she is the most beautiful little girl that he
has ever seen, with her "cheeks almost as white
as the pillow" and her hair "like threads of
gold spread all about over the bed." Compared to
her, Tom thinks of himself as a black ape.
Little Ellie is at the seashore with Professor
Ptthmllnsprts, a great naturalist, when he
captures Tom in a net. Tom bites him and slips
back into the sea. Ellie is sure that Tom is a
water-baby, an exotic creature in whom she
believes and the Professor does not, and in an
effort to retrieve Tom she slips, falls, and
hits her head on a sharp rock. About a week
later, the fairies come, bring her a pair of
wings, and take her away with them. She becomes
a water-baby, too, and a good friend and teacher
of Tom. Ellie is a charming child, if a shallow
type as a character.

ELSIE WAINWRIGHT (*Handles**), L. C. Wainwright,
proprietor of Mercury Motor Sales in the tiny

industrial park in the town of Polthorpe not far
from Hall Farm Cottage, where Erica Timperley is
vacationing with her Myhill relatives, Auntie*
Joan, Uncle* Peter, and their son, Robert*. A
teacher who left the profession because he
failed to connect to his satisfaction with both
superiors and students, Elsie loves people and
enjoys socializing more than work. He has an
astute eye for character and a liking for
language, which he combines in giving nicknames,
or handles, to friends and customers, names not
always understood or appreciated. He becomes a
romantic hero to Erica, who thrills to the
handles and wishes she had one, too, and loves
his glamorizing such mundane things as the crack
in the street, which he calls the San Andreas
Fault. Elsie's wife considers his motorcycle
business not quite respectable and would like
him to return to a more socially recognized
occupation. His daughter, about Erica's age, is
a prissy snob. Much as she likes him, Erica
comes to see that she must take what he says
with a grain of salt and that she must not let
her liking for him color her judgment about what
is proper behavior. Elsie is the book's most
interesting character and is slowly and
effectively revealed to the reader.

EMILY GARLAND (*The Maplin Bird**), fifteen-year-
old orphan who becomes a housemaid for a wealthy
family and becomes involved with the son, a
dashing young gentleman smuggler, Adam* Seymour.
Intelligent and strong-willed, Emily wants to
make a home for herself and her brother, Toby*,
and works very hard for the opportunity.
Although she is smart enough to see Adam's
faults and knows that he is using her and Toby,
she cannot help loving him for the way he treats
her as an equal and is overwhelmed by the
unaccustomed emotion. Her good sense, however,
keeps her from becoming physically involved with
him, and even when she is wildly weeping at his
arrest and sentencing, she realistically tells
herself that she would never have meant anything
to him anyway.

EMILY GREENGRASS (*The Peppermint Pig**), mother
of Poll*. Emily is a fine storyteller, particu-
good at the scary and bloody stories that Poll

and Theo* most enjoy. She is a woman of gumption
and sets out to earn what she can for the
family by sewing when her husband goes off to
America. Though she remains loyal to him, she
sees his weakness and has some moments of
bitterness at being put in a position of
dependence upon his sisters. She also has a
generous heart, taking an interest in Annie
Dowsett, though she at first disapproves of
Poll's friendship with Annie, and even arranging
that Annie go to work for Lady March so that the
old lady will have a good girl in the house
instead of her disrespectful servants, even
though Lady March has tried to cheat her into
sewing at cut rates for her. It is clear that
Poll gets her spirit from her mother.

EMILY MOBY (*Charlotte Sometimes**), 10, Char-
lotte* Makepeace's sister when Charlotte is
Clare Moby in 1918. Emily is much like
Charlotte's own sister, Emma, a rebellious,
adventurous, outspoken girl who likes to do
things. She is not always satisfied to have
Charlotte as her sister, and occasionally she
blames Charlotte for not keeping her (Emily)
from misbehaving, insisting she should be more
moral and assertive, like Clare. It is Emily's
idea that Charlotte enter the boarding school
at night and try to sneak into the wheeled bed
in order to return to her own time and bring
Clare back. After the two girls do return to the
boarding school, Emily falls ill of flu. While
she is in the sickroom, Charlotte manages to
sleep in the wheeled bed again and go back to
her own time. Emily is an interesting, fairly
well-developed character.

EMILY'S VOYAGE (Smith*, Emma, ill. Margaret Gordon, Macmillan, 1966; Harcourt, 1966), talking
animal fantasy, sequel to *Emily: The Story of a
Traveller*. The charming protagonist, a guinea
pig named Emily, leaves her comfortable home
where she cares for her bachelor brother,
Arthur, and goes on a journey. Although she
worries about Arthur's welfare, she is moved by
a desire to travel and agrees to a trip arranged
by the weasel. She takes with her a kettle,
teapot, and spirit stove, her green umbrella,
and other necessary equipment for travel. She

finds herself on a ship crewed by a group of inexperienced, seasick rabbits, captained by an incompetent hare, who is more interested in writing poetry than in running the ship, and steered by a cheeky water rat named Tiffy, who is really the cabin boy. Fortunately the weasel has stowed away, and with his help Emily and Tiffy manage the ship. For some time all goes well, until a storm wrecks them on an island inhabited by noisy but friendly monkeys and parrots. Emily keeps busy writing in her diary and conducting a school for the young monkeys, but she is homesick and worries about Arthur. In the meantime, Arthur, left to himself, is having a fine time with his cronies eating and drinking up the supplies and turning Emily's neat house into a shambles. When a message comes by a brown owl (who got it from a sea gull), he recognizes it as a page from Emily's diary telling of the shipwreck. Somewhat reluctantly, Arthur sets out to rescue her. He hires a tug-boat run by an otter, who takes him, seasick all the way, to the island where Emily greets him with a display of fireworks, the impractical cargo favored by the captain. Arthur likes the island and wishes they could stay, but Emily now feels the need to get home. Tiffy is taken on as an assistant by the otter, and the weasel joins them; the captain and all the rabbits decide to stay. Although the house has been cleaned in Arthur's absence, Emily finds things not quite right and is glad to take over again. The story is simple but has considerable charm. Emily is a maiden lady, precise but with a spirit of adventure and practical competence in emergencies. The matter-of-fact tone contrasts amusingly with the bizarre happenings. Fanfare.

EMMA IN WINTER (Farmer*, Penelope, ill. James J. Spanfeller, Chatto, 1966; Harcourt, 1966), fantasy set for about two months in the contemporary period in an English village, which explores the nature of time and of dreaming, is a sequel to *The Summer Birds** and *Charlotte Sometimes**, and features Emma of the former book. Two years after the summer in which the school children of the unnamed village learn to fly, Charlotte* is away at boarding school and Emma still lives with abstracted, unconcerned

Grandfather Elijah and lazy, uncaring Miss
Gozzling, their housekeeper, in big, rambling
Aviary Hall. Emma is lonely; she feels abandoned
by Charlotte and friendless and unwanted at
school. Several times at night she dreams of
flying again, over a snowy landscape and with
Bobby Fumpkins, a fat boy who has been babied by
his mother, is taunted and disliked by the
village children, and eats when he feels frustrated and rejected. In her dreams, Emma teases
and belittles him, as she also does later while
out sledding in the real world. An unusually
cold, hard winter sets in, disrupting normal
activities and causing some hardship in the
village. In school, kind, firm, no-nonsense Miss
Hallibutt appoints Emma and Bobby head girl and
boy, since they are now the oldest children in
the school, and they become the objects of envy
to some of their schoolmates. Thrown together,
the two gradually become friends, sharing tea
and even celebrating Bobby's thirteenth birthday
at a party put on by his overprotective mother.
Emma feels sorry for deriding Bobby and treats
him with more respect as she comes to see that
he is a gritty, resourceful, intelligent lad.
Bobby blossoms, for the first time in his life
having a real friend, and becomes more assertive and surprisingly the leader of the two.
Emma discovers that she and Bobby have been
dreaming the same dreams, and, as the cold
intensifies and they spend more time together,
they dream themselves backward in time, through
the days of dinosaurs, where their experiences
are harrowing, and right into the Ice Age. The
dreams variously embody the people and conflicts of their real lives. Bobby, the more
bookish one of the two, discovers in a book of
Grandfather Elijah's a concept that intrigues
the children: that time is like a bedspring
with various dimensions into which people can
sometimes think themselves. After Emma is
caught making unkind drawings of Miss Hallibutt, the two dream their final dream, going
back in time to the beginning of the world.
There they are surrounded by leering, angry
faces, including that of Miss Hallibutt. They
are saved from being trapped in that dimension
when Bobby insists that they wish themselves
back into their proper time frame. The cold

spell breaks, and the dreaming stops. Emma looks forward to spring and Charlotte's return from school. Bobby, neglected by Emma and again an outsider without friends, reverts to consoling himself by eating. A perceptive study of social misfits, the story moves unevenly in plot but exhibits good characterization and a pleasing style. The idea of time as a coil is inventive, but the children inhabiting or sharing the same dreams strains belief, the dreams do not mesh well with reality, and the ending is a letdown. Choice.

EMMA TUPPER (*Emma Tupper's Diary**), 14, highly intelligent schoolgirl from South Africa who spends her holiday in Scotland with relatives. Emma is sensible and stable compared to the McAndrew cousins and displays courage at crucial moments. She also feels compassion for the repellent creatures they discover, enough so that she agrees to keep the discovery a secret rather than endanger their survival. She is keeping a diary as a school assignment, hoping to win a prize for the best one for the holiday.

EMMA TUPPER'S DIARY (Dickinson*, Peter, ill. David Omar White, Gollance, 1971; Atlantic/Little, 1971), novel that shares the characteristics of realistic fiction and science fantasy, about a discovery rather like the Loch Ness monster, in the West Highlands of Scotland in the mid twentieth century. Emma* Tupper, 14, a girl from South Africa going to school in England, arrives in Scotland to spend holidays with distant cousins she has never met. Their father, Major McAndrew, is at a conference in Switzerland. The family at hand consists of three McAndrews--Andy*, 22, an engineering student, Finn* (Fiona), 18, an artist, Roddy* (Roderick), 14--and a very beautiful, vague woman of twenty-six, who is called Poop* Newcombe. The McAndrews have just been to the annual shareholders meeting of McAndrew's Infallible Liniment, a scalp lotion, and have learned that the company, which is the family's major support, is doing badly. They decide to use the two-man submarine invented by their mutual Victorian ancestor to fake a monster in

their loch, hoping to interest the television
people and become a tourist attraction. Andy
also hopes to rekindle a romance with an
attractive assistant producer he knows. With
great energy and ingenuity they tackle the
project, Andy getting the ancient submarine,
*Anadyomene**, into working condition and Finn
designing a dinosaur-like head and tail to
attach to hoax the TV people. The continual
acrimony between imperious Andy and clever,
hot-tempered Roddy erupts, and Roddy refuses to
be part of the project any longer, a situation
that forces Emma into the place of the second
man on the sub. Although she is terrified every
time they submerge, Emma agrees in order to ease
the family conflict, and they manage a couple of
runs which Finn films. Before the TV crew
arrives, having fallen for the bait of Finn's
film, Roddy insists on taking the sub at night
without Andy knowing, to prove he can do it.
Emma agrees to go with him if he will then stop
his continual needling of Andy. To their
astonishment, when they are submerged they see
strange creatures, not huge but long, with
lizard-like head and flippers, which attack the
Anadyomene and react to the searchlight with
fear and strange, wildcat-like cries. Following
them, they get the false head of *Anadyomene*
stuck and have to go on into an underwater
cavern, the source of the hot springs that feed
the loch. It is full of creatures and their
horrible stench. Because they have used the
searchlight so much, *Anadyomene's* batteries give
out, and Emma and Roddy must climb up through
twisting passages, finally, after extreme
effort, coming out on the mountainside where
their ancestor built a monument to Darwin,
locally known as Darwin's pimple. Though sick
with dread and fatigue, Emma agrees to go back
with Andy, who brings new batteries and tools
to cut the fiberglass head off so they can get
the submarine back out of the cavern. Andy is
full of plans to exploit these actual ancient
monsters (obviously creatures from before the
ice age which have survived because of the hot
springs in the lake) as a tourist attraction,
and Emma, thinking that they must reserve the
find for science, plans to sabotage the show
they are set to put on for the TV people. In

the process, she almost drowns in *Anadyomene* and is saved by Poop, an expert swimmer, whom she then persuades to send for Major McAndrew. When he arrives they have a family meeting and vote down the tourist idea; then the Major persuades Emma that scientists will also spoil the lake and destroy the fragile environment that supports the creatures. He shows them parts of a journal and a skull that he found in the safe, proving that their Victorian progenitor had also discovered the creatures and had opted to keep them secret. Emma starts to burn the diary she has kept of the strange experience, but the Major persuades her to keep it locked up with the skull and the old journal so that the story will not be completely lost. Each chapter starts with a short passage from Emma's diary and then slides into narrative, a technique that uses the journal idea without the constraints of of pretending that everything, including the dialogue, is reported by a teen-aged diarist. The pace is fast and the plot ingenious, but so many bizarre elements are included that it is hard to take the story seriously. Characters are well differentiated and interesting, if somewhat extreme, and the setting is strongly evoked. Fanfare.

THE EMPEROR'S WINDING SHEET (Paton* Walsh, Jill, Macmillan, 1974; Farrar, 1974), historical novel of the fall of Constantinople in 1453 under the last Emperor Constantine*. A starving, emaciated English boy falls from an orange tree into a garden at Mistra just before a delegation arrives to offer the crown of the Roman Empire of the East to Constantine, Despot of the Province of Morea. The delegation is followed by an old man dressed in black, who relates a dream which is interpreted to mean that as long as one who is at Constantine's side at that moment is with him, the city, Constantinople, cannot fall. Although the old man, Plethon, who represents the western church interests and so is hated by many of the Greek citizens, intends that he shall be always by Constantine's side, the clever Despot produces the English boy, whose real name is Piers Barber but whom they call Vrethiki*, which means "a lucky find," and vows that the boy shall not leave his side. Piers is

a young boy probably not more than eleven or
twelve who has shipped on a Bristow vessel, been
shipwrecked, seized by Turkish pirates and so
cruelly treated that his mind rejects the
memory. He then escaped and made his way over
the Taygetus mountains. Thus he becomes an
unwilling member of the emperor's household,
tied to the Lord Constantine because of the
superstitions of the people. Since Vrethiki
knows no Greek, he can communicate in his
schoolboy Latin only with Stephanos* Bulgaricos,
Eunuch of the Bedchamber and Constantine's
devoted slave, to whom the boy is an ignorant
barbarian but a necessity to his master.
Gradually he learns that the city, and therefore
the empire, is threatened by Turks, and that
Constantine is trying to make his church bow to
Rome so he can get help from the Pope. Before
he is formally crowned he must write the creed
in his own hand, and the churchmen are split
over the inclusion of a single word,
"Filioque," added to the Latin Creed and
strongly resisted by the Greek church. Though
homesick, furious at being forced into virtual
slavery, and afraid of the threat of the Turks,
Vrethiki becomes part of the official retinue of
Constantine, following a few steps behind him on
all public occasions, through his coronation
and his entrance to Constantinople. The city at
first strikes the boy as a wonder of lavish
beauty and richness, but later he sees that
much of the wealth is sham and that the past
splendors are crumbling with neglect. He comes
to understand some of the complex intrigues and
conflicts in the city, not only between
churchmen, but also between various Greek
factions and between Venetians and Genoese, all
of which the emperor must handle with patience
and firm tact. Some of this information he
learns from English-speaking John Inglis, one
of the emperor's Varangian Guard, which is made
up of mercenaries from many nationalities.
Although Vrethiki clings to his hatred for the
emperor for having entrapped him in a place and
quarrel both foreign to him, gradually he comes
to admire and eventually love the quiet,
serious man. During a couple of years, while the
Turkish forces move closer and eventually
surround and lay seige to the city, Vrethiki

THE EMPEROR'S WINDING SHEET

attends all the formal meetings, the
innumerable church services, the councils of
war, and the elaborate ceremonies with
Constantine, understanding what Stephanos
patiently explains and some little that he can
glean from observing and from a smattering of
Greek he has picked up. There are some hopeful
times, like the arrival of Justiniani* from
Genoa, who becomes commander of the land walls
and whom Vrethiki almost worships as the ideal
heroic figure, and when the Turkish effort to
bridge the boom, a huge chain strung across the
Golden Horn, is thwarted. There are more
discouraging times, as when the number of
fighting men is tallied at perhaps nearly 7,000
in the city to oppose more than 100,000, and
when the Turks, unable to bridge the boom, bring
their ships overland. Throughout what always
seems like a doomed effort, the emperor works
tirelessly to oversee the work, settle quarrels,
and encourage the people, and he refuses to
leave the city for a place of greater safety, as
he is often urged to do. In the end when it
seems as if, miraculously, the major massed
attack may be beaten off, Justiniani is wounded
between the inner and outer walls and insists on
a gate being opened so that he can be brought in
to be treated. The Turks follow and overrun the
city, and Vrethiki sees Constantine, his royal
garments discarded, fight alongside two of his
faithful retainers and then fall. When the wave
of Turks has passed over to loot and burn the
city, Vrethiki creeps down, pulls the piled
corpses off the body of Constantine, and removes
the undershoes that mark him as the emperor, so
that his body won't be desecrated. Then, after
hiding in a dry well overnight, he makes his way
to the seashore, sees the ships from Venice and
Genoa leaving the ravaged city, and plunges in
to swim to the nearest ship or drown. The strong
current sweeps him to the lead ship, which
ironically is that of the now dying Justiniani
and is bound for Italy, from where the boy can
get an English ship home. Although the book has
a very full canvas, the intrigues are labyrin-
thine, and the events of the seige and fall of
the city are detailed, interest does not flag
in the story, and the problems and strategies of
the resistance efforts are clearly delineated.

Vrethiki is more than an adequate observer of
events. His gradual change from sullen despair
to devotion to both the emperor and the city is
convincing, but the strongest characterization
is that of Constantine himself, no plaster hero
but a troubled, dedicated leader working against
insuperable odds to save his empire. The novel
has a somber tone and gives a memorable picture
of a dramatic and important time in history and
the decaying but still marvelous Constantinople.
Carnegie Com.; Fanfare; Whitbread.

AN ENEMY AT GREEN KNOWE (Boston*, L. M., ill.
Peter Boston, Faber, 1964; Harcourt, 1964),
fantasy, fifth in a series of novels set at
Green Knowe, an old house in England, this book
detailing events a year or two after those of
A Stranger at Green Knowe*. Mrs.* Oldknow has
let the cottage made from the chapel vaults to a
scholar of ninth-century manuscripts, a Mr.
Martland Pope, but she firmly refuses when a
pushy woman, Dr. Melanie* Delia Powers, asks to
rent the guest room as a study for her work for
the Philosophical Society of Jerusalem. Mrs.
Oldknow has recently told her great-grandson,
Tolly*, and Ping*, a displaced Chinese boy who
has become like an adopted great-grandson, the
story of Dr. Vogel, the scholar and alchemist
who was tutor for an Oldknow boy in 1630 and
who, after dabbling in black magic, became so
terrified that he burned all his books and
disappeared. Melanie, as the boys refer to her,
is seeking any of Dr. Vogel's remaining books,
and though on the surface she is sweet and
ingratiating, she seems to the boys not only
pushy but also sinister. The refusal of the room
infuriates her, and immediately thereafter a
series of unpleasant and inexplicable events
occur. As they row down the river, Mrs. Oldknow
suffers an attack in which she becomes very
unlike herself, laughs evilly and says she
doesn't care what happens to the boys. Ping,
sure that she has become a vehicle for demons,
slips over her neck the horsehair ribbon
attached to a stone he has brought her from
Fydlyn Bay and which they think is a Druid
stone, since the last of the Druids were driven
into the sea there. This snaps her out of her
strange condition, but when they return they

find Melanie waiting with some legal papers, on
which she asks Mrs. Oldknow to witness her
signature. Actually, as they discover in time,
it is a receipt for the sale of Green Knowe to
Melanie. The boys fasten the witch ball, an
ancient globe made of reflecting glass which is
supposed to ward off demons, in the garden where
Mrs. Oldknow likes to sit, and they take the
Persian looking glass, which reflects predicted
events, to their room to study. Because they
realize that Melanie is particularly interested
in the roof of Mr. Pope's cottage, they decide
to explore the space between the ceiling and the
roof. There they find a network of dry
traveler's-joy vines, and, after cutting some
away, they discover a sort of book made from a
dead bat with the witch's alphabet, Crossing the
River, written on it, and, exploring further, an
old leather-bound volume, badly rat eaten. They
take it to Mr. Pope, who recognizes it as a
ninth-century copy of a very ancient book of
magic. They are then besieged by a series of
plagues, first one of repulsive maggots eating
the garden, on which Mrs. Oldknow's many birds
feast; this is followed by an invasion of cats,
which kill a large number of the birds, but
which seem to be scared away by the ghost of
Hanno*, Ping's gorilla friend, which he conjures
up. The next is a plague of snakes, which the
boys destroy by finding the source, a snake's
egg with a magic spell written inside. Tolly
throws it in the river, and all the snakes
follow. Shortly after, Melanie invites the boys
to come that evening to The Firs, the
neighboring house she has rented, to see an
execution. Reconnoitering ahead of time, they
discover a pole with the letters the alphabet,
Crossing the River, carved widdershins in a
spiral down it, and they realize it is the name
of the devil and his daughter: MELUSINE
DEMOGORGONA PHOSPHER AND LORD BELIAL. Before
they can use this power of knowing Melanie's
true name, several other frightening things
happen, including a piece of stone from the roof
nearly hitting Mrs. Oldknow as they watch an
eclipse of the sun. The boys, armed with mailing
tubes as megaphones, hide in a tree until
Melanie comes out and then chant a spell
using her true devil's name and starting,

"Vaunt! Hence, begone!" At this, she seems to be broken in two, as if some abominable presence has pulled itself out of her, and she is left a harmless, tottering woman. A cable announcing that Tolly's father is coming for a short visit from Burma and bringing a friend has almost been forgotten in the latest excitement, but when the boys start to hang the Persian glass back in its original place, they foresee that the friend will be Ping's father, assumed to be dead in guerrilla fighting some five or six years earlier. The connection with the people living at Green Knowe in earlier periods is more tenuous than in earlier books of the series, and the boys are not as individualized, but the powers of evil magic become frighteningly real. The plagues, particularly the maggots and the snakes, are described memorably in loathsome sensory detail. The feeling of the old lady and the two boys (Mr. Pope is too preoccupied to be an ally) being under seige is strong, and their determined courage despite setbacks provides the theme. Choice.

ESCA (*The Eagle of the Ninth**), slave gladiator whom Marcus* buys for a body servant and then frees so they can go as companions to hunt news of the lost Ninth Legion. Son of a Clan Chieftain of the Brigantes, he was taken in an uprising against the legions and sold as a slave. As a child, he saw the Ninth Legion marching north. Like the other warriors of his tribe, he is tattooed on the breast and shoulders, and he acts more like a warrior than a slave, retaining his pride and dignity. After their adventures, he is granted Roman citizenship and plans to work as a freedman on the farm that Marcus has been granted.

ESDRAS (*The Namesake**), battle-maddened monk who leaves Thornham with young Alfred* Dane-Leg carrying two blood-soaked arrows from the body of the martyr, King Edmund. When they reach the West Saxon army, he binds the two arrows together to form a cross and goes into the forefront of the battle naked, "bare sark", and apparently impervious to weapons. This wins him a reputation as lucky for the army and a place by King Ethelred's side. He never washes, his hair grows long and tangled, and he soaks his robe in the blood of Christians who have died in battle. It is he who brings word of King Ethelred's death. Later he reappears in the story, now evidently completely insane and able to make only hideous noise, his tongue having been cut out by the Danes.

ESTELLA (*Great Expectations**), beautiful daughter of Miss* Havisham, whom Miss Havisham has adopted in a deliberate attempt to get revenge on men by training her to break their hearts. Estella recognizes that she is being used for this purpose, but she has been so well trained that she feels no pity for her victims nor any love for her adoptive mother. She marries a man for whom she has no love or respect and who mistreats her. By a convoluted twist of plot, she is revealed to be the true daughter of Magwitch*, Pip's* convict benefactor, and Jaggers's* housekeeper. At the end her hard life has softened her heart. She is not a very convincing character.

ETHEL FEEDBAG (*Which Witch?**), a comic figure, one of the Todcaster witches who compete for the hand of Arriman the wizard. She is a country witch who resembles her familiar, a pig, in appearance, and who is most conscpicuous for her manure-smelling Wellington boots. She also gets hiccups on parsnip wine. When it is her turn to compete in the contest, she makes a mess of putting a grocer and his wife and daughter inside trees and garners few points toward winning.

EUSTACE SCRUBB (*The Voyage of the "Dawn Treader"**; *The Silver Chair**; *The Last Battle**), cousin of the Pevensie children, Peter*, Susan*, Edmund*, and Lucy*, whose full name is Eustace Clarence Scrubb (Lewis says that "he almost deserved it") and who involuntarily accompanies Edmund and Lucy on the trip with Caspian* to find the seven exiled lords of Narnia*. At first he is thoroughly disagreeable, bossy, bullying, lazy, snide, and spiteful, a child spoiled by permissive parents who consider themselves progressive and their methods of child rearing up to the minute. Since Lewis*

points out what kind of people Uncle Harold and
Aunt Alberta are early in the book, the reader
dislikes Eustace, as do the Pevensies, but also
makes excuses for him. His nastiness is not
really his fault, but the responsibility of his
deluded parents and teachers. He also has not
been given the right books to read but only
instructional material. It seems Eustace represents Lewis's comment on contemporary education
and parenting. After the dragonish Eustace
literally becomes a dragon, he improves considerably and is quite agreeable and helpful
for most of the rest of the trip. After his
return, we are told that people talk about how
he has improved, except for his mother, who
thinks he has become tiresome and commonplace
and blames it on the Pevensies. He puts some of
the experiences of the *Dawn Treader* voyage in
his diary, in a detailed account that reveals
more about Eustace than he probably would have
liked the reader to see. He doesn't contribute
much to the action of the story after his
reformation, but does serve as an excellent foil
for the Pevensies, who are obviously the right
sort of children. He shares duties as protagonist in *The Silver Chair*, where he and
Jill* Pole seek Caspian's lost son, Prince
Rilian*; free him from the wicked Queen, the
Lady of the Green Kirtle; and restore him to his
father and the throne. Eustace in this book is
much like the Pevensie boys, obedient, responsible, spirited, capable, and courteous. His
levelheadedness contributes in *The Last
Battle*, where he and Jill help King Tirian*
against the evil Shift the Ape. Tirian teaches
Eustace the arts of battle, and he fights
valiantly with the scimitar against the
Calormenes. He appears in the same book at the
end as one of the Seven Kings and Queens of
Narnia. He is a well-drawn, dynamic figure.

THE EXETER BLITZ (Rees*, David, Hamilton, 1978;
Elsevier, 1980), historical novel of the German
blitz which, on May 4, 1942, attempted to
destroy the English town of Exeter with its
famous cathedral in retaliation for the fire
bombing of Lubeck. Colin Lockwood, 14, is more
concerned with his annoyance at the Cockney
evacuee from London, Terry Wooten, who shares

his desk in the overcrowded boys' school, and
the aging history master, Mr. Kitchen, who has
been called up from retirement, than with the
bombing raids, until the night when he is bribed
by his mother to serve refreshments at the
fashion show sponsored by the store where she
works. He performs creditably, even when Mr.
Kitchen shows up with his wife, but while he
watches the slide show narrated by the fashion
expert from London, Lorna Wimbleball, he finds
it so hilarious that he has to leave. He stops
at Exeter cathedral to pick up his jacket which
he left in the tower on an afternoon visit with
his father, the head verger. He is in the tower
when the air raid starts. In vivid scenes, the
story follows each of the Lockwood family
members through the raid and the next few days.
June, 10, (Colin's younger sister) and his
father crouch in the makeshift shelter under the
stairs while their home crashes around them.
Mary, 18, his older sister, and her boyfriend,
Lars, a half-Swedish ballet dancer who is about
to be called up to service, leave the movie they
are watching and take refuge in the underground
passages which date from medieval times and have
now been converted into bomb shelters. Mrs.
Lockwood searches frantically for Colin while
the customers are herded into the store's
underground shelter and joins the Kitchens and
Mrs. Wimbleball, all of whom are then trapped in
the descending elevator. Colin witnesses, close
up, the fire bombing of the city and the strikes
on the cathedral, then dashes for a shelter
where he finds Terry Wooten and makes the first
overtures of friendship. Mary, a nursing
student, finds her way through the burning city
to the hospital, where her mother and Mrs.
Wimbleball are eventually brought in among the
injured. June and Mr. Lockwood emerge uninjured.
Although the book gives a vivid picture of the
bombed and burning city, its emphasis is more on
the effect on the people, their acceptance of
the changes in their lives and the way they cope
with the destruction around them. June sees that
her mother's recovery is more important than the
loss of all her possessions. Mary realizes that
she loves Lars more than he will ever love her,
and she stoically accepts that fact. Colin
asserts his independence and helps Terry, whose

widowed mother ran a fish-and-chips shop, cook fish and bake potatoes for the homeless, and at the story's end he has matured through the experience. In a humorous but touching scene, Mrs. Wimbleball entertains the hospital ward with her fashion slide show, even though she is now paralyzed from the waist down, symbolizing the theme of survival in adversity. An introduction supplies historical information about the Exeter raid. Carnegie Winner.

F

THE FAIRY DOLL (Godden*, Rumer, ill. Adrienne
Adams, Macmillan, 1956; Viking, 1956), brief
story for younger children about how Elizabeth
gains self-confidence with the help of the fairy
doll that tops the Christmas tree. When
Elizabeth is four, she is short and fat with
straight hair and grey eyes, unlike her three
siblings, Christabel, 8, Godfrey, 7, and Josie,
6, all of whom have long legs, curly hair, and
blue eyes. Moreover, Elizabeth is always
breaking things, forgetting things, and failing
to do what is expected. When she is six, she
gets a new bicycle for Christmas to replace her
old tricycle, but she can't learn to ride it,
nor can she learn to read or to recite her
multiplication tables. When she is seven,
Great-Grandmother comes to visit for Christmas.
Elizabeth is to make the presentation of white
roses in a crystal basket, but as the children
are singing a carol she becomes fascinated by
the dewdrop at the end of the old lady's nose,
and she drops the gift, shattering the basket.
She hides on the floor behind the chest where
the Christmas tree ornaments are kept and weeps
until Great-Grandmother sends for her and
suggests that she needs a good fairy, just as
the fairy doll falls--or flies--down from the
tree. Although Josie, particularly, is scornful,
Elizabeth takes the idea very seriously. Because
Mother says some people think fairies were the
first people, she makes the doll a cave home
using her bicycle basket, lined with moss and

sawdust for fairy sand to cover the floor. She
makes her a bed from a sea shell, a table and
desk of sections cut from a branch, and stools
from toadstools, and finds suitable "fairy
things" for clothes and food. Whenever Elizabeth
needs to remember anything, she seems to hear a
"ting" in her head, and soon she is no longer
forgetting to brush her teeth or how to say the
seven-times table. In the summer when the fairy
doll seems listless, she realizes that it must
be wanting to fly, so she ties it to her
handlebars and determinedly learns to ride the
bicycle. Then, late in the fall, the fairy doll
is lost. All the family hunts for it, but it is
not found. Elizabeth once more hides behind the
chest and cries, but because Great-Grandmother
is coming for Christabel's twelfth birthday, she
comes out, washes, and joins the party. She
discovers that the "tings" continue even without
the doll. At Christmas, when they decorate the
tree, Elizabeth feels bad, but something tells
her to look in the chest, and there is the fairy
doll, not bedraggled as she had become, but just
like new. They put her on the top of the tree.
Elizabeth gets a new baby doll and is willing to
have the fairy doll go back after Christmas with
the other ornaments. The story is simple, sweet,
and slight. The main interest is in how the
older children's perception of Elizabeth changes
as she gains confidence. Carnegie Com.

FALCONER'S LURE: THE STORY OF A SUMMER HOLIDAY
(Forest*, Antonia, ill. Tasha Kallin, Faber,
1957), third in a series of novels about the
large Marlow family, the first of which is
Autumn Term, a boarding school story. In *Falconer's Lure*, whose main character is Nicola, 13,
the family has come back for the first time
since World War II to Trennels Old Farm where
they used to spend holidays. The owner, their
great uncle, has died, but their father's cousin
Jonathan is in residence and is acting as test
pilot for experimental planes being designed and
built at a nearby airfield. The eldest Marlow
son, Giles, is on naval sea duty in the
Pacific, but all the others are present: Karen,
18, about to enter Oxford; Rowan, 17, expected
to be games captain at boarding school next
term; Ann, 16, who is musical and soft-hearted;

Ginty (Virginia), nearly fifteen; Peter, 14;
and Nicola's twin, stage-struck Lawrie. Their
father, Geoff, a naval officer, has just been
promoted to captain. Their mother manages the
large household, but the cook, Mrs. Herbert,
does most of the real work. The meandering story
is held together by two central threads, an
interest in falconing and the various events of
the festival competition. Nicola becomes
involved with a local boy, Patrick Merrick, 15,
who has been helping Jonathan keep and train
three hawks. When Jonathan is killed in a crash,
the estate, which is entailed, cannot be sold
and must be inherited by Nicola's father. Since
it is heavily in debt, it appears that he will
have to resign from the Navy to run it and that
the whole family will live there, it being too
expensive to keep up the house in London, as
well. Patrick is more shaken by Jonathan's death
than are and of the Marlows, and he is also
worried about what will become of the hawks,
since his father, a member of Parliament,
expects to move to London. The goshawk, Jael,
can be trained to do her own hunting and
released. The friendly little merlin, which he
calls The Sprog, in his opinion is not important
enough to worry about. The falcon, Regina,
however, will need constant care and training.
He and Nicola hatch a plot to keep Regina at her
boarding school, and Mrs. Marlow writes and gets
permission from the headmistress. This only
confirms the problem that Nicola has foreseen of
financing the food and care for the bird. In
hope of winning enough in prize money, she
enters singing and riding events in the Cole-
bridge and District Summer Festival competi-
tions. All the others also enter, Karen in
swimming, Rowan in horseback jumping, Peter in
sailing and diving, Ann in piano, Ginty
(reluctantly) in swimming, Lawrie in elocution
and swimming, and Patrick against Peter in the
diving and against Rowan in the jumping. Peter
is also involved in a photo contest, for which
he takes Patrick's suggestion that he get a shot
of the eyasses in a wild peregrine falcon's
nest. With Nicola and Patrick he climbs the
cliff and gets the shot, but on the way back he
freezes, overcome by his old fear of heights,
and Patrick must hold him while Nicola climbs by

a more dangerous route and calls the Coast
Guard. Since Patrick was nearly killed two years
before while climbing at the same spot, both
sets of parents are greatly alarmed, and the
rivalry between Peter and Patrick, already
kindled by Patrick's preference for Nicola's
company, is fanned into flame. It becomes much
deeper when, while shooting rabbits, Peter
accidentally kills Jael. In the festival
competition Nicola is overcome by the meaning of
the song about death which she is singing and
loses her place, but gets commendation for her
voice and style. Lawrie, who aspires to be an
actress, has so often made fun of the assigned
poem, Stevenson's* "Foreign Lands," that she
cannot say it seriously and is scolded severely
for mimicking the last girl to recite; Lawrie,
however, has managed to scoot out and, in a case
of mistaken identity, it is Nicola who must stay
to be lectured and to apologize. Later, with
Nicola to back her, Lawrie goes to explain to
the formidable actress judge. She recites her
serious poem so well that she is invited to tea.
Before the other events occur, Nicola and
Patrick lose˙ Regina, find her again, then stay
out all night and sleep in a haystack to keep an
eye on her. In the morning, finding that she is
caught in a net, Patrick disentangles her and
frees her permanently. He is not enthusiastic
about letting Nicola take the merlin to school,
but Nicola thinks that if she can get enough
money to support the bird she can persuade him.
Peter wins the sailing, Karen the swimming, and
Ann does creditably in the piano contest, but
Ginty deliberately disappears and can't be found
at the time of the swimming competition. In the
diving contest, Peter and Patrick are the
finalists, and Peter wins by conquering his fear
of heights enough to do a "dead-man's drop" off
the high board. Patrick, a thoroughly decent
sort, congratulates him, and as they become
friends Peter tells him that he has won the
photo contest for his picture of the falcon's
nest. The remaining event is riding. Nicola
wants desperately to win, using one of the
Merricks' horses, because she needs the prize
money for hawk food, but she is deliberately
fouled by the girl whom Lawrie mimicked.
Although the girl's brother later offers her the

prize money, she refuses and puts her trust in Rowan, who has promised her half the prize if she wins in the jumping. Rowan and Patrick are finalists, but this time Patrick wins. Torn by conflicting emotions, Nicola rides his horse home for him and meets his father, who, she finds, has sold a little book on hawking that she bought for Patrick at a used book stall and gives her the proceeds, a very substantial sum that will easily serve to finance the hawk's needs during the school term. The question of her father's career is solved when Rowan persuades him that she wants to leave school and learn to run the farm at Trennels. The story has an old-fashioned feel, not just because of the boarding schools, ponies, and servants, but because of the "holiday adventure" atmosphere that echoes the books of Arthur Ransome*. The youngsters, who are clearly but rather arbitrarily differentiated, seem much younger than teenagers of the late twentieth century or even American teenagers of the 1950s. Much of the story is told, quite skillfully, in dialogue, and the whole festival competition is kept interesting, even though only Nicola has any stake in it more than personal and family pride. A good deal of information about falconry is included. Carnegie Com.

THE FAMILY FROM ONE END STREET AND SOME OF THEIR ADVENTURES (Garnett*, Eve, ill. author, Muller, 1937; Vanguard, 1939), episodic family novel set in the 1930s in the small working-class town of Otwell, England. The family of Jo* and Rosie* Ruggles, steady, hardworking dustman and laundrywoman, live in a very old and very small house near the middle of town not far from Woolworth's and the three cinemas. Though short on money, the family, in particular the older children and Jo, are long on ideas and have a full share of good times and sometimes surprising adventures. After the author introduces the parents and explains how the seven children, four boys and three girls, got their names, the remaining nine chapters (most of them also self-contained) revolve mainly around the lively, spunky children, starting with the eldest. Lily Rose, 12, a stocky, capable child, "Helpful in the Home," and an aspiring laundress motivated

by the Girl Guide motto to do good deeds,
accidentally burns up with a too-hot iron the
green silk petticoat belonging to one of Mrs.
Ruggles's best customers, Mrs. Beasley, who
fortunately takes the mishap in good part.
Bright, ambitious Kate, 11, wins a scholarship
to secondary school, creating no small amount of
consternation over the matter of appropriate
clothes. Jim, 9, the elder of the twin boys,
longs for excitement, and, as a Daring Deed to
impress the members of the Gang of the Black
Hand, seeks the source of the Ouse which flows
past Otwell, stows away in a drain tile loaded
on a barge, and is almost transported as cargo
to France. John, his twin, accepts a job
watching a car, crawls inside when it starts to
rain, and is unwittingly driven off by the
owners. They graciously invite him to their
son's ninth birthday party, where he cleverly
wins the scout knife in the treasure hunt. Baby
William distinguishes the family in the eyes of
the community when he takes first prize in the
local baby contest, and, in a less
well-developed adventure, little Jo, who loves
the cinema, sneaks in early and falls asleep.
The last three chapters revolve around the
packet of money that Mr. Ruggles and his partner, Mr. Bird, discover while collecting the
trash of Mr. Short, an abstracted author. The
family is featured in the newspaper and later
use the reward to pay for a long-awaited trip to
London to visit Uncle Charlie and his family.
Uncle Charlie's dustcart and horse take first
prize in the annual dustmen's parade, and, after
food, fellowship, and a few simple mishaps, the
Ruggleses return to Otwell having enjoyed a
perfect day in the big city. The author seems
now and then to be poking fun at the working
class, but the parents, other adults, and the
older children are distinctly drawn and very
likeable. In addition to the convincing characters, an affectionate tone, a warm and easygoing, generously detailed style, believable if
felicitously solved plot problems, and a very
vividly realized setting produce a consistently
interesting, highly appealing portrait of a
loving family. Sequels. Carnegie Winner.

FAND (*The Stronghold**), fifteen-year-old

daughter of Nectan* (the chief of the Boar people), sister of Clodha*, and good friend of Coll. She is Coll's ally in attempting to get her father to allow the youth to construct the tower of defense against the Romans. She figures chiefly in the scenes in which she is to be sacrificed to the god Belanos at Beltane, May 1. No whiner, she meets her fate bravely and is saved when Bran* casts himself under the knife in her place. She is a strong person but less distinctively drawn than her older sister.

FANNY'S SISTER (Lively*, Penelope, ill. John Laurence, Heinemann, 1976; ill. Anita Lobel, Dutton, 1980), short, realistic period novel which takes place one Sunday somewhere in England in 1865. Less an account of action than of family relationips and a child's coming to terms with self and situation, the story tells of the discontent of little Fanny, 9, the eldest of seven children, at the birth of still another baby. Fanny wakes in the morning to the new-born's mewling and the servants' activities in the bustling Victorian household, in which their distant father reigns supreme and her almost as distant mother is again not to be bothered. Nurse scolds, the teacher insists that Bible verses be mastered, and Fanny is tidied up and rushed off to the church while the Younger Children go for a ride in the donkey cart. In church, Fanny's vexation erupts in the form of a prayer: may God provide cherry tart for dinner and take her new baby sister back to heaven. Vexation turns into fright when cook serves up a mouth-watering cherry tart for dinner. Fanny fears God will answer the other part of her rash prayer, too, and will take away the baby. In horror at what may transpire, Fanny decides to solve her problem in storybook fashion by running away and taking service as a kitchen maid. She applies at the house of her vicar, certain that this elevated worthy will not recognize her. He does, however, but keeps his knowledge to himself, accepts her application at face value, and sets her to work. She struggles valiantly if ineptly to wash dishes and prepare tea, and, conscience-stricken when praised for her efforts, pours forth her tale of woe. The kindly old vicar sets her mind at ease about God

and her sister, relates some of his own childhood misfortunes at being the youngest of ten,
and delivers her home in a much more agreeable
state of mind. Ever afterward little Ethel is
Fanny's favorite sister, but Fanny can never
again tolerate cherry tart. This warmly told,
subtly humorous story is rich in character
revelation, human nature, and irony and offers
some insights into what an upper-class, well-off
Victorian household may have been like. Sequels.
Fanfare.

FANTASTIC MR. FOX (Dahl*, Roald, ill. Donald
Chaffin, Allen, 1970; Knopf, 1970), short,
comic, talking-animal fantasy novel set in a
valley in the English countryside recently.
Three mean and grasping farmers angrily lay
plans to catch and kill the fox that has been
stealing their fowl: Boggis, an enormously fat
chicken grower, who eats three boiled chickens
every day; Bunce, a grotesque, potbellied dwarf,
who raises geese and ducks and lives on
doughnuts and mashed goose livers; and Bean, a
turkey and apple grower as thin as a pencil, who
lives on apple cider. The three men fail to kill
Mr. Fox as he attempts to emerge from his hole
at the foot of a tree on the nearby hill, where
he lives with Mrs. Fox and their four small
kits, instead blowing away his splendidly lush
tail. Furiously angry, they decide to dig the
foxes out. At first they employ conventional
shovels and then two enormous caterpillar
tractors with mechanical diggers affixed to
their fronts. They dig for days, upturning most
of the hill in the process, while inside,
resourceful, courageous Mr. Fox comes up with
what Mrs. Fox terms a fantastic idea: to tunnel
deeper and deeper into the hill. In their
frantic efforts to capture the animals, the
humans destroy the entire hill, leaving in its
place an immense open crater. Then they surround
the hill with hunters armed with guns, seating
themselves within the crater, absolutely determined to starve the foxes out. Mr. Fox gets
another notion: he and the kits tunnel to
Boggis's chicken house and raid it and then go
to Bunce's giant storehouse of hams, bacon, and
dressed fowl, along the way encountering respectable, gentlemanly Mr. Badger, who reports

that all the underground animals are very much
disturbed by the humans' destructive intrusions
into their territory. After raiding the storehouse, the animals tunnel to Bean's cider
cellar, where they help themselves to cider over
the protests of rude and drunken Rat. The book
climaxes with a grand feast for twenty-nine
displaced animals at Mr. Fox's new underground
house. Mrs. Fox declares, "My husband is a
fantastic fox," to choruses of joyful claps and
loud cheers of agreement. Ironically, while this
is going on, the three farmers are still perched
outside the foxes' old lair, in the crater, in a
driving rain, still certain that they have
trapped the animals within and that they will
starve them out. The slapstick and sometimes
crude and clumsy humor of this zippily told,
utterly preposterous tale seems directed at
later elementary youngsters accustomed to the
obvious entertainment of comics and Sat-
urday-morning television cartoons. Choice.

THE FAR-DISTANT OXUS (Hull*, Katharine, and
Pamela Whitlock*, ill. Pamela Whitlock, Cape,
1937; Macmillan, 1938), episodic family novel
with adventure story aspects set near the seacoast at Exmoor in Devonshire in the early
1930s. The Hunterly children--Bridget*,
Anthony*, and Frances*--arrive in August to
spend the rest of their summer holiday at Cloud
Farm with elderly Mr. and Mrs. Fradd. They are
delighted to find that Mr. Fradd has ten horses
in his stables and more in a herd on the moor.
After exploring the moors on their ponies,
Talisman, Timothy, and Treacle (ridden by
Bridget, Anthony, and Frances respectively), at
bedtime they discover under Bridget's pillow a
note inviting them to an adventure at a secret
rendezvous the next night down by the river.
They sneak out after ten, stealthily make their
way to the appointed place, a timber yard, and
there meet Maurice*, a sturdy boy with a jet
black pony named Dragonfly and a Labrador named
Ellita, and the Cleverton children, Peter* and
Jennifer*, with their ponies, Gray Owl and
Goosefeather. They discover that in a spirit of
adventure Maurice and the Clevertons have given
Persian names out of "Sohrab and Rustum" to
various local places, among them the river,

which they call the Oxus; Cloud Farm is
Aderbaijan; the local mountains, the Indian
Caucasus; the Cleverton place, Siestan; and the
local town, Cabool. They learn that Maurice has
plans for building a log hut where the Cloud
Farm tributary meets the Oxus. After a good deal
of difficult carting of timber from the yard
overseen by Maurice and construction directed by
Peter that night and subsequently, the hut is
completed and outfitted, and a sort of tree
house built in a nearby oak. The children call
the place Peran-Wisa, settle in with hammocks
and blankets, and spend the night there.
Maurice, who seems to have no home, makes the
place his headquarters and lives in the hut,
which the children have made quite cozy with
stools, bookshelves with favorite books like
Swallows and Amazons* (which *Oxus* obviously
resembles), and similar amenities of home life.
Various small adventures follow--discovering a
herd of wild horses with a beautiful foal which
they name Rukush and later rescuing the foal
during the annual roundup; helping with the
wheat harvest; enjoying a glorious sleep-out in
the Fradds' new straw-stack, among others--
which are prelude to the great adventure that
consumes about half the book: their week's
expedition by raft and pony down the Oxus to
the sea. Their elaborate preparations for the
expedition include constructing a raft for food
and camping equipment which they take turns
poling with the current. They camp on shore
every night, sleeping in hammocks and sharing
the work of preparing hearty meals which are
described in mouth-watering detail, and have a
grand time with only a few mishaps to add spice
to the journey. The most serious situation
occurs while Maurice and Frances are rafting.
They choose the wrong branch at a fork, dead-end
into a lake, and must tie up the raft and hike
some distance back to where the others have
camped. As they proceed coastward, the Oxus gets
dirtier and the countryside dingier. They skirt
a dismal iron manufacturing town just before
arriving at what they call the Aral Sea on the
evening of the third day. They camp on the rocky
coast, where they enjoy swimming and have pony
races complete with handicaps and colors and
assisted by Mr. Fradd's brother who owns a farm

in the area. This Mr. Fradd comes to the rescue
when they realize they can't punt the raft
upstream to get home again. He loans them his
donkey and cart for their gear, and, after
exploring the local resort town of Seabridge,
Maurice brands the raft as a memorial and sets
it adrift, and they all head home. In spite of
running out of food on the way because they
forgot to stock up before the stores closed on
Saturday and enduring a steadily drizzling rain
on Sunday, they arrive home Monday noon, one
week after departure, happy and satisfied with
their escapade. Then Maurice organizes a final
adventure to mark the end of the holidays.
Under his direction, the children gather wood
and tinder to construct a beacon on the highest
peak of the Indian Caucasus, Mount Elbruz.
After dark they ride to the peak, Maurice
plunges a flaming bracken torch into the pile
of fuel, and the blaze lights up the entire
mountain. Then to the children's surprise and
delight, Maurice sets afire five more beacons
that he has secretly built, his farewell to his
five vacationing friends and to their glorious
holiday together. After a slow start devoted to
a discussion of the attributes of ponies, the
book continues to amble along with lots of
discursive conversation and little tension. A
problem introduced late, occasionally reverted
to, and providing some unity and a little
low-keyed mystery--who Maurice is, and where he
comes from--is never resolved, and the dark
youth slips away at the end as mysteriously as
he arrived early in the novel. Nevertheless, the
book is full of the kind of activities and
subjects good-natured, fun-loving children enjoy
doing and talking about: sleeping out at night
on their own in the company of other amiable,
active children; details about the behavior,
riding, and grooming of horses; secret names,
passwords, and similar "clubby" paraphernalia;
good food; the joy of planning; getting away
with things that probably adults would forbid if
they knew about but that are not morally
wrong--the authors picture life as happy,
intelligent, healthy youngsters would like it
to be. They create somewhat idealized yet real-
seeming children, although they seem shallow
types lacking in personal identity and described

in cliches ("shattering smile"). The children's ages are never specified, except in relation to one another, that is, with Bridget and Maurice being the eldest, Frances and Jennifer the youngest, and the others in between, and thus no reader should have trouble finding one of the six to identify with. The children get on extremely well together, the older ones looking after and making allowances for the younger ones quite agreeably, and no tizzies or tantrums spoil the interlude. The windy moor and late summer heat of the river setting are vivid and also idealized, and the effect of the whole is every child's dream of adventure come true. Sequels are *Escape to Persia* and *Oxus in Summer*. Fanfare.

FARJEON, ELEANOR (1881-1965), born in London; for more than seventy years a prolific writer of novels, stories, poetry, plays, and nonfiction for adults and children, with some 100 publications to her credit, some under the names of Tomfool and Chimaera and some in collaboration with other writers. She was born into a literary family, the daughter of an actress and the popular novelist Benjamin Leopold Farjeon, the sister of writers Herbert and Joseph Jefferson Farjeon and the composer Harry Farjeon, and granddaughter of American actor Joseph Jefferson, who was famed for his stage role as Rip Van Winkle. Since the Farjeon home was the gathering place for literary and dramatic figures of the day, she grew up among famous people and was taken to the theatre and opera from the time she was four. She was privately educated, because her father had little respect for formal schooling, and was largely self-taught in her father's extensive, personal library. She began turning out stories, poems, and plays at an early age, and by seven could not only read but also type and proof copy. By sixteen she had written the libretto for an opera, "Floretta," which was set to music by Harry Farjeon and produced by the Royal Academy of Music in London in 1899. There followed a grand array of publications from her versatile pen and fertile imagination. She wrote rhymes, games, and articles for *Punch* and then a set of stories intended for adults,

Martin Pippin in the Apple-Orchard (Collins, 1921; Stokes, 1922), which girls enjoyed and took over and which was widely praised. Its sequel is *Martin Pippin in the Daisy-Field* (Joseph, 1937; Stokes, 1938). She wrote other collections that were popular in the early part of this century but have mostly not endured. The Martin Pippin books are still occasionally read, as are *The Little Book-Room* (Oxford, 1955; Oxford, 1956), also a collection, which received the Carnegie Medal; *The Glass Slipper* (Oxford, 1955; Viking, 1956), a prose version of a musical play adaptation of the Cinderella story she did with Herbert; her *Poems for Children* (Lippincott, 1931); *The Children's Bells: a Selection of Poems* (Oxford, 1957; Walck, 1960); and the humorous verse biographies *Kings and Queens* (Gollancz, 1932; Dutton, 1932) and *Heroes and Heroines* (Gollancz, 1933; Dutton, 1933), also done with Herbert. She also wrote *The Hamish Hamilton Book of Kings* (Hamilton, 1964, as *A Cavalcade of Kings*, Walck, 1965) and *The Hamish Hamilton Book of Queens* (Hamilton, 1965, as *A Cavalcade of Queens*, Walck, 1965), both coedited with William Mayne*. Her *The Silver Curlew** (Oxford, 1953; Viking, 1954), a prose version of the musical-play adaption of the old story "Tom Tit Tot," for which Clifton Parker wrote the music, was named to the Fanfare list. It is lively with incident and quaintly charming but seems overplotted and condescending in tone to late-twentieth-century tastes and is seldom read any more. Farjeon received the international Hans Christian Andersen Award and the first Regina Medal from the Catholic Library Association for the body of her work. She never married and lived in a cottage in Sussex until 1940, when she moved to London to be near her brothers. After the war, she sold her Sussex house and moved to Hampstead where she died. She also wrote eleven novels, nine books of poems, two books of short stories, and seven plays, among other works for adults.

FARMER, PENELOPE (1939-   ), born in Westerham, Kent; teacher and author best known for her poetic, complexly plotted dream and time fantasies about the sisters Charlotte* and Emma Makepeace: *The Summer Birds** (Chatto, 1962;

Harcourt, 1962), in which lonely Charlotte and
Emma are taught to fly by a strange little boy
who is also an outsider; *Emma in Winter**
(Chatto, 1966; Harcourt, 1966), in which Emma
and a new school friend inhabit the same dreams;
and *Charlotte Sometimes** (Chatto, 1969; Harcourt, 1969), in which, while at boarding
school, Charlotte is transported back in time to
1918. *The Summer Birds* was commended for a Carnegie Award and is listed in *Choice* and Fanfare; *Charlotte Sometimes* appears in Fanfare;
and *Emma in Winter* in *Choice*. Farmer's family
and early home life have influenced her work.
Born just before World War II, Farmer has said
she retains strong memories of the air raids and
bombings, events that may account for the
underlying dark tone of her writing. As a child,
she enjoyed putting words to paper and attempted animal stories in imitation of Beatrix
Potter, and she and her twin sister wrote and
put on little plays. Charlotte and Emma have
their prototypes in Farmer's mother and her
sister, and their settings are the Downs of Kent
where Farmer grew up. After a private education
and then graduation from St. Anne's College,
Oxford, with a B.A. with honors in history and
from Bedford College, University of London, with
a Diploma in Social Studies, she married Michael
Mockridge, a lawyer. After the birth of two
children, they were divorced, and she married
Simon Shorvon, a neurologist. Before and after
the university she tried various jobs while
writing at the same time, working as a mother's
helper, charwoman, waitress, office clerk, post-
man, and teacher in the East End of London from
1961-1963. She published a book of stories for
adults and a television play before she began
writing for children, which she did at the
suggestion of editor Margaret McElderry, then of
Harcourt, who had read some of her stories. Her
first book to attract critical attention was
The Summer Birds and a dozen novels followed,
among them the fantasies *The Magic Stone*
(Chatto, 1965; Harcourt, 1964), *William and Mary*
(Chatto, 1974; Atheneum, 1974), and *A Castle of
Bone** (Chatto, 1972; Atheneum, 1972), a
Fanfare-selected dream and time magic book about
a boy's experiences with a cupboard that
converts things and people to earlier states of

being. Recently she has also turned to oral
tradition for her material for young readers,
editing a collection of myths, *Beginnings:
Creation Myths of the World* (Chatto, 1978; Atheneum, 1979), and writing a series of picture
books from Greek mythology done in close collaboration with the illustrator, among them
Daedalus and Icarus (Collins, 1971; Harcourt,
1971) and *The Story of Persephone* (Collins,
1972; Morrow, 1973). She has also written
Standing in the Shadow (Gollancz, 1984), *Eve:
Her Story* (Gollancz, 1985), and *Away from Home*
(Gollancz, 1987), which are novels for adults.
While some critics have complained that her
fantasies for children are overplotted and that
her ingenuity lacks control, others praise them
as richly imaginative, highly personal, daring
in conception and execution, and deeply involving.

FARMER GILES OF HAM (Tolkien*, J. R. R., ill.
Pauline Baynes, Allen & Unwin, 1949; Houghton,
1950), literary tale of the rise of a simple
farmer to be king of the Little Kingdom, in the
valley of the river now known as the Thames, in
some legendary time before the days of Arthur.
Aedigius de Hammo, familiarly known as Giles of
the village of Ham, is a home and comfort loving
farmer until a giant wanders down from the
mountains of the northwest and stomps on his
favorite cow. Awakened by his dog, Garm, Farmer
Giles loads his blunderbuss with all the old
nails, bits of wire, and pieces of broken
pottery that are handy and climbs the hill above
his farm to see what is going on. When the
giant's face appears suddenly in front of him,
he pulls the trigger in panic. The giant is not
only stupid, like most giants of old stories,
but is also nearsighted and deaf, and, thinking
the nail that pierces the skin of his nose is a
stinging fly, he turns and stomps back to higher
ground where the insects are not so fierce.
Roused by the excited comments of Garm (dogs
spoke English in those days), the other
villagers cheer and crowd into Giles's house to
drink his health with his ale. News soon spreads
as far as the king, who sends Giles a
commendation written in red on white parchment
and a gift of an old sword that had been

gathering dust in the armory. News also gets
around in the mountains, where the giant tells
of rich lands in the southeast where cows can be
picked up in any field and there is never a
knight to be seen, and eventually this news
reaches a dragon named Chrysophylax Dives.
Although dragons have become scarce and the
custom of a knight providing a dragon tail for
Christmas dinner has been formalized into the
cook creating a pastry tail, the dragons that
remain are hungry, and Chrysophylax sets out to
see if the giant's stories are true. Garm, who
has been wandering far from home, again raises
the alarm, but Giles is not concerned until the
dragon comes right into his neighborhood. The
appeals of the people to the king for a
dragon-slaying knight have gone unanswered, and
now they appeal to Giles, particularly the
miller, who is his rival, the blacksmith, who
loves gloomy news, and the parson, whose
counterpart in a nearby village has been eaten.
The blacksmith is prevailed upon to provide
metal rings and pieces of chain to be sewn on a
leather jerkin and pants as ring-mail, and the
parson, examining the old sword with its archaic
inscriptions and epigraphical signs, discovers
that it is Caudimordax, known in the vulgar
tongue as Tailbiter, a sword which will not stay
sheathed if a dragon is within five miles.
Pushed into action at last, Giles sets off on
his old mare with Garm reluctantly accompanying
him. When they meet the dragon, Garm bolts, but
Giles has a conversation with him. The wily
dragon, at first anticipating a nice fat farmer
for dinner, is terrified of Tailbiter and,
crippled by the sword's blow to one wing, runs
until he collapses just outside the church of
Ham. There the village people bargain with him
for his treasure in return for his freedom.
Promising to bring it on the feast of St.
Hilarius and St. Felix, and swearing sacred
oaths, the dragon leaves, never intending to
return. News, however, has once more reached the
king, who arrives with his retinue to await and
claim the treasure. After the dragon does not
bring it, the king sends his knights off to slay
the dragon, with Giles reluctantly at their
head. When they meet the dragon, those knights
who are not immediately killed flee, and Giles,

with Tailbiter, takes up the matter of the broken promise with Chrysophylax. This time he is not easily fooled. He forces the dragon to bring out a large portion of his treasure and then ties it on the beast's back and makes him cart it not to the king's court, but to Ham. Since he has allowed the dragon to keep a portion of his treasure in exchange for his lifelong friendship, Giles has a powerful ally when the king comes to claim the spoils for his exchequer, and the king has no great fighting force, many of his knights already having defected to Giles with whom the pay is more certain. Giles becomes king of the Little Kingdom, often known as Lord of the Tame Worm, or just of Tame, which becomes corrupted to Thames. The story has a playful tone, with clever use of the folktale pattern, but does not attempt to tell serious adventures as do Tolkien's longer works. Choice.

THE FATE OF JEREMY VISICK (Wiseman*, David, Kestrel, 1982; *JEREMY VISICK*, Houghton, 1981), time fantasy set in the old copper-mining country of Cornwall, in the late twentieth and the mid-nineteenth centuries. When Matthew Clemens, 12, calls history "rubbish," his teacher, George Williams, assigns him special homework, which is to find and copy the inscription on the Martin family grave in the cemetery at Gwenap, just across the road from where he lives. With the help of his neighbor and classmate Mary Thomas, he finds the Martin inscription. In the process he is unusually drawn to another stone that records the burial place of Reuben Visick and his sons, Charles and John, all three of whom were killed in the Wheal Maid mine in 1852, and that was set also as memorial to Jeremy Visick, 12, "whose body still lies in Wheal Maid." Matthew, usually a physically boisterous youngster, begins to have periods of quiet and seeming absentmindedness, and he keeps finding himself returning to the Visick grave. One night his mother and older sister, Janet, who has heard him go out, find him curled against the stone, asleep. A bump on the back of the head that he receives in rugby seems to intensify his odd experiences. Mary's father, a farmer interested in local history, tells them about

the mines, gives Matthew a copper-bearing rock
found at the 150-fathom level of Wheal Maid, and
tells him that the cottage where the Clemens
family live is on the old Visick land. Matthew
realizes that the stone-walled shed behind his
house was the Visick home, and more than once he
sees the Visick father and sons going off to
work before daylight. With Mary he goes to the
site of the Wheal Maid, but when he is drawn to
climb down among the old shaft openings, Mary
protests at the danger, and they go home. One
night he follows the Visicks part way in his
pajamas; another time, dressed in old clothes,
he goes all the way to the shaft opening with
Jeremy but is afraid to follow him down the
ladder and runs home in panic. The next time he
goes all the way into the mine with Jeremy,
invisible to the older Visicks. He helps Jeremy
load and haul off the slag rocks and watches
while the older Visicks set the charge for
blasting. When it does not go off, they advance
cautiously and are caught under the crashing
rocks as it goes off belatedly. The blast has
extinguished the candles and blocked the
passage. Matthew and Jeremy, hand in hand, feel
their way through other passages, finally
finding a winze, a sloping passage to the next
level. At first Matthew becomes exhausted, but
when Jeremy gives up hope, Matthew leads and
drags him along, keeping him going. In the
meantime, Matthew's parents have become alarmed
at his absence and have alerted the Thomas
family, Mr. Williams, and finally the police.
Mary realizes where he must have gone, and they
begin a search, which is aborted at dark but
resumed at first light. Matthew wakes to see
light and realizes he has come to an audit, a
tunnel for water to escape, but when he tries to
wake Jeremy he finds only yellowed bones. He
crawls painfully out the audit, Mary sees his
hand, and he is rescued. When the authorities
retrieve Jeremy's bones to bury beside his
father, they bring the remnants of his canvas
croust bag, with his name stitched on, and a
piece of stone whose face exactly matches that
of the stone Mr. Thomas gave Matthew. The
gradual control by the past over lively,
extroverted Matthew is skillfully handled, as is
his father's impatience and lack of

understanding of his son, which mask a deep love. Other characters are not so well realized but are adequate for their parts. The mine itself and the long journey by the two boys in the dark is especially effective. Choice; Fanfare.

FATHER (*The Stone Book**; *Granny Reardun**), Robert, Mary's father and Joseph's* grandfather, who helps to rear him; Robert's great-grand-father; and William's great-great-grandfather. Father is a proud craftsman, who has built most of the village of Chorley in Cheshire and realizes, when he is old, that the good stone has been used up and stonemasonry is a dead craft. He sometimes drinks too much and must be fetched home. When drunk, he quotes from the Bible. He plays the ophicleide, gently for Mary's mother and loudly for drinking tunes, and ironically belts out temperance songs. He has a Macclesfield pipe that falls to the ground unbroken and that he then buries, to be dug up generations later by William, his great-great-grandson, in the last book, *Tom Fobble's Day**; this is one of several motifs that bind the books together. In *The Aimer Gate**, his grand-son, Joseph, describes him graphically and mem-orably as "a proud, bazzil-arsed devil. But he was a good un." Father is a strongly drawn, convincing figure.

FATHER GONZALEZ (*Jeremy Craven**), elderly, kind, ascetic-appearing priest of Taxco, whom Jeremy meets on the ship from England to Mexico. He urges Jeremy to "feel the heartbeat" of his new country. His respect and obvious liking for the Mexican people make a lasting impression upon the boy and influence his thinking and atti-tudes toward his adopted countrymen. Father Gonzalez affects Jeremy's story at several points, in particular in his efforts near the end of the book to keep Uncle Titus* from regaining custody of the youth.

FATHER MORTIMER (*Noah's Castle**), Norman Morti-mer, father of Barry*, Geoff, Nessie*, and Ellen, and husband of May, called Mother*; fifty-two-year-old, hardworking manager of a chain shoestore. A "compact, dapper man, a little below average height," he moves with a "neat, slightly military step," a vestige of his World War II experience when he entered the service as a non-commissioned officer, became a valued quartermaster, and rose to second lieutenant. He enjoys making decisions, commanding, and taking control, evidently elevating himself in his own esteem and to his way of thinking in the esteem of others by dominating. A male chauvinist, he is a good provider but has little respect for his wife's intelligence or feelings, assuming automatically that he has the better judgment. A child of the Depression and of a profligate father who drank and did little for his children, he seems determined not to repeat his father's mistakes, but in the process he alienates his children. A working-class man, he feels inferior to Mr*. Gerald Bowling, the former owner of the shoestore, and displays an almost childlike appreciation when "Mr. Gerald" visits. He refuses to believe that Mr. Gerald could be acting out of selfish motives. At the end, though resigned to losing all the supplies that he has borrowed millions in inflated money to buy, he remains positive that he acted correctly both morally and practically. After a blackmarketer tries to blackmail him into selling or donating the supplies, Father fortifies the house with lumber and sandbags and dons his World War II uniform, ready to do battle to protect his family as he had done in the conflict against the Germans. Father is a complex character and the most fully developed and interesting figure in the story.

FATHOM FIVE (Westall*, Robert, Macmillan, 1979, Greenwillow, 1980), spy mystery continuing the story of Chas* McGill of *The Machine Gunners** in Garmouth on the east coast of England. This novel is set in 1943, several years after the earlier book. Now sixteen and in the sixth form, Chas has grown tall and seems destined for the university despite his working class background, but he still scavenges in the litter of the riverbank with his friend Cem* (Cemetery) Jones. There he finds two interesting things: an upper crust girl from his sixth form, Sheila* Smythson, whom he has admired from a distance, walking her dog, and a large enamel bowl

containing a cardboard box, a gold watch with
the hands fixed to jam when they pass each
other, a nearly empty cigarette package, and a
gray cylinder that he later identifies as an
oscillator. Sheila, a lonely child of a mother
who suffers from nerves and a self-important
father, is surprisingly friendly, and together,
with the erratic help of Cem, they start to
investigate what Chas has decided is a spy
signal system to German U-boats alerting them to
ships with strategically important cargoes,
several of which have been blown up close to the
harbor at Garmouth. To check this theory, Chas
and Cem go through a great mound of garbage to
retrieve the cigarette packet, which Cem has
discarded after smoking the contents, and they
find a message written in German. To translate
it, they enlist the help of Audrey* Parton, who
has left school and works as a reporter on the
local paper. She reads the German and is also
able to discover that the ship named is in
harbor with a cargo of ball bearings; this is
highly secret information. Chas and Cem are
convinced that the bowl must have been dropped
through one of the trap doors in the Low Street
buildings that stick out over the water (trap
doors that are rumored to sometimes disgorge
bodies of those murdered by the Maltese thugs on
Low Street) and carried by the tide out past the
harbor patrols, with the oscillator set to send
radio signals to lurking U-boats. To test this
theory, they build a crude raft and, with Chas,
Cem, and Audrey aboard, paddle it up under the
buildings, dropping off marked basins at various
points, while Sheila waits on the beach to check
which basins are carried past her. The rafters
are chased by a sinister Maltese, nearly run
down by a tanker, almost sucked into the
propellers of another ship, and rescued by the
tug, *Hendon*, whose skipper, Dick Burley, is
something of a local hero. With some relief,
they tell Dick the whole story, are advised to
leave it alone, and are rowed ashore by his
helper, a Norwegian named Sven*, who seems far
more bitter about the Germans than Dick and who
urges them to come to him if they get more
information. The whole episode seems to be
worthless, since all the basins except the one
lost in mid-river when their raft is wrecked are

just washed ashore with the other flotsam. The
youngsters are still determined, however, and
trace the watch to a pawn shop, where the
proprietress makes a strongly sexual play for
embarrassed Chas. They also trace the cardboard
box to a spice shop owned by a Greek named
Xenophon Kallonas. Cem and Chas break into the
shop at night hunting for more evidence, are
discovered, and end up telling the whole story
to Kallonas and his worried wife. Their other
detective work is equally bumbling, but their
clues all point to a foreign sailor who wears a
narrow silver ring on his right hand. To hunt
for him, the two boys pose as workers who grease
ships' engines and the two girls as tarts. After
a couple of unconvincing sallies into the rough
bars of Low Street, they are followed and
attacked by a group of Maltese. Chas is hit on
the head and knocked out, Audrey fights her way
out, escapes, and manages to alert the police,
Cem gets away in a row boat and eventually is
picked up by the *Hendon* again, and Sheila is
taken to the madame of the local brothel,
Nelly* Stagg, on the assumption that she is
trying to cut into the local trade. Nelly is
appalled that they have kidnapped the daughter
of a town councilor, and Sheila, realizing that
her family will break up her friendship with
Chas, coolly makes a deal to keep quiet to the
police about what has happened if Nelly will
help Chas solve the spy mystery. In the ensuing
months Chas does visit Nelly, who treats him in
a friendly, almost motherly way, and then gives
up on tracing the spy until he and Cem find
Nelly's purse and Nelly's little dog, killed and
stuffed into a plastic bag, among the other
flotsam on the river bank. Hearing that Nelly
had spread word, as a ruse to get the spy to
reveal himself, that she had information for
Chas, he realizes that she, too, must by now
have been murdered, and he narrows down the
suspects to Dick Burley. He goes to Sven, tells
him his suspicions, and they row together to the
Hendon, where they find the basins and oscilla-
tors. Then Sven, the real spy, shuts Chas into
the slop chest, opens the seacocks, and leaves
him to drown. Chas is able to get a porthole
open and cut through the mooring rope, sending
the boat careening down the river. When he

wakes, the boat has gone aground, Dick Burley
is leaning over him with the River Police
inspector and a doctor, and Chas is able to
convince them of his story. With the help of
Cousin* Robert McGill, commander of a convoy
escort group, the ship scheduled to be torpedoed
is detoured, the *Hendon* drags an old hull out to
the position the ship should have been in, and
when the German submarine attacks, they are
able to capture it. It is all, however, top
secret, so the part that Chas played is not
acknowledged. He is able to watch the ceremony
when all the town bigwigs, including Sheila's
father, are lining up by the captured U-Boat. As
he watches the German sailors being marched
off, Chas recognizes Sven among them, but he
realizes that his resentment of the snobbish
upper-crust officials is greater than his anger
toward Sven, and he does not point him out. The
complex plot is fast-paced and full of clever
twists, but the characters are far less convincing than in the earlier book. The exceptions
are Chas's parents, minor but important figures,
with his mother treating him like a little boy
and blaming all his troubles on his advanced
education, and his father grimly realistic,
convinced that the real struggle is between the
working class and the bosses but still proud of
Chas for his brains and his ability to attract
a girl like Sheila. The setting in the grimy
industrial town, with its filthy river bank and
the lowlife of sailors' bars and brothels, is a
strong element. Fanfare.

FEBRUARY'S ROAD (Verney*, John, ill. author,
Collins, 1961; Holt, 1966), mystery-adventure in
which a teenage girl helps to thwart a plan to
build a highway across the South Downs which
would cut off her farm from the best riding land
and make illegal millions for some local
speculators. February Callendar, 13, narrates
the story, which occurs during the Christmas
holidays some eighteen months after the
adventures of *Friday's Tunnel**. Three social occasions mar the haphazard but relaxed post-
Christmas days of the large family at Marsh
Manor for February and her brother, Friday, 14.
The first occasion is a party at Fitchetts, the
house on the Chichester road newly occupied by

Captain Gumble, to which they are invited with
their parents since the Gumble's nephew, Peter
Blow, is visiting. Friday sees this as social
disaster, since Peter is head boy of his house
at boarding school, but at the party they are
virtually ignored by Peter, who spends his time
with Helen Ponton, a stupidly pretentious girl
from February's school who has been adopted by
the wealthy neighboring Sprocketts. February is
rescued by Adam Henry, 18, son of the local
doctor and an old friend, but she is shocked to
see her very honest father, Gus (Augustus)
Callendar, a newspaperman, swipe a letter from
Captain Gumble's desk. The second occasion is
the first fox hunt of the year, which is
participated in by February, who is a fine
rider, and her next younger sister, Gail, 11.
February manages to stay close to the front
along with Peter, and when they are both thrown
as they try to jump a river, she rescues him,
ties up his bleeding head, and helps him home.
The third social event is a young people's
dance, planned by her mother for their barn and
dreaded by both Friday and February. Before this
occurs, bulldozers move up to the quarry above
Marsh Manor, ready to start the road, and the
youngsters learn that their father had agreed,
before the road was announced, to sell half the
paddock to pay off the mortgage. February
enlists the editor of her father's newspaper,
the *Messenger*, and the American-born columnist
Mike Spillergun in the fight to prevent the road
from spoiling the downs and their farm, and she
tells them her suspicions that there is collusion between Captain Gumble, Lord Sprockett, the
Downland Preservation Company, Ltd. (which
bought back the piece of paddock), and Jasper
Blow, M.P., Peter's father. Rather than help
decorate the barn, February walks up to the
quarry, where she surprises Adam practicing
Othello for his repertory company. There she
idly pulls an old saucepan out of the water,
where it has been partly frozen in. The next
morning breakfast is interrupted by two furious
workmen who accuse the Callendar family of
sabotaging the construction by pouring water in
the exhausts of the road machinery. Later that
day, a local policeman and a plainclothesman
arrive and question February, who foolishly

denies having picked up the saucepan, which, it
turns out, has her fingerprints all over it.
They are followed by reporters, and in a few
days February is something of a local celebrity.
Mike Spillergun's next column hints at the
collusion, and Gus Callendar is assumed to have
written it or been behind it, an embarrassing
situation since he has been strongly in favor of
better roads and is assumed to have changed
sides when his own land was threatened. The
plainclothesman returns, and February rightly
guesses he is from Scotland Yard, actually
investigating the huge claims for insurance for
the machinery, which has been wrecked again,
this time with sand poured in the engines and
one of the watchmen knocked out. Suspicion
falls on various people, including Gail, who,
thinking February did the first damage, has
sneaked out at night hoping to emulate her
sister and has overheard some revealing
conversation. Another overheard conversation,
this time by February and Adam's sister, Sasha,
provides further clues. Eventually it is proved
that Captain Gumble (along with some local
people) is the main culprit, and that, having
been given an ultimatum by Peter (who is
concerned for the family honor) he is trying to
flee the country when he is stopped. The road is
clearly going to follow a more sensible route,
if it is not to be cancelled completely. The
letter Gus Callendar took from Captain Gumble's
desk was his own letter agreeing to sell his
land. The dance is no longer an occasion to be
dreaded, since their mother put the wrong date
on all the invitations and both young people
will be back at school by then. The story has
more characters than are easy to keep track of;
they are adequate for the plot but not highly
developed. There are enough false leads and red
herrings to keep a reader guessing about who
actually did what. A good deal of lively family
humor lightens the suspense, and all is wrapped
up plausibly in the end. Carnegie Com.

THE FELLOWSHIP OF THE RING (Tolkien*, J. R. R.,
Allen & Unwin, 1954; Houghton, 1954), first of
the three-volume novel, *The Lord of the Rings*,
which is often called the Tolkien trilogy.
Picking up the story of the hobbits* and The

Shire some sixty years after the return of Bilbo* Baggins from his travels in *The Hobbit**, the novel starts on his "eleventy-first" birthday, which is also the thirty-third birthday of his cousin and heir, Frodo* Baggins. Bilbo has kept the ring but has used it little, and now, though he is unchanged in appearance, has become tired and decides to depart from The Shire, leaving his belongings, including the ring, to Frodo. For the next seventeen years Gandalf* appears occasionally at Frodo's house, in between his wide travels and deep studies in the lore of the wise, and has come to realize that the ring is far more important than even he guessed and that it is, actually, the Great Ring of Power, the one forged by Sauron, Lord of Evil, eons before to control the power of the other great rings. As soon as Gandalf is certain of this, he urges Frodo to leave The Shire since he knows Sauron has grown strong again, has begun to dominate the lands around his own land of Mordor, has learned that the ring has reappeared, and suspects that it is in The Shire. Frodo sells his house to relatives and lets it be known that he intends to return to Buckland where he grew up, but actually he starts off with his gardener and faithful servant, Sam* Gamgee, and two young cousins, Pippin* Took and Merry* Brandybuck (who insist on coming along), heading for Rivendell, home of Elrond the half-elf and his people. Even before they leave The Shire they are followed and threatened by Ringwraiths, spirits of humans subverted to be servants of Sauron, who appear as Dark Riders, and on the trip they have several encounters with these evil creatures, as well as being captured in the Old Forest by the ancient willow tree and on the barrow downs by a barrow wight. They also have some unexpected helpers, including Tom Bombadil, ancient, singing, happy earth-spirit, and Strider*, a Ranger they meet at the inn at Bree and who becomes their guide. At Rivendell they take part in a council called by Elrond and attended by representatives of all the major peoples of good will, at which is considered what to do with the ring. The ring cannot be discarded or destroyed except by casting it into the fire where it was forged, in Mount Doom in the land of Mordor, and it cannot be used for good since it corrupts its users; yet it must be kept from Sauron, for with it he would control the whole world for evil. Frodo courageously takes upon himself the task of trying to take the ring to Mordor, and with him go the other three hobbits; a dwarf, Gimli, son of Gloin of Bilbo's adventure; an elf, Legalos, son of the king of the Wood-elves of Mirkwood; Strider, whose real name is Aragorn, son of Arathorn; Boromir*, a man from Gondor, the land just west of Mordor, who has come north seeking help and advice; and Gandalf, the wizard, making up a fellowship of nine. After a long, hard journey they encounter their first great challenge at Caradhras, a mighty peak. There they try to cross the mountains and are forced back by a terrible snow storm. Gandalf then leads them by the only alternate route, through the Mines of Moria, a journey of several days by winding corridors and vast chambers, which are partly dwarf-wrought and partly more ancient. There they find evidence that Balin and those who went with him to try to reopen the mines were killed by orcs, and they themselves are attacked by a combined force of orcs and trolls. They narrowly escape and are almost at the eastern entrance to Moria when a more horrible creature, a Balrog, appears. It fights Gandalf on a narrow bridge over a fiery chasm, and pulls the wizard with it when the bridge breaks. They crash into the flames. Heartbroken at the loss of Gandalf and with Frodo wounded, they go on to Lothlorien, land of the Lady Galadriel and one of the last havens of the elves, where they are healed, refreshed, and given elven cloaks, elven bread (or lembas) for their journey, and boats, in which they can float down the River Anduin to the point where it runs between Mordor and Gondor. There they must decide how to proceed, and as Ringbearer, Frodo must make the decision. Reluctant to take anyone with him into Mordor, where he knows he must go, yet afraid to start alone, he goes off by himself to consider. There Boromir follows him and tries, first by persuasion and then by force, to get the ring from him. Terrified, Frodo slips the ring on his finger, which causes him to disappear, and runs for the boats, intending to

leave alone before the ring can corrupt others.
Sam, however, guesses what Frodo has in mind,
jumps for the boat, and almost drowns before
Frodo can pull him out, and together they start
across the river to the land of Sauron. The
other two volumes tell the adventures of the
others in the fellowship and of the final,
terrible journey through Mordor which is made by
Frodo and Sam. The story is far longer, darker,
and deeper than *The Hobbit*, and it was originally published for adults, though older children
often read it with fascination. In the 1960s it
became extremely popular and gained the status
of a cult novel on college campuses. It is
usually considered one of the major works of
fantasy of the twentieth century and is credited
with reviving a popular interest in the genre.
Choice.

FENODYREE (*The Weirdstone of Brisingamen**),
dwarf instrumental in enabling Susan and Colin
to carry Firefrost* to Cadellin* the wizard
before Selina* Place and Grimnir* can get it.
Fenodyree is the leader in their quest, having
"the same qualities of wisdom, of age without
weakness, that they [Colin and Susan] had seen
in Cadellin, but here there was more of
merriment, and a lighter heart." He is a
stereotypical "good guy" figure and interesting
as a plot functionary.

FERGUS (*Children of the Red King**), son of
Cormac, King of Connacht, who at seven is
rescued from the Norman-held Abbey of Athenmore
Athenmore and elected official heir to his
father over the challenge of his uncle Felim.
When Duncormac is destroyed by the Normans and
he and his sister, Grania*, are taken by the
Norman noble, Sir* Jocelin de Courcy Rohan, he
is at first truculent and unwilling to be
friendly to either Sir Jocelin or his lovely
wife, Lady Blanche, but when Sir Jocelin
proposes that he study with an Irish hermit,
Brother Colman, he gratefully gives his word
that he will not attempt to escape. This resolve
is put to the test when Brother Colman gives him
a message that a rescue mission will try to get
him away, and he agonizes about his divided
loyalties to his father, who he thinks is

attempting his rescue, and to his oath to Sir Jocelin. He decides to say nothing and nearly pays with his life when the rescue actually proves to be his uncle's ambush to kill him. A slight, blond boy, he seems to his big red-haired father to be more Norman than Irish when they meet again.

FESTE (*The Children of Green Knowe**), fine horse belonging to Toby* Oldknow, a chestnut with a white nose and four white feet. Although he has been dead for nearly three hundred years, his stall is kept empty and he is often heard to neigh in the evenings. On Toby's ride through the flood to the doctor, he refuses to cross the bridge, plunging into the river and swimming instead, and reaching the other side just as the bridge collapses. When Black Ferdie tries to steal one of the horses, Feste appears and chases him, causing him to break his knee. Tolly* longs to see him and leaves sugar cubes on the edge of his stall. Eventually he hears Feste neigh, and on Christmas morning he feels him and hears him crunching up the apple he has brought, but he never actually sees him.

FEZZIWIG (*A Christmas Carol**), jolly businessman to whom Ebenezer* Scrooge was apprenticed. Described as a "slight old fellow in a Welsh wig," he is seen at the Christmas dance he gives for his apprentices, his servants, and some of his neighbors, at which he prances with the younger people in high good spirits, the soul of friendliness and generosity. The attitude of Fezziwig in this the merriest scene introduced by the Ghost of Christmas Past is in sharp contrast to the way Scrooge treats his employee, Bob Cratchit.

FINLAY, WINIFRED (1910-   ), born in New-castle-upon-Tyne, Northumberland; teacher, col-lege lecturer, lecturer on books to school-children and librarians, and author of more than three dozen novels, books of retellings, and radio plays for children. She attended High School for Girls, Whitley Bay, Northumberland, and received her M.A. in English with honors from King's College, University of Newcastle, in 1933. She married Evan Finlay, a college lecturer, in 1935, and has one daughter. She began her career as an author by writing novels for her own daughter when, during World War II, suitable books were scarce. She wrote first for young children and then for teenaged girls as her daughter grew older. Her stories are set in real places which she knows well, and include local lore and history for interest and authenticity as well as accurate geographic detail. She has said she strives always to show how actions affect character and character actions. Her novels tend to follow a formula: youth on holiday become involved in local mysteries. Some novels are set in the British Isles, like *Cotswold Holiday* (Harrap, 1954) and *Mystery in the Middle Marches* (Harrap, 1964), and *Danger at Black Dyke** (Harrap, 1968; Phillips, 1968), which received the Edgar Allan Poe Award and in which three boys playing Roman soldiers near Hadrian's Wall hide a mysterious youth involved in international intrigue. Other stories take their protagonists abroad, like *Judith in Hanover* (Harrap, 1955), *Alison in Provence* (Harrap, 1963), and *Adventure in Prague* (Harrap, 1967). Her later novels show a marked departure from their predecessors, being time fantasies involving magic and mythological motifs, like *Singing Stones* (Harrap, 1970) and *Beadbonny Ash* (Harrap, 1973; Nelson, 1975). In mid-life and mid-career, she changed her approach dramatically owing to health problems. Because of complications following a pneumonectomy she became unable to work or travel. She turned from writing novels to retelling legends, ghost stories, and ballads, using notes she gathered on her trips and drawing largely on the lore of the border country of her childhood. Some of these books are *Folk Tales of the North* (Kaye, 1968; Watts, 1969), *Tales from the Borders* (Kaye, 1979), and *Vampires, Werewolves and Phantoms of the Night: Demonic Tales from Different Lands* (Methuen, 1983). She has lived in a seventeenth-century house in a village in the English Midlands.

FINN, PATRICK (*The Winter of the Birds**), flamboyant, affected in dress, articulate, and perceptive; a jovial giant of an Irishman of indeterminate age who stops when Alfred* Graves hails his vehicle, which was once a taxi but is no longer used as such. He delivers Alfred to Liverpool harbor as he requests, saves him from attempted suicide, takes him to the Haunton home of his sister, Lily* Flack, to retrieve his suicide note, gets caught up in Mr.* Rudge's problem of the steel birds, and proves himself a hero, at least in the eyes of young Edward Flack, for his undaunted courage in the face of great obstacles. The reader never learns where Finn has come from or much of anything personal about him, but at the end Edward says Finn will leave St. Savior's Street now that his heroic mission is accomplished. An irony of the story is that so unlikely a hero should affect so much change so deftly. He is an interesting but never convincing character.

FINN MCANDREW (*Emma Tupper's Diary**), Fiona, 18, artistic daughter in the highland family that tries to fake a monster to attract tourists to their loch. Although she really doesn't want to spoil their isolated home with development, Finn goes along with the plan, designing and making the creature's head from fiber glass and taking the films to be sent to the television people because she vainly hopes that if her brothers are busy with the project they will not fight as much as usual. At the family meeting she gives her proxy to Emma* Tupper and is accused by her brothers of abdicating responsibility.

FIRE AND HEMLOCK (Jones*, Diana Wynn, Methuen, 1985; Greenwillow, 1985), complex fantasy involving variations on the ballads of Tam Lynn and Thomas the Rhymer and elements from Fraser's *The Golden Bough*, set in the English town of Middleton in the late twentieth century. Polly* Whittacker, at nineteen, looking at a book she has read before, suddenly realizes that she remembers it differently, that, in fact, she has two distinct sets of memories covering the last nine years. Her suppressed memories, which she gradually dredges up, start at Halloween when she was ten, staying (along with her friend, fat Nina* Carrington) with Granny* Whittacker because her parents are having marital problems. The girls have been playing High Priestess in old black dresses of Granny's, and Polly wanders

by accident into a funeral at Hunsdon House, the
mansion at the end of Granny's street. There a
tall, bespectacled man rescues her from the
reading of the will, and they have an interesting conversation in the garden about imagining
things. He introduces himself as Tom* Lynn and
also shows her two urns bordering a door, which
can be spun on their pedestals, so that the
lettering on them seems sometimes to say
NOW-HERE and sometimes NO-WHERE. She helps him
pick out six pictures, which are his legacy, by
mixing up the stacks of those he may choose from
with those that his ex-wife, Laurel*, has told
him are too valuable to go out of the familly.
He gives her one choice, a framed photograph
named *Fire and Hemlock*, showing a haystack
burning in a field with a hemlock plant in the
foreground. Shortly afterwards she receives a
long, badly spelled and typed letter from Tom
Lynn, expanding on the adventure they imagined
in which he is really Tan Coul, a hero, disguised as an ironmonger named Thomas Piper, she
is his assistant, named Hero, and together they
defeat a giant in a supermarket. About this time
Nina says that two people Polly saw at the
funeral, Morton* Leroy and his son, Seb*, 14,
are taking turns watching her, but when Polly
boldly confronts Seb, he says it is she they are
watching and not Nina, and warns her to stay
away from Tom Lynn; if not, either Morton or,
worse, Laurel (whom Morton plans to marry) will
"see to" her. Despite this warning, Polly is
delighted when Tom, who is a cellist with the
London Philharmonic, invites her to have tea wth
him in London. On this occasion and every time
they are together in the next five years, the
things they have made up seem to happen in a
bizarre and often dangerous way. Tom continues
to write Polly letters and, as the orchestra
travels, to send her cards and books from
distant parts. After some time he leaves the
orchestra to start a string quartet; the other
quartet members are both real-life Philharmonic
musicians and figures in the fantasy adventures.
They seem to know what is happening on both
levels, and, unfortunately, so does Morton
Leroy, who somehow is orchestrating the most
threatening episodes. During this period,
Polly's parents are divorced and her mother,

Ivy*, takes in a series of lovers as "lodgers," each of whom is eventually disturbed enough by her over-possessiveness and suspicions to leave. Irrationally, Ivy blames Polly and sends her off to Bristol to live with her father, Reg*, and his new wife, Joanna. After she arrives it becomes clear to Polly that Reg has not told Joanna that she was coming or that she is expecting to stay. To save both herself and her father the shame of explaining, Polly pretends she is there for just a brief visit and goes off toward the station with no money for a ticket or food. Through a seeming coincidence, she is rescued by the string quartet and goes to live permanently with Granny. Seb, who attended a posh boys' school in Middleton, also figures in both sets of memories, in the ordinary-life ones having met her at a party the year she started college and pursued her until they have become engaged, and in the other memories as the boy she met at the funeral and knew while he was at school. As she remembers, she realizes that she did something dreadful to Tom four years before when she was fifteen. Driven nearly frantic because she does not understand the relationships between Tom and Morton and Laurel, and prodded by Seb to ask Tom about it, she uses the *Fire and Hemlock* picture and a photo- graph of Tom as a boy, which she stole once from Hunsdon House, to perform a bit of witchcraft, thereby unwittingly giving Laurel power over her. When, a little later in a confidential chat, Laurel tells her that Tom has cancer and only four years to live and that he has been embarrassed by her crush on him, she promises to forget him. Now, on Halloween four years later, she realizes that her promise has made her and nearly everyone else forget that she ever knew Tom Lynn, and that it has been nine years since the last funeral at Hunsdon House, the prescribed period between sacrifices of olden times intended to keep the king vigorous. She also realizes that Tom will be the next sacrifice. She catches the bus for Middleton, where Granny helps her sort out what she must do and then goes to Miles Cross to wait, just as the girl in the legend waits to claim and save Tam Lynn. In a final, fantastic scene in the frozen garden of Hunsdon House, Tom and Morton battle psychologically for their lives in the presence of Laurel, Seb, Leslie* Piper (Tom's nephew, who is Laurel's newest boy recruit), Leslie's father, who has been masquerading as an ironmonger for nine years, the other quartet members, and an audience of elegant men and women. Seb is obviously afraid that if Tom somehow gets away, he will be the sacrifice instead or will have to replace his father as Laurel's mate. As Polly tries to help Tom, she sees that it makes him lose ground, and she realizes that she can only help him by giving him up, renouncing him completely. With that, Morton disappears into nothingness. In a brief coda, some hope is held out that, together, Tom and Polly can defeat Laurel's logic and find happiness. The many threads of plot are so intricately woven together that it is difficult to sort out just who has understood how much of the otherworld aspects of the situation and at what time in the story. A second, careful reading proves that the various strands tie together logically, but the demands on the reader are considerable. The characterization, however, is strong, and even minor characters stand out clearly as individuals; furthermore, the tone of mixed impending doom and delight is very effective. Some knowledge of the ballads and the principle of the sacrifice for the king, while not essential, will help a reader better understand events. Fanfare.

FIREFROST (*The Weirdstone of Brisingamen**), the droplet-shaped jewel on Susan's bracelet which she calls her Tear and which Cadellin* calls Firefrost, the Weirdstone of Brisingamen. At times it emits a special light that Susan notes resembles the light in the cave of Fundindelve. This is the chidren's clue to the identity of the stone as Firefrost, Cadellin's magical token for protecting the Sleepers, the knights that lie sleeping in Fundindelve.

FIREWEED (Paton* Walsh, Jill, Macmillan, 1969; Farrar, 1970), realistic novel of two young people on their own during the worst of the bombing of London in World War II. The narrator, who gives his name only as Bill and admits that it is really something else, is sent at fifteen

as an evacuee to Wales, mostly because his
father has gone into the army and his aunt, who
has grudgingly raised him, doesn't want to be
bothered with him. His host family lives far up
the mountain, speaks little English, and has no
money or desire to buy him essential clothes for
winter. When his father sends him five pounds,
he simply leaves and heads back to London.
There, coming out of a subway that serves as an
air-raid shelter, he spots Julie, a girl perhaps
fourteen or fifteen, who is also on her own, and
he teams up with her. She had been on a ship of
children being evacuated to Canada which was
torpedoed; when she was returned to England, her
parents didn't want to see her while she awaited
a new ship, and so, disillusioned and hurt, she
walked out of the shelter. Since she has fifty
pounds to pay Canadian expenses, they buy some
blankets and jackets from the Salvation Army
store and continue sleeping in air-raid shelters
until some school teachers start rounding up
stray youngsters. They then move to the basement
of a bombed-out house that belongs to Julie's
aunt. There they have a short, idyllic period
and are comparatively comfortable with a
fireplace, a primus stove, cold running water,
and the aunt's cook's ration book. After one
particularly bad night's bombing, they notice a
young child sitting on some rubble and crying.
Several times during the day they see him, and
eventually, after a cold rain has begun, they
take him in, warm him, and feed him, but they
can't get him to say anything except "Dee-kee,"
although they heard him talking to a woman
earlier in the day. Dickie, as they call him,
becomes ill, and they realize how precarious
their system and their happiness have been. Bill
goes out into a raid to try to find milk for the
child, discovers the dairy store bombed and the
lunch counter he frequented destroyed, and
finally takes a pitcher of milk which was
sitting in front of a dead woman whose shattered
house he passes. When he gets back to their
hideout, he finds that the explosions nearby
have made the remains of the upper stories
collapse, burying Julie and Dickie. Horrified,
he contacts the air raid warden and persuades
him that there were people in the basement. A
rescue crew digs through the rubble for hours.

Julie is brought out, seeming at first to be dead but actually only injured and in shock. Dickie is found peacefully asleep. Bill spends a couple of days finding the hospital where Julie is recovering, a search complicated because they have never exchanged last names, and then is told that no one but relatives may see her. When he finally is allowed to go to her room, her mother, Mrs. Vernon-Greene, and her older brother are there; both are obviously of much higher social status and suspicious of him. The brother suggests that the relationship is inappropriate and, when Julie assures him that there was nothing between them, Bill runs out, feeling betrayed and desolate. The story is narrated by Bill some years later; consequently, it is clear that he survived and that he never saw Julie again, though he still is deeply in love with her, and only after some time has he begun to wonder if she said what she did only to keep her brother from interfering. The love between the two young people is well evoked, and their scheme of living without being apprehended by the authorities is perfectly plausible, although they both seem more naive than young people of the late twentieth century. The strength of the novel is in the scenes of war-torn London and of the reactions of people under the increasingly desperate conditions. Choice; Contemporary Classics; Fanfare.

FIVE BOYS IN A CAVE. See *The Cave.*

FIVE CHILDREN AND IT (Nesbit*, E., ill. H. R. Millar, Unwin, 1902; Dodd, 1905), amusing, episodic family fantasy set in the countryside of turn-of-the-century Kent. Four children-- Cyril*, sometimes called Squirrel, about four- teen, and his younger brother and sisters, Robert*, Anthea* (sometimes called Panther) and Jane*--liken the White House, the large, old place to which the family has just moved, to a fairy palace and are certain they will be happy there. Less than a week after they arrive, their adventures start. While digging for Australia in the sand in a nearby gravel pit, they find a Psammead* (pronounced Sammyadd), or Sand-fairy, a brown, fat, furry, feisty creature that can grant wishes. The book's eleven chapters des-

cribe their adventures in coping with what
happens as a result of their several usually
hasty or casual wishes. Their first adventure
results when Anthea wishes them as beautiful as
the day and they become so handsome that the
servants do not recognize them and shut them out
of the house. As the day wears on, the children
wonder what will happen at evening, fearing they
will turn to stone. To their great relief, sunset brings the restoration of their old, comparatively plain appearances, and they realize
that the Psammead's work lasts only for a single
day at a time. The next day, in spite of the
Psammead's warning, they wish "to be rich beyond
the dreams of...avarice." The Psammead fills the
gravel pit with millions in gold coins, and,
since the children did not think to specify
their wealth, the coins are unfortunately a
foreign currency that no one will accept as
legal tender. When the children try to purchase
a horse and cart, the dealer summons the
"pleece." Sunset saves them, however, since the
gold coins and thus the evidence in the case
disappear as the sun goes down. The next day
Robert becomes so irritated with Lamb, their
baby brother for whom they are to care, that he
wishes "everybody wanted Lamb so they'd [his
siblings] get some peace." Soon wealthy Lady
Chittenden becomes enamored of Lamb and takes
him home, and her coachman and footman come to
blows over him. Fortunately sundown intervenes
before gypsies make off with him, and the spell
is broken. A particularly humorous set of misadventures ensues when Anthea suggests they
request the Psammead to give them wings. After
flying about the countryside, the four children
alight in a church tower, fall asleep, and
awaken after sunset to find their wings gone and
the tower door locked. Their shouts for help
attract the attention of the vicar and his servants, who at first think lunatics are attacking
them. In other adventures, the White House
becomes a great, black, medieval castle under
siege; Robert wishes he were bigger than the
baker's boy, who has just trounced him, becomes
a giant, and is displayed as a sideshow at the
local fair; when Cyril rashly wishes Lamb were
adult, the children are chagrined by their
little brother's pseudosophisticated behavior as

a handsome youth in gray flannels and green tie;
and, after reading *The Last of the Mohicans*,
Cyril wishes for Red Indians, and the children
are taken captive and almost roasted alive. The
last adventure--and the farewell to the Psam-
mead--arises out of Jane's dreamy wish that it
would be lovely if Mother might have all the
jewels that were stolen from Lady Chittenden's
house the night before, and they appear in
various places in Mother's room. When Mother
insists on going to the police even though Cyril
suggests waiting for Father, who will return
after sundown (and find the jewels gone), Anthea
takes charge. She goes to the sand pit, grabs
hold of the Psammead, and refuses to let it go
until it grants several wishes that put everything to rights. In return, the children promise
never to ask it for another wish. The Psammead
is well-drawn, with a history going back to the
age of dinosaurs and an irascible yet accommodating manner, but the children are almost
indistinguishable from one another, and the
adults are types, functionary figures who exist
for the sake of the plot. The episodes are
lively with humor of action, conversation, and
character and are full of the kind of detail
that is true to the nature of the young and thus
makes what happens seem very real. The tone is
breezy, the style energetic, and the pace rapid.
Though not as highly regarded as the author's
stories about the Bastable children, this novel
has two sequels, *The Phoenix and the Carpet* and
The Story of the Amulet, and is considered a
classic in the fantasy-family story genre. Children's Classics; Choice.

FIVER (*Watership Down**), small, intuitive rabbit, brother of Hazel*, and the one under whose
direction the group leaves Sandleford Warren,
arrives at Watership Down, and gets does from
Efrafa, the totalitarian warren under General*
Woundwort. Fiver's ability to see into the
future and to intuit good and bad events is
vital to the plot. He demonstrates the importance of the psychic.

FLAMBARDS (Peyton*, K. M., ill. Victor Ambrus,
Oxford, 1967; World, 1968), period novel set
shortly before World War I in Essex, on a

decaying estate called Flambards where the over-
riding interest is in horses and fox hunting.
Orphan Christina* Parsons, 12, is summoned to
live with her Uncle* Russell and his two sons
at Flambards, because, she realizes, she will
inherit a large amount of money when she is
twenty-one and her uncle plans to have her
eventually marry the elder boy, Mark*, 14, in
order to restore the fortunes of the place,
which has become run down by his extravagance
and lack of interest in anything but horses.
Uncle Russell has been crippled in a riding
accident, a condition that has only increased
his violent temper and heavy drinking habit. On
the day of her arrival, the younger son,
William*, 13, (also called Will) is thrown from
his horse and breaks his leg, an accident caused
by Mark's recklessness in jumping. Christina is
shocked at the callous lack of sympathy both
Mark and his father show for William, but she is
used to living as an unwanted child with
relatives, and she keeps her own counsel. Uncle
Russell himself is shocked because she does not
know how to ride, and he turns her over to the
stable boy, Dick* Wright, 15, with orders that
she shall learn by hunting season. Dick is
patient and gentle, and a marvelous rider, and
to her own surprise Christina becomes an
excellent rider and loves it as well as her
clever mare, Sweetbriar. The tensions in the
house, however, are difficult to live with. Mary
the housekeeper is overworked and not allowed
enough money to keep the house in good
condition. Violet, Dick's sister, who works in
the kitchen, is much less clever than her
brother and is sweet on Mark. William, who hates
riding, has deliberately walked on his broken
leg before it is healed, knowing that it will
cripple him and that he will no longer be forced
to join the fox hunting. Mark, who takes after
his father, can be charming but is also
unfeeling and brutal to both horses and people.
In one hunt, when Dick has brought up the second
horses but Mark's has gone lame, he switches
saddles and rides Sweetbriar, leaving Christina
furious on a tired horse. With his usual
impatience, he puts Sweetbriar to an almost
impossible jump over a hedge instead of opening
a gate. The gallant horse tries but crashes,

throwing Mark and injuring herself seriously. Uncle Russell, who has no interest in a horse that cannot jump, orders that Dick take her over to the keeper of the hounds to be butchered for dog meat. Christina, appalled, consults William, who cautiously suggests that he might find a home for Sweetbriar if she can persuade Dick to turn her over to them. Dick, who has fallen in love with Christina, agrees, though he realizes it is a risky decision. Will and Christina take her to the home of Mr. Dermot, an eccentric gentleman who is building an airplane. She discovers that Will has been working with him secretly and that he is the test pilot for the frail aircraft, *Emma*. Mr. Dermot welcomes Sweet-briar, and all seems well until Mark remarks to his father that the hound keeper was surprised when he mentioned the mare; thus, the truth comes out. Uncle Russell is furious, fires Dick, throws his crutch at Christina, and viciously beats William with his cane. Christina learns that Dick was the main support of his bedridden mother and that without references from Uncle Russell or Mark he can't get another job. The old groom, Fowler, who has trained Dick, blames Christina, and in an ill-advised attempt to help she goes to see Dick in the miserable village cottage where his family lives. He is embarrassed, and she feels helpless, realizing her mistake. Some time later he joins the army, and Violet is dismissed for becoming pregnant. When Dick reappears in uniform and intercepts and beats Mark thoroughly, Christina realizes that it is Mark's child. She deplores the violence, but the others, particularly Fowler, seem to see it as the natural course of events. When she is seventeen, the point-to-point (the main competition in the hunt club) is interrupted just when Mark seems about to win by the arrival of *Emma* with William at the controls and looking for a place for an emergency landing. Mark is furious, and Uncle Russell, who has known nothing about William's interest in flying, rages that he will send him to British Columbia. Before he can be turned out, Will leaves, but he tells Christina that he will be back to take her to the Hunt Ball, to which he asked her a year earlier. Mark has assumed that she will go with him, although when he had taken her the previous year he had gotten drunk and she had had to find another ride home. Aunt Grace, a dressmaker with whom Christina had lived before moving to Flambards, sends her a lovely gown, and, though she dares not expect William to come, he does arrive in Mr. Dermot's Rolls Royce. At the dance, Mark, who has been very angry that she is not going with him, asks her to marry him. When she refuses, she realizes that she can't go back to Flambards. William suggests that she marry him instead, and they drive through the night together to Aunt Grace's home in Battersea. The book gives a picture of a kind of life that was largely erased by World War I, characterized by big estates with many servants living almost as serfs, and the gentry spending recklessly to satisfy their habits, and, more specifically, a family caught in an obsessive love of horses and hunting. The Russell men are well drawn, and Christina, living amidst their conflicts, is a naive but sturdy character. The best scenes are of Flambards itself, the dilapidated house, the neglected fields and the polished stables, and of hunting, where the excitement in the descriptions is contagious. Boston Globe Honor; Carnegie Com.; Choice; Fanfare; Guardian.

FLAMBARDS IN SUMMER (Peyton*, K. M., ill. Victor Ambrus, Oxford, 1969; World, 1970), third in the *Flambards* trilogy, this one set during World War I, starting shortly after William* Russell (also called Will) has been killed in air combat, and his brother, Mark*, having been declared missing in action near Gaza, is given up for dead. Christina* Parsons Russell, now twenty-one and having come into her inheritance, returns to Flambards determined to bring the dilapidated estate back to life with her money. She finds the place even more run-down than she remembers, with only old Fowler the groom and Mary the housekeeper left to cope and with both of them resigned to the decay. At first she is about to give up, but shortly after she arrives, she discovers that she is pregnant, and she decides that she must restore the place for this child which is Will's. The only workers she can hire are two village boys, Stanley, a sharp-faced,

insolent youth, and Harry, who is retarded.
Fowler, after opposing her schemes, becomes
enthusiastic when she starts buying horses.
Remembering that some six years earlier Violet
Wright, the kitchen maid, was dismissed for
becoming pregnant by Mark, Christina decides to
try to bring his child, whom she envisions as a
pretty, fair-haired girl like Violet, to Flambards. To her surprise, she rather easily finds
Violet in a London slum, now the mother of four,
and she literally buys the child from her for
five hundred pounds. It is not a girl but a
dark, glowering Russell boy named Thomas Mark
and called Tizzy*. Mary and Fowler are both
shocked at her taking in a bastard, and the
neighbors ostracize her. Tizzy, who has spent a
lot of time at the brewery helping the carters
with the dray horses, soon settles in, missing
only his uncle, Dick* Wright, who, he says to
Christina's surprise, lived with them in London.
Christina hunts up Dick in a tavern and asks him
to come back to Flambards, but he hesitates,
reluctant to dredge up the past and unable to do
heavy work, having been invalided out of the
army with tuberculosis caused by a shell
fragment through his lung. He agrees to come in
the spring if he feels better. The farm work is
too much for her motley crew, and Christina
applies, over the protests of Fowler and Mary,
for some German prisoners. She is sent only one,
a small, middle-aged man named Wilhelm, who
turns out to be a real farmer but speaks no
English. In early spring, Christina's child is
born, a girl whom she names Isobel after Will's
mother. Just as it all seems too much for her,
Dick arrives, able to do light work and to
direct the others, and, best of all, able to
speak German to Wilhelm, having picked up a bit
in the hospital. With the work at last beginning
to take shape, the war seems far away until a
German Gotha crashes and explodes in a Flambards
field. Dick and some of the village men save two
of the crew, but the accident, to which
Christina is the first at the scene, brings back
all her grief at Will's death and, after a
violent spell of weeping, helps her get over it.
Responding to a telegram for transport from the
station, which Christina assumes is from Aunt
Grace, she finds with a great shock that it is

Mark, who has been in a Turkish prison for some
eighteen months and is now home on leave. His
presence greatly complicates life at Flambards,
bringing with it the discord which is in his
nature and in particular his antagonism to Dick.
Mark is astonished at Tizzy, but sets about
charming him immediately. He even lets Tizzy
ride Christina's horse Pheasant, which has
always fascinated the child but is very erratic,
the reason she was able to buy him for a
bargain. When Pheasant returns without the
child, they all turn out to hunt for Tizzy and
find him lying in some trees, suffering from a
concussion but no broken bones. The incident
makes Christina realize how much she depends on
Dick, and after the doctor goes, she slips down
to the stables and they declare their love for
each other. When she returns, Mark, who has been
drinking too much, picks a fight and points out
to her that it is his house and if she is
interested in Dick she will have to get out. She
tells him that she will take the children and,
until she can make other arrangements, they will
stay in the farmhouse where Dick has been
living. She then turns to see that Tizzy has
come downstairs and overheard their quarrel. The
next morning Tizzy has disappeared, and riding
out to find him she discovers that the farmhouse
is on fire. She, Mark, and Dick, along with the
other hands and many villagers, fight the fire.
It destroys the farmhouse but they do save the
horses and the newly harvested crops. Dick, who
is suffering from smoke inhalation, tells her
that the fire was deliberately set with a
bundle of straw placed under his bed. At home
she finds Tizzy innocently in bed, but with
smoke in his hair and clothes, and she realizes
that he tried to prevent a move by destroying
the farmhouse. Hardly are they back at the house
than the family solicitor appears, having made
an appointment to discuss finances with Mark.
The debts left by Mark's father are so great
that the only way he can survive without working
is to sell Flambards. Christina offers to buy
it. Mark, discovering that Tizzy set the fire,
beats him with a belt and damages the fine
rapport between them. Just before Mark is to
return to France, Dorothy* Saunders, a former
love interest, turns up, having been a nurse in

Europe. The two go off together. At the end they are to be married, leaving Tizzy to Christina, who plans to marry Dick and live at Flambards. Christina develops as a more interesting character than in the two previous books, taking positive action to determine her own future and fighting actively for Flambards and the children. The reversal in social roles for Dick is made acceptable by the changes the war has caused, and Mark, who represents the old conventions, is not only infuriating but pictured as out of step with the new society. A sequel, but not part of the original trilogy, is *Flambards Divided*. Fanfare; Guardian.

FLEMING, IAN (LANCASTER) (1908-1964), born in London; journalist and writer of espionage novels. He was educated at Eton, the Royal Military Academy at Sandhurst, the University of Munich, and the University of Geneva. From 1929 to 1933 he was Moscow correspondent for Reuters, Ltd.; from 1933 to 1935 he was associated with Cull and Co., merchant bankers; and from 1935 to 1939 was a stockbroker in London. In 1939 he went to Moscow as a reporter for *The Times* and unofficially as a representative of the foreign service, and until 1945 he did secret service work for naval intelligence. His journalistic career also included a period from 1945 to 1959 as foreign manager for Kemsley Newspapers and from 1949 to 1964 as publisher of the bibliophilic magazine, *The Book Collector*. He also wrote a column for the *Sunday Times* under the pseudonymn Atticus. He is best remembered, however, as the creator of the character of James Bond, Agent 007, whose adventures made him one of the best-known espionage figures in literature. Among the Fleming novels that have been made into movies are *Casino Royale* (Cape, 1953; Macmillan, 1954), *From Russia, With Love* (Macmillan, 1957), *Doctor No* (Macmillan, 1958), and *Goldfinger* (Macmillan, 1959). For children he wrote only one book, *Chitty-Chitty-Bang-Bang, the Magical Car* (Cape, 1964; as *Chitty Chitty Bang Bang*, Random, 1964), the story of a wonderful flying automobile, which was filmed by United Artists in 1968.

FLETCHER, DAVID (LESLIE) (1918-   ), born in

Devonshire; artist and author of a variety of
books for children. He was educated in history
at Corpus Christi College, Cambridge. During
World War II he served in a corvette on convoy
duty in the North Atlantic and the Mediterranean. He studied painting and has traveled extensively. Two of his novels were named to the *Horn
Book* Fanfare list, *Angelo Goes to the Carnival**
(Hutchinson, 1956; as *Confetti for Cortorelli*,
Pantheon, 1957), a story for younger children
set in Sicily, and *The King's Goblet** (Constable, 1964; Pantheon, 1962), a mystery thriller
for older children set in mid-twentieth-century
Venice. Among his other books are *Mother o'Pearl*
(Pantheon, 1970), a collection of three literary
tales using folktale conventions and patterns
but adding modern wit and turns of phrase, and
The Children Who Changed (Michael Joseph, 1961;
as *The Village of Hidden Wishes*, Pantheon,
1960), a fantasy about two girls who get tricked
into changing places with their dolls and
discover that it is not a pleasant life. He has
made his home in Brighton, Sussex.

FLICK (*Travelers by Night**), young hoodlum who
leads a band in Yald Forest which steals from
campers and hikers and fancies it to be in the
Robin Hood tradition. After they capture
Charlie* and Belle* Marriot, Belle convinces
them that the elephant, Tessie, is very
dangerous and gets them to release Charlie and
return their money. Flick admires her spirit and
even her scar, which seems like a badge of
honor, and he suggests that she come back in a
few years when she's old enough for him. Flick
and his brother, Billy, have been in an orphan
home, though they have a mother who, before they
ran away, expected Flick to get a job and
support her. Flick is cynical about society, but
he is concerned for his younger brother and
worried by Billy's cough.

THE FLIGHT OF THE DOVES (Macken*, Walter, Macmillan, 1968; Macmillan, 1968), realistic novel
set in Ireland in the mid twentieth century.
Fed up with the brutal treatment by their
stepfather, "Uncle" Toby (Tobias) Morgan, Finn
Dove, 12, takes his sister, Derval, 7, and heads
for the home of his Granny O'Flaherty in western

Ireland. Unfortunately he can't remember the
name of the village where his grandmother lives
and has only vague memories of his last trip to
see her, which was when he was about Derval's
present age. While Uncle Toby is at the pub,
they make their getaway and board the mail boat
by mingling with a large family. On the Irish
side they are helped by a number of people: a
boy named Poll, whom they meet in the street,
and his father, who gets them a ride in a lorry
heading west; the lorry driver Nickster, who
unfortunately is arrested for receiving stolen
copper for resale; a detective named Michael,
who takes his vacation time to trace and aid the
children; a gypsy boy named Moses, who helps
them get across the Shannon River as part of his
family, under the very eyes of the police, and
later helps them get away from his father,
Powder, who plans to turn them in for the
reward; and various nameless people. They are
pursued by the police, who have been alerted; by
Uncle Toby's boss, an attorney, who has learned
that the children have been left a large legacy
by a great-uncle; by Uncle Toby himself, now
crying crocodile tears; and by a mysterious
stranger named Nicko, who turns out to be sent
by an uncle in America who is determined to get
control of the children so he can profit from
the legacy or, if it comes to that, to do them
in since he would then be the beneficiary. Finn
discovers from newspaper reports of the search,
which has become a major story, that Granny
lives in the village of Carraigmore. They make
their way all across Ireland, sometimes hitching
rides, and arrive at Carriagmore almost simultaneously with Uncle Toby, Michael, Nicko, newspaper reporters, and the police. Granny and her
two sons, with the help of the villagers, are
prepared to hold off the law. Michael, however,
fetches the judge from his fishing vacation.
Since Michael has made inquiries about Uncle
Toby and the legacy, the judge is able to
persuade the stepfather to avoid a court fight
that could bring unpleasant facts to light and
to give up his claim and allow the children to
stay with their grandmother. Though the children
are believable and several of the Irish
characters are well drawn, the story depends too
much on the unlikely attitude of Michael, who

hovers like a guardian angel but, because he is a policeman, does not give Finn and Derval the direct aid that would get them to their grandmother speedily and avoid the other threats. With the press convinced that Uncle Toby is a loving guardian and a reward of 100 pounds offered, it is hard to believe that so many people would give aid without informing the police. Fanfare.

THE FLOOD AT REEDSMERE. See *The Great Gale.*

FLORENCE BONE (*A Long Way from Verona**), Jessica* Vye's best friend, a sensible girl who is very good at mathematics. She also has the ability to put things in their proper perspective and a good sense of humor, being inclined to break into impromptu songs composed of titles and first lines of poems and books. She is described by an understanding teacher as "droll." When the school has been bombed and she is sent to the posh school, The Gables, she begins to talk like the boarding school girls, using words like "spiflicating," while Jessica at the local school of St. Wilfred's is picking up a working-class vocabulary. Steady Florence is a good foil for emotional Jessica.

A FLUTE IN MAYFERRY STREET (Dunlop*, Eileen, ill. Phillida Gili, Oxford, 1976; *THE HOUSE ON MAYFERRY STREET*, Holt, 1977), mystery novel set in Edinburgh, Scotland, in the 1970s. When Colin Ramsay, 11, and his sister, Marion, 16 (who is confined to a wheelchair as the result of a traffic accident) are cleaning a bookcase, they find folded into a book a letter dated January 24, 1914, to Charles Ramsay from Alan A. B. Farquhar, saying that his work is now finished and he is leaving a small trunk in the hands of Charles's servant. Partly because she has so little to interest her, Marion becomes intensely curious about these figures from the past. She gets Colin to begin a search through their large, rambling house, which still contains belongings of several past generations of Ramsays. Clues lead to other clues, though some seem to appear fortuitously: Colin finds a photograph of Charles Ramsay, which has slipped between two floorboards in an upper room; in an attic he finds the lap desk which was shown in the photograph; in the desk are scraps of paper which, pieced together, form a letter from Charles to Alan, telling that the servant, Watt Davie, has stolen the trunk and did not deliver the letter; in an attic room, formerly occupied by the servants, he finds an old coat that belonged to Watt Davie; in the coat pocket is a newspaper ad for an antique shop in High Street; at the High Street address Colin finds the granddaughter of the 1914 owner, who looks up records which show that Davie sold some stolen items there, but not the trunk; and so on. Gradually they piece the story together, and as they do both of them begin to hear flute music, culminating in a complete dream-vision which they share when they spend the night in one of the upper rooms. In the meantime, Colin has earned a coveted place in the school orchestra only to find that he must acquire his own flute, a purchase far beyond the means of his widowed mother. Marion's confined life is made somewhat brighter by their lodgers, a student couple named Jan and Jake Taylor, who arrange treats and share an interest in the mystery. Colin finally finds a small trunk, evidently stashed by Watt Davie under a second-story floorboard, and they discover that it contains a flute and a musical manuscript written by the well-known composer Alasdair Balfour, the professional name for Alan A. B. Farquhar. Inspired by the music and the discovery, Marion gets up and walks for the first time since her accident. They send the manuscript to the composer and are later favored by a call from his grandson, who falls in love with Marion and brings back the flute as a gift to Colin. Although the ending is too pat, the story itself has unusual depth for a mystery, with good characterization of the principal figures and a strong sense of setting. IRA Honor.

FOOTSTEPS. See *John Diamond*.

FOREST, ANTONIA, born in London; author of a large number of novels for young people, at least twelve of them about the big Marlow family. Four of these, including her first, *Autumn Term* (Faber, 1948) are boarding school

stories; the others are holiday adventures, a-
mong them *Falconer's Lure: The Story of a Summer
Holiday** (Faber, 1957), the third in the series,
in which Nicola, one of the twins who are the
youngest of the eight children, helps a neighbor
boy care for and train hawks. *Peter's Room**
(Faber, 1961), the fifth in the series, is more
genuinely a family story, telling of how several
of the children make up and seem to live out an
elaborate romantic fantasy during a Christmas
holiday. Her books have been praised for good
dialogue and a flair for characterization. The
Marlow family stories reflect a life of boarding
schools, servants, and fox hunts. *The Thursday
Kidnapping** (Faber, 1963; Coward, 1965), in
which youngsters in charge of caring for a baby
find him missing when they emerge from the
public library where they have left him in his
carriage, seems set in a more modern world. This
and a couple of her Marlow books were commended
for the Carnegie Medal.

FORGERY!. See *Gold Pieces*.

FORMULA 86 DELAYED-ACTION MOUSE-MAKER (*The
Witches**), the mixture invented by the Grand
High Witch to shrink children and turn them into
mice. At the witches' meeting she gives the
directions for making it: take the wrong end of
a telescope and boil it until it gets soft,
because the wrong end of a telescope makes
things look small; then take forty-five brown
mice, chop off their tails with a carving knife,
fry the tails in hair oil, and simmer the bodies
in frog juice for one hour; then add an alarm
clock set to go off when the mixture is supposed
to take effect and roast it in the oven until it
is crisp and tender; finish by mixing in the
claw of a crabcruncher, the beak of a blabber-
snitch, the snout of a grobblesqvirt, and the
tongue of a catspringer. The result, according
to her, will be a "marvelous-looking green
liquid," one drop of which will turn a child
into a mouse in exactly twenty-six seconds.

THE FOX IN WINTER (Branfield*, John, Gollancz,
1980; Atheneum, 1982), sensitive novel of the
friendship between a teenaged girl and a man of
ninety, who is one of the patients of the girl's

mother, a district nurse in Cornwall. Frances*,
called Fran, is about fifteen. She has never
been much interested in the demanding, often
hectic job her single mother handles with a
mixture of devotion, humor, and anger--anger at
the doctors who play god and won't take
suggestions, at the other district nurse who is
just out of school and won't adjust to Cornish
customs, at the patients who call her for grave
emergencies and small errands because they don't
want to disturb the doctor or their relatives.
When Nancy* (usually called simply Nurse by the
country people) gets a call to go to isolated
Penhallow Farm one snowy night, Fran, accompanying her mother, meets Tom* Treloar, who lives
down a track impassible by car near the head of
a narrow coastal valley, and his wife, Lettie,
who has suffered a slight stroke and has
fallen. Fran is impressed with the fiercely
independent, outspoken old man, and on
subsequent visits she listens to his description
of the cave on his beach where seals come in and
of the various birds that inhabit the valley. To
complete an English assignment to interview an
old person, Fran chooses Tom Treloar, and they
have an interesting talk interrupted by Lettie's
second seizure. Thereafter he keeps sending Fran
messages through her mother and even a painfully
written letter about the farm, until she goes
back and shows him the written interview.
Impressed by her "proper writing," he wants to
dictate his memories to her. She resists this
further involvement, but eventually finds
herself regularly recording his memoirs on her
cassette recorder, bringing him library books,
and even going through the many drawers in the
house, helping him sort the jumble of letters,
papers, photographs, and other memorabilia that
Lettie has squirreled away over the years. Both
Nancy and Fran are distrusted by the Treloars'
grandson, Desmond, a greedy man cowed by Tom's
vigorous rage but clearly waiting, with his wife
and daughter, to get his hands on Tom's money.
Tom likes to tease Desmond by references to
changing the will and to imply that he might
leave his money to Nurse and "the maid," as he
refers to Fran. When Tom has a fall and both he
and Lettie are taken to the hospital, Goonlaze
House (the former workhouse which he has

dreaded) Fran visits him and finds him delighted
with the attention and the service, but they are
soon moved to a very inferior private nursing
home where Lettie is neglected. Nancy helps Tom
get in touch with his cousin Winifred, who
agrees to come and help care for them on a trial
basis in exchange for the farm if she should
decide to stay. This arrangement lasts only one
day and ends with Lettie back in the hospital,
Cousin Win leaving in a huff, and Tom trium-
phantly back in his own house and in charge.
Fran and a school friend, David, explore the
seal cave, and Tom is intensely interested in
every detail of Fran's careful description. He
teaches her a board game called fox- and- geese,
which the miners used to play, and tells her of
finding a set of beautifully carved pieces for
the game in one of the old tin-mine tunnels in
the valley. She and Dave enter the old mine to
hunt the pieces, which he had rewrapped in their
oilskin and left on a ledge, but they find a
cave-in has blocked the passage and buried the
pieces forever. As her school activities take
more time, Fran sees Tom less often, but then,
feeling guilty, she returns. For his ninetieth
birthday she makes him a cake, which is shared
warily by Desmond and his family. When Lettie
dies, Tom gets out to go to the funeral and is
moare concerned than ever to finish recording
his memories. Near the end of the last tape, he
makes an excuse to get her away, and when she
returns he switches off the recorder and tells
her it is finished. He also tells her he has
thought of leaving her the farm, an idea that
shocks her, but that he has decided that it
should go to Desmond because he is family. He
dies the next day. Later Fran learns that he has
left a hundred pounds each to her and to her
mother, a legacy that Nancy thinks, for
professional reasons, they should contribute to
the nursing fund, but more important to Fran,
he has left her his mother's amber necklace and
all the letters and photographs that she helped
him sort out. At the end of the last tape he has
thanked her for her attention and told her that
she has given him something to live for in his
last year. The relationship between the old man
and the girl, strong characters both, is
touching and believable. She recognizes that he

is manipulative, but she genuinely loves him for his humor, his appreciation of language and nature, and his proud spirit. The descriptions of the old people's disabilities are frank and unsentimental, and the glimpses of Tom's ninety years on the Cornish coast give a strong sense of setting. Carnegie Com.

FOX OF FURROWFIELD (*The Song of Pentecost**), one of the book's most interesting characters and one whose courage and wit enable the refugee mice to reach their destination safely. A large, handsome creature with a lavish, red brush tail, he pretends to be caught in a trap to entice Pentecost* but then so admires the little mouse's bravery and persistence that he decides to help the mice. He is a poet, a thinker, and a good family man. A moral sort, he confronts the Cockle-Snorkle* Bug about the Bug's duplicity, asserting that the Bug just likes to "see folks suffer." His excellent running skills in avoiding hounds enable him to create the diversion that gets the mice through Weasel Woods safely. Fox indirectly brings about Pentecost's* death: the spiteful Bug has told the mice that Fox is dead, and when Pentecost sees Fox on the hillside and realizes that his friend is alive, he exposes himself to the hunters and is killed by the shot intended for Fox.

FOXY WILLIAMS (*Owlglass**), aristocratic fox, a member of the club who rarely attends but is much admired. Extremely clever at getting away from the hounds, Mr. Williams leads a life of leisurely ease except on hunt days, when he matches his wits against the Others. After he leaves the club meeting, Brock*, the badger, tells "The Story of How Foxy Became Mr. Williams," in which is related the time Foxy was cornered in a shed and escaped the hounds by running up the fireplace flue, and then, finding himself trapped on the roof, dropped down another chimney and came out in a locked room. Discovering him there, the owner, a Mr. Williams, courteously led him to the front door and bowed him out, and, in respect, Foxy took his name from then on.

FRANCES (*The Fox in Winter**), daughter of the
district nurse in a coastal village in Cornwall.
An independent teenager, Fran gets along well
with her mother but has never been attracted to
her profession or interested in her patients
until she becomes involved with the formidable
old man, Tom* Treloar, through a school
assignment to interview an old person. Gradually
Fran learns more about Tom's life and comes to
understand his fierce determination to keep
control of it despite his ninety years. When he
gives her a metal "F" that he took from a
wrecked ship, she is pleased, but she is
genuinely shocked at his suggestion that he
might leave her his farm, partly because she
knows that his grandson would contest the will
in court and partly because she does love the
farm and in some ways covets it. Although she is
concerned for his welfare, she also recognizes
that he loves to get his own way, as when he
wins at the game of fox-and-geese, and she is
feisty enough herself to enjoy winning and to
keep him from dominating her completely. She is
not distressed when he asks her about her father
and is amused at his embarrassment when he
realizes that evidently her mother was never
married.

FRANCES HUNTERLY (*The Far-Distant Oxus**), along
with Jennifer* Cleverton, one of the two
youngest of the six children who undertake an
"expeditionary force" down the Oxus to the sea.
She is almost indistinguishable from Jennifer,
although we are told that she has a natural
gift for conversation and friendship, and she
does seem more outgoing than Jennifer. She
likes to read and can be very persuasive.

FRANCIS SHELLEY (*Windfall**), son of wealthy
diamond merchant Peregrine Shelley, who owns the
racing yacht *Good Fortune*. Francis admires Matt*
Pullen for his skill in sailing his fishing
smack and longs for the sort of practical skill
he sees among the working sailors. After Matt
has been crewing on the *Good Fortune*, Francis
persuades his father to let him live with the
Pullens in Marshfield and help on Matt's fishing
boat. His father believes this hard work and
rough living will break him of his romantic

notions, but he sticks to the job and insists on going back for more in the winter, when fishing is more backbreaking and dangerous. The high point of his life is when Matt sends him alone in the *Reward* to get help while he stays on the abandoned *Rose in June* to claim it as salvage. Although Francis has traveled abroad, studied with a private tutor, and is to go to Oxford soon, he considers sailing the only really worthwhile thing he has learned.

FRIDAY'S TUNNEL (Verney*, John, ill. author, Collins, 1959; Holt, 1966), mystery adventure set in Sussex in the mid twentieth century, concerned with the ramifications of international intrigue on an eastern Mediterranean island. February Callendar, 12, and her brother, Friday, 13, have just come home for holiday from boarding school when their father, Gus (Augustus), a journalist, must leave for the island of Capria, where a coup has been reported and both American and Soviet forces are lining up to gain influence. Since Gus once wrote a book on Capria, *The Uncrowned Kingmaker*, and knew both the president, Umbarak, and his half-brother, Zayid, in World War II, he is drafted for the assignment not only by his newspaper, the *Messenger*, but also by a high government official, Hal Fawcett (General Sir Harold Vesey-Fawcett), even though he now does little foreign correspondence work, having settled at the farm, Marsh Manor, with four daughters younger than February and another baby on the way. While he is gone, Fawcett's son, Robin, 20, an engineering student, is to stay at the farm as a summer tutor, an idea both February and Friday deplore at first. Complications develop even before Gus leaves: when she is out riding on her horse, February runs into a foreign-looking man at Deans, a house on the other side of Querbury Beacon, the hill behind their farm, who is angry at her appearance and tries to grab her bridle; their car is shot at on the way to the airport; February sees a last-minute package tossed onto the baggage cart and loaded into the chartered plane; and her father appears concerned to see some packing cases marked "Sunrise Cigarettes Ltd. Returnable Empty." Robin, who has met them

at the airport, drives the youngsters home and
soon becomes part of the family. He is deeply
interested in the tunnel Friday has been
building for some years into the hill behind the
farm, and is helpful with the younger girls. He
is not much good at formal lessons, but is
fascinating on his favorite subject, old canals
in the area. He is also interested in the
gypsies named Spiro who live nearby, about whom
Gus once wrote a book and who are actually
descendants of Caprians imported to work on a
canal tunnel in the eighteenth century. Although
Gus's article debunking the idea of an uprising
or coup is datelined Capria, they all know that
it was written before he left, and when they
learn that his plane has crashed, evidently
blown up by a bomb in the luggage, they are
terribly worried. They are even more concerned
when it seems that he never boarded the plane,
and they hope to keep that knowledge from
whoever seems to be trying to kill him. February
learns about the mythical metal caprium, said to
be found on the island, which has the potential
to supply power greater than nuclear fission by
its property of repelling explosively if two
minute fragments get within a foot of each
other. This, surprisingly, is much the situation
in her favorite comic strip, *Wheazy-Fidgett*,
which is carried in the *Messenger*. She also
comes to realize that the foreign-looking man at
Deans is Lord Sprockett, a ruthless, high-
powered financier, who, it later develops, was
one of the Spiros. A postcard from Gus,
obviously in some sort of code, confuses
everyone, but February figures it out, and, at a
meeting with Robin, his father, and the
Messenger editor John Gubbins, she insists on
learning the facts that the adults are keeping
from her in exchange for her interpretation. In
the meantime, Friday's tunnel has broken
through into a bricked chamber that proves to be
the remains of an old canal tunnel going right
through Querbury Beacon to Deans. In an
exciting climactic scene, February realizes
that Sprockett is using the tunnel to store
caprium that has been illegally imported with
Fawcett's knowledge in order to keep it out of
the hands of both the Americans and the
Russians. She rushes off to follow and warn

Friday and their younger sister Gail, who are
exploring the tunnel. Coming upon Sprockett,
who threatens to kill her, she bashes him
unconscious with her lantern, and with her
siblings finds her father and Umbarak shut in
the tunnel, unable to get out of the closed
entrance at the Deans end. Friday digs a
passageway big enough for February to squeeze
through, and she rides a gypsy pony to get help.
In the end a war has been averted, an
assassination attempt on Umbarak by his half
brother has been thwarted, and it has been
revealed that Zayid had conned Sprockett by
substituting silver-paper covered candy called
gob-stoppers for the caprium which was
supposedly wrapped in a special silver asbestos
cigarette paper. The plot is ingenious, full of
false leads, sudden reversals, and a variety of
villans, but the characters are never more than
cardboard figures. The book is ostensibly
written in the first person by February, who,
after all the wild adventures, has broken her
pelvis sliding down the bannisters, but the
style is not convincingly that of a twelve-year-
old. Long passages of dialogue give information
essential to the plot, a clumsy stylistic
technique and one that lacks verisimilitude.
The book is dated more by its tone and the
treatment of the children than by its
references to World War II events as being in
the recent past. Sequel is *February's Road**.
Carnegie Com.

FRODO BAGGINS (*The Fellowship of the Ring**),
younger cousin whom Bilbo* Baggins of *The Hob-
bit** adopts as his heir and who thereby becomes
the bearer of the great and perilous ring of
power which must be destroyed so that it will
not fall into the hands of Sauron, Lord of Evil.
Frodo, like other hobbits*, is of tougher fiber
than he appears, and he carries out the nearly
impossible task, his greatest strength being
shown in his resistance to the power of the ring
itself, which corrupts its users and proves
irresistible even to men of good intentions.
Before he reaches Rivendell, in the early part
of the adventure, Frodo is wounded in the attack
by the Ringwraiths on Weathertop, and though he
is healed by Elrond, his hurt recurs even after

the ring has been destroyed and he has returned to The Shire, so that he becomes ill each year on the anniversary of his wound and realizes that he must leave Middle-earth and go with the elves into the West. Having lived with Bilbo as a young hobbit, he has learned some Elvish and many of the songs that the old hobbit has written and transcribed, and so he starts out with some useful knowledge and less naive than Bilbo was at the beginning of his adventure in *The Hobbit*. Frodo is unassuming and modest, but but he inspires devotion, particularly in his servant, Sam* Gamgee, and his two young cousins, Pippin* Took and Merry* Brandybuck.

FROG (*The Song of Pentecost**), one of the animals that accompany Snake* and the Harvest Mice on the journey to Lickey Top and a new home. He lies so much he can't tell the difference between truth and fiction, and he says whatever he thinks his audience wants to hear. Because he lies so much, he has become very tense and suffers severe shooting pains down his sides. Snake loses his home in Oily Green Pond because Frog supports Cousin* Snake's assertion that Snake's father left it to him. Frog sees the light, however, and reforms, and thereafter he is a worthy member of the expedition. Under cross-examination at the trial over the owner-ship of the pool, he is intimidated by Cousin and reverts to type, telling confusing stories that support both Snake's and Cousin's claims.

FYSON, J(ENNY) G(RACE) (1904-   ), born in Bromley, Kent, the daughter of a government administrator of education. She was educated by a governess at home, in a private village school, and at St. Swithun's School in Win-chester. She has been a painter and weaver, a playwright, and author of children's books and a radio play. When poor health kept her out of school in her late teens, she turned to reading, painting, archaeology, and literature, her special interests being historian Edward Gibbon and Sir James Frazer's *Golden Bough*. Later, when she was left a widow with a young son and began to write to supplement the family income, she drew upon this incidental knowledge to produce her two published novels, which were both historical, set in ancient Mesopotamia, and commended for the Carnegie Medal: *The Three Brothers of Ur** (Oxford, 1964; Coward, 1966) and its sequel, *The Journey of the Eldest Son** (Oxford, 1965; Coward, 1967). They received critical approval for the skill with which Fyson evokes the times of Abraham and interweaves exciting action with the religious, economic, and artistic life of the ancient Mesopotamians, and for their Biblical but never heavy style. Her radio play, *Saul and David*, also set in ancient times, was produced in 1952. She has made her home in Kent.

G

GANDALF (*The Hobbit**; *The Fellowship of the Ring**), known as Gandalf the Grey, wizard of Middle-earth who marks the door of Bilbo* Baggins with a sign that means "Burglar wants a good job, plenty of Excitement and Reasonable reward," and thereby starts him on an adventure with thirteen dwarfs to regain their home and treasure from the dragon, Smaug*. In *The Hobbit* he is shown as a clever wizard with some magical powers who is able to slay the chief goblin (or orc) in the mountains, to summon the eagles to rescue them from the wolves (or wargs), and to foresee the coming of the goblins and their allies in the Battle of Five Armies. In *The Fellowship of the Ring* and the two volumes that follow it, he is revealed as a character of much greater power, one of the truly Wise of Middle-earth, who for eons have fought against the power of evil. In his studies in the archives of ancient lore, he has learned enough to suspect that Bilbo's ring is indeed a great ring of power, in fact, the one ring made to control the others, and he tests this theory by getting Frodo* to hand it to him and then casting it into the heart of the fire so that Elvish letters show up along both outside and inside. In the early part of the fellowship's journey, Gandalf is the leader, but just as they are about to emerge from the Mines of Moria, he fights with the horrible Balrog so that the others may escape and is carried with it into the fiery chasm and evidently lost for good. In

the later adventures, he reappears at the edge
of Fangorn Wood, having gone through a sort of
death and been reborn into Gandalf the White,
more powerful and more ethereal than before. He
is present at the collapse of the power of
Isengard and is important in the defense of
Gondor. In the end he leaves for the West across
the seas with Bilbo and the last of the elves.

GARDAM, JANE (PEARSON) (1928-   ), born in
Coatham, Yorkshire; librarian, editor, and
author of fiction for both adults and children.
She attended Saltburn High School for Girls and
Bedford College, London, where she received a
B.A. in 1949 and did graduate study from 1949
to 1952. She organized hospital libraries for
the Red Cross, served as subeditor of *Weldons
Ladies Journal*, and later as assistant library
editor of *Time and Tide*. Her husband became a
Queen's Counsel and they traveled and worked
in Singapore, Hong Kong, the West Indies,
Indonesia, Bangladesh, and Europe. She has won a
number of distinguished awards for writing,
including the David Higham Prize for a book of
short stories, titled *Black Faces, White Faces*
(Hamilton, 1975), and she was named a fellow
of the Royal Society of Literature in 1976. Most
of her books for children are said to be
intensely autobiographical, and all are written
with a deft touch and economical language. In
A Few Fair Days (Hamilton, 1971; Macmillan,
1972), a little girl grows up through a series
short pieces that have the ring of memories. *A
Long Way from Verona** (Hamilton, 1971; Macmillan, 1971) is set in Yorkshire during World War
II, and is a story full of humor and subtle
insights. *The Summer After the Funeral** (Hamilton, 1973; Macmillan, 1973), a *Boston Globe-
Horn Book* honor book, and *Bilgewater** (Hamilton,
1976; Greenwillow, 1977) are also stories of a
girl growing up. All four have similar
protagonists, or at least show different aspects
of the same bright, unconventional female
character. In all four the protagonist has a
remote but important father who is either a
schoolmaster or a clergyman. *The Hollow Land**
(Macrae, 1981; Greenwillow, 1982) departs from
this pattern, being the chronical of the
friendship between a Yorkshire boy and a younger

London boy who comes to the area for holidays, and is told in a series of episodes during which both boys grow up. It won the Whitbread Award and was a Carnegie Highly Commended book. Gardam has also written shorter books for early readers, including *Bridget and William* (Macrae, 1981) and *Horse* (MacRae, 1982), and has published novels and books of short stories for adults.

GARFIELD, LEON (1921-   ), born in Brighton, Sussex; novelist and reteller of myths. He attended Brighton Grammar School, studied art, and served in the Royal Army Medical Corps from 1940 to 1946. From 1946 to 1969 he worked as a biochemical technician at Whittington hospital, London, and since then he has been a full-time writer. He is married to Vivien Alcock*, also a writer and artist. He has written more than twenty books of fiction for children, but is also noted for his unusual treatment of nonfiction, including the two books of Greek myth and hero tales that he wrote with Edward Blishen: *The God Beneath the Sea* (Longman, 1970; Pantheon, 1971), which won the Carnegie Medal, and *The Golden Shadow* (Longman, 1973; Pantheon, 1973). Both are told with the tension and concrete detail of fiction. He also wrote *The House of Hanover: England in the Eighteenth Century* (Deutsch, 1976; Seabury, 1976), *Tales from Shakespeare* (Gollancz, 1984), and *Child o' War: The True Story of a Boy Sailor in Nelson's Navy* (Collins, 1972; Holt, 1972). *Child o'War* is a biography told on three levels: the actual memoirs of a man who joined the British navy as a child, fictionalized scenes of his dictation in his elderly years of these memoirs to a bored family, and passages giving a broader historical picture of the events. Garfield's fiction has been widely commended. It has been described as Dickensian, and as having "a combination of comedy, high adventure, romance, mystery, and an eye for intriguing detail." Notable in most of his novels is an ironic tone and a strongly evoked setting, usually in the eighteenth century. Among those that have won critical acclaim are *Devil-in-the-Fog** (Constable, 1966; Pantheon, 1966), which won the Guardian Award; *Smith** (Constable, 1967; Pantheon, 1967), the

story of a twelve-year-old pickpocket, thought
by many to be his best novel, and which, among
other honors, was awarded the 1986 Children's
Literature Association Phoenix Award for a book
that has stood a twenty-year test of time; *Black
Jack** (Longman, 1968; Pantheon, 1969), whose
main figure is a gigantic man cut down from the
gallows and revived; *The Drummer Boy** (Longman,
1970; Pantheon, 1969), a haunting tale of return
from the wars; *The Sound of Coaches** (Kestrel,
1974; Viking, 1974), a semi-picaresque tale of
an orphan seeking his fortune, which brings the
protagonist back to his starting point; and
*John Diamond** (Kestrel, 1980; as *Footsteps*, Delacorte, 1980), a story of desperate intrigue and
danger in the back streets of London. Another
book set in eighteenth-century London is a group
of slightly interrelated stories, *The Apprentices* (Heinemann, 1982; Viking, 1982). Two of
his novels, both examples of his most rollicking
humor, are set in the nineteenth century: *The
Strange Affair of Adelaide Harris** (Longman,
1971; Pantheon, 1971), and its sequel, *Bostock
and Harris; or, The Night of the Comet** (Kestrel, 1979; as *The Night of the Comet*, Delacorte, 1979). Garfield is also noted for ghost
stories, including *Mister Corbett's Ghost** (Pantheon, 1968), *The Restless Ghost* (Pantheon,
1969) and, a somewhat longer and deeper work,
The Ghost Downstairs (Longman, 1972; Pantheon,
1972), in which the protagonist, selling seven
years of his life to the devil, thinks to trick
him by selling the first seven rather than the
last, and is haunted by the child of those lost
seven years. Several of his novels have been
chosen for the *Horn Book* Fanfare list and cited
in the *Choice* magazine list of books for an academic library. Garfield has also written picture
books, mostly retellings of Bible stories; among
them is *King Nimrod's Tower* (Constable, 1982;
Lothrop, 1982), illustrated by Michael Bragg.
For adults he has written *The House of Cards*
(Bodley, 1982) and a completion of the novel by
Charles Dickens*, *The Mystery of Edwin Drood*
(Deutsch, 1980; Pantheon, 1981). In 1981 he was
Britain's nominee for the international Hans
Christian Andersen Award.

GARNER, ALAN (1935-   ), born in Congleton,

Cheshire; author of books and plays for children, highly acclaimed for the inventiveness of his work. He grew up in the village of Alderley Edge, where his family has lived for hundreds of years, and attended primary school there. The village and the great hill also known as Alderley Edge have provided the location for his stories, which excel in a sense of place. Confined to his bed with meningitis for a long time, he lived with his grandmother, entertaining himself by reading her old Victorian books. At grammar school in Manchester on a scholarship, he distinguished himself both academically and as a sprinter. After grammar school he spent two years in the Royal Artillery, achieving the rank of lieutenant, and then won a scholarship to Oxford University to study classical archaeology. He later developed interests in Celtic lore and archaeology, areas that have also provided raw material for his writings. In 1957, before graduating, he left Oxford to return to Cheshire and take up writing professionally; he had beome interested in writing while he was in service through a chance reading of *Lord of the Flies*. Two weeks after finishing the book, he began the novel later published as *The Weirdstone of Brisingamen** (Collins, 1960; as *The Weirdstone*, Watts, 1961), his first book, which is listed in *Choice* and was named to the Lewis Carroll Shelf. In it and its sequel, *The Moon of Gomrath* (Collins, 1963; Walck, 1967), children of Alderley Edge become involved with characters from Celtic and Norse mythology in exciting encounters with good and evil. Celtic lore and good and evil are emphases in other books, too, along with the interconnectedness of the generations, the dignity and worthiness of hard and hand labor, and the value of good craftsmanship. Most notable of his other books are *Elidor** (Collins, 1965; Walck, 1967), a Contemporary Classic and Carnegie Commended book, in which magic and otherworld characters affect the lives of some Manchester children; *Red Shift** (Collins, 1973; Macmillan, 1973), a *Choice* book of complex plot that interweaves stories in three time frames: one a contemporary love story, another set among acculturating Roman legionaries, and the last unwinding during the English Civil War; and The

Stone Book Quartet, four novelettes, which, in order of events, are: *The Stone Book** (Collins, 1976; Collins, 1978), *Granny Reardun** (Collins, 1977; Collins, 1978), *The Aimer Gate** (Collins, 1978; Collins, 1979), and *Tom Fobble's Day** (Collins, 1977; Collins, 1979). They trace the history of a single family through five generations, are set in Cheshire, celebrate craftsmanship and craftsmen (in particular, stonemasonry), and appear in *Choice* and on the *Horn Book* Fanfare list. His most highly regarded novel is *The Owl Service** (Collins, 1967; Walck, 1968), which is set in a Welsh village, is based on a legend from the *Mabinogion*, won both the Carnegie Medal and the *Guardian* Award, and was later named to Fanfare and *Choice*. Garner has also written the texts for picture books and the scripts for a dozen and a half plays for stage, radio, and television, with some of them, like *The Owl Service* and *Red Shift*, adapted from his own stories, and others presenting completely original material. He has also published books of his own retellings of legends and folk tales, among them *The Guizer: A Book of Fools* (Hamilton, 1975; Greenwillow, 1976) and *The Lad of the Gad* (Collins, 1980; Philomel, 1981). Considered a ground-breaking and highly individual writer, he makes his home in Cheshire with his wife and six children and is much in demand as a speaker for organizations concerned with literature for the young and writing.

GARNETT, EVE, born in Worcestershire, her father an English lieutenant-colonel, her mother Irish; freelance writer of fiction and nonfiction and of social commentary for adults and children, illustrator, and painter, who has made her home in Sussex. After schooling in Devon and Worchestershire she attended Chelsea Polytechnic School of Art, where she won a five-year scholarship to the Royal Academy Schools in London. After only two years of study, she received the Creswick Prize and Silver Medal for landscapes. She intended to make landscape painting her vocation, but experiences in the East End slums changed the direction of her life. She was appalled and angered by the conditions in which she saw children living

there and was determined to do what she could
to change their hard lot. She took sketches of
what she had seen to an editor, who commissioned
her to illustrate Evelyn Sharp's *The London
Child* (Lane, 1927). She decided to continue to
try to focus people's attention on the working
poor, and a mural at The Children's House, Bow,
London, and several books resulted. *The Family
from One End Street and Some of Their Adventures** (Muller, 1937; Vanguard, 1939) is a
humorous, realistic account of the everyday
lives of the several members of the Ruggles
family, the father of whom is a dustman and the
mother a washerwoman. After being rejected by
eight publishers as unsuitable for children,
since it deviated from the usual antiseptic
middle-class fare, it won the Carnegie Medal
and led to sequels: *Further Adventures of the
Family from One End Street* (Heinemann, 1956;
Vanguard, 1956) and *Holiday at the Dew Drop Inn:
A One End Street Story* (Heinemann, 1962;
Vanguard, 1963). In addition to books of short
stories for children which are also about
working-class families, she edited an anthology
of poems for children, *A Book of the Seasons*
(Oxford, 1952; Bentley, 1953), and for adults
wrote *To Greenland's Icy Mountains: The Story of
Hans Egede, Explorer, Coloniser, Missionary*
(Heinemann, 1968; Roy, 1968), a biography that
was stimulated by her several trips to the
Arctic Circle; *"Is It Well with the Child?"*
(Muller, 1938); and *First Affections* (Muller,
1982), a book of reminiscence. She illustrated
her own books and books for other writers,
among them an edition of Robert Louis
Stevenson's* *A Child's Garden of Verses* for
Penguin (1948). Her paintings have appeared in
shows in various London galleries.

GARRET BYRNE (*The Green Bough of Liberty**),
eldest brother and therefore owner of Ballymanus, the family farm in County Wicklow, Ireland.
A bookish type, Garret studies good farming
methods and works hard, but abandons the place
eagerly to take part in the 1798 rebellion to
rid the country of English rule. After a series
of disastrous encounters, he leads the last of
the holdout rebels in their inaccessible
mountain camp but eventually must negotiate to

surrender when their supplies run out in the
bitter weather. He is then given safe passage to
Germany.

GENERAL WOUNDWORT (*Watership Down**), the
dictator-leader of the totalitarian warren at
Efrafa, which comes into conflict with the
democratic warren at Watership Down. Orphaned in
infancy, Woundwort grew up wild, big, and
savage. Terrible in combat, he forced a small
warren to accept him as Chief Rabbit. He then
established the Efrafa Warren as a closed
society to make extermination difficult. He
created a ruling Council and Owsla (fighting
force) that for years accepted his decisions
without question. They impose their will on the
warren, which operates under very strict rules
for all aspects of life. At the time the
Watership rabbits come into contact with Efrafa,
Efrafa has become overcrowded, and dissatisfaction is rife and quelled only by severe
strong-arm tactics. After the defeat at
Watership Down, General Woundwort disappears and
becomes a legendary "bogey-man" figure among
the area rabbits. He is a foil for the
democratic Hazel*, with his warren a symbol of
repressive tyranny and its effects.

GENEVA (*Songberd's Grove**), lively, black-
haired, resourceful girl of about twelve, who
becomes friends with Martin* Singer and helps
him against the bully Lennie* Byre. She lives
with her mother, La* Golondrina, at No. 7
Songberd's Grove in the flat directly above
Martin's. Martin meets her under inauspicious
circumstances: she enters his room uninvited to
search for the shawl he took from her when she
made a hasty trip up and down his fire escape to
get herbs for her mother from Martin's garden.
Geneva helps Martin fix up the garden as a place
where they can be in peace and get away from
Lennie's badgering and thugs. Because she gets
the idea to plant grass, the two leave the
garden by the garden door, are set upon by
Lennie's thugs, and flee to the canal, where
they find the house in which John* Pollard and
John* Pim live. This leads to the restoration of
Songberd's Grove as a historic area and the
breaking of Lennie's hold on the inhabitants.

Geneva's mother is a former Spanish dancer who has fallen on hard times, and their apartment is an exotic conglomeration of memorabilia and pungent spices and herbs. Geneva looks after her mother; she has become a take-charge child. As a character she is sympathetic, credible, and engaging. She is a foil for Martin and Lennie.

THE GENTLE FALCON (Lewis*, Hilda, Oxford, 1952; Criterion, 1957), historical novel set in England and France in the late fourteenth century during the reign of Richard II. At fifteen, Isabella* Clinton, the first-person narrator, is a spirited, country-bred girl who prefers working in the fields with the peasants to learning to be a lady, although her English father was a gentleman and her mother is kin to the French king. Then a summons comes from court stating that she is to be a lady in waiting and companion to Isabella*, daughter of the king of France and child bride of the English King Richard. A neighbor, Sir Geoffrey Cobham and his son and squire, Gilles*, 18, are to escort her to London. Isabella Clinton gets off to an immediate love-hate relationship with Gilles, whom she finds overbearing but fascinating. On the trip, just as it seems they are becoming friends, they come upon a minstrel girl, Jehanne*, who joins their party and whom Isabella resents because Gilles's attention is diverted to her. At court Isabella is coached by Lady Standwich, and she is appalled and angered to find that lady, along with many others, speaking against the king and his French marriage. As she stoutly defends her king, Richard himself overhears. Lady Standwich is banished from court, but Isabella is approved by the king and accompanies the party to France where the wedding, already formalized by proxy, is to be reenacted in fact. Isabella is worried because Jehanne, disguised as a page, is also with the party. Isabella is much impressed by the seven-year-old princess, who behaves with quiet dignity beyond her years, and in the next months she watches the child's love grow for Richard, who treats her with gentle kindness. Unfortunately, the French Lady de Coucy, a woman with no love for either Richard or young Queen Isabella, has been appointed the royal

governess, and Isabella Clinton clashes with her
in a number of minor ways. In the next seven
years she serves the young queen and watches the
court intrigue, led by the king's uncle, the
Duke of Gloucester, and sees the growing
extravagances and wild behavior of Richard turn
much of the court and the people against him.
She also observes that the young Queen Isabella,
though gentle, is very strong and determined in
her quiet way; hence the book's title. When
Bolingbroke (later King Henry IV) returns from
exile to lead a revolt against Richard, she
learns that Gilles is of Bolingbroke's party and
that Jehanne, who reappears, is a spy dedicated
to the welfare of the young queen. Although
Gilles and Jehanne have planned an escape for
the queen, Madam de Coucy returns and takes her
away. Gilles then turns his attention to
Isabella Clinton, who will be executed if
caught, and lends her his horse, planning to
send her to France hidden in a load of his
father's wool. When this plan goes awry, she
must find her way to the coast afoot, disguised
as a boy. With several close calls, but aided by
a young girl who gives her shoes, an innkeeper
who covers her hair with dark grease, and a cook
who hides her with a girl suspected of having
the plague, she gets to the coast and finds that
Cobham's ship has waited for her. In France she
is interviewed by the king and spends some time
with the greedy queen, Ysabeau, a woman who
spends extravagantly but neglects and almost
starves her own children. She waits while France
tries to get Queen Isabella back with her dowry
and Henry tries to get the young queen to marry
his son, later to be Henry V. Eventually Queen
Isabella returns and, after some time, marries
her cousin, Charles of Orleans. She brings the
news that the Clinton estate has been forfeited
to the crown and given, at his request, to
Gilles. He arrives in France and persuades
Isabella to marry him, thereby returning her to
the country home she loves. Although the story
deals with a dramatic period and centers on the
little-known but interesting figure of the
French Isabella, the fictional story of Isabella
Clinton, Gilles, and Jehanne is not strong
enough to maintain the interest through long
passages concerned with Richard's failing

fortunes. Isabella's eventual marriage to Gilles is predictable, but he never seems an attractive enough character to make it satisfying. The historical story is more compelling, and the disappearance of Queen Isabella from the story at a critical time weakens the novel. Fanfare.

GENTLEMAN GEORGE (*Tumbledown Dick**), one of the street salesmen and beggars who sleep at the "Guv'nor's kip," a sort of flophouse in Manchester. George dresses in a neat suit and tie and apparently spends most of his time in the free library, reading and thinking up confidence schemes to extract money from gullible but charitable clergymen. Actually, he proves to be son of the new rector near Dick's home, acting a part so tht he can get material for a book on the street people of his day. He takes Dick and Alf Eckersley skating and proves to be skilled at the sport.

GEOFFREY TINKER (*The Weathermonger**), sixteen-year-old who rescues England from the Changes, a five-year period in which it has turned into a machine-hating, witch-baiting society much like that of the Middle Ages. For some reason, Geoffrey has acquired along with the Changes the power to cause weather conditions and has used that power to become the wealthiest man in Weymouth, so that, although the antimachine frenzy has either bypassed or left him and his uncle, he has not been willing to escape to France. As the story opens he has been caught drying the magneto for his boat's motor in the oven and is about to be drowned as a witch with his younger sister, Sally*, but because he has been hit on the head, he cannot remember any of the past five years. Sally tells him that their uncle has been stoned to death for trying to build a loom run by water power.

GEORDIE BICKERSON (*Danger at Black Dyke**), George Bickerson, ten-year-old Northumberland schoolboy. Three years before the story starts, he was taken in by Gran* Ridley after his mother died and his father abandoned him. A natural leader, he has a commanding manner, a gift of gab, a quick mind, and tremendous energy. He is proud of his position as centurion in the boys'

Mithraic society, and the others defer to his leadership. His confidence is superficial, with his authoritative manner masking a deep fear of losing friends and being abandoned again.

GEORDIE MONROE (*The Battle of Wednesday Week**), Scots boy of eight or so who lives near the Lattimer croft and hangs around the place, watching the children and occasionally playing with Lucy* Graham. He is too quiet and shy to interject himself into the children's activities because there are simply too many of them and they are bigger than he. On the mountain by himself, however, he is confident, sure-footed, and quick, like a young mountain goat. He seldom speaks to anyone, let alone the Lattimers and Grahams, but when Lucy falls into the fissure on the mountain he quickly races for help and speaks in sentences that are quite atypically intelligible. Later, when Charlotte* Lattimer reproaches him on another matter, he again retreats into monosyllables. Though he seldom affects the action, he is an interesting and winning figure.

GEORGE BATCHFORD (*Hobberdy Dick**), local cattle-man hired by the city-bred Puritan Mr.* Widdison to oversee the farm at Widford Manor. Unlike his employer, George knows the importance of the old ways and believes in the ghosts and hobgoblins that inhabit the old houses. George organizes the forbidden Christmas festivities, helps Martha* Widdison color Easter eggs, and hangs bored flints over the mangers to protect the horses against witches on Midsummer's Eve. Martha turns to George to help her find the Culver treasure when Hobberdy* Dick has put the clues into her mind. Anne* Sekar gives George one of the bags of coins so that he can marry the servant girl Charity, who is always in danger of being dismissed by bad-tempered Ursula Biddums.

GEORGE OVERS (*A Likely Lad**), rough-and-tumble brother of Willy* Overs. Two years younger and completely different in temperament, George has no interest in school and does not worry as Willy does, but when roused he fights fiercely with fists and words, even attacking his larger and older cousin, Stan* Sowter. Not plagued by conscience as Willy is, George plays with the neighborhood boys in the alley although his mother has forbidden it, and admits to reading the sort of books that so shock his mother when they circulate secretly in school. He serves as a foil to Willy's character.

GEORGE PONTIFEX (*Up the Pier*), Kitchener's* father and Ellen's* husband, an easygoing, philosophical man. He keeps cool about the Pontifexes being in 1971 instead of 1921, confident that they need only humor Samuel* and things will turn out satisfactorily.

GEORGE REYNOLD (*The Cave*), boy who proves most level-headed in the nearly disastrous expedition. From a poor and disorganized family, George has low status in the club at the start, but he takes over leadership when Alan* Hobbs loses his nerve and, despite a badly burned hand, leads the boys to eventual safety. He says little but responds to beauty in nature more strongly than do the others.

THE GHOST OF THOMAS KEMPE (Lively*, Penelope, ill. Antony Maitland, Heinemann, 1973; Dutton, 1973), lighthearted, action-filled fantasy set in England in recent times. The Harrisons-- somewhat irresponsible James*, about ten, Helen, a little older and inclined to be prissy, and their caring and opinionated parents (this is how James sees all three)--move into East End Cottage in Ledsham, Oxfordshire, unaware that workmen renovating James's attic room have released the spirit of a seventeenth-century sorcerer, Thomas Kempe. The story, told from James's point of view though not by him, relates the events of the next several weeks as Thomas's inability to adjust to a new time dimension disrupts first the life of James and his family, and then that of the village. This proves to be a period of considerable difficulty for James as he attempts to avoid being blamed for the notes Thomas leaves in old-fashioned handwriting, spelling, and phraseology, as well as his various pranks, and to get rid of Thomas before he causes real trouble. Thomas is upset at finding that things are no longer done as they were in his time and that other people like the minister and the pharmacist are doing tasks he considers his prerogatives. In particular, he resents old Mrs.* Verity, the busybody who lives next door to the Harrisons and who he insists is a witch and has caused Mrs. Harrison's allergies. He twitches off James's bed-quilt at night, causes mysterious drafts, and disrupts television programs, among other minor acts of disturbance, and, among more serious ones, he alters prescriptions and smashes things. When matters don't go his way, Thomas flies into rages and rips through the house. Convinced that he is dealing with a poltergeist, James consults Mrs. Verity about ghosts and learns about exorcism. He learns, too, that Bert* Ellison, the local carpenter, is said to be able to exorcise ghosts. Bert's first attempt, trying to lure Thomas into a bottle, results in immediate failure. While investigating a refuse heap for helpful information about the cottage, James discovers an old diary telling how young Arnold* Luckett was aided by the rector in getting rid of Thomas by luring him into a bottle. Knowing that Thomas is too intelligent for them to try that method again, James is still hopeful that he may be gotten rid of in some other way. Bert's second try, with magical scrawls, a rowan twig, and a brass ring, is interrupted at the most inopportune moment by Mrs. Verity. When Thomas paints "Widdow Veritie is a Wytch" on her fence, the Harrisons are finally convinced that these unfortunate happenings are not James's doing and attribute them to local "louts." More pranks follow--trouble at a local archaeological dig, a scurrilous message on the fire station door--until things come to a head when Thomas sets fire to Mrs. Verity's house. At the school's centennial, Thomas begs James in a note to find his resting-place. Apparently he has grown weary of this lonely, anachronistic existence and longs for peace. When he can't find Thomas's grave in the local cemetery, James again consults Bert, who discovers a crypt bearing his name beneath the church floor. James places Thomas's pipe and spectacles on the headstone, and Thomas disappears into his grave in a wavering, gradually dwindling blue light.

James walks contentedly home, reflecting on the continuity of life and the unexpected dimensions of the human character. Characterizations are skillful, and even the minor figures have distinct personalities, for example, Simon*, James's blase school friend, and Mr. Hollings, James's exuberant teacher. James himself can be seen from several perspectives. Family relationships are accurate, and the adults are sympathetically if flatly presented. Touches of ironic humor, generous amounts of authentic dialogue, and the story within the story contribute color and texture. The result is a fresh and lively fantasy worked out with wit, precision, sensitivity, and inventiveness. Carnegie Winner; Choice; Contemporary Classics; Fanfare.

GILBERT D'ASSAILLY (*Knight Crusader**), friend and companion knight of Philip* d'Aubigny, who joins the forces of Philip's father, Sir Hugo, at Blanche Garde. Like Philip, he is captured in the ill-fated march against the Turks at Tiberias, is imprisoned at Damascus, escapes with Philip, and eventually goes with him to England. Gilbert has come from Normandy because he is a nephew of the Grand Master of the Hospitallers, but he prefers to make his own way. He is a quiet, awkward young man, devoted to Philip, but not his peer in feats of courage and arms.

GILES (*The Wool-Pack**), Master* Thomas Fetterlock's faithful shepherd, at whose house Nicholas* Fetterlock was a fosterling when very young. Ever zealous for his master's interests, Giles is the first character to suspect that Leach is up to no good and so informs his employer, who characteristically refuses to believe anything bad about a friend or business associate.

GILLES COBHAM (*The Gentle Falcon**), overbearing youth who mistakes Isabella* Clinton for a servant girl at their first meeting and threatens to have her whipped for her saucy tongue. When Richard II's fortunes begin to fall, Gilles sides with Harry Bolingbroke (later Henry IV) but risks being thought a traitor to

his own side by trying to get Richard's child
queen, Isabella* of France, safely out of the
country. When she will not go and is taken away
by her traitorous ex-governess, Gilles
concentrates on getting Isabella Clinton,
companion to the young queen, to France and
safety. After her escape, when her lands are
forfeit to the crown, he asks for them as his
reward and loses the king's favor by forcing him
to pardon Isabella and allow her to return to
England if she will marry Gilles, which she
eventually does.

GILLES THE OUTLAW (*The Writing on the Hearth**),
renegade who helps Lys* reach Meg's* cottage
when she flees from Odo* the Plowman and the
Earl* of Suffolk's hounds, and to whom Stephen
goes for help in saving Meg from the
interrogators who think she is a witch. Gilles
lives in a makeshift hut in the wooded hills
overlooking Ewelme. Once a French monk studying
in England, he took to the hills when the French
monasteries were closed during the wars with
France. Since then, he has been living a kind of
Robin Hood existence outside the law, helping to
provide food, espcially venison illegally taken
from the earl's estate, for those in need. He is
a stock figure.

GINGER (*Black Beauty**), emotional, tall,
chestnut mare, who is Black Beauty's stable- and
teammate at Squire Gordon's. At first surly
toward Beauty because she has been turned out of
her box to accommodate his arrival, she
eventually becomes Beauty's good friend and
honest companion in harness. She is easily
fretted and has a tender mouth because she was
abused with whip and bit in her youth by her
breaker, a headstrong young man named Samson,
who often mishandled her. Ginger tells Beauty
the story of her life, during which she had
many other abusive masters before arriving at
Birtwick Park. After she is sold to the Earl of
W-------, along with Beauty, she is subjected
again to the tight checkrein, a contemporary
fashion she greatly hates and which the author
presents as especially reprehensible, and one
day, when the Countess orders that Ginger's
check-rein be tightened still more, the mare

rebels, rearing up and kicking out in her pain and frustration, and is consequently passed on to another master. After that, she falls on increasingly hard times, finally being sold to a very hardhanded London cabbie. Beauty last sees her when, having dropped dead from overwork and abuse, her bony old body is being carted away for disposal. The author uses Ginger to illustrate what will happen to horses that are not humanely cared for.

THE GIRL IN THE GROVE (Severn*, David, Allen & Unwin, 1974; Harper, 1974), suspense fantasy set in Wethershaf, a village near Croon, England, in modern times. After the death of her financier father, which may have been a suicide to escape prosecution for fraud, Jonquil* Darley, 15, and her mother, Isobel, move to a cottage he had bought but never used, and her mother goes to work for Jonquil's Uncle Tim. Isobel's life is made interesting by a neighboring widower, Bernard* Hunter, who owns a fruit farm, but Jonquil is at first annoyed by the hostility of Bernard's son, Paul*, 16, who warns her not to walk around on the farm or the adjoining closed manor house, of which the Hunter land was once a part. Irritated and bored, Jonquil persists in her walks and meets a girl in the grove on the hill near the manor. She is a girl of about thirteen, dressed in old-fashioned clothes, and acts alternately teasing and sad. Only after a second encounter with the girl does Jonquil realize that she is the spirit of Laura* Seccombe, who died some sixty years earlier. Paul is much involved with Laura, jealously possessive and concerned about her, so much so that he disappears from his boarding school to bring a cake to the girl on her birthday. Jonquil guesses that he might be meeting Laura, goes to the manor house, and meets him and Laura there, but they are interrupted by the caretaker and Bernard, who assumes that Paul and Jonquil have arranged a rendezvous. Paul is sent back to school and Jonquil banished to live with her Uncle Tim. Complications arise: Isobel and Bernard Hunter become romantically involved; a wealthy young man, Henry Johnson, becomes interested in Jonquil; and Paul's grandmother, who was Laura's nursemaid in her youth, gives

Jonquil a desk she took from the manor, and concealed in its back are letters written to her by Charles Seccombe. Through what Laura has told her and memories of some local people, Jonquil knows that there was a romance between this older brother of Laura and the nursemaid, and that when it was discovered she was dismissed and he left for America, never to return. Paul, having figured out the less than nine months between this event and his father's birth, is sure his real father was Charles Seccombe. Jonquil is worried about Laura's hold on Paul and also about how to get Laura's spirit to rest. Old Mrs. Hunter recovers partially from an attack, and, alerted that Laura is reappearing by news reports of a wild party the neighboring young people have in the manor, at which Jonquil and others see her, she faces the story calmly and asks Jonquil to meet her at the church to pray for Laura, whom she has never ceased to love even though she now knows that the girl in jealousy had hidden the letters meant for her so many years before. Standing at Laura's grave with Jonquil, the old woman is startled by the sight of a young American serviceman and dies of a heart attack. Her death seems to give Laura's spirit the chance it needs to go to rest with the only person who ever really loved her. The serviceman proves to be grandson of Charles and, through complicated evidence, is related to Jonquil rather than to Paul. The thriller plot is well crafted and the main characters interesting, if somewhat typecast, particularly Paul's parvenu father. Poe Nominee.

GIRL WITH A LANTERN (Kyle*, Elisabeth, ill. Douglas Relf, Evans, 1961; *THE STORY OF GRIZEL*, Nelson, 1961), historical novel set in Scotland and in the Netherlands during the reigns of Charles II and James II of England and William and Mary of Orange, who become joint rulers of England and Scotland in the "Glorious Revolution" of 1688. The story follows the varying fortunes of the historical family of Sir Patrick Hume of Redbraes, who incurs the enmity of Charles II for resisting the king's efforts to impose English forms of worship upon the Presbyterian Scots. Events are seen mostly from the point of view of staunch, courageous,

resourceful Grizel, eldest of Sir Patrick's five
children and seventeen when the novel begins.
Her father in hiding and her mother in failing
health, Grizel runs the household with the help
of Jamie Winter, her father's faithful groom.
Although Grizel sometimes feels sorry for
herself, she realizes where her duty lies and
accepts her circumstances with good spirit.
After her father is declared an outlaw and his
property is confiscated by the crown, the family
escapes by Dutch ship to Utrecht. They live
quietly for three years among the sympathetic
Dutch, hoping that a change in the political
climate in England, now ruled by Catholic James
II, will make it possible for them to return
home. Grizel continues to supervise the house
and lessons of her siblings, while her father
earns a modest living as "Dr. Wallace," a
dispenser of medicines. Patrick, the eldest son,
gets a position in the Palace Guard, as does
George Baillie, the son of the executed Lord of
Jerviswood, which is not far from Redbraes, and
the family is befriended by Maarten Van
Mierevelt, a wealthy Dutch merchant. Further
interest arises from Grizel's relationships with
three men: handsome young Lieutenant John
Neville of the British Dragoons, a Devon youth
who is shot by George Baillie while he is trying
to prevent Sir Patrick from sailing; George, who
gradually comes to command her respect and
affection; and kind Maarten, who proposes
marriage and whose suit her family favors. When
Mary, who becomes Queen of England after James
II is deposed, offers Grizel a position as
lady-in-waiting, the girl declines, and the conclusion finds Sir Patrick serving as Chancellor
of Scotland, with his estate restored, while
Grizel looks forward to marrying George and
becoming the lady of Jerviswood. Duty and
loyalty to family and conscience play a strong
role in the story, and the sense of the period
and its problems is strong. Grizel is a
sympathetic and likeable heroine with convincing
dilemmas and choices, and the style is pleasing,
with just enough Scots dialect to have a good
effect. Suspense is high while the family
remains in Scotland, but the shift in the last
half of the book from the family's fortunes to
Grizel's determination of her personal, and, in

particular, her romantic destiny is bland and
unsatisfying in comparison. The multiplicity of
events at the end makes the conclusion confusing. Grizel's three suitors are obvious
foils, and Queen Mary's appearances seem gratuitous. Grizel's lighthearted and light-headed
sister, Christian, who dies of a fever just
before they return to Scotland, is an
interesting minor figure. Fanfare.

GODDEN, (MARGARET) RUMER (1907-   ), born in
Sussex; novelist and author of nonfiction for
both adults and children. When she was nine
months old, she was taken to India, where her
father was a steamship agent in Bengal, and she
lived there until 1919, when she was sent with
her three sisters to boarding school in England,
a very unhappy move for her. After attending
five schools in a short time, she settled at
Moira House, Eastbourne, Sussex, but she
returned to India in the 1930s and directed a
children's ballet school in Calcutta. Her first
literary success was with her novel for adults,
Black Narcissus (Davies, 1939; Little, 1939),
which was made into a movie that she disliked
intensely. She has published about twenty other
novels for adults, some of which are often read
by young people, among them *Episode of Sparrows*
(Macmillan, 1956; Viking, 1955) and *Greengage
Summer* (Macmillan, 1958; Viking, 1958). One of
her best known books for children is the brief
story *The Mousewife* (Macmillan, 1951; Viking,
1951), based on a story found in the journal of
Dorothy Wordsworth. Many of her books for children are doll stories, including *The Dolls'
House** (Joseph, 1947; Viking, 1948), *Miss Happiness and Miss Flower** (Macmillan, 1961; Viking,
1961), *Little Plum** (Macmillan, 1963; Viking,
1963), *Home Is the Sailor** (Macmillan, 1964;
Viking, 1964), and *The Fairy Doll** (Macmillan,
1956; Viking, 1956). Although these all contain
a fantasy element in which the dolls' thoughts
and wishes are known, the main plot usually
concerns the problems of the human children.
Among her other novels for children are *Operation Sippacik* (Macmillan, 1969; Viking, 1969),
an adventure story set in Cyprus; *Mr. McFadden's
Halloween* (Macmillan, 1975; Viking, 1975), a
horse story; *The Kitchen Madonna** (Macmillan,

1967; Viking, 1967), a story of a boy who tries
to design a shrine for his kitchen to make the
Ukranian maid happy; and *The Diddakoi**, a story
of a half-gypsy orphan, which won the Whitbread
Award. Two of her novels were commended for the
Carnegie Medal, and several have been included
on the *Horn Book* Fanfare and *Choice* magazine
lists. Godden has also written two books of
verse for children, and edited *A Letter to the
World: Poems for Young Readers*, by Emily Dickinson (Bodley, 1968; Macmillan, 1969). Among her
several books of nonfiction are biographies of
Hans Christian Andersen and Beatrix Potter. Although many of her books have a tendency toward
sentimentalism, her writing is deft and sensitive.

GODMAN, GROVER (*The Iron Lily**), husband of
Lilias and father of Ursula, a cold, hard, dour,
and apparently sometimes abusive man, ironmaster of Froreden foundry. He is much respected
for his skill, fairness, and industry and was
the one-time business partner of Sir Henry
Sydney of royal connections. Godman's marriage
to Lilias was arranged by the Sydneys as a
reward for faithful service. Though apparently
Lilias and Godman are fond of each other, it is
only as her father lies dying, his chest crushed
in a terrible foundry accident, that Ursula for
the first time sees the two exchange a sign of
affection. Though most of his ironwork is
utilitarian in purpose, Godman crafts decorative
pieces with great skill in his spare time, among
them an iron lily, which is the symbol of his
high regard for Lilias and of his assessment of
her character. This is the device she eventually
hangs above her door at Strives Minnis.

GOLDENGROVE (Paton* Walsh, Jill, Macmillan,
1972; Farrar, 1972), sensitive story of two
weeks in which a young teenager, visiting her
grandmother's seaside home, discovers the truth
about her background and anticipates the
difficulties of growing up. Madge Fielding
comes, as she has each summer, to Goldengrove,
her grandmother's home at Godrevy in Cornwall,
at the same time her slightly younger cousin
Paul is visiting, but this time, because of her
mother's interference, it is in the fall rather

than mid-summer. Both youngsters realize that their parents have feuded but that Gran wants them to know each other, and they have always had a marvelous, carefree time together. This year, however, there are some changes. Gran is older, frailer, and inclined to be forgetful and to fall asleep in her chair; Madge has "gone different around her middle somewhere," Paul thinks, and she is put in the best guest room instead of with him in the big attic room they have always shared before. The biggest change is that Gran has rented the little cottage on her land to Ralph Ashton, a professor of English literature who was blinded in the war and whose wife has recently left him. Madge, attracted by the idea that she can do a kindness and also by her need for a father figure, offers to read for him. She begins to spend part of every day with him, with various consequences. Paul is hurt at her lack of interest in the old boat, which they had decided to clean out and paint, and jealous of the time she spends with Ralph. Madge herself has mixed feelings, a growing attraction to Ralph, whom she begins to think of as Mr. Rochester, annoyance at the amount of time the reading takes and boredom with the scholarly books he wants read, and guilt because of her boredom and because she knows she is neglecting Paul. When, just a few days before their holiday is over, Gran suggests that Paul may be feeling left out, Madge casually says that Paul always understands and that she will probably marry him for that reason. This precipitates a phone call by Gran to Madge's mother and a subsequent letter from her to Madge, explaining that the girl's father was not killed in the war, as she has always been told. Furthermore, she writes, he is really Paul's father as well, and Paul is Madge's brother. When their marriage broke up, her father insisted on taking Paul. Madge, already feeling uncomfortably in the way with her mother and stepfather and having idealized the memory of her own father, is devastated by the news that he rejected her but insisted on keeping his son. She also feels terribly cheated by being kept from having a brother through her whole childhood. Desperately she turns to Ralph and proposes that she stay and live with him, taking care of him, reading to him, and being his lover, if he doesn't want another wife. Trying to be kind but firm, he rejects her offer, but not as gently as he intends. Humiliated, Madge runs down to the beach, fits the ancient mast and sail she has found into the newly painted boat, and pushes it off, telling herself she intends to sail to the lighthouse, but perhaps unconsciously attempting suicide. When she gets far enough off shore for the wind to catch the sail, it rips the decayed material to shreds, and as she tries to bail, the rotten boards in the boat's bottom collapse. Paul finds her on the beach and helps her up to Gran's house. Because she is very ill, she stays at Gran's, where her mother and Ralph and finally Paul, who has returned to school, come to visit her. Paul admits that he always thought she was his sister and exults that now their parents will have no excuse to keep them apart. He doesn't understand when Madge says it is too late, that there are some things that can't be put right. Although there are a few peripheral characters--Amy, the girl who looks after Gran, and her American soldier boyfriend, Walt, Jeremy, the fisherman who takes them out in his boat, and others--the story has essentially four characters, each drawn with skill and sympathy. Paul is a practical, straightforward boy who will always land on his feet. Gran is aging, remembering the fights that broke up her son's marriage and dreading the same sort of emotional crises for Madge. Ralph is slightly bitter and withdrawn from affection to keep from being hurt again. Madge is an intelligent, sensitive girl, just growing out of childhood, vulnerable to the pain of adulthood without its understanding. The setting in time is unclear, but when one takes the sequel, *Unleaving**, into account, it is apparent that the war in which Madge's father was supposedly killed and in which Ralph lost his sight must be World War I and that the action of the book, therefore, occurs in the early 1930s. There are some vivid scenes, like that in which Madge, trying to feel what it is like to be blind, lets Paul blindfold her and steer her into a dark storeroom and then panics when she pulls off the blindfold and discovers it is still dark. The style is unusual, all told in present tense, with the point of view shifting continually from one character to another, a tricky technique that is made to work well. Choice; Fanfare.

THE GOLDEN KEY (MacDonald*, George, Crowell, 1906), literary tale which appeared first in *Dealing with the Fairies* (Strahan, 1867), set in the timeless world of fairy land. Mossy, a young boy, having heard from his aunt that at the end of the rainbow is a golden key, follows a rainbow into the forest and sleeps on the mossy bank that marks its end. In the morning he finds a little golden key, with sapphires set in the handle. He comes to a cottage where a beautiful lady is singing to a little girl named Tangle, a child who has been neglected by the servants supposed to care for her and driven into the forest by the fairies. The lady has washed and dressed Tangle in lovely clothes and fed her upon the "air-fish" that led her to the house. From the cooking pot emerges the spirit of the fish, now a little human form with wings. The next morning the lady sends the children off together, and they travel through a strange landscape and cross a plain covered with shadows, though they cannot see what casts them; they suspect that the key may be to the land from which the shadows come. They grow gray and wrinkled as they cross this plain and then are mysteriously parted. Tangle wanders on and encounters her air-fish, now an aeranth, a sort of fairy, which leads her through mountain passages to the Old Man of the Sea. He doesn't know the way to the land of the shadows, but sends her on to the Old Man of the Earth, who strangely is both an old man and a youth of marvelous beauty. He in turn shows her the way to the Old Man of the Fire, which is through a large hole that she must throw herself into, to be carried by water and through great heat to a cool, mossy cave, where she is suddenly gifted with an understanding of all that has happened. She sees a little naked child playing with balls of various sizes and colors, arranging them in patterns on the floor. She watches him for seven years before she asks if he is the Old Man of the Fire. He leads her to an egg, breaks it open, and tells her to follow the serpent that emerges. In the meantime, Mossy, now an old man, has found the Old Man of the Sea, and at his direction sets off walking across a raging sea, his feet making no holes. He goes on and on until he reaches a cliff, which he climbs half way until the path stops and he finds a keyhole into which his key will fit. This opens a great door into the mountain, and he follows the passage to a room full of stones shining in rainbow colors. There he finds Tangle. Together they discover another keyhole in one of the pillars of the room which opens a door and reveals a stairway to the land from which the shadows come. Both young again, they ascend hand in hand. Some critics have interpreted the story as an allegory for the journey of the religious life. It is an example of MacDonald at his most mystical, a work which appeals to a rather special taste. It has neither the genuine quality of folktale nor the grounding in realistic detail and character development of modern fantasy. A 1967 edition (Farrar) is illustrated by Maurice Sendak. Choice.

GOLD PIECES (Bentley*, Phyllis, Macmillan, 1968; *FORGERY!*, Doubleday, 1968), historical novel with murder-mystery aspects set in Yorkshire in 1769, told by fourteen-year-old Dick (Richard) Wade, a weaver's son, with hints of old-time, country speech. While picking bilberries on Erringden Moor, Dick rescues a frisky English sheepdog pup whose paw is caught under a rock. On his way home, he stops to ask directions at Bell House, the home of the Hartleys, who are blacksmiths. The Hartley brothers and Jamie, the son of one of them and about Dick's age, behave strangely when they see the dog, and Dick notes that the dog obviously dislikes them. A little later, "clipped" coins turn up in the region. Clipping involves chipping away edges of gold coins so that new ones can be forged out of the chips. Even Joe Wade, Dick's father, who is known and respected throughout the area for his honesty, integrity, and weaving of very high quality, passes one quite innocently when he sends Dick to pay the monthly rent. Mint authorities offer rewards for information about the coiners and declare coining a treasonable offense punishable by hanging. Dick becomes friends with Jamie Hartley, a handsome, saucy youth who is often in trouble and whose father beats him. Dick picks up some of Jamie's ways, and once gets a good scolding for throwing a stone at John Wesley when he preaches in the village. Then someone tries to kill Sam, the dog, and Amos, the old gamekeeper, warns Dick to stay away from the local inn and to get rid of the animal. Things come to a head when Mr. Kay, a businessman from Lancashire, identifies Sam as his lost dog. It turns out that, while passing through the village, Mr. Kay happened to see David, Jamie's father, coining. David attacked him, and Sam rose to his master's defense and later became lost. Then a revenue agent is shot and killed, evidently because he was mistaken for Mr. Kay. Dick knows that old Amos the gamekeeper shot the agent, coerced into the deed by the Hartleys, but Dick keeps mum about it. David Hartley is convicted and hanged for forgery. At the end, Dick tries to persuade Jamie to mend his ways, and there is some hope that Jamie will respond. Mr. Kay, who has invented the flying shuttle, gives one to Joe in appreciation for Dick's rescuing Sam. The plot is exciting but overforeshadowed, and most characters are cardboard figures, unconvincing as people and only going through the appropriate motions. The plot blends well with the period, but is clumsily constructed and spun out. Poe Nominee.

GOLLUM (*The Hobbit**; *The Fellowship of the Ring**), also known by his original name, Smeagol, creature with whom Bilbo* Baggins plays the riddle game in the depths of the goblins' mountain and from whom he obtains the ring. Gollum is wizened, with long arms and enlaged eyes from having lived so long in the dark, and he speaks with a hiss and a sort of gulp, which gives him his name. His intention is to eat Bilbo, but he cannot resist talking to him first since it is so long since he has had contact with anyone he can talk to, and when he realizes that Bilbo has found the ring he becomes distraught with fury and consternation. In *The Fellowship of the Ring* it is revealed that he is from a branch of the hobbits of ancient times, that he murdered his cousin for the ring

and then hid in the tunnels deep in the mountain
to protect it, and that he has lived many times
the life span of his kind because of his
possession of the ring. This possession,
however, has consumed him, until he is really
the servant of his "Precious," as he calls the
ring, and is in such agony without it that he
has emerged from the mountain and made his way
to Mordor, where he has been tortured for
information and then expelled. Gandalf* has
found him, extracted the story from him, and
given him to the elves of Mirkwood to guard.
He has escaped from them, however, and somehow
has managed to trail the fellowship to where it
dissolves, and then to follow Frodo* Baggins and
Sam* Gamgee until they capture him and he
becomes their treacherous and unpleasant guide,
even going into and through Mordor. In the end
he is instrumental in the destruction of the
ring, biting off Frodo's finger and, stepping
too far in his dance of victory, toppling into
the chasm of Mount Doom. He is a despicable and
pitiable character.

GOODBYE, DOVE SQUARE (McNeill*, Janet, ill. Mary
Russon, Faber, 1969; Little, 1969), realistic
novel, sequel to *The Battle of St. George
Without** and set about two years later after
the church has been torn down and almost all the
residents of the square have moved to a housing
project known as the Flats or the Happy Land.
The crowd of youngsters has scattered. Henry*
Mickle is now a flunky in an office, Gwen* is in
nurse's training, Madge* works at a supermarket,
the older Flints have left home, Sidney Lumba is
a housepainter and plays in a dance band, and
only Matt* McGinley is still in school. When by
chance he meets Madge lurking in an unused train
station rather than going to the Youth Club
dance at the Community Center, Matt impulsively
suggests that they go back to look at Dove
Square. Their dismay at the rubble and the empty
buildings turns to astonishment when they meet
Shaky* Frick with his two little dogs and learn
that he is still living, unauthorized, in one of
the old buildings. With considerable caution,
he takes them to his hideout and shares with
them his supper of fish and chips. After they
leave, Madge berates Matt for eating so much of

Shaky's dinner. They quarrel, and she goes off
on the bus alone. Conscience-stricken, Matt buys
another package of fish and chips and is about
to take it to Shaky when he runs into a man whom
he calls the Salesman, a sinister, smiling
character who has been hanging around the Flats
asking questions. Chased by him, Matt inadvertently leads him to Shaky's basement and then
overhears him threaten to tell the authorities
that Shaky is squatting unless he gives
information about where some mutual acquaintance
is living. Worried, Matt tells Henry. They go
together to Dove Square and explore some of the
empty buildings, including the one where Madge
lived with her Cousin Maudie. There they find
the linoleum carefully peeled back in one
corner, revealing an empty hole under the floor
boards. Madge has already told Matt that Ma
Flint recently walked out on the family, as she
has done periodically, so when Gwen sees Pa
Flint being brought to the hospital as an
accident victim, the girls organize to care for
the Flint family. This proves exhausting. When
a welfare worker calls, surveys the chaos, and
sees Sammy, the youngest, who does not speak
well and may be retarded, Madge calmly says
that their grandmother is arriving tomorrow to
take over, and then sets Matt the job of finding
a plausible grandmother. Henry, sleuthing in the
apartments, has discovered where Miss* Queenie
Harrison lives. Having been bored and isolated
in the Flats, she is delighted to come and care
for the Flints. Matt has seen the Salesman
several times, and when Madge shows up wearing
the watch with which he tried to bribe Matt,
the boy puts two and two together and confronts
Cousin Maudie. She admits that the Salesman is
Madge's father, who has been in jail ten years
and who left stolen money in her care, and that
she is really Madge's mother. Knowing that,
when he fails to find the money in the old Dove
Square kitchen, the Salesman will blame Skaky,
Matt rushes off to Dove Square, where he meets
Madge hunting for Sammy Flint, who, reminded of
the place by the Christmas decorations, has
returned to his old home. Together they see the
Salesman threaten Shaky, Sammy try to clobber
him with a bottle, and the old stove go over in
the ensuing melee. As they watch the house go up

in flames, Madge translates Sammy's garbled tale
of how some time earlier he saw Cousin Maudie
looking at the money and then took it himself
and hid it in his own old apartment, which is
now burning beyond saving. The Salesman disappears, Madge realizes who her parents are, Ma
Flint returns on Christmas morning, and Shaky,
his little dogs in a kennel, has Christmas
dinner with Miss Harrison. Though the action of
the young people is not as directly exciting as
in the earlier story, it is psychologically
more interesting. Despite the threat posed by
the Salesman, the plot is unsensational. The
gritty city life is more depressing in the
Flats than it was in Dove Square, and the tone
of the story is generally gloomy, though the
main characters are depicted as survivors.
Choice.

GOOD-BYE TO THE JUNGLE. See *Widdershins
Crescent.*

GOOD NIGHT, MR. TOM (Magorian*, Michelle,
Kestrel, 1981; Harper, 1981), realistic novel
concerned with a case of child abuse and set
during World War II in the English country
village of Little Weirwold. The Billeting
Officer is slightly hesitant to drop off an
evacuee child at the cottage of crusty,
reclusive Tom* Oakley, who is sixty-plus and
caretaker of the church, but the mother of
William* Beech has insisted that he should be
placed near a church and the harassed officer is
running out of possibilities. Although almost
nine, Willie, as Tom calls him, is as small as a
six-year-old, terribly frightened, and, as Tom
discovers that evening, covered with bruises and
sores. His carrier bag contains almost nothing
except an old Bible, a leather belt with a steel
buckle, and a letter from his mother explaining
that the belt is "for when he's bad." The next
few days, Tom, trying to cope with the child, is
continually surprised: when he picks up the red
hot poker, Willie almost faints, thinking he is
about to be branded; seeing the bed prepared for
him, he crawls under it, never having slept in
one; he is terrified of the friendly black-and-
white collie, Sammy, and does not know what a
cow is; he vomits almost everything he eats and,

persuaded to sleep in the bed, wets it regularly. Tom buys him boots and clothes and when he
discovers that although Willie can't read he
loves to draw, gets him paints and sketch pads.
The other village people are surprised at Tom's
involvement, and they help out, with Dr. and
Mrs. Little offering advice and witch hazel for
the sores, Mrs. Fletcher knitting a heavy jersey
and a balaclava hat, Mr. Fletcher and his older
sons helping dig an air-raid shelter, and
George Fletcher reluctantly asking Willie to
join a blackberrying picnic with him and the
Thatcher twins, Carrie* and Ginnie. Another
evacuee, Zach* (Zacharias) Wrench, an uninhibit-
ed boy of Jewish theatrical parents who is
billeted with the Littles, invites himself along
and soon becomes the leader of the five and an
idol to Willie. With encouragement and the
healthy village atmosphere, Willie begins to
blossom, learns to read, develops his real
drawing skill, and even is chosen to act
Scrooge in *A Christmas Carol* when the original
choice, an evacuee, returns to London. He has
begun to run, play, and chatter almost like
other boys when a letter comes from his mother
saying she is ill and needs him home for a
while. With apprehension but a little hope, he
goes by train back to London loaded with
presents from his Little Weirwold friends, only
to be accused by his mother of stealing them and
lying, and to find, when his mother sneaks him
into their apartment, that she has a new baby
whose mouth she has taped shut to keep the
neighbors from discovering her. After a month of
hearing nothing, Tom is so worried that he
takes the train for London, with Sammy, and
eventually hunts up the Deptford slum where the
Beeches live. The air-raid warden says that he
has seen nothing of Willie and a neighbor says
Mrs.* Beech has gone away, but Sammy scrabbles
so frantically at the door that a policeman
finally lets them break it down. They find
Willie tied in a closet beneath the stairs, in
his own vomit and excrement, holding the body of
the dead baby, whom he calls Trudy. Tom goes
with him to the hospital, and when he realizes
they are going to keep Willie sedated and send
him to a home for mentally ill children, he
kidnaps the boy and takes him back to Little

Weirwold. There William gradually recovers, with
Zach and the other youngsters lending support.
When he forces himself to go see his beloved
teacher, Mrs. Hartridge, whose baby has been
born since her husband was declared missing, he
is able to ease the guilt he has felt for the
death of Trudy. Tom takes him and Zach with the
old cart and horse to the sea for a holiday.
Organized by Zach to explore the haunted
cottage, Spooky Cott, the youngsters discover a
young amputee veteran, Geoffrey Sanderton, who
is an artist, living alone to try to heal his
shattered nerves. When Willie returns home, he
finds a policeman, the warden from his block in
London, a psychiatrist, and female social worker
all talking to Tom. The woman tells him that
his mother has committed suicide and that he
will be taken to a children's home. He protests
and, when he is sent from the room, decides to
hide out with Lucy, a younger child who has
always embarrassed him by her adoration, but
before he can make his get-away, the strangers
leave and he learns that Tom is planning to
adopt him. Zach's father is injured in a bombing
raid, and he returns to London to see him;
while he is there he and his parents are
killed. Grief-stricken, William is helped by
Tom's understanding, by Geoffrey, who gives him
drawing lessons, by his own determination to
learn to ride Zach's bike and to act more like
his exuberant friend, and by Carrie, who was
also very close to Zach. At the book's end, he
has begun to realize that he is growing up and
Tom is growing old, and that their roles will
change. Although the plot is basically the same
as that of many Victorian novels--a
misunderstood child redeems a cranky old man and
brings light into both lives--the details of
William's abuse and the evocation of emotions--
his fear, his mother's demented rage, and Tom's
growing involvement--are so strong that the
story seems fresh and is moving. The villagers
may be a bit too universally supportive to be
completely believable, and Zach is not entirely
plausible, but William's gradual change in the
warm and decent atmosphere is convincing.
Carnegie Com.; Fanfare; Guardian; IRA Winner;
Jr. High Contemporary Classics.

THE GOON (*Archer's Goon**), huge, smelly, seemingly dim-witted fellow who shows up at the Sykes's house saying he came from Archer* and demanding the 2,000 words that Quentin* Sykes has been sending in quarterly. He has enormous feet and a little, round head with fair hair, and speaks in brief disconnected phrases. He has a way of tearing open doors and pushing his way past guards and through meetings as if he is oblivious to anything except his goal, but Howard* soon realizes that he is not as daft as he pretends to be. After he has been part of the Sykes household for some time, he seems to develop a great fondness for Howard, deep respect for Howard's mother, Catriona, a desperate crush on Fifi, their live-in college girl, and tolerance for Awful* Sykes. Eventually it is revealed that he is Erskine, the next-to-youngest of the seven wizards, who "farms" drains and sewers and who wants to break the power that keeps them in the city because he likes to travel. Though the family comes to treat him like an enormous, not very clean dog, he retains some of his potentially threatening aspects.

GOPAL (*The Devil's Children**), Sikh boy who becomes chief translator and explainer to Nicky* Gore when she joins the group. A slight boy with a thin face and silky soft skin, he seems a bit girlish to Nicky at first, but she soon finds that he is hardy and brave as well as good-natured. He accompanies her to the village at night to get information after the robbers come, and acts as lookout. In the battle he courageously jumps out to protect Uncle* Chacha Rahmta against three hoodlums and kills one of them with his sword. Like all Sikh men, his last name is Singh, which means "Lion."

GOUDGE, ELIZABETH (1900-1984), born in Wells, Somersetshire, later living in Devonshire and Oxfordshire; educator, artist, and author best known for her books for adults. She was the only daughter of Henry Leighton Goudge, who became Regius Professor of Divinity at Oxford, and there is a strong religious element in her writing. After Grassendale School in Hampshire she took a degree from Reading University

School of Art. Though it had been her ambition
from childhood to become a writer, her parents
felt that the profession was too risky and urged
her to complete art training in order to have
something to fall back upon. When her first
writings failed to sell, she taught applied art
and design for ten years, continuing to write in
her spare time. Her break came when she was
thirty-two with the Sunday night performance of
her play *The Brontes of Haworth* (London, 1932).
A novel for adults followed, *Island Magic*
(Duckworth, 1934; Coward, 1934), and her career
was launched. In 1938 she took up writing full
time, and the next forty years saw the
publication of ten books for children, fifteen
novels for adults, and two dozen plays and books
of short stories, verse, biography, and autobiography, and anthologies, some of a spiritual
or inspirational nature. Her stories for both
adults and children have a strongly romantic and
mysterious atmosphere (some critics termed it
sentimental or saccharine); are lush with
incidents, characters, and local color; and are
highly moralistic. Two of her novels for young
readers have received critical citations; both
are fantasies: *Smoky House** (Duckworth, 1940;
Coward, 1940), a Fanfare book, and *The Little
White Horse** (U. of London, 1946; Coward, 1947),
a Carnegie Medal winner and a Fanfare book. In
the former work, the arrival of a mysterious
Fiddler spells trouble for an English seacoast
village (whose inhabitants are inveterate
smugglers) when he turns out to be a customs
agent. *The Little White Horse* tells how tiny,
red-haired Maria Merryweather rights old wrongs
in a secluded valley on the coast of Devonshire
with the help of a little white unicorn. Goudge
also published several other novels for
children, among them *The Valley of Song* (U. of
London, 1951; Coward, 1952), and *Linnets and
Valerians* (Brockhampton, 1964; Coward, 1964);
some short stories for the Christmas season; and
God So Loved the World: A Life of Christ
(Coward, 1951). The most famous of her many
books for adults is *Green Dolphin Country*
(Hodder, 1944; as *Green Dolphin Street*, Coward,
1944), which won the $125,000 MGM Literary Award
and the Literary Guild Award and was made into a
movie.

GRAHAME, KENNETH (1859-1932), born in Edinburgh, Scotland and died in Pangbourne, England; author and editor. Grahame was the third of four children; his mother died when he was five and the family was moved to the home of a maternal grandmother at Cookham Dene in Berkshire and later lived with other relatives. His father drifted away and died an alcoholic. Grahame attended St. Edward's School, Oxford, from 1868 to 1875, and then worked for four years in the office of his uncle, a parliamentary agent; then until 1908 he was employed by the Bank of England, London. During this period his writing career began with two autobiographical volumes, *The Golden Age* (Lane, 1895; Stone, 1895) and *Dream Days* (Lane, 1898), both of which are books for adults but unusual in their child's view of the world and events. *The Reluctant Dragon** (Holiday, 1938), published as a book for children, is a story that originally appeared in *Dream Days*. He also edited *Lullaby Land: Songs of Childhood by Eugene Field* (Lane, 1898; Scribner, 1897) and later *The Cambridge Book of Poetry for Children* (Cambridge U. Press, 1916; Putnam, 1916), but he is known essentially for one book, *The Wind in the Willows** (Methuen, 1908; Scribner, 1908), which is acknowledged to be one of the classics of children's literature. It began as bedtime stories for his son, Alistair, and in its quiet appreciation for nature it reflects his home in Berkshire. It has been dramatized many times, notably by A. A. Milne*.

GRAMPER PONTIFEX (*Up the Pier**), old man known to his family and to his public as "the Last of the Magicians." One of his spells goes awry, perhaps with some help from Samuel* Pontifex (who also has magical powers), or perhaps because of overconfidence, and his family finds themselves in 1971 instead of 1921, which is their proper dimension. Gramper becomes very depressed after this unfortunate happening, and can make no spells of force for a while. Victory in a contest to control the storm restores his faith in himself, however. He enlists Carrie's* aid in returning the Pontifexes to their own time. The family occasionally calls him Ponty.

GRAN-AT-COALGATE (*Gran at Coalgate**), Annie

Dunham, warm-hearted, strong-spirited maternal grandmother of Jinnie Friend, who accepts the bigoted, disapproving man Jinnie's mother (her daughter Kate) has married just as she accepts Aunt* Polly Dunham, the scandalous woman married to her son Davie. A woman respected by her neighbors and loved by all her family, she works hard but does not deny herself or her family pleasures in life, and she understands Jinnie's need for attention and sympathy.

GRAN AT COALGATE (Cawley*, Winifred, ill. Fermin Rocker, Oxford, 1974; Holt, 1975), novel of a girl's sudden growth in awareness of both the joys and sorrows of life during a few days' vacation away from her self-righteous and disapproving father in the industrial northwest of England in the late 1920s. Because she has been so worried about her exams and about whether her father will allow her to attend Secondary School, which is essential to her ambition of being a teacher, Jinnie (Jane Ann) Friend, 11, has vomited at school three days in a row, and her mother uncharacteristically not only insists on taking her, against Dad's wishes, to the doctor (who advises a "real holiday"), but also contrives that Jinnie will go not to puritanical Gran-at-Barton as the girl dreads, but to her own mother, Gran-at-Coalgate*. In this warm, loving household, many of Jinnie's certainties are jarred. Dad (Josiah* Friend) doesn't hold with strikes, dancing, or women having opinions, and as a storekeeper he feels himself a cut above the pitmen in his wife's coal-mining family. Gran (Annie Dunham) keeps house for her youngest son, Jamesie, for one of her sons-in-law, Uncle Bob Lunn, and for a granddaughter she is raising, Nan, 14. At first Jinnie is aware only of having the full attention of her understanding grandmother, which on their previous brief visits she has shared with her mother, Kate, and her younger brother, Robbie, but, gradually, disturbing elements intrude. Nan seems to have changed since she started at the Secondary and to be more interested in lads than in her younger cousin. Talk of the impending strike casts a shadow on the whole community. Most disturbing, Aunt* Polly Dunham, a vibrant, dark-haired woman who

speaks out in public, is somehow involved with
Tot Bourke, a giant of a miner and a friend of
Jamesie, while her husband, Uncle Davie Dunham,
is spending too much time and money (even for
Coalgate) in the pub, and her oldest son, Will,
is bitter and resentful and even, Jinnie
realizes, has beer on his breath when they meet
at the fish-and-chips shop. When she goes on an
errand for Gran to Aunt Polly's, she witnesses a
family fight in which Will smashes the fancy
cake his mother has been decorating, Polly
throws a knife at him, and Uncle Davie emerges
from the bedroom, slaps his wife, and rudely
tells Jinnie to get out. Nevertheless, the week
is full of unexpected and delicious new
experiences: wonderful meals at which she does
not have to eat bread first to tamp down her
appetite, as Dad insists; the Pictures (Dad
disapproves of movies); and even a dance (which
Jinnie tries to tell herself is a Church
Social). She even learns to dance herself, and
is willing to try when a boy asks her, even
though the preacher at Chapel has said that
dancers' ankles thicken by one and a half
inches in a fortnight. She is fascinated by
Nan's friend Betsey Smeaton, who, she decides,
is a Vamp and who does the Charleston (showing
her garters), and she watches with only partial
comprehension as Betsey tries to steal Will from
nice, quiet Nora Whitehead. At the dance, Aunt
Polly, arriving with Tot, is the center of
attention and has a verbal sparring match with
Betsey, at which Will blunders off in fury.
Later Jamesie calls for his girl, Dottie. He
brings news that a woman has been found murdered
out on Robson's field and says that the
youngsters had better walk home in a group.
Before Jinnie is up the next morning, Gran is
called out, and throughout a very strange day
she pieces together the story: it is Aunt Polly
who was thought murdered but is really in a
hospital badly injured; Will has disappeared;
the police are questioning everyone, including
Jinnie; and Uncle Davie is being arrested.
Jinnie is expected to take care of Aunt Polly's
little boy, the glum and unappealing George.
Will returns, is freed from suspicion, and makes
up with Nora. Gran is taking her savings, meant
for Nan's education, to hire a lawyer, and

Dottie breaks up with Jamesie when he promises
the money he has saved for their marriage to
help out. Before Jinnie can really sort
everything out her mother arrives, sent by Dad
to bring her out of this pit of iniquity even
though her promised week is not yet up. Jinnie
goes home with the assurance, gleaned from bits
overheard at Gran's, that Mam will somehow
persuade Dad to let her go to the Secondary, at
least if she wins a scholarship, and with some
new ideas about what constitutes goodness and
sin. A brief epilogue gives two bits from the
Newcastle *Mail*, one announcing the Northumberland Scholarship Winners, with Jinnie's name
among them, and one telling that Mrs. Polly
Dunham, having regained consciousness, has
described her assailant as a foreigner, age
about thirty. The reader is left to speculate
about whether this is true or whether she is
protecting either Tot or Uncle Davie. The main
strength of the book is in characterization,
with even many of the minor characters fully
drawn and memorable. Jinnie herself is an
appealing child, with a tendency to think in
capital letters about problems of Sin and her
inability to Speak Out and to Dare to be a
Daniel, but also with an instinctive
recognition of the love and generosity that
holds the Coalgate family together. It gives a
strong sense of the period and of life in a
mining town. Carnegie Com.; Guardian.

GRAN BELL (*No End to Yesterday**), small, self-
righteous woman who controls her husband, her
family of ten grown children, their spouses, and
their offspring with an iron will. Suspicious,
small-minded, and unrelentingly respectable, she
believes that none of her sons can do wrong,
none of their wives and girlfriends is worthy of
them, and nothing that her grandchild Marjory*
Bell can do will keep her from going wrong and
turning out like her disreputable mother.
Marjory believes her mother is dead. Gran
continually berates Marjory for being ungrateful
for the good home she has been given, and she
saves up an accounting of the child's sins to
tell her father when he comes home on weekends.
A woman of inflexible habit, Gran expects all
the family to come to dinner every Sunday, and

like a martyr insists on such duties as making
every bed in the house, a ritual of airing the
sheets, making the bed, and finally turning it
down before bedtime, even for her married
children who still live in her house. She has
managed to break up romances repeatedly for
her youngest son, Uncle* Ron, and destroys the
relationship of Marjory's father, Henry*, with
the attractive young woman he brings home for
inspection. Her antagonism to Marjory is at
least partly the result of her belief that
Marjory's mother, being pregnant, had trapped
Henry into marriage, and that Marjory may not be
Henry's child, although there is a strong
resemblance. As an adult, looking back, Marjory
admits that, of the whole family, the only one
she thoroughly hated was Gran.

GRANDAD BARTON (*Comfort Herself**), Comfort's
mother's father, who lives with Comfort's
Granny* in Smithy Cottage in the village of
Penfold in Kent. He understands children better
than Granny does and is patient and sensible. He
gives Comfort a part of his garden for her own
to grow flowers, thinks it is good for her to
play with the children of the village
("Children need other children to knock their
corners off," he says), and takes her for walks.
Granny thinks he spoils her, and they argue
about it at night after they think Comfort is
asleep. He is an engaging figure. He has no
African counterpart in the story, although
Comfort does have an African grandmother.

GRANDAD HEWITSON (*The Hollow Land**), owner of
the cottage, Light Trees, where the Batemans, a
family from London, come to spend vacations.
Living with his son's family, he maintains his
independence and his interest in the world, even
coming to the hilltop to see the eclipse of the
sun in 1999. In the story, the oil reserves have
been depleted, and the world of his nineties has
returned to many of the ways of the world of
his boyhood. It is Old Hewitson who rescues his
grandson, Bell* Teesdale, and Harry* Bateman
when they are trapped in an old mine. It is he
who has shown Bell the rare sight of the frozen
waterfall and understands the marvel that makes
Bell set off with Harry in the snow to see it

again. It is he who solves the question of ownership of Light Trees by leaving it in his will to Anne Teesdale, his great-granddaughter and Bell's daughter. Only he suspects that Anne has decided to marry Harry, who is thirteen years her senior.

GRANDMA BAGTHORPE (*Ordinary Jack**), the matriarch of the overachieving, eccentric Bagthorpe clan. She has a grudge against Uncle* Parker because he recklessly ran down Thomas, her beloved cat, with his car. She hopes that Jack's Pronouncement about a Brown Bear foretells Thomas's resurrection. When the story begins, the family is celebrating her seventy-fifth birthday at a party during which Daisy* Parker burns, among other things, the "Birthday Portrait" Rosie* has painted of her grandmother. During the rest of the book, Rosie and Grandma are engaged in making a replacement, which never satisfies the old lady, until Atlanta, the Danish maid, completes it by adding Thomas to the picture.

GRANDMA LIZZIE WHITE (*Ravensgill**), grandmother of Bob* and Dick White and widow of Clifford Patrick White, who was accused of the murder of her father, Abraham Dinsdale. Grandma White, also often referred to as Lizzie, is eccentric, demanding, and imperious. Erratic and unpredictable in behavior and in dress, she may fuss and fume over real or imagined slights, deliberately trying to make her family feel guilty, and she may dress quite fashionably on occasion and on others haul out long out-of-date attire. Sometimes her hair is blue and sometimes ginger colored. She is tart-tongued and inclined to decorate facts. She enjoys the cinema, is a haphazard housekeeper, likes to go on outings, and has tried hard to bring up the boys properly. Just what part she played in the death of her father and in her husband's escape and subsequent death is left open in the novel. She is the book's most interesting character.

GRANDMOTHER (*Comfort Herself**), Comfort's father's mother, a staunch African matriarch who rules her large family with an iron hand. She can be imperious, sulky, posturing, demanding,

and self-righteous. She insists the children be
obedient, industrious, and respectful. She is
much like Granny* Barton, her counterpart in
England. Comfort likes her and tries to please
her, yet the girl realizes that to do the things
she wants to do, like going to market to get
out of the confinement of the village, she will
have to be as crafty and wily as the old woman.
Grandmother is uneducated by white standards,
yet has managed to provide well for her family
and accumulate property and is considered
wealthy. The reader never learns the source of
her disappointment with Mante*, Comfort's
father, but it has something to do with his
marrying Margaret and not sending his nephews
and nieces to school.

GRANDMOTHER HOLBEIN (*The Robbers**), widow of a
famous general who lives by Queen's Grace and
Favour in an apartment in a castle. An imaginative woman, she has raised Philip since he was
an infant, entering into his make believe and
being sensitive to his strong emotions but she
has also taught him to behave and to think for
himself. When her son remarries and decides to
take Philip, she feels she cannot stand in his
way, but after Philip gets into trouble and his
father plans to send him to boarding school, she
comes to London, accuses her son of being a
bully, reclaims her grandson, and does her best
to patch up the break with the family of his
friend, Darcy* Jones.

GRANDPA (*Kept in the Dark**), past eighty, father
of the children's mother who has so disapproved
of her marriage to a Jewish actor that he has
never met her children until their father's
illness makes it necessary that they go to live
with him. A former soldier and a self-made
wealthy man, he orders people about and tells
the children, "In Rome you do what Romans do
[and] I'm the Chief Roman." When David*, his
grandson by a former marriage, arrives and
begins to manipulate everyone in the household,
Grandpa becomes strangely passive, blackmailed
by his fear that David will somehow hurt the
children, and he comes near to having a heart
attack when trying to prevent David from taking
Bosie* off in the car. When David flees the

police on the motorcycle he has   forced Grandpa
to buy for   him, the old man   resumes his former
manner.

GRANDPA BAGTHORPE (*Ordinary Jack**),   the patri-
arch of the family, who, Uncle* Parker suggests,
has S. D., Selective   Deafness. He makes off-cue
remarks, watches TV   a   lot,   and is generally
oblivious to the zany activities going on around
him.

GRANDPA FITCH (*A Dog So Small**),   Ben Blewitt's
kind, loving,   nonassertive grandfather, husband
of Granny* Fitch and   father of Mrs.* Blewitt. A
workingman of limited   earnings, now retired, he
took a   pledge not to   drink after the birth of
his first child and   henceforth always turned
over his paycheck to his wife, who managed their
resources capably. He continues   to defer to her
judgment, occasionally attempting to temper what
seems   to   be   a   harsh decision   or   remark   by
adding   a   short   postscript   to   a   letter   or
furtively making a statement from behind a
gnarled hand. He had half-promised Ben a dog for
his   birthday, and after Granny sends a wool-
work one instead, Grandpa   tries in various ways
to   make it   up to   Ben. Ben's understanding of
his   Grandpa's guilt   and his   attempts to
alleviate it   provide some   of the   story's most
moving moments. At the end, Grandpa helps Ben to
see that Ben   must accept Brown for   what he is.
If Ben   is going to keep   Brown, this acceptance
will be necessary, an   attitude, of course, that
reflects his   own philosophy of   life with
Granny. Grandpa is   well   drawn, likeable,   and
convincing.

GRANDPA   JOE   (*Charlie   and   the   Chocolate
Factory**),   one   of Charlie   Bucket's   four
grandparents. He and the other grandparents
spend all   their time in   bed, with two   at each
end of the   only bed in the   poverty-stricken
household.   Grandpa Joe   is   ninety-six   and
one-half years old   and has not been   out of bed
in   twenty   years, but,   when   Charlie   wins   a
ticket to Willy* Wonka's Chocolate Factory,
Grandpa Joe jumps to the floor and does a
victory dance in his pajamas. Earlier he gave
Charlie the last few coins from his old leather

purse for "a fling at finding the last ticket."
Grandpa Joe is chosen by the family to accompany
Charlie on the factory tour and finds it very
exciting. Like the other figures in the book, he
is too distorted to be credible as a person in
his own right, but, since everything that goes
on in the story is on the level of an extended
comic book, he fits the nonsense. Some have
found Dahl's* depiction of the aged offensive,
however.

THE GRANGE AT HIGH FORCE (Turner*, Phillip, ill.
W. T. Mars, Oxford, 1965; World, 1967), mystery
novel set in the Midlands district of England in
the mid-twentieth century. Three boys, Arthur*
Ramsgill, son of a sheep farmer, Peter* Beck-
ford, the youngest son of the rector of All
Saints Church at Darnley, and David* Hughes, son
of a cabinet maker (all of whom appeared in
Turner's previous mystery, *Colonel Sheperton's
Clock*), become interested in the question of
what happened to the statue of Our Lady which
was supposedly taken from the church at the time
of Henry VIII. When they visit the deserted and
badly deteriorating Church of Little St. Mary at
High Force, they run into the new occupants of
Folly Grange, retired Admiral* Sir John
Beauchamp-Troubridge and his man-of-all-work,
Guns* Kelly. They not only make temporary
repairs on the Yellow Peril, the bike that
mechanically inclined Peter has damaged on the
mountain roads, but also show the boys around
the Grange, give them tea, and tour with them
the pigeon-infested Little St. Mary's. Soon they
are all involved in cleaning and restoring
Little St. Mary's, which Peter's father has had
to take under his wing. All of this angers the
owner of the Grange, Miss* Cadell-Twitten, an
eccentric elderly bird lover who lives nearby in
Bird Cottage. They find a picture of All Saints
Church in 1790, at the time Miss Cadell-
Twitten's ancestor had a lovely Doom window
replaced with a gaudy Queen Charlotte window by
his architect, Gothic Adams, who lived at the
Grange and evidently removed the clerestory
arcade and the statue at the same time. The
arcade they find lining the staircase at the
Grange, but although there is a niche which
might have held the statue, it is filled in and

plastered over. Miss Cadell-Twitten hints that
she knows the whereabouts of the statue, but she
won't tell them because their noise scares her
birds. Later research in the library and church
records proves that Sir Joshua Cadell and Gothic
Adams quarrelled, that Sir Joshua smashed the
Doom window, and that Adams left the statue to
All Saints Church but only to whoever could find
it, since he didn't trust Sir Joshua to hand it
over at his death. Equally interesting to the
boys, the admiral, and Guns is the problem of
how to test-fire the ballista the boys have made
and the eighteenth-century cannon owned by the
admiral. With the ballista they have a satisfying afternoon demolishing an old calliope Guns
has rigged for a target, but the cannon
presents a bigger problem, since Sergeant
Macintosh, the local police officer, has warned
them that it is illegal to make or set off
explosives. They finally settle on hauling the
cannon to a pond near a quarry and timing their
shots to coincide with the blasts. By the time
they have wrecked and sunk the "battleship" made
of junk by Guns and the boys, a storm has begun,
and they make their way with difficulty back to
the main road and the Ramsgill farm. There they
find a crisis situation: most of the sheep are
down from the high pastures but not yet in
shelter, and one sizeable bunch still needs to
be brought in from High Barn. Arthur hitches the
snow plow to the tractor and with David and Guns
sets off on the difficult rescue mission, while
the others help Mr. Ramsgill at the farm. The
next day they try to get the admiral's Rolls
Royce back to the Grange, with Arthur plowing a
path ahead with the tractor. When they reach a
place so drifted over that they have to blast,
the admiral sends David, the only one who can
manage snowshoes, ahead to see if Miss
Cadell-Twitten is all right. He finds her
cottage almost snowed under and has to enter
through an upper window. He discovers the old
woman disoriented and without food or fire. He
gets supplies from the Grange and, when the
others get there, helps her on a plank path they
build to get across to the Grange. Revived by
the warmth and food, Miss Cadell-Twitten
gratefully tells them where the statue is:
still in its niche in the Grange, plastered

over by Gothic Adams so that Sir Joshua could
not find her. This is a peculiarly flaccid
mystery, predictable and without great interest
in its main question. It is difficult to believe
in three boys, apparently junior-high age, being
so involved in finding a statue, and almost as
difficult to accept the total involvement of the
adults in firing the ballista and the cannon.
The tone is less like a mystery than an Arthur
Ransome* holiday adventure, with the grown-ups
joining the children in a jolly game of
make-believe. Still, the descriptions of the
churches, the Grange, the countryside, and
particularly the trips through the storm to
rescue the sheep and Miss Cadell-Twitten are
strong and vivid. The boys, especially Arthur,
speak in a very British slang that is often
genuinely funny. Carnegie Winner.

GRANIA (*Children of the Red King**), daughter of
Cormac, the Red King of Connacht in thirteenth-
century Ireland. A girl with flaming red hair
and high spirits, she rides disguised as a boy
to rescue her younger brother, Fergus*, when she
is nine, and at twelve she leads him in a
dangerous night journey through the bog to her
father's secret camp to persuade Cormac to make
his peace with the Normans. She has inherited
something of her father's quick temper and as a
young child has difficulty holding it in check
when goaded by her disagreeable and jealous
cousin, Mairi.

GRANNY BARTON (*Comfort Herself**), Comfort's
mother's mother, who lives with Grandad* in
Smithy Cottage in the village of Penfold in
Kent. Comfort's social worker, Miss Hanker,
arranges for Comfort to live with the Bartons
after her mother dies. Granny is out of tune
with children, self-pitying, self-righteous,
overly conscious of appearances, snobbish, judgmental, and yet thoroughly devoted to Comfort
and to making Comfort happy. She is afraid of
spoiling Comfort. Evidently, she and Grandad
disapproved of their daughter's "hippy" way of
life and her marriage to Mante*, and Granny
doesn't want Comfort to turn out the same way.
She doesn't want Comfort to play with the
village children, but relents when she sees how

important friends are to Comfort. She is a mixture of contradictory qualities. Her counter-part in Africa is Grandmother*.

GRANNY FITCH (*A Dog So Small**), Ben Blewitt's pragmatic, frugal, strong-minded grandmother, Grandpa* Fitch's wife, and Mrs.* Blewitt's mother. The mother of eight, she made do on a workingman's limited salary and now sees to it that they get along on their small pension. She can be fussy, for example, about Young Tilly making the linoleum dirty, and Grandpa tends to cater to her. She has poor eyesight, so Grandpa and Ben read to her, often from the Bible, in scenes which contribute a pleasant, warm, sometimes humorous, and occasionally symbolic note to the story; for example, after reading the story of Noah to her, Ben awakens to a rainbow. Arthritic, she no longer can write, so Grandpa does that for her, adding little notes that she never sees that succinctly express his point of view about things. She is a woman of conscience who truly feels sorry for Grandpa's impulsive half-promise of a dog but also comes to see that her substitution of the wool-work Chihuahua dog, though it was one of her most precious possessions, was wrong, too. When she visits the pigsty while Ben is playing with Young Tilly's pups, the reader can see that she is not cold or domineering but tries to be fair and open-minded. When Ben leaves with Brown, she perceptively sums up matters: "People get their heart's desire...and then they have to begin to learn how to live with it." Next to Ben, she is the most interesting figure in the book, a well-drawn, convincing character.

GRANNY RANDALL (*The Way to Sattin Shore**), stubborn, domineering, secretive, astute, physically infirm matriarch of the household, grandmother of Kate*, Ran*, and Lenny* Tranter, and mother of Kitty* Tranter. Her room opens off the front hallway, and everyone who enters must pass by it: "as long as the door stood ajar, Granny was there, the watcher." After receiving the note in violet-colored ink from Nanny* Tranter saying that Fred Tranter has returned to Sattin from Australia, Granny somehow accumulates a large sum of banknotes,

intending to buy him off. She stores them in the
loft and manages to get them down herself, but
not without shutting Syrup the tomcat in the
loft, where he makes cat-messes that anger
Kitty. Kitty blames Lenny, and family rows
ensue. At the end, Granny gives Kate the big
old tray that Kate used to slide on during the
February snowfall. She gives it to her,
instructs her not to slide with it though she
knows Kate would love to, and then spitefully
tells her there won't be any snow in Australia.
Since Granny is behind so much of the past and
present action and is such a potentially malign
influence, she is the most interesting figure in
the novel. Her foil is Nanny* Tranter.

GRANNY REARDUN (Garner*, Alan, ill. Michael
Foreman, Collins, 1977; Collins, 1978), short,
realistic novel of family and neighborhood life,
second in the quartet of books that "form a saga
tracing four generations of a working class
family in Chorley, a small town in Cheshire,
England." Joseph*, son of Mary, grandson of
Mary's Father* (the stonemason of *The Stone
Book**), and a "granny reardun" (a child
possibly illegitimate raised by grandparents),
has reached his last day of school and knows he
must declare his choice of occupation. Though he
admires Grandfather's craft, which can be seen
throughout the village, he knows that he cannot
follow in Grandfather's footsteps. While Grandfather struggles to build a wall with inferior
stone (all that remains to be quarried), and
Damper Latham, the carrier, and Grandfather belt
out temperance songs to the tunes Joseph plays
on his cornet, Joseph knows he approaches
closer to having to make a decision. As he
stands on the school porch and gazes outward
through the stone arch that frames it, he sees
the steeple his grandfather built and knows the
answer--that though the steeple bears the
imprint of Grandfather's chisel, the golden
cock that crowns it is the work of the smith
and the smith's work always tops Grandfather's.
Later, while proud, imperious, beer-drinking
Grandfather finishes the wall with worthy stone
from the house of the ousted Allmans, Joseph
announces his decision, prodded by Damper--that
he wishes to be apprenticed to Jump James, the

smith. He is amazed when Grandfather approves
of his choice and reason--that Joseph must get
"somewhere aback of you"--and so announces it
to the world. The strong old man, who, as Mary's
father, dominated the first book, rules this
one, too, even though the story is primarily
Joseph's, with his demand for worthy stone, his
boisterous singing, and his "who-whoop" by
which he summons Joseph home echoing through the
village. The story can stand alone as the
account of a momentous day in which a youth
makes a life decision but also contributes
significant fleshing-out details for the other
three books. There is some humor of situation
and irony, and the understated, poetic style of
the first book, punctuated with local terms,
persists, making the reader work more than is
usual in children's books but adding greatly to
the book's impact and distinctiveness. Choice;
Fanfare.

GRANNY WHITTACKER (*Fire and Hemlock**), Polly*
Whittacker's no-nonsense grandmother, who takes
her in when both her parents have essentially
rejected her. Granny is unduly angry that Polly
has wandered into Hunsdon House; she is
suspicious of Tom* Lynn and dislikes Seb* Leroy;
but it is not until the final day that Polly
discovers that Granny knows more about the
otherworldly nature of the place and people, her
own husband, a violinist, having been a victim
of Laurel* Leroy's fatal attraction and the
nine-year sacrifice in lieu of the king. Because
of this knowledge, she supports Polly in her
effort to free Tom from the spell.

GRANPA UTTERY (*Annerton Pit**), retired mining
engineer who spends his time following up ghost
stories and other reports of the paranormal in
order to debunk them. A quiet, rational man, he
has been particularly interested in how his
blind grandson, Jake* Bertold, senses presences
in a room, knows people's intentions from their
voices, and has other seemingly impossible
perceptions. Because he and Jake have been very
close, the boy is especially worried to find
Granpa cold and ill in the caravan where he is a
prisoner, particularly because he is susceptible
to pneumonia. After they have escaped from the

mine, Jake longs to have a good talk with his grandfather, hoping the old man can explain or at least help him deal with the memory of the presence he has felt in the mine at the spot where the victims of the 1837 disaster were found.

GRAN RIDLEY (*Danger at Black Dyke**), Geordie* Bickerson's grandmother, who took him when his mother died and his father abandoned him. He has been living with her for three years. Perceptive and intelligent, she quietly keeps tabs on the boys' activities and knows more about what is going on at Black Dyke than they think. She is wise in country ways and knows the Northumberland area well, since she grew up there and has lived there all her life. At the end, it is revealed that she and her playmates had also played in the old farmhouse and had searched for treasure there. Finding none and being ordered from the place for their safety, she and her friends put together a box of their precious childhood possessions and left it in the passage to be found "millions of years" in the future. Geordie and his friends discover the box. Gran is a good character, convincing and likeable.

A GRASS ROPE (Mayne*, William, ill. Lynton Lamb, Oxford, 1957; Dutton, 1962), realistic novel of family life that takes place one week recently in the Yorkshire Hills, in which some schoolchildren unravel the mystery behind a local legend involving a lost treasure. Little Mary* Owland, about six, who believes firmly in fairies, her sister, Nan*, perhaps twelve, of a more practical bent, and Adam* Forrest, Head Boy at Thornton, Nan's grammar school, who is painting the trim and signboard of the Dyson family's Unicorn Inn that stands over the pass from the Owlands' Lew Farm, decide to see if there is anything to the old rumor that treasure lies under Yowncorn Yat (Unicorn Gate), the great cliff that dominates the region. The treasure is said to have been attached to the collars of a pack of hounds and a unicorn magicked into the Yat by a Dyson ancestor who was courting an Owland girl whose father opposed the match. The girls and Peter* Dyson, about

eleven and also in awe of Adam, help Adam clean
up the inn signboard and in the process discover
clues that seem to support the legend: four
layered, rampant unicorns, the names of the
hounds, Hewlin and Balanter, and most important,
a hunting horn that still works. While Mary
believes staunchly in the old tale, Nan doesn't
but plays along to spare Mary's feelings, and
Adam, who has a bet going with the Headmaster
over the treasure, seeks a scientific explanation. He appears to be on the way to one when
one night Peter blows the horn, and it can be
clearly heard over the pass at Lew Farm,
apparently through an echo phenomenon. Then
Peter's mother mentions the old belief that
maidens can catch unicorns with grass ropes, and
Mary fashions a rope. Late one moonlit night she
sneaks out alone, determined to capture the
unicorn. She crawls into the Yat through a
tunnel that lies under the waterfall where old
Dyson drowned digging for the lost treasure and
which connects with an abandoned mineshaft, the
area she is convinced is fairyland and where the
hounds and unicorn must be. There, in a small
moonlit glade, she encounters a fox cub and
fashions for it a collar and chain out of thin
metal material she finds, believing it is one of
the lost hounds. The family find her not long
after her disappearance, and Mr. Owland explains
the legend--that the hunting horn, echoing
through the hills, drew the hounds up the pass
and over the rim of the cliff, where they
plunged to their deaths in the water-filled
mineshaft, thus supporting Adam's conviction
that the story has a rational explanation.
Moreover, the collar and chain Mary attached to
the baby fox seem to be made of silver. Mary
appears to be right to some extent, however,
because the stick she tethered the baby fox to
looks very much like a unicorn's horn. Some
subtle humor, much of it adult; real-sounding
conversation, through which much of the action
is revealed; strong local color and sense of the
geography of the region; well-delineated
characters, some of whom employ local dialect;
an easygoing style; an affectionate tone; and
warm, convincing interpersonal relationships all
make for an unusually effective story. Carnegie
Winner; Choice.

GRAVELLA ROLLER (*The Piemakers**), ten-year-old only child of Arthy*, respected piemaker of Danby Dale, and his wife, Jem*. Gravella sometimes dreams of becoming a famous actress, but "the plain truth of it was that whenever another pie was on the go she could feel her own heart treacherously thudding and her tongue aching to ask questions about it." She knows she'll probably follow in her father's footsteps. She already has an important responsibility in the family business, preparing the seasonings. She doesn't really like her name, yet is grateful that she wasn't a boy because then her name would be Gravy. She affects the action little, being mostly an observer, but she thinks she may have been the cause of Arthy's failure with the king's pie and she feels guilty about it. She fears she may have miscopied the king's recipe and thus caused the pie to be over-peppered. She is a little ashamed of the possibility that her mother may be descended from a witch, and she doesn't much like her cousin Bates, a fat, disagreeable boy who eats too much. Her observations about the behavior and attitudes of her parents, her Uncle Crispin, Aunt Essie, and Cousin Bates are shrewd and humorous, but never unkind.

GRAY, NICHOLAS STUART (1922-1981), born in Scotland; stage actor and director, author of humorous, inventive fantasies for children, and best known for his plays for the young. After attending various private grammar schools, he abandoned formal education at fifteen for the stage, publishing his first play when he was seventeen. Most of his plays are based on folk tales or stories by Hans Christian Andersen, like *The Tinder Box* (Oxford, 1951), *New Clothes for the Emperor* (Oxford, 1957), and *The Marvelous Story of Puss in Boots* (Oxford, 1955). *Over the Hills to Fabylon** (Oxford, 1954; Hawthorn, 1970), his first published novel, was commended for the Carnegie award. It is a happy, marchen-type story of original concept and many incidents and characters set in a magical city which, when endangered, can be moved to another place. Among his dozen other books for middle-grade readers are collections of short stories: *Mainly in Moonlight* (Faber, 1965; Meredith,

1967), *The Edge of Evening* (Faber, 1976), and *A Wind from Nowhere* (Faber, 1978); and the novels *Down in the Cellar* (Dobson, 1961), about how a mystical woman helps some children hide an escaped convict; *The Seventh Swan* (Dobson, 1962), about a young man who has a swan's wing for a right arm; *The Apple-Stone* (Dobson, 1965; Meredith, 1969), about an apple that talks; *Grimbold's Other World* (Faber, 1963; Meredith, 1968), about an orphaned boy and a talking cat; and *The Stone Cage* (Dobson, 1963), a reworking of the Rapunzel story. He acted in repertory theaters in London and throughout England and included Hamlet and Iago among his roles. He also published a novel for adults, *Killer's Notebook* (Dobson, 1976). He lived in England and Scotland and died in London.

GREAT AUNT SOPHY (*The Borrowers**), old woman in whose house the Clock family of Borrowers lives (Pod*, Homily*, and Arrietty*) and who is visited by the boy* who makes friends with the Clocks. Great Aunt Sophy has been bedridden in her upstairs room for many years. Pod often borrows from her room. She enjoys watching him and talking to him about bygone days. She believes that he comes out of her decanter of fine Old Pale Madeira wine. She adds humor and a dimension of credibility to the story.

THE GREATEST GRESHAM (Avery*, Gillian, ill. John Verney*, Collins, 1962), novel of a very traditional and repressive London Victorian household and the changes wrought when two unconventional youngsters move in next door. All three Gresham children are urged (commanded actually) by their martinet father, Captain Gresham, to live up to their "great name," a requirement that sits easy upon Amy, 8, worries Henry, 10, who always feels such exhortations as a reproach, and kindles in Julia, 12, a burning desire to be famous, though she has no idea how to proceed. When the Holts move in next door, the first other children on a street mostly of cranky old maids, Julia and Henry realize right away that Captain and Mrs. Gresham will probably think them unsuitable and forbid them to play together, but they are really fascinated by Kate, who is about Henry's age and leads a rich

imaginative life he envies, and Richard, an
older boy studying for a scholarship at Christ's
Church College, Oxford, who treats them
patronizingly but has exciting ideas. Richard,
who spends most of his time reading and is
adored by his younger sister, whom he calls
Woggle, decides to take the Greshams in hand and
help them develop a little independence of mind.
He proposes that they start the Society for the
Achieving of Greatness, Broadening of Horizons,
Enlarging of Ideas, and the Cultivating of
Independent Minds, to be called SAGBOHEICIM.
Each of them will have to pass a test for
membership, starting with Amy who, Richard
decides, must give up her cuddler, or security
blanket, and Mrs. Vonnister, her disreputable,
earless stuffed rabbit. Eager to be part of a
secret society, Amy hands over her shabby
treasures, and Richard bundles them together
with a leash from Kate's imaginary wolfhound,
swings them about his head, and lets them fly.
They land in the chimney of the house belonging
to Miss Moule, whom they call the Old Dame.
Julia's test is more complicated: to lay a
wreath on the tomb of Lord Byron in Westminister
Abbey. She makes a limp and wilted wreath, and
without permission she goes with Kate and
Richard. At the Abbey the man in a black gown of
whom she asks the location of the tomb is
incensed that she suggests that such a man would
be buried there, the Ladies of the Putney Bright
Hour, on tour, try to adopt her for the morning,
and she finally leaves her wreath in one of the
banner-covered stalls lining the chapel. On the
train back, trying to read a book of Byron's
poetry that Richard has loaned her, she finds
that the woman next to her is shocked at her
choice and discovers that it is the Old Dame.
Henry's task is to climb the large apple tree in
the Holt's yard, a tree he has always yearned to
climb, but at the critical moment his father
sticks his head out the window, Henry goes weak
in the knees, is shamed before them all, and is
roundly scolded for being a sniveling weakling
by Papa. In fact, Papa is so enraged by Henry
that he rather lightly passes over the Old
Dame's complaints about Julia. Richard then
presides over the SAGBOHEICIM initiation in the
cellar of the Holt house, in which each victim

is roped to a stone table and Richard, shrouded
in an old window curtain like some ancient
Druid, pretends to disembowel the initiate, a
ceremony that amuses Amy and excites Julia, but
turns imaginative Henry into a screaming
hysteric. Mild, scholarly Mr. Holt rescues him,
and the Gresham maid hustles them home, where
they learn that a chimney sweep at Miss Moule's,
exploring the reason for a smoking fireplace,
has discovered Mrs. Vonnister. Henry takes the
blame for throwing it, since they want to keep
the Holts out of their father's notice. When
Richard next decides to take them in hand, he
decrees that, because she cares too much about
what people think, Julia shall ride around the
neighborhood on the milkman's cart dressed in an
old white gown of her mother's from the
dressing-up box. Though she finds the idea
horrifying and the milkman uncooperative, Julia
bravely carries out her assignment, only to be
reported again by the Old Dame. Papa is so
enraged that she is locked in the guest room for
several days, with Henry and Amy forbidden to
open the door or talk to her. Since nearsighted
Julia reads at every opportunity, one of the
reasons she and Richard interest each other, the
hardest part of her imprisonment is that there
are no books in the guest room, but Henry
manages to smuggle in some reading material,
including the only book he could buy for a
penny, *Remarkable Instances of Early Piety.*
These sad stories of children's deaths make her
weep, and her parents, finding her sobbing,
think she has repented and release her. She has
a hard time keeping up her vow of piety, but she
rather enjoys her father's embarrassment when
she kneels to beg his forgiveness and says
things like, "Yes, indeed, dear Papa, let it be
as you will." Just before Richard is to take his
exam for the scholarship, Henry is recuperating
from severe measles and Amy from chicken pox, so
Julia is the only one to respond to the message
from the Holts for a party to pour a libation to
the gods. Since Papa has forbidden her to visit
the Holts or to allow them to come to the
Gresham house, they stay on their own sides of
the fence, but Julia passes a mixture of oil,
vinegar, Worcester sauce, and brandy through the
hedge for the libation and watches Richard's

elaborate ritual, after which he downs the rest of the mixture. Kate announces later that he was sick all night, must have failed the examination, and will probably kill himself. After Julia reports this to Henry, he rushes off by himself to the school in Fareham to check the examination results posted on the gate. On the way home, feeling far from well, he is taken in hand by the Holts' Aunt B, a dressmaker who haphazardly keeps house for them, and Julia, who has guessed where he is, arrives at the station just in time to see them accosted by the Old Dame. Aunt B stands up to the Old Dame, calls her a nagging busybody, and effectually scares her off, but this time Henry is very ill. Papa is in Scotland on a hunting holiday, and Mamma does not want to worry him by telling him of Henry's condition. Amy, realizing that Mamma is as afraid of Papa as Henry and Julia are, sends a telegram telling him to come home. When he arrives, Henry is too scared to look at him, and just as Amy is explaining to him that everyone except her is afraid of him, Aunt B enters and in her hearty way convinces him that Henry has been heroic, rushing off to try to save Richard by finding that he did, indeed, win a scholarship. Richard has even found a medal from a dog collar and had it inscribed, "SAGBOHEICIM Medal for Greatness," for Henry. In a highly amusing and convincing way, the novel recreates the 1890s from the point of view of properly brought-up but lively children. The greatest strength is in characterization of timid, worried Henry, dreamy Julia, matter-of-fact Amy, and their "ragey" Victorian Papa. Carnegie Com.

GREAT EXPECTATIONS (Dickens*, Charles, Chapman, 1861; Peterson, 1861), chronical of the strange rise and fall of the fortunes of a country boy in Victorian England. Pip* (Philip Pirrip), the first-person narrator, is an orphan, brought up "by hand," as she repeatedly reminds him, by his bad-tempered sister, wife of the blacksmith Joe* Gargery. When he is still very young—able to read but not yet nearly old enough to be apprenticed—he comes upon a convict on the marsh near his home who has escaped from one of the prison ships anchored nearby. Under the man's terrible threats, Pip steals food and a

file for him and then lives in fear of both the
convict and his conscience. Some time later Pip
is summoned to the home of Miss* Havisham, a
local lady of wealth and mystery, who has
communicated to Joe's Uncle Pumblechook that she
wants a boy to come and play. Unusual as this
request seems, it is not as odd as her home,
which is kept almost entirely dark and exactly
as it was years before on the day she was to be
married and was jilted, even to the table set
with wedding cake, which is crumbled to dust and
covered with cobwebs. Miss Havisham herself
still wears her wedding gown and veil, now
yellowed with age. There he meets Estella*, a
girl about his own age, who treats him with
scorn but at Miss Havisham's direction plays
card games with him and with whom he falls
immediately in love. This visit is repeated
every few days for some time, with Miss Havisham
lavishing extravagant praise on Estella,
watching with evident delight as she beats Pip
at the games and insults him, and urging her to
"break their hearts, my dear." The repeated
visits cause Pip's sister and Uncle Pumblechook
to speculate that Miss Havisham is planning to
"do something for the boy," but what this is,
they don't know. After some months or years, she
suddenly appears to notice that Pip has grown
taller. She directs him to bring Joe with him at
his next visit, arranges the papers for his
apprenticeship as blacksmith, gives Joe twenty-
five guineas for the time Pip has spent
"playing" at her house, and makes it clear he is
to expect nothing else from her. Pip's view of
another way of life, however, has spoiled him
for his new role, and though he works steadily
for Joe, who is simple but thoroughly good, his
heart is not in it. After about a year, Pip's
sister is attacked by an intruder, struck with a
convict's leg-iron which has been filed apart,
and thereafter remains an invalid and unable to
talk. Biddy*, a girl not much older than Pip,
who has helped at his village school, comes to
care for her and the household, and she and Pip
continue to study when they can. In the fourth
year of his apprenticeship, a lawyer named
Jaggers* appears and tells Joe and Pip that an
undisclosed person has directed him to say that
Pip has "great expectations" and to arrange that

he be educated as a gentleman. Pip's family and the local people assume, of course, that Miss Havisham is his benefactor, and in the ensuing years her occasional requests that he escort Estella somewhere convince Pip that she intends him eventually to marry this adopted daughter, though the girl continues to be cold to his devotion and cruel by her attentions to other men in his presence. Pip first studies with Mr. Matthew Pocket, a relative of Miss Havisham, and lives with his son, Herbert, who calls him Handel and who is himself "looking about" for a position in a cheerfully ineffectual way. Together they live a largely idle life and run up a considerable debt, though Pip secretly invests the 500 pounds that Jaggers hands over to him on his twenty-first birthday in a partnership in a business for Herbert. Pip shamefully neglects Joe and, on the rare occasions when he visits the family, he patronizes Biddy. When Pip is twenty-three, a filthy, seafaring man appears one night at his lodgings, and Pip recognizes him as the convict he helped in his childhood. To his horror, he learns that the convict and not Miss Havisham is his benefactor, and has come back from Australia to see how his protege is shaping up as a gentleman. Since this man, Abel Magwitch*, was transported as a convict, he is a fugitive, and Pip must hide him and make arrangements to get him safely out of the country. Magwitch, however, has an old enemy from the days before he was in the prison ship. His enemy alerts the police to Magwtch's presence, and he is recaptured just as Pip and Herbert are about to get him aboard a ship for Hamburg. He is tried and sentenced to death, but dies before he can be hanged, and Pip's expectations die with him, Magwitch's fortune being forfeit to the crown. Pip is trying to give up his rooms and arrange to work for a living when he is struck ill and also arrested for debt. Good, honest Joe comes, pays Pip's debt from his savings, and nurses Pip back to health. Pip thinks he might mend his life by marrying Biddy, but arrives home just after Biddy and Joe have been married. Thereafter, Pip goes to work for Herbert's firm, rises to partner, repays Joe and Biddy, and becomes a devoted uncle to their son, whom they name Pip. The book has been published with two different endings. In the more popular one, Pip eventually revisits the site of Miss Havisham's house, meets Estella, whose brutal, worthless husband has since died, and, the experience having softened her heart, finds true love with her at last. In the more artistic ending, he remains a bachelor and meets Estella only once, by chance, when he is walking with little Pip. She has married a second time to a doctor and shows she has softened her heart by kissing the child, thinking he is Pip's son. The book's theme, that it is disastrous to want and expect undeserved money and social position, is overshadowed by Dickens's gallery of memorable characters, some of which have only a tangential relationship to the main plot: Uncle Pumble-chook, who always claims credit for Pip's rise in fortune, quite without reason; Mr. Wopsle, the clerk at the village church who becomes a delighted third-rate actor; Mr. Jaggers, Pip's guardian; Mrs. Pocket, who is the daughter of a knight and whose social pretensions cause her to neglect her children and ignore the chaos of her family life; Mr. John Wemmick*, Jaggers's clerk; Bently Drummle, the spoiled, sulky, proud rich boy who marries Estella; Clara Barley, who marries Herbert; Clara's drunken father; and many others. The convoluted plot ties these characters together through a series of unlikely coincidences. The novel is rich in satiric comments and scenes of life of both the wealthy and the poor of the period, and remains a favorite among Dickens's novels, despite the unlikely premise that a convict would devote his fortune to a boy he met in a chance encounter and despite, or possibly because of, the grotesque scenes at Miss Havisham's house. Choice.

THE GREAT GALE (Burton*, Hester, ill. Robin Jacques, Oxford, 1960; *THE FLOOD AT REEDSMERE*, World, 1968), historical novel about the great flood that ravaged the east coast of England in the winter of early 1953. The village of the story and all the characters except one, Rod* Cooper, are fictitious; the general events are true. Two schoolboys, Ned Brewster and Mark* Vaughan, skip school one Thursday late in Janu-

ary and carelessly let out one of Farmer
Claypoole's cows. The animal plods and browses
her way to Reedsmere Gap in the narrow strip of
dunes along the North Sea, where she paws at the
rotting sandbags that form part of the defense
against the sea, tearing holes in them so the
sand trickles out and endangering the village
that lies beside the lake called Reedsmere
Broad. A violent wind comes up in the northwest
and joins with an unusually high tide, and on
Saturday night the village of Reedsmere is
flooded, the sea waters plunging through and
widening the breach of the disintegrating sand
bags. Mark and his sister, Mary*, 13, are home
alone that night in their comfortable house by
the Broad while their doctor father and nurse
mother dine with friends in a neighboring
village. The children observe sea water flowing
into the house under the door but keep their
wits and quickly move upstairs such perishables
as books and records, get out the family boat,
Donovan, and with considerable expertise,
pluck, and hard work, row over to the small
cottage of an elderly couple who live by the
Gap, Jim* and Hepzie* Foulger, and rescue them.
They all first take shelter in St. Mary's
Church, where quick-thinking, practical Canon
Crowfoot organizes games and singing to keep the
refugees and the choir boys warm and calm. When
rising waters flood the church, the villagers
move by boat to Reedsmere Hall, the residence
of Sir Bartlett and Lady Spekes. Fortunately
situated on higher ground, the Hall becomes
home for most of the village for several days.
Many people are transported there by Rod Cooper,
an airman from a nearby American base. A tall,
lanky youth in a rubber water suit, Cooper
heroically evacuates two or three people at a
time in a rubber dinghy. Mary has anxious
moments: she is separated from Mark and Jim,
whom Cooper later rescues from a roof top, and
the mother of her best village friend, Myrtle*
Beamish, suffers a bad head injury when her
house is swept away by the flood. Mopping up
operations involve many hours of very hard work.
Doctor and Mrs. Vaughan tend to the sick and
injured, caring for those they can and seeing
that others get to the hospital. For a while,
Mark helps the sandbaggers repair the breach at

the Gap, Mary scrubs the Vaughan house and cooks for refugees and workers, and both she and Mark help clean the Foulger place and paint and repair it. The Vaughan house becomes refuge for several nights for a homeless young couple with a new baby, the Throwers, and the sandbaggers sleep there. Spirits in the village rise enormously when the Queen pays a surprise visit to the Hall, an event that the reader does not witness but learns about through dialogue. The Saturday night after the flood sees Reedsmere Hall resounding with dancing and singing as the whole village celebrates the joy of their survival, and Monday morning finds Mary and Mark on the train returning to boarding school, more mature in outlook because of the harrowing experiences of the past week. The author builds up to the flood well, and the episodes set during the catastrophe are dramatic and exciting. At the book's midpoint--where mop-up begins--the pace flags in comparison. Such activities as sandbagging, cleaning out debris, and fixing food for workers, such activities have less intrinsic emotional appeal, although they are true to the facts of the situation. The last half of the book, however, depicts well the challenges facing the survivors of a flood, such problems as lack of food, potable water, and medicines, disrupted communication and transportation systems, hordes of well-meaning but nuisance-causing sightseers, divided families, and the stench and filth from the ooze that the receding waters leave behind. The book also shows well the encouragement people gain from cooperative effort, and the importance of a few strong leaders. There is some humor, for example, the efforts of Ned Brewster and his pal, Jimmy Bell, to rescue the Brewster hens and another neighbor's pet guinea pigs, and Mary's problems when she puts too much rice in the cooking pot and too much disinfectant in the wash water. The book's greatest strength lies in the author's matter-of-fact tone and her careful attention to homely detail. These factors anchor the events firmly in reality and convince the reader that they could indeed happen to real people. Views of English village life are clear, and the country dialect, spoken by all but the Canon, the Squire, and the

Vaughans (all of whom enjoy a higher social status) adds to the sense of location, gives the reader a sense of village society, and contributes liveliness to the narrative. This is a substantial novel in which the characters transcend the needs of the plot, and history and story blend well. Carnegie Com.

GREAT-GRANDMOTHER SCHOLAR (*The Haunting**), at eighty-eight the matriarch of the "papery" Scholar clan, Barney Palmer's dead mother's family. She has sharp, unfriendly eyes and a fetish for neatness, and no one in the family dares to cross her. She suspects that Barney may be a magician, the only one of his generation in their family. She herself was born a witch, but hated her ability, suppressed it, and kept it a secret. She was determined that the similar ability of her son, Great-Uncle* Cole, also be suppressed and that he become an ordinary, well-behaved boy like his brothers. He rebelled and ran away, severing ties with all the family and only contacted Barney in recent years. Mrs. Scholar represents overcontrolling parents.

GREAT-UNCLE COLE SCHOLAR (*The Haunting**), Barney Palmer's great-uncle on his mother's side, the black sheep of the family and the one Great-Grandmother* Scholar does not want anyone to talk about because he refused to suppress his magical powers as she wanted him to. He ran away from home and held odd jobs, turning up again after the death of his brother Barnaby in hopes of maintaining contact with his family through Barney. Once the story of his mother's ability as a witch comes out, the family has more sympathy for him, and he stays around, becoming friends with Troy* and often visiting the Palmers. He is at first an unlikeable character who becomes sympathetic in the course of the story.

GREAT-UNCLE GUY SCHOLAR (*The Haunting**), the Palmers' great-uncle on their mother's side. He is one of the first to notice that something special is happening to Barney and one of the first to think that Barney is a magician, the only one of his generation. When Tabitha* consults him in his capacity as a pediatrician about Barney's problems, he first suggests Barney may be struggling with his own peculiar psychological concerns, perhaps arising from guilt over being the cause of his mother's death (Barney's mother died when he was born). As a character, Guy is a functionary, the means by which readers are given information vital to the plot.

THE GREEN BOUGH OF LIBERTY (Rees*, David, Dennis Dobson, 1979), historical novel of the 1798 rebellion in Ireland, based on lives of the author's ancestors, who took part in the uprising. In County Wicklow, the Byrnes of Ballymanus are gentry, descended from the Lords of Ranelagh but now reduced to a living on a single farm owned by the eldest brother, Garret*, and worked by him and his two brothers, Billy* and young Ned*, 18. Their grandfather, their sister, Fanny, and Garret's wife, Mary, and infant son, Dermot, also live there, but it is understood that, since the place cannot support more than one family, Billy will become a priest and Ned, when he is twenty-one, will go off to become a soldier, not for the hated English but on the continent, probably for France. Ned is in no hurry, since their neighbor and distant cousin, Ellen Kennedy, has recently caught his fancy. Without knowing any of their inner secrets, Ned is aware that his brothers are part of the Society of United Irishmen, a group planning a revolt against English rule when French help arrives. Before that event, Cornelius Sinnott, a draper from Wicklow, brings word that the local leaders of the group have been found meeting at the home of Oliver Bond (the Leinster delegate to the National Directory of the United Irishmen) and have been arrested. Garret sees that this necessitates an immediate uprising. He and Billy leave, insisting that Ned, much to his chagrin, stay to protect the women and their home. He agrees with the proviso that if they decide to seek shelter with their relatives at Cabinteely, a wealthier branch of the family with English connections, he will escort them there and then be free to join the rebels. When a party of English soldiers arrives, Ned stops his grandfather from blasting them with his old musket, thereby preventing

them from all being arrested or shot, but he
refuses to give them letters from Garret and
Billy and is tied to the triangle, a wooden
structure the troops carry with them, and given
two lashes, a punishment which leaves his back
bleeding but is relatiavely mild, since many men
are beaten to death. The soldiers then set fire
to the thatch. Although Grandfather will not
leave the badly damaged house, which is
partially saved by a downpour of rain, Ned takes
the others, including Ellen and her mother, on
an arduous journey to Cabinteely. Before he
leaves to find his brothers, Ned gets Ellen to
promise to marry him when the war has been won.
As he makes his way across country, he comes
upon a conflict in Kilcullen and sees a terrible
massacre from his hiding place in a tree, which
he has climbed to get a better view.
Surprisingly, he finds both Garret and Billy in
the rebel camp at Hacketstown. He fights with
them in a couple of battles but is captured when
government forces attack the camp. After many
weeks in a miserable, filthy dungeon, he is
brought before General Dundas, who informs him
that he has been offered as a trade for Colonel
Tedford, a prisoner in the rebel camp now
directed by Garret. After months of waiting, he
and the English are both surprised by a sudden
successful rescue raid, led by Garret. At the
new rebel camp in the mountains, Ned finds
Ellen, who insisted on coming when she got news
that Ned was a prisoner. He marries Ellen and,
sickened by the war, leaves with her to try to
get back to Ballymanus. There they find
Grandfather, who has managed to repair the house
and who insists that Ned take over as manager.
Before long Fanny returns with bad news: Garret,
unable to hold out longer in the bitter weather,
has surrendered and is to be allowed to leave
for Germany, and Billy has been captured and is
to be tried. Ned and Fanny are not permitted to
attend the trial where he is sentenced to be
hanged, but they are allowed to visit him before
the execution. After several months of hard work
at Ballymanus, during which Grandfather dies and
Ellen becomes pregnant, Ned is summoned before
the English authorities and informed that since
the place belonged to Garret, it is forfeit to
the crown and will be seized, with all that is

in it, in a few days. Though Ned is bitter and rebellious, Fanny sensibly starts packing all their possessions and arranging for neighbors to help cart them away at night and store them. The morning before the English arrive, the family leaves Ballymanus for good, heading for Dublin and possibly intending later to join Garret in France. The disaster of the uprising is shown not only in what happened to this one family but also in vivid descriptions of the brutalities on both sides, particularly the floggings that laid bare the backbones of the Irish and the practice of giving "pitch caps," covering the hair with tar and setting it afire, a practice that did not kill but permanently deformed and often deranged the victim and was done frequently enough to give rise to a new class of people known as "croppies." The book is illustrated with drawings from the period. The strength of the novel lies more in its depiction of actual events than in characterizations, though Ned is adequate as a fiery young man who learns from experience and Billy emerges as a memorable figure. Other.

GREGORY THOMAS (*The Kitchen Madonna**), intense nine-year-old who decides to provide a "good place," a household shrine, in their London kitchen for their Ukrainian-born maid, Marta. An intelligent, self-absorbed boy, thin and with glasses, Gregory has never voiced the need for security and continuity that his professional parents have not given him and that Marta provides. Having to talk with people in his pursuit of the makings of his kitchen Madonna, he falls back on bookish phrases--"there is no other course open to me"; "could you make sure that a goodly proportion of those shiny jewelly-paper ones go in?" and to the salesclerk in Rostov's jewelers, haughtily, "I was told that you sell icons." To the surprise of his whole family, he makes several new friends during his endeavors.

THE GREY KING (Cooper*, Susan, ill. Michael Heslop, Chatto, 1975; Atheneum, 1975), fantasy novel set recently in Wales, fourth in The Dark Is Rising series. The story continues Will* Stanton's quest for the objects that will

eventually enable the Old Ones to destroy the
Dark. This time he follows clues found in the
inscription on the side of the Grail. Will is
sent to recover from a bout with hepatitis at
the farm of his uncle and aunt in the mountains
of northern Wales. There he initiates the search
for the golden harp with which he can awaken the
Six Sleepers whose help the Old Ones need to win
the final battle against the Dark. Will makes
friends with Bran* Davies, a white-haired youth
of mysterious background who is ostensibly the
son of a farmhand, Owen Davies. Together the two
boys travel an old pilgrim trail, Cadfan's Way,
and enter the mountain, where they win the harp
by correctly answering riddles put to them by
three blue-robed figures, one of whom is
Merriman* Lyon. They are opposed by the Grey
King, who, among other obstacles, causes a fire
on the mountain, sends his foxes, the legendary
migwn, to attack them and the sheep, and bodily
takes over a mean-tempered, neighboring farmer,
Caradog Prichard, inducing him to kill Cafall,
Bran's beloved white dog with silver eyes, and
to attempt to kill even Bran himself. Will is
persistent, however, and with the help of the
kindly, capable shepherd John Rowlands*, finally awakens the sleepers and learns from Owen
that Bran is the Pendragon, true son of King
Arthur. Dialogue is extensive and suits the
story in vocabulary and tone. Characters are
distinctly drawn, and, though the plot is
mechanical, incidents seem plausible and are
adventurous. Suspense is particularly high at
the end. Bran is the most interesting character,
much overshadowing Will, the protagonist. As in
the previous books in the series, Celtic
folklore strengthens the plot, which is not in
itself very compelling, contributes to setting,
builds atmosphere, which is the book's strongest
feature, and gives the story its sense of
dealing with important, timeless, universal
matters. Other books in the series are *Over
Sea, Under Stone* and *The Dark Is Rising**.
Carnegie Com.; Choice; Fanfare.

GRICE, FREDERICK (1910-   ), born the son of a
miner in Durham in the northern part of England,
the locale of his most convincing novels;
educator and writer best known for his

historical novels for young adolescent readers. Drawing heavily on his origins is the novel *The Bonnie Pit Laddie** (Oxford, 1960; as *Out of the Mines*, Watts, 1961), which was nominated for the Carnegie Medal, won the Other Award, and was named to the Fanfare lists. It describes vividly and believably the life of a colliery family like his own, focusing on strife between the miners and their oppressive bosses as seen from the vantage point of the twelve-year-old boy, Dick. Other novels set in the north country are *The Oak and the Ash* (Oxford, 1968) and *The Courage of Andy Robson* (Oxford, 1969). Of his other half-dozen novels, *Johnny-Head-in-Air* (Oxford, 1978) tells how the direction of a boy's life is influenced by finding the remains of a flying machine, a story that derives from Grice's experiences in the RAF, and *The Moving Finger* (Oxford, 1962; as *The Secret of the Libyan Caves*, Watts, 1963) relies on his service experiences in World War II in North Africa. *Aidan and the Strollers* (Cape, 1960; as *Aidan and the Strolling Players*, Duell, 1961), his first novel, recounts the experiences of traveling players during the British Regency. Grice's writing has been described as pleasingly romantic, loosely and inconsistently plotted, strong in characterization, and highly entertaining. He was educated at Johnston School in Durham and at King's College in the University of London, where he took a B.A. in English with honors. He received his teacher's diploma from Durham University and became assistant master at Dawson School in Durham. During World War II, he served as a lieutenant in the Royal Air Force and then returned to education to become Head of the English Department at Worcester College of Further Education until 1972. He married, became the father of two daughters, and lived in Worcester. His first publications were books of folktales. He has also written readers and books of verse and biography for adults. He has published some thirty books, most of them for youth.

GRIFFITHS, HELEN (1939-   ), born in London; writer noted for her unsentimental, keenly observed animal novels for middle-grade readers. Born just before World War II, she was evacuated to the north of England where she spent a happy childhood roaming farms and moors and developing the love for animals that is evident in her writings. Though her ambition was to become a farmer and she even worked on a Bedfordshire farm when she was sixteen, she took up secretarial training and held various office positions before 1959 when she met and married Pedro Santos de la Cal, a young Spaniard in the hotel business. The couple had three daughters and lived in Switzerland, Mallorca, and Madrid, as well as in London, before he died in 1973. After his death, she taught English in Madrid for a while. She published her first novel at sixteen, and by the time she was twenty-one and her first child was born she had published three more and had a contract for a fourth. Her first two books, *Horse in the Clouds* (Hutchinson, 1957; Holt, 1958) and *Wild and Free* (Hutchinson, 1958), and two later ones, *The Wild Heart* (Hutchinson, 1963; Doubleday, 1964) and *Stallion of the Sands* (Hutchinson, 1968; Lothrop, 1970), all about wild horses on the South American pampas, resulted from a book she read on Argentina. Several of her books have Spanish settings, among them *The Wild Horse of Santander** (Hutchinson, 1966; Doubleday, 1967), about the love between a blind boy and an intractable colt, which was commended for the Carnegie Medal. In addition to horse stories, she also wrote about dogs in such novels as *Leon* (Hutchinson, 1967; Doubleday, 1968), *Pablo* (Hutchinson, 1977; as *Running Wild*, Holiday, 1977), and *The Dog at the Window* (Hutchinson, 1984; Holiday, 1984); and about cats in *Moshie Cat: The True Adventures of a Majorcan Kitten* (Hutchinson, 1969; Holiday, 1970). Altogether she has published some two dozen novels for young readers and a novel for adults, *The Dark Swallows* (Hutchinson, 1966; Knopf, 1967).

GRIMNIR (*The Weirdstone of Brisingamen**), the Hooded One, enemy of Cadellin*, Susan, and Colin, cohort of Selina* Place. He dies at the end, killed with a double-edged sword at the hand of Cadellin, who, it turns out, is Grimnir's brother. Grimnir's real name is Govannon. Once a proper man, he studied the old lore and became a lore-master of renown, but "in his lust for knowledge he practised the forbidden arts, and the black magic ravaged his heart, and made a monster of him. He left the paths of day, and went to live, like Grendel of old, beneath the waters of Llynd-dhu, the Black Lake, growing mighty in evil...." Grimnir is the stereotypical wicked sorcerer, representing pure evil.

GRIZEL MAXWELL (*Kate Crackernuts**), mother of Kate Maxwell, who is called Kate Crackernuts. The widow of a noble, she lives like a peasant until she comes to the attention of Andrew Lindsay, the widowed laird who has a beautiful daughter, Katherine. Although she has never treated her own daughter well, when Grizel marries Andrew she becomes obsessed with the idea that Katherine will outshine Kate, and she employs an old local witch woman to cast a spell on her stepdaughter. Handsome and efficient, she is able to act the part of a good wife and at the same time secretly be a leading member of a witches' coven, which on full-moon nights engages in wild revels, including sexual orgies, which are not explicitly described. Her character is made up of contradictions: even her fierce love for Kate is matched by antagonism toward the girl, and her main desire seems to be for power.

GRYPHON (*Alice's Adventures in Wonderland**; *Alice's Adventures under Ground**), eccentric, blunt-spoken character who escorts Alice* to visit his friend, the lachrymose Mock* Turtle. The Gryphon is not described; Carroll* merely states, "If you don't know what a Gryphon is, look at the picture." The Gryphon is casual about the zany events that go on, taking them all in stride and commenting succinctly in a kind of cockney dialect. He helps keep the Mock Turtle concentrating on the task of relating his history and participates with him in demonstrating the wild dance called the Lobster-Quadrille. Like the other characters, he is a comic figure.

THE GUARDIANS (Christopher*, John, Hamilton, 1970; Macmillan, 1970), futuristic science fiction novel set in London and the English countryside in 2052 A.D. England is divided into Conurbs, congested, highly populated areas of high-rise apartments, electricars, holovision, and state-run spectator sports to keep the masses occupied, and the County, a quiet, pastoral, pre-World War I world, where gentry live in spacious farmhouses lit for effect by oil lamps (though Conurb technology functions for most practical purposes), travel by horseback or in horse-drawn carriages, stage fox hunts, archery contests, and lavish, dress-up garden parties, and are waited on by cadres of well-trained and willing servants. After his father, a Conurb electrician, dies under suspicious circumstances, his father's closest friends, the Kennealys, refuse to take him in, and he is abused verbally by masters and physically by older students at the austere state-run boarding school at Barnes to which he has been sent, Rob Randall, 14, runs away to the County, where his mother lived before she married his father. Rob has harrowing experiences before locating and crossing the Barrier, the twelve-foot high diamond-meshed wire fence that separates Conurb from County. Once having burrowed beneath it, he encounters a yellow-haired youth on horseback a little older than he. This is Mike Gifford, who out of sympathy and curiosity about the Conurb hides Rob in a cave in the woods and brings him food, clothes, books, and a reading lamp. When astute, kind-hearted Mrs. Gifford discovers what is going on, she takes him in, passing him off as a distant cousin, Rob Perrott, from Nepal. A beautiful summer follows, as Rob learns County ways (really those of country gentlemen), and grows to like the Giffords: matriarchal but kind Mrs. Gifford, their pleasant daughter, Cecily, companionable Mike, and agreeable, vague Mr. Gifford, who spends his time growing bonsai trees in a special greenhouse. Rob learns to ride, attends a regatta, cricket matches, and similar social funcions, and wins in an archery meet. At school with Mike in September, he notes early that the boys are trained for authority and not submissiveness as at Barnes. He discovers, too, that Mike is friends with a youth named Penfold, who maintains that comfort does not justify loss of freedom. At Christmas the boys visit the Penfold home, where they meet Penfold's older brother, Roger, an even more ardent revolutionary. Though the Penfolds recruit Mike to their cause, Rob resists, out of loyalty to the Giffords who have been so kind to him, a sincere appreciation for his new way of life, and doubts about the rightness of the Penfold cause. During the next school holiday, a rebellion breaks out in Oxford, where Mike has gone ostensibly to buy a horse, and the family soon learns he is involved. The insurrection is quickly quelled, with some loss of life, but Mike gets away safely and returns to Gifford House that night. He asks for help from Rob in escaping and receives it, since Rob remembers how willingly Mike had helped him. Mike leaves for the Conurb, planning to join a cell of rebels there. The next day Rob is taken for questioning to Sir Percy Gregory, Lord Lieutenant of the County, at elegant Old Hall, where he is treated with the utmost civility but nonetheless grilled. Athough Rob does his best to protect Mike, Sir Percy soon breaks down his defenses by informing him that he and the other authorities have known his true identity all along. Sir Percy also indicates that the authorities feel that Rob has the qualities of initiative, resource, and intelligence needed to become one of them, the guardians who govern society, who aim for peace, plenty, and happiness for the greatest number by making all important decisions and by channeling the impulse for violence and dissent into spectator sports and athletic contests. Rob accepts his offer and returns to live with the Giffords, looking forward to a good education at state expense and an easy life afterwards. He changes his mind abruptly, however, when Mrs. Gifford reprimands him for not turning Mike in on the night he returned and sought Rob's help in escaping. She says the tiny operation on the brain that Mike would have received to stifle his impulse for dissent would not have mattered at all and that Mike would soon have been home with his family and happy. She says that Mr. Gifford had received such an operation in his youth and that it has not prevented them from having a good marriage. Appalled by the corruption that turns people into puppets and makes them like it at the same time, Rob decides he cannot himself in good conscience become a master of puppets and chooses to leave and return to the Conurb to join in the fight for freedom. The accent is on action and suspense in the first half of the book and then shifts to ideas when Rob takes up life in the County. The author effectively draws the contrast between life in country and city and leads gradually to the revelation of how the nation is governed and why it is set up as it is. Since the reader learns along with Rob how things are, the impact on the emotions is all the greater. The terse, understated style makes such sensationalistic aspects as the mind-bending operation palatable. As in most books of this literary form, ideas take precedence over character development, and characterization is the minimum needed for the plot. Suspense arises from both conflict and ideas and is well maintained, but there are fewer technological gimmicks and less talk about technology than is typical for the genre. Christopher; Guardian.

GUDGEON, TOM (*Midnight Is a Place**), half-mad sewer "tosher," or scrounger for refuse; Lucas* Bell's master when Lucas works as a tosher. He is a "big bony fellow with a leaden complexion, pale bluish eyes, and a broken nose." He is "remarkably dirty" and exudes a "most extraordinary stench." He lives in a kind of houseboat down by the river. His helpers soon come to bad ends because Gudgeon is paranoid and quickly grows suspicious of them. He attacks Lucas and leaves him on the riverbank for the tide to carry off, where Lady* Eulalia Murgatroyd and Anna-Marie* discover him just in time to rescue him. Gudgeon becomes less rational as time goes by and, when last seen, raves in semiaccurate Biblical quotations.

GULLIVER'S TRAVELS (Swift*, Jonathan, Motte, 1726; originally entitled: *TRAVELS INTO SEVERAL REMOTE NATIONS OF THE WORLD, BY LEMUEL GULLIVER*), classic fantasy novel which purports to be the memoirs of a very early eighteenth-century traveler, set mostly on the high seas. It consists of four parts, of which the first

two, Gulliver's voyages to Lilliput and
Brobdingnag, are the best known. Lemuel Gulliver, ship's surgeon on the *Antelope*, is sailing
from Bristol for the South Sea in 1699 and is
shipwrecked by a storm. He swims for his life to
an island, falls into an exhausted sleep, and
awakens to find himself in Lilliput, a country
of miniature people six inches high, who take
him prisoner but otherwise treat him hospitably,
and throughout his stay feed and clothe him
quite satisfactorily. They first restrain him by
ropes tied to stakes and then transport him by a
specially prepared machine to the capital city,
Mildendo, where they quarter him in an ancient
temple. Though some object, most approve of the
mild disposition of Quinbus Festrin, the Man-
Mountain, as they call him, and gradually lose
their fear of him. The nobles entertain him with
acrobatic exercises and feats of skill, the
emperor visits him, and learned men teach him
their language. Assured that he will not harm
them, they set him free and allow him to roam
freely about the area. While Gulliver holds in
his hand the tiny statesman Reldresal, principal
secretary of private affairs, he gives the
visitor a quick overview of the country's
political situation. He informs Gulliver that
there are two struggling parties, the Tramecksan
and Slamecksan, called so from the high and low
heels on their shoes, with the Slamecksan, or
Low Heels, being currently in favor. He says
that Lilliput is threatened with invasion from
the Island of Blefuscu, "the other great empire
of the universe," the dispute between the two
countries probably originating over which end
of an egg should be cracked first. With the
Little-Endians currently in power, many Big-
Endians have sought asylum and help from
Blefuscu. Gulliver captures the entire Blefuscu
navy, linking the fifty men-of-war together
with cables and towing them to Lilliput. In
reward, the emperor makes him a Nardac, the
highest possible title of honor in Lilliput and
urges him to subdue Blefuscu. When Gulliver
refuses, an intrigue against him begins between
the emperor and some courtiers, among them,
Flimnap, the Lord-High Treasurer, and Bolgolam,
the High-Admiral, who are jealous of him. When
a friendly courtier informs him privately that

they are preparing to indict him for treason,
blind him, and starve him to death, he escapes
to Blefuscu, where he discovers a boat off the
northeast shore of the island, retrieves it and
repairs it with the help of the Emperor of
Blefuscu, who is grateful to him for not
implementing the Emperor of Lilliput's plans for
conquest, takes on provisions, and is bidden
farewell with great ceremony. September 24,
1701, nine months and thirteen days after
arrival, Gulliver sets sail, is soon taken
aboard an English vessel plying those seas. He
returns home on April 13, 1702, and makes a good
profit by exhibiting the miniature animals he
has brought back with him. Two months later, on
June 20, 1702, lured by the desire for more
adventures, he sets sail upon the merchant ship
Adventure, bound for Surat, and the second part
of the novel begins. The *Adventure* proceeds
without notable incident until the following
year, when she encounters a violent storm off
Madagascar and is blown and buffeted mightily
by the wind. The captain puts in at an
unfamiliar land and sends some crewmen,
including Gulliver, for water in a long boat.
Gulliver explores, is left behind, and soon
discovers he is in Brobdingnag, where the
inhabitants are twelve times his size. Thus he
is in the same size relationship to these people
as the Lilliputians were to him. He is captured
by a reaper, who takes him to his master, a
farmer. The farmer, his hands, and his family
consider the miniature Gulliver an interesting
curiosity and treat him kindly. The farmer's
nine-year-old, goodnatured daughter, small for
her age at about forty feet tall, gives him her
doll's cradle for a bed, washes his clothes,
teaches him the language, and lavishes care and
affection on him. She calls him Grildrig, or
mannikin, and he calls her his Glumdalclitch, or
little nurse. Gulliver remarks that the two
"were never parted while I was there." The
farmer senses an opportunity for financial gain
and exhibits Gulliver in the town as a public
spectacle. Two months after Gulliver's arrival
in Brobdingnag, his master takes him to the
country's metropolis, Lorbrulgrud, or Pride of
the Universe, where the queen is so impressed
that she buys him from the farmer for 1,000

pieces of gold. The king orders that he be
treated specially and that Glumdalclitch be
added to the royal household as his companion. A
special little chamber is fitted out for him
with furnishings his size and a hinged ceiling.
In a little traveling box created just for his
comfort, he accompanies the royal couple in
their travels about their realm. His small size
brings dangers, too, at the farmer's from rats,
and at the court from a malicious dwarf, who
plays tricks on him; and he is almost kidnapped
by a monkey as large as an elephant. He plays
the spinet with cudgels to entertain the court,
and his descriptions of England lead the king to
conclude that the English are a "pernicious race
of little odious vermin." In an effort to
elevate his country in the King's opinion,
Gulliver tells him about gunpowder. To Gulliver's surprise, its destructive potential
horrifies the king, who forbids Gulliver to
mention it again. Gulliver feels that these
people are intellectually stunted and provincial
in their thinking. After two comfortable years
in Brobdingnag, Gulliver is out by the sea one
day in his small carrying box taking the air
when he is borne away by a very large bird,
possibly a giant eagle, and dropped into the
sea. He is rescued by a passing ship, whose
captain and crew disbelieve his fantastic story
at first but later are convinced by artifacts he
shows as proof. He arrives in England on June 3,
1706, about nine months after rescue, still
adjusting to the small size of his surroundings
after being among the giants for so long. For
his third voyage, Gulliver joins the *Hopewell*,
which sails August 5, 1706, and a little later
becomes master of a sloop, which is captured by
pirates, among them a malicious Dutchman who
sets Gulliver adrift. He arrives at some land,
soon observes an inhabited flying island drawing
near his location, makes contact with it, and is
drawn aboard. This is Laputa, Floating or Flying
Island, an exactly circular body of 10,000 acres
of land 300 yards thick. The Laputans often
become so absorbed in their own deep thoughts on
various intellectual concerns that they block
out everything else and must be brought back to
reality by specially assigned servants called
flappers. When it is apparent that the masters

have become overly abstracted, the flappers gently strike them on the mouth and ears with bladders to awaken them. The people also constantly worry that the world may be destroyed. Gulliver discovers that they have made great advances in astronomy and that they have what is called the Astronomer's Cave, in which there is a mighty loadstone with which the king causes the island to rise and fall and with which he can keep the occupants of the earth beneath under his control by threatening to blot out the sun and rain. Treated well but regarded as their intellectual inferior, Gulliver stays for two months and then begs leave of the king to depart, is let down to the continent of Balnibarbi again, and walks to the metropolis of Lagado, where he is given hospitality by a noble named Munodi. Although the city is one-half the size of London, the houses are in disrepair, and the people ill-clothed. He learns that some years ago an Academy of Projectors was formed to develop new economic and social schemes, which have not yet been implemented even though the old order was not continued. Gulliver visits the academy and talks with the scientists there, among them one who has contrived a new method of building houses starting from the top down and another who employs hogs in plowing by burying at intervals acorns, dates, and the like to encourage the animals to root, systems that seem sound in theory but have proved impractical. Other specious endeavors include a scheme for shortening discourses by leaving out verbs and participles and another for abolishing words altogether and substituting for them the things themselves. Leaving Lagado, Gulliver travels to Maldonada on the coast and then takes ship for the little island of Glubbduddrib, the Island of Sorcerers or Magicians, where the governor has the power to call up ghosts to wait on him. Gulliver observes such historical personages as Hannibal, Caesar. Pompey, and Alexander the Great, who assures Gulliver that drink not poison did him in. He then goes to Luggnagg, an island southeast of Japan, where he finds the inhabitants polite and generous. He discovers an interesting phenomenon there, the Struldbrugs, or Immortals, people who are born with red circles on their foreheads and who age but never

die. Upon reaching eighty years, these persons
are regarded dead in law, the Luggnaggians'
means of guarding against the immortals'
accumulating too much power and money. From
there Gulliver sails to Japan, where he takes
ship to Amsterdam and on April 16, 1710, reaches
home. Assuming the captaincy of the *Adventure*
launches Gulliver upon his fourth and final
series of exploits. He sails from Portsmouth on
September 7, 1710, and within a few months his
men have conspired to seize the ship, taken him
prisoner, and put him ashore on an unknown
strand. Exploring, he discovers the area is
controlled by the Houyhnhnms, horses who behave
much like humans. They employ monstrous, hairy
humanoids called Yahoos as beasts of burden. The
Houyhnhnms consider Gulliver a brute animal,
too, of the class of Yahoos, and are surprised
he wishes to learn their language. He has a kind
Master, a learned dapple gray, who treats him
well, helps him learn the language, and listens
to the story of his adventures and the
description of his country and of Europe. His
Master receives the information incredulously
and shows indignation about the role of the
horse kind in the outside world. Gulliver learns
that falsehoods are unknown among the
Houyhnhnms, and that they believe in being
governed by reason. They consider friendship and
benevolence the two main virtues. All their
literature is oral, and they are great poets.
Gulliver lives for three years very happily with
his dapple gray Master and his family, until one
day his Master tells him that the Houyhnhnms
have taken offence at his treating a Yahoo, a
brute animal, like a Houyhnhnm, and insist that
he either employ Gulliver properly or tell him
to swim back to where he came from. With the
help of his Master's sorrel nag he builds a sort
of Indian canoe and sadly departs. He reaches
New Holland, where he is wounded by natives, and
is helped by friendly Portuguese to get to
Lisbon, all the while experiencing problems of
readjustment to life in a world run by Yahoos.
He arrives in England December 5, 1715, having
spent a total of sixteen years and seven months
in travel. He concludes by saying that he has
adhered strictly to the truth in setting down
the record of his experiences, his intention

being to inform and instruct for the "public good," a task he is eminently qualified for since he has had the advantage of living among the exemplary Houyhnhnms. Gulliver's account lacks suspense and approaches the essay more than the novel when judged by late-twentieth-century narrative standards. It gains its force from the great seriousness with which Gulliver speaks, even when he is poking fun, and everything is worked out with careful, sober attention to details of appearance and purpose. Intended for an adult audience as political satire, the book has long been popular with children, in particular the section on Lilliput, and is regarded as a forerunner in the fantasy-adventure genre. Although it is long and compact with descriptive detail, it is not too hard for good readers. Editions recommended by the citation committee are: ill. Arthur Rackham, Dutton, 1952; retold Padriac Colum, ill. Willy Pogany, Macmillan, 1962; New American Library, Signet Paperback, n.d. Children's Classics.

GUMBLE'S YARD (Townsend*, John Rowe, Hutchinson, 1961; *TROUBLE IN THE JUNGLE*, Lippincott, 1969), realistic novel of suspense with detective story aspects set in the 1950s in a ghetto in a city called Cobchester in northern England. Orphaned Kevin* Thompson, 13, who tells the story, and his sister, Sandra*, 12, live with their shiftless Uncle Walter*, his fat, slovenly companion, Doris*, and Walter's two children, Harold*, 8, and Jean*, 6, in a run-down house on Orchid Street in the Jungle*, so called because the streets are ironically named after tropical flowers. The half-a-week's action starts on a Saturday, when Walter and Doris simply walk out and leave the children to fend for themselves. Since the youngsters are afraid they will be parceled out to foster homes, take-charge Dick* Hedley, a neighbor youth of fourteen, suggests they move to Gumble's Yard, the most tumbledown part of the Jungle, an area of abandoned warehouses and four row cottages a few blocks away by the canal. With Dick's help, Kevin and Sandra pull off a daring midnight "flit," moving the barest of living essentials in a baby carriage and along the way narrowly avoiding police and a light-colored van driven by a mustached man

(who is one of the criminals who figure later
in the story). They set up housekeeping in the
attic of one of the cottages, which they reach
through a trap door or by shinnying up a
drainpipe. Complications soon crop up. While
selling firewood to earn money, Kevin and Dick
are set upon by toughs from the ghetto over the
hill and are rescued by curate Tony* Boyd, who,
with his fiancee, Sheila, takes an interest in
the children's welfare. Tony agrees to help
them but insists that more permanent arrangements be made by week's end. Then the boys
discover that packing cases are being delivered
to and taken from the area mysteriously by van
and barge and that Walter is one of the movers.
Dick's curiosity impels them to open one, and
they discover pressing irons used for counterfeiting and later also a passport, from which
Dick concludes that they have stumbled on a
smuggling operation. While Kevin seeks out his
Uncle Bob in Ledyard, whom he luckily finds
despite great odds, Tony and Sheila take over
the younger children and Dick continues
sleuthing. All the story strands come together
in a smashing scene at the end, when the boys,
Tony, Uncle Bob, and the police capture the
thieves, among them an escaped convict, Flick
Williams, who planned to use the fake passport
to flee the country. It turns out that Uncle
Walter helped transport the contraband but was
not involved in the actual theft. He agrees to
return to care for the children, Tony arranges
for charges against him to be dropped, and the
family moves back to the house at Orchid Grove
Street, with hope but no assurance that the
future will be better and that Walter and Doris
will mend their irresponsible ways. Skillful
characterizations, Kevin's usually matter-of-
fact reporting of what happens, and careful but
not elaborate descriptions of the children's
living arrangements before and after the "flit"
and of the "flit" itself lend credibility to an
unlikely plot. Although the diction occasionally
seems to be that of the writer and not Kevin,
the story is suspenseful and moves quickly, and
the conclusion seems appropriate to the events
and the characters as presented. The children
are distinctly drawn--practical Sandra; resourceful Dick, who comes up with the ideas

that springboard the action; pathetic little Harold, who most misses Walter; little Jean, a romantic who adjusts readily to their new life; and Kevin, rather passive, a follower and the mouthpiece, who likes to tell stories and tells this one about the seamy side of urban life well. (Mr.* and Mrs. Hedley) Sequels. Choice; Fanfare.

GUNS KELLY (*The Grange at High Force**), servant and long-time friend of Admiral* Sir John Beauchamp-Troubridge, who rents Folly Grange while he writes an official history of convoys. Guns was the admliral's gunner on the destroyer during World War II and retired with him. He is a man-of-all-work, equally efficient at reroofing the church, mixing explosives, or washing dishes, wearing a frilly apron. A familiar type, he has never-failing admiration for and loyalty to his employer.

GUS POSSIT (*The Circus Is Coming**), uncle of Peter* and Santa* Possit, who works as an auguste, an acrobatic clown. Because his sister Rebecca has been a lady's maid for a duchess and has acquired snobbish attitudes, she has never mentioned Gus to the children, and they know of him only because a card arrives from him every Christmas. Gus is well meaning, but he is irritated by Peter's politeness and by both children's way of keeping their clothes clean and their gloves on, as they have been taught. Because he has lived happily alone in his little caravan, he is more annoyed than grateful at Santa's efforts to help him keep house. Whenever he speaks sharply to one of them, as he frequently does to Peter, he is sorry, but he is naturally outspoken and abrupt, and he has no idea how the children might be feeling or how to make them feel comfortable in their new environment.

GUS ROPER (*The Plan for Birdsmarsh**), tough, enthusiastic friend of Paul* Fairfax, who yearns to sail but is forced by his hard-drinking fisherman father to go to work as an apprentice mechanic in a garage. Somewhat scornful of Paul's awkwardness and lack of sailing expertise, Gus continues their friendship largely be-

cause Paul owns the old smack *Swannie*. Although
Gus's family and social circumstances are far
worse than Paul's, he is not an introspective
boy, and he has the ability to get what he
wants in life. The prospect of Birdsmarsh being
turned into a marina and resort hotel means the
possibility of finding a job doing what he
loves, and he feels little sympathy for what he
considers Paul's sentimental love of the land.
When Paul is lost at sea, Gus is uncharacteristically smitten with guilt, a feeling that
doesn't last long after Paul's rescue.

GUTHORM (*The Namesake**), historical figure (also
spelled Guthrum), Dane who breaks his oath to
leave Wessex and marches to capture and set up
base at Exeter. There, because the Danish fleet
of Hubba has been wrecked in a storm, his force
is besieged and brought to terms by Alfred* the
Great. In the novel, he is pictured as
ambitious, brave, and venturesome, but not as
clever as he thinks he is.

GWEN (*The Battle of St. George Without**; *Goodbye, Dove Square**), pretty, self-dramatizing
hirl, who is part of the group of youngsters
living in Dove Square and later in the housing
project. Confident with boys, she is not sure
she wants the life of her older sister, the
house-bound mother of twins, and she seeks a
cause to give her life meaning. In the second
book she has left school and is in nurse's
training.

GWENDOLEN CHANT (*Charmed Life**), young witch who
dominates and, it turns out, uses without
principle the magical powers of her younger
brother, Cat*. A fair-haired, blue-eyed child,
she looks all innocence and sweetness but is
really self-centered and spiteful and, in the
end, genuinely wicked. She is determined to be
recognized as talented by the enchanter
Chrestomanci* and inventively produces a series
of disasters in an effort to gain his attention.
On a more childlike level, she engages in a
battle of wills with Chrestomanci's daughter,
Julia, involving marmalade in Julia's face, hot
chocolate pitchers poised over Gwendolen's head,
and other displays of their contending magical

abilities.

GWENDOLYN SWAMP (*Which Witch?**), comic figure, a thin, pale witch who comes from a family of banshees and who plays the harp in the Todcaster Palm Orchestra. Her sheep familiar, Percy, gets measles, and she catches them from him. She is replaced in the contest for the hand of Arriman the Wizard by Madame* Olympia, the black enchantress.

GWYN (*The Owl Service**), intelligent, often surly Welsh youth who aspires to leave his family's valley and to make something of himself, and who sees education as the way to accomplish his goal. He is sensitive about being Welsh and knows the English people who own the house in which he and his housekeeper mother, Nancy*, are working look down on him. Although warned by Huw* Halfbacon, who is revealed as his father, not to let his passions get the better of him, he persists in his pursuit of Allison* and in his notion that she thinks he is not good enough for her because he is Welsh. In reality, she is simply weak and easily swayed by her parents, who want her to aspire to a youth of her own social set. Nancy uses the threat of taking Gwyn out of school as a way of controlling him. He can be sneaky and manipulative, and sometimes he steals cigarettes for Nancy in order to get her to do what he wants by getting her in a good mood. He is a well-rounded figure.

H

HAL (*The Wool-Pack**), foster-brother of Nicholas* Fetterlock and son of Giles*, Master* Thomas Fetterlock's chief shepherd. He is a sharp-eyed, sharp-eared youth, good-natured and quick-minded. Because he gets around a lot, he brings Nicholas information about Leach's activities. He secures the key to Leach's barn while his uncle, the barber, is pulling Leach's infected tooth, helps put feathers into the wool bales, keeps tabs on Leach, and informs Nicholas when Leach and the Lombard, Toad Face, are removing the stolen wool from Leach's barn. He is a type figure, necessary for the plot.

HAL (MacGibbon*, Jean, Heinemann, 1974), realistic novel set in the slums of London in recent times. Looking from the back window of the tenement where he lives with his mother, Barry* Padgitt, fourteen or fifteen, has watched the local youngsters sneak into the Bute Street Site, an area between the canal and the Bute Institute so full of underground railroad tunnels that it is has been considered not suitable for building and therefore has been allowed to grow wild. There the children play a game that started out as Flags but has progressed to something else, an exciting war with sexual undertones, led on one side by a boy that Barry calls "The Spaniard" and on the other by a dark-skinned girl he names "The Indian Queen." Since he has been ill, Barry does not go to school and is afraid to go out alone, having been bullied in other neighborhoods by bigger boys, but, while his mother works, he waits daily for the game and becomes intensely fascinated. One day, fearing the Queen will be surprised and taken, he throws a flower pot from the window as warning. Thus alerted to his presence, the girl, Hal* (Glory) Piercy, who is of West Indian parentage, starts to worry about him and comes to his apartment, trying to get him to come out. He refuses, but later, having seen the Spaniard, whom he now knows as Crimp Watson, coming in by the institute with a man, he drags himself down the stairs and over the wall to warn her, fearing that Crimp has alerted the police. The man turns out to be Tim Black, lately laid off from the institute because of lack of funds for his project. He has investigated the area and suggests that they start an adventure playground, of which he will apply to be play leader. With varying degrees of enthusiasm the young people agree, and Barry gradually becomes involved and stronger as he gets some exercise in the fresh air. Hal continues to worry about him and enlists the aid of her unconventional teacher, Miss Camperdown, who meets Barry and tells Hal she will have him in her class if he will come to school. At first he refuses, but when he discovers that his mother is proposing that he start at Cranmere College, a boarding school, as arranged by one of her sewing clients, he is so appalled that he begs Hal to see if he can't come to Jefferson, her school. Under Hal's protection, he starts school and even originates the idea for their Open Day program, a sort of musical about the slave trade, with the children from Africa and the West Indies contributing their ethnic dances and songs. The two Greek boys, Dimitri and Andreas Georgiou, act as whip-wielding guards, and Barry, the best actor, is the rich slave owner. The program is a great hit with the parents in the ethnically mixed neighborhood, but the success coincides with disaster for the site, where it develops that Crimp's father and an associate have bought the land and persuaded the Council that with new techniques it can be built upon. Mr. Watson gives them a smarmy talk about how they can continue to have a small piece for a garden, but the bulldozer operators move in, recklessly smashing the "caff," Hal's special lunch counter, and the wall of the greenhouse, where the little children have kept their pets. Tim weakly gives in; Crimp, who hates his father, hides out in the tower he has built; Barry persuades Hal to sneak out at night to go once more to the hill in the "jungle" of thorn bushes and weeds before it, too, is bulldozed away. As they lie together in the tall grass, Crimp comes upon them and warns them that the guards are patrolling the place with a dog. Since they can't get back the way they came, he leads them to his tower, but Barry, seeing that he must distract the guard so Hal can get away, runs back toward the wall where they entered and is attacked by the dog. When he is brought home by the guard, shaken and sick from the encounter, his mother keeps Watson, whom she has been dating, from filing trespassing charges, and uses the occasion to pressure Barry to start at Cranmere College. As they leave in the taxi, Miss Cramperdown and Tim follow, try to talk to Mrs. Padgitt at the station, and get her attention only when Barry vomits all over his new school clothes. In the end Mrs. Padgitt gives in, planning to marry not Mr. Watson but another suitor who has been courting her and to let Barry live with the Georgiou family during the term. All does not end happily: Hal's good friend, Mary Malone, is pregnant, presumably by Crimp though she won't admit he is responsible; Crimp has run away; and the site will be made into "rich people's flats"; but there is a sense that the tough kids are survivors and that Barry will not slip back into his invalid's self-absorption. Although these are young people in a disadvantaged neighborhood, there seems to be less sense of danger and crime than in American urban novels and no suggestion of drugs or alcohol among the youngsters. Neither is there any indication of racial prejudice, except a feeling of Barry's mother against "foreigners" in general. The result is a novel that is absorbing but seems naive and old-fashioned. Barry and Hal, and to some degree Barry's mother, are well drawn characters. Other.

HALCYON ISLAND (*The Islanders**), the place that provides the ironic setting for the novel.

Remote, isolated, windswept, infertile, it is a demanding home to about 100 people, who dislike newcomers and hold to the instructions in the Book of Teaching that has been handed down by word of mouth from the Deliverer. When Charlie* Herrick reads their Book to them, the first time they have actually heard what it says, they discover that the ancestor they have revered, Joseph Kane, was the sole survivor of eight mutineers and murderers, who with an equal number of women from the island of Rikofia originally settled Halcyon. It appears that the island's name has never described life there as it really has been, neither in the past nor in the present, and it appears, too, that the future will be no better. It seems the "halcyon" existence has only been illusory.

HAL PIERCY (*Hal**), really named Glory, tall, self-assured West Indian girl in the slums of North London who draws invalid Barry* Padgitt out of his self-imposed isolation and into the life of the polyglot neighborhood. Although she is responsible for her two younger sisters, having to get them up and fed, and take one to Infants School and the other to a day-care center before her own school day and to care for them after school, she has concerned parents who are careful to keep track of her and see that she gets an education. Barry has called her (to himself) the Indian Queen and has remarked that she moves like a cheetah. She is both drawn to him and impatient with him when he is emotionally dependent upon her, yet is irritated when he gains in self-assurance and makes other friends. Her own infatuation with Tim Black, the director of the adventure playground, gradually subsides when she discovers that he is engaged to her favorite teacher.

HAM (*The Moon in the Cloud**), Noah's* conniving, unscrupulous second son, who tricks Reuben into fetching the animals Noah has instructed Ham to acquire for the ark because Ham is too cowardly and lazy to do it himself. Ham has another reason for wanting to get rid of Reuben; Ham lusts for Thamar, Reuben's pretty young wife. Noah says Ham is "work shy," and he and Mrs. Noah have deep misgivings about their son's veracity and fidelity to the traditional religion, and rightly so, since Ham values trinkets and believes his father is a little crazy. A vision impresses him with the truth of Noah's story about the impending flood but doesn't change his character or behavior. At the end, Ham gets what he deserves; he is squashed flat by an elephant.

HAMISH MACLEISH (*Danger at Black Dyke**), friend of Geordie* Bickerson and Tim* Charlton and a cofounder and member of the society of Mithras. He is good-looking and outgoing and is well-liked by the girls. His friendship with Connie enables the boys to keep informed. He enlists Connie's help in keeping track of the two strangers who are seeking Bud* Riley.

HANDLES (Mark*, Jan, Kestrel, 1983; Atheneum, 1985), realistic novel of family and neighborhood life with girl's growing-up story aspects, set in rural England in contemporary times. City-bred, motorcycle-crazy schoolgirl Erica Timperley, 11, feels little enthusiasm when Mum unexpectedly informs her that she is to spend her summer holidays with the family of her Auntie* Joan Myhill on their farm near the village of Calstead. Erica finds Hall Farm Cottage uninteresting, her Auntie Joan hard-driving and acid-tongued, her Uncle* Peter dull, and her cousin Robert*, who is about her own age, unpleasant, lazy, and lumpish. She uncomplainingly settles in, however, sensibly trying to make the best of things. She assists Auntie Joan conscientiously with the vegetable stall that accounts for a good share of the Myhills' income, but she misses the busyness of home. She sometimes thinks about sneaking back on the bus but refrains for fear of upsetting Auntie Joan. One day Erica runs an errand for Uncle Peter on Auntie Joan's ugly, willful bicycle into Polthorpe to the machine shop of a certain Elsie* Wainwright. To Erica's surprised delight, it turns out to be a motorcycle repair shop. Several weeks of joy follow as Erica becomes involved with the lives of Elsie, his helper, and friends. She savors their good-natured banter, appreciates Elsie's assistance in selling Auntie Joan's vegetables, thrills to the

opportunity to work on engines, and above all
longs for a handle, or nickname, like those
that people-loving, word-loving, observant
Elsie whimsically bestows on intimates. These
include Bunny, his fat mechanic; Kermit, who
looks like a frog on a Honda; Gremlin, Kermit's
mischievous son; Yerbut, who argues; and Arrow,
the plumber whose real name is Bowen. She
eagerly rides into town on the Iron Cow, as she
dubs the bicycle, dressed in yellow oilskins
against the rain, calling herself the Dreaded
Yellow Jelly Mould, an epithet she hopes Elsie
will bestow on her but doesn't. So happy is she
with her newfound friends that she wishes she
had never posted her complaining letter to her
mother. She intercepts the mail for her mother's
reply and neglects her duties around the house
and yard, provoking Auntie Joan to reprimand
her. The glamor of life with Elsie diminishes
somewhat when Erica learns that her romantic
hero has a shrewish wife and prissy daughter.
Then the Myhills discover that she has been
etching pithy and not always kind slogans into
the marrows (squash), an idea she got from
Elsie. They are furious with her because they
now realize what she really thinks of them, and
tension builds. Fortunately, the reopening of
school brings the holidays to an end. When Erica
bids farewell to the shop, she discovers that
Elsie has indeed given her a handle, Eroica
Symphony, in appreciation of the way she
contrasts with Elsie's spoiled daughter. Erica
hops the bus for home, and passes by the
industrial park where Elsie's shop stands. She
spots for the first time the sign over the door,
Mercury Motor Sales, Proprietor, L. C. Wain-
right, and the puzzle of where Elsie got his
handle is solved. She has learned the folly of
judging by appearances and the need for weighing
the consequences of one's actions. The author's
strong points are her ability to show interpersonal relationships with warmth and understanding and to get with conviction into the
mind of a strong, sensible, modern schoolgirl.
The characters of the two main settings have
clearly individualized personalities. The style
is detailed and leisurely, and the author makes
extensive use of striking figures: Auntie Joan's
"remarks came in short rows of words, like

lists," the bicycle's creaking sounded like "the pitiful moans of some creature that was dying from a loathsome disease of the lungs," and "the lorry would burst murderously out of its strait-jacket." Conversation reveals the clipped effect associated with British speech and uses much contemporary slang; and language, situations, character, and irony all serve as sources of understated, subtle humor. Erica's sometimes naive, frequently astute, internal musings contribute much of the story's interest. Carnegie Winner.

HANNO (*A Stranger at Green Knowe**; *An Enemy at Green Knowe**), thirteen-year-old gorilla who escapes from the London Zoo and lives for a few days of freedom in the thicket behind the old house at Green Knowe. Before he was captured as an infant, Hanno lived a life of freedom in the African jungle. A huge and powerful beast, he differs from the other apes in the zoo in that he has not given up. He seems to accept the boy Ping* as a young gorilla, to be tolerated and cuffed into obedience. In *An Enemy at Green Knowe*, Ping conjures up Hanno's ghost, which scares off the plague of cats that are killing Mrs.* Oldknow's birds.

HARE-WOMAN (*On the Edge**), one of the two terrorists from the Free People revolutionaries who kidnap Tug* Shakespeare and hold him hostage in an effort to get the British government to set up community homes for all children under sixteen. The Free People are dedicated to abolishing the family unit, which they regard as the government's instrument of repression. Jinny* Slattery dubs her the Hare-woman because she is thin, lanky, and furtive and has big, pale hazel eyes like a hare. Though for no good reason except frustration she once beats Tug mercilessly about the head, she at other times treats him quite maternally and protects him from Doyle*; he calls her "Ma" and becomes curiously fond of her. The Hare-woman, who is also referred to in the novel as the Woman, is a former child abuser whose maimed child was taken from her. At the end she is unable to shoot Tug and is herself shot by police.

HARI (*The Village by the Sea**), second in the poor village family of Thul and one year younger than Lila*. Not as hard a worker as his sister, Hari dreams of ways to get a job and runs off to Bombay with the other protesters of the fertilizer factory not so much to take part in the rally as to escape the hopeless situation with his ill mother, his drunken father, and his frightened sisters. In the city he is at first terrified, but when, by good luck and the kindness of a stranger, he lands at the Sri Krishna Eating House, he buckles down and works as he has never worked at home and saves all his meager wages to take back to his family. Clearly a bright boy and more given to emotional swings than Lila, he hates his father whose drinking and debt have almost ruined them, nearly gives way to despair and homesickness in the city, and responds eagerly to the friendship and education offered by Mr. Panwallah. Although it is Lila who has kept the family alive and saved her mother's life while Hari is gone, it is his plans and training that offer hope for the future.

HARMAN, HUMPHREY, educator, writer of several books set in Africa. In World War II, he went to Africa and spent most of his time with African soldiers there and in Madagascar and the Far East. After the war, he became a schoolmaster, joined the Colonial Education Service, and went to Kenya, where he lived for more than ten years before publishing his first book, serving as a District Education Officer and training African teachers. This first book, *Black Samson** (Hutchinson, 1965; as *African Samson*, Viking, 1966), is a fictionalized retelling of an oral Luo version of a story that seems to be authentic history grafted onto myth and which is known from the Congo to Kenya. He has also written *Tales Told Near a Crocodile: Stories from Nyanza* (Hutchinson, 1973; Viking, 1967) and *More Tales Told Near a Crocodile* (Hutchinson, 1973). *Men of Masaba* (Viking, 1971) recounts myths, legends, romances, tall tales, jests, and moral tales of the Bukusu people of Kenya.

HARNETT, CYNTHIA (MARY) (1893-1981), born in Kensington, London; educated at a private school

in Eastbourne in Sussex and at Chelsea School of
Art in London; author and illustrator of books
for children and young people and highly
respected in particular for her historical
novels, a genre in which she broke ground for
young readers, peopling her books with ordinary
folk instead of mainly rich and famous ones. As
she was growing up she developed a strong sense
of the importance and pleasure of history.
During her childhood she saw Queen Victoria, who
had a palace in Kensington and was then well on
in years, out riding in her carriage and pair.
She often played with an older brother, who
loved history, the two exploring ruins and he
telling stories of olden days that he made up
for her. She began to paint after World War I,
then turned to writing as a more lucrative
profession. During the late 1930s and the 1940s
she collaborated with her art teacher, G. Vernon
Stokes, who was also her cousin, in producing a
series of jointly written and illustrated books
for younger children, mainly picture books about
country life. After World War II, she switched
to writing historical novels, hoping to transmit
to young readers something of her own love for
past times. She decided to concentrate on the
effects of events on common people, a departure
from the current fashion. Her first historical
novel was *The Great House* (Methuen, 1949; World,
1968), about an architect who in 1690 pulled
down old houses to build new ones. Later came
Ring Out, Bow Bells! (Methuen, 1953; as *The
Drawbridge Gate* by Putnam, 1954), about Dick
Whittington. Three of her historical novels have
won awards or been named to lists of critically
approved books. *The Wool-Pack** (Methuen, 1951;
as *Nicholas and the Woolpack*, Putnam, 1953) won
the Carnegie Medal and was named to the Fanfare
list. About a Cotswold wool merchant's son who
helps foil a trade plot to ruin his father, it
projects a keen sense of the period's culture.
*The Load of Unicorn** (Methuen, 1959; as
Caxton's Challenge, World, 1960), was commended
for the Carnegie and selected for Fanfare and is
about a London boy apprenticed to William
Caxton* who uncovers a plot to keep Caxton from
securing the paper he needs for his press. *The
Writing on the Hearth** (Methuen, 1971; Viking,
1973), another story of intrigue and her last

novel, is set in the mid-1400s in London and
environs during the reign of Henry VI and is
also listed in Fanfare. She wrote other novels
and several books of nonfiction, and edited an
anthology of prose and verse. She illustrated
her historical novels herself with detailed
drawings of costumes, activities, and places, a
practice that gave her the opportunity to
combine what she said were her three great
pleasures: writing, drawing, and history.
Exciting adventure stories, her books also
project a vivid picture of their times, and
much of their reading pleasure comes from the
author's extensive use of descriptive detail.
She was known and admired for her lengthy
research and her painstaking efforts to insure
that every detail, no matter how small, be
absolutely accurate. During both world wars
Harnett served with British Censorship. She
made her home in Henley-on-Thames.

HAROLD THOMPSON (*Gumble's Yard**; *Widdershins
Crescent**), son of Walter*, brother of Jean*,
and cousin of Kevin* and Sandra*, a little,
thin, fair-haired, dreamy boy. In *Gumble's
Yard*, he is mostly sad and on the fringes of
things because he misses his father so much. He
endangers their "flit" when he runs home for his
coveted space helmet. He hopes one day to become
a famous scientist. In *Widdershins Crescent*, he
is revealed as a far brighter than average youth
and wins a scholarship to Cobchester College.
The whole family is very proud of him,
especially his father, and, at the end of the
book, the entire neighborhood gathers to see him
off for the first day of school. Kevin gives up
school so that Harold can have the chance for a
good education. Harold is a winsome boy, a round
and dynamic character, with flaws as well as
virtues.

HARP OF TEIRTU (*The Whispering Mountain**), the
Telyn Teirtu, a golden harp that legend says
Kilhwch, son of Prince Kelyddon, got his cousin
King Arthur to help him steal for the Princess
Olwen. It was crafted by the Children of the
Pit. Later it comes into the possession of the
monks of the Order of St. Ennodawg. Owen's
grandfather finds it in the ruins of their

monastery. There is a very complicated verse
prophecy associated with it which eventually
comes true. It turns out that the harp really
belongs to Tom* Dando.

HARRIS (*Owlglass**), rat whose near fatal attack
by Old* Beak and Claws starts the effort to get
spectacles for the owl. A younger member of
the club, Harris hopes to be voted into full
membership after he tells his story, "The Story
of How My Great-Great-Grandfather Sang before
Queen Victoria," a tale of how his ancestor
struck a bargain when he was starving with a
food-rich Sicilian puppeteer, whereby the rat,
who had a beautiful tenor voice, became a live
puppet in the Punch and Judy Show. Having been
discovered by Lord Melbourne, the show is
summoned to the palace, where Victoria, then a
young queen, makes the rat her favorite and
eventually names him Steward of the Spent Candle
with the right to reprocess and sell the partly
burnt candles that were never relit at
Buckingham Palace. Harris is a member of the
three-man deputation to the owl to investigate
the delicate subject of the attack and of Beak's
failing eyesight.

HARRIS (*The Strange Affair of Adelaide Harris**;
*Bostock and Harris; or, The Night of the
Comet**), quick-thinking boy who is the horror of
his ancient history teacher, Mr. Brett, but the
idol of his slower classmate, Bostock*. Harris
has a scientific interest in a variety of
questions. In *The Strange Affair of Adelaide
Harris*, he has heard the story of Romulus and
Remus, and in the interest of seeing whether a
wolf will foster an infant abandoned in the
wilds, he persuades Bostock to help him kidnap
his youngest sister and leave her on the
commons, thereby starting a series of interre-
events far beyond his imaginings. In *Bostock and
Harris*, he manages to get his friend Bostock
into complicated trouble and create a complex
of misunderstandings, never realizing that he
is to blame. He confidently guarantees
Bostock's success in attracting the love of his
sister Mary, basing his advice on a learned
article on the mating habits of animals. The
only son among a number of daughters, he has

mostly contempt for his sisters and for females
in general and covets for himself not love but
Captain Bostock's telescope, dreaming that he
will gain fame by discovering new stars and
planets. Harris is also a supporting character
in the title story from *The Restless Ghost*.

HARRIS, MARY K(ATHLEEN) (1905-1966), born in
Harrow, Middlesex; author of some of the best
school stories of the mid-twentieth century.
She attended Harrow County School for Girls from
1915 to 1922. A convert to Roman Catholicism,
she wrote several books published by the Catholic press, Sheed and Ward, including *The Wolf*
(Sheed, 1946), *Elizabeth* (Sheed, 1961), and
Helena (Sheed, 1964). Most of her eleven books
of fiction for children are boarding-school
stories, although some of the later ones are set
in day schools. Her first novel, *Gretel at St.
Bride's* (Nelson, 1941) is about a refugee from
Nazi Germany in an English girls' school where
others think only of sports, food, and other
shallow matters and are unconcerned with
catastrophic international events. Her only book
told in first person, *Seraphina** (Faber, 1960),
has a protagonist who makes up a mother and
says she is an explorer in Central Africa, to
replace the actual one who deserted her shortly
after birth and finds herself caught in a tangled web of deceit. *The Bus Girls** (Faber, 1965;
Norton, 1965) concerns the on-again-off-again
friendships of a group of girls who ride the
same bus to their girls' school. *Seraphina* and
The Bus Girls were both commended for the Carnegie Medal. Her last book, *Jessica on Her Own*
(Faber, 1968), is about the daughter of a
Cambridge-graduate mother, and depicts home life
as equally important as the Secondary Modern
school she attends. The same types of girls
tend to appear in the different novels, but they
are sharply characterized and involved in lively
but plausible plots. Harris also wrote three
novels for adults.

HARRIS, ROSEMARY (JEANNE) (1923-   ), born in
London, the daughter of an officer in the Royal
Air Force; critic and writer of novels and
picture books for children and young people and
of novels for adults. Since her father's assign-

ments required the family to move frequently,
she grew up in various places. She served in
the Red Cross Nursing Auxiliary in London during
World War II and attended the Chelsea School of
Art and the Courtauld Institute, both in
London, to study art restoration. She became a
picture restorer but left that for full-time
writing with the publication in 1956 of her
first adult novel, *The Summer-House* (Hamilton). She published several more books for
adults, some of them thrillers, and then completed a book for young readers begun years
before, *The Moon in the Cloud** (Faber, 1968;
Macmillan, 1969), which won the Carnegie Medal
and is listed in *Choice* and Fanfare. Inspired by
objects acquired by her parents during a trip to
Egypt, it is a humorous and clever improvisation
of the Noah story. The hero, Reuben, a conscientious animal tamer, is assisted in his quest
for passengers for the ark by several independent-minded, talking animals. *The Shadow on
the Sun* (Faber, 1970; Macmillan, 1970) and *The
Bright and Morning Star* (Faber, 1972; Macmillan,
1972) complete what is known as Harris's
Egyptian trilogy. She has also written *The
Seal-Singing* (Faber, 1971; Macmillan, 1971), a
contemporary novel set in Scotland that builds
on local legend; the futuristic companion novels
A Quest for Orion (Faber, 1978) and *Tower of the
Stars* (Faber, 1980); and the texts for several
picture-story books, including *The Flying Ship*
(Faber, 1975), *Green Finger House* (Eel Pie,
1980; Kampmann, 1982), and *Mr. Bear's Picnic*
(Walker, 1987). She has completed television
plays and published retellings of folk tales and
legends and an adaptation of Spyri's *Heidi*
(Benn, 1983). She credits her artist's training
for the strong visual quality of her style and
is noted for her wry humor and gift for
invention in both substance and style.

HARRY BATEMAN (*The Hollow Land**), London boy
who, at four, is brought for vacation to Light
Trees, a farm in the Cumbrian fells, and who
loses his heart to the place. A self-absorbed
child, he is perfectly happy by himself, singing
tunelessly, or with Bell* Teesdale, a local boy
who is four years older. He complains that
nothing happens in London, and as he grows older

he becomes more and more one of the Cumbrian
people.

HASTINGS-BENSON (*Bilgewater**), English and mathematics master at St. Wilfrid's School, who acts
as an uncle to Bilgewater, though he is much
older than her father. He owns a Rolls Royce,
and she calls upon him to rescue her from the
horrible weekend at the Roses'. He has an
unfortunate characteristic of falling violently
in love with almost any female available, the
first one evidently having been Bilgie's mother,
and when he is inevitably rejected, he tries the
patience of all his friends by weeping and
talking endlessly about the affair. On the
Thursdays when he and his companions regularly
call upon Bilgie's father, he is the one who
always calls for the opening of the wine and, in
fact, often fortifies the evening with his own
hip flask.

HATHAWAY (*Archer's Goon**), fourth in the family
of seven wizards who control the city. Hathaway
has opted to live in the past, in the sixteenth
century, where he has a pleasant wife and two
children and controls transport in the modern
city by electronic communications. At one time
he stayed too long in the past and now is unable
to leave it without becoming ancient and
decrepit, and he carefully warns Howard* and
Awful* Sykes to stay no more than an hour when
they visit him so that they will not be affected
by the change. Besides controlling transport, he
"farms" records and archives and thereby
discovers that Howard is adopted and realizes
that he must be Venturus. By tracing the records
of his children, he discovers that they are
ancestors of both Catriona and Quentin* Sykes
and therefore that Awful is descended from him
on both sides. She is extremely attracted to
him. Of all the wizards, he is the best adjusted
and happiest.

HATTY MELBOURNE (*Tom's Midnight Garden**), the
staunch, high-spirited, little Victorian girl
with whom Tom* Long plays in their
almost-idyllic garden at the back of Uncle*
Alan and Aunt* Gwen Kitson's apartment house.
When Tom first meets Hatty, she pretends she is

a princess, her fairy-tale compensation for her aunt's cruelty and her cousins' scorn. She accepts Tom readily because he plays companionably with her. She grows up as the story in the garden goes on, while Tom stays young, but, at the end of the novel, her dreaming and Tom's sharing those dream memories with her indicate that she and he inhabit the same dimension of experience though separated by more than fifty years of age. Hatty has grown up to become Harriet Bartholomew, the owner of the apartment house in which the Kitsons live and behind which the garden appears during the night.

THE HAUNTING (Mahy*, Margaret, Dent, 1982; Atheneum, 1982), fantasy of magic and ghosts with mystery story aspects in a family setting, which takes place recently in a city of undisclosed location. Shy, withdrawn Barney Palmer, 8, whose real name is Barnaby, is the youngest in his close-knit family, which includes his father, John, who is often away but who his children know loves them deeply, Claire, his warm, understanding, and affectionate stepmother, and his two older sisters, aloof, silent, fanatically neat Troy*, 13, and bossy, garrulous, self-assured Tabitha*, about ten, who is an aspiring writer. Events start when Barney sees a vision on the way home from school one Friday afternoon, a ghostly child in a blue velvet suit who announces mournfully that Barnaby is dead and that he feels lonely. Terrified, Barney assumes that the vision foretells his own imminent demise, and is greatly relieved to discover when he gets home that his Great-Uncle Barnaby Scholar on his dead mother's side has passed away. Again that evening, Barney hears the ghostly voice, and the next day, when the family visits the Scholar relatives to pay their respects, still another haunting occurs, this time one that Tabitha observes. Family conversations reveal the startling information that the Scholars have a family skeleton, a black sheep relative, Great-Uncle* Cole, who had supernatural powers that brought him into conflict with his imperious mother and who ran away while still quite young and is presumed dead. The hauntings continue,

leaving Barney pale and wan. He confides in
Tabitha that he is convinced that Cole intends
to take him away, and Tabitha consults Great-
Uncle* Guy, a pediatrician, who says he thinks
Barney is a Scholar magician--there has been
one in every generation; Cole was the magician
in his time--and that the family has discovered
that Cole is still alive and had been in
contact with Great-Uncle Barnaby, unbeknownst to
anyone. The mystery intensifies, and the climax
occurs when Cole arrives at the house to claim
Barney as friend and associate in dead Barnaby's
place. A battle of wits and magical powers
ensues, and, when the Scholars also arrive,
conversation becomes quite acrimonious as old
hostilities surface. When, to put a stop to the
arguments, Barney makes the sacrifice and
offers to accompany Cole, surprisingly Troy
speaks up. She reveals the shocking information
that it is she and not Barney who is the
magician in their generation and that she has
inherited her special powers from Great-
Grandmother* Scholar. The old woman loathed the
talent with which she had been born, had
submerged it, and was determined to make Cole
over into her image of what a young man should
be. Barney is delighted to be completely
ordinary, and Cole and Troy become friends. For
the first time in his life, Cole has a family
that appreciates him for what he is. The
characters are well-drawn, and Barney is a
convincing and winning protagonist. That the
Palmers should be unaware of such a juicy item
of family history as a black sheep seems
unlikely, however, and Troy's change in personality is altogether too sudden, dramatic, and
felicitous, but these shortcomings fade in view
of the skillfully sustained atmosphere of light
suspense, the touches of comic relief, the
richness of the underlying ideas, the deft
psychological touches, and the accuracy and
inventiveness of the diction. Although an artful
mystery on the first level, this is primarily a
story of family relationships, which suggests
that people cannot be made over and that it is
important for all members of the family to be
loved and appreciated for what they are, themes
that emerge gradually without explicit statement. Carnegie Winner.

HAZEL (*Watership Down**), Chief Rabbit at Watership Down; leader of the survivors of the destroyed Sandleford Warren. A calm, unassuming, usually sensible yearling, he is steady, compassionate, and observant. Without him the group would not have made it to Watership or continued to exist after they got there. He listens to ideas and advice and never pretends to know everything. Occasionally he makes bad decisions, as when he decides to get rabbits from Nuthanger Farm, but mostly he shows good judgment. At the very end, in an epilogue, the reader is told that, many springs later, Hazel is summoned by a shining stranger rabbit, probably Lord Frith, the rabbit god. This evidently means that he dies. A well-developed figure, he serves as a foil to General* Woundwort, the dictator of the Efrafa Warren.

HECTOR (*A Little Fear*), Mrs.* Tucker's feckless, mostly beagle dog, obtained from the pound to keep her company and give her some protection in her new home on the old Bright place overlooking the swamps along the Broad River. Hector contributes comic relief and tension to the story. He is aware before the old woman is that potentially dangerous creatures lurk in bush, tree, swamp, water, all about the place, but to the Njimbin* and most of the others he remains a figure of fun, to be teased and tormented for their pleasure. Hector wins the reader's sympathies early for his good intentions, his growing allegiance to his mistress, and the way he rebounds after his terrifying experience on the water when the Njimbin tricks him into the rowboat and then takes him for a harrowing ride downriver, where he leaves him tied to a tree and where a passing farmer discovers him and brings the terrified and dispirited animal home. After that Hector begins to snarl and growl at the shadowy Njimbin, which he can see but Mrs. Tucker can't at first, and at the other creatures the Njimbin occasionally commands.

HELEN EDGINGTON (*The Lark on the Wing**), sensible, plain childhood friend of Kit* Haverard and Pony* Cray, who plays games of pretend with them

when they are young and later shares a flat with
them in London, where she has a scholarship to
the London School of Economics. Daughter of a
socially ambitious mother and an ineffectual
father, Helen has suffered by comparison with
her two popular, frivolous older sisters and has
had to fight to do what she wants with her life.
Kit's cousin, Philip Kitson, admires her.

HELL'S EDGE (Townsend*, John Rowe, Hutchinson,
1963; Lothrop, 1969), mystery-detective novel
set in the late 1950s in the Yorkshire
manufacturing city of Hallersage, also known as
Hell's Edge from its furnaces and smoky
atomsphere. Spunky, romantic, resourceful Ril*
(Amaryllis) Terry, 15, moves with her father,
Robert, a pleasant, bespectacled resident tutor
and widower, to Hallersage from southern
England. They soon establish a friendship with a
distant relative, Fred Clough, a workingman, his
wife, Florrie, and their son, Norman*, who is
almost sixteen. Florrie tells them the story of
their mutual early nineteenth-century ancestor, Caradoc Clough, who led an unsuccessful
rebellion against the local large landowner, Sir
George Withens, after Sir George fenced in the
town Common for himself. They learn also that
local folklore has it that Sir George became
reconciled with Caradoc in later life, relented
of his deed, and decided that the land should
revert to the city. No will or deed to that
effect was ever found, however. When Ril learns
that the students at the school she will attend
must travel by trolley across town to their
playing fields even though the old Common lies
adjacent to the school plant, she decides to
investigate the old rumor to see whether the
land can be reclaimed. Norman, at first aloof
and disapproving of her because he thinks she's
stuck-up, becomes interested in the enterprise
and serves as a staunch ally, in spite of his
father's commands otherwise. Great-Aunt Martha,
a centenarian, gives them a "message" that has
come down in the family from her grandfather
about the Withens's Common: "It's safe behind
the night thoughts." The message makes no sense
to anyone until a bright but plain school friend
of Ril's, Hilda Woodward, suggests that "night
thoughts" might refer to a long, philosophical

poem of Caradoc's period published in book form.
This leads Ril to investigate surreptitiously
and unsuccessfully Sir George's library, when a
few days later, Miss Celia* Withens, beautiful
heiress to the Withens mansion and millions and
a school governor, invites her to tea at
Withishall. Then Norman suggests they break into
Withishall at night, and this time behind a
sliding panel Ril discovers an envelope
containing a document. The two make a harrowing
escape from the hall, certain of victory. When
they read the document, they are delighted to
discover that Sir George had indeed wished the
property returned to the town, but they are
dismayed to learn that, since the document was
unwitnessed, it has no legal force. Before they
turn it over to Miss Withens, whose property it
is, Norman makes a copy, which he cleverly turns
over to old Sam Thwaite, a school governor also,
a self-made millionaire, and the one other most
powerful person in the district. Sam "blackmails" Celia and her lawyer with the threat of
bad publicity unless she agrees to sell land
from the old Common to the school at a fair
price. Proud and afraid people will think she's
a soft touch, Celia refuses and takes off for
vacation in Nice, driving at a terrific speed in
her bright red Jaguar. In Sam's Rolls Royce,
Ril, Sam, Norman, and the lawyers for both sides
pursue her, and a harrowing chase ensues during
which Celia crashes her car and the others
rescue her. In the hospital she gives in and
reluctantly agrees to the sale. Ril rejoices for
the town and the school, delighted that she has
been able to be of benefit to the town she has
come to regard as her home. Characters, though
interesting and appropriate for the plot, are
conventional types--idealistic, romantic Ril;
proud, moral, upwardly mobile Norman, sensitive
about his working class background; haughty,
distant, beautiful, vulnerable, poor-little-
rich-girl Celia; self-made, blustery, heart-of-
gold philanthropist Sam Thwaite; absent-minded
professor Robert Terry; fast-talking, dishonest
car salesman Roy Wentworth, whose attempts to
woo and win Celia's millions are found out and
cause her to strengthen her resolve to retain
the Common; maternal Florrie; and plain Hilda,
who blossoms through association with more

outgoing Ril. There is some sense of Hallersage as a dirty, smoky factory town, an old urban area badly in need of renewal. The book is mostly composed of fast-moving plot, with the familiar conventions of the mystery-detective genre, and almost everything for predicting the outcome lies near the surface. Carnegie Com.

HENRY (*The Night Watchmen**), imaginative school-boy who, having been ill for a month, is given another month out of school to recuperate. Bored and lonely, he discovers two eccentric tramps, Josh* and Caleb*, in the park and makes friends with them, delighted to be associating with people his mother would disapprove of. Henry is instrumental in helping the two tranps escape from the Greeneyes, the villains who are jealous of do-as-you-pleasers and who wish to discover the secret of whistling up the night train and traveling to There, the place where do-as-you-pleasers live. At the end, whether the adventure with the tramps really happened or was the result of Henry's imagination is left to the reader to decide.

HENRY BELL (*No End to Yesterday**), Marjory's* father, who works in another city and returns only for weekends. Having been deeply hurt when his wife left him for another man while he was in the army during World War I, he has turned his child over to his mother and lacks the imagination and sensitivity to see how she is being psychologically abused. It never occurs to him to doubt the reports of his mother and sisters about Marjory's misbehavior, her difficult personality, and her "hardness" and ingratitude. Marjory's cousin Teddy* Bell refers to him as "old stoney-face," and Marjory is both afraid of him and pathetically eager for his approval. Though he allows his mother to destroy his relationship with the first young lady he brings home for inspection, he is elated when on his second try Dolly Hawthorne refuses to let Gran* or his sisters intimidate her, and the triumph that he and Marjory share at that time is the first real understanding they have ever had. Later, however, he is so disapproving when Marjory falls in love with a married man that he turns her out, and it is some fifteen years after her lover's divorce and their marriage before he will see Marjory and her children.

HENRY BIRKINSHAW (*Tumbledown Dick**), uncle to Dick, who owns a pet shop in Tib Street, Manchester. A large man with a heavy mustache and a melancholy air, he cares deeply about the animals he tends, especially the tropical fish, which feed his fantasies about a life in the South Sea Islands. His forearms are tattooed in a marvelous pattern of snakes, so realistic that when a real snake is found in a market basket and brought to him, in the newspaper photographs reporting the incident it is hard to tell the real from the tattooed snakes.

HENRY HOLBEIN (*The Robbers**), television news personality, father of Philip*. Although he has rarely come to visit Philip and has never bothered to think of his needs and interests, he decides after he remarries to take the boy to live with him and his new wife, Maggie*. Charming and generous when so inclined, he is self-centered and insensitive and, when the boys get into trouble, rude and arrogant to the poor family of Darcy* Jones. His mother accuses him of being bored with Philip and suggesting a boarding school so he can pay someone else to take the responsibility, and his blush shows Philip that the charge is true.

HENRY MICKLE (*The Battle of St. George Without**; *Goodbye, Dove Square**), show-off and rather lumpish friend of Matt* McGinley, who becomes involved in the effort to save the old church in Dove Square. He figures to a lesser degree in the sequel. Henry is always eating candy and is sweet on Gwen*, an unrequited feeling.

HENRY'S LEG (Pilling*, Ann, ill. Rowan Clifford, Viking, 1985; Viking, 1985), amusing, realistic novel with mystery-story aspects, set in Darnley, England, in the 1980s. Henry Hooper, 11, freckled and big for his age, has a great love for junk, collects it compulsively, and stores it mostly in his attic room in Fir Grove, the dilapidated house he and his mother, Ivy, have shared since his father walked out to live with his girlfriend, Sheila Howarth. Henry's

biggest rival in scrounging junk from dust bins
is Danny Crompton, a filthy old ragpicker with
one peg leg, whom Henry thinks of as Desperate
Dan. One evening Henry gets into a horror movie
by pretending to be with the older brother of
his friend, Nev Hodgkinson, but all he can think
of is the mannequin's leg he has seen sticking
out of a trash barrel behind a store. He hears a
crash and some sirens, and as soon as he can he
walks out of the movie thinking he will pick up
the leg on his way home. To his surprise, the
leg seems to be gone, but then he spots it under
a parked car. As he carries it under his arm,
Desperate Dan lurches up and tries to wrest it
from him. Henry shoves him away and runs for
home. His mother tells him she has found a job
on a newspaper and also says they are renting
the other half of the attic to Cousin Noreen,
who is studying art at the Poly, the local
college, an announcement that fills Henry with
gloom since he wants the whole attic to himself.
Before he goes to bed he sees two figures
talking in the rain near the gate; they are
Desperate Dan and a beefy young man with a
motorcycle. The next day Desperate Dan waylays
him in their driveway and offers him three
pounds for the leg. When Henry hesitates, sure
there is something very special about the leg if
Dan wants it so much, the old man attacks him.
Henry is saved by Fred Holt, Noreen's boyfriend,
who is delivering some of her belongings in a
van. Noreen proves to be a surprise, wearing
enormous mirror glasses, very tall, and dressed
like a punk, all in black and white with her
face floury, her hair closely shaved at the
sides, flat on top, and dyed in black and white
squares. She also proves sympathetic and
remarkably interested in Henry's junk, which she
sees as a goldmine of raw material for her
"sculpt" for a local art show. She particularly
covets the leg. In the meantime, Henry has been
exploring ways to get money, badly needing it to
replace his bicycle, which is decrepit, and,
more urgently, to replace the school uniform,
consisting of purple shorts and a reddish purple
shirt, which his mother has bought second-hand
and which is far too small for comfort or
appearance. He has been collecting dead
hedgehogs from the roads, hoping to sell them to

a scientist at the Poly who has advertised that
good prices will be paid for frozen specimens.
Since their refrigerator is no longer freezing
even ice, Henry has made a deal with the boy
next door, Graham Snell, to hide the hedgehogs
in the freezer in his garage, under the sprouts.
He also tries to sell a non-running gold watch
he has found to his friend Mr. Schofield, but he
finds the old man very upset, more than he
usually is when his store has been robbed, and
Henry can't bring up the subject. The next night
he wakes to find a face looking in his attic
window; it is the motorcyclist, whom he starts
to call The Blob, obviously standing on the old
fire escape. The next afternoon he returns home
to find the leg missing and little dents in the
linoleum from Dan's peg leg. Furious, he goes
directly to Egypt Street in the derelict part of
town where Dan lives, finds the old man asleep,
and steals back the leg, now in two pieces since
Dan has cut the foot off. He gives it to Noreen,
who has painted her attic room white and is
constructing an all-white sculpture employing
many of Henry's wire coat hangers and egg
cartons. Several times he has seen lights in the
old Spring Mill from his window, and once,
poking around, he has been warned off by The
Blob, who pretends to be a security guard.
Worried, he tries to get in touch with his
father, but finds no one home at the high-rise
apartment and, peering through the keyhole, sees
dirty dishes and a shirt draped over a chair, a
view that makes him think that Sheila, always
one for neatness, is no longer there. Information he gains by spying and through Norene
connects The Blob with the robbery in Mr.
Schofield's store (in which some valuable jewels
there for appraisal were taken) and the old
man's subsequent sudden death by a heart attack.
When he again sees flickering lights in the mill
at night, he decides to investigate. He climbs
through a drainage hole in the wall and works
his way up into the mill basement, where he
finds the remnants of a thieves' hideout with
lots of empty merchandise boxes as well as old
cans and mattresses, and a great pile of
miscellaneous things in one corner. Drawn as
usual to the fascination of junk, Henry examines
a few of the things and uncovers the heel of a

leg. When he tugs it out, the piles comes down
with a clatter, and he looks up to see The Blob
at the top of a flght of stairs. After a wild
chase through the mill, Henry, still clutching
the leg, gets out, followed by The Blob, who
sets off the burglar alarm by accident. Henry
pelts along the canal bank, The Blob in hot
pursuit. Henry slips, falls into the canal, and,
thinking he is drowning since he can't swim,
sees the leg float off just as The Blob hauls
him out. After that he is very ill for some time
and only later learns that the police arrived on
the scene and arrested The Blob, who is now
cooperating with them by giving information on
the rest of the gang he was once part of, the
gang that robbed Mr. Schofield's store, were
chased by police, and stuffed the bag of jewels
into the manequin's leg before they got away, an
action Desperate Dan had witnessed. Eventually,
the police retrieve the leg from the now-frozen
canal and find a small bag of valuable jade
pieces stuck in the ankle. Mrs. Schofield is
saved from the demands of having to pay for
them. She gives Henry a reward of 200 pounds.
Noreen and Fred take Henry to the art center to
see her sculpture on display, an all- white sea
of objects named "Afterwards," from which the
leg sticks out, the foot attached at an odd
angle. He finds it oddly disturbing, but he is
more interested in getting home because he has
seen his father approaching Fir Grove on a bike
just as the van was leaving for the exhibit. He
hurries home on foot, past all sorts of
fascinating junk that fails to interest him, and
finds both parents eager to greet him. While the
mystery of the leg carries the plot along, the
main attention of the story is on Henry's
blunders and his depression at his mother's
disorganization and his father's absence. There
are some very funny scenes, as when Graham's
mother, a fanatic for cleanliness, discovers the
hedgehogs in the freezer, and when the
substitute teacher tries to organize a band.
Though no permanent reunion of the parents is
promised, the ending is hopeful. Guardian.

HEPZIBAH GREEN (*Carrie's War**), housekeeper for
Dilys Gotobed at Druid's Bottom, a decaying
mansion that once had a whole staff of servants

and gardeners. Hepzibah came to Druid's Bottom as nursemaid for retarded Mister* Johnny Gotobed when he was a boy and she was not much older, and she now takes care of the poultry, helps in the hayfield, cares for dying Dilys, and provides food and love for Albert* Sandwich and, when they can get there, Carrie* Willow and her brother Nick*. Faced with being evicted because Dilys has evidently neglected to make a will, though she had intended to leave her the house and land, practical Hepzibah starts seeking a remote farm that will take her and Mister Johnny and doesn't waste time or energy blaming Mr.* Evans. Locally, she has a reputation for knowing folk medicine and having second sight, and the children half believe it when Albert calls her a good witch.

HEPZIE FOULGER (*The Great Gale**), old village woman whose arthritis makes it hard for her to get around. She and her husband, Jim* Foulger, are liked and respected by the villagers in Reedsmere, the town they live just outside of, and Mary* and Mark* Vaughan are especially fond of them. Hepzie appears in several strong scenes as genial, accommodating, and warm: being rescued during the flood by her husband, Mark, and Mary through a hole cut in the thatched roof of the cottage at the edge of Reedsmere Broad; sitting by Jim's bed in Reedsmere Hall when he lies ill of pneumonia and reporting the gist of the conversation between him and the Queen; and giving her heirloom locket to Rod* Cooper in appreciation for his rescuing Jim and other villagers. A strongly realized figure, she is neither sentimentalized nor caricatured.

A HERD OF DEER (Dillon*, Eilis, ill. Richard Kennedy, Faber, 1969; Funk, 1970), adventure story of a boy who gets caught in the middle of a feud between Connemara natives and the rich foreigner who tries to live on land he has bought in the district. Peter Regan, 15, is unwilling to work for a sheep farming cousin in Roscommon. Instead he walks to Galway and is robbed on the way by a family of tinkers (gypsies) named Burke. He is befriended by Michael Joyce, from Argentina though of an Irish father, who has come to Connemara and bought a

home, thinking he will raise deer on his land
which is marginal for any other farming or stock
raising. He has hired a Scottish herdsman used
to deer, but now two bucks and three does are
missing, and the local people are not friendly.
He proposes that Peter pose as a city boy off
for a camping holiday and see what he can find
out. After buying Peter a tent, sleeping bag,
and cooking stove, he arranges a meeting place
in an old shepherd's hut near the sea. Peter
pokes along for a couple of days, striking up
conversations where he can, but he doesn't find
out much until he stops at the farm of Ned
Hernon, east of Salleen, and gets permission to
put up his tent in the wood across the way.
Ned's youngest son, John, who is about Peter's
age, asks him to go shark fishing the next day,
his first experience in a currach or even on the
sea, though he has rowed often on a lake. By
luck and an impulsive act, Peter makes possible
the catching of two sharks at once, so
delighting the Hernon men and the others on
shore, particularly Ned's old father, Tadhg,
that he is a something of a hero and is treated
as one of the family. They pay no attention to
his presence when they discuss moving the stolen
deer from a piece of land belonging to Colman
Donnelly (the ne're-do-well who has sold his
family holdings to Mr. Joyce) to some safer
spot. The next day Peter goes out with John to
set lobster traps with the shark meat and learns
that Patsy Carroll of the village at the edge of
Mr. Joyce's land will move the deer to Inish
Goill in the night. The next day Peter walks on
to Mr. Joyce's place and, when asking permission
to camp, is rudely warned off by the gun-toting
Scotsman. In a rage he stomps back to the tiny
shop in the village, where the men drinking
porter welcome him, and Patsy Carroll, who, it
turns out, is the shop owner, offers him a
camping place in his field. Pretending to go
for a stroll by the sea, Peter heads for the
shepherd's hut and meets Mr. Joyce, to whom he
tells what he has learned. He is troubled by his
role as a spy but thinks he may be able to
prevent Mr. Joyce from calling in the Guard and
instead to bring about a reconcilation somehow.
The next day he learns that three men, old Tadhg
Hernon and two friends from the old Black and

Tan days, have threatened the Scotsman at night and scared him into leaving the country. Inadvertently, Peter lets out to Colman Donnelly where the deer are now, Inish Goill being an island just off the shore in Lough Corrib, which is reachable by a causeway and a plank bridge. The men comes up with the surprise suggestion that Peter and John Hernon go to Inish Goill to see how the deer are faring, since if the Guard are called, all the grown men must be at their own places. There the boys find not only the Burkes, come to mend a still on the island, and the deer, but also Colman Donnelly, who has come to look at the deer, too, and who at first tries to get them to go home at once, and then suggests that he will ride back with them in the morning. They check the deer again that evening, and in the morning plan to check again, and, to their surprise, Colman will not wait for them. They are further surprised and dismayed to find that the deer are nowhere on the island, though they know the plank bridge had been taken up during the night. Back at Patsy's, suspicion suddenly turns on Peter, who admits he told Colman where the deer were hidden, and he must prove he's really a country boy by milking the cow. Reinstated in their confidence, he is pressured into writing a threatening letter to Mr. Joyce, since he has been to school most recently and his handwriting won't be traced to the local men. They send him and John to deliver the letter. Outside Colman's house they grab one of the Burke children, drag her to the shepherd's hut, and read the message she is carrying in her hair, which is a demand for more money or if they don't want the deer turned loose. John goes to try to dicker with the tinkers, to exchange the deer for the child, while Peter guards her, but when Mr. Joyce comes along, the child overhears them talking and then darts away, saying she'll tell on them. At Colman's house they learn from his wife that he and Burke have gone up to his land at Screeb. Peter and Mr. Joyce follow, discover that the tinker has shut the deer in an old barn, where the buck has gored the three does and is threatening Colman and Burke. While Peter distracts the buck, Mr. Joyce grabs its antlers and throws it, allowing the two men to get out

of the way before it escapes off into the
darkness. Then all the men from Patsy's converge
on the scene, more furious at the boy who has
spied than at Colman, but when they see the dead
deer and learn that Mr. Joyce is not thinking of
prosecuting them, they are abashed. After a
little time to think it over, they decide
Peter's part is not shameful but rather that of
a hero for bringing both sides to an understanding. From then on he works for Mr. Joyce every
summer. The adventure in itself is interesting
but it is the pictures of the country life and
the shark fishing that stand out in the book as
well as the sharply drawn country people, with
their suspicions and their easy friendships,
their strong superstitions and their practical
good sense. Their reasons for trying to force
Mr. Joyce to stop raising deer are a complex
mixture of the history of landlords in Ireland
and the men's sense of tradition, which become
clear to a reader who sees the situation through
Peter's eyes. Peter is adequate in his role and
is strongest as a vehicle to reflect the beauty
of the countryside and the customs of the
Connemara people. Lewis Carroll.

HERR JAKOB VOGEL (*Children of the Book**), fat,
short Viennese baker, father of Anna*, who is
presented as a loving and caring, if authoritative, husband and father. When, after the
Turks arrive, panic hits Vienna and many people
flee, he elects to remain, motivated by loyalty
to the city he has spent his life in and to his
neighbors and friends, who will need his trade
more than ever. Inclined to make all the
decisions at first, he gradually comes to see
that his daughter and her fiance have good heads
and even defers to them occasionally. He is a
proud member of the militia.

HILDICK, E(DMUND) W(ALLACE) (1925-   ), born in
Bradford, Yorkshire; teacher and novelist. He
attended Wheelwright Grammar School, Dewsbury,
Yorkshire, and received his teaching certificate
from Leeds Training College, Yorkshire. He also
served in the Royal Air Force from 1946 to 1948
and worked at a variety of jobs, including
public library assistant, clerk in the Leeds
truck repair depot, and laboratory assistant for

the Admiralty Signals Establishment in Surrey and Yorkshire, before becoming a teacher of retarded boys from 1950 to 1954. Since 1954, he has been a freelance writer, producing more than sixty books for children, most of them fiction, and a number of novels and nonfiction books for adults. His first six books for children are set in the industrial working-class north of England, starting with *Jim Starling* (Chatto, 1958). These were followed by some whose main character is Lemon Kelly, all of which employ a setting influenced by the seven years Hildick lived in New Town of Stevenage, near London. More recently, his stories have had American settings, the first of these being *Manhattan Is Missing* (Stacey, 1972; Doubleday, 1969). Most of the American books feature assertive Jack P. McGurk and his band of ten-year-olds who solve crimes and employ humor and lively dialogue, and are designed for less able readers, among them *The Case of the Secret Scribbler** (Hodder, 1978; Macmillan, 1978). Hildick was at one time a visiting critic and associate editor of the *Kenyon Review* at Kenyon College, Ohio, and has lived in Canada with his wife, who is also his agent.

H. O. BASTABLE (*The Story of the Treasure Seekers**), Horace Octavius Bastable, eight-year-old youngest child in the large and lively Bastable family, which seeks to restore the fallen fortunes of their "ancient house." He clumps around after the others in his big boots, a happy tagalong the older ones indulge but also respect for his ideas. They are determined he will become the right sort of boy. As Oswald* says, they "are not going to let it be our fault if he grows up a milksop." They include him in most of their escapades. He is a pleasing figure, a happy little fellow and a good foil for the others.

HOBBERDY DICK (*Hobberdy Dick**), hobgoblin who has guarded and guided Widford Manor for time out of mind and who has kept the secret of the hiding place of the Culver treasure until it is imperative that it be found to aid his favorite humans, Joel* Widdison and Anne* Sekar, the last of the Culvers. Visible to only a few humans, mostly children, and then only rarely, Dick is nevertheless important in their lives, deft at finishing their tasks, clever at manipulating events, and capable of speaking into the sleeping minds of mortals. Both the evil of witches and the power of Christianity are threats to Dick and the other old spirits, but to protect his humans Dick challenges both these other forces and even crosses running water, a painful and debilitating experience.

HOBBERDY DICK (Briggs*, K. M., Eyre, 1955; Greenwillow, 1977), fantasy set in 1652 in an old English manor in the Cotswolds under the care of its resident hobgoblin, Hobberdy* Dick. For centuries Dick has looked after Widford Manor, home of the Culvers and the Sekars, but finds new problems when the Puritan Widdisons buy the place, city people with no feel for the customs and traditions of the area. Mr.* Widdison is a good man but severe and unimaginative, with his mind on business and acquiring wealth. His second wife is a social climber, a foolish woman who is prejudiced against her stepson, Joel*, 17. Gentle, intelligent Mrs. Dimbleby is the mother of Widdison's first wife. The children are three little girls: Rachel, 10, Martha*, 8, and Diligence, about six, their little brother, Samuel, and a baby. Of the servants, sharp-tongued, disagreeable Ursula Biddums has come with them from the city, but George* Batchford, the cattleman, is local and understands both farming and the importance of the old ways, including the existence of Hobberdy Dick. Deft, clever, and helpful to his favorites, Dick is seldom seen by humans, but he is much involved in their lives, sometimes planting ideas in their sleeping minds, often finishing tasks for those he favors, and even protecting them against ghosts and other spirits as far as his powers will permit. Joel and young Martha take to the country immediately, but Mrs. Widdison influences her husband to send Joel back to the city to keep an eye on the business there. Discontented Mrs. Widdison engages young Anne* Sekar, a well-born orphan, to work as her "gentlewoman," a sort of companion-servant to her, and longs for acceptance by the neighboring gentry who

ignore her until Dick causes the breakdown of
Madam Fettiplace's coach near Widford and gives
the Widdisons an excuse to be hospitable. The
old lady remains stiffly aloof, but her young
daughter-in-law is more gracious and becomes
friendly to Mrs. Dimbleby and later to Anne.
When Mrs. Dimblelby's health begins to fail,
Mr. Widdison thinks of sending for Joel. He
hesitates, and then writes a letter but doesn't
send it. Dick, knowing time is short, takes it
to Fettiplace's and, disguised by the dark,
asks that it be sent to town with their
dispatches. Joel comes home in a storm, able to
reach Widford only because Dick, neighing like a
mare, entices his horse across the ford and to
the manor. At Christmas, though celebration is
forbidden by the Puritan master, George Batchford organizes a party in the old oasthouse, to
which all the servants and children sneak out.
When Mr. Widdison almost discovers them, Dick
leads him a merry chase in the mist, and he
returns so befuddled that his wife accuses him
of drinking. For Easter, with the help of Dick
and George, Martha finds and dyes eggs for all
the children, and they secretly join the village
youngsters in an egg roll before dawn on
Fulbrook Hill. Joel has been sent to Oxford, as
his grandmother wished, though not before he has
become much attracted to Anne. At Midsummer's
Eve, Martha sneaks out to join a village girl
to watch the gypsy bonfire, and on the way home
she is captured by the witch, Mother Drake, who
also has attempted to subvert Dick to her
service by magic. Dick rouses Anne and George,
and they hunt through the night. When they do
not find her, Mrs. Widdison sends for Joel, her
husband havng returned to the city. Dick
organizes all the friendly spirits and imps of
the countryside to search, and they conclude
that the witch is holding Martha in Skipton
Barrow. With the help of Grim, the venerable
hob of old Stow churchyard, Dick manages to
defeat the witch, but he needs humans to free
Martha from the spell. He finds Anne dozing and
tells her to search the scriptures and hurry to
the scene. Finding Joel there hunting, she
gives him the Bible, and by reading Luke 10:
17-20 they deliver Martha from the enchantment
and carry her home. Mr. Widdison, called home

because of this event, reveals to Joel that he is planning a match for him with the daughter of a Puritan business acquaintance and is much put out when Joel is not pleased. This precipitates Joel's realization that he is in love with Anne, and, afraid that he will reveal himself by his anger when Mrs. Widdison mistreats her, he arranges that Lady Fettiplace will ask to have Anne serve her instead. Mrs. Widdison is afraid to cross her noble neighbor, and Anne realizes her love for Joel is ill-fated and goes sadly but willingly. Dick, upset by this change, sends dreams to Martha of the Culver treasure (of which he alone knows the hiding place) since Anne is the last of the Culvers and he knows Mr. Widdison will never agree to a betrothal between her and Joel unless she has a valuable dowry. After the treasure is found, it seems at first as if Mr. Widdison will claim it, but he is an honest man, and when it is proved to him that Anne is the true heir, he gives it to her and is pleased that she still wants to marry Joel. In gratitude, Anne makes three gifts for Hobberdy Dick to choose from: a broom, which will keep him in service to the manor for the indefinite future, a suit of green, which will release him to fairyland, and a suit of red, which will presumably send him to Christian heaven. With some wrenching, he chooses the red suit and disappears, having left his favorite humans well fixed financially and emotionally. The story is rich in folklore, with many minor characters of spirits and impets, and with customs from pagan times that were still followed secretly in Puritan England. Dick is a charming little fellow, and the humans are well characterized, so that a reader cares about their problems and believes in Dick's influence in their lives. The author skillfully makes it seem plausible that those characters who believe in Dick understand his efforts and even, particularly the children, see him occasionally, while those who don't believe can attribute his actions to other causes. Choice.

THE HOBBIT (Tolkien*, J. R. R., Allen & Unwin, 1937; Houghton, 1938), fantasy based on the quest pattern, subtitled *There and Back Again*, peopled mainly by creatures from the northern

European oral tradition and set in a land and era called Middle-earth. Bilbo* Baggins, one of the more well-to-do and respectable hobbits* of The Shire, is surprised to find himself entertaining thirteen dwarfs and astonished to learn that they are expecting him to join as the fourteenth member of their expedition to retrieve their ancestral home and treasure from Smaug*, the dragon of the Lonely Mountain. He does not know that the wizard, Gandalf*, has marked his door with a sign identifying him as a burglar in want of a job. He has no intention of taking part in anything as uncomfortable and disreputable as this enterprise, but as they talk and sing some previously hidden spirit of adventure wakens in him, and soon he finds himself on the road, worried mostly because he has forgotten his pocket handkerchief. On the way they run into various difficulties and hazards. They are captured by trolls, attacked by goblins (or orcs), harried by wolves (or wargs), waylaid and almost killed by huge spiders, and thrown into the dungeons of the Wood-elves. They also have unexpected and fortuitious aid. Gandalf, by clever ventrilo-quism, keeps the trolls arguing until sunrise, which freezes them in stone and frees Bilbo and the dwarfs. A long rest in Rivendell, land of the half-elven people, refreshes and restores them. The most unusual help comes from a situation that appeared destined for disaster. Gandalf routs the orcs by a great flash from his staff which kills their chief, but in the ensuing confusion Bilbo is dropped by Dori, the dwarf who is carrying him, and, when he regains consciousness, finds himself alone in a seemingly endless tunnel, where he discovers a ring and puts it in his pocket. He comes upon an underground lake and meets a strange, slimy creature called Gollum*, who plans to eat him, but, afraid of Bilbo's little sword, Sting, stalls for time by proposing a game of riddles: if Bilbo is the winner, Gollum will do what he asks; if Gollum wins, he will eat the hobbit. When Bilbo runs out of ideas for riddles, he asks what he has in his pocket, and Gollum cannot at first guess, but when he paddles back to his rock in the lake, intending to get his ring, which makes him invisible, and then to

strangle and eat Bilbo, he finds it missing and
realizes   the   answer   to   the   last   question.
Furious, he chases Bilbo, who slips the ring on
without thinking and so escapes and finds his
way out of the mountain. Great eagles summoned
by Gandalf save the company from the wargs and
set   them   down   near   the   home   of   Beorn,   a
shape-changer, who is a man by day and a bear by
night. There they get rest and provisions and,
when   they   start   through   the   dread   forest,
Mirkwood, Gandalf leaves them. By using the
ring, Bilbo is able to free the dwarfs from the
spiders   and   avoid   being   shut   in   the   elven
king's dungeons, and eventually with its use and
considerable   ingenuity he   works out   a way   to
free them by getting the guards drunk, stealing
the   keys,   and   packing   the   dwarfs   in   empty
barrels to   be   floated down   the   river to
Laketown. Unable to nail himself into a barrel,
he must follow, clinging to a barrel, sometimes
on top and sometimes beneath, arriving soaked,
bruised, and miserable, but free. The men of
Laketown provide them with supplies and ponies,
and they set off to the mountain, where they use
a map and a key that Gandalf had provided to
find a secret entrance to a small tunnel. Bilbo,
in his role as burglar, sneaks down and steals a
single goblet from the sleeping dragon, and, on
a   second   trip,   engages   in   a   riddling
conversation with the great beast, discovering
the   vital   information   that   Smaug   has   a
vulnerable spot free from the armor of diamonds
that   protects   most   of   his   soft   underside.
Aroused   to   fury,   Smaug   almost   catches   the
company outside the tunnel and then smashes the
cliff, destroying their entrance, and flies off
to attack Laketown. A thrush that has overheard
Bilbo warns the captain of the archers, Bard,
who is   able to bring Smaug   down with a
well-placed   arrow.   The   town,   however,   is
wrecked. Bard sends messengers to the elves, who
come in a great force and join with the men, who
blame the dwarfs for stirring up the dragon and
want recompense for their losses. The leader of
the   dwarfs,   however,   Thorin*   Oakenshield,   has
become more greedy and stubborn as he has come
closer to his treasure, and now he barricades
himself in   the mountain, sending   for his
relatives   from   the   Iron   Hills   for

reinforcements. Bilbo, seeing the futility of all these actions, takes the beautiful Arkenstone of Thrain, which he has picked up secretly from the dragon's hoard, and sneaks away to give it to Bard as a bargaining chip, knowing that it is more valuable than all else to Thorin. In Bard's camp he finds Gandalf, just returned, and they are able to avert a war between the dwarfs on one side and the men and elves on the other in time to join forces against the orcs and wargs, who sweep down hoping to take the treasure for themselves. In the great battle Bilbo slips on his ring and is hit on the head, so he takes almost no part in the fighting. He wakes to find the two youngest dwarfs, Fili and Kili, killed, and Thorin mortally wounded. He and Gandalf return to The Shire uneventfully, in time to find Bilbo's relatives auctioning off his possessions, assuming him to be dead. Except for Balin, who is the friendliest to Bilbo, and Bombur, who is very heavy, the dwarfs still alive at the end are not developed into distinctive characters. Bilbo, however, changes during the adventure from a timid, comfort-loving hobbit to one with considerable courage and self-confidence. The style in the early portion of the book has an almost condescending storytelling quality, but it sharpens as the adventures become more serious. The book is generally agreed to be one of the most important fantasies for children of the twentieth century. Its sequel, the three-volume *Lord of the Rings*, is much longer, deeper, and darker, and was published for adults, though it is often read by children. Books Too Good; Children's Classics; ChLA Touchstones; Choice; Fanfare.

HOBBITS (*The Hobbit**; *The Fellowship of the Ring**), an unobtrusive but ancient people of Middle-earth, between two and four feet in height and therefore also called Halflings. They resemble men in appearance, except for their feet, which are hair-covered and have hard, leather-like soles, and they have round, cheerful faces, curly hair, which is usually brown, and long, clever fingers. They also speak the languages of men and are similar to men in their interests and desires, being particularly fond of bright colors, notably yellow and green, and of eating, as well and as often as possible. A merry and generous people, they like parties and giving and receiving presents, and they prefer a comfortable, well-ordered life, being suspicious of adventures, unconventional ideas, and any kind of machinery more complicated than a water mill. Although they seem soft and naive, they have a tough streak that often surprises their enemies, and when put to the test show they unexpectedly strong fibre, both physically and emotionally. Unlike most of the types of characters in these books, which are drawn from the oral tradition, hobbits seem to be Tolkien's* own invention.

HOBEKINUS (*The Devil on the Road**), actual historical character from the seventeenth century, whose real name was Matthew Hopkins and who styled himself the Witchfinder General. From an ultra-conservative Puritan family, he studied in Amsterdam at a time when hundreds of witches were being executed, and he returned to England and set himself up in the business of finding and trying witches, for which he was paid handsomely. He is credited with causing the death by hanging of 500 women and of thus amassing a fortune. In the novel he is pictured as a man of very slight build, skilled at swaying a crowd by impassioned accusations. When John* Webster appears in his motorcycle clothes and creates a series of explosions, Johanna* Vavasour introduces him to Hobekinus as her master, the devil, and forces the witchfinder to kiss his boot. Afterwards, Hobekinus becomes mentally unbalanced and soon dies.

HODGES, C(YRIL) WALTER (1909-   ), born in Beckenham, Kent; artist, stage designer, and historical novelist. He was educated at Dulwich College and Goldsmiths' College School of Art, both in London. Except for the period of 1940 to 1946, when he served in the British Army, he has since 1931 been a stage and exhibition designer, mural painter, and freelance book, magazine, and advertisement illustrator. Among his other positions he has been designer of productions, for Mermaid Theater and St. George's Theater, London; art

director for Encyclopaedia Britannica Films,
Chicago; Judith E. Wilson Lecturer at Cambridge
University; design consultant and adviser for
the Globe Theater Reconstruction Project; and
Adjunct Professor of Theater, Wayne State
University, Detroit. He received the Kate
Greenaway Medal in 1965 for *Shakespeare's Theater* (Oxford, 1964; Coward, 1964), and an honorary doctorate from the University of Sussex,
Brighton, in 1979. Besides illustrating more
than seventy books by other authors, he has
written and illustrated both fiction and
nonfiction with historical subjects. *Columbus
Sails* (Bell, 1939; Coward, 1939), retells the
famous voyage from three viewpoints: those of a
monk, a sailor, and an Indian in Spain. Among
his best known books are *The Namesake** (Bell,
1964; Coward, 1964), which was commended for the
Carnegie Medal, and its sequel, *The Marsh King*
(Bell, 1967; Coward, 1967), which tell the story
of Alfred the Great. Another work that received
high critical acclaim is *The Overland Launch**
(Bell, 1969; Coward, 1970), the dramatic tale of
a real 1899 effort by a Devonshire lifeboat crew
to rescue the men of a foundering ship. Other
books are on the Norman Conquest, Magna Carta,
the Spanish Armada, the English Civil War, and
England from the War of the Roses to the age of
Shakespeare. He also wrote a book of short
stories about actors and playwrights in
Shakespeare's time, *Playhouse Tales* (Bell, 1974;
Coward, 1974). His historical novels, his nonfiction, and his illustrations are all noted for
solid realism, dramatic action, and accurate research.

THE HOLLOW LAND (Gardam*, Jane, ill. Janet Rawl-
ins, MacRae, 1981; Greenwillow, 1981), episodic
novel of two families set in the Cumbrian fells
and spread over about twenty years from 1979 to
1999. A London family, the Batemans--the
parents, a crowd of "great boys," of whom only
James is identified by name, and little Harry*,
4--have rented the old farm of Light Trees for
a vacation home. This starts a long association
with the Teesdale family--Bell*, 8, Eileen, his
older sister, the parents, and Grandad*
Hewitson--an association which is almost broken
off at the outset by misunderstanding when Mr.

Bateman, a writer, objects to the noise of the
haying in the home field around Light Tress and
which is saved only by the friendship of Harry
and Bell. Through the years, Light Trees becomes
Harry's true home as he is one of the few
"incomers" who ever really belongs to the area.
He and Bell explore one of the abandoned mine
shafts and are trapped by a cave-in; and later
they go off on their bikes in the winter snow to
see a waterfall turned to ice, a marvelous
sight, and have a terrible time getting back.
Harry, a quiet, self-contained boy, makes
friends with the strange, Puritanical "egg
witch," after deliberately smashing her three
dozen eggs on her doorstep and having to go back
the next day and scrub her whole walk, and he
lures her mother, Granny Crack, who took to her
bed seven years before though she is physically
well, out into the sunshine. In another
episode, a television personality, a "Household
Word," comes to consult with Mr. Bateman,
bringing her daughter, Poppet, who appears to be
hating every minute but actually has fallen in
love with the place, is thrilled by the
excitement of the flood, comes back to visit
Eileen, and eventually marries Bell. Other
characters include Kendal* the sweep, who takes
the older Bateman males on an exhausting fishing
trip in the rain, and then stays the whole
evening telling stories of local ghosts, to the
dismay of all but little Harry, and Jimmie
Meccer, lamed by a quarry accident, who is set
by the villagers to guard the houses from
gypsies and is robbed of his old table from his
back kitchen, a table for which a dealer gives
1,000 pounds, a sum which comes to Jimmie when
the thieves are caught. Jimmie has his legs
repaired by modern surgery and moves to South
America. The opening episode is narrated in the
first person by Bell; the last, set in 1999, is
partly narrated by Anne, eleven-year-old
daughter of Bell and Poppet. Oil reserves having
run out, the farm life has reverted and now is
much as it was in Grandad Hewitson's youth, with
horse-drawn vehicles and harvesting by scythe. A
wealthy distant cousin from South America
arrives claiming Light Trees and planning to
destroy the house and mine the land for the
silver left in the old workings and for the

possibility of oil. Harry, now a man of about
twenty-four, is stunned, Bell is sullenly angry,
and Anne, who has already decided that she will
marry Harry when she is older, is heartbroken.
In a memorable scene, when all the villagers
gather "up Nine Standards" to see the eclipse of
the sun, Grandad Hewitson announces that he has
consulted solicitors and found that the will in
which he will leave Light Trees to Anne, with
Harry having the right to rent it all his life,
takes precedence over the South American
cousin's claims. In a very compressed, economical style, the rural life is evoked and the characters delineated sharply and with considerable
humor. Dialect is used deftly, with a clever
twist when Bell corrects Harry, and later his
daughter Anne, for talking as he does. Although
the last chapter is in the future, there is no
feel of fantasy. Carnegie Highly Com; Choice;
Whitbread.

HOLLY (*Watership Down**), captain of the Owsla,
or peace force, at Sandleford Warren; one of the
two survivors of the ill-fated warren. He and
Bluebell, the jester-rabbit, make their way to
Watership Down and join Hazel's* warren. As
strongly as he had once opposed the request of
Fiver* and Hazel to get the rabbits out of the
Sandleford Warren, so staunchly does he become
a supporter of the new warren. He bravely
undertakes the expedition to Efrafa to get does,
a very dangerous enterprise. He is one of the
novel's strongest figures, appearing in many
scenes as a leader and fighter.

HOLY JOHN (*The Dancing Bear**), saint for the
household of Lord Celsus, an ascetic who sits or
kneels on a pillar in the courtyard, taking
pride in not having washed for twelve years. He
belongs to the Christian sect of the Monophys-
sites and disputes other beliefs with the convoluted logic dear to the hearts of the Byzan-
tines. The raid by the Huns seems to him a sign
from God that he is to give up his life of denial of the flesh and set off to convert the Kutrigurs, and he sees signs that Silvester* and
Bubba* must be part of the journey. A former
soldier, he has more worldly wisdom than he
appears to have, and though he is subject to

epileptic seizures, he also can fake trances for effect or to gain time. He is a mixture of innocence and guile, and though he is primarily interested in his own quest to convert the heathen, he saves Silvester from disaster several times.

HOME IS THE SAILOR (Godden*, Rumer, ill. Jean Primrose, Macmillan, 1964; Viking, 1964), doll story set in Penlelig, Wales, in the mid-twentieth century. The Llewellyn family, made up of the parents and Sian, 8, her sister Debbie, 18, their brother Kenneth, 11, and their Welsh maid, Blodwen Owen, have a doll house that was once Debbie's and is, now mostly Sian's. It is peopled by the Raleigh family: Mrs. Raleigh and Miss Charlotte, the governess, both with porcelain heads and cloth bodies; Dora, the eldest child, all of porcelain; Opal and Pearl, twins of thicker china; Bundle, a baby made of pink stockinette; Morello, a gloomy maid with a white china face and a limp body; Mrs. Lewis, a Welsh doll servant of celluloid; and the newest arrival, Curly, a seven-year-old sailor doll of sturdy china. Gradually, Curly learns of the fate of the two other men of the doll household: Captain Raleigh, the father, was lost in the sand at the beach years before, and Thomas Hood Raleigh, the grown-up brother naval officer doll, was given by Sian's mother to a visiting French girl named Arlette. Curly vows to find Thomas and accidentally begins his quest by falling out the window into the path of a troop of marching Sea School boys. Sian sees one of them pick him up and march on. The story switches at this point to be mostly about Bertrand Lesseps, 16, the very bright and arrogant French boy whose British uncle, tired of being advised and corrected by his nephew, has sent him to the Sea School, most of whose students are working-class boys a couple of years older than Bertrand. At first Bertrand makes himself as thoroughly disliked at the Sea School as he has been in most other places he has lived. At the school, however, the boys are quick to let him know his faults and to show their contempt. When he picks up Curly, his group is on their way to sea duty aboard the *Golden Galleon*, the school's instruction ship.

He keeps Curly for a mascot, and his luck does
seem to change. For the first time he is not
seasick and clumsy, and he begins to get along
with the other boys. Just as they are coming
in to dock, Curly falls out of Bertrand's pocket and over the ship's side into the estuary.
Without hesitation, Bertrand dives in after
him and, being an excellent swimmer, manages
to retrieve the doll amid the cheers from his
mates. Since it is against the rules to swim
without permission, he is assigned to duty
watch after being confined to bed with a bad
chill, and so is unable to return Curly to the
house of the Llewellyn family as he had
intended. Since Curly looks much the worse for
his adventure, he writes his sister, Marie
France, to ask her to send a sailor doll from
her collection to "the little girl with dark
hair who looked out of the window when the doll
dropped," a doll whose arrival is a great
surprise and mystery and who appears to be the
long-lost Thomas. In the meantime, Sian quite
by chance has found the even longer-lost
Captain Raleigh in the sand of the dunes. When
he is again free, Bertrand, a reformed character, brings Curly back to Sian, Charlotte
marries Thomas and has twins, and all ends
happily. Despite clever writing that tells
the story sometimes from the point of view of
the humans and sometimes from that of the
dolls, the book suffers the problem of many
doll stories that, since the characters cannot
act without human assistance, it is difficult
to forget that their adventures and emotions
are make-believe. The story of Bertrand's
difficulties in the Sea School dominates
Curly's story. The plot is skillfully woven,
however, and is not sentimental. Fanfare.

HOMILY CLOCK (*The Borrowers**; *The Borrowers
Afield**; *The Borrowers Afloat**; *The Borrowers
Aloft**; *the Borrowers Avenged**) bony, untidy,
self- and family-important, house-proud, emotional, appearance-conscious Borrower woman,
fond mother of Arrietty* and loyal and loving
wife of Pod*. In the first book, her desire for
creature comforts and nice things leads to the
family being discovered by Mrs.* Driver. Because
she doesn't want to emigrate after Pod is

"seen," she suggests teaching Arrietty to borrow. This leads to the crucial scene in which Arrietty meets the boy*. Along with Arrietty, the reader learns about family and Borrower history from her conversations with Pod, about the other Borrowers who used to live in Great* Aunt Sophy's house but disappeared: the Overmantels, who lived in the morning room, the Rain-Pipes, Uncle* Hendreary, his wife, Aunt* Lupy, and their daughter, Eggletina, who was probably eaten by a cat, the Sinks, and the Harpsichords, among others. Homily herself was a Bell-Pull before she married into the Clocks. Homily can fly off the handle, complain bitterly, and discover the darkest clouds, but she can also rise to the occasion, and does so numerous times throughout their wanderings. She always does her part. Her tense relationship with Aunt Lupy, to whom she serves as a foil, adds dimension to both their characters as well as contributing to the plot and providing some comic relief. Homily is an interesting, well-rounded, dynamic figure.

HORATIO BERESFORD (*Thursday's Child**), six-year-old orphan whom Margaret* Thursday takes under her wing when his older sister, Lavinia*, must leave him at St. Luke's so she can become a scullery maid for Lady Corkberry. He is a lovely, blond child, angelic looking and polite but sturdier and more dependable than one would expect from his age. When Margaret plans the escape from the orphanage, he follows her instructions carefully, and when he becomes a "legger" for the canal boat, he leads the horse for miles without complaint, even in miserably rainy weather. At the orphanage, he fares somewhat better than the others, because the pupil-teacher at the village school is fond of him and gives him extra things to eat.

THE HORSE AND HIS BOY (Lewis*, C. S., ill. Pauline Baynes, Bles, 1954; Macmillan, 1954), adventurous fantasy set in the mythical land of Narnia*, fifth novel published and third novel in chronological order in the series. The action takes place while the Pevensie children, Peter*, Susan*, Edmund*, and Lucy*, reign at Cair Paravel. It begins far to the south in the

country of Calormen, a powerful realm of
Oriental splendor, which is ruled by a tyrant
called the Tisroc. Calormen is a land where
slaves do most of the work and whippings and
burnings are common, society has polarized into
the very rich and privileged and the very poor
and exploited, weapons are swords and scimitars,
transportation is by foot for most or horseback
and sedan chair for the wealthy, and intrigue
and immorality rule at court. Shasta*, a
fisherman's boy of twelve or so, runs away from
his cruel master on a conceited, talking Narnian
horse named Bree*. On their way north to Narnia,
they are joined by a girl dressed in armor and
riding another talking Narnian horse, a shy mare
named Hwin*. The girl, Aravis*, daughter of a
Calormene noble, is fleeing from an undesirable
arranged marriage. The four make their
precarious way overland mostly by night, part of
the time pursued by a ferocious lion, to the
capital city of Tashbaan, agreeing to meet if
separated at the Place of the Tombs across the
river spanned by the city's bridge. They enter
the city disguised as peasants, and all proceeds
well until Shasta is mistaken for the truant
Prince Corin of Archenland, a scapegrace who is
traveling with Queen Susan and King Edmund of
Narnia. Shasta is taken to their quarters and
manages to get away, but not before he learns
that the Narnians will soon secretly sail home
to avoid Susan's having to reject openly the
suit of disagreeable Prince Rabadash of
Calormen. During this time, Aravis falls in with
an old friend, the muddleheaded Lasaraleen, in
whose company she overhears Rabadash and his
father, the Tisroc, plan war against Archenland
and Narnia, using Susan's abrupt departure as an
excuse. Most of the rest of the novel is taken
up with the race to get the news to King Lune in
Anvard of Archenland so he can prepare to
repulse the Calormene attack. The four travelers
rendezvous at the tombs and then make their
weary way across the desert. They cross the
Winding Arrow River into Archenland just ahead
of Rabadash's army, are pursued by a lion who
wounds Aravis, and are given refuge by the
mystical Hermit of the Southern March. He orders
Shasta to continue, and after a hard run on
foot, the boy encounters King Lune and delivers

the vital message. Separated from the king's group and despairing, he falls in with the lion, who reveals himself as Aslan*, informs Shasta that he has been watching over him all along, bucks the lad up, and stays with him until he has entered Narnia. There Shasta runs into talking animals, one of whom, a Stag, delivers the news of the impending invasion to the Narnian monarchs. King Edmund and Queen Lucy arrive the next morning, and a terrible battle ensues at Anvard in which the Calormenes are decisively defeated. Shasta is revealed not surprisingly by this time as Prince Cor, the twin of Corin and the true son and heir of King Lune, who was kidnapped as an infant, and Aslan turns Rabadash into a donkey for his persistently asinine behavior. The sequential plot depends upon coincidence and has more action than most of the Narnia books. The question of Shasta's identity adds a mild mystery. Characters are flat types, and there is some comedy. The reader sees that Narnia is only one country in a large world and gets a clearer picture of the landscape. Aslan appears as preserver and sustainer. Since so much of the story consists of superficial action, this book is less satisfying than its predecessors. Carnegie Com.; ChLA Touchstones; Choice.

HOTEL CONTINENTAL (*The Other Way Round**), cheap London hotel owned by Frau Gruber and catering to refugees, at which Anna*s parents live. When it is wrecked by a bomb, Frau Gruber buys a house in Putney which was owned by a maharajah, and the refugees move there.

THE HOUSE AT POOH CORNER (Milne*, A. A., ill. Ernest Shepard, Methuen, 1928; Dutton, 1928), second of two episodic fantasies (following *Winnie-the-Pooh**) about the author's son Christopher* Robin and his friends, Pooh* Bear, Piglet*, Owl, Rabbit, Eeyore*, and Kanga and her baby, Roo, all of whom are based on the boy's stuffed animals and live in the forest surrounding the Hundred Acre Wood. Unlike the first book, these stories have no external frame and there is no mechanism by which the toys come alive. They simply exist and enjoy various, mildly complicated adventures, from which they are usually rescued by Christopher Robin. The title story occurs in the winter, when Pooh and his great friend, Piglet, decide to build a house for gloomy Eeyore, the old gray donkey, and for materials unwittingly use the sticks which make up Eeyore's present house. Several of the episodes deal primarily with Tigger, the cheerfully bumptious new animal in the forest. The animals attempt to get him breakfast, each trying his own favorite food as Tigger assures them that tiggers like everything except, in turn, honey, "haycorns," and thistles, until he finally visits Kanga and tries Roo's strengthening medicine, Extract of Malt, which turns out to be what Tiggers really like best. Tigger is also happily sure that tiggers can fly, jump, swim, and climb trees; when he sets out with Roo on his back he proves this last to be true, but he forgets that tiggers don't know how to climb down again. Christopher Robin and several of the others hold the boy's tunic like a blanket, catch Roo, and are almost flattened when Tigger loses his hold and crashes down. When Eeyore appears floating down the river as the others are playing Poohsticks, Tigger is the culprit, having "bounced" at him and made him slip down the bank. Rabbit, who likes to take charge, organizes a plan to "unbounce" Tigger: he, Pooh, and Piglet will take Tigger to an unfamiliar part of the forest and lose him there until he is properly chastened. Unfortunately, the three give Tigger the slip but then become lost in the mist, while Tigger easily finds his way back to Kanga's, where he lives. Rabbit also organizes a search for Small, one of his "friends-and-relations" whose real name is Very Small Beetle, and Pooh and Piglet both fall into their old Heffalump trap, where Piglet finds Small climbing up Pooh's back. Piglet is the hero when Owl's tree blows down while he and Pooh are visiting. Since a branch blocks the front door, which is now in the ceiling, Piglet is hoisted up on a string worked like a pulley to the letter box, where he squeezes through and goes for help. Later, when Rabbit organizes a search for a new house for Owl, and Eeyore, who has seldom ventured out of his damp, gloomy corner of the forest, proudly discovers Piglet's house, Piglet again shows his pluck by saying he thinks it is the perfect house for Owl and taking up Pooh's invitation to come and live with him. The animals stay forever the same age, but Christopher Robin is growing up. Rabbit takes charge of finding out what Christopher Robin does in the mornings, and they discover that he is "instigorating Knowledge, becoming Educated." In the last of the ten episodes, the animals discover that Christopher Robin is going off to school. They all sign a "Rissolution" and give it to him, and he and Pooh go off to the Enchanted Place at the top of the forest, where he knights Pooh and tries to explain. The stories are perhaps more carefully developed than those in the first book, but still have the same whimsical charm and spontaneity. Children's Classics; ChLA Touchstones; Choice; Lewis Carroll.

THE HOUSE IN NORHAM GARDENS (Lively*, Penelope, Heinemann, 1974; Dutton, 1974), realistic novel with fantasy overtones set from January to March in the early 1970s in North Oxford, England. Clare Mayfield, 14, lives happily with her kind, vague, scholarly great-aunts, Aunt* Susan Mayfield, 80, and Aunt Anne Mayfield, 78, maiden ladies of low income and high reputation, in a rambling Gothic Victorian house in Norham Gardens. While she is searching for a blanket for Maureen* Cooper, 28, a lodger, the two come upon artifacts collected many years before by Clare's deceased Great-Grandfather Mayfield, an anthropologist who worked in New Guinea, among them a wooden slab carved and painted with primitive designs. Shortly thereafter, Clare dreams about the tribesmen to whom the slab belonged and awakens fearful and tense, with a sense of unfulfilled obligation hanging over her. The dreams persist, leaving Clare feeling washed-out and even suspended in time, hearing things and seeing strange striped figures. She becomes convinced that the little brown men of her dreams wish the slab returned. As she pores over old photos and reads family records about New Guinea, her sense of connection with the past intensifies, though her relationship with her great-aunts remains as satisfying as ever. She visits the Pitt Rivers Museum, to which her grandfather gave his artifacts and there meets

John* Sempebwa, a friendly, outgoing Ugandan
student, who later takes a room in the house. He
discovers that the slab is a *tamburan*, a New
Guinean ceremonial shield and a kind of tribal
coat of arms. Talkative, stylish cousin Margaret
(who is obviously intended as a foil) comes to
visit. Up to the minute on everything, she
deplores Clare's having to live with such
elderly people, a sentiment Clare definitely
does not share. At school Clare seems increasingly abstracted, and at home Maureen and John
become concerned about her. Clare sets the
tamburan on the doorstep for the little brown
men, but Mrs.* Hedges, the day-lady, unwittingly
brings it back inside. Confident that modern
medicine will put Clare to rights, Mrs. Hedges
sends her off to the doctor, who does nothing
for her, and later Clare spends a lovely,
carefree day with John in London, exploring the
history of the country in art and architecture
and visiting the zoo. She continues to have
dreams and visions, one in which the Norham
Gardens house stands vacant and desolate. She
becomes reluctant to leave the place, since she
identifies so closely with it. One day she
comes home from school to find her aunts
unexpectedly and atypically absent. Panic-
stricken, she bikes off to Mrs. Hedges's house,
skids on the ice en route, and is struck by a
car and hospitalized with bruises and a broken
arm. There she dreams that she visits the tribe
and offers them the shield, which they refuse
because they no longer recognize it, since
modern civilization has changed them. Home
again, Clare decides to give the shield to the
museum and plants a tree for Aunt Susan's
eighty-first birthday, just the kind of present
she knows her aunt would most like and one that
both connects them with the past and gives a
grasp on the future. Two stories develop
simultaneously. One story, in a factual, more
objective style, appears in italics at the
beginning of each chapter. It relates the
history of the Stone Age tribe that Clare's
grandfather discovered and from whom he received
the *tamburan*, beginning with the time the shield
was made and coming up to the present, when
schools and modern technology have arrived and
the tribesmen no longer want the *tamburan*

because they have forgotten why they once needed it yet have not come to see that they need something to replace it. Action is subordinated to atmosphere, and the plot, though engrossing, seems to offer a grab bag of themes--time, growing up, materialism, aging, the effect of modern technology, the need for roots and knowledge of self, to name a few--and leaves the reader perplexed about what to carry away. The plot also is not entirely clear: Have the occurrences all been the result of tension Clare feels because she faces important exams? Is she experiencing growing-up pains? Is she simply an overimaginative adolescent? (She is not presented in this way at the outset, being rather coolly collected and self-possessed like her aunts.) What is the connection between what goes on and the weather? (With the cessation of cold weather the problems with the *tamburan* cease.) This is, nevertheless, a rich, haunting book with good characterizations, a keenly realized psychological setting, and a polished, highly figurative but never florid or bookish style. It is a novel about an unusual young woman, not told by her but recounted convincingly from her point of view. Fanfare.

THE HOUSE ON MAYFERRY STREET. See *A Flute in Mayferry Street.*

HOWARD SYKES (*Archer's Goon**), school boy who becomes involved in the machinations of the seven wizards who control the city and their attempt to force his father to write the 2,000 words that are his quarterly payment in lieu of taxes. Howard is large for his age, a straightforward thirteen-year-old whose only passion is for designing spaceships. He is fond of his parents and his spoiled little sister, but he sees their faults and weaknesses clearly. When he discovers he is Venturus, he is appalled, and he decides to grow up into a much more decent wizard than he has been in the past.

HOWKER, JANNI, student and author. Although her childhood was spent in Norfolk, Suffolk, Lincolnshire, and Cambria, her parents and grandparents came from Lancashire, and she has lived there as well. She received her B.A.

degree from Lancaster University and has
recently been studying for an M.A. in creative
writing there. She has also worked with the
elderly and mentally handicapped and as an
assistant on an archeological site. Her first
book, *Badger on the Barge* (MacRae, 1984; Greenwillow, 1985), a collection of short stories,
won the International Reading Association award.
The Nature of the Beast* (MacRae, 1985; Greenwillow, 1985), a novel of a boy in a Lancashire
town where the mill, the major source of employment, closes, was listed as Highly Commended by
the Carnegie Award committee and cited on the
Horn Book Fanfare list. Turning back some
eighty years, *Isaac Campion* (Greenwillow, 1987),
tells of the twelve-year-old son of a horse
dealer yanked from school to do the work of his
older brother who has been tragically killed, a
story of poverty and strained family relationships at the turn of the century. Howker's
characters typically are working-class, rough
but determined, a far cry from the boarding-
school adolescents in much earlier English fiction.

HOWL (*Howl's Moving Castle**), wizard who is reputed to eat the hearts of young girls and suck
out their souls. When Sophie* Hatter, under a
spell as an old woman, acts as cleaning woman in
his castle, she finds he is a young man in his
twenties, with dyed blond hair and glassy green
eyes, who "slithers out" of any responsibility
or any definite decision. When they go through
the door after setting the knob to the black
blob, they come into his twentieth-century home
town in Wales, where Howl's sister, Megan Parry,
treats him with contempt because he does not
conform to the respectable pattern of the
family, but his niece, Mari, and his nephew,
Neil, both adore him. There he is known as
Howell Jenkins, a man who studied folklore at
the University and then disappeared. He seems to
feel real grief at the death of Mrs.
Pentstemmon, a witch who was his tutor in
Kingsbury, but it is not until Sophie retrieves
the heart he has given, in compassion, to the
fire demon, Calcifer*, that he is able to truly
love a real woman.

HOWL'S MOVING CASTLE (Jones*, Diana Wynne, Greenwillow, 1986), complex fantasy set mainly in the fairy-tale kingdom of Ingary but moving through time and space travel to various other fictional lands and to present-day Wales. When their father dies, Fanny, his young wife and stepmother of the two eldest Hatter girls, arranges that Lettie*, the beautiful middle girl, shall be apprenticed in the cake shop; that Martha*, the youngest, who is her own child, shall go as student and assistant to Annabel Fairfax, the witch of Upper Folding; and that Sophie*, the eldest, will stay and work in the hat shop, which she will eventually inherit. After some months during which the hat shop thrives but Sophie is both overworked and bored, she goes to visit Lettie, who confesses to her that she is really Martha, having learned a spell to disguise herself and having traded places with Lettie, to the relief of them both. Sophie, less contented in the hat shop than before, is astonished when the Witch of the Waste appears and casts a spell on her, turning her into an old woman. She hobbles out of the town of Market Chipping, befriending both a dog and a scarecrow as she stumps along and becoming so exhausted by nightfall that when the moving castle of the Wizard Howl* comes along, she commands it to stop, goes in, and sinks down in the chair in front of the fire. Though she has heard that Howl eats the hearts of young girls and sucks out their souls, she feels safe in her present form. In the middle of the night, the fire, or the fire demon, Calcifer*, makes a bargain with her: he will try to remove the spell she is under if she will break the contract that binds him to the castle. To do this she must stay at the castle, posing as the new cleaning woman, and live with Michael Fisher, the apprentice of doubtful ability, and Howl, a self-centered young man adept at squeezing out of answering any question or making any commitment. Nothing in the story is quite what it seems. The castle itself seems on the outside to be a huge structure made of large, black, coal-like stone, but inside it is just a central room, a bath, and two small bedrooms upstairs. Above the door is a knob, with a different-colored blob of paint on each

side. If the red blob is at the bottom, the door
opens to Kingsbury, the city where the king
lives; if the blue blob is down, it opens to
Porthaven, a town of wharves and sailors; green
opens to the hills above Market Chipping; and
the black, she discovers later, opens to Wales,
where Howell Jenkins lived before he studied
magic and became the Wizard Howl. She discovers
gradually that in the castle Calcifer does all
the strong magic and Michael the hackwork, while
Howl gads off catching girls, not literally
eating their hearts but pursuing them until they
fall in love and then dropping them promptly for
a new quest. In an extraordinarily complicated
series of events, Sophie and Michael use
seven-league boots to try to catch a falling
star, accompany Howl to Wales where they meet
his family and his nephew's teacher, Miss
Angorian, visit the king in his palace, observe
a battle of witchcraft in the skies over
Porthaven, and have numerous other encounters
with magical powers. In the end most of the
actors in the drama turn out to be something
other than they seem. Calcifer is really a
falling star; Miss Angorian is really the Witch
of the Waste's fire demon; Lettie's young man,
who has been under a spell as a dog, is really
the Wizard Suliman and also Benjamin Sullivan,
of the same town in Wales as Howl; the scarecrow
is Prince Justin, the king's brother. Martha and
Michael are united. Sophie retrieves Howl's
heart, which he had given to Calcifer. She frees
the fire demon from his contract and, with her
newly discovered magic powers, grants him
another 1,000 years to live. With his heart now
in place, Howl can love the woman who loves him,
and with the spell of old age removed, that
woman is Sophie. The story moves at a rollicking
pace, full of humor and unexpected twists that
are almost too involved to follow. There is
great fun in the use of traditional folk motifs
and magic elements in new contexts. The whole is
held together by good characterization, particularly of Sophie, who is both a sweet, patient
girl and a wickedly self-serving old woman,
sharp-tongued and practical. The various
settings are described with such richness and
life in Howl's castle in such concrete detail
that there is a sense of reality even in the

fantastic and bizarre story. Boston Globe Honor.

HUGH (*The Blue Boat**), English boy of about eight, who with his brother, Christopher*, has adventures with two circus performers, one extremely tall and the other a dwarf, on a lake near the coastal village of Withern. Hugh discovers the blue boat in which they paddle about the lake. The boys use the boat even though they have not asked permission, because Hugh has wished for a boat and the two half believe the boat has appeared in answer to his wish. Later, the boys discover the boat belongs to the dwarf, whom they call the goblin. Hugh is a willful, independent boy, inclined to be babyish. His brother thinks he is uncommonly lucky, because interesting things just seem to happen to him, like being invited inside a train cab to see what's there. Hugh doesn't like Mrs. Wrigley and wishes he were back in Africa with his mother and father. He initiates the boys' imagining adventures. Hugh is a likeable if somewhat naughty boy. Like his brother, he is a well-drawn character who remains the same in spite of his experiences.

HUGHES, TED (EDWARD JAMES HUGHES) (1930-   ), born in Mytholmroyd, Yorkshire; prolific, versatile, and highly acclaimed writer of poetry, plays, and short stories for adults, who also writes fiction, poetry, and stage, radio, and television plays for children. His short surrealistic novel for children, *The Iron Man: A Story in Five Nights** (Faber, 1968; as *The Iron Giant: A Story in Five Nights*, Harper, 1968), appears in *Choice*, and his *Moon Bells and Other Moon Poems* (Chatto, 1978) won the *Signal* Poetry Award. Also for children he published *How the Whale Became and Other Stories* (Faber, 1963; Atheneum, 1964) and almost a dozen other books of original poems, including *Meet My Folks!* (Faber, 1961; Bobbs, 1973), humorous verse, and *Season Songs* (Faber, 1976; Viking, 1975). Some of his plays for the young are *The Tiger's Bones* (1965), *Orpheus* (1971), *Beauty and the Beast* (1965), and *The Pig Organ; or, Pork with Perfect Pitch* (1980), and with poet Seamus Heaney he edited *The Rattle Bag: An Anthology* (Faber, 1982). Best known as a poet for adults, he has

won many awards, including a Guggenheim
Fellowship, the Somerset Maugham Award, and the
Queen's Gold Medal for Poetry. He attended
Mexborough Grammar School in Yorkshire and
Pembroke College, Cambridge, on a scholarship,
receiving his B.A. and M.A. in archaeology and
anthropology. From 1948 to 1950, he served in
the Royal Air Force. He has married twice, the
first time to the American poet Sylvia Plath,
who died in 1963. In the 1950s he held various
jobs, teaching from 1957 to 1959 at the
University of Massachusetts. He has made his
home in Devonshire. Two of his many books of
poetry for adults are *Lupercal* (Faber, 1960;
Harper, 1960) and *Crow: From the Life and Songs
of Crow* (Faber, 1970; Harper, 1971). He has
edited and translated extensively. Critics have
praised the striking imagery and vigorous,
electrical style of his work for the young, and
some object to the violence and the bleakness of
the tone, but generally they applaud his
imaginative and distinctive handling of his
subjects.

HULL, KATHARINE (1921-1977), born in London,
coauthor with Pamela Whitlock* of adventure
novels for children. Daughter of Sir Hubert
Hull, she was educated at St. Mary's Convent,
Ascot, Berkshire, and at Lady Margaret Hall,
Oxford. She served in the Women's Royal Air
Force in World War II, attaining the rank of
captain. She married Paul Buxton, a diplomat.
*The Far-Distant Oxus** (Cape, 1937; Macmillan,
1938), a Fanfare selection, was written when she
was fifteen and Whitlock was sixteen. In the
summer term of 1936, the two girls, friends from
school, were caught in a storm, took shelter
from the rain, and thought up the idea of
writing together an adventure novel about children, ponies, and moors. By Easter they had
completed a draft, which they sent for approval
to Arthur Ransome*, whose adventure stories
they enjoyed, suggesting that his characters
might like to read it. The manuscript was carefully written throughout in two different
hands. Ransome thought it excellent fare and
sent it on to Cape, who published it and its two
sequels, *Escape to Persia* (Cape, 1938; Macmillan, 1939) and *Oxus in Summer* (Cape, 1939;

Macmillan, 1940). The two women also cowrote *Crowns* (Cape, 1947), about an imaginary world invented by four cousins. Although regarded by critics as better crafted, it never attained the popularity of the first book, which, though naive technically, is full of the subject matter children find interesting: lots of action, youths on their own, camping, ponies, boating, and mystery.

HUMPTY DUMPTY (*Through the Looking-Glass**), volatile, easily insulted, sharp-tongued, proud character, who appears to be a humanized egg. Alice* encounters him sitting on a wall, in a scene that improvises on the familiar nursery rhyme and the old proverb, "Pride goeth before a fall." Like most of the characters in the book, he is rude to Alice, and she has difficulty following his reasoning. He engages her in a perplexing discussion on the meanings of words and gets angry about her innocent remarks on his shape and her calling his cravat a belt, an item he says he received as an un-birthday present. He explains the "Jabberwocky" poem to her, recites a long nonsense poem about fishes, and makes such uncomplimentary remarks about her appearance as "Your face is the same as everybody has." He insists that if he does fall from the wall, the king and his men will repair him. Though exaggerated to zaniness, he is one of the most memorable and beloved characters in the books about Alice.

HUNTER, MOLLIE (MAUREEN MOLLIE HUNTER MCVEIGH MCILWRAITH) (1922-   ), born in Longniddry, East Lothian, in the Lowlands of Scotland; regarded as one of the most gifted of contemporary novelists for young readers. Since the publication of her first book for the young in 1963, *Patrick Kentigern Keenan* (Blackie; as *The Smartest Man in Ireland*, Funk, 1965), she has written some two dozen books of mainly two kinds, historical fiction for teenagers and fantasies of magic and folklore for middle-graders, all employing her Scottish heritage. Her father Irish, her mother Scottish and a talented storyteller, Hunter has recalled that her Scottish childhood as the third of five children was joyful and satisfying. After her

father died when she was nine, the family was
plunged into poverty, and at fourteen she was
forced to leave home and school to work in
Edinburgh. At eighteen she married Thomas
"Michael" McIlwraith, a hospital catering
manager, who comes of the Highlands' Clan
Donald; they had two sons. She was determined to
become a writer and wrote features for newspapers and plays. She made up stories for her
children, later working them up into novels and
eventually assisted by the boys and her husband
with substance and historical accuracy. Her own
youth serves as background for *A Sound of
Chariots** (Hamilton, 1973; Harper, 1972),
regarded by many as her masterpiece, which was a
Child Study selection, was named to the Fanfare
list by the editors of *Horn Book*, and appears in
Choice and Contemporary Classics. Loosely autobiographical, it describes Scottish Bridie Mc-
Shane's efforts in the years following World War
I to overcome poverty and become a writer. Its
sequel is *The Dragonfly Years* (Hamilton, 1983;
as *Hold on to Love*, Harper, 1984), in which
Bridie faces conflicts between love and career.
The Third Eye* (Hamilton, 1979; Harper, 1979), a
story of suspense and of a girl growing up in
early twentieth-century Scotland, was named to
Fanfare. Two of Hunter's historical novels have
won awards: *The Stronghold** (Hamilton, 1974;
Harper, 1974), a powerful narrative about the
resistance of Celtic Scots against Roman
slavers, which won the Carnegie Medal and was
named to *Choice* and Fanfare, and *You Never Knew
Her as I Did!** (Hamilton, 1981; Harper, 1981),
about efforts to free Mary Queen of Scots from
her island prison. This latter book also appears
on the Fanfare list. *The Kelpie's Pearls**
(Blackie, 1964; Funk, 1966) and *A Stranger Came
Ashore** (Hamilton, 1975; Harper, 1975) are,
respectively, humorous and suspenseful improv-
isations on Scottish lore. They appear in
Choice, and the second work also was a *Boston
Globe-Horn Book* honor book and cited in *Books
Too Good to Miss*. More recently she has pub-
lished another girls' growing-up novel, *I'll Go
My Own Way* (Hamilton, 1985; as *Cat, Herself*,
Harper, 1985), about the daughter of wandering
Scottish tinkers, and a set of picture books
with illustrator Marc Simont called the Knight

of the Golden Plain series, which consists of short, light fantasies made up for her grandchildren. For adults, she has published plays and *Talent Is Not Enough: Mollie Hunter on Writing for Children* (Harper, 1976), a book of philosophy and personal experience. A much honored writer, she is in demand as a speaker and lectured in the May Hill Arbuthnot series in 1975. She lives in the Scottish Highlands near Inverness.

HURLY BURLY (*When Shakespeare Lived in Southwark**), right-hand man to the robber captain, Cock* Lorel. Having been a soldier and down on his luck, Hurly was branded as a vagabond with a V on his thumb, thus assuring that he could no longer earn an honest lving. He protects Miles Francis and Nat* Marlowe from Cock's murderous rage when they have attempted to escape, but whips them soundly himself. He explains to Miles the laws of the brotherhood and so impresses him that when Miles later has a chance to betray him the boy refuses to speak, though it might save his own future. When Nat and Miles are escorting Lord Lumley to safety and escaping themselves, Hurly sees them but pretends not to recognize them. Later, having fallen out with Cock, he prevents Numps from attacking Mistress Susan, and Numps murders him.

HURREE BABU (*Kim**), Hurree Chunder Mookerjee, hulking, obese Bengali who is a member of the Indian Secret Service and listed as R.17. By his own admission a fearful man and one who hates physical discomfort, he nevertheless gets himself into many "dam'-tight places" and suffers cold, rain, long foot journeys over the mountains, and other hardships as part of his work, for which he has real zest. He has an M.A. degree from Calcutta University, and his secret longing is to be made a Fellow of the Royal Society for his ethnological notes.

HUW HALFBACON (*The Owl Service**), seemingly half-witted handyman on an estate located in a Welsh valley not far from Aberystwyth and owned by the English girl to whom Gwyn*, Huw's son, is attracted. Huw tries to inspire Gwyn to break the power of the curse that haunts the valley

and goes all the way back to ancient times and
the myth of Blodeuwedd*. Evidently this must be
done through forgiveness and love, and Gwyn
doesn't prove up to it. Huw apparently is the
hereditary lord of the indigenous inhabitants
of the valley and is regarded by them with
respect. Though the English think he's a
half-mad babbler, his conversations with Gwyn
reveal him as knowledgeable, clear-thinking,
and straight-talking. He was the one who covered
the painting of the woman of flowers in the
billiard room with stucco and hid the dishes
with the owl or flowers pattern in the loft in
an unsuccessful attempt to stop the ancient
power from working again. He is one of the most
interesting figures in the novel, enigmatic and
complex to the end.

HWIN (*The Horse and His Boy*), shy, talking
Narnian mare, captured as a foal and taken into
service among the Calormenes, whose comments
about Narnia to her mistress, Aravis*, induce
the girl to seek refuge there from an undesirable arranged marriage. At first Hwin is modest
to the point of timidity, but she gradually
learns to put forth her good ideas and several
times acts to facilitate their safe arrival in
Archenland. At the end, the reader is told that
Hwin lives happily to a ripe old age in Narnia,
as she had hoped to do, and often visits Shasta*
(now Crown Prince Cor) and Aravis in Anvard.

I

IBBOTSON, EVA (1925-   ), born in Vienna, Austria, her father a physiologist and her mother a writer; researcher, teacher, and writer. She received her B.Sc. degree from Bedford College, University of London, in 1945, and later took a diploma in education from the University of Durham. Primarily a writer for adults, her inventive and lively comic fantasy *Which Witch?** (Macmillan, 1979), about a wizard's efforts to find a bride, was commended for the Carnegie Award. For children she has also published *The Great Ghost Rescue* (Macmillan, 1975; Walck, 1975), about a boy's efforts to provide a sanctuary for ghosts displaced by urban sprawl, *The Haunting of Hiram C. Hapgood* (Macmillan, 1987), and *The Worm and the Toffee-Nosed Princess, and Other Stories of Monsters* (Macmillan, 1983). She has written novels and short stories for adults, television plays, and many articles for periodicals. She married Alan Ibbotson, a university lecturer, and has four children.

IDA BIGGIN (*The River at Green Knowe**; *A Stranger at Green Knowe**), eleven-year-old niece of Dr.* Maud Biggin, who rents the old house for the summer. Very small for her age, Ida is nonetheless self-reliant, a leader of or at least equal to the two boys in their adventures by day and by night. Though honest and generally polite, she has a bit of her aunt's bluntness. She does not appear in *A Stranger at Green*

Knowe, but she writes a letter suggesting that Mrs.* Oldknow invite Ping* to stay with her for the summer, and since Tolly* is not able to come, the old lady takes up Ida's suggestion, giving Ping a second summer at Green Knowe.

INGEBORG NYGAARD (*When Jays Fly to Barbmo**), daughter of a Norwegian farmer and a Lapp mother, who endures most of the German occupation during World War II on their island farm north of the Arctic Circle. Although she does not know the story about her dead mother until after her father's death, she has always felt an intense interest in the Lapps who bring their herds to summer pasture on the island, and when her farm is destroyed and the Germans are driving out all the settlers and villagers, she makes an arduous and dangerous winter trip to join her Lapp grandfather's family. She lives with them, accepted and happy, for some months.

THE INTRUDER (Townsend*, John Rowe, ill. Graham Humphreys, Oxford, 1969; Lippincott, 1970), novel of mystery, suspense, and some detection, set in the late twentieth century in Skirlston, a dying village at the sandy estuary of the River Skirl somewhere in northern England. Arnold Haithwaite, 16 and on the dull side, lives with elderly Ernest Haithwaite, the only Dad he has ever known. Old Ernest operates Cottontree House, a general store and bed-and-breakfast, on lease, like other properties in Skirlston, from the Duchy of Furness in return for a single bunch of violets a year. Arnold helps about the place, and, to bring in a little cash, he traps fish and sometimes serves as Sand Pilot to guide tourists across the tidal flats for old Joe Hardwick. Joe also holds the office of Admiral, a duchy appointment of long tradition but currently of minor practical importance. The people of the area confidently expect that some day Arnold will take over Ernest's business and will take Hardwick's place as Sand Pilot and Admiral, too. Trouble enters this sleepy microcosm with the arrival of a skinny, sharp-tongued, walleyed little stranger who says his name is Arnold Haithwaite and claims he's the son of Ernest's dead cousin Tom. He poses a clear threat to Arnold's

well-being and identity. Also known as Sonny
Smith, the stranger has big plans for turning
the area into a resort. He quickly insinuates
himself into Ernest's favor, insisting that the
old man needs care and implying that Arnold has
been remiss in his responsibilities. He moves
into Cottontree House and soon dominates the old
man, urging Ernest to spend his days resting in
bed, cooking for him, and even bringing his
fiancee, Miss Valerie Binns, to help him keep
the place clean and fix it up. Arnold, who feels
increasingly threatened by the man, confides his
apprehensions to the Ellison children, Peter,
13, and Jane, 15, whose family is living
temporarily at Skirlston Manor, the home also
of Miss Katharine Hendry, another longtime
resident of Skirlston. When Ernest gets sick
and becomes steadily weaker and Arnold becomes
disconsolate about his own situation, Peter
decides that they need to find out who Sonny
and Arnold really are. Finding out about Sonny
comes to nothing. Peter follows the man to a
derelict cottage in Gumble's Yard, a seedy part
of the city of Cobchester, is caught by Sonny,
and is probably saved from being murdered by the
chance arrival of Miss Binns. Miss Hendry at
first refuses to give Arnold information about
himself and then suggests that Arnold contact a
certain hairdresser in Irontown. Peter goes in
Arnold's stead and discovers that Arnold is the
illegitimate son of the hairdresser's sister and
a Cardiff sailor and was taken in by Ernest as
an infant since Ernest assumed Arnold was the
child of his dead son, Frank. Peter and Miss
Hendry try unsuccessfully to get Mr. Blackburn,
the ducal agent, to intervene on Arnold's
behalf. Mr. Blackburn finally agrees to go to
Cottontree House when he discovers that Sonny
has decided to turn the place into the Bay View
Private Hotel and to cut down the cotton tree,
an area landmark. The agent discovers Ernest
quite ill, probably from poison, and summons the
doctor. Sonny attacks Arnold, who flees to the
sands, where he manages to escape from Sonny. In
the darkness, Sonny meets death from the gale
winds and rapidly incoming tide. Arnold reaches
safety in abandoned St. Brendan's Church, where
earlier Jane Ellison was marooned by the tide.
Arnold's ingenuity and courage get them both

through the highest tide of the year, and they
are rescued about midnight. The Admiral advises
Arnold to stop moaning and pick up his life
where it was before Sonny arrived, noting that
everything is really the same as it always was,
and Arnold eventually accepts that. Much more
skillfully written than most thrillers, the
book's power comes from the author's ability to
create and sustain tension and draw exciting
scenes without lapsing into melodrama or using
shock appeal. Contributing to the apprehensive
mood are the crisp style of mostly short, simple
sentences, the frequent use of sentence
fragments, and the foreshadowing, in particular
of adverse changes in the weather. The seaside
setting functions as backdrop and almost as
character. It provides the constant of sand,
sky, and sea, which Sonny unwittingly and
tragically proposes to change for financial gain
and which inevitably claims his life. As
character, the setting not only affects the
fates of those who live there but also protects
its own against those who would violate them.
The characters, if type-cast, are individualized, serve the story well, and are carefully
contrasted for deeper revelation. There is some
social comment. The plot grips the reader from
the beginning, from the moment when Sonny on
first arrival attempts to kill Arnold, a scene
that ironically heralds and balances the final
one involving the two characters. Interest holds
through to the ironic conclusion, where it is
suggested that identity and belonging involve
more than names, for at the end the reader
learns that Sonny is in fact exactly who he says
he is--Arnold Haithwaite. An additional value of
the book comes from its sensitive portrayal of
Arnold, who is shown as mildly retarded yet
valued and plucky yet diffident in the presence
of the malicious Sonny, who represents the
terrors and venality of the outside world.
Arnold is respected and protected in the
community despite his illegitimacy (which
everyone except Arnold knows about) and his
handicap, or perhaps even because of them.
Adding still another dimension is the parallel
between the way the community takes care of
Arnold and the way the sea and sand protect the
inhabitants of the area who respect and value

them. The matter of identity is crucial in the
story—both literally and metaphorically, and
the conclusion clearly suggests that identity
and worth transcend names and origin. Boston
Globe Winner; Carnegie Com.; Choice; Contemporary Classics; Fanfare; Poe Winner.

IRELAND, TIMOTHY (1959-   ), born in South-
borough, Kent. His first-person, realistic
novel, *Who Lies Inside** (Gay Men's, 1984),
about a husky, eighteen-year-old schoolboy's
struggles to identify and come to terms with his
homosexual orientation, received the Other
Award. Previously he published the novel
Catherine Loves (Bodley, 1980), in which a girl
tries to hold her threatened family together.
Ireland lives and works in London.

THE IRON GIANT. See *The Iron Man.*

THE IRON LILY (Willard*, Barbara, Longman, 1973,
Dutton, 1974), richly crafted historical novel
with elements of mystery and romance set in the
Ashdown forest in Sussex south of London at the
time of Elizabeth I and fourth in the
Mantlemass* series of which *The Lark and the
Laurel** is the first. Her mother and half
brother dead of the plague and her cruel,
over-churched sister-in-law taunting her with
the discovery of her illegitimacy, gently reared
Lilias Rowan, 15, runs away and takes a position
as a housemaid at Penshurst, the manor of Sir
Henry and Lady Mary Sydney, who have royal
connections. Lilias's only clues to her real
identity are a gold ring bearing a lark and
laurel crest and the name Medley following hers
in the parish baptismal record. Plain and
crooked-shouldered, Lilias has a strong instinct
for survival, earns a reputation for industry,
wins Lady Mary's favor with a soothing balm for
her smallpox-ravaged face, and is rewarded with
a husband, Grover Godman*, a skilled ironmaster.
The narrative then leaps ahead some dozen years
to Godman's death in a foundry accident and
Lilias's resolution to earn the epithet bestowed
upon her by Godman, "the iron lily," not only by
maintaining his Froreden foundry but also by
establishing one of her own. She determines also
to discover who her father was and whether she

is any relation to the family now living at
Mantlemass whose surname is Medley. As she
establishes her foundry at Strives Minnis in
Ashdown forest, the Medleys generously offer
help, even though they realize she will be a
fierce competitor and indeed has secured through
her powerful royal patron, Sir Henry, the very
site for her foundry that Richard* Medley had
wanted for his. Gradually the Godmans and
Medleys become friends, and on a visit to the
manor house, Lilias sees the lark and laurel
motif in an embroidered picture over the hearth,
which reinforces her conviction that there may
be a family connection. When the men of the
forest refuse to work for a woman, and a
crooked-back one at that, Lilias hires Welsh
laborers. In retaliation, the local men come at
night intent on wrecking her foundry. Richard
(himself a hunchback) and Lilias outface the
attackers together. Now accepted as master (a
term she insists upon), Lilias soon must
confront a greater problem, one arising from her
ambition to better the station in life of her
daughter, Ursula, by marrying the girl against
her will to the heir of an iron fortune, Christy
Willard. To her dismay and anger, Lilias
discovers that Ursula has fallen in love with
Robin, the ward of Piers* Medley, Richard's
brother. Fearing that Piers Medley may be her
real father, that Robin is his illegitmate son
as rumored in the district, and that a marriage
between the two youths might perpetuate the
family handicap, Lilias puts Ursula into service
with Lady Mary Sydney. Ursula, her mother's
daughter in determination and resourcefulness,
runs away and returns to Mantlemass. Faced with
the need for information, Lilias confronts Piers
and learns that, while she is indeed his
daughter, Robin is only his ward. She also
learns the secret of Mantlemass: that the family
is descended from Richard III, with whom the
family's physical deformity originated. The way
is clear for the two young people to marry, and
the tribulation of almost losing the daughter
she loves so much tempers Lilias's ambition and
leaves her wiser, more understanding, and more
compassionate. Although overplotted and melodramatic (for example, Ursula comes upon the
scene just in time to aid her sweetheart as he

and Christy batter each other bloody over her) and overforeshadowed, the characters act and talk like real people. Even less important figures linger in the memory: Deborah, Lilias's girlhood friend grown old and gap-toothed in her early thirties, who aids Ursula in her flight from Lady Mary's; Susannah Mallory, a Medley cousin, the warm, maternal, spinster mistress of Mantlemass, who gives Robin the clue to Ursula's whereabouts; prim, pious, self-righteous Catherine Medley, Piers's daughter, who reacts with anger to Ursula's innocent question about Robin's parentage; and even the bashful, newly married Mantlemass groom, Will Bunce, whose very obvious infatuation with his silly, lisping, young wife sets in relief both Ursula's character and her budding romance with Robin. Details of everyday life are clear and contribute well to the story, and the author skillfully weaves the larger historical issues into the lives of the characters, especially showing how Elizabeth's Spanish wars feed the fires of Lilias's amibition and compound her personal problems. Dominating the book is Lilias, proud, sturdy, and determined that life not beat her down, whose hopes and dreams, well-intentioned though they may be, almost destroy what she loves most in all the world. Lilias is the strongest and most memorable of several strong women in this series of novels and the personification of the iron lily symbol of her foundry. Although Lilias remains inarticulate about her feelings, having learned to repress them in her youth, she does come to see the need for understanding and accepting the wishes of the daughter she loves so much and letting the girl live life in her own way. Such motifs as the crooked shoulder, the lark and laurel, a particular knife, the iron, and the forest recur in the novels and provide unity as well as considerable story interest. Guardian.

THE IRON MAN: A STORY IN FIVE NIGHTS (Hughes*, Ted, ill. George Adamson, Faber 1968; *THE IRON GIANT: A STORY IN FIVE NIGHTS*, ill. Robert Nadler, Harper, 1968), short, surrealistic, poetic fantasy involving humans, an anthropomorphized machine, and a space being, set in modern times, beginning probably in the English

countryside and then shifting to Australia. The
Iron Man arrives, origin unknown, at the top of
a cliff. He gazes toward the sea he has never
seen before, steps forward, and topples head
over heels downward, crashing to pieces on the
rocks. Sea gulls inadvertently bring together
his hand and eye, and these parts gradually
reassemble his body. This happens the first
night. The second night, Hogarth, the farmer's
son, sees the Iron Man on the cliff and reports
to his father, who encounters the monster while
driving and manages to topple him with his car.
Nevertheless, the next morning the farmers
discover that their steel and iron machinery has
disappeared. They dig a "colossal hole," and
Hogarth lures the man into it. The farmers come
with bulldozers and earth-movers and cover him
over, mounding the dirt high and packing it down
hard. Months pass, and, while a family picnics
on the hill, the ground splits open, and the
Iron Man comes out. He resumes eating barbed
wire, hinges, tin cans, and other items made of
iron that he finds in the countryside. At
Hogarth's suggestion, the farmers make a pact
with the giant: he can eat all he wants from the
local junkyard in return for not eating the
metal from their farms. For the first time the
Iron Man is completely happy; for the first time
his eyes glow blue instead of red, and his body
is no longer rusty. Then a monstrous space-bat-
angel-dragon flies down from a distant star and
lands in Australia, covering the whole of the
continent, and demands to be fed living beings.
All the war machines that humans can muster fail
to defeat the monster. Hogarth gets the idea of
asking the Iron Man to help, reminding him that,
if the space monster destroys life, the giant's
supply of scrap iron will cease, too. The Iron
Man heroically challenges the space monster to
a test of strength, with the winner to become
the other's slave. Two times the Iron Man is
heated white hot on flames the engineers
prepare, and two times the space monster flies
to the sun to be heated on flames there. The
third time the Iron Man orders the engineers to
prepare a fire for him, the space monster gives
in, saying that he can no longer bear the sun's
flames. A star-spirit responsible for making the
music of the spheres, he found the war cries of

humans attractive and decided to come down to
enjoy them better. The Iron Man orders him to
make sphere-music again. Having bested the
space-monster, the Iron Man is proclaimed a
hero. The world becomes wonderfully peaceful as
the soft, eerie space music alters the behavior
of humans. They stop making weapons because they
just "wanted to have peace to enjoy this
strange, wild, blissful music from the giant
singer in space." This didactic antiwar story
lacks logic. The first chapter bears little
relationship to those that follow, nor is it
clear how such a dreadful monster could make
beautiful music, or why the music should make
people peaceful; and only the first two chapters
of the total of five involve the nights of the
title. The atmosphere is dreamy at first but
then becomes almost comic in the heroic portion.
The author's use of language is the best part of
the story; it is euphonious, rhythmical, and
descriptive with imagery and figures of speech.
Choice.

ISA (*Talking in Whispers**), Isabel, dominant
twin in the team of marionetters who aid Andres*
Larreta. Isa is both quicker witted and more
sensible than her brother, Beto*, but after she
falls in love with Andres she is more willing
than he to run risks. She contacts the American
newspaperman to give him the copies of
photographs incriminating the regime, and she
introduces the puppet General Zuckero into the
show in the market at San Miguel, although this
satire on the president of Chile could easily
mean torture or death for her.

ISABELLA CLINTON (*The Gentle Falcon**), narrator
of the story and companion and lady in waiting
to Isabella* of France, child wife of Richard II
of England. Isabella is involved with some
exciting action when Richard loses his crown and
his wife is taken prisoner. As the queen's
companion and supporter, Isabella Clinton finds
her life is forfeit. Disguised as a boy, she
first hides in a load of wool; then, when it
appears she will be discovered, she escapes and
trudges across the country, several times
narrowly escaping capture, until she reaches the
coast where a ship to France awaits her. For

most of the book she follows the fortunes of
young Queen Isabella and is more an observer
than an active participant in the action. Her
own romance with Gilles* Cobham takes second
place in interest to the dramatic historical
events.

ISABELLA OF FRANCE (*The Gentle Falcon**), second
wife of Richard II of England, married as a
child of seven, and the central historical
figure of the novel. Although neglected and even
abused as a child by her mother, greedy Queen
Ysabeau of France, she is a grave, dignified
child who responds to Richard's kindness with a
deep devotion that lasts beyond his death when
she is fourteen. Although the usurper of the
throne, Henry IV, wants her to marry his son
(later to be Henry V), she steadfastly refuses
and finally is allowed to return to France
where, at sixteen, she marries her cousin,
Charles of Orleans, himself a child several
years younger than she. At twenty-one she dies
in childbirth.

THE ISLANDERS (Townsend*, John Rowe, Oxford,
1981; Lippincott, 1981), fast-moving, realistic,
sociological problem novel with adventure- and
survival-story aspects set at an unspecified
time, perhaps at the turn of the twentieth
century. The arrival of two teenaged castaways,
Otipo and Mua, in a storm-tossed outrigger canoe
(their home island of Rikofia having been
destroyed by a volcano) spells change in the
lives of the 100 residents of Halcyon*, a small,
remote, infertile island somewhere on the South
Pacific high seas. Among the residents are the
Reeves family, which includes diffident Dick,
the father, capable Hester, the mother, and
their children, sensitive Thomas*, big, solid
Molly*, both in their teens, and Beth, about
twenty, and Beth's sweetheart, Adam* Goodall,
22. Their leader, William* Jonas, also called
the Reader because he has been entrusted with
passing on the Teaching of the Book left by the
Deliverer, Joseph Kane, who settled the island
100 years earlier, insists that the Law requires
that the youths be transported to nearby barren
Kingfisher* Island. Moved by compassion for the
youths and not sure William is passing along the

received wisdom accurately, since, like the
other Halcyonites, the Reader is illiterate,
Adam persuades the villagers to vote to keep the
children, who are then taken in by lonely Abel*
Oakes, a widower of advanced age whose own
children are dead. When ten more survivors from
Rikofia arrive and storms devastate the potato
crop, bickering breaks out over the propriety of
allowing them to remain. The villagers decide to
transport them to Kingfisher, where they will
most certainly die of starvation. When Abel,
Molly, Thomas, Adam, and little Jemmy Kane
decide to take supplies to the unfortunates,
they discover on Kingfisher Charlie* Herrick, a
shipwrecked sailor, and bring him back to
Halcyon. Now Reader in William's place, Adam
insists Charlie read the Book of Teaching aloud
to the islanders. To their astonishment and
dismay, the narrative presents not the moral
teaching and philosophy they expected but a tale
of deep violence, mutiny, and murder among their
ancestors, some of whom were also from the
island of Rikofia and whose descendents the
Halcyonites have ironically doomed to starvation
on Kingfisher. The islanders discover that the
Deliverer, Joseph Kane, was not the righteous
hero their traditions have pictured. Mutiny
occurs again when fringe elements persuade most
of the island's able-bodied men to strike out
for the mainland with them and steal the
islanders' only canoes and guns and most of the
supplies to do it, also forcing Charlie, who has
navigational instruments, to accompany them. The
remaining islanders face possible starvation in
the months that follow, since without canoes
they cannot fish, and a plague of rats,
offspring from pets of Charlie's that the
mutineers released, destroys the crops. Under
Adam's leadership, the Reeves family and the
others are managing to survive when help comes
from an unexpected source--the transported
Rikofians who have seen the smoke from the
signal fires Molly has suggested they light. The
following spring Charlie Herrick returns with a
schooner, bringing supplies and the news that
most of the mutineers have come to bad ends. The
story is told in four sections, each of which is
introduced by an italicized "Wave" in the
author's voice that provides essential infor-

mation or summarizes less important action. The fifth Wave tells of the arrival of present-day business interests and tourism. The typecast characters suit the story, which moves energetically if unevenly with acceptable coincidences and much dramatized action, excitement, and clear-cut conflict. Themes include the survival of body and spirit, compassion, the difficulty of deciding where right lies, and the effects of greed, selfishness, and violence. The numerous ironies and ambiguities strengthen the uncomplicated, linear plot, but leave the reader let down and puzzled about the meaning of it all. The physical setting, way of life, and worldview of the islanders are strongly drawn. Christopher; Fanfare.

AN ISLAND IN A GREEN SEA (Allan*, Mabel Esther, ill. Charles Robinson, Dent, 1973; Atheneum, 1972), realistic novel of family life and a girl's growing up set on the Outer Isles of Scotland (Hebrides) in the late 1920s. Mairi Gilbride, now nineteen and a college student, looks back upon the two years in her childhood when Isobel* Darroch boards with the Gilbrides in their small croft-house. Times are hard, the soil of their small holding is very lean, and Mairi's widowed mother can scarcely make a living for her four children and their aged grandmother. Mairi is eleven when her two older brothers, Martin and Neill, emigrate to Canada, following the example of many island youth. Scarcely has Mairi adjusted to their loss when she learns that Father Donald, the parish priest, has secured a position as live-in maid in Glasgow for her sister, Jean. Isobel's arrival not only helps the family financially but also eases the pain of the departures and, a little later, of the grandmother's death. This wealthy, educated young Englishwoman has come to learn Gaelic so that she can write a book about the islands. Kind, generous, and hardworking, she pitches in with the many tasks about the croft, making herself one of the family and soon earning the admiration and respect of the islanders. Ros* MacBride, 27, a neighbor, helps acquaint her with Gaelic literature and gather songs and stories from the elderly islanders for her book. Mairi listens to their discussions,

tags along on the collecting jaunts, and loses
herself in the books Isobel loans her. For the
first time she observes the pleasures of
intellectual conversations and experiences the
power of the well-written word. When Isobel
takes her along on a visit on the mainland to
Isobel's Uncle George, a writer, Mairi gets her
first view of the world beyond the islands.
Finding Jean happy in her situation reaffirms
Mairi's growing understanding that good people
can be found away from the islands and even
among the wealthy. After Jean returns to marry
Ros, Mairi's mother decides to emigrate to
Canada to join her sons. Her two years with
Isobel have matured Mairi sufficiently so that
she can face leaving the islands. Here is a rich
picture of the ways and thinking of the Outer
Islanders from the viewpoint of a young girl,
who comes to see that change is an inevitable
part of life and who, through the help of loving
friends and relatives, develops the courage to
try to make the most of whatever the future may
hold for her. Glimpses of everyday life in the
croft-houses, labor in the fields, and travel by
foot, bicycle, and sail, as well as rich,
sensory language describing the wind and weather
and the changing seasons make the setting so
intrinsically a part of the story that it
functions almost as another character. Characterization is strong and sympathetic, though
Isobel's future fiance is slightly too shallow
and, as a newcomer, Isobel herself is a trifle
too compatible with the close-knit community
and too much a contrast to the absentee
landlords. Mairi's second sight introduces a
gratuitous psychic complication, but the plot
flows well otherwise, and the style is simple
and direct, flavored with just enough Gaelic
words and turns of phrase for atmosphere. Boston
Globe Honor.

ISLAND MACKENZIE. See *The Nine Lives of Island
Mackenzie.*

ISOBEL DARROCH (*An Island in a Green Sea**),
wealthy, educated, young Englishwoman, who comes
to the Outer Isles of Scotland (Hebrides), the
home of her ancestors, where she boards with the
Gilbrides, living with them in their small

croft-house while she learns Gaelic and gathers material for a book on the islands. By example, patient encouragement, and careful planning, she helps Mairi overcome her antipathy for change and for the world outside the islands. At the end of the novel, she decides to marry Colin Forbes-Cowan, a talented and well-known young painter whom she has known for many years. As Isobel is presented (that is, from Mairi's point of view and in her words), this match does not seem suitable for Isobel. Colin, a self-engrossed, rather callous and often arrogant man, paints Mairi sitting in front of her croft-house.

IVY WHITTACKER (*Fire and Hemlock**), discontented mother of Polly*, who manages to alienate her husband and a series of lovers by being overpossessive and suspicious. Ivy is given to moods and discontents and keeps insisting that she deserves "a little share of happiness" in life. She suspects that the gifts Polly is receiving from Tom* Lynn are either from her father or from David, Ivy's current lover, and is infuriated by what she considers their secretiveness. She comes to think that Polly has invented Tom, and ascribes her overactive imagination to her father, Reg*, whom Ivy accuses, with some justification, of living in an imaginary world and not facing facts. She also irrationally accuses Polly of breaking up her romance with her first lodger, and sends her off to live with her father, telling her she needn't try to come back. She is an unpleasant character, yet pitiful, the creator of her own unhappiness.

J

JACKUS, COLIN (*The Dark Behind the Curtain**), youth enrolled in Mr.* Garner's school who is forced by Headmaster Garner to join the cast of the class play, *Sweeney Todd, the Demon Barber of Fleet Street*. He is regarded as rebellious and troublesome by the other youths, but really behaves in an antisocial way because he feels inferior. He got caught stealing tape recorders from the school, a deed that Colin Marshall* put him up to for self-gratification. He helps Ann* Ridley send the spirits back to their own dimension. At the end of the book he has matured enough to no longer strive to win Marshall's approval.

JACOB (*The Chimneys of Green Knowe**), little slave boy whom Captain* Oldknow buys in Barbados and brings home to be a companion to his blind daughter, Susan*. When the captain first sees him, Jacob is cleverly avoiding being sent to America along with other slaves following a West Indian slave mutiny, and Jacob himself proposes that the captain buy him. He is far more perceptive about Susan's abilities than any of her family or the servants have been, and he goes to great trouble to provide things for her to touch and feel that will give her understanding of the world around her. Thinking that Tolly*, whom he sees occasionally, is the ghost of a sailor boy come to haunt them, he plans a juju dance in front of the statue of St. Christopher to exorcise the spirit, with Susan beating the African rhythm on the drum, an effort that shocks the pious grandmother. When Sefton*, Susan's arrogant older brother, bullies and ridicules him, he gets even in crafty ways, often "borrowing" one of Sefton's cuff links, a silver button from his coat, or an embroidered slipper, and passing it to Susan, so that when searched, he seems entirely innocent. Technically freed, because the captain doesn't believe in slavery, Jacob is a loyal slave for Susan but also independent and spirited.

JAGGERS (*Great Expectations**), imperious and sinister lawyer who becomes Pip's* guardian. Secretive to the extreme, he refuses to let Pip ask any questions about his benefactor, though he knows that the boy naturally and wrongly assumes it is Miss* Havisham. In his practice he is highly successful and treats his clients with brutal scorn. It is eventually revealed that his housekeeper, to whom he is callously cruel, was once the wife of Abel Magwitch* and is the mother of Estella*, and that Jaggers arranged that Estella be adopted by Miss Havisham while her mother was being tried for murder. He tells Pip frankly that he disapproves of the fortune Pip has been told to expect and acts only as an intermediary between the boy and his benefactor. He illustrates the heartlessness of the legal profession.

JAKE BERTOLD (*Annerton Pit**), blind twelve-year-old boy whose ability to make his way in the dark leads his brother and grandfather to escape from the terrorists who have imprisoned them in the old mine. Jake not only has seemingly impossible physical accomplishments, like riding a bicycle along a strange road guided only by sounds, but he is very perceptive about people's personalities and intentions, judging accurately by nuances in their speech whether they are telling the truth or withholding information. In his relationship with his impulsive brother, Martin*, 17, he is the stable force, understanding Martin's moods, and he is able to judge when the older boy is about to blow up or when his enthusiasms are carrying him away. After his strange experience in the mine, when he felt a

presence and was aware of actually seeing
himself crawling along the tunnel, he longs to
talk with Granpa* Uttery, his rational and
intelligent grandfather, to whom he is very
close but who is recovering in a hospital.

JAMES AND THE GIANT PEACH (Dahl*, Roald, ill.
Nancy Ekholm Burkert, Allen, 1967; Knopf, 1961),
comic fantasy of magic, talking animals, and
absurd happenings, set in the mid-1900s in the
English countryside not far from Dover, on and
over the high seas, and in New York City. Since
his parents died, James Henry Trotter has lived
with disagreeable, selfish, lazy relatives, fat
Aunt Sponge and bony Aunt Spike, who make him
work very hard, often beat him, and refuse to
allow him to have any friends. One day a funny
old man gives James a bag of slimy, green
crocodile tongues, instructing him to swallow
them as soon as he can. James trips and falls,
spilling the sack, and immediately the squirmy
green things burrow into the ground beneath the
old peach tree that stands in the yard. Almost
immediately a peach appears on the wasted
branches and grows rapidly to the size of a
small house. The aunts see economic possibilities right away and sell tickets to sightseers. Told that night to clean up the litter
left by gawkers during the day, James spies a
hole in the ground near the peach, enters the
hole, and discovers a tunnel that leads into
the very heart of the peach. In the peach's
stone he finds living in a strange greenish
light and in human fashion with sofas, beds,
and overstuffed chairs several giant talking
insects: Old-Green-Grasshopper, Ladybug, Miss
Spider, Centipede, Silkworm, Earthworm, and
Glow-Worm, anthropomorphized creatures who put
on airs and mostly trade insults, having been
metamorphosed by the magic of the slimy, green
crocodile tongues. The next morning, Centipede
bites through the stem connecting the peach to
the old tree. The peach crashes through the
fence around the tree and rolls downhill,
squashing Aunt Sponge and Aunt Spike flat as two
paper dolls. It bounces down the slope, picking
up speed as it goes, careering over villages and
through fields, flattening everything in its
path and tumbling finally over the white cliffs

of Dover into the sea, a truly nightmarish ride
for James. The water around them boiling with
sharks, the creatures look to James for safety,
an attitude that persists throughout the story,
and James always proves inventive and resourceful. He attaches silk strings spun by Silkworm
to sea gulls one by one, using Earthworm as
bait, until 502 gulls lift the peach high over
the water, drawing it like a golden balloon
through the sky over the ocean. It passes over
the *Queen Mary*, whose captain reports what he
sees through his telescope, prompting his
officers to declare he's been at the whiskey
again. On top of the peach, Old-Green-Grasshopper entertains his crew-mates with concert
music, and James learns a good deal about
insect anatomy, habits, and contributions.
Centipede also entertains with nonsense songs,
as he does at other points in the story. There
are some ticklish times, for example, when
Centipede falls overboard, when wispy Cloud-Men
hurl hailstones down on them, and when the peach
gets trapped in a rainbow and they are almost
captured by the Cloud-Men. When dawn breaks one
morning, they realize they have drifted to
America and are sailing over the city of New
York. The peach lands on the pinnacle of the
Empire State Building, creating a state of panic
among officials and populace, but James assures
the Americans that he and his friends are not
invaders and introduces his fellow-travelers in
a long nonsense poem. The travelers are escorted
to City Hall, where the mayor makes a great
speech of welcome and treats them to a
ticker-tape parade. Boys and girls of the city
eat up the peach, but the travelers live on,
becoming rich and successful, each in an
occupation specially suited to his or her
peculiar talents. The enormous peach stone is
set up as a monument in Central Park. Inside it
lives the now famous and celebrated James Henry
Trotter. The once-despised and lonely youth now
has myriads of friends for whom he spins the
tale of his travels. Eventually he sets the
whole story down in a book, "And that is what
you have just finished reading." The fast-
moving farce seethes with absurd, imaginative,
action-filled scenes, in the preposterous manner of a Saturday morning television cartoon.

Some satire contributes adult humor. Characters are one-dimensional caricatures distinguishable only by traits that may be peculiar to their species, except for Centipede, who is the clown of the crew and constantly susceptible to catastrophe. James is a modern-day Cinderella, rising from a state of utter abjection to fame, fortune, and acclaim, though one can hardly identify with him. Events are described with James in the center but narrated by the story-teller speaking as "I." Choice.

JAMES BUBB (*Castors Away!*), actual historical figure of the period of the Napoleonic Wars whose life was saved in a manner much like that in the novel. In the story, he is a former wheelwright's apprentice who was tricked into joining the British army while drunk and who served admirably in Egypt against Napoleon's forces, rising to the rank of sergeant. He was left on board the Twenty-eighth Regiment trans-port ship that is wrecked off Suffolk because he was drunk and subsequently was washed overboard and carried ashore by the waves. At this point he comes into contact with the Henchmans. He is found and presumed drowned but is revived through the intensive efforts of Dr.* Henchman and his family. He is then arrested and sentenced to 300 lashes, helped to escape by the Henchman children in a thrilling episode, and then, on board Captain Henchman's ship, *Pericles*, at Trafalgar, he acquits himself with honor against the enemy. On the *Pericles*, during the critical engagement, he saves Tom* Henchman's life by kicking him down some steps and out of harm's way. A head injury during the same engagement leaves James deaf. He later marries Betsy* Farr, becomes Dr. Henchman's coachman, and makes furniture. He has a cheerful and positive attitude toward life, tells the children stories about the war, acknowledges his weakness for the bottle, and sets out to conquer it. He is loyal, honest, and brave, a likeable, convincing character.

JAMES HARRISON (*The Ghost of Thomas Kempe*), protagonist of ten or so, who finds in Thomas Kempe a lively and intelligent antagonist. James is embarrassed by things his parents do and say.

He is willing and obedient sometimes and yet is often quite difficult and irresponsible, and mostly at odds with his older sister, Helen, with whom he bickers and whom he teases--he is a typical preadolescent. He is imaginative, mischievous, and unreliable enough for his parents to doubt his motives and truthfulness. He takes the blame for the incidents Thomas causes with less acrimony and fussing than most boys his age probably would, however. He is a likeable youth, convincingly presented as persevering and intelligent.

JAMES HOWARD (*Black Beauty**), nineteen-year-old stable boy, who works for Squire Gordon while John* Manly is coachman. Gentle, pleasant, hard-working, and conscientious, the epitome of stable boys, he leaves the Squire to take a position as a groom and is highly recommended for the job by his master. Before he leaves, however, he proves a hero by saving the lives of Beauty and Ginger* when a careless worker's pipe starts a hotel stable on fire.

JAMES SMITH (*The Warden's Niece**), youngest of the three boys who live next door to Maria* Henniker-Hadden's uncle at Oxford and with whom she has lessons. James continually asks questions (usually the most embarrassing possible at the moment), romps wildly indoor and out, and plays on the sympathies of his mother with abandon. Although his two older brothers constantly try to quell his spirits and his strong self-image, James refuses to be subdued. When his mother thinks he is coming down with scarlet fever, James insists that he is not and is triumphant and self-satisfied when he is proven right, though he has made a good thing of his illness by getting all the sympathy and attention he can. The new tutor, Mr.* Copplestone, frankly controls him with bribes.

JAMIE ANDREWS (*Ask Me No Questions**), six-year-old child from Drouet's school who is first seen eating garbage from the pigs' trough. In the terribly unsanitary conditions of the institution he has contracted an eye infection and a rash and is nearly starving, but he obediently does what his brother Will* tells him to do,

even sucking from the cow's udder   like a calf.
Because   he gives   a   nurse his   name before   he
dies,   his   body   is   autopsied,   and   Drouet   is
charged   with   his   death   in   an   unsuccessful
effort to bring the man to justice.

JAMIE RAMSAY (*The Thursday   Kidnapping**), Jame-
sina,   third child   in the   Ramsay family   and a
very   independent-minded   girl. A beautiful
youngster, she   prefers to   dress in   shabby and
ill-assorted   clothes,   usually   pretending   to
herself   that she   is   a gunslinger   in the   Old
West. When her mother insists that she wear her
yellow   taffeta party   dress to   the party,   she
puts up a big fuss with tears and door-slamming,
but   both she   and her   sister, Ellen*,   realize
that this   is a pro forma   protest, though their
mother takes it seriously. Because she has been
watching Bart outside the library and is the one
who actually leaves him alone,   she feels guilty
when he disappears,   but she is mostly surprised
when she   discovers that she is   the major cause
of a three-car accident and a motorcyclist being
injured.

JAN   (*Red Shift**),   girlfriend   of   Tom* who   is
studying nursing in London   but who meets him in
Crewe   station for   a few   brief, tortured days
together. Jan   is the daughter of   two psychologists   or psychiatrists   whom   she seldom   sees.
They communicate   by leaving messages on   a tape
recorder, as   do most of their   patients. In the
past Jan   had an   affair with   a married   man in
Germany, out of loneliness, but she is genuinely
in love   with Tom.   Even her   comparative stability, however, seems to   be insufficient to keep
him in balance.

JAN (*The Silver Sword**), excitable, inscrutable,
suspicious Polish refugee boy of perhaps ten who
accompanies   Ruth*, Edek*,   and Bronia* Balicki
across Europe from Poland   after World War II to
join the Balicki parents in Switzerland. He is a
living   link,   along   with   the   silver sword
Joseph* Balicki gives   him, between the children
and   their parents. He   is clever   and sly,   an
accomplished   pickpocket   whose   ability   at
sleight   of   hand   frequently nets   them needed
items like   food but whose   near-total amorality

also gets them into trouble. For him, survival takes precedence over almost everything. He hates soldiers, Germans especially, and he refuses to talk about his past, probably because it is too painful. His need to love and be loved is revealed by the pets he acquires, at different times getting a bony gray kitten, a feisty cock named Jimpy, and an old Bavarian farm dog named Ludwig. He alone is able to gentle and capture the escaped chimpanzee, Bistro, while in Berlin. In Switzerland he gradually begins to lose his wildness and settle down, and, the author tells us at the very end, becomes a worthwhile member of society. On the journey he is both a help and a hindrance. He taxes Ruth's patience, in particular. He is the book's most interesting figure, the only really memorable one.

JANE (*Five Children and It**), youngest of the four children who discover the Psammead* and have adventures with the wishes it grants them. Jane is an imaginative, dreamy little girl, who likes to be good and tends to worry about rules. She sometimes cries, for example, when the children are imprisoned in the church tower and she wants her tea. The episode in which she figures most prominently involves her wish that her mother could have Lady Chittenden's jewels and the subsequent appearance of the jewels in her mother's room. She participates in all the children's adventures as the younger sister they all love, look after, and depend upon, and who occasionally comes up with good suggestions. She is more of a typecast character than the others.

JANET CHANT (*Charmed Life**), girl from our world drawn by magic into the world of Cat* Chant because she is the double of Cat's wicked sister, Gwendolen*. Janet is a tomboy in jeans, cheerful in the face of a series of predicaments and practical when she finds she is doomed to stay in Cat's world, away from her mother and father who haven't noticed that she has been replaced by another double, who is an orphan and eager to take her place in a family.

JANET THOMAS (*The Kitchen Madonna**), open-hearted, friendly seven-year-old sister who helps Gregory when he makes a decorated mother-and-child picture for their Ukranian maid, Marta. Unable to sustain an intense interest like Gregory's in the project, she nevertheless insists on sharing his disobedience and willingly runs his errands and contributes her pocket money to buy supplies.

JANE WOOD (*The Scarecrows**), little sister of Simon* who adores her stepfather, Joe* Moreton. Although her age is not given, she may still be in pre-school, since she sucks her thumb and frequently insists on being carried, but she is precocious in her sexuality and clearly is trying to make Joe her property. Since her father was killed before she was born, she does not share Simon's idealized memories of him. Seen mostly through Simon's perceptions, she seems a spoiled and manipulative child, but he cares enough about her to destroy the female scarecrow to protect her.

JANEY HOGGART (*The Witch's Daughter**), blind sister of Tim. Independent and confident, she resents being babied by the hotel-keeper's wife and asserts herself by demanding coke with pickled onions and cheese in the bar instead of the warm milk in the lounge she has been offered. When she has been able to lead the other children out of the cave where they have been stranded without lights, she points out repeatedly, "It was terribly clever of me."

JEAN THOMPSON (*Gumble's Yard**; *Widdershins Crescent**), a round-faced, curly-haired little girl, sister of Harold*, daughter of Walter*, and cousin of Kevin* and Sandra*. Romantic in nature, she readily adjusts to life at Gumble's Yard and thoroughly enjoys the novelty of the experience. In *Widdershins Crescent* she refuses to leave the Jungle* at first because Walter has said she must get rid of Pussy, the decrepit old tomcat to which she has become very attached. It is partly because she later runs away with Pussy that the children take their problems to Dick* Hedley, who suggests they again consult Tony* Boyd, the vicar. At Tony's suggestion, Mr. Widdowson hires Walter, which eventually results in the weak-willed Walter being convicted of arson. Jean is a well-drawn, likeable figure.

JEHANNE (*The Gentle Falcon**), French spy sent to keep an eye on those who will be near the young French princess who has married Richard II of England. Posing first as a wandering minstrel girl, then as a page, and then as a male court minstrel, Jehanne is a mysterious figure, evidently in the pay of the king of France. After Richard's death she is imprisoned in the Tower and bluffs her way out by making Madam de Coucy think that all France will be closed to her once Isabella* Clinton reports that she has kept Jehanne prisoner.

JEM ROLLER (*The Piemakers**), housewife, mother of Gravella*, and wife of Arthy*. She assists Arthy in making pies and is very proud of their reputation for being fine craftsmen. Jem's particular responsibility is raising and blending the herbs. She is excitable, sharp-tongued, status- and appearance-conscious, and judgmental. She enjoys gossip, and though she maintains that she doesn't like her sister-in-law, Essie Roller (the wife of Arthy's brother, Crispin), because she says Essie and Crispin can't be trusted and only visit to snoop, Gravella observes that when Essie comes the two jabber contentedly with Danby and Gorby gossip as though they had never ever had cross words. Gravella marvels "at the two-facedness of grown-ups." For recreation in the evening, Jem and Arthy read pie recipes, and Jem often reads them in bed when she has trouble dropping off. She has a good many charms and remedies that she inherited from her grandmother, leading Gravella to suspect that her great-grandmother may have been a witch.

JENNIFER CLEVERTON (*The Far-Distant Oxus**), along with Frances* Hunterly one of the two youngest of the six children who embark on the "expeditionary force" down the Oxus to the sea. She serves as lookout, picks flowers for bouquets, and is the literary one, remembering lines from poems that she shares with the others. A pleasant child, she is almost indistinguishable from Frances.

JEREMY CRAVEN (Collin-Smith*, Joyce, Hodder, 1958; Houghton, 1959), historical novel set in Mexico during the revolutionary years of 1910 to 1913, at the end of the administration of the dictator President Porfirio Diaz* and involving the actual insurgent leaders Emiliano Zapata, Pancho Villa, and Francisco Madero*. An English orphan named Jeremy Craven, about twelve, becomes the ward of his uncle, garrulous, expansive Titus* Carver, ostensibly a sugar-grower in Tepoztlan, Mexico, but actually a gunrunner. On Titus's hacienda, the lonely and frightened boy enjoys security, good food, adequate clothing, and kind treatment for the first time in his recent memory. In spite of Titus's mercurial temperament, mysterious actions, questionable reputation, and obscure remarks about the boy's future usefulness to him, the two develop a mutual fondness. Jeremy makes friends with Julio*, a Mexican boy of about his own age who lives on the hacienda and through whom Jeremy learns much about the culture and history of the Mexicans, a people whom he increasingly likes and respects. Chance and Uncle Titus's schemes to profit by the political climate thrust Jeremy into contact with important revolutionary figures and events. Separated from Julio during the Festival of Our Lady in Cuernavaca, Jeremy falls in with Emiliano Zapata, who returns him to the hacienda and later buys guns from Titus. On a trip to Mexico City with Titus, Jeremy discovers revolutionary fervor running high against President Diaz, now old and regarded as oppressive and reactionary. While Jeremy and Julio are sightseeing in Chapultepec Park with Father* Gonzalez, a kindly, elderly priest from nearby Taxco, they observe a soldier shot in the streets and are detained for a brief time in prison for questioning. There they encounter Francisco Madero, who is being temporarily incarcerated by Diaz and whose gentle warmth and low-key idealism Jeremy appreciates. When *rurales* (hired assassins who function as a state police) raid the hacienda, Uncle Titus, Jeremy, and Julio escape to the camp of Madero, who is now head of a force in the north near Ciudad Juarez and to whom Titus unsuccessfully tries to sell arms. When Jeremy rashly attempts

to persuade Pancho Villa, Madero's partisan, to
cease fighting the Federales, he is shot in the
arm and his elbow broken. For days he suffers
great pain and fever and is cared for by Titus
who, ironically, is extremely remorseful for
endangering the boy. Later they accompany the
Maderistas to Mexico City, where Titus, true to
form, again opportunistically tries to make a
deal with Diaz. Disillusioned by Titus's greedy
wheeling and dealing, Jeremy flees to Father
Gonzalez in Taxco, and, some months later, when
Titus unexpectedly demands his return, goes to
the hills. A dream vision motivates him to share
his life with both Gonzalez and Titus, each of
whom needs him and offers him possibilities for
realizing his ambitions for helping his new
countrymen. Although the plot seems overly
dependent on coincidence, and the dream
sequences jar, this richly conceived, capably
written book combines a well-characterized
protagonist, who grows up realistically during
turbulent times under morally equivocal circumstances, a complicated, likeable villain, much
excitement, some suspense, and, in particular, a
sympathetic, clear, and unbiased picture of the
historical leaders and times, which is obviously
based on extensive research. Fanfare.

JEREMY VISICK. See *The Fate of Jeremy Visick.*

JERRY BARKER (*Black Beauty**), Jeremiah Barker,
London cabbie who represents the finest of his
kind. A high-principled man, he treats his
horses well, consistently gives his customers
good service and never overcharges them, and is
a loving and patient husband and father to
Polly, Harry, and little Dolly, who are an
ideal family. Jerry refuses to work on Sunday,
unless there's an emergency, is fond of making
up happy little songs, refuses to speed his
horses to satisfy customers' whims, and
vigorously speaks out against strong drink,
which the book presents as one of the period's
greatest social evils. When he falls ill of
bronchitis, Jerry is forced to give up cabbying
and to sell Beauty, who soon comes upon very
hard times.

JESSICA VYE (*A Long Way from Verona**), frank,

perceptive schoolgirl during World War II. Inclined to be emotional, disorganized, and very outspoken, Jessica is the despair of her more conventional teachers, partly because she seems to know what other people are thinking. Her account of her thirteenth year is extremely witty, but she carefully leaves out any discussion or even mention of two events that affect her deeply: the deaths of Miss Philemon, her favorite teacher, and of two children she saw playing together in Dunedin Street before the bombing. Although she tells Miss Philemon about meeting the Italian prisoner, she keeps to herself his saying to her, "You very pretty," an incident that has left her with ambivalent feelings, both fear at the sexual threat from which she has run at top speed but also pleasure at his recognition of her as old enough to be interesting.

JILL POLE (*The Silver Chair**; *The Last Battle**), spirited schoolgirl, who in *The Silver Chair* accompanies Eustace* Scrubb on the quest for Prince Rilian*. When first seen, she is weeping bitterly because she is being bullied by her spoiled and undisciplined schoolmates. At the end she and Eustace are vindicated by their successful adventure and by Aslan's* ordering them to beat the obstreperous and cruel school-children. At book's beginning Jill acts stubborn and shows off, but Aslan reforms her, and, though reluctant to embark on adventures, she proves adequate to all events and is Eustace's equal, at least, on every occasion. Her guile, in particualr, enables them to escape the Giants. In *The Last Battle*, she and Eustace help King Tirian* resist the evil forces led by Shift the Ape. Much more confident now, she leads on occasion, fights skillfully as an archer, and is alert, quiet as a cat in guerrilla activities, and clever at seizing opportunities. At the end of *The Last Battle*, she has become one of the Seven Kings and Queens of Narnia. She is much like Lucy* Pevensie, a dynamic, well-rounded, and interesting character, but more assertive than Lucy.

JIM DALTON (*The Nature of the Beast**), father of Bill* Coward's best friend, Mick*, and union

representative in the Stone Cross Mill. After
years of trying to persuade the workers to
organize he is the only one who foresees that
the workers will be made "redundant" and the
mill closed. At first the other workers blame
him, and the worry over that coupled with
concern at the betrayal by the company
unbalances his mind. His frantic wife comes to
Coward's door to beg Ned* to help her get him to
come home because he is standing at the bus stop
in the snow, wearing only his undershorts. Ned
wraps a coat around him and gently persuades him
to come in by the fire. At the hospital it is
discovered that he is diabetic, and his family
is relieved because this seems more treatable
than mental illness.

JIM FOULGER (*The Great Gale**), elderly husband
of Hepzie*, who lives with her in a little
shingle cottage with a reed-thatched roof just
north of Reedsmere Gap, outside the village of
Reedsmere. He explains to Mary* and Mark*
Vaughan how the tides and gales can come
together to cause floods along the Norfolk
coast. A village fixture, liked by all, he
maimed his left hand in a poaching accident.
Hepzie reports that, when the queen visits after
the flood and pays him special attention because
he has pneumonia, she assumes that he was
wounded in war. He quietly corrects her, saying
that his injury was an occupational accident.
He and Hepzie are delighted with the way the
children fixed up and decorated their cottage
after the flood.

JIM HAWKINS (*Treasure Island**), young hero and
narrator for most of the novel. Although his age
is never given and he could be anywhere from ten
to eighteen, he seems to be fourteen or a little
younger, and is a lively, adventurous lad with
good intentions but sometimes poor judgment.
Though crucial to the action at several points
and adequate for his role, he is not highly
characterized.

JIMMY DEAN'S COUSIN (*The Battle of Bubble and
Squeak**), schoolboy who gives his pet gerbils to
Sid* Parker because his family plans to move to
Australia, thus starting the squabbles between

Mrs.* Sparrow and the rest of the Parker-Sparrow family over whether or not Bubble* and Squeak may stay. Jimmy Dean's cousin, who is never named, appears once only in the story, near the end, when, his family having returned from Australia, he wishes to take back his gerbils from the Parker children. He soon realizes that the Parker-Sparrows have grown fond of the creatures and have gone through a lot with them. Though obviously displeased about the situation, he gives the animals up without whining and recovers his spirits when Peggy suggests that they raise gerbils so everyone may have some pets. When he says he is afraid his parents won't allow it, Mrs. Sparrow, with perhaps her own experience in mind, informs him that they'll just have to put up with it.

JIM SMITH (*The Rough Road**), orphan who is abused by his foster parents, the Bruces, and their brother, Finlay, and who almost worships Alasdair* MacAskill, cattleman on the Isle of Skye. Underfed, poorly dressed, overworked, and often beaten, Jim has become sullen at home and a trouble-maker and bully at school, but he is a responsible worker and quick learner under Alasdair's direction. When Alasdair is injured and Jim must take the cattle on to market alone, he is terrified, having never been out of his small community nor on a train before, and since he has no money, he almost starves before a cobbler rescues him; at the sale, however, he is shrewd and reliable, getting the prices he knows Alasdair expected. After he stands up to his foster mother, Sarah* Bruce, and she trips and is hurt, he runs from home and hides out at Alasdair's empty house, but then is crushed when Alasdair himself brings the police to get him. Although Alasdair later realizes his mistake, Jim has been badly hurt and is cautious about trusting anyone again.

JINNY SLATTERY (*On the Edge**), thirteen-year-old eldest child of Gypsy Joe and Bella Slattery, who have moved their family from London to the Derbyshire countryside so that Joe will have a more peaceful atmosphere in which to pursue his craft of jewelry making. The entire family must pitch in to run their little farm and make ends meet. Among other chores, Jinny milks the cow, and she and her younger brother, Oz, pick berries. Jinny often feels overworked, and her need for some time to herself is not under- stood. In her efforts to discover whether Liam Shakespeare, called Tug*, is being held captive in the cottage, she learns that she has greater control over her life than she had thought. She learns that her parents and other adults will pay attention to her if she makes clear the reasons for her actions and prove they are mature and well thought-out. She is both attracted to and repelled by the Hare-woman*, and she fears Doyle*, both of them Tug's captors. She is a well-drawn and sympathetic character and serves as a good foil for Tug.

JOANNA SEDLEY (*The Black Arrow**), ward of Lord Foxham and heir to a large fortune, whom Sir* Daniel Brackley has abducted and intends to marry to his ward, Dick* Shelton, thereby getting control of her inheritance. When Dick first meets her, she is dressed as a boy and goes by the name Jack Matcham. Dick finds Jack an unmanly sort of fellow and at one point is about to beat him with his belt for his unthankfulness and cowardice, but he desists. When Dick first sees Joanna dressed in feminine attire, he is overwhelmed by her beauty. Having failed to control Dick, Sir Daniel tries to sell Joanna to another, settling upon old Lord Shoreby. At the end, when she is about to be married to Dick, Richard* of Gloucester offers to arrange a much better marriage for her, but she refuses.

JOE AND TIMOTHY TOGETHER (Edwards*, Dorothy, ill. Reintje Venema, Methuen, 1971), nine short episodes for preschool children about the people who live in a tall, racially integrated house in a big smoky town. Timothy lives in the basement with his parents and his baby sister, Dawn Gloria. Joe lives at the top, with his father who works on the roads and his young mother, and Jessie, a Jamaican girl, lives about half way up with her father, who drives a bus, her mother, several of her brothers, and her old grandfather. Most of the episodes occur in or around the apartment building. Mrs. Lemon, an

older woman with bad legs, has heard all about
the wonders of the launderette from the
children. When her grown son comes to take her
for a ride, that is where she chooses to go,
taking Joe, Timothy, and Jessie with her, and
she is so entranced that her husband gets a
notion and arranges with a friend who drives a
van to take her once a week, with the laundry
from all the other families, so she can meet her
friends there and "make a day of it." One lonely
day, Timothy, who has always been afraid of
clowns, calls on the old Christopherson couple
and learns that Mrs. Christopherson, who is now
an invalid, was a trick rider in a circus and
that Mr. Christopherson was a clown. In this way
he realizes for the first time that clowns have
real faces underneath their makeup. The three
children visit the room where two of Jessie's
big brothers live, there being no room in the
family apartment; they learn about working
nights, when they have to be very quiet so Arnie
Lambert can sleep; they learn about parting and
death when Jessie's Cousin Rosa goes back to
Jamaica and when Mrs. Lemon's old father dies;
and they have a wonderful Guy Fawkes celebration
watching the bonfires and fireworks from the
roof and playing with the sparklers that
Timothy's dad provides. The roof is also the
scene of their big scare, when they hear a cross
voice shouting at them from the skylight of Mrs.
Smithers's apartment and learn only later that
it was Mrs. Smithers's old grandad's parrot.
When the milk company makes a special ohffer of
colored pens, all their mothers buy extra milk,
and each child draws his own sort of picture,
with Joe filling pages of a blank drawing book
with tiny pictures of trucks, buses, and trains,
Timothy making an enormous picture of the park
and everything that goes on there on a roll of
wallpaper, and Jessie, after much deliberation,
drawing a huge, multicolored "gob-stopper" candy. The book ends with a party given by the
whole apartment house to celebrate Joe's
mother's twenty-first birthday. The domestic
adventures are very quiet, ordinary events that
loom big through the eyes of under-five-year-
olds, with some interest arising from the
details of urban life. All the adults are
friendly, the children are good, and there is a

cheerful tone. The stories are dated by their determined integration; Jessie is referred to in almost every episode as a "little brown girl." The language of the boys and Jessie, while not of Dick-and-Jane simplicity, does not sound much like that of such young children. Other.

JOE GARGERY (*Great Expectations**), blacksmith and husband of Pip's* terrible-tempered sister. Long-suffering Joe insists that his wife is a "Fine Figure of a Woman," though he admits that she does "Ram-page," and he tries to save Pip from the worst of her fury, which is often administered with a stick she calls the Tickler. Simple but thoroughly good-hearted, Joe has willingly taken on his wife's young orphaned brother and is more companion to him than master or father. After Pip leaves to be educated as a gentleman, Joe visits him and insists on calling him "sir," and in the ensuing years he never resents Pip's neglect or airs. After Pip has lost his expectations and is ill and about to be arrested for debt, Joe pays what he owes and nurses him. His wife finally having died, Joe marries Biddy*. He represents the honest, uneducated but genuinely good man who has no pretensions of rising above his original status.

JOEL WIDDISON (*Hobberdy Dick**), eldest son of the Puritan who buys Widford Manor. Although city bred, Joel takes quickly to country ways and is sympathetic to the old traditions of the area. Because his stepmother now has a son of her own, she resents Joel, but he still tries to follow his grandmother's advice to be patient and dutiful. When he falls in love with Anne* Sekar, his mother's gentlewoman, Joel realizes that his father will not approve the match, and he contrives that Anne should be asked to work for a higher-class neighbor family so he will not cause her further trouble by protesting when his stepmother treats her badly. Though more imaginative and sensitive than his father, Joel is just as honest and high-principled.

JOE MORETON (*The Scarecrows**), artist stepfather of Simon* Wood. As a caricaturist of real talent, Joe has become well known and has made a

great deal of money, but he is also a serious
artist, and evidently a good one. He is looked
down upon by Simon and his schoolmates as a
"yob," not the social equal of Simon's mother,
and by the Cheshire villagers as an outsider,
brought as a child from a slum in Manchester by
a mother who claimed to be a widow but showed
no marriage license. Perhaps because of this
insecure background, he insists on marrying
Simon's mother though she thinks having an
affair would be more sensible. A fat, good-
natured man, he is the opposite of the handsome,
macho, emotionless father whose memory Simon
worships.

JOHANNA VAVASOUR (*The Devil on the Road**), young
seventeenth-century woman who exhibits powers of
good witchcraft and with whom John* Webster
becomes involved. Daughter in a family of
gentry, she is adored by the villagers, whom she
helps in time of need, but when she tries to
save some old women being tried as witches, she
herself is put on trial. When John helps her
escape hanging and come into the twentieth
century, she continues to practice her
witchcraft. The villagers refer to her as the
"harb mother" and treat her with deference. It
becomes apparent that she has reappeared at
Vasers' barn (which was really the Vavasour
house) at intervals through the years, but
despite the local efforts to pin a young man
down for her, she has never found one who would
love her enough to enable her to stay. She is a
young woman of slight build, small enough so
that John originally takes her for a child and
later thinks of her as a kitten.

JOHN DIAMOND (*John Diamond**), alias Mr. Robinson, the sinister son of William Jones's
father's partner. Pretending to seek John
Diamond, he leads William on a wild-goose chase
through low-life pubs and out onto London
Bridge, and when he finds that William knows
nothing of the 10,000 pounds his father is
reputed to have hidden, he signals his band of
savage street boys to attack William, whistling
them up with his special tune, "I care for
nobody, no, not I, / And nobody cares for me!"
Having discovered where William came from, he

goes to Hertford and sets the Jones's home on fire, hoping to kill the family and get the revenge he has been desiring for twenty years.

JOHN DIAMOND (Garfield*, Leon, Kestrel, 1980; *FOOTSTEPS*, Delacorte, 1980), eighteenth century period and mystery novel set mainly in London. Night after night, William Jones, 12, has been awakened by the sound of footsteps in the room below as his dying father paces the floor. Stricken by conscience, he believes his father is "dying of a worthless son." Hearing the steps suddenly stop one night, he creeps down, only to be startled to find his father, fully dressed, standing behind the door. His distress is only increased when his father gives him his gold watch and confesses that he is weighted down by a long-concealed sin: he cheated his friend and partner, Alfred Diamond, and fears he may have caused Diamond's death. The next day he is dead, and William's obnoxious Uncle* Turner accuses the boy of stealing the watch. Frantic with grief and hatred, William runs off to London, determined to find Mr. Diamond, who, he is sure, will somehow vindicate him. In London he becomes involved with a number of Dickensian characters: Mr. K'Nee, the attorney whose name his father had given him; Seed*, a malicious dwarf who becomes his self-appointed keeper; Jenkins, clerk to K'Nee, who is sure William has information about the 10,000 pounds his father is reputed to have hidden; Mr. Robinson, a gentleman Jenkins assures him will lead him to Diamond's son, John*; Shot-in-the-Head*, a disreputable street boy who exists by picking pockets; and an assortment of blowzy women. Naively, William blunders through sinister intrigues and ludicrous situations. He narrowly escapes death when Mr. Robinson, who is actually himself John Diamond, sets his pack of animal-like street boys on him, being saved by Shot-in-the-Head, whose life he had somewhat inadvertently saved earlier. His father's watch, which he manages to keep though he is robbed and cheated out of his money, finally yields a clue in the form of an address on a slip of paper folded inside. Following this lead, William is led to K'Nee who is calmly playing cards with Alfred Diamond, a white-haired old gentleman who

has long ago dismissed Jones's deception.
Diamond realizes that his son, however, is bent
on revenge, and they pile into a coach and drive
madly for William's home near Hertford only to
find it blazing fiercely. William's mother, his
two sisters, Uncle Turner, and the cook-
housekeeper, Mrs. Alice, are safe, but John Diamond is caught inside. Impulsively William dashes in and pulls John to safety, cutting his
hands badly as he does. All ends well with a
reconciliation between John and his father, a
disagreement and parting between William's
mother and Uncle Turner, and the arrival of
Shot-in-the-Head, who has miraculously escaped
the vengeance of the other street boys and
followed William, to be taken in by William's
family. As with other Garfield novels, the
setting and plot, though melodramatic, are fascinating, and the characters, though often grotesque, are memorable. William, whose first-
person narration depicts him as far from perfect, is a sympathetic character. Garfield's
style is highly individual and skillful, full of
unexpected figures of speech. Boston Globe
Honor; Fanfare; Whitbread.

JOHN FITZWILLIAM (*Lost John**), twelfth-century
boy who runs away from a home usurped by his
stepfather and at barely fifteen joins the
outlaw band of Sir* Ralf the Red. A boy of
courage and quick temper, John is a favorite of
Sir Ralf and contrasts with cool, thoughtful
Alain* de Farrar, Sir Ralf's son. John is
tormented by conflicts when he discovers that
Sir Ralf, whom he has adopted as a hero and
father figure, is his father's murderer and the
man he has sworn to kill.

JOHN FOWLER (*Red Shift**), leader of the men who
plan to resist the attack of the invaders from
Ireland (many of whom are actually local men)
during the English Civil War. John is a man who
craves power and has been teaching Thomas*
Rowley to read and who actually provokes him to
epileptic fits in a sort of perverse need to
control. John's main conflict is with his
father, the rector, who gathers all the people
into the sanctuary of the Barthomley church but
cannot protect them from massacre. When the

attackers insist that he identify himself, John stays silent as other men are killed in his place, until he forces his father to identify him, a sacrifice that proves futile because all the men are murdered anyway.

JOHN GOODRICH (*The Load of Unicorn**), father of protagonist Bendy Goodrich. Now an old man, he has turned his scrivener business over to his two elder sons, Bendy's half brothers Matthew and Cornelius, and works at St. Paul's as a public scribe. He has a strong moral sense and is instrumental in helping Bendy get away from the Crowing Cock (particularly from Matthew, who has no patience with the boy) and into employment that he knows has a future. John has good business sense, but he never lets economics sway his judgment and can stand up to his elder sons when he feels he must.

JOHN MANLY (*Black Beauty**), Squire Gordon's coachman, the epitome of the finest of his kind. He understands and likes horses and is uniformly gentle with them and solicitous of their needs. He cures horses that are fractious with what he jokingly refers to as "the Birtwick horseballs," that is, "patience and gentleness, firmness and petting." He disapproves of such practices as blinkers, reports cruelty to animals, and often delivers short, moralistic homilies. Beauty has a good life with him.

JOHN PARGETER (*Time of Trial**), Meg's older brother, an unstable youth who has failed in every situation in which his father has placed him and who longs for the glory and excitement of military life. After Mr.* Pargeter is sent to prison for sedition and libel, John leaves for the army, having secured a commission and eventually becoming a captain. He serves with the detachment sent to Herringsby to investigate the death of the customs officer and round up the smugglers. John is a typecast character, a foil for the studious, less self-centered Robert* Kerridge.

JOHN PIM (*Songberd's Grove**), small, thin architect, whom Martin* Singer and Geneva* meet when they flee from Lennie* Byre's thugs and who helps them defeat Lennie and fix up Songberd's Grove. He lives and works with John* Pollard, the painter, with whom he has been friends since childhood. He is a famous authority on the restoration of old buildings. When he helps the children return safely to Songberd's Grove after they have fled Lennie's thugs, he notices that Songberd's Grove has unusual architecture. Later, while employed by Lord* Simon Vigo, who is the trustee of the estate that owns the area, he persuades Lord Simon that the area contains fine examples of Georgian architecture and should be restored to its former elegance. He is tinged with the comic and seems eccentric, like most of the novel's adults, but he is an agreeable sort and the children like him.

JOHN POLLARD (*Songberd's Grove**), stocky, under-standing painter whom Martin* Singer and Geneva* meet when they flee from Lennie* Byre's thugs and who helps them defeat Lennie. He lives and works with John* Pim, the architect, with whom he has been friends since childhood. He is an enormous success as a portrait painter, particularly with fat women, whom his spidery style flatters. At the end, he agrees to do the portrait of the now thin and beautiful La* Golondrina, which he hopes will liberate him from having to do any more paintings of fat ladies. Like most of the adults in the novel, he is slightly eccentric and comic but is likeable, helpful, and accommodating to the children.

JOHN SEMPEBWA (*The House in Norham Gardens**), Ugandan student who becomes Clare Mayfield's friend. Outgoing but never intrusive, he meets Clare at the Pitt Rivers Museum, where he learns about her interest in New Guinea culture and about her great-grandfather's work there. He accompanies her home and meets her elderly Aunt* Susan and Aunt Anne Mayfield, with whom he has tea. They react favorably to his not incon-siderable charm and discuss African politics with him. He later moves in as a lodger, and through him Clare learns something about the concept of time and the importance of family in primitive culture. He informs her that the wooden carving is a *tamburan*, an old New Guinean ceremonial shield. He appears to correspond to the tribesmen about whom Clare dreams but who, unlike them, has made a more skillful adjustment to the inroads of white culture.

JOHN WALKER (*Pigeon Post**; *Swallows and Amazons**; *We Didn't Mean to Go to Sea**), eldest of the four Walker children who are featured in a series of twelve holiday adventure novels. A devoted sailor, he has learned his skills from his Naval Commander father and in *Swallows and Amazons* he is determined not to be a "duffer" as he takes charge of the *Swallow* in their adventures on the lake. An awfully upright sort, he is distressed at being accused of "messing" with Captain* Flint's houseboat. In *Pigeon Post* he does not have a partcularly distinctive role, but in *We Didn't Mean to Go to Sea* he is clearly the main protagonist, reaching decisions, setting sails in the storm and piloting the *Goblin* all the way across the North Sea with only a little help from his sister Susan*. In his role as eldest he is always the captain, with Susan as mate, and the younger siblings in lesser roles; somewhat unrealistically, he never suffers from any dissension among his "troops."

JOHN WEBSTER (*The Devil on the Road**), engineering student from University College, London, who starts on a holiday motorcycle trip to the beach and becomes involved with time travel and a seventeenth-century witch trial. A large young man, John is always ready for a physical skirmish and inclined to use his fists at the first provocation, but he has a gentle aspect exhibited in his protective devotion to the undernourished kitten he adopts. After he saves Johanna* Vavasour from being hanged as a witch and returns with her to the twentieth century, he is uneasy and unable to bring himself to make love to her, though he has had casual affairs with young women at school and is in some ways much attracted to Johanna. Before he has figured out the time-travel aspect of his adventure, he is baffled by the way the local villagers call him "Cunning," a name that he traces back to a nineteenth-century cobbler named Cunning Murrell who was said to have been a white or blessing witch.

JON AMEND-ALL (*The Black Arrow**), name adopted by Ellis Duckworth when he seeks revenge upon those who have ruined him. With his first black arrow, he kills old Nick Appleyard and sends a message attached to the shaft, stating in rhyme that he also intends to kill Sir* Daniel Brackley, Bennet Hatch, Sir Daniel's right-hand man, and Sir* Oliver Oates, a priest attached to Sir Daniel's household. The rhyme accuses Sir Oliver of having cut the throat of Dick Shelton's father and Hatch of having burned Grimstone, Duckworth's home. Later Dick joins Duckworth's group, which acts as a sort of guerrilla force for the Yorkists, and sends another message signed Jon Amend-All, this time to Lord Shoreby, warning him not to marry Joanna* Sedley. Duckworth's men later shoot Shoreby. At the end only Sir Oliver remains of Jon Amend-All's intended victims, and when Dick urges Duckworth to pardon the priest, he refuses to forgive but agrees not to seek out Sir Oliver further.

JONATHAN CODLING (*"Minnow" on the Say**), ancestor of Adam* Codling. Before he left to join the British forces against Philip of Spain in 1588, he hid the family jewels and taught his daughter, Sarah*, a rhyme that contained clues to their location. The rhyme has come down in the family, but no one before old Mr.* Codling had been able to decipher it. From Jonathan's rhyme, which was recited for them by Miss* Codling, as well as from objects in the painting of him that hangs in the Codling house and from local history, Adam and David* Moss deduce where Jonathan must have hidden the jewels. They find the place, only to discover the treasure gone. Later they realize that the same clues also apply to the new location, which is in fact where Mr. Codling has hidden the jewels.

JONATHAN MEREDITH (*The Team**; *Prove Yourself a Hero**; *A Midsummer Night's Death**), sensitive, self-contained son of a wealthy business man and a domineering, horsy woman. In *The Team*, he is pressured by his mother, who manages the Pony Club Team, into riding as one of the four team members, because he is an excellent horseman. He

is reluctant, since he likes riding for fun and
hates riding in competition. In *Prove Yourself
a Hero*, he is kidnapped and ransomed and then
suffers   great   guilt   and   mental   trauma,
reenforced by his mother's attitude, which
pushes him to risking a talk with one of his
kidnappers, whom he has subsequently recognized
at a horse meet by his voice. His self-control,
intelligence, and courage in this book make him
seem   more   mature than he does in *A Midsummer
Night's Death*, which is set later in time but in
a traditional wealthy boarding school at which
he has a hero-worshipping admiration for a
teacher much like a schoolgirl's crush on her
athletics mistress. He is also the protagonist
in *Free Rein*, in which he is seduced by and
fathers a child with neurotic Iris Webster,
escapes on his motorcycle from disgrace at the
school and his mother's wrath, joins up with
Peter* McNair, and camps out in a derelict
mansion, where they train a difficult racehorse
for the Grand National. Jonathan, who has had
long practice in hiding his feelings as the
best method of passively resisting his mother's
abrasive domination, finds it difficult to
express emotion, but girls think his reserve,
coupled with his good looks and essential
kindness, very appealing.

JONATHAN MORLEY (*The Chimneys of Green Knowe*),
son of the parson who is hired by Captain*
Oldknow to tutor his blind daughter, Susan*.
Reserved and likeable but unimaginative,
Jonathan does his best, but it is not until
Jacob*, the little black slave from Barbados,
arrives and applies his inventive mind to
Susan's problems that she begins to fulfill her
potential. Although his father taught Susan's
brother, Sefton*, along with Jonathan when both
were younger, they are very different types and
have never been friends. When ordered by Sefton
to flog Jacob for putting on a *juju* dance in
the garden, he directs the boy to scream and
vigorously beats the chair. A utilitarian but
undeveloped character, Jonathan helps Jacob
rescue Susan via the chimney when the house is
on fire and helps rescue Fred Boggis when the
boy is caught poaching. In the end Jonathan
marries Susan.

JONES, CORDELIA, artist and writer. Her first book, *Nobody's Garden** (Deutsch, 1964; Scribner, 1966), is set in the part of London where she grew up and tells of an unusual friendship between a refugee child and an unpopular Londoner that centers on their interest in developing a garden in a bombed-out site. *A Cat Called Camouflage* (Deutsch, 1970; Phillips, 1971), which she illustrated herself, is set in Yorkshire and is about a cat that helps a girl face her parents' divorce and life in a new town. In *The View from the Window* (Deutsch, 1978), a teenaged girl with rheumatoid arthritis must watch life from a hospital window and eventually meets the people she has observed from a distance. Her books have been criticized for a lack of drama but have been commended for a flowing style and sharp realism.

JONES, DIANA WYNNE (1934-   ), born in London; novelist of original, complex fantasies. She attended Friends' School, Saffron Walden, Essex, and St. Anne's College, Oxford, where she received her B.A. degree in 1956. Starting in the mid-1970s, she has produced more than twenty fantasies, many of them using traditional fantasy and folk elements in new combinations and settings. Most of her writing has been for young people, much of it with strong comic elements, but she has also published a novel for adults and several plays. Three of her books are known as the Chrestomanci* cycle after their major sorcerer character: *Charmed Life** (Macmillan, 1977; Greenwillow, 1977), which won the Guardian Award and was a Carnegie Commended book; *The Magicians of Caprona* (Macmillan, 1980; Greenwillow, 1980); and *Witch Week* (Macmillan, 1982; Greenwillow, 1982). Three others are set in the imaginary feudal kingdom of Dalemark, which is rather like medieval Iceland, and use elements of mythology: *Cart and Cwidder* (Macmillan, 1975; Atheneum, 1977); *Drowned Ammet* (Macmillan, 1977; Atheneum, 1978); and *The Spellcoats* (Macmillan, 1979; Atheneum, 1979), which explores the legendary past of Dalemark. Some of her novels are highly comic, like *Howl's Moving Castle** (Greenwillow, 1986), which uses folktale elements in wildly inventive ways, and which was an honor book for the *Boston Globe-*

Horn Book award. Some mix the comic and the serious, like *Dogsbody** (Macmillan, 1975; Greenwillow, 1977), a book commended for the Carnegie Medal, in which the spirit of the star Sirius is born into the body of a puppy on earth, and *Archer's Goon** (Methuen, 1984: Greenwillow, 1983), an honor book for the *Boston Globe-Horn Book* award, about a struggle among contending wizards to take over control of a city. Even in her most serious novels there are highly amusing scenes, as in *Fire and Hemlock** (Methuen, 1985; Greenwillow, 1985), a complex fantasy that places the ritual killing of the king from Fraser's *The Golden Bough* in a modern setting. Many of her books have a main character who is unaware of possessing magical powers and discovers the fact as the story progresses, and in most cases the reader discovers only gradually what the story is really about. Though her books are not easy, she is considered one of the most innovative of recent fantasy novelists.

JONQUIL DARLEY (*The Girl in the Grove**), fifteen-year-old who becomes involved with the spirit of Laura* Seccombe. "Jon" is in something of a state of shock since the death of her financier father, whose plane crash in France coincided with the investigation of his activities for fraud. She can't help resenting her mother's interest in Bernard* Hunter and has difficulty accepting it when Bernard's son, Paul*, tells her that her parents had been about to separate before the crash. She not only has to adjust to no longer being wealthy, but also to being without friends her own age in her new home, except for Paul, who is rude and even hostile to her. When she first meets Laura, she thinks the girl must be slightly mad. It takes her some time to realize that Laura actually died some sixty years before and that she is seeing her spirit. Her feelings toward Laura change from fear to rivalry for Paul to pity.

JO RUGGLES (*The Family from One End Street**), the father in the Ruggles family, a dustman. He is a little slow in thought sometimes, undereducated, and talkative, but is also honest, hardworking, and fond of his family. He tends to be more practical and even tempered than his overdramatizing, excitable wife. He hopes to fence off part of their back yard and raise a pig to supplement the family income.

JOSCELIN D'AUBIGNY (*Knight Crusader**), older cousin to Philip* d'Aubigny, who plays to the extreme the effeminate fop in the Outremer society which is full of overdressed, fastidious young nobles. Under this facade, however, Joscelin is a tough and skilled fighter, and he rides deliberately to his death after the Turks kill his father.

JOSEPH (*Granny Reardun**; *The Aimer Gate**; *Tom Fobble's Day**), the son of Mary of *The Stone Book**, in which he does not appear, the boy who in *Granny Reardun* decides to become a smith and so announces to his stonemason Grandfather (Mary's Father*, Robert) who has helped to rear him. In the same book, he pitches stones through the windows of the Allmans' house, from which they have been "flitted" (ousted) so the stone can be used to erect a wall around the Rector's garden. Joseph plays the cornet, perpetuating a musical motif that recurs in the books. In *The Aimer Gate*, he teaches Robert, his son, about clocks, sharing his knowledge with pride, and tells him about his great-grandfather, the stonemason, whose namesake he is. In *Tom Fobble's Day*, he builds a sled for his grandson, William, closes shop for good, reminisces about Robert, and, when last seen, is lying in bed, having suffered a stroke or heart attack. He is a character of considerable depth.

JOSEPH BALICKI (*The Silver Sword**), former schoolteacher and father of the Warsaw children who make their way across Europe at the end of World War II to join him and their mother in Switzerland: Ruth*, Edek*, Bronia*, and their waif-friend Jan*. The story begins in 1940 when Joseph is in the German prison camp of Zakyna in southern Poland. He escapes by his wits a year later and returns to find his family gone and his house blown up by the Germans. He gives a paper knife in the form of a little silver sword to Jan, an urchin whose "pitch," or area of salvage, is the Balicki ruined house, and extracts from the boy the promise that he will tell Joseph's children that he has gone to Switzerland and show them the little sword as proof, should he encounter them. Joseph makes his way to Switzerland, traces his wife to a concentration camp through the Red Cross, and then traces his children to the refugee camp near Lake Constance to which their long journey has brought them in 1945, after Jan has given them Joseph's message. Joseph is shown as a brave and determined man, a type but appropriate for the plot.

JOSH (*The Night Watchmen**), amiable, bearded tramp, brother of Caleb*, whom Henry* meets and helps escape from the Greeneyes. Caleb is suspicious of Henry, but Josh immediately accepts him, insisting that children are "natural born do-as-you-pleasers--leastways, till they're twelve or thereabouts." Josh is writing a book, for the sheer joy of creating, and as Joshua M. Smith, he writes letters of introduction to the mayor, churches, and other people seeking interviews for his book. Josh is more outgoing, optimistic, and trusting than Caleb, who thinks he needs to protect his brother.

JOSH (Southall*, Ivan, Angus, 1971; Macmillan, 1972), tense novel of a visit by a modern Australian city boy to the remote town founded by his great-grandfather some 100 miles from Melbourne. Although his cousins have told him great stories about the place, Josh Plowman, 14, has never been to Ryan Creek, partly because his mother doesn't want to join the family rush to butter up Aunt Clara, the only remaining Plowman in the town, in hope of inheriting her wealth. When he arrives, exhausted from the long train trip and from his apprehensions at meeting new people, he finds his great-aunt abrupt and censorious, and he falls asleep without undressing or unpacking. In the morning he is appalled and furious that she has unpacked his bag and taken his book of poems which are private writings he has brought with him mostly to keep his father from prying into them in his absence. His anger when she admits she has read them starts them off on a bad footing. At Sunday

School, the first he has ever attended, he is
embarrassed that all the young people know all
about him and surprised at how they seem to
adore his aunt, clustering about her, carrying
her books, and vying for her attention. In his
first meeting alone with the local young people,
after he has stormed off to keep from crying in
front of his great-aunt, he is horrified to find
they are scornful of his cousins, who have
visted previously, and make snide remarks about
Aunt Clara. Ashamed, he returns, apologizes to
Aunt Clara, and has one small victory when she
uses his real name, Josh, instead of calling him
Joshua. The next morning he is surprised that
the boys call for him to take him shooting, as
they have promised Aunt Clara they will, but
they trip him at the gate, heap scorn upon him
(although Harry Jones tries to get them out of
earshot of the house before they do), and go off
without him. He wanders off by himself, comes
upon the boys who have just caught a rabbit in a
trap, and breaks into tears as they kill it. Now
having real reason to scorn him, they leave him
alone, and he wanders down to the muddy pond by
the dam where Harry's fat, somewhat simple-
minded sister, Laura, is swimming and waiting
for him. She is suffering from a crush on him
and comes on too strong for a boy like Josh who
has never had a girlfriend. To impress him, she
climbs to the bridge and, although he tries
vainly to stop her, jumps off, though the only
person previously known to have tried it was
killed. To get her to leave, he agrees to come
to her house for a lunch of pancakes after he
dries his clothes, which he got wet trying to
help her out after she jumped, but he goes to
sleep instead. The next day Aunt Clara reminds
him that the boys have said he was to play
cricket with them (or perhaps she has told the
boys he would) and insists that he run over to
Bill O'Connor's house to find out what time they
will play. Reluctantly he does so and is greeted
hostilely at the door by Betsy, Bill's sister
whom he really admires, and then with equal
hostility by Bill, but their mother insists that
he come in, have tea, and be included in the
cricket game, which turns out to be a real match
with an out-of-town team from Croxley. Hoping to
edge him out, Bill insists that he wear proper

whites, but his mother intervenes to say that
Bill will borrow some for him. Before time for
the match he encounters Rex, Bill's younger
brother, and he discovers some complicating
factors: Laura and a little boy called Sonny who
was hanging around the day before have been
lying and twisting their accounts of events to
say that he chased Laura up to the bridge,
forced her to jump off, and then threatened to
beat up Sonny; Aunt Clara is spending her money
to send all the brighter youngsters in town,
including Harry, Bill, and Betsy, off to high
school, and letting families live free in the
houses she owns; Rex blames Josh and his cousins
for coming and sponging off her; and finally,
Rex is losing his position as wicket-keeper
because of Josh entering the cricket game. When
he returns to the house, he finds that in
revenge Bill has borrowed clothes from someone
much shorter and twice as heavy as Josh, so that
even with them pinned up he looks ludicrous.
Roused to real fury, Josh marches out, confronts
Bill, shrilly accuses him, and starts a fight,
only to get knocked down repeatedly. The fight
is broken up by the schoolteacher, who is there
to act as umpire for the match. Back at Aunt
Clara's, Josh is told that they will accept him
at the match dressed in his own clothes, but
that if he refuses to play Bill will not be
allowed to play either, and Bill's team will
boycott the game. Josh refuses to let them
pressure him and locks himself in his room. Aunt
Clara tells him through the door that she will
send him home on the morning train. Thinking
this over, he decides he would rather walk home.
He leaves a note, and sneaks out, but by the dam
pond is waylaid by Harry, who beats him up for
standing up Laura, threatening Sonny, making
eyes at Betsy, and, obscurely, for worrying Aunt
Clara, but he doesn't get any opposition from
Josh until he tears the poems, which Josh has
been taking with him. Then, when the other kids
discover where they are, Harry tries to protect
him while both cricket teams converge on him and
rip his clothes off, bounce him in the brush,
and throw him into the pond, where he almost
drowns since he can't swim. The Croxley team,
pulling him out, suddenly turns on the Ryan
Creek kids, and there is a terrific rumpus, with

Josh crouching in the middle, kicked by both sides. He is rescued by the schoolteacher, who, with Aunt Clara, takes him to the doctor. His aunt tells him that the truth has come out, and furthermore, that the boys are all ashamed of themselves and want to make it up to him by a new cricket match and a picnic in his honor. Josh finally is able to assert himself and retain a bit of self-respect by insisting that he is walking home, starting in the morning. This is an initiation story, and Josh is clearly meant to triumph in the end. He is characterized as a sensitive boy, and a poet, who brings on part of his troubles by his impulsiveness and clumsiness. The hostility of the local kids is presumably explained by their feeling of obligation to Aunt Clara and their resentment at having to entertain the other cousins on previous occasions, but it seems extreme and too sudden. Much of the story is told in an inner monologue which starts at such a pitch of tension that it is wearying and loses effectiveness before the reader reaches the strong scenes on the third day. Carnegie Winner; Contemporary Classics; Fanfare.

JOSHUA SMITH (*The Warden's Niece**), second of the three boys who live next door to Maria* Henniker-Hadden's uncle and with whom she has lessons. Joshua, who is just Maria's age, is kind-hearted and sensitive; he is very worried when they get into scrapes and embarrassed at the behavior of his brothers and their eccentric tutor, Mr.* Copplestone. Of the three boys, he is the nicest to Maria, and she feels most confident of his help and understanding, but she admires his older brother, Thomas*, more.

JOSIAH FRIEND (*Gran at Coalgate**), Jinnie's straightlaced father, a small shopkeeper who considers himself a cut above the miners in his town and in his wife's family. A narrow-minded, bigoted man, he disapproves of movies, dancing, short skirts, drinking, swearing, strikes, wasting money, playing on the Sabbath, women who speak out, answering back--there seems no end to the list of things he finds sinful. He doesn't believe in cosseting children, and his refusal

to say that he will pay the added expense to
send Jinnie to the Secondary School, even if she
wins a scholarship, has so worried her that she
is vomiting in school. When she overhears Mam
speaking up to him at night and her fear causes
her to vomit again, he says it is "naught but
hunger" and urges her to have a piece of bread
with butter. Opinionated and self-righteous, he
is in the Guild at Chapel and is a thoroughly
unlikeable man.

JOSSIE MILBURN (*The Bonny Pit Laddie**), old
miner whose pickax Dick and Kit swipe when they
are down in the abandoned pit. They are trapped
there when the bottom ladder, which is made of
wood, collapses. They explore the tunnel,
discover Jossie working by himself, take his
pick, and with it create foot and handholds to
clamber out. When Jossie can't find his pick, he
thinks the mine is haunted and becomes something
of a figure of fun in the town. Later, when the
pithead collapses and the 200 miners are
trapped, Dick and Kit among them, Dick notices
Jossie, realizes that Jossie must have been
working that seam when the boys swiped his pick,
and confides in Kit and in the foreman, thus
enabling the miners to get to safety.

THE JOURNEY OF THE ELDEST SON (Fyson*, J. G.,
ill. Victor G. Ambrus, Oxford, 1965; Coward,
1967), episodic historical novel with adventure
story aspects set in Mesopotamia, the Land
Between the Two Rivers, 4,000 years ago. At the
beginning of this sequel to *The Three Brothers
of Ur**, Shamashazir, 14, the eldest son of
Teresh the Stern, a respected, wealthy trader,
has achieved his fondest wish--to accompany one
of his father's caravans to the dangerous White
Mountains that lie north of Ur. Once there,
Shamashazir takes authority as the master's son,
consults the Teraphim (the Teresh family's
household god) about the routes, and chooses the
one he feels will yield danger and glory, though
he knows it is wrong and is against the wishes
of Serag, his cousin and the expedition's
leader. Trouble follows quickly--Shamashazir
tumbles over a steep, tall cliff and is presumed
dead by his caravan. His battered body is found
by a small tribe of about forty wandering Hiberu

under the leadership of gentle, resourceful
Ishak (chief) Enoch, whose wife, the Ishakeen,
is skilled at medicine, sets the boy's badly
broken leg, and nurses him to health. When the
tribesmen and the Ishak's proud son, Enoch, who
is also fourteen, demand that Shamashazir be put
to death because he has learned the secrets of
their worship to the Great Spirit, or Lord of
All the Earth, the Ishak saves his life by
convincing them that the tribe of Enoch and the
people of Ur must have a common ancestry because
they have similar traditions, for example, their
legends about the flood. Shamashazir adopts the
Lord of All the Earth as his god, is instructed
in his worship, and, before long, through
persistence and patience, he wins the friendship
of the aloof and contemptuous Enoch. The
tribesmen teach him the ways of mountain life,
and they are thrilled and amazed at his accounts
of the wonders of Ur. The tribe makes its way
over the mountains, while Shamashazir, Enoch,
and two retainers visit the valley village of
Kenan to buy corn. They arrive as the Kenanites
are preparing for the Feast of the Corn Dingir
(god), to whom, they are horrified to discover,
Shaul, ten or eleven and the son of the
village's Ishak, Moab, is to be sacrificed. In a
series of unlikely but hair-raising and heroic
episodes, they rescue him and his younger
brother, Zepho, 7, who is next in line for
sacrifice. Soon joined by Ishak Moab, who has
fled the village because he now rejects the
practice of human sacrifice, and by eight other
youths, each of whom fears that his father may
be chosen as the next Ishak and that he may thus
be sacrificed, they have some problems but
successfully elude pursuit. They encounter a
small band of coppersmiths from whom they hope
to secure a kettle to facilitate food preparation and learn to their surprise that the
group's leader is Ishak Moab's uncle, Irad, who
years before had fled Kenan to escape being
sacrificed. They soon discover that Irad's
people are related to the tribe of Enoch through
Irad's wife, Ruth. Enoch has a vision that they
are sure indicates that the Lord of All the
Earth has lifted the curse of Cain, the ancestor
of the Kenanites whose action in slaying his
brother, Abel, started the practice of human

sacrifice among them. Upon hearing this, the old Ishak, Irad, dies of shock. His now leaderless people choose to join Enoch's tribe, and the others go on to Ur with Shamashazir. The meeting with Enoch's tribe and the passage to Ur are left entirely to the reader's imagination. The stage shifts abruptly to Ur, where Shamashazir finds that a hearty welcome awaits him. His brothers, Naychor and Haran, and his sister Sarah have given him up for dead, and only his sister Dinah has remained certain he would return. Grief has tempered Teresh's sternness, and, upon hearing of Shamashazir's adventures, he informs his son that he has known about the Lord of All the Earth all along and that he set aside that worship of his ancestors because he had thought the Teraphim more appropriate for life in Ur. Now he decrees that henceforth his family will follow the Lord of All the Earth, the god who has guided his son, and the Teraphim is removed from the family chapel. The book offers enough problems, action, and characters to fill several novels, and something is always happening. Motivations, however, are not entirely clear, situations sometimes violate logic, elude credibility, happen too rapidly, or are underdone, and melodrama abounds. For example, Shamashazir's conversion seems precipitous; it does not seem reasonable for the proud Kenanites to choose to go to Ur, where they will be enslaved, just because they're interested in its wonders and because Shamashazir tells them the Urites are humane; and the escape of the brothers occurs altogether too fortuitously. Characters exist for the sake of the plot and are not adequately differentiated, and Enoch and Shamashazir mature predictably. There seems to be no identifiable climax, and the ending seems rushed, as if inspiration had failed. Nor does the author make clear the relationship between Shamashazir's selfish choice of the route at the beginning of the novel and the family's adoption of the Lord of All the Earth at the end. Although the book is consistently interesting, the period's scenery takes precedence over the story. The reader is left with a good idea of what life in ancient Mesopotamia and (possibly) eastern Canaan might have been like in the old days, but without a clear sense of what of thematic significance is to be gained from the story. Carnegie Com.

JOURNEY TO JO'BURG: A SOUTH AFRICAN STORY (Naidoo*, Beverley, ill. Eric Velasquez, Longman, 1985; Lippincott, 1986), realistic novel of home and community life set in contemporary South Africa. Their gold-miner father dead of coughing sickness and their mother employed as a maid in distant Johannesburg, Naledi, 13, her younger brother, Tiro, 9, and their little sister, Dineo, live with their granny and aunt 300 kilometers west of Johannesburg in an unnamed village, which, according to the map in the front of the book, lies near the Botswana border. Since Dineo has been suffering from a fever and seems near death, Naledi persuades Tiro to accompany her to Johannesburg to inform their mother of their sister's plight. On their own, the two set out with provisions given them by a neighbor girl, a couple of sweet potatoes and a bottle of water. They trudge the dusty-red earth road to the tar highway, then go through a small town, always keeping a lookout for policemen, who, they know from conversation, are dangerous. When they pass an orange orchard, a young worker chances a whipping by giving them some fruit to eat and an old shed to sleep in that night. The next morning a friendly truck driver, bound for the city, picks them up and takes them to Johannesburg. He gives them money for the bus to the Parktown sector, where Mma works, because he says it's much too dangerous for them to walk there. When they innocently almost board a whites-only bus, they are saved from trouble by a young woman named Grace Mbatha, who also offers them shelter for the night. They take a non-whites-only bus and soon arrive at the large, pink house where Mma works and communicate their problem to her. When Mma's Madam coldly insists that Mma care for her little girl that night while she and her husband attend a party, the two children go to Grace's house, experiencing on the way a police "pass raid," during which blacks are arrested and herded into a van for violating the law that says they must at all times carry identification. At Grace's they learn that her older brother emigrated to an unnamed foreign country

after being imprisoned for demonstrating for
black rights. The next morning they meet Mma at
the train station and return to their village.
Mma hires a car to take Dineo to the hospital,
and Naledi accompanies them there. They must
wait hours in line along with many other parents
and ill people; Mma endures the delay with
patience. One woman's baby dies before they see
the doctor, and the grief-stricken woman carries
the tiny body out wrapped up in a plastic bag.
The doctor hospitalizes Dineo and tells Mma to
come back for her in three days. When Mma brings
the little girl home, Dineo is much improved,
but Mma must return immediately to Johannesburg.
If Mma does not get back by the time the woman
has said she must, Mma will lose her job and,
without a good reference from her previous
employer, will not be able to get another one.
Mma leaves worrying about the debt to the
hospital and about how to provide the fruit,
vegetables, and milk the doctor says Dineo needs
to thrive. Naledi is discouraged but hopeful.
She would like a good education and draws
courage from knowing that Grace and others like
her have the same aspirations and are working to
improve conditions for blacks. She realizes that
her journey to Johannesburg has been a valuable
learning experience. The characterization is
minimal, scenes are undeveloped, and dialogue
sounds stilted, contrived, and instructive.
Since the author does so little with Naledi's
character and fails to exploit incidents
adequately, it is hard to feel much sympathy for
Naledi as a person, and she remains a type
figure. Whites are uniformly presented as
unfeeling and abusive and blacks as abused and
suffering. Style and narrative technique are
naive, and the book often sounds like a reading
textbook. Consisting of thinly veiled sociology,
it gives middle- and later-elementary readers
some idea of the problems produced by apartheid.
Naledi seems older than thirteen in the illustrations. Glossary. Other.

JOWETT, MARGARET (1921-   ), born in Ipswich,
Suffolk; educator and theater history
specialist. She attended Princess Mary High
School, Halifax, Yorkshire, and Leeds University, where she received her B.A. in English and a

diploma in education in 1943. She was English Mistress at Withington Girls' School, Manchester, until 1950, after which she spent a period as a freelance researcher and teacher, then became Senior Lecturer at Bretton Hall, Wakefield, for ten years. After 1957 she also was a lecturer at the College of Education, St. John's College, York, and Principal Lecturer in Drama at the College of Ripton. For young people she wrote two novels, both about theater history: *A Cry of Players* (Oxford, 1961; Roy, 1963), which is set in the late sixteenth century at the beginning of Shakespeare's career, and *Candidate for Fame** (Oxford, 1955), which was commended for the Carnegie Medal. The latter is a story of the rise of a young actress in the provincial and London theaters of the late eighteenth century. Both have been praised by critics for thorough and accurate research.

JULIO (*Jeremy Craven**), Mexican youth whose character and stories inspire Jeremy with affection for the Mexican people. Julio becomes Jeremy's good friend and loyal companion. At first Jeremy is the follower of the two, but, as he grows in physical strength and self-confidence, Jeremy gradually assumes the leadership. Jeremy learns from Julio that Uncle Titus* is a gunrunner.

THE JUNGLE (*Dan Alone**; *Gumble's Yard**; *Widdershins Crescent**), a tumbledown district in the city of Cobchester, where for five years the Thompsons, Walter*, Doris*, Kevin*, Sandra*, Harold*, and Jean*, as well as Mr.* and Mrs. Hedley and their son, Dick*, live before moving to Widdowson Crescent in Westwood Estates in another part of the city when the Jungle is pulled down for slum clearance. Ironically, the dirty, run-down area is so called because the streets are named after tropical flowers. The Thomspons live at 5 Orchid Grove Street, while the Hedleys live on Brazil Street just on the other side of Hibiscus. Gumble's Yard lies at the foot of Hibiscus, consists of abandoned warehouses, cottages, and empty ground, and is bounded by Canal Street, the canal, and the railway sidings. The carefully delineated setting makes the plots more believable.

THE JUNGLE BOOKS (Kipling*, Rudyard, ill. J. Lockwood Kipling and others, Macmillan, 1894, 1895; Century, 1894, 1895), episodic fantasy of the life of Mowgli*, a boy raised by the wolves of the Seeonee pack in India, presumably in the late nineteenth century. First published in two books, there are fifteen stories, some earlier printed in *St. Nicholas* magazine, with nearly half of them unrelated to the Mowgli story, but it is the tales of the jungle boy, which have often been issued in separate collections, that are most memorable and have put the books on award and citation lists. The first story, "Mowgli's Brothers," tells of the coming of the baby, just able to walk, to the wolves' cave, followed by Shere* Khan, the lame tiger, who demands the child as his quarry. Mother Wolf drives him off and lets the little brown baby suckle with her cubs. When they can run a little, they are all taken to the pack meeting on the Council Rock led by Akela*, the gray Lone Wolf, to be admitted to the group. When Shere Khan questions the right of Mowgli, as Mother Wolf calls him (meaning little frog), to be admitted and several wolves echo his question, Akela asks who will speak for the man-cub, and is answered first by Baloo*, the sleepy brown bear who teaches the Law of the Jungle, and then by Bagheera*, the Black Panther, who offers one bull, newly killed, as the price for Mowgli's admittance. The second half of the story takes place some ten or eleven years later, after Akela has become old and a new generation in the pack incited by Shere Kahn has grown to resent the man cub among them. Bagheera warns Mowgli and directs him to steal some of the Red Flower, fire, from the nearest village, to nurse it carefully with dried branches, and to bring it to the Council Rock, where Akela, who has missed his kill, is no longer the leader. When Shere Khan, with no right in the wolf pack, openly speaks up, Mowgli challenges him and drives him and his followers among the wolves away by swinging blazing branches; left alone with Bagheera and the few wolves who have taken his part, he weeps for the first time and then turns to the village to meet

men. Some of the other Mowgli stories occur in
the interval between his   admittance to the pack
and his leaving it.   In "Kaa's Hunting," Mowgli
is kidnapped by the Bander-log, the monkey
people, who are frivolous, have no law, and may
idly drop   him from   the   trees   when their
attention lapses. Baloo and Bagheera enlist the
help of Kaa*, the great Rock Python, whom the
Bander-log fear, and follow them to the Cold
Lairs, an old lost city almost buried in the
jungle, where the monkeys have taken the boy.
The three then rescue him. Later Kaa, having
become a great friend to Mowgli, takes him back
to the Cold Lairs and shows him the abandoned
treasure room, which is still guarded by an
ancient cobra, and because it catches his fancy,
he takes a jeweled ankus (an elephant goad)
though the rest of the treasure means nothing to
him. When Bagheera tells him what it is, he
throws it away, then sleeps and later follows
the trail of the man who picked up the ankus and
was murdered for it, and of three others who
successively kill and are killed for the
beautiful piece. In "How Fear Came," in a time
of drought the animals gather at the Peace Rock
under the Water Truce, where all animals may
come to the river without danger, and Hathi, the
Wild Elephant, tells of how the first tiger
brought killing into the jungle.   In
"Tiger-Tiger!" Mowgli, a herd boy after he has
been taken in by Messua (a village woman whose
child was stolen by a tiger), organizes his
wolf-den brothers to separate the water buffalo
bulls from the cows and to trap sleeping Shere
Khan in a ravine between them, and then stampede
the bulls to trample the tiger. He skins the
great cat and pegs his hide to the Council Rock.
The villagers believe he deals in magic, and
they plan to burn Messua at the stake for taking
him in. "Letting in the Jungle" tells of how
Mowgli sends Messua and her husband off through
the night to an English settlement, protected by
his animal friends, and then calls on Hathi to
trample the crops, destroy the huts, and drive
the villagers away forever. In "Red Dog," a pack
of wild dogs from the plains invades the jungle.
Helped by Kaa, Mowgli works out a plan to
infuriate them, and then lead them along the
cliffs where the wild bees nest. By running very

fast, and then diving into the river below, where Kaa catches him, Mowgli escapes the stings which kill most of the dogs or drive them into the river. There they are carried down to the wolf pack which waits to destroy them below. The last story, "The Spring Running," occurs when Mowgli is nearly seventeen. He has been living in the jungle for years but for the first time the mating season in the spring brings him an awareness of his sexuality, and, thinking he is perhaps dying, he takes a long run and comes by chance to a hut where Messua now lives with a young son. There he briefly sees a girl and is torn between the jungle and life among men, into neither of which he will ever fit completely. All the Mowgli stories are distinguished by a serious, tense, dramatic tone, full of poignant emotion. While the jungle and the animals are realistic and not generally anthropomorphized, the stories posit a Law of the Jungle more codified than any natural law, and of course the verbal communication between species and the jungle boy is fantasy. Among the non-Mowgli stories the best known are "Rikki-tikki-tavi," about a mongoose that saves an English family from cobras, and "Toomai of the Elephants," about the son of a trainer who sees the rare and secret dance of the elephants. Some of the stories are strange, cynical, and very adult in concept, but in Mowgli and his animal friends Kipling has created memorable and appealing characters. Poems precede and follow most of the stories. Books Too Good; Children's Classics; ChLA Touchstones; Fanfare; Lewis Carroll.

JUNO (*Masterman Ready**), the young black girl from the Cape of Good Hope who serves as nanny to the children of Mr*. and Mrs*. Seagrave and who, with the Seagrave family, is marooned on the unnamed desert isle after the *Pacific* falls prey to a South Seas hurricane. Although Juno is a capable and willing worker and contributes her share to the family's survival, she is regarded as being inferior in intellect and resource to the whites and speaks in "darky" dialect.

JUSTIN (*The Silver Branch**), Junior Surgeon Tiberius Lucius Justinianus, who is posted to Britain in one of the efforts of the Roman

forces to bring Carausius back under the control
of Rome. Justin, who has a bad stammer, has
always felt himself a disappointment to his
father and has been physically unable to meet
the standards required of a Centurion in the
legions. Dark-haired and ugly, with ears that
stick out on a large head and narrow shoulders,
he is nonetheless a skilled surgeon and devoted
to his calling. When he and Flavius must escape
from their posts and go underground, he sends a
letter to his father saying that he has done
nothing shameful, and after their distinguished
service in defeating Allectus, he receives a
letter from his father showing that he has at
last made the older man proud.

JUSTINIANI LONGO (*The Emperor's Winding Sheet*),
volunteer from Genoa who becomes commander of
the land walls in the defence of Constantinople
against the Turks. A soldier of fortune, he
brings with him 700 well-armed men and a
reputation that buoys up the spirits of the
defenders, even though he frankly states that
Genoa officially remains neutral and he warns
them not to count on help from Venice or the
Pope. Stocky and thick-set, he has a jaunty air
and a frank manner that disarms even the
Venetians, who are usually suspicious of anyone
from Genoa. Vrethiki* is at once attracted to
him, and after Justiniani sends the boy a
beautiful Italian dagger, Vrethiki worships him.
His disillusionment is great when, at the
critical point in the Turkish attack,
Justiniani, wounded, insists on having one of
the gates to the inner wall unlocked so that he
can be taken within to be treated, thereby
allowing the Turks to enter and overrun the
city. Vrethiki throws the dagger at his feet
with contempt. When at the end Vrethiki swims
out to the ships that are leaving the fallen
city and is thrown a rope from Justiniani's
ship, he is at first bitter toward the man, but
his hatred lessens when he hears the dying
Justiniani blame himself for his cowardice and
say that the courage of the Emperor Constantine*
will be remembered forever.

K

KAA (*The Jungle Books**), great Rock Python
thirty feet long with a beautifully mottled
brown and yellow skin. Baloo* and Bagheera*
enlist his help in rescuing Mowgli* from the
Bander-log, the monkey people, because the
monkeys fear him alone of all the jungle people
since he can travel to the treetops where they
sleep. In the Cold Lairs he hypnotizes the monkeys, and even Baloo and Bagheera come under his
spell until jolted out of it by Mowgli. Though
they have asked his help, neither animal feels
comfortable with Kaa, but after that incident he
becomes a great friend of Mowgli, leading him
to the treasure room in the Cold Lairs and working out the plan to defeat the terrible invading wild dogs in the story, "Red Dog."

KATE (*The Watcher Bee**), first-person narrator
who has been brought up by her aunt and uncle
and feels that she never really belongs in the
activity of her village or at her high school.
For years she treasures a secret fantasy
concerning Sir George St. Orbin, whom she has
briefly seen once, a fantasy that is dampened
when he marries a pork heiress, and finally dies
when she learns that he has been killed in the
Spanish Civil War. She always writes, usually
secretly, and while she is at Fulford High
School, her former teacher at the village school
produces for a local festival a play she wrote.
Although she is thrilled, she gets only negative
criticism at high school, where her headmistress

considers it inappropriate and chides her. Kate is intelligent but naive and inclined to speak too frankly. Even though she sees through Lucy* Denham-Lucie's pretensions and realizes that her aunt has far more true worth, she can't help enjoying her glimpses of Lucy's less restricted life. Her one triumph at the "hockey school," as she calls Fulford High, is that she was once granted special permission to take a later train from Welham Station because she had conjunctivitis, and she continues to take the later train for years, since the permission is never withdrawn--a token of independence that she cherishes.

KATE CHANT (*The Changeover: A Supernatural Romance**), mother of Laura* and Jacko. She is a sympathetically drawn figure, warm, loving, disorganized, and at times torn between her needs as a woman and her responsibilities as a mother. Divorced, Kate barely makes ends meet on her salary as manager of a local bookshop. When Kate allows Chris Holly to spend the night, Laura's resentment of the young librarian grows, but Kate is at that point too worried about what is happening to Jacko to pay much attention. Later her mind returns to Laura, and she cautions her daughter against Sorry* Carlisle. Married at a young age herself, she frets about Laura's growing relationship with Sorry. At the end, Kate and Chris are contemplating marriage. By that time, Laura has come to appreciate Chris's caring and support and understands her mother better.

KATE CRACKERNUTS (Briggs*, K. M., Alden, 1963; revised, Kestrel, 1979; Greenwillow, 1979), novel that retells the folk tale of the two Kates as a seventeenth-century historical romance set in Scotland and Yorkshire. Although they have known and loved each other from early childhood, Katherine Lindsay, gentle, fair-haired daughter of Andrew, the widowed Laird of Auchenskeoch, has been brought up very differently from Kate* Maxwell, the dark, roughly treated daughter of a strong-willed widow, Grizel*. When the girls are twelve and thirteen, Andrew marries Grizel, mistakenly thinking she will make a good mother for his

daughter. Although she masks her hostility, it
is suspected by her daughter and by Andrew's
faithful man Gideon Ibbotson, who acts as tutor
to the girls. Katherine, docile and innocent,
fears Grizel but does not foresee her evil
intent. Kate, known fondly by her stepfather as
"Crackernuts" from her habit of climbing trees
and hoarding the nuts, is used to roaming free
and wild over the hills, and she is both shocked
and fascinated when she follows her mother one
night to a witches' meeting and sees that she is
a leader of the outlaw group. Twice she thwarts
her mother's plan to have old Mallie Gross cast
a spell on Katherine, but when Andrew has gone
to aid the king, Charles II, in the Civil War,
Grizel gets a false message to Gideon that asks
him to visit his relatives in Yorkshire and
lures Katherine, fasting, to Mallie's hut where
the old witch casts a "spell" on her, convincing
her that she has a sheep's head over her own.
Katherine flees in horror to the hills, where
Kate finds her and, knowing that Katherine's
life is in danger, arranges with a fisherman to
take them to England. Their boat is followed by
one carrying Mallie and Grizel, which sinks. The
girls make their way to Yorkshire, with
Katherine both mentally and physically ill. Kate
gets a job as domestic help in the home of
Squire Roger Frankland, whose son Will is under
a spell that forces him to dance with the
fairies whenever the Seven Whistlers call him on
the night of the full moon. Kate volunteers to
sit with him, and when they hear the Whistlers
and she cannot restrain him, she goes with him.
In the limestone cave, they find the witches,
gypsies, and a few of the "fairies," the small
people who are probably cave dwellers, in a wild
revel. With one of the fairy children she trades
nuts for pebbles which, when dropped into the
Lady's Well, will lift the spell from Katherine,
and she is able to leave with the greatly
weakened Will. Gideon, having escaped from a
gypsy ambush instigated by Grizel, returns, and
with Katherine watches Will on the next
full-moon night, but Kate returns alone to the
cave and obtains from the same child a draft
that lifts Will's spell. At the book's end she
is to marry Will, Katherine is to marry Gideon,
and Andrew is home safely from the wars. Such a

summary does little justice to an intricately woven plot, in which hypnotism and superstition explain the "spells" in a believable way, the political struggles between the Royalists and the Covenanters are intrinsic, and the survival of old religions is intertwined with the practice of witchcraft. Characterization is well defined and subtle. Choice.

KATE LUCAS (*The Other People**), thirteen-year-old who is sent to spend her vacation with her Aunt Poppy, proprietor of the shabby Sea View Guest House in Sunny Bay, while her mother honeymoons with her new husband, Godfrey Pennington. Kate's expectations having been raised by postcards of Sunny Bay, she is terribly disappointed by the run-down reality and is uneasy among the strange assortment of guests at the Sea View. Gradually, however, she becomes interested in them as individuals and is partially instrumental in solving some of their problems. At the same time she begins to come to terms with the changes that her mother's new marriage will bring in her own life.

KATE MAXWELL (*Kate Crackernuts*), known as Kate Crackernuts, a strong female character, wild and free but loving and steadfast to her stepsister, Katherine Lindsay, who believes that a witch has placed a sheep's head over her own. In seventeenth-century Scotland witchcraft is condemned but practiced widely, and Kate, taken to a witches' meeting by her mother, is both attracted and repelled by the revels. Later, following Will Frankland to a revel in a cave, she is able to keep her head and see the evil in the practices that are gradually killing him. Despite her fear of her mother and her strong protective feelings toward Katherine, who is the target of her mother's enmity, Kate has a great desire for her mother's love, and, in a touching scene, grieves when she hears of her mother's death, not for the loss, which is in many ways a relief, but because they were never able to share the true love of a mother and daughter.

KATE TRANTER (*The Way to Sattin Shore**), schoolgirl of about ten, quiet, independent, and secretive, who sets out to learn the family history behind her father's disappearance. Her friend Anna Johnson says Kate is "like a cat sometimes...friendly one minute, and the next you go off all by yourself and have secrets." Unlike the more evenly disposed Anna, who seems hardly bothered by her parents' impending divorce and even suggests that maybe Mr. Johnson and Kate's mother, Kitty*, might get married, Kate becomes moody and her schoolwork suffers while she's puzzling over the problem of her father. She instinctively dislikes Arnold West, whom she first sees at Sattin Shore. Later he tells her he moved Bob Tranter's body below tideline, where Bob subsequently drowned, casting suspicion on Kate's father, who then fled the area. Kate tells no one what Arnold has told her. She does, however, tell Nanny* Tranter that she dislikes Arnold, but Nanny Tranter, who may or may not know of Arnold's involvement, says he's an unhappy person who has been like a son to her and that she will eventually go to live with him. Kate gives Nanny her beloved tomcat, Syrup, as a keepsake. Though she changes little in the story, Kate is an interesting, likeable, and well-drawn protagonist.

KATHLEEN O'BRIEN (*Dogsbody**), Irish girl who comes to live with her uncle, his wife Duffie*, and their two sons, because her activist father has been sent to prison. A patient, loving child, she puts up with her aunt's unkindness and the teasing of her cousin, Basil* Duffield, and does almost all the housework as part of the bargain that allows her to keep the puppy she found half-drowned. As Sirius grows, Kathleen is the only one who realizes that he understands people's language, and she talks to him and reads aloud to him at night, a practice that helps her overcome her loneliness but also gives him valuable information. When she gets a letter from her father saying he will be out of prison in about a month, she is delighted, but when she hears on the radio about the prison break, she is not surprised that he is one of the escapees. When he is killed, not by the police or army but by the opposing faction, she is both sad and enraged, a feeling she expresses by smashing Duffie's pots. At the end, when her dog, Leo, is dead, she accepts the fact that the luminary she talks with is his spirit, but that does not make up to her for the loss. She goes to live with Miss* Smith, the ex-schoolteacher, and gets one of Patchie's puppies, not to replace Leo but to keep Miss Smith company.

KATHY FISHER (*The Thursday Kidnapping*), disagreeable next-door neighbor to the Ramsays who kidnaps the baby, Bart. Both neglected and spoiled, Kathy not only tries to lie her way out of every bad situation, she also convinces herself that her lies are the truth. When she is caught shoplifting, she is more angry at the store employee who apprehends her than guilty at her crime, and when Jamie accuses her, she at first denies it, then tries to laugh it off, and then declares that it is the fault of the store for leaving merchandise around in the open. She knows how to manipulate her mother, but there is clearly no love between them, and Kathy fears her father, who has threatened to send her to boarding school. Ellen* Ramsay, who has been annoyed by Kathy pretending at school to be her friend, sees that she is to be pitied and realizes that she must do something to help her. Kathy is an unpleasant but convincingly drawn character.

KATIA. See *Little Katia*.

KAYE, GERALDINE (1925-   ), born in Watford, Hertfordshire; teacher and for more than thirty years a prolific writer of novels and readers for youth, mostly about children in different or cross-cultural situations. The daughter of a surveyor, she served in the Women's Royal Naval Service during World War II, then took her B.S. with honors in economics from the University of London School of Economics and Political Science in 1949. She married Barrington Kaye, a lecturer and writer, in 1948, and had two daughters and one son. She was a scriptwriter for the Malayan Film Unit in Malaya from 1951 to 1952 and taught in a Methodist girls' secondary school in Singapore from 1952 to 1954 and at the Mitford Colmer School in London from 1962 to 1964. She has also lived in Africa and writes about children there as well. Her earliest publications

were readers for use in Africa, published by
Oxford. In 1960 she turned to general fiction,
making use of her knowledge of Africa and Asia
here as well as in her books for a younger
audience. She has also written for teenagers,
especially for reluctant teens, focusing on
social issues and family problems. Though her
output has been large and her stories popular,
only one has received an award, and that among
her most recent publications, *Comfort Herself* (Deutsch, 1984; Deutsch, 1985), which won
the Other Award. Comfort, the daughter of a
racially mixed marriage, must decide whether to
live with her father's family in Ghana or with
her deceased mother's people in Kent. The book
is consistently interesting if sociological, and
Comfort is well drawn, but her experiences seem
too deliberately contrived to contrast life in
Africa and England for easy credibility. Earlier
Kaye wrote the novels *Billy-Boy* (Hodder, 1975),
Children of the Turnpike (Hodder, 1976), *The
Day after Yesterday* (Deutsch, 1981), and *A
Different Sort of Christmas* (Kaye, 1976). Recent
publications are the novel *The Call of the Wild
Wood* (Hodder, 1986), several forty-eight-page
illustrated stories for a younger audience, and
some readers.

KEITH HESELTINE (*Earthfasts**), grammar-school
youth who hears a strange noise while out on Haw
Bank overlooking Garebridge, enlists the help of
his friend David* Wix in investigating it, and
observes an eighteenth-century drummer boy,
Nellie Jack John Cherry, come out of the hill.
Not as strong-minded or assertive as David,
Keith relies more on intuition than intellect.
At first he is mainly interested in seeing how
John will react to situations, while David is
more concerned about John's feelings, but
later, after David's disappearance, Keith begins to understand what it means to be alone in
another dimension. He never seems to be afraid
to return the candle, simply appearing to accept
the task as something he must do, nor does he
seem to be hypnotized by the flame as David is.

KELPIE (*The Kelpie's Pearls**), proud, strong-
minded, somewhat mischievous, and quarrelsome
water spirit, who has lived in Morag* MacLeod's

pool for many years. Because he gives Morag pearls as payment for helping him, he sets in motion a chain of events that makes it impossible for her to continue living in the area and results in his pool being dynamited. When he calls up the Loch Ness monster to satisfy Morag's curiosity, the region is flooded with sightseers and scientists. Thus he further fuels the fires of suspicion that Morag is a witch. He finally bears her away to Tir-nan-Og, because he says there is no longer a place in this world for her. Here she will always be an object of curiosity or laughter. The kelpie is an interesting, well-rounded figure.

THE KELPIE'S PEARLS (Hunter*, Mollie, ill. Charles Keeping, Blackie, 1964; ill. Joseph Cellini, Funk, 1966), fantasy that improvises on Scottish folklore, set in the mid-1900s in Scotland on the hillside above Loch Ness not far from Inverness. Old Morag* MacLeod, 72, lives alone and contented on her small croft through which runs a burn (brook). In its pool for 200 years there has lived a kelpie*, a shape-changing water spirit. When Morag frees his foot, which has gotten stuck between some stones, the kelpie rewards her by giving her a pearl necklace and scattering pearls in the pool. When Alasdair*, an unscrupulous local poacher, inquires about the necklace, Morag candidly tells him her story, and he immediately decides to steal the pearls from the pool. Attacked by the kelpie in the form of a huge, threatening, black horse, Alasdair is saved when Morag places a binding spell on the kelpie, one she learned from her white (good) witch grandmother. Then Alasdair spreads the rumor that Morag is a witch. Only Torquil* MacVinish, a lonely orphan who lives on the croft down the way with the disgruntled Old* Woman, continues to think of her as a kind, caring person. More trouble comes when the kelpie raises the Loch Ness monster for Morag and she candidly answers the questions of a newspaper reporter, whose story attracts droves of curious spectators and scientists to the region and increases local suspicion. Thrill-seekers so disrupt Morag's way of life that she employs a spell of her grandmother's to call up a three-day storm that sends the curiosity-seekers scurrying. The storm also destroys a dam that Alasdair has constructed to drain the pool and get the pearls. Thwarted, Alasdair decides to dynamite the pool and is later arrested for his act. Just in time, the kelpie, who realizes that Morag will never again be accepted by her neighbors, assumes his black horse form and bears her off to Tir-nan-Og, the Celtic Land of Heart's Desire. Both Torquil and the Old Woman see them leave. Torquil reports to the police, when they investigate Morag's disappearance, that she looked young and happy, while the Old Woman asserts that she was weeping. Ironically the Old Woman's statement casts doubt upon the idea that Morag was a witch, because it is commonly believed that witches cannot weep. This dramatic and suspenseful story of goodness and love conflicting with selfishness and greed combines clear characterization, plenty of atmosphere, incisive descriptions, some humor, and ironic comment on contemporary mores. Mostly narrative and understated, it projects a stong oral storytelling flavor. Gaelic terms and old customs and beliefs contribute texture and support the setting and the world of the fantasy. Choice; Fanfare.

KEMP, GENE (1926-   ), born in Wigginton, Staffordshire; teacher and author of books for older elementary-grade readers. She was educated at Wigginton Church Primary School, Tamworth Girls' High School in Staffordshire, and the University of Exeter, where she received her B.A. with honors in English in 1948. She married twice, the second time to Allan Kemp, a bus driver and union official, and has two daughters and one son. She taught in private and public secondary schools and at Rolle College in Devon before becoming a freelance writer in 1979. Since 1972 she has published some fifteen books, many of them with school settings, about friendships, or with unorthodox protagonists; they are briskly entertaining works. *The Turbulent Term of Tyke Tiler** (Faber, 1977), set in a primary school, rollicks along to a surprise ending, where the spunky, obstreperous, narrator-protagonist is revealed as a girl. Generally conceded to be her best book, it won both the Carnegie and Other awards. *Gowie Corby Plays Chicken* (Faber, 1979) concerns a skeptical primary-school boy who has trouble making friends, while *No Place Like* (Faber, 1983) switches to a college setting, where a youth's negative attitude makes college difficult at first. Her first books were fantasies, a series about Tamworth, a crusading pig. She turned to novels then and also did a book of short stories, *Dog Days and Cat Naps* (Faber, 1980), and edited an anthology of poems, *Ducks and Dragons: Poems for Children* (Faber, 1980). Recent titles include *The Well* (Faber, 1984), about a girl's adventures growing up in an English village before World War II, *Jason Bodger and the Priory Ghost* (Faber, 1985), a time fantasy, *Juniper: A Mystery* (Faber, 1986), in which school becomes a refuge for a child with a troubled family life, and *I Can't Stand Losing* (Faber, 1987). She has made her home in Devon.

KENDAL (*The Hollow Land**), chimney sweep and proprietor of a fish-and-chip shop in the Cumbrian fells, cheerful under all circumstances and blissfully unaware that his friends and neighbors do not always share his attitude. Superstitious, he is a great source of local lore, especially stories of ghosts, candles made of dead hands, frozen bodies in the dairy, and other fascinating horrors.

KENNEMORE, TIM, writer of fiction for older elementary and junior-high ages. Her third book, *Wall of Words** (Faber, 1982), was commended for the Carnegie Medal. A story of contemporary family life, it uses a light touch to deal with the serious problems of an irresponsible father and a dyslexic daughter. Critics have praised its wit, humor, sprightly style, snappy, and authentic dialogue, and realistic sisterly tensions, but have taken umbrage at its didacticism. Her first novel, *The Middle of the Sandwich* (Faber, 1981), also a domestic novel of the here and now, tells of a London girl's problems while staying with her aunt in the country and adjusting to a new school. *The Fortunate Few* (Faber, 1981; Coward, 1982) is a fantasy set in the future that postulates a

society in which girls are trained as gymnasts
from the age of five. The fourteen-year-old
protagonist enjoys the status of being the
highest paid athlete of her day.

KEPT IN THE DARK (Bawden*, Nina, Gollancz, 1982;
Lothrop, 1982), chilling mystery set in rural
England in the last third of the twentieth
century. Noel*, 14, Clara*, 12, and Bosie*
(Ambrose), 10, having come to live with their
mother's parents because their actor father has
had a mental breakdown, have learned, with some
difficulty and a good deal of care, to adjust to
the elderly couple they had never met before
because their grandfather had disapproved of
their mother's marriage. Then David* shows up;
he is an older half cousin from America whom
neither they nor their absent mother had heard
of. Their grandmother, Liz*, clearly dislikes
the young man, and Grandpa*, usually given to
barking orders and being obeyed instantly, is
strangely passive, even frightened. When David
turns his charm on the children, Bosie
immediately becomes his willing slave, and
Clara's quick sympathies are caught by this poor
orphan who says he wants to be part of a real
family, but Noel, always a loner, is suspicious.
Gradually David begins to control them all. When
Clara tells him how the maid, Batty* (Mrs.
Battle), plays mean tricks on Liz by hiding
things to make her think she is losing her
memory, David takes the opportunity to fire
Batty and assigns Bosie to be the cook and the
other two to do all the other work. He insists
on driving Grandpa's carefully preserved
Bentley, and smiles strangely when Grandpa makes
the condition that he must never take the
children for a ride. Then David lures Bosie into
the car, almost runs down Grandpa, who tries to
interfere, beats up Noel, who attacks him, and
refuses to leave when Grandpa tells him to go.
Liz, who has taken to her bed, suddenly changes
tactics and is charming to David, trying to
placate him to protect Grandpa. The children's
mother visits and doesn't understand their
problem at all, finding David attractive and
accusing them of being petty when they try to
explain the situation. David terrorizes them,
threatens Noel with a gun, and digs an

"asparagus bed" in the front garden, a hole shaped suspiciously like a grave, which is possibly for Liz's beloved but aging dog and possibly for other victims. In a naive effort to get money to bribe David to leave, Bosie starts a scam at school, sneaking, for a price, into the principal's office to erase the names that misbehaving students are forced to write in the conduct books. When he finds the office locked, he gets a ladder and goes in the window, where he accidently spills ink. He then messes up the office to look like a robbery and is caught as he comes down the ladder. Strangely, this solves their problem. At the sight of the police car bringing Bosie home, David takes the motorcycle he has gotten from Grandpa through blackmail and flees. By the time their mother and their recovered father come to visit, things are back to normal. The characters are strongly differentiated and believable. David remains a mystery, certainly willful and perhaps an imposter but possibly really a lonely young man in need of a family, or possibly a sinister, or even insane, criminal. This ambiguity is acceptable because the story is told from the perceptions of the three children, and they gradually change in their attitudes toward David. The feeling of foreboding and the growing sense of terror and helplessness are effective. Poe Nominee.

KERR, (ANNE) JUDITH (1923–   ), born in Berlin, Germany; illustrator and writer of both picture books and autobiographical novels. She was the daughter of writer and drama critic Alfred Kerr, who was forced to flee Germany with the rise of the Nazi party in 1933. With her older brother and her musician mother, Kerr lived in Switzerland and France and came to England in 1936, where she became a naturalized citizen in 1947. She attended the Central School of Art, London, and served as secretary for the Red Cross in London, a teacher and textile designer, and a reader, script editor, and scriptwriter for BBC-TV. She married writer Nigel Kneale and has a son and a daughter, for whom she started her novels, in order to tell them about her early life which was so different from theirs. Her younger years were the subject for *When Hit-*

*ler Stole Pink Rabbit** (Collins, 1971; Coward, 1972) and her adolescent life in England was used for *The Other Way Round** (Collins, 1975; Coward, 1975). Both were chosen for the *Horn Book* Fanfare list. She has continued the story of her life in *A Small Person Far Away* (Collins, 1978; Coward, 1979). In addition she has written and illustrated several picture books, including *The Tiger Who Came to Tea* (Collins, 1968; Coward, 1968), *When Willie Went to the Wedding* (Collins, 1972; Parents, 1973), and several about a cat named Mog, the first being *Mog, the Forgetful Cat* (Collins, 1970; Parents, 1972).

KERRY TATE (*Wall of Words**), eight-year-old younger sister of Kim*, third of the four Tate sisters and Kim's favorite. Though apparently bright, she is unable to read and write, doesn't know right from left, and is unusually awkward and ungainly in her movements. A succession of psychologists and experts haven't been able to figure out why she can't learn and why she gets sick every time she goes to school. Mrs. Hanrahan suggests that the child may be suffering from dyslexia, and at the end of the book Kerry is seen walking her English sheepdog along the graffiti wall in the park, where beneath the inscription "Dyslexia Rules K.O." she writes, "Oh No, It Doesn't! Kerry Tate," words that indicate that she is learning to cope with her disability. She also has developed some self-confidence. A quiet child, thin and with coppery red hair, she has kept to herself, loving pets and quiet activities. When Mrs. Tate's employer asks that she present a bouquet to the Duchess who will assist at the opening of the new Sports Centre and Anna carries on because she hasn't been chosen, Kerry, who is naturally retiring, bargains away the responsibility for a share of Anna's Saturday Kidsline wages, money she uses to buy a longed-for sheep dog. She is an unsentimentally presented handicapped child.

KEVIN THOMPSON (*Gumble's Yard**; *Widdershins Crescent**), youth who tells the story, brother of Sandra* and nephew of Walter* Thompson. He tends to be a follower and usually leaves decisions to Sandra and Dick* Hedley. In the first book, however, he seeks out Uncle Bob on his own, an act of courage and perseverance, and in the second book, it is his idea to quit school and go to work to keep the family together and enable Harold* to go to Cobchester College. He describes himself as being skinny and poorly dressed and not as good at ideas as Dick or as good at managing things as Sandra, both of whom he admires. He enjoys telling stories and sometimes entertains the children that way. He is less clearly drawn than the other characters, but his narrative about the events that happen in the Jungle* and at Widdershins Crescent seems objective and honest.

KEWAL (*The Devil's Children**), young Sikh man, cousin of Gopal* and Ajeet*, who provides much information to Nicky* Gore when she joins their group. It is Kewal whom Nicky, affected by the Changes, tries to knife when he starts a stalled bus, but he does not hold this against her. A lively, curious man, he likes to find out the reasons for things, and gives the best explanations for what the Changes have done to the English and for how Arthur* Barnard has been able to make himself master in the village. Nicky notices that, though he is quick and clever, he is also lazy and vain, with a preference for wearing good clothes that become a reason for not doing any dirty work. He has a squint so that one eye does not focus in tandem with the other, but this does not destroy his good looks. He has spent most of his life in England and was a university student when the Changes came, and he admits to Nicky that, though he speaks Punjabi fluently, he thinks in English.

KIDNAPPED (Stevenson*, Robert Louis, Cassell, 1886; Scribner, 1886), historical adventure novel set in Scotland in 1751, dealing in part with the Jacobites some six years after the defeat of Bonnie Prince Charlie, the Young Pretender, at Culloden. The narrator, David* Balfour, 17, sets off with a letter left him by his recently deceased father to his Uncle* Ebenezer Balfour of Shaws, of whom he had never previously heard. At Shaws he finds a house with large portions unfinished and the rest in a dilapidated state. His Uncle Ebenezer proves to be a surly, suspicious miser, who grudgingly lets him in and shares his meager meal but refuses to let him have a fire or a light. The next night he suddenly gives David a substantial sum of money, and then sends him through the dark, stormy night up a flight of steps in the unfinished section of the house to get a chest of important papers. A flash of lightning, briefly illuminating the stairway, reveals that it ends not in a room but in a sheer drop-off, and saves David from certain death on the stones below. When he returns and surprises his uncle, the old man has a heart seizure, but with the medicine David administers he recovers. The next morning a boy named Ransome comes to the door from the ship *Covenant* with a message from Captain Hoseason, and Uncle Ebenezer, apparently relenting, proposes that David go with him to the inn where he is to meet the captain to transact business, and then go on to the lawyer, Mr. Rankeillor, who knew David's father and can apprise him of his rights. After conferring with Uncle Ebenezer at the inn, Captain Hoseason lures David aboard the *Covenant*, where the boy is clubbed and bound in the hold while the ship takes off for the Carolinas, where he will be sold as a slave. The brutal mate, however, kills Ransome, and David is pressed into service as ship's boy. As they beat their way around the north of Scotland in a fog, they run down a boat and pick up the only survivor, a smallish man, who is pockmarked and wearing a pair of pistols, a sword, and a well-filled money belt, and who turns out to be a Jacobite messenger named Alan* Breck Stewart, who is taking a second rent which was levied on the highlanders of Appin to the Young Pretender in France. Having overheard the captain plotting with some of his men to murder this stranger, David warns him, and together they defend the roundhouse against the crew's attack. They manage to wound the captain and kill several others, and force the survivors to come to terms. Since the one officer who could pilot has been killed, however, the ship is soon in difficulties, and just as the lifeboat is being lowered, David is washed overboard and, clinging to a spar, is carried to an islet where he lives in misery for several days until some

fishermen indicate that he can easily cross the
water to the main Isle of Mull at low tide. He
then makes his way along, getting help from the
local residents and following a trail left by
Alan Breck for "the lad with the silver button,"
which is one from Breck's his own coat, a button
he gave to David after their roundhouse fight.
After he arrives in Appin, David encounters a
group led by Colin Roy Campbell of Glenure, who
is called the Red Fox. He is the hated king's
factor and is evicting local people from their
long-held homes. As David is being questioned, a
shot rings out and the Red Fox is killed. David
runs after the man who fired the shot and is
therefore thought to be in league with him. As
he runs, he encounters Alan Breck carrying a
fishing rod, and together they make a speedy and
harrowing escape. They soon learn that they are
both wanted for the murder, with a large price
upon their heads, and they make a long and
gruelling journey, mostly at night, through the
Highlands to the Firth of Forth, having many
adventures on the way: they visit Cluny
Macpherson, the outlawed chief of the clan
Vourich, in his mountain hideout; David falls
ill and is nursed in the home of Duncan dhu
Maclaren in the Braes of Balquidden, where Robin
Oig (son of Rob Roy) and Alan come near to
having a duel by swords which is diverted by
clever Duncan into a contest by bagpipes. Alan
is bested, and they part friends. When they come
to Forth, they cannot pass over the river
bridge, which is guarded. Alan neatly arouses
the pity of the landlord's daughter at the inn,
pretending that David is ill, and gets her to
row them across the Firth. In Edinburgh David
goes to the home of the lawyer, Mr. Rankeillor,
convinces him that he is indeed David Balfour,
and learns the story he has never known: how his
Uncle Ebenezer and his father both loved the
same woman and how his father won the woman but
left his rightful claim to Shaws to his younger
brother, Ebenezer, and became a schoolmaster,
never telling David that he would be the heir to
a large estate. With Mr. Rankeillor (and his
clerk as a witness), David and Alan go to Shaws,
and there Alan poses as a messenger from Highlanders who have captured David, and tricks
Uncle Ebenezer into admitting that he had the

boy kidnapped aboard the *Covenant*. Mr. Ran-
keillor forces Uncle Ebenezer to settle with
David out of court, and, with money available,
David expects to be able to help Alan return to
France. Their further adventures are told in a
sequel, *Catriona* (as *David Balfour* in the United
States). Many of the Highland characters as
well as the Red Fox are historical personages.
Although the political allegiances of the
Highland clans are somewhat confusing and the
book assumes a knowledge of the Jacobite
movement, the adventure alone can carry the
interest, the style is skillful, and the pace of
the plot never falters. David is adequate as a
hero, but other characters are more memorable,
notably Uncle Ebenezer and Alan Breck.
Children's Classics.

KIM (Kipling*, Rudyard, ill. J. Lockwood
Kipling, Macmillan, 1901; Doubleday, 1901),
novel of India in the late nineteenth century,
showing the richness and diversity of life
there as seen through the eyes of a street
urchin who becomes part of the great Indian
Secret Service. Although he is English, the son
of a soldier of an Irish regiment and a
housemaid in a colonel's family, orphan Kim*
(Kimball) O'Hara, 13, has grown up as a native
on the streets of Lahore, posing as a Hindu, a
Muslim, or whatever suits his fancy, begging and
earning a bit executing commissions of intrigue
for men of fashion, and sometimes trailing men
who have nothing to do with horses for the
red-bearded Afghan horse-dealer Mahbub* Ali, in
what is obviously intrigue of another sort. He
loves the bustle of the city and the excitement
of the chase, and he is known to all the native
quarter as Little Friend of All The World. When
Teshoo* Lama from Tibet comes seeking the Wonder
House, the Lahore Museum, Kim sees in him a new
adventure and becomes his *chela* (disciple) to
beg for him and travel with him as he seeks a
sacred river that will free him from the Wheel
of Life. Kim, too, thinks up a quest, a search
for a Red Bull on a Green Field which, along
with 900 devils, will bring him fortune, all
that he can remember from his father's opium
ravings about his regimental colors and fellow
soldiers. The boy carries in an amulet around

his neck the papers, which he cannot read, that are all his father left him--his birth certificate, his father's Masonic membership certificate, and his mustering out papers from the army. Together Kim and the lama start on their way, stopping at Umballa where Kim executes a commission for Mahbub Ali, which is to take in a very secret way the pedigree of a white stallion to a certain Colonel Creighton, and then (though this was not part of Mahbub's plan) watching from hiding while the colonel confers with the commander-in-chief who orders up 8,000 men, with guns. When they come upon an army unit encamping, Kim, always full of curiosity, crawls near and sees to his astonishment that their flag is a red bull on a green field. He returns that night to see more, bidding the lama wait nearby, and is captured as a thief by the Anglican chaplain, Mr. Bennett, who wrenches the amulet from his neck. Amazed at the garbled story Kim tells, while trying to get back his amulet papers, Bennett calls in the Catholic chaplain, Father Victor, and to verify his story Kim summons the lama. When the old man discovers, from Father Victor's incredulous comments translated by Kim, that the boy is a sahib, an Englishman, and that they will send him to school at the Masonic Orphanage in the hills, he inquires what is the best school for sahibs and the cost, and after brief meditation, announces that he will send the money for that school. He then rises and disappears into the night. The lama is as good as his word, and Kim is sent to the school at Lucknow, but not before he has appealed by letter to Mahbub Ali, who rides onto the parade ground, rescues Kim from a drummer boy who is beating him, and talks in riddles about him to Colonel Creighton, arousing the interest of this director of the spy network in the boy, who is naturally suited for the service. For nearly three years Kim is at school, learning to read and write English and also learning mathematics and the rudiments of surveying, but disappearing every vacation into the great stream of native life, at first by himself, and later in the company of Mahbub, traveling to the far reaches of the country and working as a minor player in various secret investigations. He is occasionally punished for

skipping school and spending a day in the
company of a street beggar, actually the lama
whom the authorities at the school do not
recognize as a man to honor or revere. By
Colonel Creighton's order he also spends some
time at Simla at the curio shop of Lurgan*
Sahib, one of the important men in the Great
Game, as the secret service is called, who
teaches him many valuable things not dreamed of
at the Lucknow school. There he also meets
Hurree* Babu, an obese Bengali, who, unlikely as
it seems, is another player in the game. When he
is almost sixteen, having passed his examinations and taken prizes in mathematics, he is
told that the colonel has found a minor post as
an assistant surveyor for him, and he goes to
join his lama, again a *chela*, as they wander
about the country seeking the lama's river, and
with Kim thoroughly enjoying himself. In a
third-class train compartment, quite by chance,
he identifies a wounded and terrified fellow
player by an unusual amulet and a series of
passwords, and by quick thinking and techniques
he learned from Lurgan changes the man's
disguise and saves him. Hurree, in the guise of
a Dacca physician, congratulates him and enlists
his aid to travel as a backup within a day's
walk in the high hills where the Babu is to find
two men traveling as hunters who are really
agents of Russia, intent on surveying and subverting the kings of some of the mountain
states. The lama is delighted to travel back in
the mountains and seems to regain his health,
striding up and down steep trails that leave Kim
breathless and exhausted. They come upon the
Russians, to whom Hurree has joined himself as
the representative of a local rajah eager to
serve them. When one of the men sees the
marvelous picture of the Great Wheel of Life
drawn and expounded by the lama, he tries to buy
it, grabs and tears it, and strikes the lama in
the face. Their bearers, hillmen all, flee in
horror with all the baggage, and Kim, after
kicking one of the Russians in the groin, gets
the lama away, leaving Hurree wringing his hands
and wailing at their "beating a priest." The
bearers help the lama, who is sick and shaken,
to Shamlegh-under-the-Snow, a village perched on
a tiny shelf between a steep mountainside and a

sheer drop-off, where the Woman of Shamlegh
orders some of her several husbands to carry the
lama in a litter back to the plains. First,
however, the bearers divide all the baggage,
giving Kim the red-topped kilta he requests,
which holds all the records and letters from
local kings that the Russians have collected in
eight months. He also gets the woman to take a
message to Hurree, who will escort the Russians,
begging and without baggage, for weeks across
the mountains, pretending great deference and
thoroughly discrediting them in all the hill
provinces. When the woman suggests, with the
boldness of a matriarchial queen, that he repay
her with love, Kim pleads his priesthood but
kisses her goodbye, congratulating himself on
being no longer treated like a child. They make
their slow journey back to the plains, to the
home of a woman from Kulu who has entertained
them before, and there Kim, overburdened with
his worry about the papers he carries and the
health of the lama, succumbs to the fever he has
been fighting off. When, after weeks of illness,
he wakes, he finds Hurree there, again as the
Dacca physician, as well as Mahbub, who has been
summoned by the Babu in case there is need for
force to get the papers away from their hostess.
Kim gratefully gives up the key to the locked
box she has provided and goes off to find the
lama, whom Hurree says he pulled out of a nearby
river where he was drowning. With beatific calm
and joy, the old man tells Kim that he has found
his river and was about to join the One when he
remembered his *chela* and wrenched his soul back
to save the boy. There is no need for haste, he
says; salvation is certain. The childish simplicity of the lama contrasts with the cynicism
of Kim and his mentors in the Great Game, and
the two stories, progressing side by side, provide plot tension, though the great strength of
the novel is in its warm and appreciative picture of the multiplicity of people and strange
life crowded into the subcontinent. Although the
book was first published for adults, its lively
hero makes it a favorite among young people who
are good readers. Choice.

KIM O'HARA (*Kim**), Kimball, urchin from the Lahore streets who becomes a member of the Indian

Secret Service. Kim is very bright and intensely
curious, a good actor and natural mimic who
loves the excitement of intrigue and, having
seen evil and violence all his life, is not
shocked or afraid in the most dangerous
situations. Although he is English and therefore
a sahib, he has scorn for most of the clumsy
sahibs who are so ignorant that they are
constantly ridiculed and cheated by the natives.
An unbeliever or free thinker to whom one creed
is as good as another, Kim attaches himself to
the Tibetan lama with love, recognizing the
genuine goodness of the old man, but while the
lama is trying to free himself from the
illusions of this world, Kim constantly delights
in the world around him, with all its color,
dirt and noise, and variety.

KIM TATE (*Wall of Words**), at thirteen the
eldest of the four Tate sisters. She is bright
at school, athletic, and much attached to Mr.*
Tate, who she is certain will soon finish his
novel on Russia and return to live with his
family. She is slower than the other children to
see that he really doesn't care enough about his
family to want to continue to live with and
support them. She feels very close to Kerry*,
her dyslexic sister, and much of the novel deals
with how she discovers the nature of Kerry's
problem. Near the end of the book the reader
learns that Kim has tested as gifted, but her
mother refused to let her be put in special
classes because she feared that Kim would turn
out to be like her father, too one-sided to
relate well to others and too introverted to
develop his talents in a worthwhile way. In the
book, Kim learns that she has to face facts.

KIM TYSON (*Brother in the Land**), girl whom
Danny* Lodge saves from a thug in nuclear-
devastated Skipley and immediately falls in
love with. Cynical and unsentimental, Kim is
far more aware of the hopelessness of their
situation than Danny, and she is also more
skilled at scrounging supplies and more willing
to kill, if necessary, to survive. Her
vulnerability shows up in her concern for her
sister's baby, which is born deformed and dies
immediately. After she and Danny leave with Ben,

she surprises two of the motorcyclists who have
attacked him. She is able to get their machine
gun and kills Rhodes* as he is about to kill
Danny.

A KIND OF WILD JUSTICE (Ashley*, Bernard, ill.
Charles Keeping, Oxford, 1978; Phillips, 1979),
realistic novel of suspense with detective-story
aspects set recently in London. Ronnie Webster,
a frightened, abused, streetwise schoolboy of
about ten, desperately takes control of his
destiny and in the process learns that some
people are indeed trustworthy. He thus begins to
think better of himself and develops some hope
for the future. Ronnie has been living "on the
edge of real fear" ever since the local crime
bosses, Roy and Bernie Bradshaw, threatened to
break Ronnie's back if his father, Steve, an
ex-race-car driver, refused to "nick" and drive
hot cars for them. Ronnie loves but distrusts
both Steve, who relieves his fear and shame with
drink, and his overdressed, shallow, neglectful
mother, Val, who urges Steve to go along with
the Bradshaws for the trinkets the money will
buy. Monosyllabic in speech, Ronnie can't read
and refuses to write. He is thought hopeless by
teachers, and, small, thin, and withdrawn, he is
shunned by his schoolmates. He considers school
a waste of time for one like himself who needs a
different sort of skill to survive on the
streets. The Bradshaw gang holds up the box
office at the City East-Arsenal football
(soccer) game. The police soon pick up Steve for
driving the getaway car because meticulous,
methodical Detective-Inspector Kingsland has
found one of Ronnie's remedial reading cards in
the abandoned car. Ronnie feels guilty for
causing his father's arrest, scared for what the
Bradshaws might do to him, and puzzled when he
gradually realizes that his mother planted the
card there. When Val walks out (Ronnie learns
later it is to join Bernie Bradshaw), old
Charlie* Whitelaw (a bus driver), Kingsland, and
the remedial reading teacher, Miss Lessor, all
offer help, but Ronnie trusts no one, and,
afraid that he will be taken "into care," runs
away, intending to sleep on the streets.
Discovering that living on the town is not as
easy in real life as on the television, he

decides to accept Charlie's offer and moves in with Charlie and his wife, Elsie, who run a small bus company. Paralleling Ronnie's story is that of another isolated and fearful child, his partner in the remedial reading class, Manjit Mirza, a Sikh girl from the Punjab. Manjit's father, also unwillingly involved with the Bradshaws, had been caught with a fake passport and deported to India. Now the Bradshaws are arranging his reentry, though for a price and with threats. Manjit's and Ronnie's stories come together for the climax when Charlie agrees to drive the bus for a senior citizen outing to Paris, during which the Bradshaws will smuggle three Indians, including Manjit's father, into England. Ronnie overhears the plan, assumes that Charlie is a willing accomplice of the two thugs, and informs on him to Inspector Kingsland, certain that the information will buy his father's release from jail. He is disappointed when Kingsland says that no arrest can be made without evidence and convinces the boy to return to Charlie's place. That night Ronnie overhears a conversation between Charlie and Elsie that indicates that Charlie is also under the thugs' thumbs. For appearance's sake, Ronnie is taken along on the trip to Paris. On the way he notices that Roy Bradshaw has a streak of purple paint on one wrist from spray used during the robbery and realizes that this will be enough to convict Bradshaw. With sudden inspiration, he also sees how he can save Charlie. He upsets the schedule to pick up the Indians by running away, knowing full well the senior citizens will not allow Charlie and Bradshaw to leave without finding him. He informs the gendarmes, who tell Kingsland, and Roy Bradshaw is arrested. Charlie is exonerated, Bernie and Val skip town, Steve will probably be released on probation to work for Charlie, Kingsland is proud that Ronnie proved his judgment of the boy's resource sound, and schoolmates and teachers develop a higher estimation of Ronnie. Kingsland has maintained his record for clever police work, and Ronnie has, as Kingsland's sidekick, Jonesy, remarks, achieved revenge, a "kind of wild justice," to quote Francis Bacon. Ronnie seems more confident of himself since he has scored a victory in "real life," but little Manjit seems as alone and separate as ever. The style is vigorous and understated and often employs dialect and street jargon. Events are related in the third person but are so severely focused on Ronnie that it seems he is telling the story. Most of the book consists of his thoughts and reactions. Here and there the point of view switches to those of Kingsland and Manjit. Characters are flat and black or gray because that is the way Ronnie sees them. Tension is high throughout the book, and there are several fine action scenes. More than just another thriller, the story presents a sympathetic look at two kinds of modern-day London social problems involving children of dysfunctional families. Carnegie Com.

KING (*The Moon in the Cloud**), ruler of Kemi (Egypt), whom Reuben serves briefly and comes to like and respect. A lonely, isolated, indulged young man, he displays a keen sense of justice and human sympathy that indicate that he may eventually become a great and good ruler, if he survives the flood, that is. During the tumult of the festival, he is busy granting petitions when a chance encounter brings him face to face with Reuben, pretending to be a beggar, and Tahlevi*, pretending to be a madman, in their effort to escape. The king quickly sizes up the situation, and, knowing from previous conversation how much Reuben longs for freedom and Thamar, gives him his royal signet ring as a token of freedom and allows both Reuben and Tahlevi to go free.

KING, (DAVID) CLIVE (1924-   ), born in Richmond, Surrey, England; lecturer, education officer, and writer of novels for children and young people. A graduate of King's School in Rochester, he received his B.A. degree in English from Downing College, Cambridge, in 1948, and later attended the School of Oriental and African Studies in London. From 1943 to 1946, he served in the Royal Naval Volunteer Reserve as a sub-lieutenant. He has had a varied career, holding positions in different parts of England and in many countries abroad. He has seen service with the British Council as an administrative officer in Amsterdam, Nether-

lands; as student welfare officer in Belfast,
Ireland; as lecturer in Aleppo, Syria; as
lecturer and director of studies in Beirut,
Lebanon; and as education officer in Madras,
India. He was a warden for the East Sussex
County Council in Rye and education adviser for
the East Pakistan Education Center in Dacca. Now
a full-time writer, he is married, has a
daughter and a son, and has made his home in
England in Norfolk. His books reflect his
extensive travels and the history and geography
of the places where he has lived: *Hamid of
Aleppo* (Macmillan, 1958); *The Town that Went
South* (Macmillan, 1959; Penguin, 1961), a novel
that reflects his life in Rye and tells of a
town that comes adrift and is carried off to
sea; *Stig of the Dump* (Penguin, 1963), about the
friendship between a boy and a man living a
Stone Age existence in a chalk-pit dump; *The
Twenty-Two Letters* (Hamilton, 1966; Coward,
1967), a historical novel about the invention of
the alphabet; *Ninny's Boat* (Kestrel, 1980;
Macmillan, 1981), a novel set in the Dark Ages;
and *Me and My Million** (Kestrel, 1976; Crowell,
1979), a rollicking farce set in London that is
is only venture into comedy and is a *Boston
Globe-Horn Book* honor book. He has also written
readers and plays for the stage and television.

KINGFISHER ISLAND (*The Islanders**), the nearby
island, which the Halcyonites also refer to as
Sin Island, a bitterly ironic name. In
accordance with received Law they maroon all
newcomers on it, presumably to keep evil from
corrupting their society on Halcyon*. Kingfisher is even more barren than Halcyon, with
very steep cliffs on the side nearest Halcyon
but with herds of wild goats farther back upon
which Charlie* Herrick and the Rikofian exiles
survive.

*THE KING OF THE GOLDEN RIVER; OR, THE BLACK
BROTHERS: A LEGEND OF STIRIA* (Ruskin*, John,
Smith, 1850; Wiley, 1860), literary tale supposedly set in a province of Austria, showing the
value of instinctive charity and respect for
nature. In a beautiful valley favored by climate
and soil and known as the Treasure Valley live
three brothers, Schwartz and Hans (both ugly men

with overhanging eyebrows and dull eyes) and
their younger brother, Gluck, 12, a fair-haired,
blue-eyed boy, who is kindly and cheerful even
though he is abused and overworked by his
brothers. One night while Gluck is acting as
turnspit and minding the roast, a strange little
man comes to the door and begs to be allowed to
come in by the fire to dry himself. This
extraordinary gentleman has a very red face with
an even redder, almost bronze-colored nose,
curling mustaches, and merry, twinkling eyes.
His dripping does more to put the fire out than
the fire does to dry him, but the mutton
continues to cook, and as it nears completion,
the old man asks for a slice. Gluck, in pity,
decides to give him the one slice his brothers
have promised him for his own dinner. Just as he
is cutting it off, his brothers return. They try
to throw the visitor out but are tossed about
themselves, and in anger they send Gluck to the
coal cellar after the little man leaves and
promises to return at midnight. That night a
tremendous storm ruins the valley, sweeping away
trees, crops, cattle, and all the gold the
brothers have amassed but leaving on the kitchen
table a small engraved card that says, "South
West Wind Esquire." There follows a drought for
several years, so damaging that the brothers
give up farming and go to the city as
goldsmiths, melting down the gold plate that is
all that is left of their fortune and mixing it
with copper to cheat their customers. Since they
drink up all the incoming money, they are at
last reduced to only one mug belonging to Gluck,
which is decorated with a fierce little face of
the reddest gold. The older brothers toss it
into the melting pot, leaving Gluck to mind it.
To his astonishment it starts talking to him,
and when he pours it out, instead of liquid
there emerges a little golden dwarf about
eighteen inches high. He introduces himself as
the King of the Golden River, tells Gluck he was
under an enchantment, which has now been broken,
and announces that whoever climbs to the top of
the mountain from which the Golden River issues
and casts into the stream at its source three
drops of holy water shall find that the river
will turn to gold, but failing the first attempt
he will become a black stone. The older brothers

first beat Gluck for the loss of the mug and then fall to fighting. Schwartz is arrested and Hans, therefore, is the first to try his luck. He steals some holy water and starts off, but finds it much harder than he expected and grows very thirsty along the way. It occurs to him that he will need only three drops of the holy water, so he starts to drink part of it. Just as he puts it to his lips, he sees a dog, dying of thirst, in the pathway. He drinks, kicks the dog aside, and goes on. The next time he stops to drink a child appears, stretched nearly lifeless on a rock, and in desperate need of water. Hans eyes it deliberately, drinks, and passes on. Next he comes upon an old man who cries piteously for water, but Hans denies having any and steps over the prostrate body. When he throws the holy water into the stream, he staggers, falls in, and is changed into a black stone. Gluck, in the meantime, gets a job from another goldsmith, earns enough to pay Schwartz's fine, and gets him out of prison. Schwartz buys some holy water from a priest, sets out, and has much the same experience as Hans, refusing water to a child, to an old man, and at last to his brother Hans, whom he sees lying exhausted by the path. With a great crash of lightning the earth gives way beneath him, the waters close over him, and he becomes a black stone. Gluck then decides to try his luck. He asks a priest for holy water and is given it willingly. When he comes to an old man he gladly gives part of the water to him. When he sees a child he decides to suffer his own thirst but revives the child with all but a few drops of the water. At the sight of a little dog dying of thirst beside the trail he tries to pass by but is so stricken with pity that he pours the last drops into the dog's mouth. It jumps up and is transformed before his eyes into the King of the Golden River, who plucks a lily that grows at his feet, shakes three drops of water from it into Gluck's flask, and tells him to cast that water into the river. Although the river does not turn into a stream of gold, it breaks through some underground passage into Treasure Valley, revitalizes the land, and makes it a fertile and bountiful home for Gluck. Although the story is based on a folktale

pattern, it is far longer and more elaborate
than tales from the oral tradition, and the
morals are spelled out far more explicitly: "And
thus the Treasure Valley became a garden again,
and the inheritance which had been lost by
cruelty was regained by love." This makes it
appeal more, perhaps, to the Victorian than to
the modern taste. Children's Classics.

THE KING'S GOBLET (Fletcher*, David, Constable,
1964; Pantheon, 1962), mystery thriller set in
Venice in the mid-twentieth century, some years
after World War II. Troubled by his father's
loss of his glass-blower's job, his mother's
overwork, their poverty, and his own aimless-
ness, Aldo* (Rinaldo) Gambadello, 15, the first-
person narrator, wanders the city and joins the
gang of Gino the Fox, but also goes for counsel
to Old* Guido Falieri, a gondolier now grounded
by a heart condition. One night he finds Old
Guido's gondola adrift and Guido dying, and can
make out only the word "letter" from the old
man's attempt to speak. Other clues cause him to
suspect this has something to do with a
marvelous ruby glass goblet, a family heirloom
and the only thing of value still owned by his
father. Made of two layers of glass, one crimson
and one vermillion, with a hunting scene in
gold filigree embedded between them, it was one
of a pair for the Doge to give to King Henry the
Third of Navarre in 1574, but was reported
broken and kept by an ancester. Aldo meets a
wealthy American boy, Al van Stratten, who is
lamed by polio, and hires out to him as a guide,
comandeering Guido's gondola to provide transportation. After some rivalry, the two boys become good friends. Gino, furious at being rejected, organizes his gang to ambush them, but
Al, an athletic boy before his illness, fights
Gino off, and they get the gondola away only to
be caught in a terrific storm. Al's father
arrives in Venice trying to find the mate for a
goblet in his extensive art collection, one of
the pair blown for King Henry in 1574, having
been alerted by a letter from Old Guido that it
is still in Venice. When Aldo takes him to see
the goblet, his parents being out of town, he is
appalled to find that it is missing and
immediately suspects Gino, who admits that he

took it, demands half the sale price, and threatens to destroy the goblet if Aldo makes trouble. Aldo reasons that the goblet must be hidden among the other ruby glass in the factory where one of the gang works, a suspicion confirmed by an American girl who joins a tourist group and spots it. Aldo and Al elude the watchful gang, sneak into the factory via a sand chute, retrieve the goblet, and escape in a wild chase, only to ground the gondola in the mud of low tide. When they finally float off, Gino and his friends ram and destroy the gondola, but Aldo jumps clear with the goblet onto the barge of a friend and is chased to the door of a church, where he trips and shatters the goblet. Thinking his chance for wealth and his father's treasure are both destroyed, he goes home to find the goblet there, his father having substituted an imitation of his own making. Mr. von Stratten, despite his great wealth, is unable to get Aldo's father to sell the goblet, but he sets him up in his own glass-blowing shop to turn out art works. Aldo gives up a chance to go to America with Al in favor of working with his father. Except for the Americans, who are in language and attitude the stereotypes seen through British eyes, the characters are convincing and the action, particularly in the second half, is fast-paced, but the main impression the book leaves is of a visit to Venice. Sometimes this description is overdone: "I shoved on my oar, thereby stirring a puddle of molten silver on the ebonized waters . . . clock towers and campaniles now floodlit for the summer season . . . glowed a luminous pink in a world of indigo blue. Blobs of a cheerful yellow from the globes of the street lamps punctuated the quays every fifty yards." Fanfare.

KINGSLEY, CHARLES (1819-1875), born in Holne Vicarage, Dartmoor, Devonshire; clergyman, poet, and author. The son of a clergyman, he grew up in Devon and was educated in Bristol and Cornwall. When he was sixteen, the family moved to London, and he attended King's College there. He received his B.A. with honors from Magdalene College, Cambridge, in 1842. He originally intended to study law, but decided instead to go into the church and was ordained in the Church of England in 1842. He was for many years Rector of Eversley, Hampshire. He was Regius Professor of Modern History at Cambridge and tutored the Prince of Wales. He was also Canon of Westminster and chaplain to Queen Victoria from 1873-1875. A man of wide-ranging interests, he had a lifelong fascination with geology and natural science. He advocated Christian Socialism, urging the church to work actively to improve social and economic conditions among the people. He himself taught his parishioners to read and write and worked to get better wages and living conditions for them. As Pastor Lot, he wrote books and published in magazines on their behalf. He also published many sermons, tracts, and poems. His best known book for young readers today is *The Heroes* (Blackie, 1855; Warner, 1855), which is considered a masterful retelling from Greek mythology of the stories of Jason, Perseus, and Theseus. Written specifically for his three eldest children, it was also intended to serve as an antidote to coy and didactic versions in circulation at the time. *The Water-Babies** (Macmillan, 1863; Burnham, 1864), was written for his youngest son. Cited in Children's Classics and selected for the Lewis Carroll Shelf, it tells of an abused chimney sweep who is turned into a water-baby and encounters numerous and varied creatures of the water. It is highly moralistic and instructional and often arch and condescending toward its audience, but it reveals a strong love for children and nature, qualities that marked Kingsley's work for the young. He also published for young readers *Westward Ho!* (Macmillan, 1855; Ticknor, 1855), *Hereward the Wake* (Macmillan, 1866; Macmillan, 1866), and *Madame How and Lady Why* (Bell, 1870; Macmillan, 1885). He loved walks, animals, and the outdoors, and was admired for his sweet and gentle disposition.

KING-SMITH, DICK (1922-   ), born in Bitton, Gloucestershire; farmer, teacher, and author. He attended Marlborough College, Wiltshire, from 1936 to 1940, and received his B.Ed. from the University of Bristol in 1975. He served in the Grenadier Guards from 1941 to 1946. For twenty years he farmed in Gloucestershire, and then from 1975 to 1982 taught at Farmborough Primary School. Since 1982 he has been a freelance writer, all his books being animal fantasies intended for younger children but engaging enough to entertain adults who are reading to the children. His first, *The Fox Busters* (Gollancz, 1978), concerns the fowls of Foxearth Farm who band together against the menace of foxes. His next book, *Doggie Dogfoot* (Gollancz, 1980; as *Pigs Might Fly*, Viking, 1982), is the story of a piglet with misshapen feet which enable him to become a mighty swimmer and to save the farm. In *The Mouse Butcher* (Gollancz, 1981; Viking, 1982), the uncouth but stout-hearted Butcher wins the heart of the Persian in the manor house and defeats the villains. *The Sheep-Pig** (Gollancz, 1983; as *Babe: The Gallant Pig*, Crown, 1985), which won the Guardian award and was an honor book for the *Boston Globe-Horn Book* award, is about a bright and determined young pig who makes a permanent place for himself on the farm and wins the sheep trials by learning the sheeps' language and replacing the old herd dog. His books are marked by high spirits and clever dialogue.

KIPLING, (JOSEPH) RUDYARD (1865-1936), born in Bombay, India and died in London; major poet, short-story writer, and novelist. The son of an English civil servant, he spent the first five years of his life very happily in India and then was sent to stay with distant and unsympathetic relatives in England where he endured six miserable years before he was removed from that environment and sent to the United Services College, known as Westward, Ho! since it had taken over an unsuccessful Devon resort of that name. Although not well suited to life in a boarding school designed for boys headed for a military career, he made friends with other nonconformists and managed to survive and in some ways beat the system, a life he later fictionalized in *Stalky & Co.* (Macmillan, 1899; Doubleday, 1899), at once a school story and a hilarious parody of the genre. When he was seventeen he returned to India and became an assistant editor of the *Civil and Military Gazette* in Lahore for five years and then worked as editor and contributor for "Week's News," on

the *Pioneer* in Allahabad, India. During this
period he published seven volumes of short
stories, starting with *Plain Tales from the
Hills* (Macmillan, 1890; Lovell, 1890) and a
volume of verse, *Departmental Ditties and Other
Verses* (*Civil and Military Gazette*, Lahore,
1886; Thacker, 1890; with additions, as *Departmental Ditties, Barrack-Room Ballads, and Other
Verse*, U. S. Book, 1890). In 1889 he returned to
England, where he became a prominent literary
figure and wrote *The Light That Failed* (Macmillan, 1891; U. S. Book, 1890), his best known
novel for adults. His best long work may be *Kim**
(Macmillan, 1901; Doubleday, 1901), the story of
an Irish orphan who lives by his wits on the
streets of India and becomes part of the British
Secret Service, which was not originally
published for children. In 1892 he married an
American woman and lived for several years in
Vermont, a period that is reflected in *Captains
Courageous: A Story of the Grand Banks* (Macmillan, 1897; Century, 1897), which is about a
spoiled and wealthy boy who falls off an ocean
liner, is picked up by a New England fishing
boat, and is rehabilitated by the hard work and
new view of life he encounters on board. After
1896 Kipling returned to England and settled
first in London and later in Burwash, Sussex. He
received many honors, including the Nobel Prize
in 1907 and honorary doctorates from McGill
University, Montreal, the Universities of Durham, Oxford, Cambridge, and Edinburgh, the Sor-
bonne, Paris, and the Universities of Strasbourg
and Athens. His books for children demonstrate
his command of style and show remarkable variety. His *Just So Stories for Little Children*
(Macmillan, 1902; Doubleday, 1902), the first
three of which appeared in *St. Nicholas*
magazine, are whimsical tales that play with
language. *Puck of Pook's Hill* (Macmillan, 1906;
Doubleday, 1906) and its sequel, *Rewards and
Fairies* (Macmillan, 1910; Doubleday, 1910),
are historical fiction set in a fantasy frame.
His best loved works are probably the serious,
dramatic stories about Mowgli, the boy raised by
wolves, from *The Jungle Books** (Macmillan,
1894–1895; Century, 1894–1895), some of which
appeared first in *St. Nicholas*. Though his
imperialistic political views made him unpopular

in the mid-twentieth century, Kipling is acknowledged as one of the great literary figures
and particularly as a brilliant stylist who
changed the pattern of the short story.

KITCHENER PONTIFEX (*Up the Pier**), son of Ellen*
and George* Pontifex and brought with them by
Gramper's* wayward spell into 1971 from their
proper 1921. A sharp-eyed, cautious youth of
twelve, he resists putting his confidence in
Carrie* until he is sure her intentions are
friendly. He tells her about the spells by which
she can see the family and fills her in on
details of his family history. In their own
time, he and his father have a ukelele act for
sightseers on the pier.

THE KITCHEN MADONNA (Godden*, Rumer, ill. Carol
Barker, Macmillan, 1967; Viking, 1967), realistic story of the relationship between a withdrawn youngster and a Ukranian maid, set in
London in the mid twentieth century. The usually
self-absorbed, quiet Gregory* Thomas, 9, who
keeps an emotional distance from everyone except
his cat, Rootles, becomes fascinated by the
stories of her Ukranian home that their new
maid, Marta, tells him and his sister, Janet*,
7. Their architect parents, busy but concerned
about the children, do not realize that Marta is
unhappy because the stylish kitchen has no "good
place" or household shrine that was the center
of life in her family home. Gregory, a highly
intelligent, bookish boy, decides that he will
provide one. The visit that he and Janet make to
the British Museum is disappointing since the
icons there are darkened by age and are not
decorated like those Marta described, but they
talk to a gentleman who suggests that they try
Rostov's, Court Jewelers in Regent Street.
Though forbidden to venture so far alone again,
they make the trip the next Saturday, and
Gregory handles the supercilious salesclerk with
dignity and finds a suitable icon, but Janet, an
open, uncomplicated child, humiliates him by
telling the clerk that they have 30 shillings
while the icon costs 438 guineas. In their haste
to get away, they are soaked in a rain and duck
into a church. There they buy a vigil lamp and
see a "dressed up picture," a Madonna that is

more like Marta's description than the elaborate
icon. Unfortunately they lose their purse, and
Gregory is temporarily stymied, but faced with
the challenge he becomes very inventive. Starting with a newspaper picture of a sixteenth-
century painting, he fashions a Madonna dressed
with bits of fine fabric which he begs from
Madame Ginette, a milliner. For a border he
needs the jewel-colored metalic papers from
toffees, and for these he tries to borrow from
the sweet-shop proprietor, using his watch as
collateral. When she hears the story, the
sympathetic woman takes his IOU instead. He even
sacrifices his precious ship picture for its
frame and the sky background. His parents are
astonished, Marta is overjoyed, and Janet, who
has been his willing assistant and has given up
her allowance without protest, is proud. The
details of Gregory's passionate concentration on
the construction of the picture are made fascinating, but the main emphasis is on Gregory's
change to a boy who can show his love. Through
his perceptions the reader can understand the
importance of providing a Madonna for Marta, who
has given a much-needed security to his life.
Though the story is brief, the characterizations
are strong. Fanfare.

KIT HAVERARD (*The Lark on the Wing**), Jane Kitson Haverard, Quaker girl who grows from a
slightly rebellious twelve-year-old in *The Lark
in the Morn* to a young woman with love and a
brilliant singing career opening before her.
Though her cousin, Laura* Haverard (who has
raised her), has always scoffed at her musical
ambitions and has insisted that she get training
to be her professor father's secretary, Kit
sticks to her hopes, encouraged by her mother's
old vocal teacher, Papa* Andreas, by his successful pupil, Terry* Chauntesinger, and by her
Kitson cousins, who understand music better than
Laura does. Kit is a very hard worker,
single-minded in her devotion to her vocal
career, and both bright and good-looking, but
she is extremely innocent and is naively unaware
that four of her young men friends are in love
with her.

KITSON (*The Member for the Marsh**), schoolboy,

David Rosley's friend, treasurer of the Harmonious Mud Stickers. He organizes the club's singing and plays the tin whistle to which the boys harmonize. He explains the club name to David. The Harmonious part is obvious; the Mud Stickers part comes from the bus on which the boys ride to school, an old stick-in-the-mud. He has a good sense of humor ("This is last Tuesday's bus...."), is distinguished by his long nose, is thoughtful, and acts as mediator in disputes. When he and Starr try to make firecrackers in Kitson's kitchen to exorcise demons from the marsh, the mixture explodes, because, Kitson thinks, something was wrong with the sulphur. He refuses to discuss the consequences he faced. He is a rounded, interesting figure.

KITTY TRANTER (*The Way to Sattin Shore**), mother of Kate*, Ran*, and Lenny*, daughter of Granny* Randall, in whose house she and the three children live, and wife of Fred Tranter, who Kate initially supposes is dead but who has really fled to Australia after the accidental drowning of his brother, Bob. Kitty works at a confectioner's and seems undemonstrative, capable, and quiet. She is close and loving with her mother yet is also afraid of her. She ordinarily does not pry into her children's lives and urges them to bring friends home, yet there is a strange tension between both her and her mother and her and her children that adds to the impact of the plot problem, which concerns Fred Tranter's whereabouts. At the end she intends to emigrate to Australia with Fred, having decided that her future lies with him. She refuses to be intimidated into staying in Ipston by her domineering mother. Kitty is an interesting, puzzling figure, one whom the reader gradually learns to know.

KIZZY LOVELL (*The Diddakoi**), orphan whose father was a gypsy and whose mother was an Irish girl. Until the death of her great-great-grandmother, with whom she has lived in Admiral* Twiss's orchard, Kizzy has been much like the traditional gypsy child, earning a bit by selling flowers and holly at back doors, living mostly in the open, and having nothing to do

with the village children. When she first goes
to school she is terrified of the flush toilet,
and even after living at elegant Amberhurst
House she prefers to eat outdoors by a fire. She
is a thin child with brown skin and brown eyes,
and wears gold rings in her ears. Although
neither she nor her Gran knows how old she is,
she is assumed to be about seven. Through all
her troubles with the children at school she is
sustained by her temper and her stubbornness,
but at the same time she is a wistful waif
longing for love.

KNIGHT CRUSADER (Welch*, Ronald, ill. William
Stobbs, Oxford, 1954; Oxford, 1979), historical
novel set near the end of the twelfth century
in the kingdom of Jerusalem, or Outremer. The
novel is in three parts. In the first, which is
the longest and best developed, young Philip*
d'Aubigny, who was born at his father's castle
of Blanche Garde in Jaffa, has grown up in far
greater luxury than Europeans of the period, but
he is also excellently trained in the combat
arts. His father, Sir Hugo, is more tolerant of
the Turks than many in Outremer are and scornful
of the intrigue at the court, particularly among
the Pullani or half-native nobility. Philip
saves a Turk, Jusuf Al-Hafiz, from bandits and
takes him to Blanche Garde, where Sir Hugo
entertains him cordially. Shortly thereafter,
Philip travels with his father to court at
Jerusalem, where he meets his cousin Joscelin*
d'Aubigny, a seemingly foppish but really tough
young noble, and his uncle, Sir Fulk. When one
of the crude Normans recently arrived in
Outremer picks a quarrel with Philip, they have
a duel in which the boy acquits himself well and
as a result is knighted by the king, Guy of
Lusignan. At the celebration dinner given by Sir
Fulk, Philip meets Sir Gilbert* d'Assailly, an
awkward young fellow newly arrived from Normandy
and a nephew of the Grand Master of the
Hospitallers. Philip persuades his father to
enroll Gilbert as one of the knights of Blanche
Garde. A year later Sir Hugo and his men are
called to join the ill-fated army at Acre,
assembled because the Turks are holding the
castle at Tiberias in siege. Against good sense,
the king listens to the aggressive head of the

Hospitallers and decides to march to Tiberias instead of waiting for the Turks, under Emir Saladin, to bring the war to them. The long march without water in terrible heat weakens both men and horses, and when the Turks attack it is disastrous. Philip sees his father, his uncle, and his cousin all killed. Wounded, he is captured and saved from death only by the intercession of Jusuf and is given to him as his captive. The second part opens in Damascus where Philip has spent for four years as a servant, secretary, friend, and nursemaid to Jusuf's aging father, the Emir Usamah* Ibn-Menquidh, who is writing the story of his life. Jusif having been killed in a later battle, the Emir offers to adopt Philip as heir if he will give up Christianity. Being respectfully refused, he gives Philip some valuable black pearls with the unspoken permission to escape if he can. Not long afterwards he is approached by a knight of the Hospitallers in the disguise of a beggar, who is actually arranging the escape of prisoners to join the new Christian forces led by Richard* I of England. Philip plans with him and insists on a second horse so that Gilbert, also a prisoner in Damascus, can escape with him. By bribing a Syrian slave, they effect the escape, though Gilbert sprains his ankle on the way. Before they can reach the Krak des Chevaliers, castle of the Hospitallers, however, they are captured by Turks who take them to the Eagle's Nest, the mountain fortress of the Assassins, a religious sect feared even by Saladin. There the Old Man of the Mountains, the Sheikh Rashid ed-Din of Basra, sends them on to Krak with orders to be ready to murder whomever he names in a message they will receive. The alternative is to be murdered themselves by the Assassins' elaborate spy system. At Krak the Grand Master urges Philip to use his influence as heir to Blanche Garde and his uncle's more extensive estates on his side in the current intrigues, holding out the offer of eventual Grand Mastership of the Hospitallers for him. Philip resists both these pressures, killing the Assassin who comes to murder him, and joins forces with Richard I in his march to Jaffa. In camp he again meets Llewellyn*, old servant and veteran from Blanche Garde, and also meets young

Peter da Chaworth of the Welsh Marches, who tells him of the d'Aubigny castle at Llanstephan, of which Philip is heir. In Part III, Philip, with Gilbert, Peter, and Llewellyn, has traveled to England. There he enters the joust at Cardiff Castle, where he acquits himself well. He learns that the d'Aubigny lands that are rightfully his have been taken over by De Braose, a distant cousin. With help from gloomy Sir Geoffrey, Peter's father, he storms the castle and then, in hand-to-hand combat, kills De Braose and claims his ancestral lands in Wales. The novel is detailed and complex, with a very full canvas of both historical and fictional characters. A foreword and a note at the end help readers who are unfamiliar with the history of the period. Characterization is adequate if conventional for adventure novels, and the action is fast-paced, but the strongest element is the picture of the luxurious life in Outremer of the twelfth century: the magnificent castles, fastidious nobles, and the incessant political intrigue; and the contrast with the blunt English, their comparatively dirty and small castles, and the cruder living arrangements Philip finds in Britain. Carnegie Winner.

KNIGHT'S FEE (Sutcliff*, Rosemary, ill. Charles Keeping, Oxford, 1960; Walck, 1960), historical novel tracing the development of a half-Saxon orphan from dog boy to knight and fee-holder during the early Norman period in England, in the last decade of the eleventh century and the first decade of the twelfth. Randal, 9, son of a Saxon lady and a Breton man-at-arms, is an orphan and much abused dog boy at the castle of Arundel. He has wormed his way to the gatehouse roof to see the new Earl of Arundel, Hugh Goch, who is called Hugh the Red. In his excitement as Hugh and his entourage arrive, he leans out and inadvertently drops a half-eaten fig, which hits the nose of Hugh's stallion, causing it to rear and plunge and creating temporary chaos. Randal flees back to his dogs and the incident might have been forgotten had not Hugh sent for his father's Irish wolfhounds and Randal been forced to take them before the new earl. Recognizing the boy, Hugh orders that he be thrashed just short of death, but Herluin, minstrel of Hugh's

brother, Robert de Belleme, intervenes, proposing that he and Hugh, an avid gambler, play a
game of chess for Randal. When Herluin wins, he
calls the adoring boy "Imp," and turns him over
to Sir Everard d'Aguillon, to be brought up as
companion to his grandson Bevis. Before he
leaves, hurt and angry at Herluin, Randal
overhears a conversation on the water-stair at
night between Hugh and another man, whom he
afterwards identifies as Sir Thiebaut de Coucy.
They are clearly plotting treason against the
king. Though terrified at the time, Randal
almost forgets the incident in the years that
follow at Dean, d'Aguillon's holding, which the
boy loves from the start. After some initial
misunderstandings, he becomes inseparable from
Bevis, who, though two years older, is an open
and generous boy, and they grow together from
varlets to squires, going with Sir Everard to
Bramber, the castle of his overlord de Braose,
where he must put in a month of guard duty each
year as part of his land-holding fee. At
Bramber they run into de Coucy again and learn
that he covets Dean for the treasure which he
supposes is buried in the old grave mound of
Bramble Hill, which the people still hold sacred
even though it is pre-Christian. Since the king
owns all land, and barons and their underlings
hold it only at his pleasure, de Coucy, who has
friends high at court, may be able to take it
from Sir Everard. Randal follows a hawking party
of which de Coucy is a member and gets a quiet
word with him, reminding him of the conversation
he overheard and pointing out that, while a boy
might not be believed, any suspicion would weigh
heavily with the king. He offers to take his
story before the Bishop for trial by ordeal to
prove the truth. De Coucy drops his demand for
Dean, but home at the manor times are uneasy
and the old religion seems to be resurfacing. A
strange friar rouses the people in the
marketplace of the nearby town into a witch
hunt aimed ostensibly at Ancret, the foster
mother of Bevis, who is a wise woman and a
healer. When the mob arrives at Dean, Sir
Everard meets them at the door with Bevis on one
side and Randal on the other, with their loyal
villeins behind them, and there is a fierce
skirmish in the midst of which Randal recognizes

the friar as de Coucy and marks him with crossed
dagger strokes on the cheek. The rabble
disappears at the sight of the suit of mail
under the friar's torn gown, but de Coucy
escapes, and Sir Everard is badly wounded. He
lives for some months, but despite Ancret's
nursing his wound proves fatal in the end. De
Braose offers to take Bevis on for the remainder
of his squirehood, and Bevis agrees only if he
will also take Randal. They serve at Bramber for
two years. Bevis is made a knight in a ceremony
which he insists must take place at Dean, and
with Randal as his squire they sail for Normandy
with the forces of King Henry against his
brother, Robert. There, in the battle of
Tenchebrai, Bevis is killed, ironically by de
Coucy who has joined Robert's side, and who in
turn is killed by Randal. As he is dying, Bevis
knights Randal. De Braose offers Dean to Randal
for a one-year trial, having promised Bevis that
he would do so in case of his death. Randal,
however, sees that they have taken Herluin
prisoner, de Belleme being on Robert's side, and
begs for his release. When de Braose offers him
a choice between Dean and Herluin, the boy gives
up what he wants most and chooses the life of
the minstrel. De Braose, considering that he has
passed the test, gives him both, and Randal
returns as the new lord of Dean, not joyfully
without Bevis but confidently determined to do
his best for the manor. There is also a red-
haired girl, Gisela, from Bramber who promises
to be part of his future. The complicated
political and military maneuverings of the three
sons of William the Conqueror and their powerful
nobles form a background to the story that illustrates the early stages of reconciliation between the Saxons and the Normans and the
persistence of the older British people as
exemplified in Ancret. The powerful barons are
well drawn and believable characters, but more
interesting are Bevis and Randal and the simple
people like Lewin, the shepherd at Dean. The
ways of life in the great castles and in the
modest manors like Dean are well described, and
the ceremonies like that of the knighting of
Bevis are impressive. Also notable is the simple
rural beauty of the countryside, to which
Randal particularly responds and which makes his

love for Dean convincing. Fanfare.

KRUGER (*Old   John**), loyal and brave Kerry Blue
terrier.   Of   the   several   talking   animals
belonging to Old John, he is most at the center
of events. He influences the   action frequently
and is Old John's steady companion, adviser, and
helper. Among   other things he discovers   that a
donkey is   stealing Old John's hay every night,
convinces Old John to help the donkey, which
has been kidnapped and mistreated by the evil
dwarf, Gruaga, and persuades Old John to ask the
prince to send his archers against the dwarf to
rescue Bainen, the fairy cat. He is the first of
the   three animals living with Old John whom
Bainen helps. She cures his broken leg, and thus
he learns the story of how the dwarf prevented
her from returning to her queen's rath before
morning and how she assumed the form of a cat to
elude him. In order to return to her rath,
Bainen has had to perform three good deeds.
Later she helped other animals, too, and thus
earned her freedom. She has elected, however, to
stay with Old John and her new friends to
protect them from the evil dwarf. Kruger and
Bainen have a warm, close relationship.

KYLE, ELISABETH   (AGNES   MARY ROBERTSON DUNLOP),
(-1982), born in Ayr, Scotland, where she
made her home; journalist and for forty-five
years a popular and prolific writer of mystery-
adventure novels for adults and children and of
biographical   fiction   for   teenaged readers,
often romantic, under the pen name of Kyle. Her
thirty-odd novels for adults are set variously,
but her books for young readers, twenty-three
mystery-adventures   and   eleven   biographical
books, mostly have Scotland as their locale and
use remembered scenes. After publishing for
adults, she began writing for youth in the
1940s and at the request of her publisher
produced books for the twelve-to-fourteen age
range, where at the time there was little of
substance. Among her most popular books were
Holly Hotel (Davies, 1945; Houghton, 1947), *The
Captain's House* (Davies, 1952; Houghton, 1953),
The Reiver's Road (Nelson, 1953; as *On Lennox
Moor*, Nelson, 1954), *The House of the Pelican*
(Nelson, 1954; Nelson, 1954), and *Caroline House*

(Nelson, 1955; as *Carolina House*, Nelson, 1955).
Of her biographical fiction for older readers,
Girl with a Lantern* (Evans, 1961; as *The Story
of Grizel*, Nelson, 1961) was selected by the
editors of *Horn Book* for inclusion in Fanfare.
It tells of the early life in Scotland of
historical Lady Grizel Hume Baillie (1665-1746)
and her flight with her outlawed father to
safety in Holland, where they live until the
accession of William and Mary restores him to
political favor. Detailed and inconsistently
plotted, it nevertheless gives fine views of an
England in turmoil and transition. She also
wrote biographical novels in a romantic vein
about Charlotte Bronte, Jenny Lind, Mary of
Orange, and Mary Stuart, among other works also
mostly about women. She also wrote *Mystery of
the Good Adventure* (Dodd, 1950) for youth under
the name Jan Ralston. The daughter of a lawyer,
she was educated privately, studied journalism
in Glasgow, contributed regularly to Scottish
newspapers, and traveled extensively in Central
and Eastern Europe between the world wars on
assignment, in particular, for the Manchester
Guardian. Her stories were praised for their
strong family relationships, vividly drawn
settings, and interesting plots. Many of her
books were broadcast on BBC's Scottish
Children's Hour, and *The Reiver's Road* was
serialized in a condensed version in *Jack and
Jill* magazine.

L

LADY EULALIA MURGATROYD (*Midnight Is a Place**), grandmother of Anna-Marie* Murgatroyd, mother of Sir Denzil*, wife of Sir Quincy, who was the founder of Murgatroyd's Carpet, Rug, and Matting Manufactury, the sweatshop upon which the economy of Blastburn depends. After the death of her husband and the presumed death of her son, she makes a living by teaching music, calling herself Mrs. Minetti and eventually moving to the icehouse on the grounds of Midnight Court, the mansion that had once belonged to her. She is living in the icehouse when Anna-Marie and Lucas* Bell move in. The epitome of grand-motherliness in personality, in appearance she is wrinkled, weatherbeaten, and work-worn, but her face radiates "authority and such goodness" that the children immediately like her. Her voice is "clear and deep" and "rang like a bell in the stone-built place."

LADY MARGARET DOUGLAS (*You Never Knew Her as I Did!**), affectionately known as the Old Lady, the dowager of the large and powerful Douglas family, mother of Sir William and George. She is the grandmother of Will, a page and the bastard son of Sir William, who tells the story, and of Ellen, who becomes lady-in-waiting to Mary, Queen of Scots, while Mary is held prisoner in the Castle of Lochleven. Lady Margaret was mistress of James V, Mary's father, to whom she bore James, Earl of Moray, who becomes regent to Mary's son, James VI, later James I of England.

Will notes wryly that "Sir William never moved a
step without *her* advice." Formidable, acid-
tongued, sharp-eyed, and a lover of good
company, she has much to do with the political
maneuvering surrounding Mary at the time.
Remarking that she has more than one son, she
astutely allows both Moray and George to advance
their plans because, although she knows that
both cannot triumph, she realizes that the
family will benefit whichever one comes out on
top, either with Moray as regent or George as
King George, should he marry Mary and Mary
regain power. Lady Margaret is a strongly and
memorably drawn figure.

LA GOLONDRINA (*Songberd's Grove**), Geneva's*
mother, a Spanish dancer. Her name, which means
"the swallow," is ironic because throughout most
of the novel she has become too fat to dance.
She was a famous dancer in Europe, who, after
the death of Geneva's father, an Englishman,
came to England because she wished Geneva to be
educated in England. Unable to get a job as a
dancer, she consoled herself by eating and
became immensely fat. She now works as a dresser
and general help in a London theatre, earning
just enough to keep herself and Geneva in food
and lodging. Geneva is intensely loyal to and
proud of her mother. Near the end of the book,
La Golondrina learns that her childhood
sweetheart and one-time dancing partner, Enrico
Ribera, is coming to London, and for the first
time she realizes how she has let herself go,
disconsolately overeats on shellfish, becomes
very ill, loses a lot of weight in an amazingly
short time, and, when he arrives in London, is
again svelte and lithe. She makes a comeback,
and marries him. A fairy-tale character, she
also serves as a foil to Mrs. Byre and Mrs.*
Dora Singer.

LAKE OF GOLD. See *The Long Traverse.*

LANG, ANDREW (1844-1912), born in Selkirk,
Scotland; distinguished folklorist, anthro-
polgist, editor, teacher, and scholar. He was
respected for his studies in mythology and
folklore, which greatly influenced the thinking
of his time. The eldest son of the county

sheriff, he was educated at Selkirk High School, Edinburgh Academy, and the universities of St. Andrews, Glasgow, and Oxford. His academic career was brilliant, and he became a Fellow at Oxford in 1868. While there, he produced his famous translation of Homer. He resigned his Oxford post after seven years to devote himself to his writing and subsequently produced a long and highly respected list of publications, including articles, poems, reviews, essays, novels, retellings, and collections of tales. He also lectured and edited series for the Longmans and Nutt publishing companies. His first story for children came out in 1884 after he was a well-established scholar, *The Princess Nobody* (Longmans, 1884), a story on the pattern of the traditional fairy tale. His love for the old Scottish ballads, upon which he was raised, produced *The Gold of Fairnilee* (Arrowsmith, 1888), Next came *Prince Prigio** (Arrowsmith, 1889), an ironically humorous fantasy along the line of the courtly fairy tale, which in a reissued edition was named to Fanfare. It and its sequels, *Prince Ricardo of Pantouflia* (Arrowsmith, 1893) and *Tales of a Fairy Court* (Collins, 1907), were later published as *Chronicles of Pantouflia* (Arrowsmith, 1932). In the year he published *Prigio* he also put out a collection of traditional stories called *The Blue Fairy Book* (Longmans, 1889). This was so successful it led to a series of similar books, twenty-five in all; these are the collections for which he is most important in children's literature today. Each book has a color in its title, and they are popularly known as Lang's "color fairy books." His wife, Leonora, often assisted him with his children's books, retelling many old tales skillfully and interestingly for him. He also published for young readers *Tales of Troy and Greece* (Longmans, 1907) and versions of the stories of Joan of Arc, Robin Hood, and King Arthur, among others. He spent his later years on Scottish history and Homeric scholarship and died near Aberdeen.

THE LANTERN BEARERS (Sutcliff*, Rosemary, ill. Charles Keeping, Oxford, 1959; Walck, 1959), historical novel set in Britain in the early

fifth century A.D., when the last of the Roman
troops are recalled and an alliance of
British-Romans and Celts are trying to stem the
tide of invading Saxons. The third in Sutcliff's
Roman trilogy, it is also a psychological study
of how bitterness can destroy a man's future.
When the order comes for the Auxiliary
Troops--all that are left in Britain--to abandon
the country and sail for Gaul, Decurion Aquila,
18, commander of a troop of Rhenus Horse-
Auxiliary Cavalry, goes "willful missing," realizing that he belongs to Britain, where he was
born, more than to Rome. On impulse, as soon as
the galleys have safely put out to sea without
him, he climbs the Rutupiae tower and fires for
one last time the great watch light that has
guided ships into harbor for centuries. At his
home, a small estate worked by freemen several
days journey southwestward from Rutupiae, his
blind father and his sister Flavia, 16, are
pleased to have him return, but their pleasure
is interrupted by a Saxon attack in which
Aquila's father and all the men of the farm are
killed, and Aquila sees his beloved sister
carried off screaming by a blond giant, son of
the leader Wiermund. Because Aquila has killed
Wiermund's brother in the fight, he is not
slain immediately but rather is bound to a tree
for the wolves to savage. The wolf howls they
hear, however, are not real but rather those of
a pack of rival raiders from Juteland, who take
Aquila for a thrall to give to his captor's
grandfather, partly because he has a dolphin,
the grandfather's good-luck symbol, tattooed on
his shoulder. For three years he is slave in
Juteland, earning some distinction for his
master because he can read the scrolls of the
Odyssey that have turned up among the booty of
the raids. After an unusually hard winter
during which the old man dies, his grandson, who
has inherited Aquila (or Dolphin, as they call
him), decides to take up the invitation of
Hengest for settlers on Tanatus, the island off
the coast near Rutupiae, and he takes his
book-reading slave with him, first having a
thrall ring hammered on to his neck so that he
can be chained at night like a dog. In
Hengest's burg, Aquila comes by chance on
Flavia, for whom he has continued to hunt, but

his sister is now married to her Saxon captor
and has borne him a son. She helps Aquila to
escape and gives him their father's signet ring,
with a dolphin carved on a flawed emerald, which
has been her bridal gift, but she refuses to
leave her husband and child to go with him.
Bitterly, he feels that life has nothing left
for him except revenge against the little
bird-catcher, who he has discovered had betrayed
the secret plot supporting Ambrosius, son of
Constantine, in which his father participated,
and had thereby brought on the Saxon burning of
his home. First he walks westward until he is
out of Saxon territory and stops at the hut of a
monk in the forest, Brother Ninnias, who gives
him food and a place to sleep, and files the
thrall ring off his neck. He also tells Aquila
two things: that on the night after the Romans
left he saw the Rutupiae Light once more flaring
and that the bird-catcher he seeks lies buried
there in the clearing, having escaped from the
Saxon torturers after betraying his fellows,
stumbled this far, and died of his injuries. He
also suggests that Aquila, having nothing else
in his life, go westward to Arfon in the
mountains and take service with Ambrosius, who
still hopes to save Britain from Vortigern and
the Saxons. Because of his good Roman training
and his total dedication, Aquila soon becomes
one of the Companions, the inner circle close to
Ambrosius, the Prince of Britain, and is with
him when the three red-haired sons of Vortigern,
the young foxes as they are called, come to
pledge their loyalty to Ambrosius, having broken
with their father because he has put away their
mother and married Rowena, the beautiful
golden-haired daughter of Hengest. With them
they bring many of the Celtic chieftains
including Cradoc, a middle-aged man from farther
south in Wales, whom Aquila is able to save in a
fight against raiding Scots from Ireland. When
Ambrosius, seeking to strengthen the alliances
with these Celtic chieftains, tells Aquila to
ask for one of Cradoc's two daughters for his
wife, he does so without enthusiasm and chooses
not the beautiful, blond, older girl but Ness,
her small, dark, younger sister. Because he has
had an emotional shell around him since he lost
Flavia, Aquila is not able to show Ness any

affection, and their marriage is one of
antagonism more than love, although after the
birth of his son, whom he names Flavian but
calls Minnow, he tries with only slight success
to break through his bitter aloofness and
establish rapport with the boy and with his
wife. When the Celtic chieftains break away from
Ambrosius and Cradoc leaves Ness free to stay or
go home with him, she chooses to stay with
Aquila, and for the first time he begins to
understand Flavia's choice. Through the years
there is fighting almost every summer between
the men of Ambrosius and the Saxons, but no
decisive victory. At last, when Minnow is almost
fifteen, on the eve of what promises to be the
life or death battle, the boy arrives with his
sword at the camp, determined to be part of the
fight and hoping to join the cavalry wing led by
Artos (Arthur, the bastard son of Ambrosius's
brother, Utha), whose charismatic charm and
genuine kindness has always made the boy his
willing slave. Aquila, hurt that Minnow chooses
to follow Artos rather than him and worried
about the fate of the untrained boy in battle,
insists that Minnow stay in his unit, but later
learns that in the middle of the battle Minnow
rode off after his hero. By then, however,
Aquila has seen the Saxon whom he knows by the
resemblance to be Flavia's son, and he hunts
unsuccessfully for him among the dead and
wounded. That night he finds Brother Ninnias
tending the wounded and, walking with him back
to his hut in the forest, stumbles over a body
which proves to be Flavia's son, badly wounded
but alive. Aquila carries him to Ninnias's hut,
helps tend him, turns away some drunken soldiers
from his own unit who would have knifed any
Saxon they found, then leaves money, a pass
through British lines, and his signet ring for
the boy. Some time later, just after Ambrosius
has just been crowned High King of Britain,
bringing Cradoc and other Celtic leaders again
under his command, the ring is returned to
Aquila, showing that the boy has made his way
safely home. Aquila takes that occasion, before
all the assembled leaders, to confess publicly
to Ambrosius that he helped a Saxon escape, and
Minnow, thinking that his father will be
censured, steps forward to share the disgrace

with him, a gesture that means more to Aquila than Ambrosius's understanding and Artos's expressed admiration. The story covers a long span of years and details in a very interesting way much little-known political intrigue and history of the period. The main focus, however, is on Aquila and his psychological problems, which stem from his horror over Flavia's capture and his bitterness that she has accepted a Saxon for her husband. His belated efforts to reach out to his wife and son are emotionally moving and tend to obscure the plot's heavy reliance on coincidence. Carnegie Winner; Choice; Fanfare.

THE LARK AND THE LAUREL (Willard*, Barbara, ill. Gareth Floyd, Longman, 1970; Harcourt, 1970), richly textured historical novel with mystery-story aspects set just after the defeat at Bosworth Field in 1485 of Richard III by Henry VII Tudor. Proud, ambitious Sir Thomas Jolland, on the losing side in the war between the Lancastrians and Yorkists, chooses exile in France. Before he leaves, he sends his pampered, pettish daughter, Cecily, almost sixteen, for safekeeping to her aunt, imperious Dame* Elizabeth FitzEdmund, holder of a manor called Mantlemass* in the Ashdown Forest deep in the Sussex countryside. As the days pass, Cecily learns the satisfaction of hard work, grows less egocentric, and gains the love of Lewis* Mallory, the nephew of Roger Orlebar, owner of Ghylls Hatch, the horse farm nearby. When she arrives at Mantlemass, Cecily is only dimly aware of her surroundings, of the bustling manor with a bakehouse, kitchen, brewery, cellars in profusion, barns, and coney yards, a little kingdom nestled in a "vast expanse that was half forest and half heath." Self-pitying, Cecily is both angry that her father has so callously disencumbered himself of her by sending her to this remote place and hurt by the realization that his chief interest in her lies in how he may use her to advance his political and social ambitions. She is appalled at the way Dame Elizabeth violates established standards of upper-class feminine propriety and mingles freely with her servants and tenants, actually working alongside them at what she regards as her fair share of the menial, everyday tasks that keep the manor running. As fall moves into winter, however, Cecily gradually learns household tasks and by Christmas is able to shoulder her share of responsibility. Her attitude toward her aunt changes, too, and she finds she loves and admires the woman for whom once she felt contempt. She continues to ponder remarks her aunt made when she arrived: "I will see you happy . . . I have only one purpose for you: to give back what has been taken away." She soon becomes friends with high-spirited Lewis Mallory, and at the end of a day's ride to the seacoast, he pledges on his father's lark-and-laurel ring to protect her always, an incident that serves as prelude to their budding romance. In the spring Cecily learns that her father intends to marry her to an influential French nobleman, who will be able to set aside a marriage contracted for her when she was five. It turns out that she and Lewis had been wed as children, and Dame Elizabeth, knowing of the match, has been acting to bring the two young people together. Cecily now understands the meaning of Dame Elizabeth's remarks. No longer a "doll," a "puppet," or a "dead thing," Cecily grasps her destiny and flees into the forest for sanctuary from her father's messengers who have come to take her away. The local weaver, Halacre, gives her refuge, and a forest family, whose son, Davy*, she sheltered earlier, take her into their rude cottage. When Sir Thomas's messengers pursue her and Lewis through the forest bogs in the story's exciting climax, one servant's horse slips, drowning the man in the lake, while the other's horse runs away. The book's end sees the two young people remarried and about to join Dame Elizabeth at Mantlemass, which they will some day inherit. Such drawbacks as the conventional characters, overplotting, and fairy-tale ending can easily be overlooked in consideration of the rich picture the novel presents of the economic, social, and political life of the period. This book serves as introduction to a distinguished series, known collectively as the Mantlemass Novels (among them *The Iron Lily**), which trace the family's history down to the time of Cromwell. They show how larger political events affected the area and the lives of the people who lived in it.

Choice.

THE LARK ON THE WING (Vipont*, Elfrida, Oxford,
1950; Bobbs, 1951), sequel to *The Lark in the
Morn*, career novel set mostly in London, telling
of Kit* (Jane Kitson) Haverard's training and
first professional appearances as a singer.
Arriving home from boarding school certain of
her musical vocation, Kit, 17, meets opposition
from her cousin, Laura* Haverard, who has raised
her and who has decided that Kit is unmusical
and should train to be a secretary to her
elderly father, a historian. Though disappointed, Kit takes the advice of her old Quaker
Quaker friend, Dr. Cray, nót "to kick against
the hurdles" but not to give up her hopes
either, and she goes to secretarial school,
studying music by herself in her spare time. Her
friend, Terry* Chauntesinger, an established
singer, is furious at her choice, but at her
first dancing party given by her cousins at
Kitsons, the restaurant part of the family
business, he forgives her. When Laura, a tireless worker on Quaker committees, is unable to
accompany Professor Haverard to the Anglo-French
Athenaeum meeting at Rosayac, Kit goes with him,
and, though her cousin is sure neither one can
manage without her, they enjoy themselves and
get to know each other for the first time.
Professor Haverard dies soon afterward, leaving
such a large legacy to Laura that Kit is
virtually penniless. Laura decides to sell the
house immediately and go to a Quaker training
school, and Kit seizes the opportunity to go to
London, get a secretarial job at the Friends
International Service Center, share a flat with
her friends Pony* (Ursula) Cray and sensible
Helen* Edgington, and take lessons from Papa*
Andreas, the fine vocal coach who taught her
mother and who teaches Terry. All works out
well. At Papa's she gets excellent instruction
and encouragement from Tánte Anna, Papa's
cousin, Lotte, the housekeeper, and Miss Fish-
wick, her old piano teacher from school, now
turned full-time accompanist. At her job she
finds the atmosphere full of fervor for Quaker
causes but the work relaxed and the workers
friendly. The apartment becomes a center for
young people: her Kitson cousins, beautiful

Milly*, plain, literary Sheila, and ever-
supportive Philip; and Kit's handsome, popular
brother, Miles; and his friends who live in the
next flat, Bob Hardcastle and his musical brother, Felix. She lets Felix, a popular singer,
talk her into taking an engagement on her vacation at the fashionable Kitson restaurant at
Belmouth without consulting Papa Andreas. Though
it pays well, it is hard on her self-esteem, because she must sing inferior music to diners who
don't listen. Later, with Papa's approval, she
sings at a fund-raising open house for a Quaker
cause, where she is mostly ignored but attracts
the attention of an old lady with an ear
trumpet. Felix fixes up another appearance for
them to sing duets with the Silverbridge
Chamber Concert Society, Kit having been reccom-
mended by the dowager, but when the date arrives
Felix has flu, and Kit, though ill herself, must
appear without him. She comes back with an offer
of an engagement at the prestigious Seahaven Pa-
vilion for the next winter, and Felix, hurt that
she has not insisted on including him, confesses
that he loves her. Kit is appalled at his attitude and further upset when she realizes that
Philip might be equally willing to marry her,
and that Bob is also in love with her, though
Pony loves him. It is not until Kit sings a new
oratorio, "The Hill of the Lord," with Terry at
Heryot Cathedral with resounding success that
she realizes that she and Terry are in love and
meant for each other. At the book's end, Bob and
Pony, both medical students, seem destined for
each other, as do Philip and Helen. Popular,
frivolous Milly, who has rejected the Quaker
zealot Laurence Cray because she does not want
to accompany him to remote Chihar, has been
changed by the news of his martyrdom and is now
determined never to marry. Both the story and
the characters are full of high-minded
sentiments, more often concerned with integrity
in art than with religion or social causes. Kit
is believable in her single-minded devotion to
music, particularly in the light of her long
antagonism to Laura's insensitive domineering,
but her lack of recognition that four men are in
love with her seems too naive, even for the
apparent period of the setting, which seems to
be the 1930s. The period is not entirely clear;

strangely, neither the first or second World War
is mentioned, yet the social setting seems
earlier than the first publication date, 1950.
The strongest element of the book is the sense
of the interdependence and mutual support of
the large family and the Quaker community.
Carnegie Winner; Fanfare.

THE LAST BATTLE (Lewis*, C. S., ill. Pauline
Baynes, Lane, 1956; Macmillan, 1956), fantasy,
last in the series about the mythical land of
Narnia*, the country of the magnificent lion,
Aslan*, and the Talking Animals and Trees. Two
hundred years in Narnian time have passed since
the events in *The Silver Chair*, and young King
Tirian* now rules. Evil afflicts the land in
the form of perfidy, corruption, and greed.
Shift, a crafty, scheming, ambitious Ape,
dresses up his dupe, a naive Donkey named
Puzzle, in a lion's skin and passes him off as
Aslan returned, quartering him in an old stable
and exhibiting him briefly on occasion to the
Narnians at midnight, bonfire-lit gatherings. He
has leagued himself with the Calormenes, a
neighboring country traditionally hostile to
Narnia, to supply them with workers and timber,
enslaving in Aslan's name the free Narnian
beasts and cutting down trees, murdering the
Dryads within them. In desperation Tirian calls
upon Aslan for help, and Jill* Pole and
Eustace* Scrubb, on a train on their way back
to school, suddenly bump down in front of him.
They release him from the tree to which he has
been bound by his Calormen captors, and the
three prepare their resistance. They rescue
Tirian's beloved Unicorn, Jewel, and Jill
bravely takes possession of the unfortunate
Donkey, but, when they rescue some Dwarfs from
Calormenes and attempt to convince them of
Shift's duplicity by showing them poor Puzzle,
they are dismayed to discover that the Dwarfs
simply don't believe them and that the Dwarfs'
confidence in leaders has been severely shaken.
They realize that other Narnians have
undoubtedly been similarly corrupted. When they
receive the bad news from Farsight the Eagle
that Cair Paravel has fallen to Calormen and
see the terrible, wraith-like god of the
Calormenes, Tash, pass through the forest, they

head for the stable and a showdown. At a
midnight gathering, Tirian calls Shift's hand,
fighting breaks out, and everyone, Jill
included, battles valiantly. Forced inside the
stable, Tirian faces Tash, who is banished by
Aslan before he does harm, and then sees the
Seven Kings and Queens of Narnia, Lord Digory*,
Lady Polly*, Peter*, Edmund*, Lucy*, and Jill
and Eustace also, who have been forced into the
stable, as well as Jewel, Puzzle, and Poggin, a
Dwarf who came over on their side. Soon they all
realize the stable is no longer there, and that
they are standing in a green, grassy world of
blue skies and beautiful atmosphere. They see a
Door, framed but without a wall, and know the
stable is much bigger than they had thought.
Aslan appears, calls, "Time!," and, in a long
descriptive passage, gradually undoes all the
creation he brought into being in *The
Magician's Nephew*. He calls the creatures of
Narnia to him, and some go off to his left into
the Darkness, while others go through the Door
on his right. Finally the sun dies, and Darkness
prevails. Aslan instructs Peter to shut the
Door, through which they have all passed, and
they see a new Narnia, warm and peaceful and
lovely, and realize (as in Plato) that the old
Narnia was just a shadow of this, the real one.
Sleek and bright-eyed, Reepicheep*, the talking
mouse of previous books, welcomes them into a
beautiful garden on a smooth, green hill, where
they see many characters from previous books,
including King Frank and Queen Helen, from whom
all the sovereigns of Narnia descended, Fledge
the flying horse, and Mr.* Tumnus the Faun. They
are given a glimpse of the England from which
they came and are informed by Aslan that they
need have no fear of leaving Narnia again. They
have been involved in a railway accident, are
all dead, and will be in Narnia forever.
Although the Christian theology is obvious, the
tone never becomes instructive, and there is
plenty of action and humor. Tirian is a brave
and lonely figure, an almost solitary and
pathetic champion of good. There is enough of
the comic and deluded about Shift to keep him
from becoming the stereotypical villain, and the
reader soon sees that Puzzle causes much of his
own trouble by using his lack of cleverness as

an excuse to not use his head at all. Small
details add pleasure and build credibility, for
example, Puzzle and Jewel talk about "things of
the sort they could both understand like grass
and sugar and the care of one's hoofs," and
Tirian and the Calormenes employ high diction.
As usual, Lewis interjects his comments and
explanations here and there, and his storytelling voice is strong and attractive. The end
is skillfully foreshadowed, and there are
several good scenes--the introductory one of
Shift manipulating Puzzle into getting and then
wearing the skin, and Jill, Eustace, and Tirian
outfitting themselves for the struggle, among
others. The whole seems rushed, however, the
battle at the stable is confusing, and the
conclusion with its long descriptive passages
becomes confusing and is touched with sentimentality. While the story provides closure for
the series, it seems less satisfying than the
earlier books. Carnegie Winner; ChLA Touchstones; Choice.

THE LATCHKEY CHILDREN (Allen*, Eric, ill.
Charles Keeping, Oxford, 1963), realistic story
of a group of working-class youngsters whose
combined efforts save their favorite place, a
nearly dead tree at the edge of the playground.
Three of the main characters, all of whom seem
to be in their early teens, are from the
low-income housing project called St. Justin's
Estate: Billandben (William Benjamin), a fat boy
who gets dizzy from heights; Froggy (Gordon
Frogley), a cutup always on the move, and Etty
(Janet Stone), the only girl and the most mature
member of the group. They are regularly joined
by Goggles (J. J. Greavey), who lives with an
aunt across the river and is the smallest and
the brightest of them all, with an ambition to
make speeches that will move crowds to action.
Gradually another boy is added to the group,
Duke Ellington Binns, a West Indian who lives in
Battersea and whom they meet in the launderette.
Feeling that they are too old to play on the
swings and the concrete ship with which the
playground is equipped, they have laid claim to
the old tree, a place to meet and climb and
where they can imagine that they are on a real
ship or a lookout point in the far west, a place

to consider their own. They are moved to action when men come with plans to chop down the tree and build a concrete railroad engine in its place. Goggles decides they should have a protest meeting and organizes the others to make posters and place them in each of the estate buildings, which are named for famous authors: Thackery, Dickens, Addison, Trollope, and Fielding. He plans to make a moving speech, after which they will all march to the Houses of Parliament and sit down in the road until their objection to the concrete engine is heard. Their meeting attracts only about a half a dozen others, all of whom drift away when it starts to rain. Undeterred, Goggles announces that the next day he is going to Parliament. The others argue that it is a local matter, and they should go to the London County Council or to some administrative body in Westminster. Etty and Billandben set off on a bus, ostensibly to ask her mother, who works for Westminster, where to complain, but they end up in Hampstead, where they find boys throwing stones at a kitten in a tree. Etty drives them off furiously, then insists that they take a ladder from a construction site and that Billandben rescue the kitten. Unwilling to admit to vertigo, Billandben goes up the ladder and gets stuck. A passing man helps him down and then gets the kitten, and when they find that he is Malcolm McCrae, a television interviewer, they tell him the whole story and interest him in the playground tree. Froggy and Duke set off for the County Hall, tagged by Buzz, a younger West Indian boy who has lost his dog. They wander through the building, unable to find the appropriate office, then give up and head for the Battersea Dogs' Home to see if they can find Buzz's dog. There, on a dare from Duke, Froggy climbs into a pen with a lot of big dogs and can't get out. Abandoned by Duke and Buzz, he is apprehended and brought home by a policeman. Goggles is the only one who actually goes to the Houses of Parliament and demands to see his M.P. Since he doesn't know who his Member of Parliament is, he is about to be turned away when a Mr. Frisby, the smiling Vicar of St. Justin's, takes him under his wing and into the gallery, where they hear a very dull speech about the price of pig feed. Mr. Frisby then introduces him to the M.P. for the St. Justin's district, Commander Brownlegg, but neither of them is interested in hearing about the playground tree and only urge Smith, the name Goggles in panic has given as his, to attend the St. Justin's Youth Club. What looks like their best hope, the television interview with Malcolm McCrae, backfires when he and his camera crew arrive at the playground and talk to some boys from the Peabody Estate, who assure them that they don't give a hang about the old tree. Billandben daringly works out a plan in which Duke will bounce his ball against the side of the estate manager's office, thereby getting the cranky manager, Mr. Jellinek, to rush out, so that Billandben can swipe the plans for the concrete engine. That idea, too, goes awry when Duke's ball breaks a window in the office and the roll which Billandben seizes turns out to be a poster instead of the plans. Goggles is so discouraged that he decides never to return to St. Justin's, and since none of the others knows where he lives, to sever all contact with them forever. He can't make himself stay away, however, and when he sees some men at the tree with saws and an axe he can't help protesting. One of the men turns out to be Duke's father, loaned from the cleaning department for the day, and having heard all about the problem from Duke, he refuses to chop up the tree. The supervisor, furious, fires him; his workmate, citing union rules, insists that they go to the union office and file a charge of unjust dismissal; and the case escalates into a strike. After about a week of the strike, Malcolm McCrae returns with his camera crew and Commander Brownlegg, who makes a speech announcing that an amicable resolution has been reached. Duke's father is reinstated, and Goggles is filmed shaking hands with the M.P. with the others grouped behind. The plans for the engine are scrapped and the tree will remain. The story cleverly works out a solution which is only indirectly brought about by the youngsters. Their main complaint, not just that the tree is to be cut down but that they are not consulted about what they want in the playground, is never quite satisfied, but they are allowed to feel that they have won. The adults are painted with rather a broad brush, but since the episode is seen through the eyes of the various young people, this seems true to their perceptions. The children are well differentiated, and some of their actions, notably the way Duke hangs around the fringes of the group, pretending to be occupied with other interests until he is accepted, shows a close perception of this age and the dynamics of a playground group which can be loosely organized but fiercely loyal. Since the harsher elements of inner-city life--drugs, crime, child abuse, and so on--are not part of the story, it seems innocent compared to much of more recent realistic fiction. Carnegie Com.

LAURA (*Ask Me No Questions**), daughter of a London minister who is sent to stay with her aunt in Tooting when cholera strikes his parish. A conscientious child, Laura is torn by conflicting obligations when she steals food from the kitchen to give to the starving children from the workhouse school next door. She both resents and envies the way her brother, Barty*, is able to forget the workhouse children's problems. She tries to tell her grown Cousin* Henry about the abusive conditions, but he is too preoccupied to listen. Though she is the only privileged person to show humanity, she is worried constantly about her wickedness in taking food and lying to her aunt and can hardly believe she is doing it, repeating to herself the nursery rhyme, "If this be I as it surely cannot be."

LAURA CHANT (*The Changeover: A Supernatural Romance**), Australian schoolgirl, 14, who becomes involved with a family of three witches, Sorry*, Miryam*, and Winter* Carlisle, and becomes a witch herself when she sets out to save her little brother, Jacko, from being drained of life by the supernatural Carmody Braque*. Laura gains in confidence and becomes less critical and more accepting as the story progresses. At first, she is afraid of the sixth sense that enables her to perceive that something extraordinary is about to happen, fearful of her body's changing sexuality, and resentful of the attraction her mother, Kate*, feels for

librarian Chris Holly. Through her involvement
with Sorry, in particular, Laura comes to terms
with the changes in her life, in addition to
saving her brother's life by dealing with Carmody Braque.

LAURA HAVERARD (*The Lark on the Wing**), domineering, high-minded cousin of Kit* Haverard,
who moved in when Kit's mother died at the
girl's birth. She has managed the house, Kit's
three older brothers, Richard, Tom, and Miles,
and Kit's elderly father with a firm hand but is
unable to control Kit's life despite her strong
efforts to do so. Though she was fond of Kit's
mother, she resents and tries to suppress any
references to her or any tendency on Kit's part
to resemble her. In particular, she asserts that
Kit is not musical, as her mother was, and
insists that she attend secretarial school instead of taking voice lessons. Laura's attachment to Kit's father has sexual undertones; she
does all she can to come between the father and
daughter, insisting that the child will upset
the frail professor. At his death, it is
discovered that in an attempt to repay Laura for
raising his family, he has left her so much of
his money that Kit is unprovided for. Always a
tireless worker on Quaker committees, Laura
sells the family home and enrolls in a course at
a Quaker summer school, where she meets and
marries a missionary. Her husband later
proposes that they give Kit a regular allowance
to help her with her studies and consider a
redistribution of the father's estate; these
are moves with which Laura grudgingly agrees.

LAURA SECCOMBE (*The Girl in the Grove**), girl
whose spirit haunts the grove and the manor
house. When she was thirteen, Laura was injured in a fall from her favorite pony, Sulei-
man, a fall caused by her favorite dog. Her
hot-tempered father shot both animals. After
she unexpectedly recovered, her father tried to
make it up by having elaborate monuments with
statues of each of her pets set over their
graves in the grove. Laura is a flirt, a spoiled
child, and a vindictive younger sister. She has
resented her brother's romance with her
nursemaid, Millicent Meadows, and has hidden the

letters he sent to Milly in her care. At the story's opening, her spirit has been unable to rest until the death of the one person who loved her despite her faults, that nursemaid who became Mrs. Hunter and who forgave her when she realized what had happened.

LAUREL LYNN LEROY (*Fire and Hemlock**), Mrs. Eudora Mabel Lorelei Perry Lynn Leroy, in the ordinary world the wealthy ex-wife of Tom* Lynn who marries Morton* Leroy, thereby becoming Seb* Leroy's stepmother. In the otherworld existence she is the queen, and either takes a new king every nine years or officiates at the sacrifice of a young man to renew the vigor of the existing king. She has many powers of a sorceress, including the ability to make bargains that trap her victims. When Tom was a boy, she has bargained with his brother, Charles, to let him go in exchange for Tom; with Tom not to keep resisting his fate as the sacrifice in exchange for not allowing Polly to be hurt; and with Polly to forget Tom rather than embarrassing them all with her crush on him when she thinks he is dying of cancer. Laurel has a penchant for musical boys, particularly with the name Tom, and has ensnared not only Tom Lynn, a cellist, but also his nephew, Leslie* Piper, a flutist, and, many years earlier, Polly's grandfather, a violinist also named Tom. Every eighty-one years she must have a female sacrifice to renew herself, the last one having been Seb's mother whose funeral Polly attended by accident. Laurel is beautiful, eternally young, and completely evil.

LAVINIA BERESFORD (*Thursday's Child**), eldest of the three orphans who are met in London by Miss Jones of St. Luke's orphanage at the same time as Margaret* Thursday. Because she is fourteen she cannot stay at the institution and is sent to be a scullery maid for the Countess of Corkberry. A refined and attractive girl, she is spotted by Lord Corkberry as looking just like the daughter of his friend, Lord Delaware, a girl who eloped with the groom and was cut off by her family. Her father, it is finally revealed, stole some money and absconded to South America. After the death of her mother, she tried to take care of her younger brothers, but there was no money, and she was unable to get a job. Her main attribute is her concern for her brothers, a responsibility she passes on to Margaret when she must leave them at St. Luke's. At the Corkberry estate she is a diligent worker.

LAWLESS, WILL (*The Black Arrow**), one of Jon* Amend-All's band, acting as cook when Dick* Shelton and Joanna* Sedley first come upon them in the forest. A man with a checkered background, Lawless has been a novice in an abbey, a sailor, and a thief, among other things. He tricks the captain of the *Good Hope* so that Dick's band can steal the ship, and he steers it in a terrible storm so that they come to shore against all odds. When he takes Dick to his den in the forest, he insists on leaving while Dick buries his valuable papers, explaining that he can't trust himself not to sell them if he knows where they are hidden. He provides the friars' disguises by which he and Dick are able to enter Sir* Daniel's mansion unrecognized, but he almost ruins the escapade by getting drunk. When it looks as if they will be executed, he responds bravely. In the end, he turns to piety and becomes a friar.

LAWRENCE, ANN (1942-   ), born in Tring, Herfordshire; teacher and novelist. She was educated at Hemel Hempstead Grammar School and received her B.A. degree from the University of Southampton in 1964. She worked for the British Trust for Ornithology in Tring for two years, and taught in Aylesbury, Buckinghamshire, and in Tring until 1971. *Tom Ass; or, The Second Gift** Macmillan, 1972; Walck, 1973), is a clever fantasy that uses folktale elements. In the decade that followed, she published a dozen books for children, among them *The Half-Brothers* (Macmillan, 1973; Walck, 1973), set in the Renaissance, *Between the Forest and the Hills* (Kestrel, 1977), set in a Roman town of the Dark Ages, and *Mr. Robertson's Hundred Pounds* (Kestrel, 1976), set in Europe in 1595, a story for older readers about a boy pursuing a thief. For younger readers, she has written several books about Oggy, a hedgehog, starting with *The Travels of Oggy*

(Gollancz, 1973). Among her fantasies are *The Conjuror's Box* (Kestrel, 1974), which carries readers across worlds and centuries; *The Good Little Devil* (Macmillan, 1978), about an imp who is educated by a monk along with the choir boys; and *Mr. Fox* (Macmillan, 1979), a romp that uses uses traditional folk characters and motifs. Her books, fantasy and realism alike, are inventive, with strong concrete detail that convinces even in bizarre situations.

LAWRENCE WILLOUGHBY (*Elizabeth's Tower**), lame stranger Elizabeth* Barnet befriends, who came to the countryside ostensibly to recover from his car accident. He first gives his name as Jeremy Fisher, an allusion to Beatrix Potter, just for fun. For a while, he thinks Aunt Rose's husband, Bill, is the one who has been smuggling secrets to the foreign spies, but the real culprit is Elizabeth's father. Lawrence tries to help Elizabeth be more understanding and to see herself as others see her, as aloof and overbearing. She grows fond of him, and they share such intellectual pleasures as poetry as well as more active pursuits. He verges on the stock.

LEFT TILL CALLED FOR. See *We Couldn't Leave Dinah.*

LENNIE BYRE (*Songberd's Grove**), spoiled, destructive bully who tyrannizes Songberd's Grove, seeking to elevate himself in his own esteem by domineering others. His father, Basher Byre, a noted boxer, was killed in World War II. His mother, determined that her son will not follow in his father's footsteps and will forget what little his father taught him about boxing, moved to a new neighborhood and told her son his father was a florist. The boy was laughed at and picked on by his schoolfellows, who derided this occupation, and sought to compensate by becoming a bully. Now about fifteen, Lennie looks like an ape, is big and burly, wears his hair long, and likes elegant, big-shouldered jackets and skinny, tight-fitting trousers. His mother is afraid of him, and he bosses her around. At the end, the reader loses sight of Lennie, who apparently is satisfied with being admitted to Lord* Simon Vigo's club, where he can be instructed in boxing and so feel better about himself. He is an overdrawn character, yet one the reader is oddly sympathetic with, a victim of circumstances not of his own making and a foil to Martin* and Geneva*.

LENNY TRANTER (*The Way to Sattin Shore**), second son in the Tranter family, about twelve. Lenny is the most active of the three children, the only one who brings friends home with him. His school chum, Brian, is an inquisitive sort, and his questions about the family and house provoke Kate's* curiosity. Lenny likes to make things, like toboggans and electric fences, and to go for bike rides. He tells Kate he biked to Sattin, and this gives her the idea of doing it, too. He has a frightful row with his mother when she accuses him of shutting Syrup the tomcat in the loft. It turns out that Granny* Randall was responsible. Lenny and Ran are the first to talk with their father, Fred, after his return. Lenny is a pleasant, likeable boy.

LESLIE PIPER (*Fire and Hemlock**), really son of Charles Lynn, therefore Leslie Lynn, but brought up as the nephew of Tom Piper, the ironmonger at Stow-on-the-Water. Polly* Whittacker first imagines him as a very disagreeable boy with an earring shaped like a skull, and is surprised when they go to the village to find that he really does wear the earring but is a friendly, cheerful type. Later, when he is going to Wilton College in Middleton on scholarship, he is notorious for skipping school and is known as Georgie-Porgie for kissing the girls. He is, however, remarkably gifted as a flute player. Although Tom* Lynn tries to warn him, Laurel* ensnares him and is obviously keeping him as a possible future sacrifice when, at the final ceremony, his father appears to demand him back. Because Morton* Leroy is destroyed and Laurel takes Seb* Leroy for her new king, she discards Leslie. He is crushed and weeps, but rallies enough to pretend to be in good spirits.

LESTER (*Which Witch?**), the loyal ogre of the wizard Arriman Canker. He is described as a "huge, slow-moving man with muscles like footballs." He has only one eye, and to keep from offending people he wears a black patch to give the impression that he has two. Before he came to work for Arriman he worked as a sword-swallower in a fair. He occasionally gulps down a sabre or such because he finds it soothing. He is a pleasant sort, who adds color to the story, occasionally affects the action, and is one of Belladonna's staunchest supporters.

LETTIE HATTER (*Howl's Moving Castle**), second and most beautiful of three sisters. After her father's death, her stepmother, Fanny, apprentices her at a cake shop, thinking that there she will meet lots of young men and soon be married off and out of the way. Lettie, however, wants to learn and go far in the world, so when her younger half sister, Martha*, discovers a spell to exchange their appearances, she willingly changes places with her and becomes assistant to Mrs. Fairfax, the witch in Upper Folding, where she can use her brains. Even there, however, she attracts young men, among them Howl*, though she is bright enough not to fall in love with him. In the end she discovers that the man she has come to love is the Wizard Suliman, who suggests that he take her on as a pupil.

LETTIE STAMP (*Comfort Herself**), girl of about Comfort Kwatey-Jones's age, 11, who becomes Comfort's best friend while Comfort stays with her Granny* and Grandad* Barton in the village of Penfold in Kent. Lettie is outspoken, quick-minded, and capable, the one who keeps the village children in line. The oldest girl in town, she has longed for a friend her age and is delighted when Comfort is finally able to play outside. She introduces Comfort to English village life. Her counterparts are Winnie, who works for Comfort's father in Accra, and Ama, Comfort's cousin-sister in Wanwangeri. Lettie is delighted to welcome Comfort back to Penfold and at the very end announces to the birthday guests that Comfort is finally back where she belongs. Lettie is an interesting if underdeveloped figure and like several others is too obviously a foil and tool for instructing the reader.

LEWIS, C(LIVE) S(TAPLES) (1898-1963), born in
Belfast, Northern Ireland, his father a lawyer,
his mother the daughter of a naval chaplain;
university teacher, distinguished theologian,
scholar, literary critic, essayist, and novelist, best known for his writings for adults. He
is noted in children's literature for his seven
novels popularly called the Chronicles of
Narnia, which now enjoy the status of classics.
In the order in which events occur within the
novels, these are: *The Magician's Nephew** (Lane,
1955; Macmillan, 1955), *The Lion, the Witch
and the Wardrobe** (Bles, 1950; Macmillan, 1950),
*The Horse and His Boy** (Bles, 1954; Macmillan,
1954), *Prince Caspian** (Bles, 1951; Macmillan,
1951), *The Voyage of the "Dawn Treader"** (Bles,
1952; Macmillan, 1952), *The Silver Chair**
(Bles, 1953; Macmillan, 1953), and *The Last
Battle** (Lane, 1956; Macmillan, 1956). The
Carnegie Medal was given to Lewis for the last
book named but was intended to honor the entire
series, which began in 1950 and came out as a
book each year after that. Collectively, they
tell of the adventures of various children in
the magical, medieval-like land of Narnia*, a
place of mythological creatures and nobly-
speaking animals, threatened occasionally by the
forces of evil. Central to the series is
Aslan*, a magnificent lion, who may represent
the Christian Trinity and certainly is a solid
and determined force for good. Aslan creates the
land of Narnia, brings it to an end, and determines who shall enter and how long they shall
stay. Humor and excitement relieve the Christian
allegory and keep the narrative from sounding
instructive. The books have a depth and conviction about them that grows as the series
proceeds. All of them have received critical
citations, and all have been named to *Choice*
and the Children's Literature Association Touchstones list, in addition to winning various
individual awards. Lewis's mother died when he
was small, and he was sent to boarding schools.
His career as an Oxford student was interrupted
by meritorious service in the infantry during
World War I. After receiving his degree from
Oxford, he became a lecturer at University College there in 1924 and then enjoyed a thirty-
year tenure as fellow and tutor in English at

Magdalen College, Oxford. He was a colleague at
Oxford of the noted scholar, J. R. R. Tolkien*.
At the time of his death, Lewis was Professor of
Medieval and Renaissance English at Cambridge
University. He also held special lectureships at
the University of Wales and the University of
Durham. He married in 1956 and was stepfather
to two sons. Best known for his numerous
Christian writings for adults, he was most fa-
mous for his witty and insightful book of
admonition and philosophy, *The Screwtape Letters*
(Bles, 1942; Macmillan, 1943). He also wrote for
adults a series of science fantasies, several
books of poems (some under the name Clive
Hamilton), and an autobiography, *Surprised by
Joy: The Shape of My Early Life* (Bles, 1955;
Harcourt, 1956), in which he tells of his rejection of and return to Christianity. Under
the pseudonym N. W. Clerk, he also wrote the
autobiography *A Grief Observed* (Faber, 1961;
Seabury, 1963). In addition to many other
honors, he received honorary doctorates from
several universities, including the Doctor of
Divinity, and was a Fellow of the British
Academy.

LEWIS, HILDA (WINIFRED) (1896-1974), born in
London; writer of historical fiction for both
children and adults. She taught in London for a
few years, then lived for many years in
Nottingham. She published four novels for
children and twenty-eight for adults, among the
latter the exhaustively researched trilogy, *I Am
Mary Tudor* (Hutchinson, 1971; McKay, 1972), *Mary
the Queen* (Hutchinson, 1973), and *Bloody Mary*
(Hutchinson, 1974). For children, her best known
book is a fantasy for younger readers, *The Ship
That Flew* (Oxford, 1939; Criterion, 1958), about
the ship given to Frey by Odin, which is magic
only if one believes, and which takes youngsters
to Asgard, to Runnymede, to the Nile, and other
places where they meet many historical and
legendary figures. Her other children's books
are *Here Comes Harry* (Oxford, 1960; Criterion,
1960), a story of fifteenth-century English
court life at the time of the child-king, Henry
VI; *Harold Was My King* (Oxford, 1968; McKay,
1970), a story of the coming of William the
Conqueror told through the eyes of an English

boy who loses everything; and *The Gentle Falcon**
(Oxford, 1952; Criterion, 1957), about the
child-bride of English King Richard II. This
last work was chosen for the *Horn Book* Fanfare
list.

LEWIS MALLORY (*The Lark and the Laurel**), high-
spirited youth exiled to Ghylls Hatch, a horse
farm in the Sussex countryside, by his Yorkist
sympathizing father, when Sir Thomas Jolland, to
whose daughter he had been wed as a child, took
up the Lancastrian cause in the Wars of the
Roses. When the story opens, Lewis has been
living at Ghylls Hatch for about seven years
quite happily, in spite of some anger and
bewilderment at having been sent away from his
family without apparent cause. He has become a
good horseman and loves the horses. He admires
and feels sincere affection for his cousin,
Roger Orlebar, who loves him like a son;
appreciates his tutor, Sir James, the local
priest; and gets along well with Dame* Elizabeth FitzEdmund, who favors him. Though he is
too virtuously drawn as an "every girl's hero"
type, his hurt at being cast out from his
family, his good sense, and his honest liking
for hard work make him a sympathetic and
individualized figure.

LIGHTNING SOAMES (*The Cave**), Harold, smallest
member of the exploration group. To compensate
for his size and for his position as the only
boy in a family of girls, Lightning is reckless,
darting ahead heedlessly and thriving on
thrills. When he and John must walk and stand in
ice water for a long period while they chip away
a rock screen, he shows surprising endurance.

THE LIGHT PRINCESS (MacDonald*, George, ill. A.
Hughes, Blackie and Son, 1890), first published
as an interpolated story in the novel *Adela
Cathcart* (Hurst, 1864), fantasy set in the
unspecified kingdom and time of the marchen. At
the christening of the long-awaited princess,
the royal couple's only child, the king has
forgotten to invite his own sister, the
disagreeble Princess Makemnoit, and she takes
revenge by putting a spell on the baby, that she
will be "light of spirit" and "light of body"

and will "crush [her] parents' heart." Immediately she becomes almost weightless, and she
grows up always laughing, even in serious or
tragic moments. Her greatly concerned parents
try many remedies, including metaphysics, but
discover that only in the water does she have
proper physical or emotional gravity. A king's
son from Lagobel, a distant land, discovers the
bewitched princess in the lake and promptly
"saves" her, almost sending her into orbit when
he lifts her out of the water with a shove, but
she fortunately catches hold of a cone in the
top of a tree and is able to work her way down.
Her anger makes her even more attractive than
usual, and the prince falls immediately in love.
When he holds her in his arms and jumps into the
lake, she has her first experience of falling
and finds it so delightful that night after
night they meet in the lake, swim, and leap in
from the rocks around the shore. After some time
the princess makes a disturbing discovery: the
lake is becoming shallower, and as the water
level sinks, she pines. The old Princess Makemnoit has caused this by conjuring up a snake
deep in a cave beneath the lake which is sucking
the water out through a hole in the lake floor.
When only a little water is left, a golden
plate is found in the last pool saying that the
hole through which the water drains can be
stopped only by the body of a living man who
willingly sacrifices himself. The prince
volunteers on the condition that the princess
keep him company until the water comes up to his
eyes. At first the princess is rather bored by
this task, but as the water rises she becomes
more concerned, and when it comes up to the
prince's nostrils, she dives in and with great
effort pulls him out and rows to the shore. With
her old nurse, she works to revive him, and when
he does open his eyes, she bursts into her first
tears--and with the tears, regains her gravity.
After she learns to walk--a difficult task at
her age--they are married and live happily ever
after. Although the theme that life must have
some seriousness to be worthwhile is very
obvious, the cleverness of the story's conception and style keep it from seeming highly moralistic. The author also makes sly digs at cures
that kill the patient and other learned non-

sense. Choice.

A LIKELY LAD (Avery*, Gillian, ill. Faith
Jaques, Collins, 1971; Holt, 1971), realistic
novel set at the turn of the century, about a
Lancashire boy, son of a small shopkeeper, and
his struggles to assert himself against his
father's overpowering ambitions for him. Willy*
Overs is named for William Cobbett, one of his
father's two heroes, Cobbett and Cobden, both
self-made men as is Alfred* Overs himself,
having pulled himself from dire poverty, married
a woman socially above him, and become proprietor of a shop in grimy Ardwick, a working-class
section of Manchester. He is very proud of this
success, but he has his eyes on better things
for Willy: first a job in the Northern Star
insurance office, where he will work himself up
to a position of authority, and eventually
knighthood and a bust in one of the niches in
Town Hall reserved for Manchester's most famous
men. Willy, a timid, undersized boy, eleven and
then twelve during most of the action in the
book, has accepted his father's ambitions
without protest, partly because they seem to lie
in the unimaginably distant future and partly
because he sees no way to convince his father
that he would prefer to go on in school and
that the idea of working his way up the ladder
at Northern Star fills him with dread. Mostly he
is content with his life in the living quarters
behind the shop, which his mother, Ellen*
Chaffey Overs, keeps spotless at the expense of
comfort. He even endures the miserable first
Sundays, which they always spend with his
mother's sister's family, the Sowters, alternating between Ardwick and Trafford, a more prestigious section where Auntie Kitty lives. He detests Uncle* Harold Sowter, his two pale,
snivelling girl cousins, and bullying Stan*
Sowter, who is about his own age, but most of
all he hates the tension of the two sisters
trying to outdo each other. He begins to sense
the ramifications of this rivalry when Stan
taunts him and his brother George*, who is two
years younger than Willy, about Auntie* Maggie
Chaffey, of whom the boys have never heard, "who
won't have nowt to do with your mum" because she
married "lower class." The news worries Willy

until one Saturday, when he wanders into the
Rusholme district and comes upon the address
Stan mentioned to him. He sees an old woman
banging on an upstairs window, and almost before
he knows it, an elderly servant has grabbed him
and prodded him up a dark, dank staircase and
into a cluttered room where an old woman is
propped in bed. She has recognized the Chaffey
"spindle shanks" and the way his hair sticks up
at the back of his head. She tells him that she
took to her bed when her niece Ellen married and
hasn't left it since, that she keeps all her
money in banknotes under her pillow, and that he
must come again the next Saturday. Although he
dreads the place, Willy's habit of obedience
makes him return as he promised. The old woman
shrieks with laughter when he admits that he
would like to kick both Stan and Uncle Harold,
and she tells him she will change her will from
Stan as being sole heir to Willy, but he rushes
out in horror and finds his way home in a
feverish daze. It is the beginning of a long
illness. When he has recovered but still is
listless, the doctor suggests a change, perhaps
a holiday by the sea. Willy's father interprets
this in his own way and buys a tandem bicycle,
certain that this exercise will build up the
boy. When they ride over to Tafford to show the
bicycle off to the Sowters, Willy is so
embarrassed that he refuses to ride again, and
George and his father are soon taking regular
Saturday rides while Willy stays home and reads
in peace. He has nothing to do with the bike
until the day his English teacher, who has given
him great encouragement, calls at the shop to
try to persuade Mr. Overs to let Willy try for a
scholarship to grammar school, and Mr. Overs
lectures him about the uselessness of Latin and
Greek and other book learning and declares that
Willy will leave school at the end of the term
for a job at Northern Star. Willy is so dismayed
and humiliated that he takes the bike and rides
madly off, hardly knowing where he is going. He
finds himself in an unfamiliar area among
mill-workers coming off shift, and when a couple
of them offer to ride the bike home for him, he
lets them have it, only realizing later that
they are probably stealing it. A carter gives
him a ride, and in his dazed condition he does

not know they are going away from Manchester until they come to the village of Staseley as it is getting dark. The carter lets him off at a small shop, suggesting that he might get a ride back with a carrier from there. He is greeted by an ancient woman as Joey. He is unable to convince her for more than a few minutes at a time that he is not her son, Joey, who is long dead, and he is so exhausted that when she gives him food and a bed he falls asleep immediately. The next morning he learns that she is Nance* Price, and she loans him a shilling so he can telegraph his parents that he is all right. Then he sets about happily trying to clean and bring order into her chaotic shop, with a vague plan that maybe he can get his father to buy the place and let him run it, thereby escaping the Northern Star. Later, taking a break from cleaning, he wanders into the countryside, the first he has ever seen, and is astonished to be apprehended by a gamekeeper, who drags him to Earl de Staseley as a poacher. The earl questions him about his school and where he is staying, and accuses him of reading bad books when he sees one that Mrs. Price has put in his pocket. Unable to get in a word of defense in the torrent of talk, Willy runs back to Mrs. Price and is finally, after another day's work, beginning to get the shop into shape when, to his astonishment, his father appears. Back in Ardwick he finally stands up to his father, mostly in frustration, and shouts that Lord Staseley is not a parasite, as Mr. Overs has said all aristocrats are, but a man very like himself, too fond of his own speechifying to listen. Mrs. Overs is so put out at the thought of an earl believing that Willy has been allowed to read rude books that his father insists that he write a letter explaining and repaying the cost of the telegram that Lord de Staseley sent to the school to alert them of Willy's whereabouts. Willy defiantly adds his comments that anyone who owns so much land should take care of the poor people there, like Mrs. Price who needs help, and he encloses his own shilling to repay Mrs. Price. He has not told his parents that he also wrote to Auntie Maggie, asking her to buy the store so he could run it for Mrs. Price. Before the boys have returned from posting the letter, Auntie Maggie's servant has come with an urgent summons. She wants to see the whole family, but Mr. Overs takes Willy alone. The old lady is insulting as usual and is gleeful to think that Willy wants to leave his father. When she tells him that she is going to leave all her money to him, he angrily refuses, an attitude that heals the break between him and his father. The interview at Northern Star looms ahead, however. On the day Willy and his father have an appointment, Auntie Kitty and the girls appear with the news that Auntie Maggie has died, and they are appalled to learn that she may have left all her money to Willy rather than Stan. Mr. Overs, however, is more interested in a letter from Lord de Staseley, praising Willy's letter and mentioning the value of education. Uncle Harold and Stan appear, absolutely nonplused to report that there is no money; the vicious watchdogs Auntie Maggie kept have eaten all the banknotes, and it was the shock of seeing this that killed her. After the funeral Mr. Overs gives the Sowters the final shock and astonishes his sons by blandly announcing that Willy is not going to leave school for a job, but will win a scholarship to grammar school and very likely to university. The novel gives a detailed and delightful picture of lower-middle-class life and pretensions in an industrial city during the very early years of the twentieth century. Characters are subtly drawn and believable. Although not told in the first person, the events are all seen through the perceptions of Willy, whose emotional turmoils are completely convincing. Carnegie Highly Com.; Guardian.

LILA (*The Village by the Sea**), eldest of the children in a poor village family and the one who shoulders the responsibility for her sick mother and her younger siblings. A girl of perhaps twelve or thirteen, she has left school and works constantly to try to feed the family, although her drunken father spends more money than he earns and her brother, Hari*, runs off to Bombay to try to get a job. Lila is stoic, but she is strongly aware of the beauty around her and takes time from her gruelling work to scatter flowers on the sacred rock in the sea near their hut and to watch the birds and the waves. Unlike Hari, she does not dream of ways to change their fortunes but only tries to meet the day-to-day challenges.

LILY FLACK (*The Winter of the Birds**), Edward's foster mother, a self-righteous, sharp-tongued, judgmental woman, who becomes more considerate of her family and more appreciative of her neighbors through associating with Patrick Finn* and Mr.* Rudge. She is a typecast character who changes predictably, but is also one of the most engaging figures in the book. She is really a very sensible person, and her letters to the editor about saving St. Savior's Church and urging people to raise pigeons to replace the birds that are dying off are practical and provide some ironic humor. Unfortunately, the humor diminishes the book's tension and diverts the reader's attention from the potential for destruction of the terrible steel birds.

LINCOLN RIDLEY (*Castaway Christmas**), perhaps seventeen, older brother of Miranda* and Pinks*, with whom he is stranded in the cottage called Little Topsails in Somerset in western England. A calm, methodical boy, he is mostly sensible and well-organized, but occasionally he slips. For example, the night he sees the light across the water on the moor, he goes to investigate without informing the girls. He assumes the "fatherly" role in the story, protecting and providing for his sisters, and they look up to him as more knowledgeable than they and expect approval from him. He finds and reads a copy of *Swiss Family Robinson*, from which he gets some ideas for their own survival. He is an interesting if shallow figure.

LINDA MORRISON (*The Third Eye**), Jinty's second sister, older than Jinty and younger than Meg*, a nice looking girl, bright, quick, manipulative, ambitious, and ruthless. Though popular at the academy, because she has a good fashion sense and always does well in her classes, she has an independent streak that sets her apart. She quickly senses opportunities for using people to her advantage, for example, when, in

return for helping Jinty select the clothes
Jinty earned working at Ballinford Hall, Linda
elicits an innocent promise from Jinty to help
her with whatever she wants in return. Linda
demands that Jinty take her to the hall to get
a letter of reference from the earl. Later,
Mam* proves troublesome about the girls' decisions not to attend the university and refuses
to let Meg marry Dave Ferguson, since Mam
considers Dave beneath Meg because he is a
mechanic. To get her way and help Meg get hers,
Linda announces that she has seen Meg's birth
certificate and that it proves that Meg is
illegitimate. Mam throws her out, which matters
little to Linda, though she had wanted to leave
home on her own terms. At the end of the book,
the hope is that Mam will also make up with
Linda as she is making up with Meg. Linda is a
round, dynamic figure, one of the most interesting people in the novel, one the reader can
understand if not always like. She is a foil to
both Jinty and Meg.

LINE, DAVID (LIONEL DAVIDSON) (1922–   ), born
in Hull, Yorkshire; editor, screenwriter and
novelist for both adults and young people. He
spent five years in the Royal Navy in the
submarine service, and from 1946 to 1959 he was
a writer and editor for several British magazines. Since 1959 he has been a full-time
writer. His adult novels, mostly adventure and
mystery stories, are published under Lionel
Davidson, his real name, while his books for
children and young adults appear under his
pseudonym, David Line, except for *Under Plum
Lake* (Cape, 1980; Knopf, 1980), a science fantasy about a technologically advanced world coexisting with ours, which was published under
Davidson. Among his novels for adults are *The
Night of Wenceslas* (Gollancz, 1960; Harper,
1960), a spy thriller set in Prague in the midst
of a People's Festival, which won the Authors'
Club Award for the most promising first novel
and the Crime Writers' Association Award for the
best crime novel of the year. Others works are
set in Tibet, the Caribbean, Bavaria, and
Israel, among them *A Long Way To Shiloh* (Gollancz, 1966; as *The Menorah Men*, Harper, 1966),
an adventure mystery of an archeological search

for the menorah (candelabra) said to have been in the Great Temple at the time of the Roman invasion. Among his books for young people is *Soldier and Me* (Harper, 1965), about an English schoolboy and an Hungarian immigrant he has befriended as they witness a murder and are chased across a snowy countryside. The same characters appear in *Mike and Me* (Cape, 1974), in which they and friends, with the help of their art teacher, thwart the plots of unscrupulous property speculators. It has been made into a television serial. *Screaming High** (Cape, 1985; Little, 1985), a thriller set mostly in Amsterdam about a black trumpet player, involves drug smuggling, jazz music, capture, and daring escape; it was a nominee for the Edgar Allan Poe Award for the best Juvenile Mystery of the year.

LINKLATER, ERIC (ROBERT RUSSELL) (1899-1974), born in Dounby, Orkney; critic, novelist, playwright and poet. He attended Aberdeen Grammar School, and studied first medicine and then English at the University of Aberdeen. During World War I he was a private in the Black Watch; in World War II he was a major in the Royal Engineers and a member of the staff of the Directorate of Public Relations for the War Office. He also served in Korea in 1951. For two years he was assistant editor for the *Times of India*, Bombay, then taught English Literature at the University of Aberdeen, and later became Commonwealth Fellow at Cornell University in Ithaca, New York, and at the University of California at Berkeley. After 1930, except for periods of military service, he was a full-time writer, producing two novels for children, and for adults twenty-three novels, six books of short stories, seven plays, and two books of poetry, in addition to many works of criticism and other nonfiction. *The Wind on the Moon**, (Macmillan, 1944; Macmillan, 1944), which won the Carnegie Medal, is an episodic novel that began as an improvisation. It has been described as being full of "rich absurdities." His second book for children, *The Pirates in the Deep Green Sea* (Macmillan, 1949), contains bizarre characters and situations but has been criticized as being less spontaneous. Linklater won many distinctions in his lifetime, including an

honorary doctorate from the University of
Aberdeen, fellowship in the Royal Society of
Edinburgh, and the title of Commander, Order of
the British Empire.

LINNET OLDKNOW (*The Children of Green Knowe**),
6, youngest of the three spirit children who
inhabit the old house at Green Knowe where
they lived before their death in the Great
Plague of 1665. A laughing, teasing, high-
spirited child, Linnet is heard and seen by
Tolly* before he sees the others, and she seems
closer to him in age. When the great yew tree
figure of Green Noah is blindly groping for him,
Tolly cries out to Linnet and she calls to the
stone statue of St. Christopher for help.

THE LION, THE WITCH AND THE WARDROBE (Lewis*, C.
S., ill. Pauline Baynes, Bles, 1950; Macmillan,
1950), fantasy novel of adventure, magic, and
good versus evil, set in the mythical, medieval-
like land of Narnia* and the first written of
the seven novels that make up the Chronicles of
Narnia. The story starts in the world of
reality when, during World War II, Peter*,
Susan*, Edmund*, and Lucy* Pevensie are evacuated to the famous old country house of
elderly, distinguished Professor Digory* Kirke.
They explore and come upon a spare room that is
empty except for an imposing old wardrobe. Lucy
enters it, discovers it has no back, and finds
herself in the land of Narnia, where by a
lamppost she meets Mr.* Tumnus, a Faun, who
addresses her as "Daughter of Eve" and informs
her that she is in Narnia. He tells her that the
land has fallen on hard times since it has come
under the control of the wicked White Witch (the
Queen* who is called Jadis in *The Magician's
Nephew*). She calls herself Queen of Narnia and
causes it always to be winter and never
Christmas. Some days later, the other children
enter Narnia, too, by the same route. Since
prophecy says that one day two Sons of Adam and
two Daughters of Eve will occupy thrones at
Cair Paravel (the capital), the Witch, suspecting that the four children may be the
fulfillment of the prophecy and determined to
maintain her control, bribes Edmund with promises of unlimited supplies of Turkish Delight

candy and of power as her prince in return for
bringing his siblings to her. Friendly, hospitable Mr. and Mrs. Beaver take the others into
their cave home and inform them that the Narnian
animals are awaiting the return of the magnificent and powerful lion, Aslan*, who is Lord
of the Wood, to get rid of the evil Witch and
set things right. They hurry to meet Aslan at a
place called the Stone Table. On the way, the
Pevensies and Beavers encounter Father Christmas
in his reindeer-drawn sleigh, a clear sign that
the Witch's power is waning. He gives them
powerful presents: to Peter a sword and shield,
to Susan a bow, a quiver of arrows, and a
little ivory horn, and to Lucy a bottle of
cordial and a dagger, implements that prove
valuable in the ensuing battle against the
Witch. As the weather goes from January to May
in just a few hours, and as flowers begin to
bloom and ice to melt, the children and animals
arrive at the Stone Table where Aslan and his
followers, dryads, naiads, centaurs, unicorns,
and the like, as well as realistic creatures,
all noble and agreeable, are gathered. The
Pevensies and Beavers arrive before the Witch
and her dread Wolf chief of police, Maugrim,
with Edmund in tow and also sleigh-drawn, can
intercept them. The Witch prepares to slay
Edmund, but he is rescued in the nick of time by
a party Aslan sends out for the purpose. Aslan
then parleys with the witch, who claims that all
traitors belong to her to do with as she
wishes, simply because they are traitors. The
two strike an agreement. Aslan turns himself
over to the Witch, whose minions beat, berate,
and make sport of him, and then tie him to the
Stone Table where the Witch slays him with her
knife. Susan and Lucy spend a miserable night
mourning their friend and then at dawn observe
mice crawling over his body and gnawing through
the ropes. At sunrise they hear a loud, cracking
sound and observe the Stone Table sundered in
two. Aslan appears to them, alive and splen-
drous. He tells the the girls that, although
the Witch's evil power is strong, the power of
the Deep Magic is even greater. The Deep Magic
says that if a willing victim dies in a
traitor's stead, then the Table will crack and
Death be undone, and this had been accomplished

by his act. He carries the girls to the Witch's palace, where he breathes on the statues of the creatures that she has turned to stone, restoring them to life, and releases the others that linger in her dungeons. All return with Aslan to join Peter's group and find Peter, Edmund, and Aslan's forces fighting against the Witch's army of hags, dwarfs, apes, ogres, afreets, wraiths, and other assorted evil beings. Peter conducts himself most nobly in the fray, and Edmund redeems himself by breaking the Witch's wand, thus preventing her from changing her opponents to stone. He turns the tide against her but sustains a terrible wound, which fortunately Lucy's cordial is able to heal. Aslan slays the Witch, and the four children are crowned kings and queens and enthroned in Cair Paravel. Aslan slips away during the ensuing revelry, and the new monarchs eliminate the remnants of the Witch's foul brood and govern wisely and well for many years. One day, while hunting, they trail a White Stag and find themselves near the lamppost and then back through the wardrobe and in the Professor's house, on the same day and hour they had left. The old Professor assures them that they'll sometime return to Narnia: how and when remains to be seen. The plot abounds with coincidence and is often sentimental, and most of the characters are types. The parallels to the story of Christ are terribly obvious, but the informal, conversational style works well to keep the story from becoming overly instructive with Christian theology, and, as in the other books in the series, Lewis often interjects comments on manners or mores, or offers casual explanations of characters' motives to maintain a genial storytelling atmosphere. Occasionally, however, one gets the sense that he simply wishes to unload some personal bias. The blending of Greek and Norse beliefs adds color and universality to the thematic problem of the struggle between good and evil and the idea that evil disrupts the social, natural, and spiritual orders. The book is filled with action and excitement and occasionally becomes dramatic; Edmund's nastiness catches the interest; and some humor plays up the drama and plays down the seriousness of the theme. Conversations are well done, and the descriptions of food in the eating scenes add a homely, comfortable touch. Books Too Good; Children's Classics; ChLA Touchstones; Choice; Lewis Carroll.

THE LITTLE BLACK HEN: AN IRISH FAIRY STORY (O'Faolain*, Eileen, Random, 1940), fantasy of talking animals, fairies, and other elements from Irish folklore set in an undisclosed time but probably in the contemporary period. Biddy Murphy, earnest old storyteller, lives alone in a "lovely snug little whitewashed cottage" in Glennashee (the Glen of the Fairies) with her three hens, Brom, Cully*, and Cully's daughter, Cossey Dearg. A "small black sleek hen with bright red legs," Cossey Dearg is a fairy hen. She was born inside the fairy hill that stands near Biddy's house, when Cully hid her nest there. As a result, the fairies have a claim on Cossey Dearg and call her to join their revelries nearly every evening. When one night Cossey Dearg ignores their summons because she does not want to miss the tasty meal Biddy is cooking, the fairies lure her away, capture her, and take her inside the hill where Cliona, the Queen of the Muskerry fairies and ruler of the region, has her arrested and imprisoned in a cell and then sentences her to serve as maid to Sammy Soup, the royal cook. Grief-stricken, Biddy confides her loss to two children, Garret and Julie, who plan to save Cossey Dearg by capturing a leprechaun on May Eve, which will fall a few nights hence. Cliona learns of their plan and decides to capture them by surrounding them with a fairy mist. Cossey Dearg bribes old Seana Thady (the leprechaun gatekeeper of the fairy hill) with many sweet dishes to send his owl to warn the children to wear their coats inside out as protection against the mist. On May Eve, the fairies have a grand festival at the fairy fort in the glen. The fairy mist rolls in, and just as Jackie the Lantern prepares to lure the children away, Grouser the owl warns them, and a soldier of Etain, Queen of the Ivelary fairies and Cliona's rival, interrupts the revelries, complaining that Cliona is luring away two mortals upon whom she has no claim since they live in the fairy area that Etain rules. Cliona has the soldier imprisoned, a

blight falls over the feast, and the fairies
sadly return home to the hill. The next day, May
Day, Cliona holds a hunt, during which she is
wounded in the shoulder by a poisoned arrow shot
by one of Etain's soldiers. She falls into a
coma from which the skill of all her physicians
cannot rouse her. Hoping to help the stricken
queen and thus gain a reward, Cossey Dearg
steals to the queen's room, accompanied by two
new friends, Rory, Garret's lost dog, and
Pishkeen Down, Julie's lost cat, both of whom
had earlier been lured into the hill.
Piskhkeen's keen eye detects a bit of steel
still attached to the wound, Cossey Dearg pulls
it out with her strong beak, and Rory licks the
remaining poison away. Cliona, who has a change
of heart and now intends to make peace with
Etain, richly rewards the three animals and
grants them a boon besides. Cossey Dearg asks
for freedom for all three, and Cliona sends them
home to Biddy to the accompaniment of fairy
music, Cossey Dearg still wearing the little
fairy mob cap she wore as kitchenmaid. Although
the story holds few surprises, the warm, intimate tone, some mild suspense, a little humor,
lively if flat and conventional characters,
Irish speech rhythms and a sprinkling of Irish
words ("she would not be said or led by me";
"stray-away cow"; "chickeen"), many folklore
motifs, and a fast-moving if uneven plot combine
for pleasant entertainment for younger readers.
Fanfare.

A LITTLE FEAR (Wrightson*, Patricia, Hutchinson,
1983, Atheneum, 1983), fantasy novel rich in
atmosphere of place and emotion set mostly in a
swampy region somewhere in the Australian countryside not long ago. The story starts in a
pleasant rest home, Sunset House, where Old
Mrs.* Tucker's daughter, Helen, has arranged for
her to live out her days in what the younger
woman considers peace and comfort. An intelligent, sturdy, hardworking farm woman accustomed to taking care of herself and making her
own decisions, Mrs. Tucker detests the place and
hates being coddled and patronized. No one,
however, knows that when her brother, John
Bright, died he left to her his isolated place
on a river in another state. Mrs. Tucker lays

her plans carefully and steals away to the
empty, rusty-roofed cottage that stands on a
ridge above the swampy flats lining the Broad
River. She gets herself a dog for company and
protection, hires an errand boy, and settles in,
rejoicing quietly in the dignity that independence brings. Trouble soon arrives, however.
In the fowlhouse nearby lives the Njimbin*, a
sly and cunning gnome, who resents her presence
and mobilizes the indigenous creatures of land
and water in what soon accelerates into a war
over possession of the place, an unrelenting
conflict that grows in intensity and acrimony
as the days wear on. The Njimbin tricks Hector*,
the water-wary dog, into going into the rowboat
and tows the terror-stricken animal far downriver; harries the chickens, turning them out
of their run and giving their mash to the rats;
builds a fire in the fowlhouse and burns up the
rat traps Mrs. Tucker has set; plants dozens of
frogs in her house; and lures the monstrous
Hairy Man out of the swamp and into her house to
eat the frogs, among other acts of spite and
trickery. Mrs. Tucker consults Ivan, the errand
boy, who assumes that foxes or similar creatures
are at work. He takes his gun and fires warning
shots into the ground at what he considers
strategic places, including, as it happens, the
Njimbin's weapons storehouse, an act that so
infuriates the gnome that he sends a plague of
midges against the old woman. At this point,
Mrs. Tucker, now aware of the identity and
formidableness of her adversary, capitulates.
She informs her daughter of her whereabouts and
cleverly manipulates her into agreeing to sell
the Bright land and buy another, less isolated
property. She has proved that she can still take
care of herself and deserves to be allowed the
dignity of independence and self-determination
as long as she is physically able to manage.
Before she leaves the Bright place, she sets
fire to the "maggoty old fowlhouse," leaving the
Njimbin with a hollow victory. Careful attention
to creating the feel of timeless mystery and the
physical appearance of the area; the painstakingly developed and sustained tension between
two equally determined, aged adversaries both
fighting for their lives; the occasional
touches of humor; much irony; skillful char-

acterizations that extend even to the "maggoty," slow-witted rats; the ironic, thoroughly
satisfying conclusion; and the bold yet understated style make for a spellbinding story
about courage and coming to terms with life that
avoids the preachiness and sentimentality of
many contemporary novels about the aged. Boston
Globe Winner; Carnegie Com.; Fanfare; Young
Observer.

THE LITTLE GREY MEN (BB*, Eyre, 1942; Scribner,
1949), fantasy of little people and talking
animals set in Warwickshire, England, in modern
times. Sneezewort*, Baldmoney*, and Dodder* are
the little, gray men--gnomes, the last of their
kind in Britain, and well equipped by nature and
appearance to blend with their surroundings.
Their bodies are covered with hair, they wear
garments made of animal skins, and they can
understand the language of the animals and birds
among which they make their homes, which are
always near water. In early spring the three
emerge from their winter quarters, and Baldmoney
and Sneezewort, the more adventurous two of the
trio, decide to go up the Folly River in search
of its source, excitement, and their lost
brother, Cloudberry, who went on a similar quest
up the Folly the previous year and never
returned. The two construct, outfit, and embark
in a gnome-sized paddle boat, the *Dragonfly*,
leaving behind Dodder, who ridicules the whole
idea, but who later changes his mind and makes
his way upriver with the help of Heron and
Otter, joining the other two and acting as their
leader. Baldmoney and Sneezewort push past Moss
Mill with Water-vole's help, avoid the fishing
Colonel, and then are capsized and carried back
into the Mill Pond. They continue along the
shore, living off the land and tucking themselves away among tree roots at night. Joined by
Dodder, they continue, with Baldmoney mapping
their route. In Crow Wood, the three discover
that Giant Crum (who keeps the woods for the
lord of the manor) shoots or snares and then
impales woods creatures. At a Midsummer Eve
meeting of the animals of the region, Dodder
invokes the aid of Pan, the woodland creatures'
god, and shortly thereafter Giant Crum is killed
when his gun explodes. After celebrating his

death, the three continue in the repaired *Dragonfly*, occasionally quarreling and here and there finding traces of Cloudberry. They avoid a boy, are cast ashore by a storm on Poplar Island when their boat is wrecked, build a coracle of frog skins, which is wrecked by a vicious pike, and then find and utilize a toy steamboat, the *Jeanie Deans*, which has gotten away from the boy. After Halloween they have a near escape from a wood dog (a red fox) and decide to go home. There they find Cloudberry awaiting them, returned, not from the source of the Folly as they imagined, but from adventures with Heaven Hounds (wild geese), and a joyful reunion ensues. Although the characters are only a peg above Disney, the tone is arch, and the plot is patently stretched out, some tense situations, the pluck the little men display, and the vivid language that gives reality to the sights, smells, and sounds of the riverbank and woods produce a charm that carries the reader along and provides superficial entertainment. This book resembles those of Grahame*, Tolkien*, and Adams*, but measures up to none of them since it lacks their substance and thematic depth. The sequel is *Down the Bright Stream*. Carnegie Winner.

LITTLE JOHN (*Bows Against the Barons**), presented in the novel as a big man and a strong fighter. A man of action from Derbyshire, he becomes Dickon's friend. He is instrumental in saving Robin* Hood, Dickon, and a dozen other survivors of the greenwood band from the barons, and leads them northward into Yorkshire. He decides to take wounded Robin to the Prioress at Kirklees. Although he tells her that Robin is merely a wounded traveler, the woman recognizes the outlaw, and, hoping to get the reward offered for him, she bleeds him too much. Little John fights his way into the convent in answer to Robin's horn, but Robin dies anyway.

LITTLE KATIA (Almedingen*, E. M., ill. Victor Ambrus, Oxford, 1966; *KATIA*, Farrar, 1967), biographical novel of the author's great-aunt, Catherine A. Almedingen (1829-1893), who became a prominent figure in Russian letters, particularly in children's literature, and whose *The*

Story of a Little Girl is the basis for this book. When Katia is five, her mother dies in childbirth and her older brother, Nicholas, becomes very ill. Although the huge house in Tver is full of servants, the little girl is neglected by them and by her strangely remote father until her mother's friend, Cousin Sophie Berquovist, arrives to claim her and adopt her, as her mother had wished. Cousin Sophie takes her by coach 700 miles to Trostnikovo, the vast estate of a distant cousin, Nicholas Mirkov, which lies near Kursk in Little Russia. There she becomes like a sister to the children of Uncle Nicholas and Aunt Marie: Kolia, who is a mischievous boy about her own age, Nina, a little older, who is immediately her dearest friend, and their slightly older brother, timid Volodia. Aunt Marie is beautiful, sweet, gentle, and utterly incompetent, and Cousin Sophie manages the household, tutors and oversees the children, and helps entertain the continual and numerous guests, a whirlwind of energy and efficiency. Two incidents mar Katia's first years at Trostnikovo: weeping, their thirteen-year-old schoolroom maid Parasha begs Nina one morning to intercede with her father to spare her brother, Andrew the carpenter, from being sent to a twenty-five-year service in the army as punishment for some slight rudeness. The girls remember a scene they interrupted some time earlier in which Aunt Marie was begging her implacable husband to "forgive the boy," and Nina, who knows her father only as fun-loving and generous, plans to ask him that evening. In the afternoon, however, they hear a shot ring out and learn that Andrew has killed himself rather than endure the military. The other incident is more personal: despite the great wealth, the children are kept on a Spartan regimen and even when the orchards are loaded with fruit they are allowed only an occasional taste. Coming upon an unattended fruit centerpiece, Kolia and Katia note that it is so abundant that some of it would never be missed, and Katia takes two plums. Discovered, she begs Cousin Sophie not to shame her by telling the family, and her cousin agrees that her punishment will come later. Weeks after this, when a neighbor has invited them for an all-day outing complete with mushroom hunts and fireworks, a rare treat, Katia is simply left behind to suffer for her earlier sin. Three or four years after her arrival, the entire family, with twelve servants and mountains of luggage, go for a visit of several months to Matzovka, the estate of Aunt Marie's mother in the Ukraine, some 500 miles from Trostnikovo. There Katia is at first delighted with the beauty of the semitropical gardens, but her happiness is soon marred by Aunt Marie's youngest sister, Nadia, a girl three years her senior, who dominates Nina's time and is rude and spiteful to Katia. Back at Trostnikovo, Katia and Nina are friends once more, but Cousin Sophie's health begins to fail, and Aunt Marie dies, presumably of tuberculosis. When Katia is eleven, Cousin Sophie also dies, and Katia is sent back to Tver to a father who has never written to her in six years, brothers she has nearly forgotten, and a stepmother she has never met. Katia soon warms to the young stepmother, who is the soul of kindness, and to her brothers, though she often quarrels with Andrew, who is something of a spoiled baby, and teases him, but her father remains almost as aloof as ever, and her stepmother's mother, Madame Khitrovo, is a great trial, overly flattering one minute and vindictively waspish the next. She insists that the family come to stay at her oppressive manor, Dubky, for weeks, a visit all the children endure but hate before they go on to Katia's father's manor, Zveitkovo. It is far less grand, containing only two villages and stabling for only ten horses, with only a few hot houses and a ballroom for only fifteen couples, but it is a place they all love. Because Cousin Sophie's tutoring has been intense, Katia is considered something of a prodigy, and her father arranges that she go to Madame Guinter's school, the best girls' school in Tver, but he also decides she must be a boarder because it is disruptive to have her at home. She spends nearly a year there before the story ends when she is sent to the Catherine Nobility Institute in Moscow, from which students are not allowed to go home even for holidays. Although an author's note states that this is not merely a translation or a condensa-

tion of the Russian book by her great-aunt, it
moves more like biography than fiction, with
sharply drawn scenes but no real climax. It is
strongest in its picture of nineteenth-century
Russian life, with its huge estates, like
countries in themselves, immense journeys over
roads in terrible condition, enormous wealth of
the rich and harsh restrictions for the less
privileged, all set in a series of scenes of
great physical beauty. Fanfare.

THE LITTLE LAME PRINCE (Craik*, Dinah Maria
Mulock, Daldy, 1875; Macmillan, 1875), fantasy
set in Nomansland, a kingdom like that of
marchen, telling of the imprisonment of little
Prince Dolor and his eventual return to claim
his rightful throne. At the christening of the
prince, one of the ladies of the court drops him
on the marble stairs, and though no one notices
it at first, he is injured and his legs are
paralyzed. Two other important things happen on
that fateful day: his fairy godmother, a little
old woman dressed in gray, appears after his
twenty-four noble godmothers and godfathers have
each given him a name, and with her kiss she
endows him with the name by which he comes to be
known, Dolor, in memory of his ailing mother,
Queen Dolores, who dies during the ceremony.
When the prince is more than two years old and
has never walked, the king dies, and his brother
becomes regent. After some time the regent
announces that Prince Dolor is being sent to the
Beautiful Mountains for his health and then lets
it be known that he has died on the way. A state
funeral is held, but actually the little prince
has been taken away to a barren plain beyond the
mountains by a deaf and dumb horseman and a
condemned woman, who is to act as his nurse and
will be immune from execution only as long as
the child lives. They are placed in the Hopeless
Tower which has no opening at ground level and
can be reached only by a ladder which the
horseman carries. There they live as the boy
grows, with the horseman bringing them supplies
once a month. One day when he is feeling sad and
lonely, Prince Dolor longs for someone to talk
to who will love him, and the little old woman
in gray appears. She cuddles him and comforts
him and leaves him a shabby cloak, which she

refers to as a traveling cloak. He saves it,
though he has no idea how to use it, until he is
ill and his godmother appears to him again and
tells him how to sit on the cloak and say the
magic words, "Abracadabra, dum dum dum," when he
wants to travel. After he has untied the knots
and spread the cloak, he sits in the center and
watches it expand around him and turn up at the
edges like the sides of a boat. When he says the
magic words, the cloak rises to the skylight,
which he is able to open, and floats out into
the fresh air outside. He soon becomes cold and
returns, but the next day he goes for another
flight, and later for longer flights that show
him something of the world and the people in it.
He is also equipped magically with gold
spectacles, with which he can see clearly things
on the ground below him, and silver ears, with
which he can hear the sounds of the world he is
passing over. He sees a shepherd boy running and
realizes for the first time that he is crippled
and different from other boys. Just as he is
about to sink into deep depression from this
revelation, a lark appears, sings, and lights on
his lap. Before he returns to his tower, he
releases it but is delighted that it has
followed him and stays near the tower where he
can hear it all through the winter. From the
books the horseman brings him he realizes that,
if he is a prince, he must be destined to be a
king, and when he asks his nurse, who has been
softened by her association with the gentle
child, she writes the story of his history on
his slate, having sworn never to say a word to
him about it. Now fifteen and determined to
learn what he will need to know as a king, the
prince travels on his cloak and even to the
palace, where a magpie shows him a peep hole
from which he can look down into the king's bed
chamber. There he sees that the king is dead.
When he returns to the tower, his nurse is gone.
For five days he stays alone, expecting that he
will die. Then a great body of lords and
soldiers arrive to escort him back to the
palace, his nurse and the horseman having ridden
out and spread the word that he is still alive.
With the good advice of his godmother and his
own sweet nature, he becomes a good king and
eventually takes one of his young cousins as his

heir. If the story interests modern children, it must be for the general concept alone, since its moralizing and sentimental tone do not suit the late-twentieth-century temper and the plot is not consistent, even for a fantasy. For example, one wonders why does the prince wait alone in the tower, expecting to die, when he can easily leave it on his traveling cloak. Moreover, it lacks the concrete detail that might bring such a story alive. The author, who continually intrudes with comments, shrugs out of such responsibility, saying, "I can't be expected to explain things very exactly," and other similar statements. It is perhaps best read now simply as a fable of the enduring power of goodness, even against great odds. Children's Classics.

LITTLE PLUM (Godden*, Rumer, ill. Jean Primrose, Macmillan, 1963; Viking, 1963), doll fantasy, sequel to *Miss Happiness and Miss Flower**, which is a story of how unhappy Nona Fell, arriving from India to live with her cousins, is finally settled in with the aid of two little Japanese dolls. *Little Plum*, also set in Topmeadow, a market town near London, occurs nearly a year later, in the mid-twentieth century. Nona, now 9, is an accepted part of the Fell family, friendly with Anne, 15, Tom, 12, and especially close to Belinda*, 8, though the two little girls are very different, Nona quiet, dark, careful, Belinda fair, lively, impulsive. When the House Next Door, long vacant, is sold, they are wild with curiosity and soon learn that the new people are wealthy Mr. Harold Tiffany Jones, whose wife has been confined to a hospital as the result of polio, his formidable sister, Agnes, and his daughter, Gem, 9, plus a number of servants. Their hopes of making friends are thwarted, however, when Miss Tiffany Jones makes it clear she thinks them inferior and particularly considers Belinda rough and bad mannered. Gem's father does stop to talk to the girls about their Japanese dolls, but Gem ignores them, though Belinda hangs about the gate and learns from servants' gossip about Gem's pony and her riding lessons, her piano lessons, her personal maid, her governess, her French teacher, and her elocution and ballet lessons. Belinda spreads the information at

school, and her classmates make remarks when
they pass Gem in the street. Though forbidden
to go next door unless invited, Belinda climbs
the ilex tree at the edge of their yard and
inches out on a branch until she can look in
Gem's window. There she sees a Japanese doll,
slightly smaller than Nona's, which she
immediately calls Little Plum. Nona makes a
coat and *tanzu*, Japanese slippers, for Gem's
doll, and Belinda delivers them to the window
sill by crawling across a precarious bridge she
has made of a ladder with one end on a fork of
the ilex tree and the other on the fire escape
of the House Next Door. With them she leaves a
note: "Can't you keep your doll Worme?" The next
day she finds the coat wadded up and thrown
into the Fell's garden and a sign in Gem's
window, "MIND YOUR OWN BUSINESS." This starts a
series of offerings, all Japanese miniature
things for Little Plum made by Nona and
accompanied, without Nona's knowledge, by a
rude note. Each gift is returned damaged or
destroyed with a scornful message, and finally
with a bucket of water rigged to pour on
Belinda, who retaliates by taking Little Plum.
When Gem comes to the house and demands her
doll back, she and Belinda have a scratching,
hair-pulling fight. Belinda is sent to bed, but
Nona, realizing that her cousin has stolen
Little Plum, sternly insists that she take the
doll back, not suspecting that Belinda goes
across the ladder bridge. Gem's maid sees her
and screams, a crowd gathers, and Belinda is
suddenly scared and dizzy. Mr. Tiffany Jones, on
the fire escape, quietly talks her across.
Thoroughly ashamed of herself, Belinda tries to
make friends, but Gem will not speak to her,
alhough Gem's father admires Belinda's spirit.
Belinda takes her problem to Mr. Twilfit,
Nona's friend, the bookseller, who suggests
having Miss Happiness and Miss Flower host a
Celebration of Dolls in their Japanese
dollhouse. At this party all differences are
reconciled, and Gem's mother, in a wheelchair,
returns from the hospital to replace her aunt.
Throughout the story, Miss Happiness and Miss
Flower comment on the actions of the girls and
wish for a happy resolution, but otherwise do
not affect the story. The fantasy element could

be eliminated with no essential change. Belinda is a lively, believable character, but Gem is not developed and Miss Tiffany Jones is implausibly overdrawn. Despite the contrived ending, the story manages to make a quarrel of two little girls have enough importance to be worth detailing and to give a reader an understanding of Belinda's thoughtless but warm-hearted personality. Fanfare.

THE LITTLE WHITE HORSE (Goudge*, Elizabeth, ill. C. Walter Hodges, Univ. of London, 1946; Coward, 1947), fantasy set in a secluded valley on the coast of Devonshire in 1842. Tiny, silvery-eyed, red-haired Maria Merryweather, 13, raised in luxury in London but now newly orphaned and penniless, accompanied by her solicitous, sixty-year-old governess, the sweet if dyspeptic Miss Jane Heliotrope, and the King Charles spaniel, Wiggins, whose chief virtue is his canine beauty, arrive by night at Moonacre Manor, the home of Maria's guardian, Sir Benjamin Merryweather, near the village of Silverydew, which "lie together in a cup in the hills." Her apprehensions about her new home diminish when, after their carriage moves through the tunnel entrance into the valley, she observes that the moon has beautifully silvered Moonacre Park, she catches the briefest glimpse of a little white horse on the hills, and she is warmly welcomed by Sir Benjamin and ushered into his comfortable if shabby house. Her first days at the manor are filled with surprises and discoveries. Her room is a small, simply but adequately furnished circular alcove at the top of a tower, whose doorway is just big enough to admit her but too small for normal-sized adults. Each morning she wakes to discover laid out for her by some mysterious hand garments that determine what she will do that day: ride, study, or go visiting. She is puzzled when Sir Benjamin refers to the estate, the village, and the area's inhabitants as hers and tells her that the people have waited many a long year to have another princess at Moonacre. She gradually meets the occupants of the house, Wrolf, the huge, tawny, protective dog; Zachariah, the imposing, black, noble-headed cat; and Marmaduke Scarlet, the clever and talkative dwarf whose domain is the kitchen and who makes up for his short stature by using very long words. She learns that he and Sir Benjamin have a long-standing dislike of women, herself and Miss Heliotrope excepted, but she is certain never-theless that there is a woman about the place. She attends Old Parson's church, where he plays the fiddle most vigorously and preaches a staunch sermon. She later learns from him the story of Sir Wrolf the Viking, the first of the Moonacre Merryweathers, who built up the estate by devious means, and also the prophecy that one day there will come a Moon Princess who will deliver the valley from the wicked Black Men who steal from the villagers and trap wild animals. Old Parson tells her that to save the valley the Moon Princess will have to humble her pride and love not a prince but a poor man. She also meets beautiful, elderly, maternal Loveday Minette, who dresses with sweet elegance in grey linen that complements her silvery eyes and hair. Loveday, who does housekeeping for Old Parson, informs Maria that she brings Maria her clothes surreptitiously because of the way Sir Benjamin feels about women. She also serves as porteress of Moonacre Gate, the entrance to the tunnel that gives access to the Kingdom of Moonacre, also unbeknownst to Sir Benjamin. On the hill-side later that day, Maria realizes that she has come to feel she belongs to the beautiful region and makes three wishes: that she might rid the valley of the wicked Black Men; that she might meet a shepherd boy and love him; and that she might be the first Moon Princess to live always in Moonacre Manor. After sprightly Robin, Loveday's son and a shepherd, helps her drive off Black Men who are stealing lambs, Maria decides that she will someday marry him. She also decides that only by righting old wrongs can she break the power of the Black Men. She persuades Sir Benjamin to give back to God the monastery on Paradise Hill, land Sir Wrolf had appropriated; this is the first step in righting the wrongs perpetrated by her ancestor, and soon thereafter spring begins to return to Moonacre Kingdom, an obvious symbol. She and Robin brave-ly go to the terrible castle of the Black Men and ask their leader, Monsieur Cocq de Noir, a villainous fellow whose pet black rooster

perches on his shoulder, to stop raiding farms
and trapping animals. He says he will do so if
Maria gives him the first Moon Maiden's lost
pearls and proves to him that Sir Wrolf did not
kill his ancestor, Black William, Sir Wrolf's
rival whose land Sir Wrolf also took. Maria
happens to discover the pearls hidden in the
Manor well, gives them to Monsieur Cocq de Noir,
and then with the help of the little white
horse, which she recognizes as a unicorn, proves
her Viking ancestor innocent of Black William's
murder. With the help of Marmaduke Scarlet she
plans a tea party for the next day, to which she
invites all the principal characters. During the
party she effects a reconciliation between Sir
Benjamin and Monsieur Cocq de Noir, who agree to
let bygones be bygones, and brings together two
sets of estranged lovers, Loveday Minette and
Sir Benjamin, and Old Parson and Miss
Heliotrope, all of whom had thought their loves
lost forever because of their prideful actions
and whose two weddings occur within a few
months. Miss Heliotrope's indigestion disappears, because, now being married to her lost
love, "there wasn't any point in having
indigestion" any longer. Robin and Maria
announce they will soon marry, delighting all
the pet animals who "roared and miawed and
squeaked and barked and whinnied with joy," as
well as villagers and gentry. The next year they
have a grand wedding, and everyone including the
sheep on the hillsides lives happily ever after
now that the Moon Princess has returned in love
and humility to live in her kingdom. All the
characters of this pleasant, overly extended,
pastoral fairy tale are flat types--the doting
governess, the overly proud contrite lovers, the
brave and pure maiden who succeeds where adults
cannot, the happy, humble shepherd, and the
villain who is reformed by persistent goodness.
The tone is affectionate and intimate, style is
leisurely and lush with detail, particularly of
personal appearance, clothing, food, and room
furnishings, material that often has interest
for its own sake, because it is so painstakingly
presented, but which holds up the story.
Episodes are predictable, and most elements for
anticipating the outcome are on the surface. The
author's voice often intrudes with moralistic

comments. The result is wholesome, mildly instructive, quaint reading for girls. Carnegie Winner; Fanfare.

LIVELY, PENELOPE (MARGARET) (1933-   ), born in Cairo, Egypt; novelist for children and adults. She lived in Egypt until after World War II, when she returned to England for boarding school. At eighteen, she enrolled in Oxford to read history. She received her degree with honors in 1956, and the next year she married Jack Lively, who became a Fellow in Politics at St. Peter's College, Oxford. The couple have two children and have lived in a sixteenth-century English farmhouse in Oxfordshire. After the children were school-aged, she had free time to explore her neighborhood and read local history and folklore. These pursuits led to her becoming a freelance writer, first, of fantasies of magic and lore for preadolescents, and later also of books for adults. Her books show her strong interest in the English landscape and folk beliefs and in historical continuity, the discovery of the past in the present. Her first novels were variously received, including *Astercote* (Heinemann, 1970; Dutton, 1971), *The Whispering Knights* (Heinemann, 1971; Dutton, 1976), and *The Wild Hunt of Hagworthy* (Heinemann, 1971; as *The Wild Hunt of the Ghost Hounds*, Dutton, 1972), but *The Driftway* (Heinemann, 1972; Dutton, 1973), her fourth, was an Honor Book in the *Book World* Children's Spring Book Festival. Her next book won the Carnegie Medal; this was *The Ghost of Thomas Kempe** (Heinemann, 1973; Dutton, 1973). Also named to *Choice*, Fanfare, and Contemporary Classics, this is the perennially popular, humorous story of a family's problems with the troublesome spirit of a seventeenth-century sorcerer. Three other critically acclaimed books followed: *The House in Norham Gardens** (Heinemann, 1974; Dutton, 1974), a dream fantasy listed in Fanfare; *A Stitch in Time** (Heinemann, 1976; Dutton, 1976), a quiet, realistic mystery involving an heirloom sampler, which won the Whitbread Award and is listed in *Choice* and Fanfare; and *Fanny's Sister** (Heinemann, 1976; Dutton, 1980), a convincing, subtly humorous period story, which was named to Fanfare and has sequels. Recently she published another novel, *According to Mark* (Heinemann, 1984; Beaufort, 1984), wrote the story for a picture book, *Dragon Trouble* (Heinemann, 1984), and completed a book of short stories, *Uninvited Ghosts and Other Stories* (Heinemann, 1984; Dutton, 1985). She has also written a work of nonfiction for children, *The Presence of the Past: An Introduction to Landscape History* (Collins, 1976), which reflects her preoccupation with interrelationships between the past and the present, as well as novels and short stories for adults, and television plays for both audiences. Her books, even the short ones, are substantial and demanding in subject matter, diction, and themes, and, since she dares to be different, she is one of the most interesting of present-day writers for the young.

LIZ (*Kept in the Dark**), grandmother of the children, a former actress now faded and aging. Possibly frightened by her brusque, domineering husband, she seldom speaks directly to anyone but addresses her comments and questions to her dog, Nero, and scuttles away, so that the children think of her as "the Lizard." Her first reaction to the arrival of David* is to take to her bed, but when she sees that he means to taunt and challenge Grandpa* to get his way, she changes her tactics, becomes charming, and even insists on getting a ride in the Bentley, which ends in an accident, all to protect her husband, who has a weak heart.

LIZZIE BROWN (*Ask Me No Questions**), pauper child who tries to keep in condition by jumping rope 500 times daily at the awful institution run by Drouet. The child of a traveling acrobat, she was the sprite on top of the human pyramid, wearing a spangled dress until she outgrew it and her father left her in the workhouse. Though she fiercely insists he will come back for her, she really fears that he has found a new sprite to fit the dress. She curtseys to Laura* and thanks her politely for the food, but she always goes off by herself in the straw to eat it. Laura's discovery of her dead body in the barn leads to the exposure of the illness and abuse at Drouet's.

LLEWELLYN (*Knight Crusader**), veteran man-at-arms and servant of Philip* d'Aubigny when he is a boy at Blanche Garde in Jaffa. After Philip's imprisonment in Damascus, he runs into Llewellyn again in the camp of the English and Norman forces under Richard* I, and the old fighter joins him and follows him to England, even though he, like Philip, was born in Outremer. Llewellyn is the typical loyal, hard-bitten follower of adventure novels set in the Middle Ages.

THE LOAD OF UNICORN (Harnett*, Cynthia, ill. Cynthia Harnett, Methuen, 1959; *CAXTON'S CHALLENGE*, World, 1960), historical novel with mystery-adventure aspects set in London and Warwickshire for several months beginning in June of 1482, which gives a fictional interpretation of how William Caxton* came to print Sir Thomas Malory's stories about King Arthur. Impulsive, inquisitive, sturdy Bendy (Benedict) Goodrich, twelve to fourteen, lives with his kindly, much respected father, John* Goodrich, now a scribe at St. Paul's, and his earnest, often scolding older half brothers, Matthew and Cornelius, at their shop, the Crowing Cock, in the scriveners' section of Paternoster Row in London. When Bendy becomes apprenticed to his father's friend, William Caxton, his half brothers object vociferously because they fear that the printing press which Caxton has installed at the Red Pale in Westminster will soon put them and others who make a living by copying out of business. Before leaving, Bendy overhears Matthew bargain surreptiously for paper carrying the Unicorn watermark with Tom Twist, a shady peddler; this is the first in a string of events that indicates that Matthew is plotting to keep Caxton from securing the paper that he needs to make a success of his business. Although Bendy shares his knowledge with no one, he does tell his friend Peterkin, who lives next door, of Caxton's need, and Peterkin, who is employed by a waterman, secures small shipments of the Unicorn brand for Caxton, apparently from Tom Twist, who is obviously a double-dealer. When Bendy learns that Caxton wishes to publish heroic stories because he fears knightly virtues are dying

out, Bendy shows him an incomplete scroll of
stories about King Arthur recorded by one Sir
Thomas Malory that Bendy won at dice. Caxton is
eager to print the stories and sends Bendy and
Dick Pynson, another apprentice, to Malory's
home in Warwickshire for the complete manuscript. At Malory's home at Newbold Revel, the
knight's grandson, Nicholas, readily gives the
scroll to Bendy, going against the wishes of
his Great-Uncle Vincent, who has become
suspicious because someone else--Bendy suspects
Tom Twist--has been inquiring about it. On the
return trip, Bendy is captured by thieves in
league with Twist, who, Bendy learns from an
overheard conversation, is not only pirating
paper but is also in league with a group
supporting Henry Tudor's claim to the throne.
Abandoned by his captors, Bendy is found by
monks who return him to London, where he tells
his father what he has learned about the paper
and Tom Twist. John accuses Matthew of
treachery, forces him to turn over the Malory
manuscript to Caxton, and makes him agree to
stop stealing Caxton's paper. This is a
generously detailed, carefully crafted novel
whose interest lies both in its plausible plot
and in the rich picture it gives of its period.
Although most characters are one-dimensional
types or exist for the story, Bendy seems real,
with just enough of both scamp and scholar about
him to keep him interesting, and John Goodrich
and Caxton are also fleshed out. The dialogue is
slightly archaic and formal, which adds to the
sense of period, and details about current
events, the city of London, and social and
economic activities link well with the story of
Bendy's involvement with Caxton and discoveries
about Malory. Carnegie Com.; Fanfare.

LOFTING, HUGH (JOHN) (1886-1947), born in Maid-
enhead, Berkshire; creator of the remarkable
Doctor* Dolittle, who can understand and talk
with animals. He attended St. Mary's College,
Chesterfield, Derbyshire, Massachusetts Institute of Technology, Cambridge, Massachusetts,
and London Polytechnic, studying engineering. He
was a prospector and surveyor in Canada and a
civil engineer on the Lagos Railway in West
Africa, but he was not happy as an engineer and

finally settled in the United States in 1912, working with the British Ministry of Information in New York City. In World War I, he served with the Irish Guards in Flanders, and it was while in the trenches in France that he started the stories of Doctor Dolittle, illustrated with drawings, in letters to his children. Wounded and invalided out of the army, he returned to the United States and from 1923 on was a professional writer, publishing seventeen books of fiction, fourteen of them about Doctor Dolittle, and one book of verse, *Porridge Poetry: Cooked, Ornamented and Served by Hugh Lofting* (Cape, 1925; Stokes, 1924). His first book *The Story of Doctor Dolittle** (Cape, 1923; Lippincott, 1920), tells how the gentle, matter-of-fact little doctor turns from human to animal practice, tutored by his parrot Polynesia*. *The Voyages of Doctor Dolittle** (Cape, 1923; Lippincott, 1922) introduces Tommy Stubbins, the little boy who becomes his assistant and accompanies him on expeditions to outlandish and marvelous places, all told in the same straight-faced, unsensational style. For the rest of his life, Lofting lived in the United States, and his books were all first published in that country.

LONG JOHN MACGREGOR (*Master of Morgana**), the smooth-spoken, one-legged captain of the *Kingfisher*, a salmon boat, and, Niall* eventually learns, master also of his own boat, the *Morgana**. Niall describes him as "like an old pirate," his face the color of "old, well-worked leather" and his hair the "black you find in a pot of boiling pitch." Long John was once a whaler, but a South Georgia accident in which he lost his left leg put an end to that and he became a salmon boat captain. He walks with a crutch, which he sometimes uses as a weapon, and he is very good with the knife. He can be cold, cruel, and ruthless, or kind and solicitous to a cause. He will brook no backtalk from his men, yet sometimes is strangely indulgent toward them. He is an enigmatic figure, a villain not as fleshed out as Long* John Silver of *Treasure Island** fame, nor as ambiguously memorable, but still a perplexing figure who is both repugnant and attractive. Niall likes him right away, not discovering until much later that Long John all

along was leader of the poaching enterprise that
resulted in Ruairidh's near-fatal fall. Just
before the game is up, Long John explains to
Niall why he took to poaching: "This is the way
of it. Six days a week I have fished the nets
for the Laird, and fished them well, let me tell
you. But on the seventh day I have fished them
for myself." Class structure plays a subtle role
in what happens in the novel.

LONG JOHN SILVER (*Treasure Island**), wily and
villainous sea cook, also called Barbecue, who
was quartermaster for Captain* Flint and is the
the leader of the pirates aboard the *Hispaniola*.
He is fifty, has amassed and invested
considerable wealth, and plans to "set up for a
gentleman" when the voyage is done. His left
leg is cut off close to the hip, and he uses a
crutch with wonderful dexterity. He is "very
tall and strong, with a face as big as a
ham--plain and pale, but intelligent and
smiling." A man of some education, he is able to
cow the ignorant and superstitious pirates and
at first to fool all the honest men except
Captain Smollett, who remains suspicious. Even
after Jim* Hawkins has overheard Long John
subverting one young crew member and saying that
he plans to kill all the nonpirates so they will
never show up later to give evidence, and
particularly claiming Squire* Trelawney to
"wring his calf's head off his body with these
hands," the boy falls under the cook's charm and
finds it difficult to believe he is as brutal as
evidence shows. Long John changes sides nimbly
more than once, being as devious and faithless
to the pirates as to the good men. He has a
parrot named for Captain Flint, which rides on
his shoulder and squawks, "Pieces of eight!
Pieces of eight!" A complex character, Long John
Silver is one of the most memorable from
nineteenth-century fiction for children.

THE LONG TRAVERSE (Buchan*, John, ill. Morton
Sale, Hodder, 1941; *LAKE OF GOLD*, ill. S. Lev-
enson, Houghton, 1941), combination of fantasy
and historical fiction, set in Canada at
various periods of the past with the frame
story in the mid-twentieth century. Donald,
about fourteen or fifteen, has gone ahead of his

family to their summer home at Bellefleurs, on the Manitou River of Quebec. There he meets his friends, Aristide Martel and his sister, Simone, their uncle, Father Laflamme, and his father's Indian guide, Negog. Donald loves movies but scorns school work, particularly history, so Negog, with the approval of Father Laflamme, starts to show him a series of episodes from Canadian history in what he calls "*la Longue Traverse* of thinking, that journeys backways," visions brought on by looking into the pools of the river when sunset has turned them to gold. In this way Donald meets a variety of figures, some historical and some fictional: Jacques Cartier, an adventurer, who has found ore he thinks carries gold; Shirras, who, with the Scottish Hope brothers (later killed in World War I) rediscovers the lode Cartier had found and opens the Hope-Shirras mine; the Viking leader Hallward, who takes his people as far as Minnesota; Cadieux de Courville, a fur trader who dies saving his party from pursuing Iroquois; Alan Macdonnell, a Scot who may have been the first white man to reach the Pacific and was buried in the Queen Charlotte Islands; West Wind, a Piegan Blackfeet, who trades for the first rifles his people get and drives off an attack of Snake Indians mounted on the first horses the Blackfeet Indians have encountered; Magnus Sinclair, an Orkney man in the fur trade who guides Simon Fraser to the Pacific at the mouth of the Fraser River after a gruelling trip through white water; and Charles Moupetit, an Oblate Father who comes upon evidence of living remnants of the Toonits, an aboriginal people of Baffin Land who were believed to have been wiped out 1,000 years ago by the present day Eskimos. Although the pattern of the book is much like Kipling's* in *Puck of Pook's Hill*, the historical passages are clumsier because they consist of not a single major episode each but often a long series of adventures telescoped into narrative passages with little scene development. Donald does not participate in the action but is the omniscient observer, knowing all that the characters do, feel, and think. Donald and his French-Canadian friends themselves are not developed, and the frame plot has little interest. While some of the historical adventures are

exciting, and brief passages are vivid, the didactic purpose dominates the book. Fanfare.

A LONG WAY FROM VERONA (Gardam*, Jane, Hamilton,
1971; Macmillan, 1971), frank, witty novel about
a year in the life of a young girl, set in
northeast coastal England about 1940 or 1941,
the early years of World War II. Having been
told when she was about nine by a famous author
that she "is a writer beyond all possible
doubt," Jessica* Vye, 12, relates the often
hilarious, often touching account starting with
her first attempt at long narrative, which her
teacher, Miss Dobbs, brands as forty-seven pages
of pointless, silly lies, to her success in a
nationwide poetry contest sponsored by *The
Times*. Crushed and furious at Miss Dobbs's
insensitive criticism, which comes on top of
receiving two undeserved "order marks," Jessica
flares back, earns another order mark, and is
banished to the cloakroom full of shoe-bags
where she is found wailing by funny old Miss*
Philemon, the Senior English mistress, who
listens to her story and finds it so amusing
that they are soon discovered by Miss Dobbs,
both shrieking with laughter. Jessica realizes
that she is not popular with most of the girls
or with the other teachers, partly because she
is always truthful and, the reader understands,
because she is perceptive, outspoken, and more
intelligent than any of them. Miss Philemon
becomes someone to turn to for advice and
understanding, for instance, when Jessica has
wandered into the Sea Wood by mistake and come
upon an escaped Italian prisoner slashing at the
dahlias with his knife. Outraged at such
destruction, she attacks him verbally and, when
he begins to sob, pats him on the head. However,
when he looks at her with new interest and says,
"You very pretty," she is suddenly afraid and
runs away. Jessica's father, formerly a headmaster in a boys' school, has recently become a
curate; this is a change of status on which he
thrives, being a writer, a liberal, and
something of a ham actor, but her mother finds
the transition difficult. When Jessica is
invited to a Children's House Party by the
snobbish family of a rural dean, the Fanshawe-
Smithes, her mother is torn by conflicting

emotions--scorn, envy, and curiosity--and Jessica reluctantly goes. She finds herself the object of ridicule by the boarding-school children and their friends and of pleased pity by their mother, but the dean, a remote, aging man, is delighted with her, and his fourteen-year-old son, Christian*, who scorns his family's bourgeois attitudes and who looks like a portrait of Rupert Brooke in a book Miss Philemon has loaned Jessica, takes a sudden interest in her, mostly because he has read her father's articles. A couple of weeks later he appears at their door to take her "to see the slums," having berated her for knowing nothing of real life. They take the train to Shields East, a ride during which Jessica suffers the joys and agony of a first date, self-conscious at the remarks of the workmen on the train and at her sweating palm when Christian holds her hand. They are wandering down Dunedin Street in the slum area near the docks, with Christian dramatically throwing his hands in the air and declaring that it must all be destroyed, when a random German plane drops a bomb on the street. Knocked down and disheveled, they are taken in by a man with a tubercular cough and have tea with an enormous legless woman, who treats the whole raid as a huge joke. Christian, whose boarding school is in the country, has never been in a raid before and is distraught, particularly when he learns that the trains have stopped running, but Jessica suggests the bus, finds the station, and, when one comes in going toward his home, puts him on it and competently gets herself home alone. Carefully not thinking about the two children who she knows were killed by the bomb, Jessica writes a poem about the Italian prisoner and goes to sleep for a couple of days, much to the concern of her parents and the doctor, who think she must have a concussion. When she wakes and reads her poem again, she knows it is not like her previous attempts for the contest but somehow right, "complete," as it is. Miss Dobbs's criticism has shaken her confidence, however, and after much shilly-shallying she gives it to Miss Philemon to read. That night the school is bombed and, though Jessica does not tell the reader, Miss Philemon and her apartment mate, Miss Craik, are

killed. Until the school can be repaired, the
students are allotted to various schools in the
area. Jessica's best friend, Florence* Bone,
goes to a posh boarding establishment where they
learn needlework and manners, and Jessica, her
name near the end of the alphabet, is assigned
to the local St. Wilfred's, which is so
overcrowded with working-class types that she
spends all her time reading novels from the
English Classics shelf at the public library.
Thus she comes upon Thomas Hardy's *Jude the
Obscure*, which has a profoundly depressing
effect on her. She is still suffering from
depression when her school opens again, and at
the first assembly it is announced that her
poem, which Miss Philemon must have posted after
she read it, has won twenty pounds in the
nationwide contest. Jessica, who has admired a
Gauguin reproduction over Miss Philemon's
fireplace, buys a large, framed painting in an
art shop window, carries it to Miss Philemon's,
and finally forces herself to look at the house
and admit that it has been bombed out. She then
thinks of taking the painting to the legless
woman in Dunedin Street and wrestles it onto the
train and off again, only to learn that the
street has been evacuated and mostly torn down.
Having finally faced the horrors she has
suppressed, Jessica lugs her picture back onto
the train and goes home, her happiness restored.
Although at first the plot seems to be loose and
almost episodic, it is actually intricately
constructed. What Jessica doesn't tell the
reader is important to the understanding of her
psychological reaction to her losses, a subtlety
that makes the book more difficult than it first
appears and shows her as a more complex
character than most teenaged heroines. On an
easily approachable level, however, the story
has some very funny scenes, notably the
end-of-term party at Elsie Meeney's tea shop
where an eccentric woman calls them "four little
English Juliets"--hence the title--and the visit
to the Fanshawe-Smithe country home. It is also
distinguished by many sharp characterizations,
among them those of Jessica's parents, her
younger brother, Rowley, and the various
teachers, and by clever ironic observations by
Jessica, who sees through pretensions with

remarkable clarity. Fanfare.

LORD FOLAN (*The Singing Cave**), one of the strongest and largest men on the island of Barrinish, given the mock title because of his slow, formal manner of speech. Calm and peace-loving, he does not rise to the continual jibes of Rooster Hernon, his rival in the annual currach races, and when Mr.* Allen has endangered his cattle, he still is first to risk the dangerous journey to the Singing Cave in a high sea to save the man. Told of Allen's duplicity, his first impulse is pity, and he insists that the injured man be taken to his house to be cared for.

LORD GOD (*The Moon in the Cloud**), presented as a disembodied, still, small voice. In righteous indignation about the wickedness of humankind, he gives Noah* instructions for making the ark and saving the creatures of the earth. When Noah expresses concern for Reuben and Thamar, who have impressed him as being good people, the Lord assures him that things will turn out as they should. At the end, the Lord God instructs Noah to take Reuben and Thamar aboard in Ham's* place, for the world to come will need good and courageous people, and Reuben and Thamar have proved themselves to be both.

LORD MALYN (*The Whispering Mountain**), the Marquess of Malyn, owner of Castle Malyn, or Caer Malyn, an evil-hearted, greedy man who owns most of the land in the Black Mountains region and who hires Bilk and Prigman to steal the harp from old Mr. Hughes. He is used to having his own way and has so many possessions that the only thing he really wants now is to continue to want. A hyperactive man, he always seems to be in motion, even when fatigued. He dislikes women so much he will not allow any around him, ever since a curse was placed upon him by Arabis* Dando's dying mother. The cruel lord had the ill woman carried from the lodge where his gatekeeper's wife was tending her because he didn't want gypsies around. It was winter, and she soon died. He is an elaborate distortion of the stock villain who eventually meets a well-deserved and dreadful end.

LORD SIMON VIGO (*Songberd's Grove**), nobleman
for whom tailor Mr.* Tom Triplett once made
suits and who inadvertently helps Martin* Singer
defeat the bully Lennie* Byre and fix up
Songberd's Grove. An impatient man in his late
sixties and inclined to bellow when he speaks,
he has gone at full tilt all his life and still
tends to attack tasks. Now responsible for Songberd's Grove, which is part of the estate of his
young cousin, the Duke of Sarrat, he hires John*
Pim to be the architect for the restoration. He
is an interesting if overdrawn character.

LORD TOM (*Smith**), swashbuckling highwayman who
is a sometime admirer of Smith's* sister, Miss*
Fanny, and an idol to the scruffy twelve-year-
old. A big, bearded man with bright green eyes,
who always dresses in green, Lord Tom is long on
drink and stories of his own glory. He plays
the part of a hold-up man of consequence,
though actually he is a rather minor figure
among the desperadoes and is mainly noted for
his accurate knowledge of timing, of how long it
will take a coach in certain weather and road
conditions to reach a certain point on Finchley
Common, which is knowledge sought after by
other, more proficient outlaws. Although he has
betrayed Smith to the two men in brown, he
redeems himself in the climactic scene by
shooting one of them to save Smith just as he,
himself, is shot by Jack Field.

LOST JOHN, A YOUNG OUTLAW IN THE FOREST OF ARDEN
(Picard*, Barbara Leonie, ill. Charles Keeping,
Oxford, 1962; Criterion, 1963), historical novel
set in Warwickshire in the late twelfth century. In the four years since the death of
John* Fitzwilliam's father, his mother has
remarried, and his stepfather, Baron Roger de
Lyddfield, along with the baron's sons, has
begun to usurp the Berkshire estate and the
rights that belong to fourteen-year-old John.
Persuaded by Tom Bowman, who is the only
survivor of the ambush that killed his father
and who has trained John as his instrument of
revenge, and discouraged by his helplessness
against Baron Roger, John sets out with Tom to
find and kill his father's murderer, Sir Raoul
de Farrar. Before they reach Warwick, they are

set upon by bandits. Tom is killed; John is left
for dead. He is found and nursed by some kindly
peasants, but when he sets out for Warwick
again, he is captured and taken to the local
outlaw leader, Sir* Ralf the Red. On a whim, Sir
Ralf takes John for his squire instead of
killing him as his lieutenant, Simon, urges, and
John soon finds himself strongly attached to the
mercurial outlaw leader. Gradually he learns
something of Sir Ralf's history: he had planned
to attack his wife's brothers, whose land lay
beside his, and, when they were dead, to claim
their estates. His wife warned her brothers, and
in his anger Sir Ralf killed her, an act for
which he has been outlawed. Known as Lost John,
the boy soon takes part in the actual raids and
witnesses the cold-blooded murder of innocent
people but also sees unexpected mercy and even
generosity to a starving widow and her children.
He settles in well until unexpectedly Sir Ralf's
son, Alain* de Farrar, turns up, a runaway from
the monastery where his father had sent him
three years before. Because the beautiful boy
resembles his mother and reminds Sir Ralf of
her, his father is furious, but he lets the boy
stay as a kitchen drudge. Although Alain is
always cheerful and good tempered toward him,
John considers him a rival for Sir Ralf's
affection and is surly in return. When it is
apparent that an informer has told the de
Wellsfonts, Alain's uncles, about an ambush and
has thereby caused the death of a number of Sir
Ralf's men, both Alain and Simon are put to test
by ordeal, picking up a red hot bar of iron, and
Alain's courage and innocence impress even his
father. Unwittingly, Alain tells John Sir Ralf's
real name--Raoul de Farrar--and John is torn
with conflicting emotions, yet still finds that
he cannot kill Sir Ralf. Shortly after, John is
captured by de Wellsfont's men. Alain daringly
goes into de Wellsfont castle disguised as a
girl, discovers John's whereabouts, and later
leads a rescue band. In a final major effort to
defeat his brothers-in-law, Sir Ralf leads a
raid on de Wellsfont castle and is killed saving
John from certain death. Depressed and
grief-stricken, John leaves the outlaw band to
seek service with some other lord and is
unexpectedly joined by Alain, who also feels no

reason to stay with the outlaws. The parallel with the Robin Hood legends is obvious, even to the huge second-in-command (named Wolf) and the somewhat less than holy priest (named Sir Martin) who serves the spiritual needs of the band. Unlike the legend, however, the life of the band is bloody and unprincipled, even for the lawless period, and Sir Ralf is charismatic but greedy and cold-blooded. Interest in the plot shifts from John to Alain in an odd manner, and Sir Ralf's self-sacrificing final act is not consistent with his character, but the action is fast-paced and the picture of life in an England where King Richard I is off on a crusade, Prince John and his lieutenants are corrupt, and violence flourishes, is compelling. Fanfare.

LOUAN (*The Singing Cave**), Breton boatman aboard the lobster boat, the *Saint Ronan*. When the captain humiliates him by commanding him to stay aboard the boat at his home port of Kerronan, Louan cheerfully quits his job, contrives to defeat the captain's dishonest schemes, and switches to working on a sardine boat. Full of stories and superstitions, Louan is nevertheless shown to be astute and honorable in a tight situation.

LUCAS BELL (*Midnight Is a Place**), thirteen-year-old orphan, ward of Sir* Randolph Grimsby and heir of Midnight Court and Murgatroyd's Carpet, Rug, and Matting Manufactury through his father, who had been Sir Randolph's business partner. After Lucas's father married, he went to India for the company, where he and Lucas's mother died. At the book's beginning, Lucas feels lonely and unwanted and only casually tends to the studies set for him by Mr.* Julian Oakapple, his tutor. To ease his loneliness, he makes up stories about an imaginary boy named Greg. He is disappointed when Anna-Marie* turns out to be a girl, because he had hoped for a companion like Greg. He learns, however, to appreciate her finer qualities of quick thinking and resourcefulness and together the two manage to survive and provide for Mr. Oakapple after Midnight Court burns and Mr. Throgmorton refuses to acknowledge Lucas. At the end he realizes that it is each person's responsibility to make a good life for himself. The expectation is that he and Lady* Murgatroyd will help the new mill owner, Lord Holdernesse, provide better working conditions and better pay for the mill-hands.

LUCY DENHAM-LUCIE (*The Watcher Bee**), woman who was the center of village fun--cycling, panto-mimes, melodramas, concerts, and then scandals-- in her youth and who returns to the village with her daughter nearly twenty years later. Though pretentious and as phony as her name (no one knows where she got the second "Lucie" or why it is spelled with an "ie"), she is fascinating to Kate*, who has never seen anyone play a role like Lucy's, which contrasts sharply with the attitude of her plain, straight-laced aunt. Lucy is continually springing surprises, little dinners with food sent in from Harrods, a wealthy boy friend from Sheffield, and, the real shocker, the engagement and marriage of the man not to Lucy, but to her daughter, Zoe Vardoe. Her presence is a catalyst for conflict between Aunt* Beth and Uncle* Ben, who both were part of her crowd as young people.

LUCY GRAHAM (*The Battle of Wednesday Week**), youngest of the Graham-Lattimer clan, sister of Nan*, Alan, and Roderick. The most determined of the Grahams not to accept their stepmother, she comes around as soon as she meets warm, motherly Sarah, her need for maternal love overcoming her hostility. While the Grahams are still in Massachusetts, she retreats to the barn loft to find comfort among her collection of scarecrows. In Scotland, she accepts Nicholas* Lattimer first because he helps her conquer the current while they are swimming but thoughtfully doesn't give her away to the other children. Later, wanting a scarecrow for company and consolation, she goes off with Geordie* Monroe to a neighbor's barn, makes one of straw, and dresses him in kilt and plaid. On the way home, she falls into a fissure on the mountainside. After the children rescue her, Nicholas names the scarecrow the McBogus, Chief of Clan Glengarble, setting just the right mood for the children to proclaim Robert their Laird, the first positive step toward reconciliation and acceptance.

Later, Lucy goes with Geordie on the school
outing and must be rescued during the terrible
storm. Lucy is the best developed character in
the novel. A typical preadolescent, she is
inclined to be stubborn and willful but is still
a thoroughly likeable character.

LUCY MOORE (*Time of Trial**), beautiful, intelligent daughter of a local farmer with whom Meg
becomes friends while she lives at Herringsby on
the seacoast. Lucy longs for a more fashionable
life and is ashamed of her country house and
rural ways, even though her father is relatively
well-to-do and is well-regarded in the area.
She and her family befriend Meg and help her
with her wedding arrangements. Lucy is attracted
to John* Pargeter. She serves as a foil for Meg.

LUCY PEVENSIE (*The Lion, the Witch and the
Wardrobe**; *The Horse and His Boy**; *Prince
Caspian**; *The Voyage of the "Dawn Treader"**;
The Last Battle*), a major character in the
Narnia* series, youngest of the four Pevensie
children, which also include Peter*, Susan*, and
Edmund*. She is the first to enter Narnia (in
The Lion, the Witch and the Wardrobe), and is
dismayed and perplexed when at first the others
refuse to believe she has had the adventure. She
is kind, curious, and adventurous in a limited
way, and seems symbolic, in Christian theology,
of "the little child who leads them." Once in
Narnia, she convinces the other children to
stay there to help Mr.* Tumnus the Faun, who got
into trouble with the White Witch (Queen*
Jadis) over Lucy. She is much the same in
character in the other books, though in *Voyage*
she yields to temptation and speaks a spell she
knows she shouldn't. She is the one of the four
children to whom Aslan* usually first appears,
and he appears to her more often than to the
others. In the concluding book, *The Last
Battle*, she appears as one of the Seven Kings
and Queens of the eternal Narnia. Although she
seems a symbolic character, she is neither
allegorized nor sentimentalized; instead she
changes and grows and is interesting and
likeable.

LURGAN SAHIB (*Kim**), black-bearded Eurasian who

keeps a curio shop in Simla and deals in jewels--and espionage for the Indian Secret Service. He is often referred to as the Healer of Sick Pearls. A man of many talents, he tests Kim* O'Hara in a number of ways, including apparent magic and hypnotism. His main role is as a teacher, training a few select recruits for the spy service in the finer points of disguise and ways of acting as any of the many types of natives which they may be called upon to impersonate.

LYAPO (*The Sentinels**), black farmer and trapper of the Oyo, or Yoruba, tribe, in what is now Nigeria; a family man who is kidnapped and sold as a slave. Tribal organization has broken down in northwest Africa to such an extent that the people have no protection against marauders, and entire villages have been laid waste by slavers. Lyapo is brutalized by both Africans and whites. Although for a time he is so dispirited that he feels he is dead and has become a ghost according to the beliefs of his people, he regains his instinct for survival. A sensible, thoughtful, courageous man, he earns the respect of the sailors on the *Sentinel* and becomes a hand. Although offered a permanent post on the warship, he declines and elects to go back to his people and become a farmer. When he and Spencer are in the jolly boat, Spencer's skill gets them to shore; then Lyapo gets them through the tough times on shore. His superior ability there raises his self-esteem considerably and thus he sees he is not inherently inferior to the whites. He and Spencer while away their extra time playing draughts, which he later teaches the blacks in the compound where they are awaiting assignment to their farmlands. Lyapo is an interesting, credible character.

LYNCH, PATRICIA (NORA) (1898-1972), born in Cork, Ireland; writer of children's books for more than forty years. She was educated at a convent school and secular schools in Ireland, Scotland, England, and Belgium. From 1918 to 1920 she was a feature writer for *Christian Commonwealth*, Dublin. Her first book was *The Green Dragon* (Harrap, 1925), and it was followed by forty-four other books of fiction and

three books of stories and legends. Most of her
work, and the best known, is fantasy based on
folklore characters and motifs, as in *The
Turf-Cutter's Donkey* (Dent, 1934; Dutton, 1935)
and its sequel, *The Turf-Cutter's Donkey Goes
Visiting** (Dent, 1935; as *The Donkey Goes Visit
ing*, Dutton, 1936), in which a great many different sorts of elements are mixed, with many
but not all from Irish story. She also wrote
some realistic fiction, as in *Fiddler's Quest*
(Dent, 1941; Dutton, 1943), in which a girl who
is a fiddler gets involved with an Irish
Republican on the run and in other aspects of
Irish nationalism, and *The Mad O'Haras* (Dent,
1948; as *Grania of Castle O'Hara*, Page, 1952),
about a girl who wants to be a painter but must
first solve the problems of her wild relatives
who live in a ramshackle castle. Lynch also
wrote an autobiography for adults, *A Story-
Teller's Childhood* (Dent, 1947; Norton, 1962).
Many of her books have been translated into a
number of languages. She was married to R. M.
Fox, a writer.

LYS (*The Writing on the Hearth**), Stephen's
sister, whom their stepfather, Odo* the Plowman,
has betrothed to a man much older than she and
who flees for help to old Meg*. Gilles* the
Outlaw and Stephen take her to the nunnery at
Goring, where for a while she serves as kitchen
wench and then becomes a nun, as old Meg had
predicted she would. All along, without knowing
it because she is illiterate, Lys has had
Stephen's copy of Dame* Alice's letter in her
shoe and has been using it as an innersole.

M

MACDONALD, GEORGE (1824-1905), born near Huntly, Aberdeenshire, Scotland, died in Surrey; clergyman and writer best remembered for his fantasies for children. The son of a farmer, he worked his way through King's College, University of Aberdeen, where he studied physics and chemistry; then, after two years as a private tutor in London, he entered Congregationalist Theological College, Highbury, London. He served as pastor of a church for a short time but had theological views too liberal for his congregation and was asked to leave. After that he was a freelance lecturer and preacher in Manchester, Hastings, Sussex, and London, and turned to writing to support his family of eleven children. From 1870 to 1872, he edited a magazine for children, *Good Words for the Young*, in which a number of his stories first appeared. Although for most of his life he suffered from tuberculosis, which killed four of his children, he wrote more than fifty books and was praised by such literary figures as Lewis Carroll*, John Ruskin*, Alfred Lord Tennyson, Charles Kingsley*, Henry Wadsworth Longfellow, Harriet Beecher Stowe, and Mark Twain. In 1877, he was granted a Civil List pension and in his later years lived in Italy. All his stories have didactic themes, though some are more heavily moralistic than others. Perhaps the best suited to modern taste is *The Light Princess** (Blackie, 1890), in which the princess's levity is treated in a playful manner; both it and *The Golden Key**

(Crowell, 1906), a more seriously handled and mystical allegory, have been republished in modern editions illustrated by Maurice Sendak. Of his longer books for children, *The Princess and the Goblin** (Strahan, 1872; Routledge, 1871), in which the miner boy, Curdie, saves the princess from the wicked goblins, and its sequel, *The Princess and Curdie** (Chatto, 1883; Lippincott, 1882), in which together they save the kingdom from evil forces, are the most popular, though many critics think that *At the Back of the North Wind** (Surahan, 1870; Routledge, 1871), in which little Diamond is taken throughout the world by his friend the North Wind, is more typical of MacDonald's allegorical symbolism and moralistic point of view. All three of these are listed as Children's Classics, and the Princess books are among the Children's Literature Association Touchstones; five of his works are included in the *Choice* Magazine list of children's books for an academic library.

MACDONALD, SHELAGH (1937–   ), born in Hampshire; editor and author. She attended grammar school at Blandford, England, and worked as a medical copywriter for Welcome Foundation Ltd., from 1956 to 1961, then as copywriter at advertising agencies through the early 1960s and as creative group head for Papert, Koenig, Lois in London. Two of her books for young people are based in Greece: *A Circle of Stones* (Deutsch, 1973) and *Five From Me, Five From You* (Deutsch, 1974). Her most noted novel, for which she received the Whitbread Literary Award in 1977, is *No End to Yesterday** (Deutsch, 1977), a searing story of a girl growing up in a repressive household which is based on her own mother's childhood.

MACEY (*Red Shift**), soldier of the Roman Ninth Legion who comes with the legion's few remnants to Mow Cop and there tries to "go tribal" to survive the danger of two different local tribes. Subject to wild fits, he is used by his companions to attack a village and destroy it in a sort of berserk trance. Of their little band, he is the only one who tries to understand the girl they have raped and crippled, and in the end he is the only one she allows to survive.

MACGIBBON, JEAN (HOWARD) (1913–   ), born in London; editor and novelist. She was educated at St. Leonard's School, St. Andrews, Scotland, and at the Royal Academy of Dramatic Art, London. From 1948 to 1954 she was editorial director for MacGibbon and Kee, publishers. Among her fifteen books of fiction for children are a historical novel, *A Special Providence* (Hamilton, 1966; Coward, 1965), a boy's view of *The Mayflower* voyage that has been described as "refreshingly irreverent toward the Pilgrim Fathers," and *Liz* (Hamilton, 1966; Scribner, 1966), among the first of the British books to exemplify the new realistic trend of the 1960s. Her *Hal** (Heinemann, 1974), a novel of a group of inner-city youngsters spearheaded by a West Indian girl, won the British Other award in 1975. Many of her books for young people have to do with boats and sailing. She has also translated *Women of Islam* by Assia Djebar (Deutsch, 1961) and *Girls of Paris* by Nicole de Buron (Blond, 1962), and has published one novel for adults. Her work has appeared in the *Times Literary Supplement*, the *New Statesman*, and *Horizon*.

THE MACHINE GUNNERS (Westall*, Robert, Macmillan, 1975; Greenwillow, 1976), historical novel set in World War II in the coastal industrial town of Garmouth (probably Tynemouth), dealing with a group of young adolescents whose war is as much against adults as against the Germans. Chas* McGill, 14, has the second best collection of war souvenirs in Garmouth, the best belonging to bully Boddser Brown. When, after a night bombing raid, Chas discovers the tail of a German bomber which has broken off and fallen on a deserted estate, he is horrified to find the gunner, dead, sitting upright and apparently watching him, but he is also determined to get the machine gun, complete with ammunition, for his collection. He enlists the aid of Cem* Jones, who brings his Guy Fawkes dummy on its wagon, while Chas pinches his father's hacksaw. They are waylaid by Audrey* Parton, a classmate bigger and stronger than

either of them, who insists on coming along.
Together they cut the gun free, hide it in the
leg of the Guy, and later conceal it in a nearly
deserted building-materials yard. Unable to show
it even secretly to the other juvenile
collectors (since Boddser has found the tail,
vandalized the body, and the police are
suspicious), Chas has another idea: to build a
gun emplacement on the Nichol estate, now an
overgrown wilderness with a view of the docks
and coastline. He and Cem enlist the aid of
Clogger* Duncan, a boy from Glasgow, who is
bigger and tougher than the others, and is now
living with an aunt in Garmouth. Together they
walk Benjamin Nichol, called Nicky*, a timid
classmate who has been routinely terrorized by
Boddser, past his gang, and thus win his
friendship and support. Nicky's father, a naval
captain, has been killed, and his mother is
drinking heavily and openly living with an
officer who, with his men, has been billeted in
their house, a situation that makes the other
parents forbid their children to associate with
Nicky and therefore makes his home far more
attractive to them. With Audrey and another
classmate, red-haired Carrot-juice Carstairs,
they start to dig a bunker in the neglected
Nichol garden overlooking the town. When the
work proves too much for them, Chas enlists the
aid of John Brownlee, a huge retarded man who
works willingly for them in exchange for an
occasional cup of tea and encouraging smiles.
Soon they have a buried air-raid shelter,
originally intended for the servants who have
departed for war work, with the gun mounted
pointing out over the town, bunks, a paraffin
heater that will boil a tea kettle and toast
bread, and a lookout platform in a tree above, a
shelter they call the Fortress Caparetto. The
night a bomb falls directly on the Nichol house,
Nicky has been restless, having dreamed about
his father, and has gone out to the fortress to
get away from the knowledge that his mother is
laughing with the officer in her bedroom. There
Chas finds him, and since he no longer has a
family and is terrified of being sent to a home,
they decide he will live in the fortress with
Clogger, who willingly leaves his aunt a note
indicating that he's gone back to Glasgow. John

digs them another room to house the black-market ·
supplies Nicky's mother's lover had been
collecting and, since the school has also been
hit and classes discontinued, the whole group
spends much of its time there. Their first
attempt to use the machine gun on a single
German plane goes wildly astray, spraying
bullets into a home in the town, throwing Chas
backward, and blasting a hole in the fortress
ceiling, but he gets his father to build a
tripod (supposedly for a telescope), swipes some
cement, and soon the gun is concreted securely
in place. The German flyer, Sergeant Rudi Ger-
lath, escapes from the crashing plane, para-
chutes not far from the fortress, and after
hiding in an outbuilding for several days with a
sprained ankle, makes his way to the Nichol
estate, trying to figure out a way to give
himself up to the army. He goes out into the
garden to relieve himself, walks directly into a
machine gun barrel, and finds himself the
prisoner of six children. His capture poses a
problem for Chas and his friends. If they turn
him in, the adults will learn about their
fortress and confiscate their gun. For a while
they guard Rudi constantly with his Luger, but
soon he becomes more a companion, builds them an
underground toilet with a ventilator, and, when
they ask him to repair the machine gun which
isn't working right, he agrees if they will get
him a boat to escape. Though Nicky thinks and
hopes this is impossible, his father had a
sailboat which they are able to fit up and
launch. The situation comes to a head on a night
when the church bells start to ring, the
prearranged signal of the invasion. Nicky gets
Rudi to the boat, and all the children escape
from their respective families and meet at the
fortress, unaware that the bells were a false
alarm. When the local policeman, Fatty Hardy,
enlists the help of the men of the Polish Free
Army, who are eagerly looking for something to
do in the emergency, to find the children, they
advance on the fortress. The defenders see
soldiers speaking a foreign language approaching, and fire their gun, fortunately missing
wildly. A soldier appears waving a white flag,
and to the astonishment of all it is Rudi, who
has decided to return. Clogger fires the Luger

at Rudi, and all the children break out of the fortress to run to their prisoner in distress. The end is inconclusive: Rudi is wounded but may live; Clogger and Nicky will be sent to a home, perhaps together; the others are retrieved by their angry parents. All of them, however, feel a sense of accomplishment. Other characters, notably Stan Liddell, their teacher who is also head of the local Home Guard, and his World War I veteran sergeant-major, who almost discover their fortress, are important, but most of the adults are so overworked and worried that the young teenagers are left pretty much on their own. The picture of wartime England, mostly from the point of view of working-class youngsters, is strong, with lively action and some very funny scenes. Boston Globe Honor; Carnegie Winner; Choice; Fanfare; Jr. High Contemporary Classics.

MACKEN, WALTER (1915-1967), born in Galway, Ireland; actor, theatrical producer, novelist, and playwright. He was educated in Catholic schools in Galway. From 1939 to 1948 he was an actor and producer in the Gaelic Theater in Galway, and from 1948 to 1951 he acted at the Abbey Theater, Dublin. For adults he published ten novels, three books of short stories, and six plays. For children he wrote two books. The first is *Island of the Great Yellow Ox* (Macmillan, 1966), in which four boys are marooned on an island on which an archeologist and her husband are obsessively searching for a golden idol and try to quiet the boys by eliminating them. His second work is better known, *The Flight of the Doves** (Macmillan, 1968; Macmillan, 1968), about the journey across Ireland of of two youngsters to escape an abusive stepfather, a story which was named to the *Horn Book* Fanfare list and was produced as a television play in 1972.

MACPHERSON, MARGARET (1908-   ), born in Colinton, Midlothian, Scotland; writer of novels that reflect the concerns and setting of the Isle of Skye. She was educated privately in Edinburgh and then attended Edinburgh University and received her M.A. degree in 1929. She married a cattle and sheep dealer, and they rented a peninsula from the Forestry Commission on Skye and raised stock as well as seven sons. She has also taught high school at Portree, Skye, and has been active in public affairs, being Honorary Secretary of the Skye Labour Party, member of the Commission of Inquiry into Crofting, Iverness, and member of the Consultative Council, Highlands and Islands Development Board. She has written half a dozen novels for older children, all set on Skye, the first being *The Shinty Boys* (Collins, 1963; Harcourt, 1963), about the struggles of a group of boys to field their team in shinty, a very fast Highlands game similar to hurley in Ireland. Among her other works are *The Rough Road** (Collins, 1965; Harcourt, 1966), a choice for the *Horn Book* Fanfare list about an orphan boy placed with an abusive family; *The New Tenants* (Collins, 1968; Harcourt, 1968), about the difficult time a girl has in adjusting when she comes from Glasgow to Skye with her city-bred family, and *Ponies for Hire* (Harcourt, 1967), in which an island family takes in tourists whose milksop son turns out to be better than they thought and even works out a way to save the farm. All these have mid-twentieth-century settings, but she has also written historical fiction in *The Battle of the Braes* (Collins, 1972), which is based on real happenings of the 1880s and deals with passionate loyalties over croft land, cattle, and houses among the Gaelic-speaking characters.

MADAME DE VAIRMONT (*Thunder of Valmy**), Pierre's mentor and noted artist of portraits of wealthy French men and women. An old woman, she has earned enough from her portraits to paint what she wishes, and so has retired to her cottage near Aulard in the Argonne. She is knowledgeable about politics in France and abroad, and in Aulard and in Paris alike she becomes the center of a circle of radicals and intellectuals. She is strong-willed and demanding with Pierre and her servants and she often argues with her faithful old retainer, Berthe, who frequently threatens to quit but never does. The two are really very fond of each other. Madame cleverly manipulates the Marquis de Morsac* into engaging Pierre to paint his niece's portrait, and thus she brings together the two young people who eventually become sweethearts. It is through Madame that Pierre, and the reader, get to Paris to view the important events of the French Revolution that occur there from 1789 to 1792. At the end Madame returns to Aulard and resumes her painting.

MADAME OLYMPIA (*Which Witch?**), villain of the story, an evil enchantress. She replaces Gwendolyn* Swamp in the contest for the hand of the wizard Arriman Canker. She "persuades" Gwendolyn to sell her property in Todcaster to her so that Madame Olympia can enter the contest as a bona fide resident of Todcaster. She is diabolically astute and clever, she steals Rover, Belladonna's familiar, and she is the leading contender with her blackest-of-the-black trick of conjuring up droves of self-cannibalizing rats, until Belladonna takes the lead by summoning Sir* Simon Montpelier. Madame Olympia has had five husbands, all of whom disappeared in odd ways after they had made her their heir. At the end, she goes off with Sir Simon, who murdered his seven wives. The reader is left to imagine what will happen to them next.

MADELEINE STUDDARD (*The Wind Eye**), second wife of Bertrand* and mother of Mike* Hendrey. Emotional and theatrical, she is a bad match for Bertrand, and their marriage is continually erupting into quarrels. She drives with such violence that none of the family is willing to ride with her. She is also very clever at baiting Bertrand, and doesn't hesitate to insult her son or her stepdaughter Beth*. When she finds herself shorn of her anger, after an encounter with St. Cuthbert, she admits to her son that she has depended on her rage to get her through the bad times after his father died, but she finds some happiness without it.

MADERO, FRANCISCO (*Jeremy Craven**), historical revolutionary leader of Mexico, who becomes president of the country in 1911. Jeremy meets him when both are imprisoned in Mexico City. Madero is accurately presented in the story as too idealistic and too concerned with principles to hold his followers, who eventually condemn him as a vacillator. After Porfirio Diaz* resigns the presidency for which the Maderistas fought, Madero becomes president. Although he has good intentions, he proves weak and ineffectual, and, in 1913, he is shot during the coup of General Huerta. Jeremy is with Father* Gonzalez when he learns the sad news of his friend's death.

MADGE (*The Battle of St. George Without**; *Good-bye, Dove Square**), red-haired, strong-willed girl who is part of the crowd of youngsters living in Dove Square and later in the housing project. Independent and inclined to be sharp-tongued, Madge is at the same time sensitive to the needs of younger children like Henry's brother, The Trailer, and Sammy Flint. When she discovers that her Cousin Maudie, with whom she lives, is really her mother and that the Salesman is really her father, returned from prison to pick up his stolen money, she does not flinch from the knowledge, though she is touchingly shaken at first.

MAD HATTER (*Alice's Adventures in Wonderland**; *Through the Looking-Glass**), zany character who participates in the never-ending tea-party at the March* Hare's house, along with Alice* and the sleepy Dormouse*. The Mad Hatter complains that the well-meaning Hare has put butter in his watch in an ill-conceived attempt to repair it; tells in a pun-filled conversation of his troubles with Time, who won't stand beating; and sings the parody, "Twinkle, twinkle, little bat!/ How I wonder what you're at!" He is a caricature, like the other figures in the novel, and one of the most famous figures in English literature. In the second book he appears briefly as Hatta, one of the White King's two messengers, the other being Haigha. Both are parodies of themselves as they appear in the first book.

MAD HATTER (*The Other People**), J. L. S. Smith, one of the boarders at the Sea View Guest House where Kate* Lucas spends her vacation. A clever, high-strung joker, he has some mystery about him, disappearing twice a day on Aunt Poppy's bicycle. Kate feels shame when she discovers that he is the comedian for the Kooky Kapers, a third-rate vaudeville show on the Esplanade, but she finally comes to know his background: that he is the son of the reclusive man for whom her Aunt Poppy was housekeeper and for whom Aunt Poppy has been caring ever since. He was rejected by his father, who has shunned people since his daughter, his favorite child, was drowned, but Kate, plus a near accident, finally reconciles the father and son.

MAGERE (*Black Samson**), legendary Joluo war leader who is thought to be impervious to weapons. Uncle of the protagonist Opio*, Magere is a youngest son and has not distinguished himself in any way when Opio brings him word of a Nandi raiding party hiding nearby on their way home with stolen cattle. His ability to rouse a reluctant band to attack and the success of this venture start him on a career as leader not only of his clan but of the whole Joluo people, now revived from peace-loving victims to aggressive warriors. Magere leads through natural ability and will power, but he is defeated through his own susceptibility to flattery when he marries the beautiful Nandi woman, Tapkesos*, who has been said to have refused all men but him. To her he tells his secret, that he can be harmed not through his body but by attack on his shadow. Called Magere the Stone because of his apparent invulnerability, he is changed into a strange black stone after his death.

MAGGIE HOLBEIN (*The Robbers**), Margaret, step-mother of Philip*. An American from Virginia, she is considerably younger than Philip's father and, having had three younger brothers, much more atune to Philip's feelings. He guesses rightly that it is she who wants to have him live with them, not his father, and he loves her even though she misinterprets some of what he says and does. Although she appears to be in love with her husband, she is aware of his weaknesses and faults. Philip has ached to ask her whether she is a Red Indian, though he is afraid it would be impolite, and he is delighted when she volunteers that she is one-quarter Cherokee.

THE MAGICIAN'S NEPHEW (Lewis*, C. S., ill. Pauline Baynes, Lane, 1955; Macmillan, 1955), fantasy novel of magic and ventures into other worlds. It draws upon characters and motifs from Norse, ancient Greek, and Christian beliefs. It is the first chronologically of seven novels set in Narnia*, the one in which Aslan*, the mighty lion, creates the enchanted realm. The novel starts in late nineteenth-century London, where a wet, cold summer drives young Polly* Plummer and her next-door neighbor, Digory* Kirke, to explore the attic that connects the row houses in which they live. They enter a little door in a brick wall and stumble onto Digory's disagreeable Uncle* Andrew Ketterley's secret workroom. Uncle Andrew has been conducting scientific experiments of a devious nature with guinea pigs and green and yellow rings, with the yellow ones used presumably to enter another world and the green to return to London, if all goes well. He tricks the children into touching the rings, and they find themselves emerging from a pool of water into a silent, attractive, green woods, which they soon discover is an intermediary world between their own and others, all reached by use of the rings and slipping into different pools. The second pool they use lands them in the ancient, dying world of Charn, a wasteland with a dull, reddish atmosphere, deserted, flat pavements, and large, still buildings, in one of which they discover hundreds of perfectly still, waxwork-like people and a square pillar supporting a little, golden bell. When Digory strikes the bell, over Polly's strong objections, he animates one of the figures, the coldly beautiful, evil Queen* Jadis, a Witch. When they attempt to get away from her by using their rings, she grabs Polly's hair and lands with them all, first, in the Wood between the Worlds, which she hates, and then in London. Uncle Andrew becomes enamored of the Witch, whose arrogance and boldness he admires. She demands service, means to conquer the world, and rampages through London. She helps herself to a jeweler's choice gems and arrives back at Uncle Andrew's, riding atop the roof of a hansom cab she has commandeered from its Cabby* and trailed by a crowd of angry and complaining citizens, in one of the book's most lively and

humorous scenes. To keep the Witch from causing
more trouble, Polly and Digory use their rings
to return her to her own dimension, and in the
process take along Uncle Andrew, the Cabby, and
his horse, Strawberry. When Strawberry drinks of
a pool in the Wood between the Worlds, all are
drawn into still another dimension, a pre-world
where they encounter Aslan, a nobly-speaking
lion, who brings Narnia into being by singing,
first, physical features, and then mythical
figures like dwarfs and animals. The process is
described in a long, lyrical passage vivid with
imagery. Since he holds Digory most responsible
for bringing evil into Narnia, Aslan sends him
on a quest for the seed to grow a tree to
protect Narnia. Polly chooses to accompany her
friend, and both mount Strawberry, whom Aslan
has given wings and youth and has renamed
Fledge, and fly to the land bordering Narnia,
where they find a tree of silver apples. They
discover that the Witch has followed them, but
resist her urgings to secure everlasting youth
by eating the apples. They return to Aslan with
an apple. He tells Digory to plant it, and it
soon grows into a towering monarch, which
renders the area invulnerable to the Witch, who
must remain in the other land. The Cabby and his
wife, who is also brought to Narnia, are crowned
the first rulers of Narnia, King Frank and Queen
Helen. The children and Uncle Andrew return to
London, Digory with an apple from the new Tree
of Life, which cures his ill mother. He buries
the core in the garden, and years later uses the
wood of the tree it grows into to build the
wardrobe through which the Pevensie children
enter Narnia. The book's adventures and action
grow naturally out of character, and, as in the
other six books, the generous use of humor
relieves the underlying, serious, Christian
message. The book's central scene--the creation
of Narnia--is a masterful reworking of Genesis
1, imitative yet unique, and one of the most
famous passages in children's literature.
Hilarity prevails in another unforgettable
episode, the one in which the Narnian animals
try to find out what sort of creature Uncle
Andrew is and plant him in the mistaken notion
he is a kind of tree. The tone is light, and, as
in the other books, the style is informal and

conversational. The author often intrudes as a congenial, avuncular commentator on events, the characters' motives and actions, and human nature in general. ChLA Touchstones; Choice, Fanfare.

MAGORIAN, MICHELLE, born in Portsmouth, England; actress, dancer and writer. She grew up in Perth, Australia, and Singapore, and has worked in numerous touring and repertory companies. She spent two years training as a mime at Marcel Marceau's world-renowned *L'Ecole Internationale de Mime* in Paris. Her first book, *Good Night, Mr. Tom** (Kestrel, 1981; Harper, 1981), which grew out of a short story about the meeting of the two main characters, is about an abused child evacuated to an English village during World War II. It won the Guardian Award, the International Reading Association Award, and was named to the Carnegie Commended list, the *Horn Book* Fanfare list, and the list of Junior High Contemporary Classics. Her second novel, *Back Home* (Viking, 1984; Harper, 1984), is about the difficulties of readjusting for a girl who returns to England after spending World War II in the United States. She has also written poetry and a television play.

MAGWITCH, ABEL (*Great Expectations**), convict whom Pip* helps on the marsh and who becomes his secret benefactor. A violent, brutal man, he terrifies Pip as a child and horrifies him when Pip is a man, yet Pip feels responsible for him and gradually becomes so fond of him that he grieves when the condemned man dies. His story of his past reveals that he has been badly used by society and by men cleverer than he, and through what he says and various other clues Pip determines that he is Estella's* father. His motives for bestowing his fortune (which he has somehow made in New South Wales) on Pip are never quite clear, but besides gratitude for the food and the file that the boy gets for him, he seems to feel that he can get back at the world by making a gentleman of a village boy.

MAHBUB ALI (*Kim**), red-bearded Pathan from Afghanistan, horse dealer who is really agent C.25.1B of the Indian Secret Service. Mahbub

has used Kim* O'Hara as a spy and courier since
the boy was a little child in Lahore,
recognizing his natural talent and zest for such
work, and is responsible for his coming to the
attention of Colonel Creighton, the head of the
service. On the night when the boy and the lama
sleep among the horse-dealer's men under the
arched cloisters near the railway station, Kim
sees a man making a minute search among Mahbub's
personal belongings and, realizing that the
white stallion's pedigree, which Mahbub has
already given him to deliver, may be the object
of the search, quietly rouses the lama and gets
away. Later, in another place, he saves Mahbub
by warning him that the same man waits to shoot
him when he returns to his camp in the night.
Mahbub is impatient with Creighton's worry that
Kim may be too young to work in espionage
operations and leads the boy into great danger
with no qualms, but he is genuinely fond of Kim
and a little jealous of Kim's love for the lama.

MAHY, MARGARET (1936-   ), born in New Zealand;
librarian and provocative, prolific writer of
fiction for children and adolescents. She was
born in the country town of Whakatane, the
eldest of the five children of a building con-
tractor and a teacher. She was educated at the
University of Auckland and received her diploma
of librarianship in 1958. After working as an
assistant librarian, she became director of
School Library Services in Christchurch, New
Zealand, until 1976, when she became children's
librarian at Canterbury Public Library. She has
two daughters and lives near Christchurch in a
house she designed herself overlooking Governor's Bay. She is currently a full-time writer,
doing scripts for television and films as well
as stories and novels for the young. She came of
a family in which reading books and story-
making were important activities. Her father was
an accomplished storyteller, and both parents
read to the children from both children's and
adult works. One of the stories her father made
up about a lion lingered in her memory and
eventually formed the basis for her first
published book, the picture storybook *A Lion in
the Meadow* (Dent, 1969; Watts, 1969). She wrote
stories from the time she was seven and

published poems in a local paper at an early
age. The first stories she published appeared
in *School Journal*, a magazine produced by the
School Publications Branch of the Department of
Education. A New York editor saw *A Lion in the
Meadow* there and recommended that it be published as a book; and thus Mahy's book-
publishing career was launched. In rapid order,
the Watts company put out several of her
stories in picture book form. Tales of humor and
fantastical happenings, these also include *The
Dragon of an Ordinary Family* (Heinemann, 1969;
Watts, 1969), *Mrs. Discombobulous* (Watts, 1969;
Dent, 1969), and *Pillycock's Shop* (Watts, 1969;
Dobson, 1969). Some three dozen books have
followed, with picture books illustrated by such
prominent artists as Quentin Blake and Shirley
Hughes, some books of short stories, some longer
stories for early readers to read to themselves, and, more recently, novels of fantasy
and the supernatural for teenagers. All show a
lively imagination, the courage to be different, a liking for the bizarre in character and
incident, and a healthy command of language.
Two novels received the Carnegie Medal: *The
Haunting** (Dent, 1982; Atheneum, 1982), a
lively and humorous story for middle-grade
readers, in which a shy eight-year-old receives
frightening mind messages and learns he may have
inherited a disturbing family trait; and, for
teens, *The Changeover: A Supernatural Romance** (Dent, 1984; Atheneum, 1984), which also
appears on the Fanfare and *Boston Globe-Horn
Book* Honor lists. It is a vibrant, suspenseful,
and surprising account of a girl who uses her
latent supernatural power to save her younger
brother, Jocko, from demon possession. Mahy's
recent publications include three more novels:
The Catalogue of the Universe (Dent, 1985; Atheneum, 1986), a tightly knit, realistic story
which revolves around a girl's search for her
father; *Aliens in the Family* (Methuen, 1986;
Scholastic, 1985), a science fiction story of
how a girl helps her stepsiblings give refuge
to an alien from another dimension; and *The
Tricksters* (Dent, 1986; Atheneum, 1986), a
powerful story of a New Zealand family on
holiday invaded by three fascinating but
sinister young men with unusual powers; a book

of short stories, *The Horrible Story and Others* (Dent, 1987); and a series of picture books of fantasy and nonsense mostly about animals and put out by Children's Press International. Considered New Zealand's leading writer for the young and one of the most interesting and inventive of those writing for a young audience today, she twice received the Esther Glen Award of the New Zealand Library Association, for *A Lion in the Meadow* and for *The First Margaret Mahy Story Book: Stories and Poems* (Dent, 1972).

MALCOLM III (*The Queen's Blessing**), historical king of Scotland in the late eleventh century. Committed to restoring a Saxon king to the throne taken by William of Normandy, he is betrayed by a Northumbrian earl and in revenge lays waste the area, burning and killing and selling the survivors as slaves. He marries the sister of the Saxon pretender; she is Princess Margaret*, a beautiful, gentle girl devoted to feeding the poor and making the rough war camp of a court into a place of culture and beauty. Malcolm is a very large man with red hair and beard, a strong war leader gentled by his wife.

MALL PERCIVAL (*A Parcel of Patterns**), narrator, sixteen in the plague year of 1665, who loses her parents, her love, and most of her friends and neighbors to the terrible illness that strikes her village of Eyam. An intelligent girl, Mall has been taught to read by her father so she can handle the contracts he manages for the lead mines, and she writes the story as both a record and a charm, ·to rid herself of the terrible memories. She has raised a small flock of sheep and spends much of her time in the fresh air tending them, a fact which may help account for her escaping the disease. When it is clear that the illness is the plague, she sends word to lover, Thomas* Torre, that she is dead in a vain effort to keep him away from Eyam. He comes anyway, and after their brief but happy marriage, dies one of the last victims as the plague peters out.

MAM (*The Third Eye**), Jean Morrison, mother of Meg*, Linda*, and Jinty, and along with the Earl of Ballinford, the most interesting figure in

the novel. Trained as a confectioner, she fell
in love with Roger Belaney, a distant relative
of the earl, in World War I, nursing him in a
hospital and becoming his lover. When he was
killed in the war, his family turned their backs
on her. She married Dad, who has always treated
Meg as his own and who was given a job by the
earl. Mam seems to be the dominant figure in her
marriage, but Dad is sensible and cool-headed
and gets his way in important matters, though he
leaves handling Meg pretty much up to Mam. She
is very concerned that her girls grow up with
good names, very conscious of appearances,
determined that there never be any gossip about
her family, and ambitious for her girls to get
good educations and good jobs, Meg as a teacher
and Linda as an accountant, positions ironically neither desires. Mam is so driven by her
hopes for them that she refuses to listen to
them and thus loses them both. At the end, she
seems to realize what she has done and visits
Meg to see Meg's baby. The most interesting and
attractive scenes involving her are those in
which she and Jinty talk when they are both
working at Ballinford Hall; these passages
reveal her warmth and vulnerability.

MAMA (*The Other Way Round**; *When Hitler Stole
Pink Rabbit**), mother of Anna* and Max*, a
pianist used to money and servants in their
Berlin home, who must cope when the family
property is confiscated by the Nazis and they
move from country to country as refugees. Highly
emotional, she contrasts with her calm,
intellectual husband, and although lacking in
any practical training, she puts her entire and
considerable energy into learning new languages
and skills. In England, where her husband
remains an outsider, she manages to get a job,
to persuade friends to arrange scholarships for
the children to private schools, and to keep the
family running on a very inadequate income. When
Max is interned as an enemy alien, she works
tirelessly to get him freed, finally writing to
a newspaperman and politician who has reviewed a
book on Jews in Germany and by this odd
connection breaks through the red tape and gets
her son released.

MANTE (*Comfort Herself**), Comfort Kwatey-Jones's father, a member of the Ga tribe in Ghana, with whom Comfort lives while in Accra, and whom her dead mother, Margaret, called a "Prince in Ghana." He was educated in white schools (though he seems uninterested in advancing Comfort's education), works as a civil servant by day and a taxi driver by night, and is writing a novel in what little spare time he has. He is good-looking and well dressed and has a resonant voice and a pleasant disposition. He teaches Comfort to speak Ga well enough so that she can function in the village of Wanwangeri when she goes to live with his mother, Grandmother*. He intimates that he needs to hold two jobs because it takes a lot of money to support his sisters' many children, yet Grandmother implies that he has been derelict in his duty to his family. He is very proud of his new wife, Efua, who was a beauty queen, and strives to please her with modern conveniences and servants. His servant, Winnie, a young mother not much older than Comfort, becomes Comfort's friend and the Accran counterpart of Lettie* Stamp and Ama. Though underdeveloped as a character, Mante gives the impression of being a weak and shallow man.

MANTLEMASS (*The Lark and the Laurel**; *The Iron Lily**), large estate received by Dame* Elizabeth FitzEdmund as a freehold from the English Crown and transmitted to her heirs. It lies in Ashdown Forest in the Sussex countryside south of London and some twenty miles from the seacoast. It is the central feature in the set of stories known as the Mantlemass or Forest novels which follow the varying fortunes of the Mallory and Medley families, farmers, horse-breeders, and iron foundrymen who intermarry and occupy it. The novels begin with the death of Richard III Plantagenet, from whom the Medleys are illegitimately descended, continue through the reigns of Henry VIII and Elizabeth I and the wars with Spain, and end during the Cromwellian conflict in the mid-seventeenth century. As the years pass and the iron industry grows, the forest diminishes, and the area becomes more open, leaving the house and its inhabitants more vulnerable to outside influence. In the last novel, *Harrow and Harvest*, political intrigue results in the manor house being burned and part of the family emigrating to the New World.

THE MAPLIN BIRD (Peyton*, K. M., ill. Victor Ambrus, Oxford, 1964; World, 1965), romantic period novel set in the late 1850s on the Sussex coast. The orphans, Toby* (Tobias), 16, and Emily* Garland, 15, are treated as slaveys by their uncle, Gideon Boat, but they endure it until he proposes to take their father's smack, *My Alice*, which has been idle since his death, fit it out, and put his bullying son, Mark, in charge of it, with Toby as Mark's helper. Together, the young Garlands sneak out of the house, with difficulty get the smack from the mud where it has been stuck, and sail it from Bradwell to Southend. There Toby falls in with a local fisherman, Dick Harvey, 17, who is good-natured though from a brutish family, and starts to fish with him. He intends eventually to rent a cottage for himself and Emily, but first he must put all his earnings into *My Alice*. Emily's attempts to get a job are fruitless, and she must wait on the shore while *My Alice* is out fishing and then spend the night in the cramped cuddy, until one evening they respond to the distress signal of a ketch and with great effort save several survivors, including a little girl whom Emily manages to pull from the water. At the dock an imperious lady takes both the girls into her carriage and to her fine house, where they are given dry clothes, food, and beds for the night. The next day, the lady, Mrs. Seymour, offers Emily a job as housemaid. There she has, at least, security but almost no freedom; the housekeeper, Mrs. Briggs, is severe and demanding; Selina* Seymour, the grown daughter, is bored and temperamental; and Adam* Seymour is a dashing young man of many sudden arrivals and departures. When the customs men call one night asking for him, Emily realizes that he is the smuggler sailing the *Maplin Bird*, a yacht of local fame, and she also knows, though she hates to admit it, that he was the looter who first boarded the wrecked ketch and refused help to the stranded passengers. Nonetheless, she cannot help being attracted to him, especially because he talks to her as an equal and not as a housemaid, and she shields him more than once. Without telling her, he has approached Toby and arranged that the boy will steal the *Maplin Bird* (which has been seized by the customs men) and sail it to a rendezvous with some of his men. Toby gets the yacht away safely, but the revenue cutter fires on him, wrecks the *Maplin Bird*, and breaks Toby's leg. Adam is suspected and the house is searched, but he hides on the roof, then gets away. Once Mrs. Seymour understands Adam's part in the affair, she insists that Emily bring Toby from the Harvey's filthy hovel to her house and that Selina, who has begged fruitlessly to be allowed to study nursing, take care of him. He nearly dies of gangrene but, largely because Selina proves to be an excellent nurse, he survives. Just as Toby is nearly recovered, Adam reappears and proposes that Toby secretly take him to France in *My Alice*. Knowing that Toby is still too weak to sail back alone, Emily insists on going along. They hit rough weather and, though within sight of lights on the French coast, must put back to Ramsgate. Chased by the customs men, they ground the smack, and Adam goes overboard before they are caught, but Toby is arrested. Emily is aided by local fishermen, all enemies of the revenue people, and when Adam is caught, Toby is allowed to go free. Emily and Toby return to Southend and call on Mrs. Seymour to explain what has happened. The old woman, knowing her son is the cause of their difficulties, takes Emily back into her service, but, since she is allowing Selina to go to college, she will not need Emily for a full-time housemaid and proposes that she allow Emily and Toby to live in a cottage she owns and that Emily work only part-time helping Mrs. Briggs. Despite her pain for Adam and her love for him which she is gradually getting over, Emily is happy to have a chance at both security and freedom. Most of the story is seen through Emily's point of view and her emotions, which are more the focus of attention than the tale of smuggling and escape. Without sentimentality, Emily's desire for freedom and her gradually developing love for Adam are made believable and interesting. Scenes of sailing, particularly

the stormy attempt to reach France, are vivid,
and the picture of life for a working class girl
of the period is convincing. Fanfare.

MARASSA AND MIDNIGHT (Stuart*, Morna, ill. Alvin
Smith, Heinemann, 1966; McGraw, 1967), historical novel set in Paris and Haiti (San Domingo)
during the revolution of 1791-1792. Black twin
brothers, slaves, are separated from each other
when the older and quieter boy, Marassa, is sold
to a French marquis and taken to Paris as a page
boy, and the younger boy, the fierce Midnight,
remains behind in Haiti on his native coffee
plantation. About two and a half years elapse
and both are involved in revolutionary activities in Haiti before they are reunited. The
story opens in Paris thirteen months after their
separation, where Marassa, 11, is abandoned by
his master, who flees to England to escape the
mob. Assaulted by ruffians in the street and
left for dead, the boy is found and nursed to
health by a red-haired, Scottish, ex-patriot
army captain and fencing master, whom Marassa
calls Tir* nan Og, after the name of the
captain's lost estate in Scotland. The captain
decides to emigrate to Haiti and takes the boy
with him. After the sale of his brother, Midnight runs away to seek him, is caught and
branded on the left shoulder, becomes withdrawn
and despondent, and is shunned and ill-treated
by the other slaves because his running away has
caused the Beke, or master, to become harsh and
restrictive with them and bring in bloodhounds
to guard them. One Saturday night, during
bamboche, the regular slave dancing time, the
boy, isolated as usual under his mango tree, is
visited by little, old Papa* Doctor, who tends
his festering wound and enlists his aid in a
revolutionary enterprise with passwords and
messages the boy doesn't understand but feels is
a link to his lost brother in Paris, where he
has heard revolution is also breeding. When he
overhears talk that the Great One is coming on
the Night of the Drums, he thinks the reference
is to Ogoun, the blacks' local god, and runs off
to join him, taking with him the master's twin
bloodhounds, which he has made his pets and
named Dove and Diamond, after the twin mountains
that overhang the plantation. Then he discovers

the Great One is really the revolutionary leader of the renegade Maroons, runaway slaves who hide out in the hills and jungle, and realizes that the Great One's activities are antithetical to those of Papa Doctor, that the Great One hates anyone who doesn't hate the whites and wishes only to kill. Midnight lives in a cave on King's Mountain, the highest peak of the region, for many months, in a kind of dream-like existence with the dogs as his only companions and his only contact with other humans the peaceful, agricultural Maroons who live on the other side of the mountain and who think he is the god. Coincidentally, Marassa arrives in Haiti on the night Midnight runs away to the hills, is caught by Midnight's master, who thinks he is Midnight, and is rescued by Tir nan Og, who shows that the boy has no brand on his back and who demands in compensation for the kidnap of Marassa the right to buy Midnight from the master. Marassa is taken to the estate of Papa Doctor's Beke, whose slaves are such in name only, and turns sullen and angry, ironically like his twin. During a great storm, he brands himself in an attempt to match his lost brother. Later, Tir nan Og, Marassa, and the overseer of Papa Doctor's Beke go seeking Midnight but fail to find him. Midnight sees them in the distance on one occasion but doesn't recognize his brother. The Maroons rise and burn, among others, Midnight's Beke's place, and murder the whites, and Midnight realizes that the evil Papa Doctor had hoped to avert is occurring. Marassa and Tir nan Og hide in the hills, sent there by Papa Doctor so they will be safe and can also spy for him on the renegade Maroons. In the twenty-sixth month of the twins' separation, the Great One attacks the peaceful Maroon village, is confronted by Midnight, whom he takes for the Ogoun, and flees, ironically in the direction of Marassa, who in the same spirit as Midnight also rises up to confront the revolutionary. The Great One and his men are so confused that in the morning the Beke army cuts them to bits. Papa Doctor, who now also leads an army in the hills, marshals his forces to bring the rule of reason to the insurgency. In the thirtieth month, Midnight's hounds scent Marassa, and, confused, lead him to Midnight, and the twins are finally reunited.

The narrative, mostly summarized and unadorned, moves rapidly, alternating points of view between the two boys, and the dramatized scenes have power. The book seems curiously disjointed, not explicit enough and not big enough for the events it tries to include and more like scenario than proper novel. The Haitian revolutionary message system is befuddling, and one must pay close attention to figure out what is going on politically. Partly this is the effect of standing at the side of the protagonists and looking at things from their uninformed and naive perspectives, and partly it is the result of the author's terseness. Characters seem either all good or all bad, and the boys' Bekes are described stereotypically as having cruel faces and cold eyes and as being greedy and unfeeling. Though the reader learns about Papa Doctor as the boys do, the old man remains too enigmatic to be fully credible, and there is an "Uncle Tom-ism" about him that dates the book. Tir nan Og exists as the wronged heroic adventurer of brave heart and good soul. There is much emphasis on the power of fate, that what will be will be. The boys' intense yearning for each other, the ironic way they grow closer together in personality, and the sense of the physical appearance of the island are the book's strongest qualities. Carnegie Com.

MARCH HARE (*Alice's Adventures in Wonderland**; *Through the Looking-Glass**), zany character at whose house Alice* participates in a never-ending tea-party along with the Mad* Hatter and the Dormouse*. He admits to trying to repair the Hatter's watch with butter, which clogs the works, and complains about the expressions Alice uses. A caricature like most of the other characters, he is one of the book's most memorable figures and one of the most famous in literature. He appears in the second book as Haigha, one of the White King's two oddly behaved messengers, the other being Hatta. The King explains Haigha's strange posturings to Alice as Anglo-Saxon attitudes, an obviously satirical comment.

MARCUS AQUILA (*The Eagle of the Ninth**), young Cohort Centurion of Gaulish Auxiliaries with the

Second Roman Legion, who is wounded in his
first command and undertakes a secret mission to
find what happened to the last Ninth Legion, of
which his father was second in command. Marcus
has always dreamed of joining the legions, and
after the death of both his parents and a period
of living with an aunt and her Roman official
husband, whom he despised, he applied to the
legions as soon as he was of age. When his wound
makes him leave the legions he is devastated and
can think of no way to continue his life except
as some under secretary to an official in
Britain. Although Roman in appearance, training,
and temperament, and for a while very homesick
for his native Etruscan hills, he has felt a
kinship with the Britons from the first and
never lets the background make a difference
between him and Esca* or Cottia*. As his Uncle
Aquila did before him, he chooses to take up his
grant of land in Britain rather than return to
Rome, having come to feel more at home in the
north than in the country where he was born.

MARGARET BRADLEY (*The Owl Service**), Allison's*
mother, new stepmother of Roger* and new wife of
Clive*. She never appears in the story but
strongly influences the action. She seems
determined to break up the growing friendship
between Allison and Gwyn*, the Welsh youth whose
mother, Nancy*, is the housekeeper. Since
Allison loves Margaret and wants to please her,
she goes along with her wishes. Clive also
strives to please her. His efforts arouse the
ire of Nancy, who looks down on him as unworthy
of his new position as gentleman of the house.
Margaret and Nancy are both controlling parents, whose possessiveness and over direction
cause trouble; they are obvious foils.

MARGARET, QUEEN OF SCOTIA (*The Queen's Blessing**), historical Saxon princess, sister of
Aedgar Aetheling, who married Malcolm* III of
Scotland after his unsuccessful attempt to
restore Aedgar to the British throne taken by
William of Normandy. A beautiful and charming
woman, Margaret changed the rather crude court
of Scotland into a place of beauty and culture,
and she was so gentle and holy that she was made
a saint after her death. In the book, she adopts

Merca* and Dag* because one of her pauper foster children has died the same morning Merca and Dag are found collapsed and starving in the road.

MARGARET THURSDAY (*Thursday's Child**), foundling left on the church steps as an infant, raised in the home of local maiden ladies, and sent to St. Luke's orphanage when she is ten. A child given to self-dramatization, she is very fond of telling everyone that in the basket with her were three of everything, of the very best quality. Gradually she expands the story until the infant clothes have all been embroidered with coronets, and the 52 pounds left in the church each year for her keep has increased to 100. Her strong sense of self-worth stands her in good stead at St. Luke's, where she refuses to be cowed by the cruel Matron. In all the adventures with Peter* and Horatio* Beresford she is the leader, and she is often exasperated with Peter for being "soppy" and unimaginative. She promises Lavinia* Beresford that she will look out for the two boys, and she takes her responsibility so seriously that she puts off her own escape until she thinks it is necessary to get Peter away from possible arrest. In the end, she gives up the responsibility with some relief and is ready to throw all her energy into acting.

MARIA HENNIKER-HADDEN (*The Warden's Niece**), proper little Victorian girl who runs away from boarding school to her Uncle* Hadden, who is Warden of Canterbury College at Oxford, and then devotes her energies in proving she is a promising scholar so he will not send her back to school. When Professor Smith, father of the boys with whom she has lessons, advises her facetiously that she had better be clever since she doesn't seem to be good, she takes him seriously and tries very hard to do some original research that will impress her uncle. Her efforts get her into numerous scrapes, which she finds very embarrassing, but to the astonishment of her uncle she does come up with a genuine historical find concerning Stephen Fitzackerley of the seventeenth century. Maria suffers greatly from shyness and from fearing that she will be scolded or laughed at, but she shows considerable courage in her quest for knowledge.

MARIA OLDKNOW (*The Chimneys of Green Knowe**), wife of a sea captain and mother of blind Susan*. A frivolous, self-centered woman, she has no interest in her daughter and is closer to her spoiled, arrogant son, Sefton*, than she is to her husband. After her jewels have been stolen, she consults a gypsy fortune teller to find out how to get them back and labors for two years to embroider the picture of the house using as thread human hair from all the people who were present and saying with each stitch, "Great Moloch, Lord of Fire, put a pearl on this point," just as the gypsy has told her to, but the jewels are not found in her lifetime.

MARJORY BELL (*No End to Yesterday**), motherless child who is raised by her grandmother in a household of grown aunts and uncles and their spouses and offspring, all dominated by Gran* Bell. Vulnerable and intelligent, Marjory is aware of Gran's dislike, and she realizes that it has somethng to do with her mother, whom she assumes is dead, but she has never dared to ask about her. Because she has learned to protect herself by hiding her feelings, Marjory is considered by her relatives to be hard and ungrateful, and she is compared continually with her goody-goody cousin Susie, four years her senior. Despite the constant harping and criticism, however, Marjory refuses to let her spirit be crushed, swallowing her many disappointments and setbacks and determinedly making a life for herself apart from her family. Their lasting influence, however, we see in glimpses of her as a matter-of-fact, no-nonsense mother of her own children, who is not unfeeling but is unable to show her emotions easily.

MARK, JAN(ET MARJORIE) (1943-   ), born in Welwyn, Hertfordshire; writer of short stories and novels for children and adolescents. She grew up in Kent, where she attended Ashford Grammar School. She is a graduate of Canterbury College of Art and received a diploma in design in 1965. She taught art and English at

Southfields School, Gravesend, Kent, from 1965-1971, and after that became a full-time writer and writer-in-residence at Oxford Poly-technic. She married Neil Mark, a computer operator, and has a son and a daughter. Her first published novel won the Carnegie Medal, *Thunder and Lightnings** (Kestrel, 1976; Crow-ell, 1979). A story of a schoolboy friendship for later elementary and preadolescent readers, it is rich in human relations and gentle humor. Seven years later she won the Carnegie again for *Handles** (Kestrel, 1983; Atheneum, 1985), a novel for young adolescents about a girl infatuated with motorcycles. Mark has written the texts for picture books, like *Fur* (Walker, 1986; Lippincott, 1986) and *Out of the Oven* (Kestrel, 1986), and books of short stories like *Feet and Other Stories* (Kestrel, 1983). In addition, she has published the novels *Under the Autumn Garden* (Kestrel, 1977; Crowell, 1979), another boy's story for middle grades; *The Ennead* (Kestrel, 1978; Crowell, 1978), a science fiction story for teens, in which colonists from a dying Earth find a new solar system and repeat their same destructive behavior; *Aquarius** (Kestrel, 1982; Atheneum, 1984), a provocative story about a water diviner caught up in the schemes surrounding an unfortunate king, which won the Young Observer Teenage Fiction Prize; and *Trouble Half-Way* (Kestrel, 1985; Atheneum, 1986), about a girl's developing relationship with her new stepfather as they drive through England. Mark's novels tackle such weighty themes as the nature of friendship, social obligations, the necessity to confront issues, and self-assertion, and she has great skill with dialogue, characterization, and depicting interpersonal relationships.

THE MARK OF THE HORSE LORD (Sutcliff*, Rosemary, ill. Charles Keeping, Oxford, 1965; Walck, 1965), historical novel set during the Roman domination of Britain, mostly in what is now western Scotland. Using the device of the look-alike, it traces the change in an ex-gladiator recruited to act as pretender to the kingship of one of the rival northern tribes and his growth in understanding and character until he is worthy of the role he has usurped. Red

Phaedrus*, born a slave son of a Greek merchant
and his native British housekeeper, has been
sold ·to the school for gladiators, has served
for several years, and has won his wooden foil,
symbol of his freedom, in an exhibition fight to
the death against his one friend among the
performers. After one day of freedom, seized
with panic at his new state, he gets drunk and
into a street brawl and lands in jail. From
there he is taken past bribed guards by Sinnoch,
a horse merchant who trades with the northern
tribes, to a secret meeting with Gault the
Strong, one of the Kindred, the Royal Clan of
the Dalriadain, a northern tribe that worships a
male sun god. He also meets Midir*, the rightful
Dalriadain king, a young man with red hair and
an appearance very like that his own except that
he has been blinded and his forehead horribly
scarred to obliterate the Mark of the Horse Lord
tattooed on his brow. The conspirators propose
to substitute Phaedrus for the maimed Midir to
rouse the Dalriadains against the Caledones, the
worshipers of an Earth Mother goddess who have
dominated them, and against their goddess-queen,
Liadhan, the Royal Woman, Midir's father's half
sister, who had him blinded and now rules the
tribe in the old ways, in which she chooses a
consort-king who dies and is replaced every
seven years. Midir, knowing he would never be
accepted in his maimed condition and wanting
revenge, coaches Phaedrus for weeks on every
aspect of the Dalriadains. Then Phaedrus travels
north with Sinnoch and meets a few of the
Kindred who are in on the plot. They agree that
Phaedrus will pass as Midir, who has been away
from the tribe for seven years, but the real
test is to be Conory*, a cousin of Midir who was
his friend and constant companion and who has
been chosen by Liadhan to be the next king.
Conory seems to accept Phaedrus for Midir, and
it is not until later that he admits he knew all
the time but chose not to raise the question for
the sake of the uprising. They plan to strike at
the king-making, when Conory is to fight and
kill Logiore, the present king, and take his
place beside Liadhan. Through a small chance,
the timing is not quite right, and Liadhan
escapes to the Caledones with the help of her
daughter, Murna*, who distracts the attackers by

wearing the Queen's headdress. Phaedrus is made
king of the Dalriadains in the old ceremony and
almost immediately must take Murna for a wife to
forestall any dissatisfaction among those who
question the displacement of the Earth Mother,
since Murna is the Royal Daughter and destined
to be the queen-goddess after her mother. In the
pattern of the ancient bridal ceremonies, the
woman is given a head start on a horse and the
man must ride her down and capture her, a ritual
that has become simply form in most marriages
but proves to be a real hunt by Phaedrus for
Murna, who first tries to escape over the pass
to the Caledones and, cut off from that route,
rides for the bog that will suck her and her
horse to death. When Phaedrus finally reaches
her and pulls her from her horse, she responds
to his kiss while reaching for his dagger to
knife him, but, defeated, then withdraws into a
cold, distant formality that he cannot
penetrate. Most of his attention, however, is
involved in preparing for the attack of the
Caledones, who far outnumber the Dalriadains and
who have been roused by Liadhan to try to wipe
out their old enemies. When the main attack
finally does come, Phaedrus is wounded with a
slash down one side of his face and tended by
Murna, who has come out with her women to fight
alongside the men, and they at last reach an
understanding and a real love. All summer she
fights with the war host, until Phaedrus finds
her sick in the morning, and she has to admit
that she is pregnant and submit to being sent
back to the dun. At the end of the summer, the
Caledones are poised in a stronghold of a pass
to sweep down and annihilate the much weakened
Dalriadains. Phaedrus and several of the others
scout the position and realize that there is
only one weapon to defeat their enemy, fire. In
the tinder-dry hills it is terribly risky, since
it can turn on them, but they take the chance,
light the brush, and in a terrible bloodletting
defeat the Caledones, but Liadhan again escapes,
this time turning unexpectedly to the Romans in
the old naval station of Theodosia. When
Phaedrus comes with the green branch of truce
and demands her back, the commander refuses.
That night, Midir, who has made his way north as
a leather worker, comes secretly to their camp

and tells Phaedrus his plan to kill Liadhan as
the Romans are taking her down a steep stair on
the water side of the fort to send her across
the firth into Valentia. If a skilled dirk-
thrower could work his way into the old sheds
along the shore, he would have one chance to
throw before she reached the boat, and Midir,
jumping up and running then, would cause a
diversion during which the thrower could get
away. Because of his training in the arena,
Phaedrus is the best dirk-thrower, and he takes
on the task himself, worming his way through the
alleys of the native huts around the fort and
finally reaching the shed where he will wait for
Liadhan and her escort, but their plan has been
overheard by one of Liadhan's priests who
followed Midir, and Phaedrus is captured by the
Romans. As he is being dragged away, Liadhan
comes to the head of the rampart stair to gloat
at his capture, and Midir, who has escaped from
an earlier imprisonment, rushes up before the
guards realize what is happening, clasps his
arms around her, and leaps to their joint death
on the rocks below. The commander, defeated in
the case of Liadhan, offers Phaedrus his life in
exchange for 1,000 young Dalriadain men to serve
in the Auxiliaries. Phaedrus demands the chance
to talk with his own men first, and he is given
the opportunity to stand on the rampart above
the Praetorian Gate where he can speak to his
men gathered below. As he tells them of the
offer, he detaches his brooch from the shoulder
of his cloak, drives the two-inch pin into the
place just to the left of his breast bone, which
he knows from the arena is fatal, and dives to
his death as the king is meant to die for his
tribe in the time of their need. The novel is
rich in depths of meaning and memorable
scenes--the king-making, the royal hunt for the
bride, and the death of Midir and Liadhan amid
the rain and the lightning flashes on the
rampart stair, among many others. Phaedrus
changes convincingly from the flashy, shallow
gladiator to the king with his responsibility to
his people outweighing his own desire to live
and see his child. Secondary characters are also
well drawn, and the life among the British
tribes is believable and fascinating. Fanfare;
Phoenix.

MARK RUSSELL (*Flambards**; *The Edge of the Cloud**; *Flambards in Summer**), cousin of Christina* Parsons whom his father expects him to marry so that her money, which she will acquire when she is twenty-one, will restore the run-down Flambards. Mark is much like his father, violent tempered, insensitive, and obsessed with fox hunting. He rides recklessly and is infuriatingly self-centered, never giving a thought to Violet, whom he made pregnant and who hence has been dismissed from her job. Though he is often callous and casually cruel, he can also be charming, and when he finally meets his son, Tizzy*, he captivates the boy with his stories and indulgence. After he is engaged to Dorothy* Saunders, he tells Christina that he would rather marry her, but then rather spoils the sentiment by admitting it is because she rides so well. In a sequel to the original Flambards trilogy, *Flambards Divided*, he returns wounded to Flambards, a very difficult patient, and then settles with Dorothy at Dermots, where he is a constant source of irritation between Christina and her husband, Dick* Wright. Eventually both marriages break up, and Christina expects to marry Mark, who has been somewhat chastened by life's difficulties but still does not hold much promise of being an easy or thoughtful husband.

MARK VAUGHAN (*The Great Gale**), eleven-year-old son of the village doctor in Reedsmere, brother of Mary*, 13, whom he calls Mooney and of whom he is genuinely fond. He is still in the collecting stage and is a little rebellious and scatter-headed. He assumes much responsibility during the flood and is a brave and willing worker. While he and Jim* Foulger are attempting to rescue old Dotty Dick, Mark fails to moor *Donovan* properly, the boat drifts away, marooning the three on Dotty Dick's roof, and Jim falls ill of pneumonia brought on by exposure. Mark blames himself for Jim's illness. He finds carrying sandbags to repair the breach too taxing, as well as boring, and throws his considerable energies into cleaning and fixing up the Foulgers' cottage. He gets the idea of swapping stew for the sandbaggers' help in shoveling out the sand, a suggestion that

proves unnecessary when the men learn that the
Foulgers need their help. Mark is a typical
schoolboy, fun-loving, mischievous, and occasionally irresponsible, but events develop inner
resources not evident in him before.

MARRYAT, FREDERICK (1792-1848), born in Westminster, London, the son of a member of Parliament; naval officer and novelist for adults
and boys of sea adventure stories, which were
widely read during the 1800s. He was educated at
Ponders End, Middlesex, but disliked school and
tried to run away to sea several times. When he
was fourteen, his father allowed him to join the
Royal Navy. The ensuing long and highly distinguished naval career as officer and commander included service in the Western
Hemisphere, against Napoleon, and in the Far
East during the Burmese War. He was several
times decorated for valor and was made
Companion, Order of the Bath, in 1826. Four
years later he retired to devote himself to his
writing. His twenty-three years of very active
service provided the material for his more than
thirty books, the earliest all for adults. Then,
in 1841, encouraged by his own children to write
a book like *Swiss Family Robinson*, he wrote
Masterman Ready* (Longman, 1841; Appleton,
1842). It tells the exciting adventures of the
Seagrave family who, when shipwrecked on a desert island, survive through the help of a wise
old sailor named Ready. Though often instructive
of morals and information, the book is filled
with action, the flavor of the sea, and details
of everyday life under struggle-for-survival
conditions. An enjoyable Robinsonnade even
today, it is more convincing than many counterparts and is listed in *Choice*. For children,
Marryat also wrote *Narrative of the Travels and
Adventures of Monsieur Violet in California,
Sonora, and Western Texas* (Longman, 1843;
Harper, 1843); *The Mission, or, Scenes in Africa*
(Longman, 1845; Appleton, 1845); *The Children of
the New Forest* (Hurst, 1847; Harper, 1848); and
The Little Savage (Hurst, 1848; Harper, 1849),
which was completed after his death by his son,
Frank. In addition to novel writing, he unsuc-
cessfully sought a seat in Parliament, tried
farming in Norfolk, and edited *The Metropolitan*

Magazine (1832-1835), in which he serialized five of his own books. Among his many publications for adults are an autobiographical novel, *The Naval Officer, or, Scenes and Adventures in the Life of Frank Mildmay* (Colburn, 1829), and *Mr. Midshipman Easy* (Saunders, 1836). He had four sons and seven daughters, one of whom was the novelist Florence Marryat.

MARSHALL, COLIN (*The Dark Behind the Curtain**), youth who plays the part of Sweeney Todd in the play of the same name. Marshall is gradually revealed as a mean, malicious youth, charming when he wishes to be but curiously manipulative and aggressive. He and Colin Jackus* have been friends from boyhood because their mothers have been friends, but Marshall has always regarded himself as superior to Jackus and made sport of him. He seems appropriately cast as Sweeney and indeed enters into the part and becomes very convincing in the role. The reader learns at the end that he put Jackus up to stealing the tape recorders, relying on Jackus to remain loyal and not give away his part in the theft. In one memorable scene in the book, he plays with his pet ferret and seems amused when the creature bites Jackus. During the early part of the book, Ann* Ridley has a minor crush on him.

MARTHA HATTER (*Howl's Moving Castle**), youngest of the three sisters and therefore, in folklore tradition, the one who should be most successful in seeking her fortune. She is also the only one who is the daughter of Fanny, and she understands her mother much more clearly than her half sister Sophie* does, seeing that Fanny is jealous of Lettie*, is exploiting Sophie, and wants to send Martha herself far away because she knows her own daughter sees through her. Martha has no desire to go far in the world. She wants to marry a nice man and have ten children. In order to accomplish this, she finds a spell that will exchange appearances, temporarily, between her and Lettie, so that she can work in the cake shop and Lettie, who has the brains, can learn magic from Mrs. Fairfax. After Sophie gets to the moving castle, she discovers that Michael Fisher (the rather bumbling assistant to Howl*) and Martha have fallen in love.

MARTHA WIDDISON (*Hobberdy Dick**), eight-year-old middle daughter of the Puritan who buys Widford Manor. A staunch, adventurous child, she sneaks out of bed at Christmas, Easter, May Day, and Midsummer's Eve to take part in the local festivities forbidden by the Puritans as pagan. She is especially fond of her little brother, Samuel, and contrives to include him in some of the fun. Of all the newcomers, only Martha sees Hobberdy* Dick, the hobgoblin who guards the manor, and she becomes a special concern of his. In the end, her brother Joel* and Anne* Sekar plan to keep Martha with them when the rest of the family moves back to the city.

MARTIN BERTOLD (*Annerton Pit**), enthusiastic older brother of blind Jake*. When he is not accepted at engineering school, Martin impulsively spends the money he has saved for college on a motorcycle, a purchase that Jake condones only because Martin's alternative is to send the money to the Green Revolutionaries, an activist environmental group in which he is far more involved than he has told his brother. When they are captured and imprisoned in the mine tunnel by the revolutionaries, Martin is torn by his conscience; the first "proposition" to which he has agreed in the organization is secrecy, but he realizes that the threat to their lives violates the other proposition of nonviolence. Although he is not as close to Granpa* Uttery as Jake is, he proposes going on the cycle to hunt for the old man, and he is concerned that his grandfather may die in the cold, damp tunnel. Emotionally, he is less mature than Jake, and he depends on his younger brother in many ways.

MARTIN SINGER (*Songberd's Grove**), skinny, shortsighted boy with "fox-colored" hair, about twelve, self-possessed for his years, though a little naive, who moves into a flat at No. 7 Songberd's Grove with his parents, and who, with wit, resource, and some luck, breaks the power of the neighborhood bully Lennie* Byre. An imaginative, thoughtful youth, Martin tends to suppress his feelings, takes his time about making decisions, and isn't afraid to appear a coward if he isn't sure that a specific action will produce the desired positive results. He has a "troublesome inner man...who was apt to speak up and dictate to him at unexpected moments," playing conscience and instructing him. Courageous, Martin chooses to handle the trouble with Lennie himself and with Geneva's* help, rather than go to his parents (and spoil their happiness with finally having a home of their own) or to Mrs. Byre. He is naive about girls and has trouble understanding why Geneva takes an immediate dislike to strikingly pretty blonde Helga, daughter of new tenants at No. 7. His discovery of the stone head, which represents confidence and stability to him, provides depth to his personality and contributes to the setting. He is a strongly drawn figure, rounded though not dynamic, much the same at the end as in the beginning of the novel. The story is told mostly from his point of view, a technique that builds credibility and contributes humor.

MARY OWLAND (*A Grass Rope**), the younger daughter of the owners of Lew Farm in Yorkshire and about six years old. She has an unusually active imagination and believes firmly in fairies and similar elements from old stories. She is lively and inquisitive and inclined to be willful and stubborn. There is much warmth in the way her older sister, Nan*, and her parents humor her, playing along with her fancies in order not to hurt her feelings. She likes to be with Charley, the hired man; loves animals; and immediately attaches herself to Adam* Forrest, much to her older sister's embarrassment. Mary is a well-drawn, vigorous protagonist.

MARY POPPINS (Travers*, P. L., ill. Mary Shepard, Howe, 1934; Reynal, 1934), episodic fantasy set in England of the 1930s in which the main character is an eccentric nanny endowed with magical powers. When the Banks family of 17 Cherry Tree Lane, which consists of Mr. and Mrs. Banks, Jane, Michael, the twin babies, John and Barbara, the cook, Mrs. Brill, the maid, Ellen, and the handyman, Robertson Ay, are in need of a new nanny, Mary Poppins appears, blown in, the children can see, by the East Wind. She immediately takes charge of the household, bullying Mrs. Banks into accepting her without references because, she says, they are old-fashioned, quelling Michael's questions with a sharp stare, and putting Jane firmly in her place with abrupt answers. She is described as looking rather like a wooden Dutch doll, thin, with black hair, large hands and feet, and small, peering blue eyes, altogether a rather odd appearance about which she is, nonetheless, very vain. The children soon learn that there is more to Mary Poppins than her discipline and looks. In nine episodes they join her in unrelated adventures, all of which have a magical quality. The children have no part only in the first episode, in which Mary and Bert, the Match-Man who is also a pavement artist, step into one of his pictures and spend a lavish afternoon. In the other adventures they visit Mary's Uncle Albert, Mr. Wigg, who is so full of laughing gas on his birthday that they must take their tea with him sitting on air up near the ceiling; they observe the dog, Andrew, belonging to Miss Lark, their next door neighbor, asserting his independence and insisting on his stray dog friend coming to live with him, all translated by Mary Poppins; and they see the Red Cow wandering outside and hear, from Mary, the story of how she caught a falling star on her horn, which caused her to dance until, at the king's suggestion, she jumped over the moon and dislodged the star. In another episode they go to the city to have tea with their father and stop to buy crumbs from the Bird Woman. They buy gingerbread from Mrs. Corry and later watch her and Mary, with the help of Mrs. Corry's two gigantic daughters, Annie and Fannie, paste the paper stars from the gingerbread onto the sky. They attend Mary's birthday party at the zoo on the night of the full moon, when everything is turned around with people in the cages and the animals feeding them. They go Christmas shopping, where they are joined by Maia, second star in the constellation Pleiades, and they help her select gifts for her sisters. In one episode, John and Barbara, not yet one and therefore still able to understand the language of the birds, the sun, and the wind, have a conversation with a starling but then become a year old and lose their marvelous ability as Jane and Michael did before them. The episode on Michael's Bad Tuesday, when he is naughty all day, has produced some controversy. They find a compass, which transports them around the world with stops among the Eskimos, the blacks of the tropics, the Chinese, and the American Indians. The depiction of the blacks, unnoticed in the 1930s, was found offensive in the 1960s and later editions changed this portion, having them visit animals of each region, like polar bears and pandas, rather than the stereotyped ethnic groups. At the end spring comes, the wind changes to the West, and Mary departs, leaving Michael the compass and Jane her picture, with a note saying "au revoir," which the children take as a promise that she will return. Except that they have the same main characters, there is no connection between the episodes and no progression among them. Some, like the laughing gas birthday tea, are just fun; others, like the party at the zoo, have a strange, magical tone. Most of the characters are stock figures: Mr. Banks goes to the city to make money; Mrs. Banks, though she has four servants, fusses about the work and lack of money to fix up the house; Robertson Ay is lazy; and so on. Only Mary Poppins emerges as a memorable character, plain, conceited, severe, quite different from the sweet movie version which became famous, but with equally marvelous powers. Several sequels present further episodes with Mary Poppins and the Banks family. Books Too Good; Children's Classics; Choice.

MARY POPPINS COMES BACK (Travers*, P. L., ill. Mary Shepard, Dickson, 1935; Reynal, 1935), second in a series of episodic fantasies starring the eccentric nanny who rules the nursery with stern discipline and magical interludes. Jane and Michael Banks and the toddler twins, John and Barbara, are flying a kite, with the help of the Park Keeper, when, to their astonishment, they reel in the string and find Mary Poppins on the end of it, looking as she always has, a stiff figure with coal black hair, bright blue eyes and a nose turned upwards like the nose of a Dutch doll. Since everything has gone badly since Mary Poppins left, the children, their parents, and the other servants are delighted when she returns and organizes the household again. All the episodes employ some

magic. When Mr. Banks's old nanny, Miss Euphemia
Andrews the Holy Terror, arrives for a visit
with a great load of baggage including a caged
lark, Mary releases the lark and inserts Miss
Andrews in the cage, which the lark then carries
through the sky and drops, so terrifying the
formidable Miss Andrews that she stomps off to
her taxi and leaves. They visit Mary's cousin,
Mr. Turvey, for whom everything goes wrong on
the Second Monday of each month, and soon they
are standing on their heads with him, eating
sponge cake. On another visit to friends of Mary
the children meet Nellie-Rubina Noah and Uncle
Dodger in a Noah's ark and later watch from the
window as Mary helps them bring spring to the
street and park. They meet the balloon woman and
all float home holding to the strings of
balloons. On Mary's night out, they follow her
into the sky and attend a celestial circus in
which the constellations are performers and Mary
is the honored guest. In one episode their
little sister Annabel is born and talks to the
starling about her long journey before she
begins to forget, as all children do. Another
adventure is narrated by Mary after they meet a
jester who looks remarkably like Robinson Ay,
the lazy handyman, and tells of how he joins the
King of the Castle and becomes the Dirty Rascal.
All the adventures are light and unthreatening
except for one on a day when Jane is feeling
very naughty and, left behind when the others go
to Miss Lark's for tea, throws her paint box
across the room and cracks the Royal Doulton
Bowl. The three little boys, triplets, pictured
on the bowl entice her into the scene and pull
her to their house, where their great-
grandfather, a strangely sinister figure, tells
her that now they have her she will have to
stay. Fortunately, Mary Poppins rescues her.
Mary has told the children that she will stay
until the chain on her locket breaks. In the
last episode they ride a marvelous merry-go-
round, then watch while Mary buys a ticket
"with a return," boards the merry-go-round, and
is whirled off into the sky while her locket,
its chain broken, falls at their feet. The
stories have much the character of those in the
first book (*Mary Poppins**) and therefore seem
less fresh and inventive. Some are directly

similar: the visit to Mr. Turvey is rather like that to Mr. Wiggs, who suffers from laughing gas; the celestial circus is like the party at the zoo; the Noahs bring spring much as Mrs. Corry, the gingerbread lady, pasted the stars to the sky; and Annabel talks to the sun and the birds as the twins did in the first book. This similarity probably does not bother the rather young readers for whom the books are intended and who may enjoy the familiarity. The Banks parents, Mrs. Brill the cook, Ellen the maid, Bert the Match-Man, the neighbors, Mrs. Lark and Admiral Boom, and the chimney sweep all make brief appearances. Sequels include *Mary Poppins Opens the Door** and *Mary Poppins in the Park**. Choice.

MARY POPPINS IN THE PARK (Travers*, P. L., ill. Mary Shepard, Davies, 1952; Harcourt, 1952), fourth in a series of fantasies about the nanny with magical powers, this one set during one of her three periods with the Banks family outlined in the previous volumes (*Mary Poppins**, *Mary Poppins Comes Back**, *Mary Poppins Opens the Door**). In six episodes Jane and Michael Banks, and frequently their siblings, the twins, John and Barbara, and the infant Annabel, have adventures created by their prim, respectable nanny, Mary Poppins, though she never admits to her part in the events, all of which occur, at least partly, in the park adjacent to their home at 17 Cherry Tree Lane. All follow patterns reminiscent of the previous books of the series. In the first adventure Mary Poppins tells them the story of the Goose-girl and the Swineherd, both of whom think they are royalty in disguise until a passing tramp points out how superior their present lives are to those they covet, and the story cures Jane of thinking of herself as an Indian princess and Michael of imagining himself a hunter in the jungle. In one episode, three princes from *The Silver Fairy Book*, Florimond, Veritain, and Amor, come with their unicorn out of the book into the park, where various adults mistake them for urchins with a horse or gypsies with a donkey, and where the question is posed but not answered: are they storybook characters come alive in Jane and Michael's world, or are they real people come into the storybook world where the Banks family members are characters? Another adventure is a size fantasy in which Jane makes a miniature park within   the park and they   all find themselves in it, visiting a relative of Mary Poppins. In another, Miss Andrews, Mr. Banks's dreaded old nanny, leaves a box of her valuables with   the   Banks   family, among   which   are   two figurines   of   lions,   one with   a   policeman lovingly clasped in its forepaws, while the other, obviously made to look the same, has lost the human figure. In the course of the episode, during which the children discover that their own favorite policeman, who keeps company with their housemaid, Ellen, was a triplet, the lion comes to the park and finds its long-lost policeman (a brother of their friend), and in the end they discover that the figurine is now complete. One story tells of the Halloween on which the shadows of all the people meet in the park and have a party in honor of Mary Poppins, until the various owners, each feeling something is missing, arrive and claim their shadows again. Only one episode has any threatening aspects, the day that naughty Michael wishes that he could be far away from everyone and goes to the cat kingdom, where he must guess three riddles or become a slave of the cat king, and then finds that he is not to be allowed to return home but must marry the cat princess and live on dead mice, bats, and spiders. He is rescued by Mary Poppins. Throughout the book, Mary   is   the   same   strict,   vain,   acerbic character, both   feared and adored   by the children.   Other   characters   from   the   earlier books--Admiral   Boom,   Miss   Lark,   Bert   the Match-Man, the Park Keeper and his mother, the Bird Woman, Mrs. Corry and her two lumpish daughters, and others--reappear in minor roles. Episodes are somewhat longer than in the first book, but, because they follow similar patterns, they seem less inventive. Choice.

MARY POPPINS OPENS THE DOOR (Travers*, P. L., ill. Mary Shepard and Agnes Sims, Davies, 1944; Reynal, 1943), third in a series of episodic fantasies, following *Mary Poppins** and *Mary Poppins Comes Back** and featuring an eccentric nanny with magical   powers. Episodes in this book are fewer and mostly longer, and they strive for a more serious underlying meaning, but they still follow the same general pattern as those in the earlier volumes. Mary Poppins returns on Guy Fawkes day, coming down instead of the shower of stars after the children have fired a rocket in the park. Mary and her charges, Jane and Michael Banks, visit her cousin Mr. Twigley, who tunes pianos and makes instruments and music boxes. He has seven wishes which, like other storybook characters who are granted wishes, he wastes, but they all have a marvelous day spinning round and round like tops on music boxes. Two other episodes occur on afternoon jaunts of the Banks children, including the toddler twins, John and Barbara, and infant Annabel, with Mary Poppins. In one they buy peppermint candy stick horses from Miss Calico and ride them home through the air, along with most of their neighbors and acquaintances. In perhaps the most touching of all the episodes, the marble statue of Neleus and his dolphin in the park comes alive, and they play with him through a golden afternoon before he must return to his pedestal again. As in the other books, one story is narrated by Mary, this time the story of Michael's china cat, who goes to visit the queen and look at the king, and who, with practical good sense, reforms the ruler and starts the country off on the right track again. In two stories Jane and Michael follow Mary at night, once to a garden party in the sea presided over by the Terrapin, the oldest creature in the world, and on New Year's Eve to the park where they dance with their toys and storybook characters, who come alive in "the crack," the time between the end of the old year at the first stroke of twelve and the beginning of the new after the last stroke. Mary Poppins has promised that she will stay until "the door opens," and after a walk in the park during which almost all of Mary's friends from earlier episodes appear and wish her a good trip, the children see her leaving by a door that opens in the reflection of the nursery in the window. No ages are given for the children, and although they do not go to school or seem to have lessons, both Jane and Michael can read. They are not highly developed characters, and the twins are not even distinguished except by sex. Mary is a stiff, no-nonsense figure, both strict and vain, but the children adore her. Although she never explains anything and treats their memories of magical events as fabrications or dreams, there is usually some tangible evidence that proves to Jane and Michael that they really occurred. Sequels. Choice; Fanfare.

MARY VAUGHAN (*The Great Gale**), thirteen-year-old daughter and elder child of the doctor in Reedsmere, the village flooded out in the great storm of 1953, sister of Mark*, 11, of whom she is genuinely fond. Most of the story is told from Mary's point of view but not directly by her. A sensitive and thoughtful girl, when the waters rise, she remembers that old Jim* and Hepzie* Foulger have no one to look after them and enlists Mark's aid in rescuing them. She also organizes the clean-up campaign at their cottage. She willingly, if ineptly, takes care of the Vaughan house while her father and mother are tending sick refugees, and cooks, cleans, and prepares sleeping accommodations for refugees. She is a musician, and, when she and Mark leave the house to rescue the Foulgers, she takes her violin with her. She plays it to lead singing on several occasions. She is a rounded, dynamic character, whose outlook matures as a result of her experiences during the flood.

MASTERMAN READY, OR, THE WRECK OF THE "PACIFIC": WRITTEN FOR YOUNG PEOPLE (Marryat*, Frederick, Longman, 1841; Appleton, 1842), historical fore-runner in the area of sea-adventure and survival novels, a book extremely popular among boys of its day. In October, sometime in the early mid-1800s, the *Pacific* leaves England bound for New South Wales carrying cargo, a short crew, and the Seagrave family as passengers. At first the voyage proceeds without incident, but soon after a brief stop at the Cape of Good Hope the ship encounters a terrible hurricane that within a few days leaves her at the mercy of turbulent seas. When kind, capable Captain Osborn is knocked senseless by a falling mast, first mate Mackintosh, a hard, much disliked man, evac-uates the crew in the only remaining lifeboat, leaving the Seagrave family to fend for itself:

Mr*. Seagrave, an Australian planter, who has returned to England for supplies; Mrs*. Seagrave, who is in ill health; William*, a clever, steady youth of twelve; Caroline, 7; Thomas, called Tommy*, a thoughtless, naughty lad of six; and one-year-old Albert, who is in the care of Juno*, a young black woman. Masterman Ready*, sturdy second mate of sixty-four years, an able seaman and man of conscience as well as knowledge of the seas and seamanship, refuses to desert them, and, as their leader, proves to be the means of their survival in the trying months ahead. The little party soon sights a small, apparently deserted, coconut tree-covered island, and run the ship aground on a windward coral reef. After Ready repairs the ship's storm-damaged small-boat, he, Mr. Seagrave, and William remove the ship's animals (sheep, goats, pigs, fowl and dogs, and a cow which is ill and later lost to sharks), food, firearms, ammunition, and sundry other materials useful for survival, and set up a fairly comfortable camp with quite adequate tents made from ship's canvas, before another gale breaks up the *Pacific*. Ready and William take the dogs, Romulus and Remus, and explore the island, blazing a trail as they go, and find on the leeward side a more suitable site for a permanent camp, on a hill overlooking a beautiful bay, where they also discover a good source of water. Eight days after the gale demolishes the ship, Ready and William move some supplies by small-boat to the bay, and the others proceed overland, carrying what supplies they can. Under Ready's capable direction, they make a new camp, and, after Ready prepares a long-range plan for survival and allocates responsibilities, the next weeks are spent digging a well, constructing a turtle pond, making a garden, starting a storehouse and a stockade to protect against possible invasion located within the coconut forest some distance from the shore, and building a log dwelling into which they move just before a big storm heralds the start of the rainy season. In the next several weeks, the tiny company also constructs a chicken house, fishpond, and salt pan and completes the storehouse between rains. At night and during the rains, they listen to Ready tell

the story of his adventure-filled life. In spite
of problems, many of which arise from Tommy's
misbehavior, the near-death of Juno when
lightning strikes the house and sets it afire,
and William's illness from sunstroke, the little
group find to their surprise that they have been
quite satisfied with their life on their desert
isle. Mrs. Seagrave's health has improved, and
the younger children for the most part are
learning responsibility. Hopes for rescue rise
when early one morning Ready sights a brig on
the horizon. He and William construct a flag-
staff and signal fire, but a sudden gale
prevents the ship from putting in, and it sails
on without them. The same storm brings more
trouble. Driven onto their shore are canoes
bearing two young island women, called
"Indians," who, after being given food and
shelter, "escape," taking with them nails and
other valuable iron materials from the storehouse. For some time the castaways are disconsolate, but Ready gives them new heart by
spearheading the effort to complete the stockade
in preparation for attack from neighboring
islands. Ready has a premonition that danger is
imminent and insists on making the stockade
habitable and defensible. After a good deal of
very hard work, they settle within the coconut-
timbered and thatched enclosure just in time.
Early one morning Ready spies 200 or 300 Indian
canoes heading their way. Some 300 or 400
war-painted "savages" land and with spears and
clubs launch several furious assaults against
the stockade without success. The situation
becomes critical when the party discovers to its
horror that Tommy has drained the water keg and
they are entirely without water. The next day,
while the attackers make plans to burn them
out, Ready sneaks out for water and on his
return is attacked by a "savage," sustaining a
severe spear wound in his lung. That night, as
Ready is dying and the attackers are about to
fire the stockade, ship's cannon are heard, and
broadsides scatter the natives, who retreat to
their canoes. Captain Osborn, who learned the
castaways' location from the captain of the brig
that couldn't land, has secured a ship from the
Australian government and arrived to rescue them
in the nick of time. In spite of the efforts of

the ship's surgeon, Ready dies, and the Sea-
graves bury him with sadness and great gratitude for his selfless devotion on their behalf.
They leave the island somewhat regretfully, for
they realize that they have been very happy
there. In spite of their isolation, they have
had all they needed for a good life. Although
the conclusion is over-foreshadowed, the plot
never lags since the author skillfully introduces new and plausible complications to hold
the attention, inserting incidents now recognized as adventure-story conventions but nevertheless entertaining. The characters are conventional types also--the all-knowing, self-
sacrificing leader; the wise father; the
home-loving, submissive, dependent mother; the
stalwart son; the irresponsible black servant
who can perform only low-level tasks and must
receive firm direction; the mischievous, babyish
younger son--, and only Ready has depth.
Conversation is stilted, often morally or infor-
matively sententious and pious, nautical
language and Biblical quotations are frequent,
and the attitudes of the characters echo the
biases of the period. Interrupting the action
are lengthy discourses on such issues as
colonial development, such phenomena as gulf
streams and trade winds, such abstractions as
theft, reason, instinct, and order, or
observations on the nature of various animals or
fauna. Excitement, action, a vigorous if sometimes dated style, and a wealth of detail that
carries the flavor of real-life experience on
the sea outweigh the didacticism and make for
top-notch escape reading. Choice.

MASTER OF MORGANA (McLean*, Allan Campbell,
Collins, 1960; Harcourt, 1959), rousing realistic adventure novel with detective story
aspects set on the island of Skye off Scotland
and lasting for about a week beginning on
Midsummer's Day probably in the 1950s. Niall*,
16, who tells the story, feels shock and
disbelief as well as fear when his sturdy,
capable, sure-footed fisherman brother,
Ruairidh, 19, is carried home near death from a
fall off the narrow bridge that spans the chasm
by the salmon fishery where he works. Niall's
suspicions that his brother's fall was not

accidental are aroused when a mysterious thin
man claims Ruairidh's clothes at the hospital;
when, after a terrific chase, Niall recovers
them and then discovers among them his brother's
diary containing code-like entries of numbers
and the mysterious name "Morgana"*; and when
shortly thereafter a bald-headed man, who says
he is from the insurance company, visits Niall's
house and steals the pages from the diary. To
help out his widowed mother and to do some
sleuthing, Niall secures Ruairidh's job with the
salmon crew and soon finds plenty more to think
about. The tough, rather ominous crew consists
of Big Willie, a local man, who warns Niall
about the ghosts that are said to haunt the
fishermen's bothy (cottage) every night; Murdo,
a surly, red-haired, lazy fellow from the
neighboring village of Harris, whom Niall for
several reasons immediately suspects of pushing
Ruairidh from the bridge; and Long* John
MacGregor, their affable, commanding, competent,
one-legged captain. Niall bravely sticks out the
ghostly voices that echo round the bothy, even
discovering that they're really Murdo's work and
not legendary haunts, and soon confides his
story and intentions to Long John's sympathetic
ears. Fueling his suspicions about Murdo is his
discovery that the bald-headed man who took the
pages from the diary is camped near the bridge,
leading Niall to believe that he and Murdo are
probably in cahoots in smuggling. Things
speedily come to a head after Niall himself
takes a dreadful tumble into the river from the
cliff above while avoiding Murdo, survives to
join Long John in the bothy, is taken prisoner
by Long John and other fishermen, and learns to
his surprise that Long John heads a poaching
ring and that the *Morgana* is Long John's own
boat used to transport the ill-gotten gain. In a
series of rapid-action scenes, Niall gets the
wheel of the *Morgana*, is attacked by a crewman,
and, when the boat founders and runs aground, is
rescued from drowning by Long John himself.
Police capture the poachers, the bald-headed man
turns out to be a detective who had been working
with Ruairidh in collecting evidence against the
ring, and Long John feigns illness and makes his
getaway. A first-rate melodramatic adventure
story, which pretends to be nothing else, the

novel is all plot, and the characters are less important than what happens to them. Conventions abound, and the plot is over-foreshadowed, but action scenes are vivid and lively with detail and so well spaced that the reader's attention never wavers. Except for Long John, clearly the most interesting figure and an obvious echo of his *Treasure Island** forebear, characters are stock (the loving, hard-working, worried mother; the bossy, nosy, younger sister; the helpful neighborhood sweetheart; solicitous neighbors; surly villains; and so on), and even Niall lacks individuality. Niall's narrative voice seems natural, however, and he speaks with a Gaelic rhythm and occasional terms that add to the sense of setting. There is a good sense of the physical landscape and the sounds and smells of the sea. Fanfare.

MASTER SIMON BRAYLES (*The Writing on the Hearth**), Stephen's master while he is in service to Dame* Alice. Master Simon is a tall, spare man, sharp of eye and abrupt of manner, who demands quick obedience and good work. He instructs Stephen in advanced Latin and takes him on a trip to Oxford, a very memorable occasion for the boy and one that gives the reader splendid views of the city and a keen sense of what the university community was like at that time both socially and academically.

MASTER THOMAS FETTERLOCK (*The Wool-Pack**), Nicholas's* respected father, a well-to-do wool merchant and grower, who not only buys and sells wool grown by others but also keeps large flocks of his own on the rolling Cotswold Hills. He has a fine stone house on the outskirts of Burford, servants, and faithful shepherds. He is a proud and loyal man, whose refusal to think ill of a business associate or retainer leads to trouble. His wool packer, Leach, and his Lombard bankers conspire to defraud him. He is a type figure.

MATT MCGINLEY (*The Battle of St. George Without**; *Goodbye, Dove Square**), inadvertent leader of the youngsters who try to save the old church in Dove Square and who partially regroup two years later in the housing development.

Having lived in the country until his father's
death, Matt has a strong feeling for animals and
a desire to be alone with more space than the
crowded city allows. He is disturbed by the way
his mother holds herself aloof from their
neighbors but has some of the same caution about
being involved himself. His feeling for Madge*
is preromantic, and while he resents her
bossiness, he is sympathetic with her shock at
discovering her parents' identities.

MATT PULLEN (*Windfall**), young Marshfield boy
who suddenly becomes the sole support of his
mother and four younger siblings when his
fisherman father is knocked off his smack and
drowned. Matt is not only a hard worker and a
skilled sailor, having been cuffed into it by
his no-nonsense father, he is also a boy of
independence and nerve. He refuses to go to work
in his uncle's cheese shop, and he manages to
finance the new smack, *Reward*, by three daring
endeavors: he rescues a man from a foundering
ship in a storm; he guides a Dutch schooner over
a dangerous shortcut so that her diamond
merchant passengers can reach London in time for
a meeting, and he wins the smack race by driving
his boat savagely across a shallow patch where
it could have been stranded. He also can keep
his own counsel, and not until after the death
of his enemy, Beckett*, does he tell how the man
was planning to lose the yacht race deliberately
or how he hired thugs to attack and kill Matt.

MAUREEN COOPER (*The House in Norham Gardens**),
28, a lodger in the home of Aunt* Susan and Aunt
Anne Mayfield, Clare's great-aunts, who serves
as a foil for Clare. Unlike the younger girl,
Maureen is very interested in styles, dates, and
personal appearance, those aspects of life that
hold little meaning for Clare's aunts or for the
girl. Maureen is the modern shopgirl type,
unintellectual yet goodhearted, reliable,
always willing to help, not crassly material-
istic yet still caught up in ephemera.

MAURICE (*The Far-Distant Oxus**), the leader of
the "expeditionary force" down the Oxus to the
sea. He is a wiry, strong boy of unspecified
age, probably in his early teens though some-

times he seems younger than that and sometimes
much older. He is a fine rider on his horse,
Dragonfly, and a tough fighter, too, laying out
a boy of seventeen who is attempting to keep the
children from releasing a foal and mother horse
caught in the annual roundup. Maurice never
tells anyone where he lives or anything about
himself, not even at school, according to Peter*
Cleverton. He is polite, optimistic, and
nature-loving, and he is liked by grownups even
though he never seems to go out of his way to
cultivate them. He organizes the children in
most of their adventures, but he forgets
important things sometimes, for example, that
they must buy food before the shops close on
Saturday and how to get the equipment back up
the Oxus. It is his idea to give Persian names
to places. His dog's name is Ellita, which he
says is Persian for "dragon." Though an obvious
type--the mysterious, admired, athletic leader
every boy would like to be--he is the best-
drawn of the six children and is an interesting
figure.

MAX (*The Other Way Round*; When Hitler Stole
Pink Rabbit**), German Jewish refugee brother of
Anna*, who escapes to Switzerland, then France,
and then England. A boy of fierce determination,
he has been lazy in school, but in France he devotes himself to achieving in his studies in an
effort to keep from being an outsider. In England he becomes indistinguishable from English
boys his age, and when, near his completion of
studies at Cambridge, he is interned as an enemy
alien, his main dismay is at being different
from his friends. When he is released, he works
hard to join the air force so he will be like
other Englishmen.

MAX MORLEY (*The Twelve and the Genii**), the
eight-year-old boy who assists the twelve
soldiers that once belonged to the Brontes to
return to Haworth. Early in the story, Max
establishes himself as a boy of integrity and a
sensitive nature. He is careful not to cause
the soldiers to "freeze" by making sudden or
careless movements, and he makes it possible
for them to descend to the main floor of the
Morley house by appropriately attaching a string

to the side of the stairway. He also rescues
them from Brutus, the family cat, and feeds
them. Throughout the story, he continues to care
for them as a Genii should, determined to keep
their lives as they would like them to be and
not let them be controlled by those who would
not show them the proper respect.

MAYNE, WILLIAM (JAMES CARTER) (1928-   ), born
in Hull, Yorkshire, the son of a doctor; for
more than thirty years the author of books for
children and adolescents which are wide-ranging
in subject, approach, and form and vigorous and
polished in style, which sometimes employs dialect. He was educated at the Cathedral Choir
School in Canterbury, the locale for four realistic novels, among them two that are critically
acclaimed: A Swarm in May* (Oxford, 1955; Bobbs,
1957) and Choristers' Cake* (Oxford, 1956;
Bobbs, 1958). Light and filled with school
atmosphere, they provide interesting views of
life in the school as well as solid entertainment. A Swarm in May is included on the
Fanfare list, and Choristers' Cake was
commended for the Carnegie Medal. Of his approx-
imately six dozen other publications, six more
novels have won citations, four of them
realistic stories. The Member for the Marsh*
(Oxford, 1956), a narrative of family and neighborhood life set in the Yorkshire marshes, and
The Blue Boat* (Oxford, 1957; Dutton, 1960), in
which two boys have adventures with a boat and
make some important discoveries about themselves, were commended for the Carnegie Medal.
A Grass Rope* (Oxford, 1957; Dutton, 1962), in
which some school children unravel the mystery
behind a local legend, is also set in the Yorkshire hills. It won the Carnegie and is listed
in Choice. Ravensgill* (Hamilton, 1970; Dutton,
1970), about how a feud between two Yorkshire
country families is laid to rest, it finely
honed and strong in local color, and is listed
in Fanfare. Two fantasies have won critical
acclaim: Earthfasts* (Hamilton, 1966; Dutton,
1967), which improvises on Arthurian legend, was
selected for the Lewis Carroll Shelf and for
Choice, and A Year and a Day* (Hamilton, 1976;
Dutton, 1976), a mystical, legend-like story
about a foundling discovered on the Cornish

coast, appears in Fanfare. Mayne entered the
Canterbury School on a scholarship and stayed
there for five years, until his voice changed.
While he was there, the school was moved to
Cornwall because of air raids. Once home again,
he attended a Yorkshire school for three years
and then embarked on a career as a writer. His
first published book was *Follow the Footprints* (Oxford, 1953), a picture book decorated
by Shirley Hughes. Mayne has made his home in a
Yorkshire village, and Yorkshire has figured
strongly in his work. Recently, in addition to
novels--among them *Drift* (Cape, 1985; Delacorte, 1986) and *Gideon Ahoy!* (Viking, 1987)--he
has produced a series of picture-book readers
about animals, like *A House in Town* (Walker,
1987; Prentice, 1988), a twenty-eight page book
about a family of foxes, and *Barnabas Walks*
(Walker, 1986; Macmillan, 1986), a twenty-four
page book about a guinea pig loose in a schoolroom. He has also edited a popular series of
story anthologies about kings, queens, heroes,
giants, and ghosts (some coedited with Eleanor
Farjeon*) for Hamish Hamilton, and has written
also under the names Martin Cobalt, Dynely
James, and Charles Molin. Though judged inconsistent in the quality of his output (some
assert he simply writes too much), he is deemed
a pacesetter among British authors for the
young.

MCLEAN, ALLAN CAMPBELL (1922-   ), born in
Walney Island, Lancashire; novelist for adults
and older children. After attending Walney
Island Elementary School and Barrow-in-Furness
Junior Technical School, he worked briefly as an
apprentice motor mechanic and as office boy and
clerk with an accounting firm. He enlisted in
the Royal Air Force in 1941 and served five
years in North Africa and Italy, rising to air-
craftsman first class. Mustered out, he married
Margaret Elizabeth White, with whom he had
three children, embarked on a career as a
writer, and settled on a small croft in the Isle
of Skye, the area that provided substance,
setting, and color for his six novels of adventure and history for later elementary and teen
readers, primarily boys. His first three books
are mystery-adventures: *The Hill of the Red Fox*

(Collins, 1955; Dutton, 1956), *The Man of the House* (Collins, 1956; as *Storm over Skye*, Harcourt, 1957), and *Master of Morgana** (Collins, 1960; Harcourt, 1959). *Master of Morgana*, about young Niall's* search for the person responsible for the near-fatal accident of his older, fisherman brother, was chosen for Fanfare. Though most characters are stock and story conventions abound, the action scenes are lively and plentiful, and the book's villain has some of the ambiguous attractiveness of his namesake, Long* John Silver. Gaelic rhythms and terms catch the attention and contribute to the sense of place, and the descriptions of the landscape are unforced and vivid, especially those of the sights, sounds, and feel of the sea. His last three novels for youth are historical, all set in Scotland at the end of the nineteenth century, when the crofters struggled against oppressive lords and unjust government officials: *Ribbon of Fire* (Collins, 1962; Harcourt, 1962), *A Sound of Trumpets* (Collins, 1967; Harcourt, 1966), and *The Year of the Stranger* (Collins, 1971; Walck, 1972). Sympathetic to the underdog, they effectively recreate the period's problems. McLean was an unsuccessful candidate for Parliament in 1964 and later moved to Inverness. His adult novels include *The Carpet-Slipper Murder* (Ward, 1956; Washburn, 1957), *Deadly Honeymoon* (Ward, 1958), and *The Islander* (Collins, 1962; as *The Gates of Eden*, Harcourt, 1962), which received the Frederick Niven Award for the best Scottish novel of 1959 through 1962. He also received the Scottish Arts Council Award in 1972. Critics generally have praised his ability to tell a good story and build setting.

MCNEILL (ALEXANDER), JANET (1907–   ), born in Dublin, Ireland; author of many books for both adults and children. When she was seven, her clergyman father moved the family to England, where she attended Birkenhead School, Cheshire. She later received her M.A. in classics from St. Andrews University, Scotland, and from 1930 to 1933 she worked as secretary at the Belfast *Telegraph*. For more than thirty years of married life she has lived in County Antrim, Northern Ireland, where she has served as a member of the Northern Ireland Advisory Council of the BBC and as Child's Guardian on the local juvenile court. For adults she has written ten novels and one play, and for children more than thirty books of fiction, three plays, and eleven readers. Several of her easier books are about Specs McCann and his friend Curly, the first being *My Friend Specs McCann* (Faber, 1955). Among her highly praised books is *Tom's Tower* (Faber, 1965; Little, 1967), a story of school life that slides into fantasy. *The Battle of St. George Without** (Faber, 1966; Little, 1966), about a group of inner-city children who try to save an old church from demolition, and *Goodbye, Dove Square** (Faber, 1969; Little, 1969), about the same children somewhat older, after they have dispersed and moved mostly to public housing projects, are both noted for being among the first British books to treat urban life realistically. Also realistic in a different setting is *The Other People** (Chatto, 1973; Little, 1970), in which a girl visiting her aunt at a seaside resort town learns some of the seamy facts of life among the tenants of her aunt's run-down boarding house. It was named to the *Horn Book* Fanfare list.

ME AND MY MILLION (King*, Clive, Kestrel, 1976; Crowell, 1979), rollicking farce set in present-day London. Young Ringo (named after "some old pop star my mum liked"), about twelve, a canny street kid none too adept with numbers and the written word though quite articulate orally, tells the story of how he visits a London museum with his older half brother, Elvis ("They gave him this soppy name after some old pop star"). Elvis gives Ringo a black bag containing a painting worth one million pounds that Elvis has stolen and which Ringo realizes is valuable but does not recognize as a famous Madonna. Instructed by Elvis to take the painting to a certain "laundrette," Ringo reads the numbers incorrectly, hops the wrong bus, and ends up in a laundrette at the opposite end of London. Wild adventures follow thick and fast over the next three days as Ringo tries, first, to get the painting to the proper laundrette, and, second, to keep away from those who would "relieve" him of his valuable cargo. Trapped for the night in the underground, he encounters a sharp-eyed hippie named Jim, who recognizes the painting, which is now in all the headlines, and who takes Ringo to the place where he and his group, the Angels, stay. When the Angels are raided by police and paraded off to the local station, all decked out in exotic masks and weird garb, Ringo escapes with the painting, only to be waylaid by another, more opportunistic hippie, An, who takes him to a racketeer. Since the painting is much too hot to fence, the racketeer turns Ringo over to his chauffeur, who takes the boy to hoods, apparently safecrackers, who instruct him to take the painting to a certain house. Again confusing the numbers, Ringo enters the wrong place, the home of an old, deaf woman, among whose religious artifacts he stows the picture. He shinnies down her drainpipe to avoid his pursuers, at the bottom quite literally falling into a canal-boat, the *Rosie*, which happens to be passing below. There Big Van, coincidentally a painter of copies and popular art, harbors him. After a particularly comic scene in which police and an art expert almost mistake a copy by Big Van for the real picture, Ringo returns to the deaf woman's apartment for the original, and he and Big Van take the boat up the canal a short way, where Ringo again encounters the hoods, and also Elvis, who is quite perturbed by his brother's failure to deliver the painting. Ringo flees through a tunnel and finds himself in the London Zoo, smack in the middle of a another plot. The hoods, not really safecrackers but crazies, plan to bomb the zoo to "liberate" the wild animals and reptiles. Black bags get switched, and Ringo flees, not with the painting but with the hoods' bomb, and reaches the canal just in time to heave the bomb into the water. He rescues Big Van from the sinking *Rosie*, returns to the zoo where he miraculously reveals the stolen painting, and in a rousing scene before police, rescue squads, newspapermen, and TV cameras is declared a national hero. What has Ringo learned from all this? That reading can be interesting, and of some use, particularly when one can read about one's own exploits in the papers. Ringo tells his story with evident relish in breezy style and modern colloquial idiom. Events happen with tremendous rapidity, and characters are very simply sketched, being obvious types. The emphasis is on plot, and, although it is often hard to keep up with the numerous sparsely drawn scenes, the book is never dull, and King manages to work in some adult humor and clever wordplay and at the same time take a few shots at both contemporary society and modern youth. Though the whole thing leaves one breathless, it is certainly never tedious or cute, nor does it project the cozy or patronizing tone of similar books of an earlier era. Boston Globe Honor.

MEATY SANDERS (*The Cave**), Cuthbert, largest boy in the cave-exploring group, who brings most of the edible supplies and whose continual mention of food provides some mild humor. Good-natured and self-effacing, he takes the blame for losing the rope which is the lifeline for two of the boys, and when Alan* Hobbs loses the good searchlight, Meaty offers him his own, which Alan in a fit of pique throws away. When Alan is afraid to go home to face his father's fury over the loss of the light, Meaty offers to go with him and say it is really his fault.

MEG (*The Writing on the Hearth**), old woman, rumored to be a witch, who helps Lys* when the girl flees from Odo* the Plowman. Cast out by her father because she bore a son out of wedlock, Meg has spent her life in a rude hut on the edge of the chalk hills. She knows much about herbs and healing and is lettered, having been taught by her father who was an apothecary. She seems to possess second sight and sees Lys as a nun and Stephen at Oxford, predictions that come true in the story. Lys insists Meg is warm and loving, and Stephen sees her to the end as sorely misjudged. It is at her house that Stephen encounters Roger Bolingbroke*, whose association with Meg remains mysterious. Meg is a stock figure.

MEG MORRISON (*The Third Eye**), elder sister of Linda* and Jinty and victim of her mother's vocational ambitions for her. She falls in love with Dave Ferguson, son of the Earl of Ballinford's chauffeur, by whom she becomes pregnant and whom, with Archie* Meikle pre-siding, she marries in the traditional anvil

wedding in Archie's smithy. At the beginning of
the story, she is a pretty, love-struck girl,
with red-gold hair and a strong wish to attend
the village parties strict Mam* thinks
unsuitable for respectable people because of the
beer and carousing. Meg is the leader of the
three sisters. As the story goes on, she becomes
more serious, though her warmth and congeniality
make her popular with schoolmates; and the story
interest shifts to Linda. Tension between Meg
and Mam increases, especially after Mam scorns
Dave's request to marry Meg. When Mam refuses to
recognize Meg's marriage and to open her
letters, Meg still tries to keep lines of
communication open with her mother. On the day
that Mam and Jinty go to the Fiscal's office for
the investigation into the earl's death, Meg
takes the bus to visit Mam. While they are
waiting for Jinty to be questioned, Mam thinks
about things and apparently decides that
forgiveness is the best policy. On the way
home, she stops at the smithy to see her
grandchild, and the two are reconciled. Meg is a
rounded, interesting, convincing figure.

MELANIE DELIA POWERS (*An Enemy at Green Knowe**),
Ph.D. scholar supposedly engaged in a study for
the Philosophical Society of Jerusalem, who
tries to get possession of a ninth-century copy
of an ancient book of magic, left at Green Knowe
in 1630 by a Dr. Vogel who tutored the Oldknow
boy of that period. Melanie speaks in a sweet,
cultivated voice and smiles frequently, but she
impertinently opens cupboards and pries into
desks when she comes to tea, and when Mrs.*
Oldknow refuses to rent her a study room, she
leaves angrily. Thereafter she sends a series of
disasters to the house and its occupants. When
Tolly* and Ping* discover her true name,
Melusine Demogorgona Phospher, and challenge her
with an exorcist chant, the demon presence that
has been directing her departs, leaving a
crumpled up, distracted woman who says she has
lost her cat and stumbles off.

MELWOOD, MARY (EILEEN MARY HALL LEWIS), born in
Carlton-on-Lindwick, Nottinghamshire; playwright
and novelist. She was educated at Retford High
School for Girls in Nottinghamshire, was married

in 1939, and has two sons. She has been a school teacher and has written several plays for children, including the technically demanding *The Tingalary Bird* (New Plays, 1964), which was produced in London and received the first Arts Council Award ever given for a play for children. Among her others are *Five Minutes to Morning* (New Plays, 1966), which was produced in London in 1965, and *The Small Blue Hoping Stone*, which was produced in Detroit in 1976. She has also written for the Unicorn Company theatrical group. Her two novels for children, though quite different, are both distinguished for evoking a strong sense of village life in the 1920s and 1930s and the often unspoken but significant ties and conflicts among family members and neighbors in a close community. *Nettlewood* (Deutsch, 1974; Seabury, 1975) is set mainly in a decaying mansion and has elements of a mystery. *The Watcher Bee** (Deutsch, 1982), a more convincing book which won the Young Observer Teenage Fiction Prize, is the story of a girl growing up, told with deft style and wry humor.

THE MEMBER FOR THE MARSH (Mayne*, William, Oxford, 1956), quietly amusing, realistic novel of family and neighborhood life set in the mid-twentieth century in a marshy area of Yorkshire. On Monday morning, March 1, David Rosley, a clever youth of eleven with an active imagination, dallies, misses his own school bus, and must then cross a scary marsh to catch another. Along the way he hears gurgling and snapping sounds and is certain that he is being pursued by monsters. He finds three older schoolboys, who are regular passengers, sitting in the rear of the bus: Clipper*, Kitson*, and Starr*. They admit him to their club, the Harmonious Mud Stickers, calling him their Member for the Marsh, because that is where he lives and boards. Clipper is president, Kitson treasurer, and Starr secretary of the club; they pool money to buy clove candy, they while away the travel time by singing old songs in harmony, and, when they have meetings, they surreptitiously share a pipe. Subsequently, David learns that they have dubbed the marsh Chorasmia, pretend it is part of China, and call the big river nearby the Yellow. The boys tell

David that it's his responsibility to watch over
the region,   and, when David asks   what Chinamen
do against devils, Kitson   informs him that they
use firecrackers. Armed with   matches in lieu of
firecrackers, David   discovers the   scary sounds
were produced   by a "dragon," a pumping machine
that   Mr.* Tuckee,   the   old farmer whose land
abuts the   marsh, has   installed to   drain water
from the   fields into the marsh.   Though David's
fears are allayed, the   boys continue the devils
game, and Clipper calls   a committee meeting for
Saturday afternoon, during   which they will hunt
for   further demons   with firecrackers   and tea.
The boys   gather, and, tagged by   Anne*, David's
younger   sister, they   "investigate," detonating
almost   all   their   forty-nine   crackers   in
exorcising   devils (putting   one cracker in the
pump-dragon   as a   joke for   the   ditchers   on
Monday),   and   generally exploring.   They sing,
smoke,   and continue   the game   of real-pretend.
They   know   they're   making   metaphors,   really
talking about people, machinery, and drains, and
they also know the   drainage is important to the
Starrs, a   farm family   whose land will   be well
served by Mr. Tuckee's   efforts. Anne takes them
to a sudden clearing,   a broad, level, open area
she's   discovered   which   she   calls   a dancing
floor. The   boys map   the region,   which Clipper
dubs Neolithic Lake Village, and have a glorious
tea at afternoon's end at the Rosleys'. The next
week the   waters begin   to rise, and   Mr. Tuckee
informs David that   the entire   area will   be a
lake   by   summer.   The   club   discusses   the
situation, pondering   the effect on   the natural
gas and on possible "tumps," mounds with ancient
artifacts, and decides to investigate further to
see if   indeed a potential national   monument is
endangered.   Their   next Saturday's   exploration
proves   inconclusive, because   they   now need   a
boat,   and David with   Daddy's   help starts   to
build a   raft. The   boys make an   agreement with
Mr. Tuckee to   keep mum   if they   find anything
valuable in return for   his letting them explore
and dig   as much as   they wish (Daddy   says it's
fields   versus   fossils).   By   the   following
Saturday,   the water   has risen   enough for   the
boys to   raft over   to the higher   ground, where
the "village"   probably was, with   tools, pipes,
and   map. Since   club   rules   forbid   female

visitors, the boys make Anne eligible by
declaring her a dog. Starr and Anne prepare a
sumptuous chicken dinner, and Kitson searches
for natural gas. He strikes it but is distracted
and doesn't realize he's done so. Kitson and
David raft about, and Clipper carries out a
fairly scientific excavation, unearthing a few
minor artifacts and concluding that the place
was once an Iron Age village. The children feast
on Starr's chicken and are joined by David's
parents and Mr. Tuckee for dessert. They sing
old songs and chat, realizing that this is the
first meal eaten on this site in 2,000 years.
When Kitson remarks that David's tenure in the
club is over because he can't reach the bus now,
Mr. Tuckee generously proposes a solution. He
will open the spill gates enough to allow the
ridge on which they sit to remain above the
water line, and David can follow it to cross the
marsh to the bus. The day and David's first
three weeks as the Member for the Marsh end to
everyone's satisfaction. Subtle characterizations, carefully focused and controlled point of
view, and low-keyed plotting require readers to
be alert for inferences and implications. The
pace is slow, and it is some time before the
book's problems become apparent. Even then, most
of the story interest comes from overhearing the
boys' plans and observations. The four youths
are distinctly drawn, individualized, and
likeable, even the inclined-to-be-touchy Starr;
and David wins approval from the beginning,
while his little-boy fears war with his big-boy
aspirations. The author projects an excellent
sense of the way children act in the club stage
of their lives, with the need to be secret, the
endless discussions over details, the horseplay,
and the emphasis on roles and rules ("Write it
down, Starr!"). David's Mother and Daddy seem
like real people, too, understanding, caring,
fun-loving (Daddy pretends he's put the soap bar
in the soup), firm, diplomatic (Daddy says David
should let Anne find out for herself that the
other boys don't think her presence is suitable;
Mother says David should have given her more
advance notice about tea), helpful, and mostly
staying in the background where children like
them to be. The style employs nature imagery,
and Mr. Tuckee and the ditchers speak in

dialect. Carnegie Com.

MERCA (*The Queen's Blessing**), Saxon girl whose parents are killed and whose home is burned by the Scots under Malcolm* III. Taking her little brother, Dag*, by the hand, she runs from the place, coming eventually to Wearmouth, where the two are captured, marched north, and sold as slaves. Fiercely protective of Dag, who is five years younger, she feels she must provide the will to survive for both of them, just as she gives him more than half their food to keep him alive. After they have been adopted by the good Queen Margaret*, she clings to her hatred of the Scots and her desire to have Malcolm killed, even though it keeps her from being happy and causes a rift between her and Dag.

MERRIMAN LYON (*The Dark Is Rising**; *The Grey King**), friend and mentor of Will* Stanton. He is ostensibly a renowed and distinguished Celtic scholar, but is in reality an Old One, one of those immortals as old as the land who have the responsibility of saving the world from the evil power of the Dark. Mysterious in his ways, imposing in demeanor, striking in appearance with thick, white hair and deep, dark eyes, he is able to go back and forth in time and represents the ageless, universal force for good. Merriman Lyon appears in every book in The Dark Is Rising series to affect the action and assist the good. In *Over Sea, Under Stone*, the first book in the series, he is a close friend of the Drew family, whose children call him Gummery or Great-Uncle Merry. Barney Drew notes the similarity between Uncle Merry's name and that of Merlin.

MERRY BRANDYBUCK (*The Fellowship of the Ring**), Meriadoc, young cousin of Frodo* Baggins who insists on going with him when he leaves The Shire both because he is devoted to Frodo and because he has grown up hearing of Bilbo* Baggins's adventures and wants one of his own, though he has no idea how serious and dangerous it will be. Merry is the only hobbit* in the group who is used to boats and, because his home is in Buckland, east of the Brandywine River, he has been inside the edge of the Old Forest

before and serves as their guide as they start
that way. He and his cousin, Pippin* Took, at
first seem to be unlikely members of the
fellowship, but both have important parts in the
final outcome. When the fellowship dissolves,
they are captured by orcs and carried off toward
Isengard, the fortress of the wizard Saruman,
but they manage to escape, get into the forest
Fangorn, meet the Ent Treebeard, and are present
at the flooding of Isengard. Later Merry pledges
his service to King Theoden of Rohan, Lord of
the Mark, rides into battle with Theoden's niece
Eowyn, and in the great battle before the gates
of Gondor he defends Eowyn by strking the chief
of the Nazgul or the Ringwraiths in the back of
the leg, severing the sinew behind the knee, a
stroke that drives away the creature but leaves
Merry's arm paralyzed. Like Pippin, Merry grows
to a great height for a hobbit, presumably from
consuming the Ents' drink, and like Pippin, he
is inclined to talk lightly in the most serious
situations, but he is slightly older and
steadier than his cousin.

MICK COONEY (*The Singing Cave**), grandfather of
young Pat, who has been so outraged at the idea
of the boy being apprenticed to a tailor that he
has taken him to share his house and farm and to
be his heir, an arrangement that suits them
both. Young at heart, he is always ready to join
his grandson in an adventure, even to sail alone
to France to pick Pat up after he has stowed
away aboard a lobster boat. His house is the
popular meeting place of the island men, and his
fairness and good sense have earned him the
respect of young and old alike. In his naive
honesty, he does not suspect the educated Mr.*
Allen of duplicity and so is hurt more than
angered when he discovers that he has been
tricked.

MICK DALTON (*The Nature of the Beast**), best
friend of Bill* Coward, son of the union
representative at the Stone Cross Mill. A boy
who has been brought up much more carefully than
Bill, he seems younger, although they are
classmates. Excitable and given to impractical
fantasies, he is less stable than Bill, and it
is he who suggests stealing their teacher's

camera and hunting the Haverston Beast. Although
his mother has some social pretensions in the
neighborhood and belongs to antihunting organizations, Bill senses a submerged delight in
violence in Mick that makes him uneasy. When
Mick's father becomes mentally unbalanced and
the boy appears with a black eye, Bill is
genuinely shocked, although he himself might get
a black eye from his father or grandfather, and
that would surprise no one.

MICK TEMPLETON (*We Couldn't Leave Dinah**),
Michael, who with his sister, Caroline*, is left
behind in the evacuation of the English Channel
island of Clerinel which was occupied by the
Germans in World War II. Older than Caroline, he
is steadier than she and a little condescending
toward her. He is less observant and not as
decisive as she but is still a sturdy and
bright boy. He figures out the code and
discovers that the writer of the messages is
Monsieur Beaumarchais, Peter's* father.

MIDIR (*The Mark of the Horse Lord**), rightful
heir to the kingship of the Dalriadains, blinded
by his father's half sister, Liadhan, who then
seized the leadership of the tribe as the Earth
Mother, goddess-queen of the older religion
practiced by their rivals, the Caledones. He has
escaped being sold as a slave because a blind
slave is considered useless, but he has learned
the harness-making trade and become a skilled
worker. Because the tribe will never accept a
blind king, whose vigor is equated with that of
the tribe itself, and because he wants revenge,
he is willing to have Phaedrus* pretend to be
Midir returned to rally the Dalriadains to throw
off Liadhan's rule, and he coaches him
thoroughly until the ex-gladiator can pass for
the young king, returned after seven years among
the Romans. Although much like Phaedrus in
appearance, Midir has a different personality
with a cruel streak, so that both his best
friend, Conory*, and Murna*, the girl who
becomes bride to Phaedrus, realize that the
imposter is not the real king, but for their own
reasons they keep the secret.

MIDNIGHT IS A PLACE (Aiken*, Joan, Cape, 1974;

Viking, 1974), realistic novel set in the
fictitious, dirty, carpet-mill town of Blastburn
on the Tidey River somewhere on the coast of
England, beginning on October 30, 1842, and
lasting several months. It is Gothic in its
mystery and melodrama and Dickensian in its
broad palette, its retribution for the wicked
and reward for the virtuous, and its social
consciousness. Orphaned, lonely, somewhat irresponsible Lucas* Bell, just thirteen, lives in
the big, shabby, gloomy mansion called Midnight
Court with two men: his guardian, Sir* Randolph
Grimsby, the churlish, hard-drinking owner of
the local sweat-shop carpet mill, Murgatroyd's
Carpet, Rug, and Matting Manufactury, to which
Lucas is heir through his deceased father and
Sir Randolph's sometime partner; and Mr.*
Julian Oakapple, a pale, ginger-haired young
man of changeable disposition. Of mysterious
background, Mr. Oakapple is a former violinist
whose left hand lacks two fingers. The action
begins on the eve of Lucas's birthday with two
events that change his life: he is introduced to
the factory, and he gains a young companion. Sir
Randolph orders Mr. Oakapple to take Lucas on a
tour of the mill, where the boy observes
dangerous working conditions, learns that children are often crushed to death by presses, and
discovers that labor unrest is afoot. His new
youthful housemate is little Anna-Marie*
Murgatroyd, about eight, the granddaughter of
the factory's founder, now also orphaned and
the ward of reluctant Sir Randolph. A willful,
peppery child, she speaks only French, which
fortunately Lucas also speaks, but she gets on
poorly with both Lucas and the few servants left
in the mansion, which has fallen on hard times
due to Sir Randolph's profligacy. Awakened one
night by smoke, Lucas capably and responsibly
saves himself and Anna-Marie. Mr. Oakapple is
severely burned in attempting to save Sir
Randolph, who deliberately walks into the
flames. Left homeless and to their own devices
because Mr. Throgmorton, Sir Randolph's shyster
lawyer, refuses to recognize Lucas as his
employer's ward, the two maintain Mr. Oakapple
in the hospital and find shelter in the grimy
attic of an old retainer's grasping sister. For
money, Anna-Marie sells cigars she fashions from

butts she gathers, and Lucas works as a tosher, one who scrounges for saleable refuse in the underground sewers, in the employ of grungy old Tom Gudgeon*, who in turn sells the refuse to Elias Hobday, a wizened, misshapen, less-than-honest *marchand de bric-a-brac*. Toshing is dangerous work, since salvagers must be alert for changing tides and for the vicious wild hogs that roam the sewers. Lucas soon mistrusts Gudgeon, whose morality is questionable and whose jealousy shows when Lucas comes up with valuable finds. Anna-Marie encounters difficulty with townschildren, who pelt her with stones. To compound their problems, the Friendly Boys, street ruffians who roam the hospital area, demand they pay "protection money" for Mr. Oakapple. For economy and safety, they move surreptitiously to the old icehouse on the grounds of Midnight Court. They discover that the place is already occupied by an old woman, who to their amazement and joy turns out to be Anna-Marie's presumably dead grandmother, Lady* Eulalia Murgatroyd, the wife of the founder of the mill, Sir Quincy Murgatroyd. They settle in happily, even building a stable with bracken fern floor for their pony—all tidy and comfortable for the winter. Lucas continues toshing, while Anna-Marie finds work in the factory cleaning wool from the carding claws, a dangerous and painful operation. Lady Murgatroyd helps her invent tongs to facilitate the work, a device that soon brings her into conflict with the avaricious Bob Bludward*, who heads the Friendly Association, the factory extortion gang, and who also demands protection money from her. Lucas's toshing comes to an abrupt end, when he is rescued from the river in the nick of time by Lady Murgatroyd, Anna-Marie, and Davey Scratcherd, the local union organizer, after he has been attacked and left for dead by the half-mad Gudgeon. Mr. Hobday, considerably prompted by Davey, turns over some found papers bearing the name of Bell to Lucas as well as a welcome cash compensation. Lucas gets a job in the factory, luckily just in time to forestall a plot of Bludward's to murder Anna-Marie. The papers from Mr. Hobday enable Lady Murgatroyd to force the lawyer Throgmorton to give Lucas the income from his inheritance.

It comes out that Sir Randolph obtained the estate and factory by fraudulent means from Lady Murgatroyd's deceased son, Sir Denzil* Murgatroyd, and that he set fire to the house to avoid paying taxes on it. Lady Murgatroyd's cousin, Lord Holdernesse, buys the mill, which he intends to run with Lucas's advice and help, and hopes are high for improved working conditions and wages for the local hands. Deliberately melodramatic, overplotted, and fullsomely cast with eccentric or stock characters, the story offers splendid entertainment. It moves rapidly and vigorously through consistently interesting and inventive twists to a thoroughly satisfying conclusion. Many scenes stand out--Lucas toshing in the sewer, factory children snatching fluff as the great press descends upon them, Sam Melkinthrope struggling for his life to get out of the glue caldron into which Bludward and his henchmen have thrust him. Dialogue is forceful and spiced with local dialect, and the theme of greed resulting in exploitation and provoking inhumane behavior is intentionally obvious. Fanfare.

A MIDSUMMER NIGHT'S DEATH (Peyton*, K. M., Oxford, 1978; Collins, 1979), mystery novel set in Meddington, an English boarding school for boys that has recently admitted a few girls to the sixth form. Jonathan* Meredith, 16 or 17, who is in his next to last year, greatly admires Charles Hugo, a mathematics teacher who has been part of an Everest expedition and who coaches the boys in mountain-climbing techniques. When Robinson, the poet who teaches literature, is found drowned, Jonathan is disturbed to remember that he had seen Hugo with him on the deck of the poet's houseboat the night before, a fact that Hugo blandly lied about to the police. Goaded on by his oafish roommate, Ashworth, who thinks his disruptive and hectoring behavior in Robinson's class has made the school blame him for the poet's supposed suicide, Jonathan shows Hugo Ashford's exercise book with a page torn out. It is obviously the page that was left as a "suicide note" on Robinson's table saying, "I think this is the best way to end it," and really referring to a scene that the class has been assigned to write and that Ashford had dragged out too long. Jonathan is appalled by his hero's cold denial. On their climbing trip in Wales, after Jonathan has discovered that Hugo and Robinson's wife are lovers, he fears that Hugo is arranging an "accident" for him on their harrowing climb together. After his return to school, Jonathan almost drowns trying to save Iris Webster, a disturbed girl who has had a crush on Robinson, and they survive only because Hugo comes to their aid. Later Hugo confesses to him that he was with Robinson on the night of his death, and that he took the "suicide note" from the exercise books in Robinson's room and placed it on the table, but that the poet's plunge into the river was an accident. The psychology of Jonathan's hero worship and its change to fear and finally understanding is sensitive. Details of the climb and of the rescue in the swirling, almost overpowering current are riveting. The immaturity of Jonathan's reactions to Iris, coupled with their night sharing a bed in Hugo's house without fear of discovery, is less convincing in this traditional school setting. Fanfare.

MIKE HENDREY (*The Wind Eye**), son of Madeleine* Studdard and stepson of Bertrand*. Sharing some of his mother's restless energy, Michael is easily bored and infuriated at the meticulous, pedantic way Bertrand approaches life. He is also clear-sighted about his mother's faults and frequently impertinent. Although he doesn't like to admit it, he is genuinely fond of his stepsister Beth*, also a teenager, and admires the way she tries to keep acrimony from breaking out. The fantasy episodes with the boat *Resurre* are just adventures to him until he thinks he has caused Beth to be lost, and then he wishes himself nowhere. Finding himself on a deserted beach, he believes his wish has been granted, and he is terribly relieved to find some twentieth-century trash that proves he is somewhere real.

MIKE TEAVEE (*Charlie and the Chocolate Factory**), bratty boy, who finds the fourth ticket to Willy* Wonka's Chocolate Factory. Mike spends all his non-school time watching television and dressing up like the characters he sees. Of these, his favorites are the gangsters. Mr.* Wonka has invented a way of sending chocolate candy bars by television. In spite of Mr. Wonka's admonitions, Mike decides to send himself by television and comes out as a midget. He goes home about ten feet tall, however, having been overstretched on the gum-stretching machine by the Oompa-Loompas*, who were trying to restore him to his proper size and overdid the process. Mike is a caricature, like the other obnoxious children.

MILD EYE (*The Borrowers Afield**; *The Borrowers Afloat**), gypsy who carries off the gentleman's boot that Pod* has patched and in which the Borrowers are living. A fat, terrifying man, he has one dark, twinkling eye and one that is paler and hazel yellow with a drooping lid. He knows the Borrowers exist, being among the few humans who do, and wants to catch them, put them in a cage, and exhibit them at the fair. Tom* Goodenough helps the Borrowers escape from Mild Eye in *The Borrowers Afield*, taking them home with him in his pocket to the cottage he shares with his grandpa and where they live with Uncle* Hendreary and Aunt* Lupy for a while. In *The Borrowers Afloat*, Mild Eye again tries to capture them. This time Spiller* and Ernie Runacre, the policeman, spoil his plans. He is the villain in both books, but not a very frightening one.

MILLY KITSON (*The Lark on the Wing**), Emily, beautiful, willful cousin of Kit* Haverard in the large Quaker family at Gramercie. Sometimes contemptuous of Kit, she often acts as a goad to push her into bold action by implying that Kit hasn't the nerve to try. Milly is starting a dramatic career when she meets "Crazy" Laurence Cray, a Quaker missionary who has been home on a medical furlough from Chihar, and they fall in love. Milly, however, refuses to go to Chihar, although the work there is Laurence's whole life. When word comes that he has been killed but that his death has brought peace to feuding factions in that frontier country, Kit gives her the ring that Laurence has left for Milly, who tells Kit that she plans never to marry.

MILNE, A(LAN) A(LEXANDER) (1882-1956), born in London; playwright and novelist. He attended Westminster School, London, from 1893 to 1900, and Trinity College, Cambridge, where he edited *Granta* and earned a B.A. degree in mathematics, from 1900 to 1903. He worked as a freelance journalist until 1906, when he became assistant editor of *Punch* magazine. In World War I he served in the Royal Warwickshire Regiment. Although he published thirty-five plays, six novels, three books of verse, three books of short stories, and many books of nonfiction, including several volumes of sketches from *Punch*, he is now best remembered for his four books for children, two of whimsical stories peopled by the stuffed toys in his son's nursery, *Winnie-the-Pooh** (Methuen, 1926; Dutton, 1926), and *The House at Pooh Corner** (Methuen, 1928; Dutton, 1928), and two of verse, *When We Were Very Young* (Methuen, 1924; Dutton, 1924) and *Now We Are Six* (Methuen, 1927; Dutton, 1927). All four are considered twentieth-century classics and the Pooh stories have been reprinted in many different combinations and translated into many languages, including Latin as *Winnie Ille Pu* (trans. Alexander Lenard, Dutton, 1960). They were included on the Children's Literature Association Touchstone list, the Lewis Carroll Shelf list, and the *Choice* magazine list of children's books for an academic library. Milne also wrote *Toad of Toad Hall* (Methuen, 1929; Scribner, 1929), a play based on *The Wind in the Willows** by Kenneth Grahame*. His story, *Once on a Time: A Fairy Tale for Grown Ups* (Hodder, 1917; Putnam, 1922), is sometimes included in children's collections.

THE "MINNOW" LEADS TO TREASURE. See *"Minnow" on the Say*.

"MINNOW" ON THE SAY (Pearce*, Philippa, ill. Edward Ardizzone, Oxford, 1955; *THE "MINNOW" LEADS TO TREASURE*, World, 1958), mystery-adventure novel with detective story aspects set on the River Say in England in the contemporary period. When David* Moss, 11, of the village of Little Barley, returns the canoe the flooded Say has lodged against his family dock, he makes the acquaintance of orphan Adam* Codling, thirteen

or so, who lives with elderly Miss* Codling (his
Aunt Dinah), and his grandfather, addled Mr.*
Codling, in their big, old ancestral house. The
once wealthy family has fallen on hard times,
and Adam informs David that he will have to go
to live with cousins in Birmingham unless he can
recoup the family fortunes by finding the
treasure his ancestor, Jonathan* Codling, hid
for safekeeping before he left to join the
British army during the Spanish threat in 1588.
The two boys set out to find the treasure,
deducing where it might be from clues in an old
rhyme handed down in the family. They dig
systematically but unsuccessfully upstream,
meeting there Mr.* Tey, the old miller of Folly
Mill, who informs them that Adam's grandfather
had come over the water to the mill on the same
quest, and a mysterious Mr.* Smith, who is
punting on the river. David persuades Adam to
search downstream, where recovering part of Mr.
Moss's lost wheelbarrow gives them the idea of
investigating the local bridge. That dead end
provokes the memory that Mr. Tey had told them
that another ancestor of Adam's had altered the
course of the channel. When they reinspect the
portrait of old Jonathan that hangs in the
Codling house, they see in the° background a
two-span bridge and a rose. Examining the bridge
over the old channel, they find the sign of the
rose, but the aperture there is empty. Taking
Miss Codling into their confidence, they learn
that years earlier Grandfather Codling had
discovered the treasure but had hidden it again,
insisting that he would disclose it only when
Adam's father, John, returned from fighting in
the war. John's death addled the old man,
however, and Mr. Codling still awaits his
return. When Mr. Codling sees Adam in the
moonlight one night, he thinks John has come
back, suffers a heart attack from the shock, and
dies, without disclosing the location of the
rehidden treasure, which now seems lost forever.
Adam falls into despair, Miss Codling puts the
house up for sale, and the mysterious Mr. Smith
makes a bid for it. David's discovery that Mr.
Smith's real name is Ashworthy-Smith, and that
he is descended from Jonathan Codling, puts a
different complexion on matters. Further
adventures and complications transpire before,

in helping to prepare for the auction, the boys
find old Mr. Codling's recipe for rose wine with
commentary in the old man's hand that implicates
Squeak* Wilson, the elderly handyman. Since
Squeak has been behaving oddly, Miss Codling
suspects why, visits his house, and returns with
the treasure. While helping Miss Codling get
ready for the auction, Squeak had indulged in an
old weakness for wine, not only drinking up some
of the wine that Mr. Codling had hidden under
the water tank under the roof but also taking
home the jar in which the old man had secreted
the treasure jewels. Now Miss Codling can
maintain the family home, and Adam can remain
with her. After a slow start, the plot picks up,
and, though convoluted, moves rapidly to the
conclusion where all the loose ends come
together splendidly. Such standard conventions
of the form as elusive clues, codes, lost
relatives who turn up, and frustrated efforts
abound. What lifts this book out of the ordinary
are its vividly descriptive style which is rich
in sensory language, the absence of violence,
episodes fleshed out with generous detail and
dialogue, the sympathetic relationship between
the grown-ups and the children, and the strong
local color. Characterization is skillful, even
minor figures seem alive, and, though the adults
are touched with the eccentric, they never seem
ridiculous, nor are the children seen as super-
clever paragons of detecting virtue. (Sarah*
Codling; Betsy* Ashworthy-Smith) Carnegie Com.;
Fanfare; Lewis Carroll.

MINNY (*You Never Knew Her as I Did!**), the kind
and gentle laundry maid in the Castle of
Lochleven, who, Will says, is "the one person in
the Castle who did trust me...who had got that
pet name for 'mother' long ago from me, because
it was she who had clucked over and cared for me
as a child." Will likes to spend time with her
because, of all people, he does not have to
playact with her. She has much to do with the
success of Will's scheme to free Mary, Queen of
Scots. At Will's request, Minny sews costumes of
the kind worn by soldiers' wives for Mary and a
lady-in-waiting to escape in. Because she
realizes that she may never see Will again, she
reveals herself as his mother. Later, after

Mary's escape, she joins him and grows old in his house. She has a good knowledge of the political struggles involving the Douglases and admires Mary. She is an interesting and likeable figure and is well drawn.

MIRANDA RIDLEY (*Castaway Christmas**), 15, untidy looking, impatient, capable sister of Lincoln* and Pinks* Ridley, with whom she is marooned in the cottage called Little Topsails in Somerset in western England. She likes to do things and gets restless when idle. She mothers her siblings, is very concerned about their feelings, and undertakes housekeeping duties even though she feels unequal to the job. She seeks approval from Lincoln in particular. Most events are seen from her point of view. She seems young for fifteen and is a shallowly developed character.

MIRYAM CARLISLE (*The Changeover: A Supernatural Romance**), mother of Sorry*, daughter of Winter*, and member of an old and established family whose land has been gradually absorbed by urban sprawl. In an attempt to protect their property, she and her mother, both witches, raised a "cone of power" over their area. To do this they needed the help of a third witch, and Miryam decided to have a baby. When Sorry turned out to be a boy, disappointed Miryam put him out to foster parents, who abused him. Ironically, however, Sorry had inherited her powers. Miryam helps Laura* through the ritual that makes the girl a witch. Miryam is a flat, not very convincing figure.

MISS BIANCA (Sharp*, Margery, ill. Garth Williams, Collins, 1962; Little, 1962), talking animal fantasy which continues the adventures of Miss Bianca, the elegant, eloquent, beautiful white lady mouse, first portrayed in *The Rescuers**. Miss Bianca organizes the Ladies' Guild of the Mouse Prisoners' Aid Society to rescue abused little Patience, 8, an orphan who has been kidnapped into the service of the cruel, odious Grand Duchess of the Diamond Palace, a magnificent, ostentatious mansion of rock crystal, set in what is evidently the English countryside. The mouse ladies set out in high spirits, confident that the ladies-in-waiting who guard the child will flee as soon as they see mice and that Patience will soon make her home with a loving farm couple in Happy Valley. Unbeknownst to the would-be rescuers, the ladies-in-waiting are not human, but actually mechanical figures. The mice flee in terror, leaving Miss Bianca to cope by herself. She tinkers with the mechanical maids' clockwork, certain that she and Patience can escape when the clock-maker arrives, but her plan goes awry when the Duchess moves to her hunting lodge deep in the forest north of Happy Valley, where she can be properly waited upon until her Major Domo has the ladies fixed. The lodge is guarded by the Chief Ranger and two formidable bloodhounds, Tyrant and Torment. The bloodhounds, caricatures of slow-witted, blindly loyal policemen, remain impervious to the blandishments of Miss Bianca, who sees immediate flight as imperative. She and Patience slip out an unfastened window their first night at the lodge and race through the dense wood with the dogs at their heels to Happy Valley, where, unable to rouse the farmer, they take refuge in his dovecot. In the morning, as they are about to be apprehended by their pursuers, faithful Bernard appears. Worried that Miss Bianca has not returned home, he has disguised himself as a knife grinder and has made his way over the countryside, tracing them through the silver chain Miss Bianca dropped as a clue at the suggestion of Patience. He valiantly flings his knife at the Chief Ranger, whose roar of pain attracts the attention of the farmer's stalwart sons. Miss Bianca and Bernard are awarded medals for bravery, and Patience lives happily ever after with her new parents. The success of this melodramatic, utterly preposterous story, amusing but less convincing than *The Rescuers*, depends on its spunky heroine and on the author's grandiloquent, often tongue-in-cheek manner of writing. Choice; Fanfare.

MISS BRIDGET (*Smith**), 23, elder sister of the pickpocket Smith*, living in the grimy slums of eighteenth-century London. By trade a seamstress, Miss Bridget and her sister, Miss* Fanny, alter for resale the clothes of men

hanged at Tyburn Hill, which are sent to them by
Mr. Jones, the hangman at Newgate Gaol.
Sharp-tongued and cynical, she predicts only
disaster for her young brother, whom she calls
"Smut," though she thinks she recognizes the
word "property" on his document and believes it
must be a deed. When he catapults into the
prison chapel after almost escaping through the
ventilator system, she thinks quickly enough to
conceal him beneath her hoop skirt and convoy
him to freedom. Turned genteel after Smith has
set them up in a house on Golden Square, she
puts up a sign, "Miss Bridget and Miss Fanny.
Court Dressmakers," not adding, as Smith notes,
that it was the criminal court at Old Bailey.

MISS CADELL-TWITTEN (*The Grange at High Force**),
elderly old maid and bird-lover, who has a
cottage with so many birds that it is covered
with their droppings. She protests the repair of
the Church of Little St. Mary because it means
driving out the pigeons and because the noise
disturbs her birds, particularly her pheasant,
Augustus. Although she knows what has happened
to the statue, she childishly refuses to tell
because she thinks the Admiral* Sir John
Beauchamp-Troubridge and the boys have been
"naughty." After she has been rescued during the
storm, she relents and tells them. She always
wears an old tweed suit and a shapeless felt
hat.

MISS CODLING (*"Minnow" on the Say**), Dinah
Codling, spinster daughter of old Mr.* Codling,
Adam's* aunt, and David* Moss's friend. Elderly,
harried, and untidy, she honors her aged,
fuzzy-minded father, loves but never pampers
Adam, and worries constantly about family
finances. She has sold off almost everything in
the Codling house that she can to keep things
going and practices such small economies as
never having cake for tea. She forbids Adam from
seaching for the family treasure because she is
convinced it is a useless effort, but she
doesn't try very hard to control his activities
so he searches anyway. She is the one who
finally finds the treasure, but only David knows
where she found it: under Squeak* Wilson's
chair. Miss Codling tells the boys the story of

Jonathan* Codling and the family jewels and gives them the rhyme that provides the basic clues. Like most characters in the novel, she barely rises above a stereotype.

MISS DUNSTAN (*A Sound of Chariots**), a teacher Bridie hates. She insists that Bridie write more conventionally than Bridie would like to, and Bridie rebels and is beaten. Both Mrs. Mackie, the headmistress, and Bridie's father, Patrick* McShane, insist she respect Miss Dunstan and do what the woman says even though Bridie may feel her teacher is wrong. It is at this point that Mrs. Mackie becomes aware of Bridie's budding talent as a writer and begins to encourage her.

MISS FANNY (*Smith**), 19, younger of Smith's* two sisters, less tart of tongue but also less quick of wit than Miss* Bridget. Miss Fanny is sweet on the highwayman, Lord* Tom, and much admires his swashbuckling ways. She thinks she recognizes the word "felonious" on Smith's document and believes it to be a confession and worth money if they can discover what it says. Softer and more romantic than her sister, she is still quite willing to profit by Smith's misfortune if she can find a way.

MISS HAPPINESS AND MISS FLOWER (Godden*, Rumer, ill. Jean Primrose, Macmillan, 1961; Viking, 1961), fantasy of how two Japanese dolls help a lonely girl from India become adjusted to her life with relatives in England. Nona Fell, 8, has done nothing much but cry since she arrived to live with her cousins, Anne, 14, Tom, 11, and Belinda*, 7. Everything seems cold and strange after Coimbatore in Southern India, where she was cared for by old Ayah. She does not like her cousins, who laugh at her clothes and the singsong way she speaks English; she is afraid of the traffic; and she finds the food strange and unpleasant. Then a package for "the Misses Fell" arrives from Great-Aunt Lucy Dickinson containing two six-inch-high Japanese dolls and a note, saying they are Miss Happiness, Miss Flower, and Little Peach. To Belinda's disappointment, however, there is no Little Peach in the box. Anne is too old to be interested and Belinda is bored with the two

girl dolls,   both of   which have   plaster hands,
feet,   and heads,   and rag   bodies, but   Nona is
fascinated.   Being   an   avid reader,   she   knows
something of Japanese customs,   and since she is
so far from home,   she has some understanding of
the dolls' worry   and loneliness. Miss Happiness
has   a round,   smiling   face   and an   optimistic
disposition;   Miss Flower   is less   secure, more
worried and nervous.   Since they cannot   talk to
humans or move independently, they can influence
action only by wishing.   Now they wish very hard
for a kind, understanding   girl to love them and
a real Japanese home. Nona responds by summoning
the   courage to   leave the   house alone   for the
first time and to go to Mr. Twilfit's bookstore,
although the other children have warned her that
he is bad-tempered. The bookseller is so pleased
to find a   child who is a   reader and researcher
that he loads her with books to borrow,   escorts
her home,   and later   gives her   miniature trees
for   the dolls'   garden. He   prods   Tom into   an
interest   in building   the   house   by saying   it
would be beyond the boy's carpentry skills. When
Tom insists   that Nona accompany him   to get the
wood, she bravely runs beside his bike. Soon she
is making other overtures: she finds a haiku in
their school   book and   tells her   teacher, Miss
Lane,   all about   the Japanese house;   to get a
cupboard for   the bedding and clothes,   she must
speak for   the first   time to Melly Ashton,   the
girl who   sits next to   her,   and she trades her
silver bangles for Melly's pencil box. Miss Lane
responds   by painting   a   tiny   scroll with   the
haiku in   minute printing   for the niche   in the
house,   and Mrs.   Ashton, though   she makes   the
girls   reverse   the   uneven   trade,   buys   an
identical pencil   box for Nona.   At the party to
celebrate the completion of the house,   Belinda,
who has   been feeling increasingly left   out and
resentful,   asserts her right to one of the dolls
and throws Miss Flower   into her   own neglected
dolls' house. Later she relents and returns Miss
Flower, and she and   Nona become friends for the
first time.   Secretly Nona writes   to Great-Aunt
Lucy,   pointing out that Little Peach was not in
the original box,   and when the tiny Japanese boy
doll arrives,   conspires   with Mother   to insert
him into Belinda's   large breakfast peach, where
she discovers him   with joy.   The book   is very

much a "little girl" story, with author asides to the reader that give it a dated tone. Detailed directions for building the dolls' house and notes on Japanese customs are included at the end. The sequel is *Little Plum*. Carnegie Com.; Fanfare.

MISS HAVISHAM (*Great Expectations**), wealthy recluse who summons Pip* to her home so she may watch him play. Many years before, she was jilted on her wedding day, and since that time she has never gone out of her house in the sunlight and has kept the house exactly as it was on that day, even with the table set for the wedding supper and the bride cake crumbling to dust in the center. She stays in darkened rooms, grotesquely dressed in her yellowed wedding gown. She has adopted Estella* and trained her to break the hearts of men (practicing first on Pip) as her revenge on the sex. Though she knows that Pip thinks she is his benefactor and that she intends him to marry Estella, she does nothing to disabuse him of this idea. When she discovers that she has made Estella so heartless that the girl feels no love even for her, she regrets her ways and tries to make amends by helping Pip pay for the partnership for Herbert Pocket, who is a relative of hers. In the end she attempts to set herself on fire. Pip saves her, but she dies as a result of the incident.

MISS LAMPETER (*The Dark Behind the Curtain**), the teacher who directs the class play, *Sweeney Todd, the Demon Barber of Fleet Street*. Forced by Mr.* Garner to take on Colin Jackus*, she wheedles, bullies, or reasons as necessary in order to get the job done. This is her first production, and she varies her attitude and behavior quite understandably, being on occasion overzealous (as in the actors' workshops she conducts), impatient, hasty in judgment, or carefully professional and inventive. Jackus likes her.

MISS MANSFIELD (*Smith**), daughter of the blind magistrate who takes in scruffy Smith* for a meal and a bed. Believed by her father to be a saint, Miss Mansfield is really angry and frustrated, often furious at her father's naive generosity and gentle trust, and vexed into a real temper with the servants by the restraints of her life as the blind man's companion. Since she keeps her real feelings from her father, she offers to teach Smith to read and is quite proud of his progress, though she doesn't trust the boy after she catches him going through the papers in her father's study. After her admirer, Mr.* Billing, is proved a villain and later murdered in prison, she accepts Smith as her father's companion and, freed from her constant attendance on the blind man, eventually finds another admirer who marries her.

MISS MARGARET ROYLANCE (*Ask Me No Questions**), schoolmistress in Tooting, the only adult who seems concerned and wants to take action to investigate the rumors of child abuse in the Drouet school for workhouse children. An orphan herself, she has been taken in by the kindly but slightly senile parson and his wife, and she tells Laura* that she hopes never to leave that happy place. Her suggestion that the church Ladies' Committee make some contact with Drouet's school is met with hostility, and it is clear that her job will be threatened if she persists. She has the courage to write to Mrs. Drouet anyway, asking if she may call, but at the book's end it appears that she has been forced out of Tooting and that the possibilities of romance with Cousin* Henry Bolinger have come to nothing.   .

MISS MAY BELLINGER (*A Pattern of Roses**), lame daughter of "Old Brimstone" Bellinger, the Edwardian vicar, and cousin of young Netty* Bellinger. Though cowed by her father and something of a figure of fun to the villagers, Miss May is a determined character. She is able to persuade Tom* Inskip's parents that she should give the boy drawing lessons and Mr. Pettigrew, the local squire, that he should reinstate Tom in his job on the farm. Through Netty, Tim* Ingram and Rebecca* learn that it is Miss May who planted the purple rose that still grows, more than sixty years later, on Tom's grave. Her answer to Tim's letter says she was a nurse in World War I in France after her father's death and later married and had a family.

MISS MENZIES (*The Borrowers Aloft**; *The Borrowers Avenged**), village woman of forty-eight or fifty with a sweet and gentle disposition, who designs Christmas cards for a living, writes children's books, and has hobbies of wood carving, hand weaving, and ceramics. She believes in fairies and at first thinks that is what the Borrowers are. She helps Mr.* Pott develop his model village of Little Fordham, making figures of little people to place here and there in the model village. In this way she discovers the Borrowers. She brings the Borrowers items that will make life easier for them just because she is kind and generous. She is so distressed by the Borrowers' disappearance that she takes the risk of making herself appear ridiculous and reports their loss to Mr. Pomfret, the constable, who, as she had feared, doesn't take her seriously. She is horrified by the destruction that Mr.* and Mrs.* Platter cause at Little Fordham and works until all hours to repair it. Arrietty* likes her very much, and, after the Borrowers have moved to the Rectory, wishes she could tell Miss Menzies that they are safe in order to ease the woman's mind. Miss Menzies is a pleasing figure and serves as a foil for greedy, insensitive Mrs. Platter.

MISS OLIVIA BROOK (*The Diddakoi**), justice of the peace who takes in Kizzy* Lovell, the gypsy orphan. Miss Brook lives in a small, rather bare cottage at the edge of the village and has been close-mouthed about herself, so that her acquaintances are astonished when she is appointed magistrate. They discover only gradually that she has been a barrister and that her father was a famous racehorse trainer. She is a woman of exceptionally good sense and patience, and Kizzy eventually comes to trust and love her.

MISS PHILEMON (*A Long Way from Verona**), senior English mistress at Jessica* Vye's school, a very small woman with grey hair, a wide smile, and a disheveled appearance, with her petticoat coming down and her hat brim uneven. She seems to be continually spilling out her battered briefcase full of exercise books and lives with the most casual housekeeping, but she is quite famous, having published books, and in serious matters she has practical good sense. Although Jessica says she despises girls who get crushes on teachers, she obviously has a strong emotional attachment to Miss Philemon, who seems to understand her, and it is only to Miss Philemon that she tells about her experience with the Italian prisoner and later shows her poem. Miss Philemon has an unconventional attitude for a teacher, seeming quite pleased when a senior girl tells her that she is going to be married rather than accept a scholarship to Cambridge, which would have been good for the school's reputation, and remarking to herself, after hearing of Jessica's terrible day in which she got three order marks, "Order marks. What nonsense!".

MISS QUEENIE HARRISON (*The Battle of St. George Without*; Goodbye, Dove Square**), spinster who grew up in Dove Square and has cared for her old father for many years. Blessed with a sort of naive acceptance of other people's foibles, she welcomes the youngsters who come to apologize for disturbing her father's funeral and two years later is surprisingly quite willing to assume the role of live-in grandmother for the wild Flint family when their mother walks out. She seems to have had a romantic feeling for Shaky* Frick, who was her schoolmate, and at the book's end has invited him to Christmas dinner.

MISS SMITH (*Dogsbody**), retired schoolteacher who feeds and shelters Sirius and to whom he takes Kathleen* O'Brien when it is clear she can't stay with the Duffields any longer. A woman of good sense as well as compassion, she tackles the problems of both dog and child with practical action. She treats Sirius as if he can understand everything she says, which of course he can; explains to him how to get in and out of the dog door in the kitchen; and then goes on with her nap. When she takes Kathleen in hand, she starts by writing letters to the mayor, police inspector, and a dozen other important people, all of whom were once her pupils.

Describing herself as independent and crotchety, she refuses to be bullied by Duffie*.

MISS WRACK (*Which Witch?**), comic figure, one of the Todcaster witches who compete for the hand of Arriman the wizard. A sea witch, she was once a mermaid, but she persuaded a plastic surgeon to turn her tail into two legs. Her familiar is an octopus named Doris. In the contest, Miss Wrack calls on the Spirits of the Deep to help her summon the Kraken. Things go expectedly awry, and what results is a dark, handbag-shaped blob, an orphaned baby Kraken, which attaches itself to Arriman, calls him Daddy, and drips all over him and the house.

MISTER CORBETT'S GHOST (Garfield*, Leon, ill. Alan E. Cober, Pantheon, 1968), long short story or novelette that later appeared in Britain in *Mister Corbett's Ghost and Other Stories*, telling a clever and chilling variation of the legend about selling one's soul to the Devil. Set in the outskirts of eighteenth-century London, the story starts on New Year's Eve in the apothecary shop where Benjamin Partridge, the overworked and unwilling apprentice, is trying frantically to get away to his home and the celebration waiting for him while his master, Mister Corbett, keeps finding one more task to delay him and insisting that he wants the boy to put his heart and soul into his work. An old, wrinkled man who exudes the damp, heavy odor of an undertaker taps at the window and demands a medicine to be mixed and delivered to him in Jack Straw's Castle, an inn some three dark and windy miles away. Seething with sullen hate for his master, the boy has almost reached his destination when he turns aside to a tall, dark house of which he has heard tales before, rumors of ways to get revenge. Partridge cries out in alarm when the door is opened by the same old man who ordered the medicine, but he follows up the stairs to the third floor to a room where one wall is made up of pigeonholes, each containing some innocuous item--a pincushion, a pair of spectacles, a child's doll--and each tied with a piece of black ribbon. Partridge gives the old man Mister Corbett's name and, since some object that the victim has

recently touched is necessary, also gives him an
empty jar, in which the apothecary has
sneeringly told him to bring back a bit of a
ghost if he should meet one. The old man ties a
bit of black ribbon to the bottle, puts it in
one of the pigeonholes, and demands a quarter of
the boy's earnings from now until he dies.
Outside the door Partridge realizes that he has
failed to deliver the medicine, but he dare not
go back, and he is hardly at the main road again
when Mister Corbett appears running toward him
and falls dead at his feet. There follows a
nightmarish period during which Partridge is
surrounded by murderers and cutthroats, each
carrying his victim and headed for the Highgate
graveyards to get them properly underground so
there won't be evidence against them. The boy
shoulders Mister Corbett's corpse and staggers
after them, but is stopped by the tollhouse
keeper and turned back, having insufficient coin
to pay his way through. When a coach comes
clattering along the road, Partridge sees a way
out and pushes the body in front of it, ready to
accuse the driver of running Mister Corbett
down, only to discover that the occupant of the
coach is the same old man in black. Then
Partridge makes another deal with the sinister
old man who fortunately has the empty jar with
him; since the boy's soul is willing, the heavy
body will be changed into a weightless ghost. To
his horror the ghost seems terrified of
Partridge and complains of being in Hell, where
it is cold, so cold. Under the turnpike keeper's
suspicious gaze, the boy is forced to take the
ghost into the inn, where a New Year's celebration is under way. He is moved to pity but also
fear, since he realizes that he can see the
candles and the fire right through Mister
Corbett, and he contrives to keep the ghost in a
dark corner or between him and the fire, until
the call comes for all to join hands to welcome
in the new year. Discovered, they are cast out
as damned, and, his desire for revenge completely spent, Partridge agrees to let Mister Corbett
have a last look at his wife and family before
they wander off to whatever forsaken places
they can find, since they are bound together
and can't live among ordinary men. As they hide
in the apothecary shop from Corbett's baffled

wife and children, the old man in black once
again raps at the window, demanding the
medicine that Partridge forgot to deliver.
Seizing on a last frail hope, the boy insists on
trading the mixture for the empty jar and
reducing his debt to one quarter of one week's
wages. Then he watches, fascinated, as Mister
Corbett's ghost reenters his body. Not aware of
all that has happened, the Corbett family drink
a health with him, and his master insists on
driving him home in his carriage, but all is not
completely rosy: Mister Corbett fines him one
quarter of his week's wages for not delivering
the medicine as ordered. Besides being a
convincingly scary ghost story, full of Gothic
conventions, this is a character study as
Partridge changes from sullen resentment to pity
and at last offers his life if Mister Corbett
can be saved. The style is suitably elaborate
and melodramatic. Choice.

MISTER JOHNNY GOTOBED (*Carrie's War**), retarded
man cared for by Hepzibah* Green. He is very
good with the farm animals and able to do odd
jobs around the place, but his language is not
comprehensible to most people, although Nick*
Willow understands much of what he is trying to
say. Shy but usually friendly with people he
knows, Mister Johnny goes into a fury when he is
teased, and when Frederick Evans mimics him he
attacks him with a pitchfork. When Carrie*
returns with her children thirty years later, he
speaks much more clearly, having been taught by
a speech therapist who was brought by Albert*
Sandwich.

MISTER TREET (*Devil-in-the-Fog**), head of the
family of strolling players, a large man, able
to project a strong feeling of dignity even
when facing irate landlords or sitting in the
stocks. Almost always optimistic, he is a sort
of Mr. Micawber of traveling actors, moving from
one stage disaster to another without looking
back, confident that fame and fortune await this
family of geniuses. His eldest son George, who
narrates the story, assures the reader that
Mister Treet is a grand man, as great in mind as
he is in body, but George gradually comes to
doubt his father and even to suspect him of

being the abductor of the Dexter infant. When it
becomes clear that Mister Treet has, in a sense,
sold George for sixty guineas a year, the boy
still does not desert him but asks Sir John
Dexter, now supposedly his father, for the
seventy pounds Mister Treet needs to emigrate
with his children, and it is only after the
Treets miss the ship (whether purposely or
through bad management is not clear) that George
begins to see his father for the bungler and
cheat he is. Mister Treet redeems himself at the
end. When Lady Dexter, who has become fond of
her supposed son, offers him 1,000 pounds for
George and Richard Dexter tries to top her with
an offer of 2,000 pounds, Mister Treet refuses
both and is forgiven by his son.

MISTRESS FETTERLOCK (*The Wool-Pack**), Nicholas's* efficient, status-conscious mother, who,
delighted at the prospect of her son marrying
into a family of noble connections, readily
agrees that Mrs. Bradshaw and Cicely* shall
visit, entertains them most hospitably, and
offers to keep Cicely on as protege. This not
only suits the times, when betrothed girls lived
with their prospective in-laws, but also serves
the plot. It gives Cicely and Nicholas a chance
to become better acquainted and also to
continue their sleuthing, which leads eventually to the discovery that Leach has been
stealing from Master* Thomas Fetterlock.

MOCK TURTLE (*Alice's Adventures in Wonderland**;
*Alice's Adventures under Ground**), lachrymose
character whom Alice* visits, escorted by the
Gryphon*, as he is sitting on his ledge of rock
by the sea. He laments no longer being a real
turtle and looks back with nostalgia on his
schooling at the bottom of the sea in an
especially funny conversation filled with
clever puns and sly implied comments on the
nature of education. He and the Gryphon demonstrate a wild dance called the Lobster-
Quadrille for Alice, and he sings his old school
song for her: "Beautiful Soup, so rich and
green...." He is an engaging caricature of a
sentimental alumnus.

MOLE (*The Wind in the Willows**), little animal

who abandons his spring cleaning, flings down his whitewash brush, and scurries out into the sunlight to begin the adventures in the book. Naive and inexperienced but intelligent, Mole soon takes to the life of the riverbank with his friend the Water Rat*, and by the end of the story has become bold enough to dress as a washerwoman, trick the Stoats guarding Toad Hall into panic, and join with Rat, Badger*, and Toad* in an attack through the secret tunnel on the banqueting weasels. The only threatening episode in the book occurs when Mole rashly sets off into the Wild Wood by himself and must be rescued by Rat. Upon seeing the Piper at the Gates of Dawn, who is Pan, the god of little wild creatures, Mole is overcome by great awe and joy, as is his friend Rat, but afterwards neither can remember the experience.

MOLLY REEVES (*The Islanders**), about fifteen or sixteen when the story begins. She and her brother, Thomas*, discover Otipo and Mua, the first of the survivors of the volcanic eruptions on Rikofia, and speak on their behalf to the islanders. A big, hefty girl of courage and determination, Molly resents having to assume the passive, subservient role of a woman and prefers chumming with Thomas, for whose fear of heights she covers whenever she can. Although she is very much attracted to Otipo, she eventually, the afterword tells, marries Dan Wilde, because, though lacking in tact and savvy, he is a hard worker, can learn from experience, and will be better able to provide for her. Dan courts her clumsily throughout most of the novel. Molly is an eminently practical, sensible girl. She appears in most of the scenes as one of the "good guys." She suggests sailing to Kingfisher* Island in the canoe the refugees arrived in.

MONSIEUR ARMAND (*Castors Away!**), intellectual who is a fugitive from the French Revolution and who becomes Nell* Henchman's teacher after the family returns to Rushby from their holiday on the Suffolk coast with Aunt Susan Henchman. He encourages Nell to use her mind and not be satisfied with conventional answers and be-lieves in her dream of exploring new lands. He and Nell meet quite by accident one day when she rebels against Aunt Julia's requirements and runs away. She rows down river, where she encounters Monsieur Armand apparently fishing. He explains that he is only pretending to fish and is really composing poetry. Since people think he is fishing, they do not bother him, and he has uninterrupted time to himself. He appears only in the latter part of the novel but has a great influence on Nell's life. His character is based on the French poet and statesman Chateaubriand.

THE MOON IN THE CLOUD (Harris*, Rosemary, Faber, 1968; Macmillan, 1969), talking-animal fantasy set in ancient Israel and Kemi (Egypt), which improvises with wit and humor on the Biblical flood story. After the Lord* God informs Noah* of his intentions to wipe out wicked humankind, Noah assigns to his second son, Ham*, the task of gathering animals for the ark. Specifically, Ham is to get two lions and two sacred cats from Kemi. Lazy and conniving, Ham offers Reuben, a good-natured, sincere animal tamer and musician, passage on the ark for himself, his wife, Thamar, and his animals in return for doing the job for him. Because he loves his wife and his animals very much, Reuben agrees, and, accompanied by his haughty, black cat, Cefalu*, his faithful, cream-colored herd-dog, Benoni, and his crotchety camel, Anak, Reuben bravely sets out on the journey across the desert to Kemi. Along the way, the little party falls in with the caravan of the High Priest of Sekhmet, goddess to whom cats are sacred, and are taken prisoner to Kemi. There, Reuben is cast into prison as a spy, the dog and camel are parceled out, and Cefalu, who is per se a sacred figure, is taken to the temple of Sekhmet. There, he meets and falls head over paws in love with another sacred cat, a beautiful, imperious, aristocratic ball of black fluff named Meluseth. Court intrigue results in Reuben's release from prison and eventual escape to freedom. While in prison, Reuben is befriended by Tahlevi*, a good-hearted tomb-robber under sentence of death, and entertains and consoles his fellow prisoners by playing his flute. In his misery, Reuben plays so movingly that the High Priest,

to ingratiate himself with the King*, into whose
disfavor he has fallen, presents Reuben at
court. The King is pleased with Reuben's music
and keeps him on as his personal musician. At
the magnificent state festival to celebrate
Tahlevi's execution, a disturbance enables Tahlevi and Reuben to escape. Reuben collects his
animals, including Meluseth (thus acquiring the
required number of sacred cats), and makes his
way back over the desert to Israel. On the way,
they encounter Thamar, who has fled from Ham's
unwanted attentions and has found a lion cub,
and they also acquire a mature lion. They return
just as raindrops herald the onset of the
deluge. Ham claims Reuben's success as his own,
but, in his clumsy attempts to get an elephant
to board the ark, he is squashed flat, and Noah
takes Reuben and Thamar in his place. Related
dramatically in a vivid, peppery, often tongue-
in-cheek style and a contemporary tone, this
thoroughly engaging story moves with originality, action, humor (some of it adult), wit, and
suspense to an appropriate ending, with success
for the good and retribution for the wicked.
Characters are drawn in bold strokes, with some,
like Noah, Ham, and the Priest, approaching
caricature. Reuben's dilemma is convincing, and
the plight of the powerful, isolated young King
is presented with sympathy and insight. The
acquisition of the second lion strikes a false
note: it seems precipitous and contrived. Some
details recall the story of Joseph, also from
Genesis. Sequels. Carnegie Winner; Choice; Fanfare.

MORAG MACLEOD (*The Kelpie's Pearls**), plain-
living, generous, kind, proud old Scottish
woman, who helps a kelpie* and is rewarded with
a gift of pearls. Because she is candid about
her relationship with the kelpie and has some
magical powers inherited from her white (good)
witch grandmother, she is herself thought to be
a witch, a bad one. Her life made intolerable by
curiosity seekers and distrustful neighbors,
she is borne away to Tir-nan-Og, the land of
Heart's Desire, by the kelpie. She is a strongly
drawn, convincing figure.

MORAY WILLIAMS, URSULA (1911-   ), born in

Petersfield, Hampshire; illustrator and author
of more than sixty books for children. She was
educated privately and at schools in Annecy,
France, and at Winchester Art College. Her twin
sister is a well known artist in Iceland,
married to an Icelandic sculptor and painter,
and she herself married the great-grandson of
the poet Robert Southey. Probably her best known
book is *The Adventures of the Little Wooden
Horse* (Harrap, 1938; Lippincott, 1939), which
has been published in many different languages
and has been dramatized and televised. Her
studies in France gave her background for a
series about a beautiful but heartless and often
maliciously spiteful doll named Marta, *The
Three Toymakers* (Harrap, 1945; Nelson, 1971),
Malkin's Mountain (Harrap, 1948; Nelson, 1972),
and *The Toymaker's Daughter* (Hamilton, 1968;
Meredith, 1969). Many of her early books were
self-illustrated, but in the late 1960s and the
1970s she wrote a number of picture books illustrated by Faith Jaques, including *Grandpa's
Folly and the Woodworn-Bookworm* (Chatto, 1974),
and *A Picnic with the Aunts* (Chatto, 1972), both
of which have been described as having an
Edwardian flavor; *Mog* (Allen & Unwin, 1969), a
zany story of two eccentric old ladies; and the
absurd and amusing *Johnny Golightly and His
Crocodile*. Her *The Nine Lives of Island Macken-
zie** (Chatto, 1959; as *Island Mackenzie*, Morrow,
1960), the story of a cat and an old maid shipwrecked on a deserted island, which was named
to the *Horn Book* Fanfare list, is for middle
readers, as are *Jeffy, the Burglar's Cat*
(Anderson, 1981) and *Bellabelinda and the
No-Good Angel* (Chatto, 1982). For older readers
she has written a number of novels, including
Boy in a Barn (Allen, 1970; Nelson, 1970), set
in postwar Europe; *The Noble Hawks* (Hamilton,
1959; as *The Earl's Falconer*, Morrow, 1961),
set in the fourteenth century; *Castle Merlin*
(Allen, 1972; Nelson, 1972), a time fantasy; and
The Line (Penguin, 1974), an imaginative story
of a magical modern invention. All her novels
have been commended for having a strong story
line with witty and satirical undertones. She
has also published four plays and a book of
verse and has served as Justice of the Peace in
the county of Worcestershire and as Governor of

County High School in Evesham and of Vale of Evesham School for Educationally Subnormal Children.

MORGANA (*Master of Morgana**), an unfamiliar name Niall* finds in the diary of his near-fatally injured brother, Ruairidh, along with some other puzzling entries, and which he later thinks must be the name of a Spanish galleon sunken in a nearby bay for whose treasure Ruairidh and Murdo had once searched as members of a reclaiming crew. Niall eventually learns that the name refers to Long* John MacGregor's own boat, the one on which he transports stolen salmon to market.

MORNING LIGHT (*Aquarius**), former traveling dancer, acrobat, and singer, who becomes king of the desert people and their rain dancer, the scapegoat king who is expected to bring rain. By custom, the people choose the outsider whose dancing brings rain and marry him to the princess who will become the next queen. Morning Light happens on the scene when the King is being selected and is the twenty-seventh man to dance; the rains come, and he is made king, even though he doesn't want the position. Since, in spite of much dancing, he never brings another rainfall, he is despised by both the queen and the people. He is a pathetic figure, who knows his position is intolerable but who tries in his inept way to make the best of the bad bargain. He lavishes love on his baby daughter, Dark Cloud, ironically singing naughty songs to her, which is all the music he knows. He is brighter and braver than is believed, recognizes that the court is a morass of intrigue and perfidy, and knows that there is no really good solution to the problems. Thus he continues his frantic dancing.

MORSAC, MARQUIS DE (*Thunder of Valmy**), cruel, selfish French noble who is lord of the manor that dominates the countryside where Pierre's family lives. He is hated and feared. He engages Pierre to paint the portrait of his niece, Pauline, a poor relation whom he intends to marry to a rich old wine merchant. After the Revolution breaks out, he schemes to keep Louis

XVI and Marie Antoinette in power, flees to England when the mob takes control, returns to continue plotting, must again flee from the mob, and is given refuge by Madame* de Vairmont. When last seen, he is stalking from her house with his customary arrogance, presumably to sneak back to safety in England. He is a stock nobleman villain.

MORTON LEROY (*Fire and Hemlock**), father of Seb* and successor to Tom* Lynn as husband to Laurel*. He is a big, portly man with a dark, pouchy piece of skin under each eye. Because he knows he needs the sacrifice of Tom to renew his vigor, he zealously keeps track of him and tries to thwart Tom's efforts to free himself from Laurel's snares. For this reason, he threatens Polly* Whittacker and at least twice tries to kill her, since it is only through her that Tom has a chance of escape. Throughout the nine years covered in the story he is a menacing figure.

MOSES BEECH (*Moses Beech**), independent old recluse who takes in Peter* Simpson when he is lost in a blizzard and who teaches him pride in physical labor and self-respect during the nine months they live together. Although he attended school occasionally as a child, Moses cannot read, a fact he keeps carefully concealed even from his employer and nearest neighbor, Charlie Bailey. He also tries to conceal his "spells," heart attacks or slight strokes, for fear some interfering do-gooder will send him to a hospital or an old people's home. Even in the age of the British welfare state, he has never registered for an old-age pension or for medical care. Despite his advanced age he works as handyman on Charlie's farm, tends his own garden, keeps bees, and cans vast quantities of vegetables and fruit. Because he had his old mother to care for he never married, and the girl he loved eventually married someone else. His stubborn independence is pictured as admirable but extreme. He acts as a foil for Peter's freeloading father.

MOSES BEECH (Strachan*, Ian, Oxford, 1981), realistic novel of a runaway in the late

twentieth century who finds himself through
his relationship to a reclusive old man.
Discouraged at not getting a job and disgusted
with his freeloading father, who has made him
quit school, Peter* Simpson, 17, has left the
Potteries and headed for Manchester, impracti-
cally underdressed for the blizzard that surprises him on the way. Although he has left a
note for his mother saying that he is clearing
out, he is afraid of the police car which he
sees at an accident site ahead, and he heads
down a little-used lane to avoid a confrontation. Blundering toward the only light he can
see, he turns his ankle, struggles on in the
blinding snow, and collapses against the window
of an old farmhouse. He wakes to find himself in
the isolated, dilapidated cottage of Moses*
Beech, a white-haired old country man who is in
his seventies, at least. Reluctantly, Moses
lets him stay while the blizzard continues, but
on the second day Peter finds him obviously very
ill. He builds a fire, nurses the old man, and
tries, in his bumbling town-bred way, to care
for the chickens. While Moses is ill, Peter
hears a news report of his absence and
disconnects some wires in the ancient radio so
that his host will not learn that he is a
runaway. After Moses recovers Peter stays on,
hoping that the interest in his disappearance
will die down in a few weeks. Gradually he
learns more about fiercely independent Moses,
and he meets the nearest neighbors, Charlie
Bailey, for whom Moses works as hired man, and
his daughter, Susan*. Although his first sight
of Susan shoveling manure in her rough clothes
and heavy glasses does not awaken his interest,
Peter changes his mind when she comes up to
bring milk for Moses and he sees she is really a
good-looking blonde about his age. When they go
for a walk Susan tells him that she had recognized him from the television and newspaper reports, and he tries to explain to her why he
left home. Through the spring and summer Peter's
relationships with both Moses and Susan develop.
To his astonishment, he realizes that Moses
can't read and that two airmail letters stuck in
a copy of *Tom Sawyer* have never been opened. At
an opportune moment, he suggests that he could
read them aloud and discovers that they are from

Moses's younger brother who ran away to
Australia many years before. Between them they
compose a letter to Joseph, but when the reply
finally arrives it is from his wife, saying that
he died still wondering whether Moses had
forgiven him for leaving him with the care of
the farm and their old mother. With Susan,
Peter's friendship grows fast but is discouraged
by Charlie Bailey, who wants Susan to go to
agricultural college and marry a farmer and who
warns Peter to stay away from his daughter or he
will report him to the police. Susan, however,
confesses to Peter that she wants to go to a
college to study Commercial Design. Through the
summer Peter works hard on Moses's garden and
learns a lot about farm life and self-respect.
Susan manages to see him or send him a note
occasionally until Moses has a slight stroke,
and her mother insists that she be allowed to
come up to help nurse him. They see the old man
through his illness, their friendship turns to
love, they go to bed together, and Susan fears
she is pregnant. In fury, her father reports
Peter to the police. The officer investigates
and sends a social worker to interview Moses.
She decides he must be taken to a nursing home.
Peter's parents, brought by the police, and the
social worker coming to take Moses arrive
simultaneously. While Peter's father is chewing
him out in the yard, they are startled by an
explosion and find that Moses has shot himself
rather than leave his home. Peter returns to
family life that is still unsatisfactory, but
more hopeful than before. He gets a job, goes to
school at night, and dreams of someday returning
to the isolated cottage, for which Moses has
left him the deed. Since Peter is seventeen and
has left a note stating his intention, the
threat of his being widely sought merely as a
runaway, on which the plot depends, seems
unlikely, particularly after the weather moder-
ates and he writes his parents saying he is all
right. If a reader accepts this doubtful premise, however, Peter's gradual growth in self-
reliance and understanding is well developed,
and the far from happy ending seems inevitable
and satisfactory. Moses is a memorable character
and both Peter and Susan are believable teenagers. Young Observer.

MOTHER BLOODWORT (*Which Witch?**), a comic figure, one of the Todcaster witches who compete for the hand of Arriman the wizard. She is old and forgetful and often turns herself into a coffee table and then can't remember how to disenchant herself. Her familiar is a Cloud of Flies. In the contest, she makes a mess of turning seven princesses into seven black swans.

MOTHER MORTIMER (*Noah's Castle**), May Mortimer, mother of Nessie*, Barry*, Geoff, and Ellen, and wife of Norman, who is called Father*. She is a pleasant, patient, once delicately pretty woman, used to catering to and giving in to her domineering husband, who provides adequately for her and the children but who has little respect for her. She never confronts him on issues but goes behind his back when she wants something badly enough. For example, when Father insists on having Peggy the dog put down to save food and the Timpsons take her in instead, she smuggles table scraps to them. When Father allows Mr*. Gerald Bowling to dominate the place, flattered by his former employer's attentions, May refuses to put up with being treated as a maid and moves out to the Timpson house, taking Ellen with her. After the raid, she returns because she knows Father needs her.

MOUSE (*Alice's Adventures in Wonderland**; *Alice's Adventures under Ground**), one of the first creatures Alice* meets in Wonderland. She encounters him swimming in the pool of tears she wept when she was nine feet tall. She innocently offends him by talking about her cat, Dinah. He attempts to dry out Alice and his friends, the Duck*, the Dodo*, and others, by reciting the "driest thing" he knows: the story of English history starting with William the Conqueror. Later he tells the "long sad tale" of his life in emblematic verse printed in the shape of his tail. Like the others, he is a flat type, an amusing and interesting caricature.

MOWGLI (*The Jungle Books**), boy raised by the wolves in the Indian jungle. He is taught the Law of the Jungle and the master words for each type of animal by Baloo*, the sleepy brown bear, and learns other skills from his friend,

Bagheera*, the Black Panther, as well as from
the wolves, particularly Grey Brother and his
litter mates. Since he develops more slowly than
the animals, they don't recognize his superiority for many years, though his skills would be
extraordinary for a boy raised among men, but
many of them are not quite comfortable at the
way he can stare them down. Although he has
devoted friends among the animals and a woman in
the village who thinks she might be his mother
takes him in lovingly, Mowgli never really fits
into either world.

MR. ABEDNEGO TWITE (*Black Hearts in Battersea**),
Simon's emotional landlord, husband of menacing
Ella Twite, and father of scrawny, tart-tongued
Dido. Mrs. Twite is the sister of the leader of
the conspirators who scheme to overthrow King
James III and put Bonnie Prince Georgie of
Hanover on the throne. Mr. Twite often sings
scurrilous songs, plays an instrument called
the hoboy in the Glee Group of musicians to
which he and his wife belong, and is fond of
making grand gestures. At the end, weary of his
"wife and her family and their burning political
ambitions," he resolves to get rid of them and
start over in a land where musicians are
respected and sets the fuse so the dynamite will
go off earlier than planned. Since he tells
Simon what he has done, he makes it possible for
Simon to save the Duke and Duchess and all the
white hats from being blown up. He requests
that a memorial be erected to Dido on Inchmore,
bearing the inscription, "Dido Twite, a
Delicate Sprite," and Simon intends to honor
his wish.

MR. ABEL POTT (*The Borrowers Aloft**), the
gentle, old ex-railway signalman who has built
Little Fordham model village as a hobby for his
own amusement. He has worn a wooden leg since he
lost his own while rescuing a badger from a
train. He works with loving care on his models,
making them as authentic as he can and letting
others like Miss* Menzies help if they wish,
but plodding quietly on as he sees fit. He
never quite believes in the Borrowers, but,
being a kindly man, he humors Miss Menzies about
them. He serves as a foil for avaricious,

sharp-dealing Mr.* Sidney Platter, whose Ballyhoggin is the typical hokey tourist-trap
display, filled with mass-produced objects.

MR. ALLEN (*The Singing Cave**), last of a family
that once owned all the islands and good land,
but who now lives in a small cottage with his
books and housekeeper. An educated man, he is
the logical person to tell of the find of the
Viking remains in the Singing Cave, but because
his own research has made him believe the
Vikings did not reach Western Ireland and he
does not want to prove his own writings
incorrect, he goes to great lengths to steal and
dispose of the important relics and to deceive
Pat and his honest grandfather. After his
duplicity has been discovered and he has been
saved by the courageous actions of Pat and Pat's
grandfather, he tries to make amends by teaching
the boy.

MR. AND MRS. HEDLEY (*Gumble's Yard**; *Widdershins Crescent**), neighbors who help the Thompson children materially and morally. Mr. Hedley
helps them move to Widdowson Crescent, assists
them in influencing Walter* Thompson to their
way of thinking, and even lends them money. Mrs.
Hedley, though penny-pinching, overly serious,
and a little house-proud, is a warm and caring
woman. She gives them food and necessities.
Dick*, the children's best friend, is the
Hedleys' son.

MR. BAGTHORPE (*Ordinary Jack**), Jack's father, a
writer of television scripts, the ideas for
which he pirates from ·letters Mrs. Bagthorpe
receives from readers of her newspaper Agony
Columns. He is very "categorical," "especially
so on subjects about which he knew practically
nothing...." He and Uncle* Parker bicker
constantly. An exhibitionist, he breaks an arm
while trying to stand on his head and thereafter
has to use a tape recorder to produce his
scripts. When he is dictating to the machine, he
hides outside in bushes and thickets, where
Zero* finds him and runs off with his taping
equipment. At the end, Mr. Bagthorpe discovers
Jack's notebook with the vital Plan of Campaign
hidden under Jack's pile of comics, to which Mr.

Bagthorpe has gone surreptiously for reading material. Although the scheme is up, Mr. Bagthorpe doesn't want anyone to know he reads comics, so he doesn't blow the whistle on Jack and Uncle Parker.

MR. BILLING (*Smith**), admirer of Miss* Mansfield. He turns out to be the real villain of the novel. An attorney in the firm that handles old Mr. Field's affairs, he has tempted and goaded Jack Field, the lame man also known as Mr. Black, to have his father murdered, thinking that they can thereby reach his fortune. Since he has been watching the murder from a nearby window, he knows that Smith* must have the document and accuses him of the murder before Mr.* and Miss* Mansfield and accompanies the boy to Newgate Gaol. There he tries by cajolery and veiled threats to get Smith to give up the document, which he believes will lead him to the hiding place of the fortune, and even arranges for Smith's escape, also arranging that the assassins will meet him as he emerges on the roof. After the climactic scene in which both Jack Field and Lord* Tom are killed, Billing runs away, but later returns to turn King's Evidence and earn a short term in prison. There, however, the old man in the fireplace, who had taken a liking to Smith and had overheard all Billing's conversations with the boy, stoves his head in during a "nightmare," an appropriate end for the wicked man.

MR. BUMPS AND HIS MONKEY (De la Mare, Walter*, ill. Dorothy Lathrop, Winston, 1942; originally called "The Old Lion" and included in *The Lord Fish and Other Tales*, Faber, 1933), fantasy set mostly in London where there were still sailing ships and horse-drawn cabs. When *The Old Lion* has sailed south along the west coast of Africa, John Bumps, second mate, buys a monkey from his friend, the chief of the Mlango-Nlango tribe, who assures him that it is no common "skittle-skattle" monkey. Mr. Bumps names him Jasper and finds him remarkably quick to learn. Jasper soon begins to talk English and, in his quiet, serious way, makes very good sense. When they get to London, in a heavy fog, Mr. Bumps leaves Jasper by a lamppost while he goes into a

pub. An animal shop owner, Mr. Moss, finds the
monkey and takes him, but, uncomfortable at
having stolen him, sells him soon to a
small-time showman, Mr. J. Smith, who bills
himself as Signor Dolcetto Antonio. Mr. Smith
and his stout wife are both kindhearted and set
up a bank account for Jasper into which they
scrupulously put half of what they take in when
he goes on the stage. He makes his debut as
Doctor Jasper at the old Fortune Theatre and
soon becomes famous and wealthy, though he
continues to miss his first friend and to be a
bit melancholy. When Mr. Bumps returns again
from sea and sees the ads for Jasper's
performance, he at once suspects the truth and
takes his wife and three children, Topsy,
Emmanuel, and Kate, up to London for a treat,
not mentioning his suspicions to the children.
At the Fortune they have front seats in the
upper balcony, where they enjoy the arrival of
the royal family in their box and all the
preliminary acts, but when Jasper appears,
dressed as the All-Excellent Ammanabi Nana Dah,
Almighty Emperor of all the Ethiopians, Mr.
Bumps cannot restrain himself from calling out,
in his forecastle voice, "Jasper!" Without
hesitation, the monkey in his robes heavy with
gold and lace patters toward the footlights,
climbs the arch that frames the stage, and
tippets along the edge of the balcony to Mr.
Bumps. In the near-riot that follows, the king
intervenes and questions Jasper, who points out
that Mr. Bumps is his "first friend," and they
are all conducted to the Royal Box. The theater
manager agrees with Mr. Bumps and Mr. Smith to
release Jasper from his contract if he will sit
for three days and greet everyone who can pay to
pass through the theater and see him. Jasper
then gives presents to all his friends, buys a
large quantity of trinkets, takes the rest of
his money in coffers, and returns to his old
country with Mr. Bumps on *The Old Lion*. There
they spread the trinkets and the money in a
clearing and put up a tent for Jasper. The
enticing dainties and the trinkets disappear,
but none of Jasper's monkey friends come near
him. Thinking the royal robes might have scared
them off, Jasper strips to his own fur and says
goodbye to Mr. Bumps. The next day he and the

robes are gone, and when Mr. Bumps calls, no voice answers him. The simple story is memorable because of the characterization of sweet-natured Jasper, with his grave, dignified ways, his movements "as quiet as flowing water and delicate as the flowers beside it," and his serious demeanor that seems to hide a great depth of spirit. It also says, by contrast, something about the shallowness of human beings. Fanfare.

MR. CANDLIN (*The Bonny Pit Laddie**), friend of Flem Fairless, father of Peter Fairless, a schoolmate of Dick Ullathorne. Mr. Candlin is a historian and archaeologist who is interested in Branton Hill, a mound that overlooks the colliery. During the strike, he hires Mr. Fairless to tunnel into the mound. There they find the skeleton of what they think is an Anglo-Saxon chief. Dick finds the whole endeavor extremely fascinating. It whets his appetite for learning. Following the strike and terrible cave-in accident, the doctor tells Dick he is well enough to return to the pits if he wishes, but Dick realizes that he has changed and no longer wants to become a miner. He confides in Mr. Candlin, who quizzes him in Latin and then arranges with Dick's grandmother, Mrs*. Ullathorne, for Dick to go into apprenticeship with the local chemist, Mr. Dorman. Mr. Candlin's friend, Mr. Fairless, leaves Branton Colliery when he is blacklisted by Mr. Sleath and can't find a job and emigrates to Australia.

MR. CODLING (*"Minnow" on the Say**), Bertram Arthur Codling, Adam* Codling's aged grandfather, whose mind became addled when his son, John, Adam's father, was killed in World War II. He still awaits John's return, refusing to accept the fact of his death and says he will divulge the hiding place of the Codling family jewels only when John returns. When he sees Adam standing in the moonlight one night, he thinks John has come back, but dies of the shock before he reveals the secret. He is a kind, befuddled old fellow, once well-known and well-liked in the community. Years before he found the Codling jewels, the ones that

Jonathan* Codling had hidden before he went off
to fight the Spanish Armada, and then hid them
again. He hid them in such a way that the rhyme
Jonathan taught Sarah* Codling also points to
the place where Mr. Codling put the jewels. Like
most of the characters in the novel, he is a
stock but still interesting figure.

MR. COPPLESTONE (*The Warden's Niece**), the Reverend Francis Copplestone, eccentric clergyman
who becomes tutor to Maria* Henniker-Hadden and
to the Smith brothers. Immensely tall and odd
looking, Mr. Copplestone has no sense of his own
absurdity and is constantly getting into
situations where his intense curiosity makes him
look like a fool. When he tries the ladder made
of rags that the boys have fashioned to climb
the pear tree, he falls through the hen-house
roof and has to be extricated by their father.
When he tries to fight the mad bull, he is
dismayed to discover that it pays no attention
to his matador technique, and he ends in the
middle of the pond. He is undismayed by the
anger and outrage that his behavior often
creates and continues obliviously with whatever
his mind is set on.

MR. CROFT (*The Trouble with Donovan Croft**),
Donovan's father, loving and caring, a black who
emigrated with his wife from Jamaica to London.
Before the novel begins, he insisted that his
wife not return to Jamaica to care for her dying
father because he felt that the money could
better be spent on a down payment for a house.
They had a violent argument, and she walked out,
severely shaking his self-confidence. Since he
had to spend long hours working, he decided to
put Donovan in a foster home. His action causes
Donovan to feel rejected and unwanted and leads
to the boy's muteness.

MR. EVANS (*Carrie's War**), Councillor Samuel
Evans, mean-spirited store owner who, with his
much younger sister, Auntie* Lou, takes in
Carrie* Willow and her brother Nick* when they
are evacuated from London in World War II.
Having seen his father killed in a mine accident
and then having worked very hard to support his
mother, Mr. Evans resents anyone who has had an

easier life, particularly Americans and his
older sister Dilys, who married into the mine
owner's family and has had a life of beautiful
clothes, travel, and servants. It angers him to
have his sister Lou or the children enjoy
anything he has not provided, and he is
niggardly with what he has, saying, for example,
that children should not have meat because it
makes them boisterous, and insisting that they
should go up and down stairs only once a day,
for fear of wear on the carpet. Although he
bullies Auntie Lou, the children are not really
afraid of him, Nick because he is fascinated by
the man's ill-fitting false teeth and Carrie
because she senses his unhappiness and feels
sorry for him, particularly since he is expecting his son, Frederick, to join him in the
store after his army service and Carrie has
heard Frederick say he has no intention of
returning to the valley.

MR. GARNER (*The Dark Behind the Curtain**), the
headmaster of the school Colin Jackus*, Ann*
Ridley, and Colin Marshall* attend. He is an
elderly man, patient, perceptive, and understanding. The youths seem to respect him. He
forces Jackus to take a role in Miss* Lampeter's
play by threatening to prosecute him for stealing school tape recorders if he doesn't. His
reasons are undisclosed. Perhaps he suspects
that Marshall was behind the deed. Eventually
Jackus takes Mr. Garner into his confidence
concerning his and Ann's suspicions about the
spirits. Jackus never tells Mr. Garner about
Marshall's part in the tape recorder matter,
however.

MR. GERALD BOWLING (*Noah's Castle**), employer of
Norman Mortimer (called Father*) before he sold
to a chain the shoestore of which Father is now
the manager and Cliff* Trent the assistant
manager. Perceptive, hard, and unscrupulous, Mr.
Gerald realizes that Father considers him of
higher social status and is in awe of him. He
takes advantage of Father's desire to please him
by simply moving in and then blackmails Father
into letting him stay on indefinitely by implying that he will inform the authorities about
Father's hoarding food and supplies. Because of

Mr. Gerald, both Nessie and Mother* leave. When
Mr. Gerald moves out, he leaves abruptly, taking with him two dozen bottles of good liquor
and several cans of choice food, and then tips
off Share Alike, a community organization,
apparently in retaliation for not being treated
as well as he thought he should have been.

MR. GRUBER (*A Bear Called Paddington**), the old
antique dealer with whom Paddington Bear becomes friends while on jaunts about the neighborhood. Mr. Gruber always addresses Paddington
as Mr. Brown and tends to speak in aphorisms.
After he tells Paddington how the great masters
would often put new paintings on top of previous
ones, Paddington decides to remove the paint
from the canvas of the real Mr. Brown (his
rescuer) to see whether a master lies below,
and, as the reader anticipates, makes a big
mess and destroys Mr. Brown's picture. Paddington quickly paints a new one and enters it in
the local contest in Mr. Brown's name.
Ironically, it wins first prize for originality
of concept. Mr. Gruber also attends Paddington's
birthday party, where he congenially helps to
make Paddington's magic tricks a success.

MR. HENRY (*The Trouble with Donovan Croft**),
Keith and Donovan's authoritarian teacher, an
ex-soldier who takes pride in having an
exceptionally orderly classroom and in making
his students fear him. After he strikes and
reviles Donovan and Donovan runs away, he
overreacts in organizing the search and goes out
of his way to be nice to the boy. He does appear
to become more sensitive to his pupils as
people. He falls short of stereotype.

MR. HOLYSTONE (*The Stolen Lake**), Captain
Hughes's steward and Dido's good friend and
protector. A slight, self-effacing, sober man,
he is very learned, speaks nine languages
fluently, and has a varied background. In a
previous life, it comes out, he was King Arthur
of England, reborn later as a noble in Roman
America, where he played as a child with Princess Elen of Lyonesse. In the course of the
story, he is hailed as the returned High King,
and, his wicked queen, Ginevra, deposed, he

assumes his rightful position as ruler of the realm of New Cumbria, the kingdom of the ancient Celts transported to the New World.

MR. JONES (*The Robbers**), father of Darcy*, who is so crippled by arthritis that he is confined to a wheel chair. Formerly a lock-keeper on the canal, he has lost his house because of his illness and now lives with his son, Bing*, and Bing's wife, Addie*. A man of some education, he quotes Shakespeare on all occasions and sings with the remnant of a beautiful voice.

MR. JULIAN OAKAPPLE (*Midnight Is a Place**), serious, ginger-haired young man, tutor to Lucas* Bell and Sir* Randolph Grimsby's assistant. Because he hero-worshipped Denzil* Murgatroyd, he accompanied him to the English seacoast on Denzil's way to France after Denzil lost the bet with Sir Randolph. Mr. Oakapple lost two fingers in a skirmish there on Denzil's behalf, and thus his career as a violinist ended. Because of his deep love for Denzil and Midnight Court and his lingering hope that Denzil might still be alive, he offered himself for the position of tutor to Lucas. When a letter came to Sir Randolph saying that Denzil had died in France, Mr. Oakapple had Anna-Marie* Murgatroyd brought to Midnight Court. After Mr. Oakapple recovers from the burns he suffered trying to save Sir Randolph after Sir Randolph set fire to Midnight Court, at Lady* Eulalia Murgatroyd's suggestion he sets out to learn to play the violin left-handed. He is the epitome of loyalty.

MR. LEADBETTER (*Which Witch?**), the loyal, efficient secretary of the wizard Arriman Canker. He was born with a small tail of which he is very self-conscious. He used to be a bank robber, but, when he realized that crime did not suit him, he took the position with Arriman. He has two main functions in the story: he organizes the contest among the witches for Arriman's hand in marriage and acts as Terence* Mugg's uncle so that the boy can live at Darkington Hall with his earthworm, Rover, which is thought to be Belladonna's familiar.

MR. MANSFIELD (*Smith**), blind magistrate whom Smith* bumps into in the night after his flight from the two men in brown and whom he leads, for a guinea, back to his house. Moved by an almost contemptuous pity, Smith sticks to the blind man and accepts his offer of a meal and a night's lodging. Blind in more ways than one, Mr. Mansfield considers his daughter a saint, not being aware that she chafes in her restricted life and loathes his generosity to the filthy child. He is also blind in his devotion to justice, not realizing how it miscarries without compassion. Genteel Mr. Mansfield learns from scruffy Smith the real meaning of kindness and loyalty, and in the end takes the boy for his friend and companion.

MR. MCNAIR (*The Team**; *Prove Yourself a Hero**), Arthur, horse dealer and hard-driving father of Peter* and two older boys. A widower, he seems to have no feeling for his sons, his only interest in them being as workers and trainers for his horses. He routs them out before six in the morning and keeps them working until after dark at night, shouting at them angrily and never thinking of paying them. When he promises Peter that he can keep Toadhill Flax, the pony Peter has trained himself and the first one he has truly loved, but then sells him at the first good offer, Peter leaves home and appears at the council office, asking to be found a foster home and refusing to return to his father. Realizing that he is deeply disturbed, they send him to live at the home of Ruth* Hollis, and Mr. McNair, jolted by the experience, takes his first holiday in years and returns married to an Neopolitan opera singer, an ample, warm-hearted woman who brings some order and comfort to the house. In *The Team*, he is persuaded not to shoot Sirius, the unmanageable pony that throws Peter, only when Ruth points out that such action could bring on Peter's mental disturbance again, but he is pleased when Peter, havng secretly trained the pony, wins individual honors at the area trials. He and Mrs.* Meredith are both unsentimental, horsy types, but when Jonathan* Meredith is kidnapped, he is able to comfort the imperious woman. McNair is known as a slave-driving boss, a shrewd judge of horses,

and a fair dealer; his second wife and the birth
of their child, Giovanni, soften his abrasive
temperament somewhat.

MR. MOON'S LAST CASE (Patten*, Brian, ill. Mary
Moore, Allen, 1975; Scribner, 1976), lighthearted, picaresquely adventurous fantasy novel
set in contemporary Wales, which improvises on
the conventional private-eye chase and examines
attitudes toward the miraculous and unusual.
The story opens on the passenger ship *Irish
Rose*, plying toward Brumble Head, Wales, where
the second mate sights what he thinks is a
leprechaun. Later a dock watchman and security
guard spy a mysterious intruder and phone the
police. Other sightings result in the rumor that
a leprechaun is in the area. Representatives of
the communication media flock in, and a street-
wise kid and budding con man, Johnny Plackham,
sensing an opportunity to line his pockets,
organizes schoolchildren into SSFTPOL, the
Secret Society for the Protection of Leprechauns, or, as it soon becomes known, SPLOT. A
flashback chapter set in Oakwood, the world of
dwarfs, explains the phenomenon. The dwarf
Nameon* crawls inside a derelict lifeboat, falls
asleep while pondering a map and journal of the
legendary Greenweed, a dwarf who once visited
the world of humans and returned to tell about
it, and awakens on the ship. The book follows
his sometimes calculated, at other times
frantic, and always eventful progress northward
to Norton Bay, where he hopes to find two
gigantic oaks which, according to Greenweed,
form the gateway linking the worlds of humans
and of dwarves. An almost equal number of
chapters detail the zealous and persistent
efforts of Mr*. Reginald Moon to apprehend
Nameon, who by luck and resourcefulness remains
one jump ahead all the way. A retired police
superintendent, Mr. Moon happens to be present
when the call comes in from the Brumble Head
dock, and, having nothing of value to do with
his life, in dubious health, curious, eager for
excitement, and open-minded, privately undertakes an investigation. Nameon hops a freight
(observed coincidentally by Mr. Moon, who thinks
he may indeed be from another world) to
Llandridnod Wells, sets off cross-country on

foot, and finds and occupies a deserted, old
cottage not far from the village of Penmoor,
where he takes meals at the Drowning Duck inn
run by capable Mr. Butler, whom Nameon pays with
ancient holly and oak gold coins he has brought
from dwarf-land and who happily adds them to his
coin collection, and by his fat, kind wife, Mrs.
Butler, who has installed for business purposes
the sole television in their village. When he
learns from watching a television interview that
Mr. Moon is on his case and later spots the
detective's car entering the village, Nameon
takes off. He treks northward for seven miles,
sheltering that night in a barn loft which he
shares with Mr. William O'Lovelife, a garrulous,
philosophical tramp in tattered formal dress who
carries with him a case full of maps. The two
proceed by foot along the River Severn to a town
called Little Wenlock, where the tramp nips
apples at Mrs. Wilkie's stall, and then to
Welshpool, where in Joe's Cafe Mr. O'Lovelife
brings Nameon's map up to date and secures him a
ride in the lorry of the kind Irishman, Paddy
Wilkie, on his way to deliver potatoes at
Lewsbury market. There Nameon gets lost among
the stalls, and, attracted by the cathedral,
enters it, inadvertently causes trouble, and
finally, resigned to the inevitable, reveals
himself to some schoolchildren on a field trip
who happen to be members of SPLOT and are eager
to protect him from Mr. Moon, whom they consider
an archvillain. One of them, clever, take-charge
Benjamin Platts, smuggles him aboard the school
bus, which gets him to Steelborough where Johnny
Plackham lives. Johnny, however, who is SPLOT's
first president, is also its first traitor. He
locks Nameon in his backyard shed, intending to
sell his story to the media since his SPLOT scam
is no longer prospering, but his virtuous
younger brother, Tobias, releases Nameon, takes
him to the local cinema, which is filled with
schoolchildren, raffles off some of his fairy
money to get train fare, and, with Benjamin's
help, whisks him off to the rail station just
ahead of Johnny's news-thirsty crews. Mr. Moon,
who has managed to stay on Nameon's trail by
luck, deduction, and the help of a nondescript
dog named Wanderlust*, catches sight of Nameon
and gives chase. Both board but end up in

nonconnecting cars. At Norton Bay, now a resort, Nameon unsuccessfully searches for the oak trees through which Greenweed had returned to his dimension; then he spies a wrecked fishing smack off shore, enters it, and disappears. Evidently the boat had been made of lumber from the no-longer-existent oaks. Mr. Moon follows Nameon's footprints to the water, climbs inside the smack, too, finds Nameon's name carved there, curls up, and, worn out by his long quest and too tired to try to figure out where Nameon has gotten to, falls asleep. The book ends abruptly; what happens next is left to the reader's imagination. Although coincidence plays a large part in the story and the reader never finds out how Nameon gets on board the *Irish Rose*, events hold the attention and seem credible given Nameon's panic and the assumption that he can read, understand, and speak English. The reader cheers on both Nameon, who is a gritty little fellow, and Mr. Moon, whom we know would never hurt Nameon and only wants to learn who he is and whether fairyland exists. Action abounds; social comment varies in subtlety; different attitudes about the possibility of leprechauns and dwarfs contrast with one another; generous detail of place, incident, emotion, and action make things seem real; the various characters Nameon meets, though types, are interesting and carefully drawn; and comic, slapstick, ironic, and verbal humor keep the mood light. Poe Nominee.

MR. PARGETER (*Time of Trial**), idealistic London bookseller, whose published plea for parish ownership of property so that the poor may have decent lodging results in his imprisonment for libel and sedition. In some ways out of step with his times, he nevertheless sees the impor-tance of providing for Meg while he is in jail. An unusually considerate and caring man, he fails to see how he is trying to mold his son, John*, into the image of an ideal son, but he accepts the youth's running away to independence in a good manner. While in prison he writes a textbook for teaching poor children to read. He urges Meg to be patient with her sweetheart, Robert* Kerridge, and to give him time to figure out a way for them to wed. Mr. Pargeter is an interesting character, likeable and sympathetic, even if he is the stereotypical idealist.

MR. PLANTAGANET (*The Dolls' House**), father in the doll family. Once a highland doll, wearing a kilt and carrying a bagpipe, he has been neglected and abused and as a result has a timid, fearful personality. When he has the security of the house and his position of postmaster in the toy post office, he is contented, though he needs frequent reassurance from the Dutch farthing doll, Tottie*.

MR. PURVES (*A Sound of Chariots**), the store-keeper for whom Bridie McShane delivers papers to local subscribers. He appears here and there throughout the novel, but figures most impor-tantly when Bridie is accused of stealing Major Morrison's peaches. Mr. Purves sticks up for Bridie, especially when the Major insists that she must be guilty because her father was a "bloody Red." Later, Mr. Purves advises her to be less outspoken, weigh her words, and watch her step. She is grateful for his help, advice, and friendship.

MR. REGINALD MOON (*Mr. Moon's Last Case**), retired Welsh police superintendent, whose dogged persistence and powers of deduction almost succeed in catching Nameon*, the dwarf. Admiring tiny Nameon's courage in leaping from the railroad parapet to the train as it speeds by below and having nothing better to do any longer, Mr. Moon quite suddenly decides to follow the small fellow, of whose identity and origin he is ignorant at that point, but whom he suspects may indeed be . a dwarf or leprechaun. Mr. Moon is thorough, observant, imaginative in a restrained way, open to new possibilities, and kind. He begins by doing research on dwarfs in the library, and as time goes by he becomes more and more involved in the chase, until he becomes obsessed with apprehending Nameon to the exclusion of almost everything else. Neglecting his appearance, he doesn't shave or take care of himself, and his health deteriorates. He gets "his man" in the end, insofar as is humanly possible, and is the epitome of the highest type of police officer.

MR. ROPER (*The Trouble with Donovan Croft**), the headmaster of Keith Chapman's school. He carefully juggles the needs and desires of parents, teachers, and pupils. He makes mistakes but sincerely tries to serve the best interests of his pupils. He placates the angry Chapmans, reasons with stubborn, authoritarian Mr.* Henry, and helps Donovan by enlisting the aid of the school psychologist even though he knows she will, as usual, patronize him. He is a sensitively portrayed, rounded figure.

MR. RUDGE (*The Winter of the Birds**), the first character the reader sees and the one whose problem dominates the book, providing the atmosphere of terror that first catches the reader's emotions. He sees, or thinks he sees, terrible steel birds that hover over and flit back and forth on the wires that cross the roofs of St. Savior's Street and that threaten the real birds and the well-being of the area. Edward Flack is the first resident to meet him (which seems strange when both have apparently lived there all their lives or at least for many years) and is the one through whom Mr. Rudge's problem is communicated.

MRS. BEDONEBYASYOUDID (*The Water-Babies**), one of the fairies who direct the water-babies at St. Brandan's Isle. She dresses in black and is very ugly, with a nose so hooked that the bridge of it reaches above her eyebrows. She represents how people should not behave, that is, by responding in kind. She knows everything that goes on and tells Tom that she will go on for ever and ever, for she is "as old as Eternity, and yet as young as Time." She says she is the ugliest fairy in the world and will continue to be so until people "behave themselves as they ought to." Then she will become as handsome as her sister, Mrs.* Doasyouwouldbedoneby. She, her sister, the Irishwoman, and Mother Carey are all aspects of the same being. By herself, Mrs. Bedonebyasyoudid is a type figure, a shallow, didactic near-caricature but still interesting.

MRS. BEECH (*Good Night, Mr. Tom**), mentally unbalanced, abusive mother of William* Beech, the evacuee child billeted with Tom* Oakley. Religiously fanatic, she has tried to beat the "sin" out of her son and has mistreated him so that he is undernourished and terrified, almost afraid to speak, and unable to read or play, though he is almost nine years old. When she has a second illegitimate child, she sends for William, evidently planning to have him care for the secret child while she works, but, unable to cope, she ties him in a closet with the baby and only one bottle and then deserts them. Eventually she is discovered to have committed suicide.

MRS. BLEWITT (*A Dog So Small**), Ben's mother, a loving mother, wife, and daughter, who is instrumental in his acquiring a dog. She is a warm, caring woman, who respects her children and sees them as individuals with particular needs of their own, yet seems unaware that she uses them to satisfy her own emotional needs. She diplomatically gets Ben to agree to visit Granny* and Grandpa* Fitch after he has rejected the wool-work picture. When May gets married and moves to north London and the second daughter, Dilys, moves with her, Mrs. Blewitt wants to move to north London, too. With contradictory logic, she says their present place is too big, and the air is fresher in north London. Her desire to be with her daughters and her lack of satisfaction with having only males in the house leads to the family's move to a more open area, and to Ben's getting the dog he longs for.

MRS. CLIPSTONE (*Danny, The Champion of the World**), local vicar's wife, whose baby carriage William* has altered so that it is big enough to cart over 100 pheasants. The carriage is extra long and extra wide, with an extraordinarily deep well beneath. The baby rides on top of the poached pheasants, which have been doped. As Mrs. Clipstone wheels the carriage with the baby and the sleeping pheasants through the village, the pheasants begin to waken. She wheels it faster and faster, arriving at the filling station on a dead run, with her baby frantically yelling his head off, frightened out of his wits by his steadily shifting mattress. When she reaches the pump, she stops abruptly, grabs her

baby, and races off to safety. With the weight
of the baby removed, the still half-doped birds
rise up in a cloud and flap their way to the
apple tree nearby, where they are perched when
Mr. Hazell drives up in his shiny silver Rolls
Royce to claim them as his property. This is
one of the novel's most hilarious episodes.

MRS. DAISY JONES (*Tulku**), eccentric botanist
traveling in China with her guide, Lung, a young
poet. After they are joined by Theodore* Tewker
and make their way toward Tibet, she tells Theo
of her childhood in a Battersea slum, her rise
as an actress, and her love affair with Monty
German, a wealthy English Jew. She also tell of
their travels to find rare plants, of his
determination to marry her and his family's
interference, at which she connives for his
good, and of her agreement to stay out of
England for ten years. She and Lung become
lovers, and the Lama Amchi decides that their
unborn child will be the next incarnation of the
Tulku of the Siddha Asara, spiritual leader for
that part of Tibet. Planning to escape, she goes
along with the lama's religious training and
gradually becomes so impressed that she decides
to stay, insisting on safe conduct and support
for Lung and Theo as part of the bargain. She is
a forceful character, a "soldier," Lung calls
her, given to rough language but capable of
drawing-room manners, able to shoot and kill one
of the bandits who ambush them but sensitive to
Theo's emotional upheaval after his father's
death and to his religious scruples, and showing
genuine concern for Lung and true love for
Monty.

MRS. DOASYOUWOULDBEDONEBY (*The Water-Babies**),
one-fourth of the composite fairy figure, of
which the other aspects are Mrs.* Bedonebyasyoudid*, the Irishwoman, and Mother Carey. All
rule the water-babies on St. Brandan's Isle and
watch over Tom, among others. Mrs. Doasyouwouldbedoneby is a very pretty lady, tall, soft, and
comfortable, unlike her sister, who is prickly
and scaly. Mrs. Doasyouwouldbedoneby especially
likes to play with babies. Tom likes her very
much.

MRS. DORA SINGER (*Songberd's Grove**), Martin's* easily distracted and often preoccupied mother, for whom cleaning is a battle waged against the evil forces of dirt. Martin's Aunt Emmeline, Mr. Singer's sister, with whom the Singers have lived for seven years because housing is so short, has made Mrs. Singer feel inferior. The author, employing a humorous and homely image, says that "happiness and relief at being in her own place and away from her sister-in-law had made her fluff out and glow like a wet hen that had just been dried off in front of a fire." She wishes to get No. 7 slicked up before Aunt Emmeline visits, but when the vandals ruin the front door which had been newly refurbished at hard labor and painted bright red, she realistically resigns herself to the situation and then suddenly realizes that, since her family is happy with the flat as it is, it doesn't really matter what fussy Emmeline thinks. She is a foil for fearful, over-protective Mrs. Byre and ineffectual, dreamy La* Golondrina.

MRS. DRIVER (*The Borrowers**; *The Borrowers Afloat**), grumbling, suspicious, sharp-eyed cook and housekeeper of the old Georgian country house, Firbank Hall, which belongs to Great* Aunt Sophy and in which the Clock family of Borrowers, Pod*, Homily*, and Arrietty* live. In *The Borrowers*, she is defensive about her role because she knows a maid named Rosa Pickhatchet was dismissed some time before for stealing. In case someone should accuse her of theft when objects in the drawing room come up missing, she spies on the boy* and thus discovers the Borrowers, of whose true nature she never becomes aware. Ironically, Mrs. Driver is honest about material things, but stints on labor and loyalty to her employer. She is the villain of the story, the one who orders the extermination of the Borrowers, but, though a type figure, she has more depth than the usual villain and reveals a comic aspect that keeps her from being merely a "baddie" for the plot's sake. She appears again briefly at the end of *Afloat*, where she and Crampfurl the gardener discuss the Borrowers. The reader realizes, but Mrs. Driver never finds out, that Crampfurl has seen the Borrowers and knows what they really are, having sighted them and Spiller* on their trip downstream to Little Fordham.

MRS. DUNNITT (*The Seventh Raven**), old liberal, former communist, who is costume designer and make-up woman for the Christmas opera when South American terrorists take the whole cast hostage. Though basically in agreement with the terrorists' political views, she is chosen to be the advocate for the woman who represents the British public in the mock tiral, and she presents a convincing defense. She is also the person who, with great presence of mind, has transformed the original target of the terrorists, the Mattean ambassador's son, from the costume of a raven to that of a handmaiden of Jezebel, thereby concealing his identity from the terrorists.

MR. SEAGRAVE (*Masterman Ready**), wise and well-informed father and solicitous husband, who, with Masterman Ready*, builds the camps and stockade and maintains his family while they are marooned on a South Seas desert isle. A government official and planter in Sydney, Australia, he is bringing his family back to Australia after a buying trip to England when the ship, the *Pacific*, becomes disabled in a hurricane. Mr. Seagrave takes cheerfully what befalls, shows a strong belief in the providence of God, defers to Ready's leadership, recognizes the old seaman's skill and wisdom, never appears to consider the man his inferior, and seems a fount of information to answer the numerous questions his children pose, which are calculated by the author to instruct young readers in various matters of learning and behavior. Mr. Seagrave epitomizes the perfect husband and father.

MR. SELWYN RAVEN (*The Strange Affair of Adelaide Harris**), inquiry agent hired by Dr. Harris to look into the disappearance of his seven-week-old daughter and the mysterious appearance of an infant gypsy boy in her place. He is a shortish, stout, quietly dressed man whose outstanding feature is his club foot, which is encased in a large black boot. Mr. Raven is deeply acquainted with the darkness of the human soul and sees corruption and evil in even the most innocent people and events, wickedness either invented or enlarged beyond recognition by Mr. Raven's own imagination. In the case of Adelaide Harris, he becomes convinced that a foul murder is about to be committed by Mr. Brett, and his interest in this far exceeds his zeal in sorting out the misplaced babies. He constructs a large diagram of the interrelation-ships of guilt and motive in the case that resembles a huge spiderweb, with Mr. Brett at its center, all of it actually in error. Although he strikes terror into both Bostock* and Harris*, he never suspects that they are the true culprits in the case, and in the end he takes the gypsy baby and leaves it on the doorstep of the family he has decided, wrongly, should be held accountable for it. He then leaves town, congratulating himself on solving the case so brilliantly.

MRS. HEDGES (*The House in Norham Gardens**), day-lady for Aunt* Susan and Aunt Anne Mayfield and friend and advisor to Clare Mayfield. A knowledgeable and practical woman, she advises Clare about meeting payments and making repairs to the house. She gets the idea of opening the house for lodgers to bring in some needed extra money. She has a dreamy, nostalgic side to her character, too, and her stories about World War II and her wedding reinforce the novel's themes of the continuity of life and the need for tangible cultural symbols.

MR. SIDNEY PLATTER (*The Borrowers Aloft**; *The Borrowers Avenged**), greedy, rat-like, sharp-dealing undertaker, builder, and decorator, who constructs a model village, Ballyhoggin, to draw customers to Mrs.* Platter's tea room. To increase business, they kidnap Pod*, Homily*, and Arrietty* Clock (this is Mrs. Platter's idea) with shrimping net and cardboard box, right out of Vine Cottage in Mr.* Abel Pott's Little Fordham model village. They confine the Borrowers in the attic of their house for the winter, intending, when spring comes, to display the miniature people at Ballyhoggin in a glass cage he constructs. When the Borrowers escape, he leads the effort to get them back. It is his

attempt to consult Lady Mullings to "find" the
Borrowers that leads to the Platters' downfall.
He is mean and unscrupulous, his villainy
relieved by the comic aspects of his portrayal.
He serves as a foil for Mr. Pott.

MRS. JACOBS (*The Seventh Raven**), professionally
called Elsie Tope, cellist and mother of Doll*
Jacobs. She is the woman who is chosen by the
terrorists to represent the British public in
their mock trial as they hold a whole children's
opera cast hostage in a Kensington church. A
woman with a background of mental disturbance,
she is probably the major victim of the
incident, not because of her hand (injured by
a terrorist's bullet but already beginning to
heal by the book's end) but because of her mind,
whose delicate balance has been upset.

MRS. MABEL PLATTER (*The Borrowers Aloft**; *The
Borrowers Avenged**), a large, lumpy woman, foil
in personality and looks to sweet, slender Miss*
Menzies, who is also middle-aged. It is Mrs.
Platter's idea to kidnap the Borrowers from
Little Fordham, but Mr.* Platter works out the
details. Later, when the tea room trade declines, she urges him to consult Lady Mullings
and provides him with garments of Homily's* for
the lady to use in "finding" the miniature
people. She approaches caricature, like her
husband, and is flat and overdrawn but still
interesting. Though Mrs. Platter is a villain
who causes a good deal of trouble, the reader
never doubts that she will be undone in the end.

MRS. MAY (*The Borrowers**; *The Borrowers
Afield**; *The Borrowers Afloat**), the seemingly
wise and ancient woman who tells the story of
the Borrowers, mostly to Kate, the spoiled and
willful little girl, who is a kind of relative
of Mrs. May's and who, as an adult, writes it
down. Mrs. May inherits the cottage near Firbank
Hall, home of old Tom* Goodenough, who passes on
the details to Kate about what happens to the
Borrowers after they are nearly exterminated at
the end of *The Borrowers*. Although she has some
personality, Mrs. May mostly functions as a
literary device by which the writer can ease the
reader into the fantasy.

MRS. MEREDITH (*The Team**;   *Prove Yourself a Hero**;   *A Midsummer Night's Death**),   Elizabeth, wealthy,   imperious   mother   of   Jonathan*   and Jessica,   a brisk,   horsy type   used to   ordering people   around   and winning in any endeavor.   In *The Team*,   she   is   the   district   commisioner, known as the D.C.,   and   she organizes   the Pony Club team   and   pressures her   son to be part of it,   even though   he is not much   interested   in riding.   She is   highly competitive,   even ruth- less,   and seems   more angry   than grieved   when Jonathan   is kidnapped in   *Prove Yourself a Hero* and,   when   he   is   home   safely,   she   is   very irritated at having been bilked by the abductors and at having lost so much money and more than a little   critical   of   Jonathan   for   not   having somehow   escaped. Although   she genuinely   loves her son,   they have never gotten   along since he resists her manipulation passively but stubborn- ly,   an attitude   that only makes her more bossy and domineering.   In   *A Midsummer Night's Death*, she   has a minor role   and   seems somewhat   more mellow,   and in   a   sequel, *Free Rein*,   she has taken in the neurotic Iris Webster and   become a fond   grandmother to Iris's   child   fathered   by Jonathan,   though she is still highly critical of her son and abrasive in her relations with him.

MR. SMITH ("*Minnow*" *on   the Say**),   Andrew Ash- worthy-Smith,   disagreeable,   rude,   middle-aged man, who   with his   subdued wife   recently moved into   the   Barley area   and   who   is often   seen punting   on   the   Say near   the   Codling   house. Early   on,   Adam*   and   David*   suspect   he   is looking   for the   Codling treasure. Greedy   and hard,   the villain (a stock one) of the novel, he refuses   to let   his daughter,   Betsy*,   live   in Barley because she looks   so much like Adam that right away   the Codlings would realize   that the Smiths were related to them. He hopes to get the Codling house for a song,   and along with it the family   treasure   in   jewels.   At   the end,   much chastened by not getting   his wish and having to own up to his devious ways, he agrees to use his considerable   business connections   in order   to get   a   good   price   for   the   Codling jewels   for Miss* Codling.

MRS. NEECH (*Time   of Trial**),   middle-aged house-

keeper who has worked for Mr.* Pargeter ever
since her mistress married the bookseller
twenty years before the novel begins. Her
mistress died when Meg was born, and since then
Mrs. Neech has devoted herself to raising Meg
and taking care of the old bookseller. She is
stern and proper and insists on obedience,
industry, and decorum. At first she resists
adding Elijah* to the household, but later on
she and the little boy grow quite fond of each
other. Meg appreciates her warm heart, deep
loyalty, and firm support during the long months
of Mr. Pargeter's trial and imprisonment and her
rejection by Robert* Kerridge's parents.

MRS. OLDKNOW (*The Children of Green Knowe**;
The Chimneys of Green Knowe*; *A Stranger at
Green Knowe**; *An Enemy at Green Knowe**), owner
of Green Knowe, the house that dates from
medieval times, and great-grandmother of
Tolly*. A small, bright-eyed woman who reminds
Tolly of a partridge, she is almost childlike
herself in her imagination and her acceptance of
remarkable events. When roused by rudeness and
invasions to her privacy, however, she is fiery
and obstinant. She knows and sees the three
seventeenth-century children whom Tolly meets in
the house and also knows Susan* Oldknow, the
blind child from the eighteenth century, and she
even hears, occasionally, a baby from a much
earlier period, all with perfect naturalness and
acceptance. She is equally accepting of Ping's*
interest in the escaped gorilla, Hanno*, and
when she sees the marvelous beast she is not
afraid but rather shares Ping's delight and
wonder. Of all the spells that Melanie* Powers
casts on Green Knowe, Mrs. Oldknow most resents
the invasion of her mind that makes her say she
doesn't care what happens to the boys, an
invasion by a demon she is able to shake off but
briefly makes her very unlike her usual crisp,
sure self. With both boys she is loving and
understanding, and she respects them as
individuals.

MRS. SEAGRAVE (*Masterman Ready**), wife of Mr*.
Seagrave, mother of Tommy*, William*, and two
other children, and mistress of Juno*, who with
her family and Masterman Ready* is cast away on

a desert isle after their ship, the *Pacific*, founders in a storm. She is presented as very womanly and stereotyped as not strong physically, easily upset, often anxious, and totally concerned with and devoted to family and husband. Her health improves while on the isle, and she performs some labor but remains mostly a passive, nurturing, dependent figure.

MRS. SHAND (*A Stitch in Time**), very old landlady of the Fosters, who dresses in oldfashioned clothes and holds to the ways of an earlier era. She is a little afraid of children, but invites Maria to her apartment to pick up a guidebook to the area. While there, Maria sees her collection of heirloom clocks and her unusual Victorian sampler, done by an ancestor named Harriet, who arouses Maria's curiosity and grabs her imagination, and the rather meager plot of who Harriet was and what happened to her ensues.

MRS. SPARROW (*The Battle of Bubble and Squeak**), a neurotic widow now married to mild-mannered, patient, understanding Bill* Sparrow, loving mother of Sid*, Peggy, and Amy Parker. She is decisive, judgmental, overprotective, and domineering and insists she will tolerate no pets in what she obviously regards as her house. In spite of her stubborn and insensitive attitude, it is hard not to feel some sympathy for her because she is hardworking, indeed probably overworked, and has not had an easy life. On the other hand, since her insensitivity and precipitous nature inhibit communication, it is in the middle of the night that she discovers that Sid has brought the gerbils, Bubble* and Squeak, home. Eventually her maternal streak impels her to help the children care for the ailing Bubble. She is a person who needs plenty of time to adjust to change, something her children learn in the course of the story, while she learns to be less rigid and stubborn.

MRS. TUCKER (*A Little Fear**), canny old farm woman, who in search of dignity and independence steals away from the nursing home where her well-meaning daughter has arranged for her to live and attempts to make a new home for herself

in an inherited, isolated cottage near a swamp
and river. There, unknown to her, the Njimbin*,
a sly, unscrupulous gnome, has lived for ages
untold. The battle for ownership of the area
between the two aged beings begins early and
proceeds relentlessly, as the Njimbin marshals
the indigenous forces of the land and water to
evict her. At first, Mrs. Tucker, admitting that
her mind is not as sharp and clear as it once
was, thinks she may be imagining things or not
remembering correctly what she herself has done,
but she deliberately collects her wits and tests
herself, arriving at the conclusion that
supernatural forces are at work. When she
realizes that the attacks and tricks will
continue and that the plagues, such as that of
the midges, could go on indefinitely, she gives
in to the Njimbin, but, having learned that the
Njimbin considers the fowlhouse his, she
deliberately burns down the filthy, ancient coop
the day she leaves. "We'll go out with a
bang....I'd like to see that old thing's face,"
she remarks with rueful triumph to her faithful
but feckless dog, Hector*. She is presented as a
very tall, large-boned woman, with white hair
"twisted into an upside-down ice cream-cone on
top of her head." She is a thoroughly convincing, consistently interesting, sympathetic
protagonist, one the reader will not forget.

MRS. ULLATHORNE (*The Bonny Pit Laddie**), Dick
Ullathorne's grandmother, a very small, hunched,
black-haired woman, who lives alone at the
fringe of the colliery. Uncommunicative and
self-sufficient, she keeps herself apart from
the miners, considering them uncouth on the
whole. Of a higher social set, she had married
a pitman but never thought of herself as a
miner's wife. She lived very frugally all her
life and is thought to have accumulated a good
deal of money. She encourages Dick to continue
in school and gives him her books to read, which
aren't many but far more than he has at home.
When Dick must go into the pits to help support
the family, she protests but doesn't argue, an
action she considers demeaning. She secretly
helps Mr*. Candlin get Dick the job as
journeyman apprentice with Mr. Dorman, and hence
she has a significant influence on her

grandson's future.

MRS. VERITY (*The Ghost of Thomas Kempe**), elderly busybody who lives in the thatched cottage next door to the Harrisons. She constantly pops in and out of their house on some pretext or other, and Mrs. Harrison ignores her as much as she can without being rude. As the story goes along, the reader comes to understand that Mrs. Verity is not so much nosy as lonely and well-meaning and is trying too hard to gain friends. She is a gossip and knows what's going on in Ledsham as well as much of the history of the place. She tells James* about Bert* Ellison and thus is instrumental in helping James get rid of Thomas Kempe. She is an interesting figure.

MR. TATE (*Wall of Words**), absent father of the four Tate sisters, Kim*, Frances, Kerry*, and Anna*, and husband of Mrs. Tate, who manages a crafts section in a department store and then gets a job in a Sports Centre to support her family. Irresponsible and immature, he has left his family and is living alone while he ostensibly writes a best-selling novel on twentieth-century Russia. When Kim visits him at his apartment, he shows her heaps of notes that she thinks are the first draft of his novel. Later she learns that he has not told her the truth. He also tells her the story of the murder of the family of the last Romanov czar, which greatly catches her imagination. He seems a pleasant, self-deluding man, unfortunate in his self-imposed exile from his family, but too weak and selfish to realize what he is missing in not assuming his paternal responsibilities. At the end Kim comes to see and accept him for what he is. He has built a wall of words between himself and his family.

MR. TEY (*"Minnow" on the Say**), talkative, old miller at Folly Mill on the Say, who appears several times in the story in a friendly fashion, most importantly when he tells Adam* Codling and David* Moss how Adam's grandfather, Mr.* Codling, searched for the treasure and that the original channel has been altered, information that is helpful in discovering the jewels.

MR. TRIPLETT (*Songberd's Grove**), frail, pink-
ish, old man, a tailor, who lives on the first
floor of No. 7 Songberd's Grove, next door to
Martin* Singer and his mother and father. He
always looks as "though he had been sleeping
inside a mattress, small bits of cloth and
thread and horsehair" clinging to his garments.
He is friendly to the Singers and warns Martin
of trouble when the Singers move in. He spent
forty years as a tailor with a leading firm, and
he was most proud of making garments for Lord*
Simon Vigo, who is his great hero. In his old
age, he thinks of no one else, remembering all
the coats he ever made for Lord Simon with
immense pride. After the firm came upon hard
times and closed, he tried to get another job
but was too old, finally taking work with a
cleaner, doing alterations and repairs, but he
speaks with longing and fondness of the old days
when tailoring was done by hand and was a proper
craft. After Lord Simon and John* Pim interrupt
the battle between Martin and Lennie's* Teddy
boys, Lord Simon and Mr. Triplett meet again,
and Mr. Triplett notices that Lord Simon is
wearing a suit that Mr. Triplett had made for
him fifteen years before. At the party to
celebrate the renovation of Songberd's Grove,
the two happily discuss the finer points of
tailoring, just as in the old days. He is a
rounded, interesting character if eccentric.

MR. TUCKEE (*The Member for the Marsh**), old
farmer of whose marsh David is afraid because he
lost his puppy, Panama, there. Now David thinks
the place is inhabited by demons and monsters.
Mr. Tuckee thinks it's all right for David to
bring his friends to the marsh, but he doesn't
want masters (teachers) there. The reader later
realizes that he fears that masters might
complain to the authorities about his flooding
the marsh and possible "tumps," ancient mounds.
He is an enigmatic figure, a combination of
relying on tradition and thinking ahead, the
latter in particular in utilizing technology. He
is not beyond doing what is illegal to further
his financial interests. He and the unnamed
ditchers he employs are the only adults in the

book in addition to Mother and Daddy Rosley, David's parents. He is an interesting, gradually revealed figure.

MR. TUMNUS (*The Lion, the Witch and the Wardrobe**), Faun whom Lucy* Pevensie meets when she first enters Narnia*. Later she persuades her siblings, Peter* and Susan*, to remain in Narnia to help him. At first he intends to obey the White Witch, Queen* Jadis, and take Lucy to her and only pretends to be Lucy's friend. He has an attack of conscience, however, and owns up to his proposed treachery with many tears and much self-reproach. The Queen imprisons him in punishment, and he is released by Aslan* after her death. Mr. Tumnus is an engaging figure, somewhat comic, who demonstrates how evil can corrupt even those who are essentially innocent. In his conversations with Lucy, he humorously misunderstands her explanation of how she entered Narnia: he thinks she has come from the far land of Spare Oom in which lies the city of War Drobe. He is an interesting and engaging character, less flat than most in the book. He appears briefly in *The Last Battle**, meeting Lucy in the beautiful garden of eternal Narnia.

MR. WIDDISON (*Hobberdy Dick**), Puritan who buys Widford Manor and tries to keep his family and servants from celebrating the old festivals and believing in the hobgoblins and imps of the area. Because the master bedroom is haunted by the ghost of a miser, Mr. Widdison is tormented by dreams of unattainable money. Although he dearly loves Joel*, his son by his first wife, he is not sensitive to Joel's needs nor sympathetic to Joel's love for Anne* Sekar. He is, however, a man of high principles, and when he is convinced that Anne is truly the last of the Culvers, he turns over to her the treasure that was found on his land and technically is his.

MR. WILLY WONKA (*Charlie and the Chocolate Factory**), the fabulous citizen of Charlie Bucket's town, who owns and operates a marvelous chocolate factory that produces sweets of a worldwide reputation for highest quality. He is a little man, who wears a black top hat, a

plum-colored velvet coat of tails, bottle green
trousers, and pearly gray gloves; he carries a
gold-headed cane, and sports a black goatee. He
has merry, twinkling eyes, is very lively and
energetic, has the reputation for being an
inventive and successful entrepreneur, delivers
moralistic lectures to the children as they tour
his factory, and sings nonsense songs. He makes
Charlie Bucket his heir because Charlie alone
has survived the tour, being an obedient and
patient lad. Willy Wonka is a familiar type,
distorted for effect.

MURDO JOHNSTONE (*The Battle of Wednesday Week**),
husband of Alison*, middle-aged neighbor of the
Lattimers in Kilmorah, who plays a fatherly role
and is a stronger father figure in the novel
than Robert Graham. Murdo helps out with manual
labor, drives the children into town when they
need supplies, and gives them advice. He predicts the big storm and organizes Lucy's* rescue
from the stranded school bus.

MURNA (*The Mark of the Horse Lord**), daughter
of the goddess-queen of the Dalriadains,
Liadhan, and therefore the Royal Woman after
her mother's departure. Phaedrus* must marry
her to strengthen his claim on the kingship, but
instead of taking part in the bride hunt as a
ritual, she tries desperately to escape and then
to knife him when he catches her. Later she
shows him a vial of poison sent her by her
mother so she can murder him and then throws it
scornfully into the fire. It is not until she
has led her woman warriors into battle alongside
the men and Phaedrus has been wounded that he is
able to penetrate her cold reserve, and then she
tells him that she fled from him and tried to
kill him from fear but now sees that he is
different. She reminds him of the time when
Midir*, whom he is pretending to be, killed her
pet otter, the one thing she loved, a bit of
casual cruelty which meant so little to him that
he didn't remember to tell Phaedrus about it.
She also tries to explain to Phaedrus how she
hated her mother and built a wall around her own
emotions to keep Liadhan from destroying her as
she destroyed her father and the subsequent
kings, yet felt compelled to save Liadhan be-

cause she was the Earth Mother. In the end Murna
is carrying Phaedrus's child, which ironically
will have the right to kingship falsely through
him but in actuality through her, as son of the
Royal Woman. It is evident from the way she
avoids calling Phaedrus Midir that she knows he
is an imposter with whom she is now in love.

MURRAY, CAPTAIN JAMES (*The Sentinels**), commander of the *Sentinel*, a British warship
assigned to antislave patrol in the Bight of
Benin off northwest Africa. His task is to
enforce international law against trade in human
beings. He is Whig in politics, religious
(called a Blue-Light by his men for his openly
religious behavior), firm, and humane. Although
he does not agree with Brooke's* harsh methods
of handling the men, he is not so foolish as to
openly oppose Brooke and thus undercut the
officer before his men. He enjoys almost universal respect. His putting Spencer in charge
of the *Phantom* is a factor in his eventual
demotion, though under the circumstances it had
seemed the wisest move. He has the *Dolphin* and
the *Esk* both burned, rather than trying to
salvage the *Esk*, which would have cost many men.
His decision leads to the court-martial of the
commander of the *Esk*, a truly brave man. Brooke
disagrees with him about burning the *Esk*.
Brooke also thinks he should discipline the men
over the revenge-massacre on the *Dolphin*, but
Murray sees what happened as understandable and
normal under the circumstances.

MYRTLE BEAMISH (*The Great Gale**), Mary*
Vaughan's best friend in the village of Reedsmere, which is ravaged by the flood of 1953.
Good-natured and fun-loving, she is very class
conscious and occasionally gets short with Mary
when she thinks that Mary is "going posh" on
her. She and her mother manage to get out of
their house and onto the roof of the coal shed
just before the house is washed away by the
flood. Mrs. Beamish suffers a severe head wound,
and it is up to Myrtle to see that she is safe
and gets help. Following the instructions of
her mother, who is village postmistress, Mrytle
gathers together important postal papers, which
she stuffs into a bag together with aniseed

candy, to which she is partial, and Catty, her pet cat. She has a well-developed sense of responsibility and struggles to keep all these safe. The papers come out somewhat the worse for being with the candy and Catty, however. While her mother is in the hospital, she stays with the Vaughans and helps in fixing up the Foulgers' cottage. She somewhat resents Mary's going to boarding school. She is a good character whom the reader sees from several sides.

MYSTERY IN WALES. See *Climbing to Danger.*